THIRD EDITION

An Introduction to Bankruptcy Law

THIRD EDITION

AN INTRODUCTION TO BANKRUPTCY LAW

Martin A. Frey
Professor of Law
The University of Tulsa
College of Law

Warren L. McConnico
Attorney at Law
Tulsa, Oklahoma

Phyllis Hurley Frey
Attorney at Law
Tulsa, Oklahoma

WEST PUBLISHING COMPANY
Minneapolis/ Saint Paul   New York   Los Angeles   San Francisco

Production Credits

Cover Image	© 1991 Frank Clarkson/Liaison International. All rights reserved.
Cover Design	Hespenheide Design
Text Design	John Edeen
Illustrations	Randy Miyake, Miyake Illustration
Composition	Carlisle Communications

West's Commitment to the Environment

In 1906, West Publishing Company began recycling materials left over from the production of books. This began a tradition of efficient and responsible use of resources. Today, 100% of our legal bound volumes are printed on acid-free, recycled paper consisting of 50% new fibers. West recycles nearly 27,700,000 pounds of scrap paper annually—the equivalent of 229,300 trees. Since the 1960s, West has devised ways to capture and recycle waste inks, solvents, oils, and vapors created in the printing process. We also recycle plastics of all kinds, wood, glass, corrugated cardboard, and batteries, and have eliminated the use of polystyrene book packaging. We at West are proud of the longevity and the scope of our commitment to the environment.

West pocket parts and advance sheets are printed on recyclable paper and can be collected and recycled with newspapers. Staples do not have to be removed. Bound volumes can be recycled after removing the cover.

Production, Prepress, Printing and Binding by West Publishing Company.

 TEXT IS PRINTED ON 10% POST CONSUMER RECYCLED PAPER ∞

British Library Cataloguing-in-Publication Data. A catalogue record for this book is available from the British Library.

COPYRIGHT © 1990, 1992   By WEST PUBLISHING COMPANY
COPYRIGHT © 1997   By WEST PUBLISHING COMPANY
                                   610 Opperman Drive
                                   P.O. Box 64526
                                   St. Paul, MN 55164-0526

04 03 02 01 00 99 98 97   8 7 6 5 4 3 2 1 0

Library of Congress Cataloging-in-Publication Data

Frey, Martin A.
    An introduction to bankruptcy law / Martin A. Frey, Warren L.
McConnico, Phyllis Hurley Frey. — 3rd ed.
      p.   cm.
    Includes index.
    ISBN 0-314-09377-X (hard : alk. paper)
    1. Bankruptcy—United States.   I. McConnico, Warren L. II. Frey,
Phyllis Hurley. III. Title.
KF1524.F74   1997
346.73'078—dc20
[347.30678]   96-1007
                                         CIP

In memory of Warren L. McConnico
our valued friend and coauthor

CONTENTS

CHAPTER SIX
THE CHAPTER 13 BANKRUPTCY (ADJUSTMENT OF DEBTS OF AN INDIVIDUAL WITH REGULAR INCOME)   325

SECTION 1
THE FILING OF THE PETITION   326

SECTION 2
THE SIGNIFICANCE OF FILING A PETITION   331

SECTION 3
APPOINTMENT AND DUTIES OF A CHAPTER 13 TRUSTEE   333

SECTION 4
MOTIONS AND COMPLAINTS AFTER THE ORDER FOR RELIEF   336

SECTION 5
THE CLERK'S NOTICE   340

SECTION 6
MEETING OF CREDITORS (THE SECTION 341 MEETING)   342

SECTION 7
THE CHAPTER 13 PLAN   342

SECTION 8
HEARING ON CONFIRMATION OF THE PLAN   347

TABLE OF EXHIBITS

TABLE OF CASES

TABLE OF STATUTES AND RULES

PREFACE

The third edition of this book and the accompanying Instructor's Manual were necessitated by numerous changes in bankruptcy law. These changes include the 1994 Amendments to the Bankruptcy Code, the 1995 amendments to the Bankruptcy Rules, and the Revised Official Forms which became effective March 31, 1995. Revised Procedural Forms became effective January 31, 1995. In addition to these changes, several United States Supreme Court decisions involving bankruptcy law have been made since the second edition was published. Although the content of the text has been altered to reflect these changes, the overall structure of the book remains the same. The following paragraphs detail this structure.

The paralegal plays an increasingly important role in the bankruptcy practices of many law firms. Duties may include interviewing clients, drafting and filing the necessary documents in a bankruptcy case, and legal research. With this in mind, we provide in-depth coverage of the practical materials needed by the paralegal, including a detailed questionnaire that the paralegal can use when interviewing a client and a step-by-step guide for preparing the forms for filing a Chapter 7, the liquidation or "straight" bankruptcy case. We emphasize Chapter 7 because it comprises the bulk of cases filed in the bankruptcy court. The forms necessary for filing Chapter 11, 12, and 13 cases are included but receive less emphasis. A sample plan for reorganization or adjustment of debts is included for each of these chapters as well.

We provide many examples and problems in this text to help the student understand how the bankruptcy process works. A quick reference guide to the filing of a bankruptcy case and the activities that take place after the filing has been added to the text for each of the "operative" chapters of the Bankruptcy Code. (An operative chapter is one under which a case is filed. Operative chapters are 7, 11, 12, and 13.) This reference guide is termed a "road map" and will be helpful both in learning about bankruptcy and in applying this knowledge to bankruptcy cases.

Not all clients with financial problems will want or need to file bankruptcy. This text includes alternatives to filing bankruptcy to aid the paralegal in working with an attorney who has clients in this situation.

Many paralegals do a substantial amount of research in all areas of the law, and a number of our readers may be generally familiar with legal research. Because researching bankruptcy law is specialized, we have included a practical guide to sources for research in this area. We have also included a glossary to assist students with unfamiliar terms. A new feature, "Basic Terms and Phrases," has been added at the end of each chapter for review purposes.

Finally, we must add a word of caution. The Bankruptcy Code is a difficult code to read and understand. Rather than approach the Code section by section, we follow the bankruptcy process for each type of bankruptcy filing. We attempt to clearly and logically present the relevant concepts. At times, we paraphrase the Code to capture a concept. At other times, we refer to the Code section itself. We trust that our readers will go back to the original source, the Bankruptcy Code itself, because the Code is the law. We include cases throughout the text for illustrative purposes, not as statements of the rule. Reading and analyzing cases is a skill that must be constantly honed, especially by those paralegals who will be involved in legal research. Cases also serve to remind us that bankruptcy deals with real people who have real problems.

We believe this text will stimulate discussion in the classroom and provide students with a solid foundation in the field of bankruptcy. We welcome your comments and hope that you will find the following materials informative and challenging.

ACKNOWLEDGMENTS

For their aid in the preparation of this third edition, we are indebted to our many friends and colleagues, both in the academic community and in the practice. They include the Honorable Stephen J. Covey, Professor Richard E. Ducey, Lonnie D. Eck, Dorothy A. Evans, Kathy Kane, Thomas M. Klenda, Professor F. Stephen Knippenberg, Cherie LaCour, Roderic L. Notzon, Professor Walter Ray Phillips, Timothy J. Sullivan, Sidney K. Swinson, Katherine Vance, Jim Wannamaker, the Honorable Mickey D. Wilson, and Gary W. Wood.

We wish to thank our friends at West Publishing Company for their expeditious handling of this project. Special thanks to Elizabeth Hannan and Patty Bryant, our editors, and to all those who worked on this book.

M.A.F.
P.H.F.

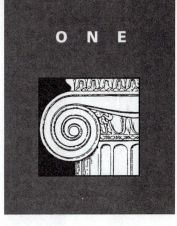

O N E

The Evolution of Bankruptcy Law

Debt collection has come a long way since the days of the Romans. Although Roman creditors were allowed by law to physically divide the debtor's body proportionately among themselves, there is no record of this ever having been done and it would hardly have helped the creditors to recover their losses. Selling the debtor as a slave was a common practice, however, and did produce some revenue. The threat of imprisonment or exile also stimulated some debt repayment. Under Roman law, debtors were obligated to pay their debts. Even if their estates were sold by creditors, the debtors received no discharge from any unpaid balance.

SECTION 1
BRIEF HISTORY OF MODERN BANKRUPTCY LAW

The word "bankruptcy" has its origin in the commercial practices of early Italian merchants, traders, and moneylenders, who transacted their business from benches in central town markets. When a merchant was unable to pay his debts, it was common practice for his creditors to break his bench as a symbol of financial failure. This practice led to the phrase "banca rotta," which is derived from the Italian *banca* (bench) and *rotta* (break). English merchants became familiar with the Italian practice and changed "banca rotta" to the English "bankrupt."

A. THE APPEARANCE OF BANKRUPTCY IN EARLY ENGLISH LAW

The earliest English bankruptcy laws, from which American law was derived, were creditors' remedies only and were quite punitive. Prior to the late 1700s, failure to pay debts was viewed as an immoral act and the debtor often faced imprisonment.

Conditions of imprisonment in the debtors' prisons of London varied considerably. Debtors lived in the prisons with their families and were not forced to work. Debtors of a higher class were able to rent apartments from the keeper of the prison. People not even connected with the prison could rent apartments or rooms there. The truly poor debtors lived in crowded wards. It was their living conditions that brought about reform. In 1829, approximately 7,000 debtors were imprisoned in London. Even as late as 1921, about 400 debtors were in London prisons.

The concept of discharge of indebtedness first appeared in English law in 1705 in a bankruptcy law available only to the commercial debtor. At this time, debtors could not bring actions to discharge indebtedness. The actions were brought by creditors to collect indebtedness, and the debtors responded by requesting discharge of their indebtedness. The commercial debtors were allowed an exemption for necessary family wearing apparel. They were also allowed an exemption of 5 percent of the estate (up to £200) if they could pay a certain dividend to their creditors.

The bankruptcy law passed in England in 1849 classified the bankrupt's discharge certificate based on fault. There were three types of discharge certificates. A first-class discharge certificate was issued if the debtor was without fault. A second-class discharge certificate was issued if the debtor had some fault, such as carelessness, but was not dishonest. A third-class discharge certificate was issued if the debtor was totally at fault due to dishonesty.

B. TREATMENT OF BANKRUPTCY IN THE UNITED STATES CONSTITUTION

During colonial days, the English colonies in North America naturally followed English law. After the American Revolution, the Articles of Confederation were passed by the Continental Congress and ratified by the 13 original states. The Articles became effective on March 1, 1781. The Articles continued to recognize the Congress as the central government of the Confederation but severely limited its powers. For example, Congress had to rely on the states for money and an army. The Articles contained no reference to bankruptcy, which meant that all bankruptcy law during this period was left to the states.

In 1789, the Articles of Confederation were superseded by the United States Constitution. Article I, Section 8, of the Constitution grants Congress power to act in enumerated areas. Article I, Section 8, Clause 4, gives Congress the power to enact uniform bankruptcy laws.

> Section 8. The Congress shall have the power . . .
>
> 4. To establish a uniform rule of naturalization, and uniform laws on the subject of bankruptcy throughout the United States.

Although the Constitution gave Congress the power to enact bankruptcy laws in 1789, it did not require the enactment of such laws. The first federal bankruptcy law was not enacted until 1800.

C. EARLY AMERICAN BANKRUPTCY STATUTES

1. THE BANKRUPTCY ACT OF 1800

The Bankruptcy Act of 1800 was a response to the financial panics of 1792 and 1797, which were caused by speculation in land, stock, and government scrip. Scrip was paper money issued in the United States in amounts of less than a dollar. These panics resulted in the imprisonment of many debtors, some of whom were quite prominent.

For instance, two signers of the Constitution had serious debt problems at this time. One signer named Robert Morris, a financier who supervised the finances of the revolutionary war from 1781 to 1784, had established the Bank of North America in Philadelphia in 1781. He lost his money in land speculation and was in a debtors' prison when the Bankruptcy Act of 1800 was passed. Morris spent three years in prison and was released after obtaining a discharge under the Act. The other, James Wilson, had a distinguished career as a revolutionary patriot, lawyer, and member of Congress. He was one of the drafters of the Pennsylvania Constitution and the first professor of law at the College of Pennsylvania, which is now the University of Pennsylvania. Wilson was appointed to the United States Supreme Court in 1789. In 1798, he fled Pennsylvania to avoid debtors' prison and died a short time later in North Carolina.

Not all debtors were prominent persons by any standard. In the generation after the Revolution, about 60 percent of the people in debtors' prison owed $10 or less. Imprisonment for debt was, however, the exception rather than the rule at this time. Even though debtors were likely to be arrested, most were not imprisoned; those who were imprisoned were generally free again in a short time.

The Bankruptcy Act of 1800, which applied only to merchants, was a temporary measure designed to expire in 1805. It was repealed in 1803. For the next 38 years, the country operated without federal bankruptcy legislation.

2. THE BANKRUPTCY ACT OF 1841

The Bankruptcy Act of 1841, the second federal bankruptcy act, became effective in 1842 in response to poor economic conditions brought about by the panic of 1837. The years prior to 1837 were a "get-rich-quick" time nationally. The Bankruptcy Act of 1841 is important historically because it provided for the initiation of bankruptcy proceedings by the nonmerchant debtor who had total debts of less than $2,000. The exemption provisions of this Act were also more favorable to the debtor. For example, clothing, furniture, and other "necessaries" not to exceed $300 in value were allowed as exempt property.

The Bankruptcy Act of 1841 lasted less than two years. For the next 25 years, the country again operated without federal bankruptcy legislation.

3. THE BANKRUPTCY ACT OF 1867

The Bankruptcy Act of 1867, the third federal bankruptcy act, was enacted after the Civil War in response to another economic crisis. It was the first bankruptcy legislation designed to be permanent. This bankruptcy law allowed the filing of both voluntary and involuntary petitions for merchants, nonmerchants, and corporate debtors. An involuntary petition is one filed by the debtor's creditors, rather than by the debtor.

The Bankruptcy Act of 1867 provided for an assignee, who was elected by creditors at the first meeting after notice of the bankruptcy petition. The assignee performed the same basic duties as today's trustee. The assignee gathered up the property of the debtor, with the exception of exempt property, and held it for distribution to creditors. Discharge would be denied for dishonest acts by the debtor.

A debtor had to have debts of more than $300 to qualify for bankruptcy under this Act. Exemptions were expanded to $500 and included necessary household and kitchen furniture, wearing apparel for the debtor and his wife and children, and other necessaries designated by the assignee, as well as property exempted by both federal nonbankruptcy law and the debtor's state law.

The Bankruptcy Act of 1867 was not repealed until 1878. For the next 20 years, the country again operated without federal bankruptcy legislation. This was the last period in American history without federal bankruptcy law.

D. THE BANKRUPTCY ACT OF 1898

The Bankruptcy Act of 1898 was the fourth federal bankruptcy act. It was divided into 14 chapters, numbered consecutively from I through XIV.

Chapter I	Definitions
Chapter II	Courts of Bankruptcy
Chapter III	Bankrupts
Chapter IV	Courts and Procedure Therein
Chapter V	Officers, Their Duties and Compensation
Chapter VI	Creditors
Chapter VII	Estates
Chapter VIII	Provisions for the Relief of Debtors
Chapter IX	Readjustment of Debts of Agencies or Instrumentalities (muncipal corporations)
Chapter X	Corporate Reorganizations
Chapter XI	Arrangements
Chapter XII	Real Property Arrangements by Persons Other Than Corporations
Chapter XIII	Wage Earners' Plans
Chapter XIV	Maritime Commission Liens

Voluntary initiation of proceedings by the nonmerchant debtor, a concept initiated in the Bankruptcy Act of 1841, was incorporated into the Bankruptcy Act of 1898. The Bankruptcy Act of 1898 also enhanced the debtor's relief by eliminating creditor consent to discharge in liquidation cases. Involuntary proceedings were also retained. Although the 1898 Act did not provide the debtor with federal exemptions, it did adopt state exemptions.

Under the Bankruptcy Act of 1898, bankruptcy courts were created as a part of the United States district courts. This gave district court judges primary responsibility over bankruptcy cases. The district court judges delegated the administration of bankruptcy cases, on a case by case basis, to "referees." These quasi-judicial officials performed both the administrative and judicial functions associated with bankruptcy cases. Over the years, referees evolved into judges and actually became bankruptcy judges under the 1973 Bankruptcy Rules.

The Bankruptcy Act of 1898 used the term "trustee" to describe the elected representative of the creditors. The Act also provided that the trustee was to be paid out of the assets of the estate.

Although the 1898 Act was substantially amended over the years, it remained in effect as the national bankruptcy law for 81 years. It was superseded by the Bankruptcy Reform Act of 1978, which became effective on October 1, 1979.

E. THE BANKRUPTCY REFORM ACT OF 1978

As the years passed, the Bankruptcy Act of 1898 became obsolete. It was not a true codification of bankruptcy law but merely a collection of bankruptcy enactments and amendments. The language was outdated, and the organization was poor. Perhaps the most objectionable features of the Bankruptcy Act of 1898 were the dual responsibilities of the office of the bankruptcy judge. The judicial function of resolving disputes was inconsistent with the administrative duties performed by the bankruptcy judge. Administrative functions usually involved contact with the litigants on an ex-parte basis, which was unavoidable and even encouraged by the administrative duties imposed upon the bankruptcy judge. Even if no impropriety existed, the administrative duties performed by the bankruptcy judge created the appearance of a bias in favor of the estate because its representatives had frequent contact with the judge.

On November 8, 1978, President Jimmy Carter signed into law the Bankruptcy Reform Act of 1978. This Act, commonly referred to as the **Bankruptcy Code** or the **Code** (not to be confused with the Bankruptcy Act of 1898, which is commonly referred to as the "Bankruptcy Act" or the "Act"), became effective on October 1, 1979, and represented the first overall reenactment of the bankruptcy laws since 1898.

The Code was originally divided into eight **chapters.** The chapters were numbered consecutively from 1 to 15, not from 1 to 8, using only the odd numbers. The even numbers were reserved for later additions. The original chapters of the Code were

Chapter 1   General Provisions
Chapter 3   Case Administration
Chapter 5   Creditors, Debtor, and the Estate
Chapter 7   Liquidation
Chapter 9   Adjustment of Debts of a Municipality
Chapter 11   Reorganization
Chapter 13   Adjustment of Debts of an Individual with Regular Income
Chapter 15   United States Trustee

Chapters 1, 3, and 5 deal with **administration, priorities,** and **exemptions** and apply to all the chapters. These three chapters are known as the **universal chapters.** Only selected sections of Chapter 3 and Chapter 5, however, apply to a case under Chapter 9. 11 U.S.C.A. § 901.

Chapters 7, 9, 11, and 13 are mutually exclusive chapters; each deals with a different type of bankruptcy case. These four chapters are known as the **operative chapters.** Selected sections of Chapter 11 are, however, applicable in a Chapter 9 case.

Chapter 7 deals with **liquidation bankruptcy,** which is sometimes called **straight bankruptcy.** The **Chapter 7 trustee** converts the **debtor's estate** into money and distributes it to the debtor's creditors. Chapter 7 may be used by individuals, partnerships, and corporations.

Chapter 9, a rarely used chapter, applies to financially troubled municipalities. A "municipality" is defined as a "political subdivision or public agency or instrumentality of a State." 11 U.S.C.A. § 101(40). The Chapter 9 bankruptcy has a history of its own, apart from the rest of the Code. A short discussion of Chapter 9 can be found in Appendix C.

Chapter 11 generally deals with **reorganizations,** usually business reorganizations. Unlike the Chapter 7 liquidation, a Chapter 11 bankruptcy is designed for filing a reorganization plan to keep a business going. In reorganization cases, creditors are usually repaid through the plan as the debtor continues its operation and not through liquidation of the debtor's estate. However, Chapter 11 cases may, by design or by circumstances, become liquidation cases.

Chapter 13 is similar to Chapter 11 in that the estate of the debtor is not liquidated. Chapter 13 deals with **debt adjustment** for individuals with regular income. It permits debtors to repay all or part of their debts over a three-year period with their disposable income.

The final original chapter of the Code, Chapter 15, initially established a pilot **United States trustee** program in 18 judicial districts. Chapter 15 had a sunset provision for automatic repeal on September 30, 1986. When the United States trustee program ceased being experimental and became a permanent part of the bankruptcy process, Chapter 15 of the Bankruptcy Code was repealed and the United States trustee system was moved to Title 28 of the United States Code. 28 U.S.C.A. §§ 581–589a.

F. AMENDMENTS TO THE BANKRUPTCY REFORM ACT OF 1978

During the years since its enactment, there have been a number of changes in the Bankruptcy Reform Act of 1978. These changes include

1. The Bankruptcy Amendments and Federal Judgeship Act of 1984
2. The Bankruptcy Judges, United States Trustees, and Family Farmer Bankruptcy Act of 1986
3. The 1990 amendments, consisting of four separate statutes: The Omnibus Reconciliation Act of 1990; The Criminal Victims Protection Act (the MADD law); The Crime Control Act; and The Judicial Improvements Act
4. The 1991 Revision of the Bankruptcy Rules and Official Forms
5. The Bankruptcy Reform Act of 1994 (which also brought about changes in the Official Bankruptcy Forms and the Procedural Bankruptcy Forms)

SECTION 2
THE DUAL NATURE OF BANKRUPTCY AS A REMEDY FOR BOTH CREDITORS AND DEBTORS

The Bankruptcy Reform Act of 1978 was viewed as highly favorable to debtors. American bankruptcy law, at least from 1978 up to the enactment of the 1984 amendments, appears to have adopted the philosophy of **bankruptcy on demand.** There are no provisions suggesting that it is morally wrong for a debtor to file for bankruptcy, and there is no requirement that the debtor be **insolvent** to file a **voluntary petition** under any chapter of the Code.

Two of the 1984 amendments, however, began to push back the idea of "bankruptcy on demand." One of these amendments required an attorney to certify that the prospective debtor whose debts were primarily **consumer debts** had been informed of the differences between a Chapter 13 case ("Adjustment of Debts of an Individual with Regular Income") and a Chapter 7 case ("Liquidation"). The other amendment allowed a bankruptcy court to dismiss on its own motion a case for substantial abuse of the provisions of Chapter 7.

Another adjustment in the balance between creditors and debtors occurred when Congress amended 11 U.S.C.A. § 707(b) in 1986 to allow the United States trustee to file a **motion to dismiss**. The amendment provides that

> (b) After notice and a hearing, the court, on its own motion or on a motion by the United States Trustee, but not at the request or suggestion of any party in interest, may dismiss a case filed by an individual debtor under this chapter whose debts are primarily consumer debts if it finds that the granting of relief would be a substantial abuse of the provisions of this chapter. There shall be a presumption in favor of granting the relief requested by the debtor.

It has been suggested that 11 U.S.C.A. § 707(b) represents a substantial shift of the balance between creditors and debtors back to the creditors' side. There is, however, no suggestion that a shift has occurred back toward the connection of moral implications to the mere filing of a bankruptcy case.

Although modern bankruptcy law originated in creditor-oriented proceedings, bankruptcy in the United States, from a public policy point of view, now has two purposes:

1. To give honest debtors a **fresh start** to assure their return to full productivity, relieved from burdensome and unmanageable debt
2. To promote the **best interests of creditors** by providing them with an **equitable distribution** equal to the liquidation value of the debtor's **nonexempt assets**

The debtor in bankruptcy has two objectives:

1. To acquire **discharge**
2. To preserve ownership of as much property as free from debt as may be possible

The trustee and the creditors also have two objectives:

1. To maximize distribution to creditors, either in property or in money
2. To assure that the debtor does not receive a discharge unless one is justified and that the debts that are **nondischargeable** according to law are not discharged through the bankruptcy proceeding

Public policy seeks to balance the interests of debtors and creditors. A constant tension exists in the bankruptcy court process and in the legislative and rule-making processes related to bankruptcy. The dual nature of bankruptcy law as a remedy for both creditors and debtors has prevailed. Although this balancing of interests between the contending parties shifts from time to time, it is continually being adjusted by legislation and judicial decisions.

Basic Terms and Phrases

Administration
Bankruptcy Code
Bankruptcy on demand
Best interests of creditors
Chapter 7 trustee
Chapters
Code
Consumer debts
Debt adjustment
Debtor's estate
Discharge
Equitable distribution
Exemptions

Fresh start
Insolvent
Liquidation bankruptcy
Motion to dismiss
Nondischargeable
Nonexempt assets
Operative chapters
Priorities
Reorganization
Straight bankruptcy
United States trustee
Universal chapters
Voluntary petition

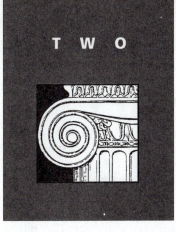

TWO

BANKRUPTCY LAW AND WHERE TO FIND IT

Legal authority may be primary or secondary. **Primary authority** is found in the Constitution, statutes, rules and administrative regulations issued pursuant to statutory authority, and case law. Primary authority may be mandatory or persuasive. **Mandatory authority** is law or reasoning that a court must follow. **Persuasive authority** is law or reasoning that a court may follow but is not bound to follow.

Secondary authority is found in all other written expressions of the law, such as legislative history, treatises, periodicals, and form books. Secondary authority is useful in understanding primary authority.

The United States Constitution is mandatory primary authority. The Bill of Rights of the Constitution protects the enumerated rights of the people from federal government action. The due process clause of the Fourteenth Amendment extends this protection to shield the people from state government action.

EXAMPLE

The First Amendment to the Constitution provides that

> Congress shall make no law respecting an establishment of religion, or prohibiting the free exercise thereof; or abridging the freedom of speech, or of the press; or the right of the people peaceably to assemble, and to petition the Government for a redress of grievances.

Although the First Amendment as drafted applies only to Congress, the Fourteenth Amendment, through its due process clause, extends the First Amendment to the states as well:

> Section 1. All persons born or naturalized in the United States, and subject to the jurisdiction thereof, are citizens of the United States and of the State wherein they reside. No State shall make or enforce any law which shall abridge the privileges or immunities of citizens of the United States, *nor shall any State deprive any person of life, liberty, or property, without due process of law;* nor deny to any person within its jurisdiction the equal protection of the laws. (Emphasis added.)

Because the Constitution is mandatory primary authority, it must be followed by all states. For example, a state cannot prohibit any person from making a derogatory statement concerning the Bankruptcy Code. If the legislature in either State A or State B chooses to enact such legislation, that statute will be in violation of the First and Fourteenth Amendments.

Article I, Section 8, Clause 4, of the Constitution gives Congress the power to act in certain enumerated areas. One of these enumerated areas is bankruptcy:

Section 8. The Congress shall have the power . . .

4. To establish an uniform Rule of Naturalization, and uniform Laws on the subject of Bankruptcies throughout the United States.

Article I, Section 8, Clause 18, gives Congress the power to enact laws that are "necessary and proper" to implement the power that has been previously enumerated.

18. To make all Laws which shall be necessary and proper for carrying into Execution the foregoing Powers, and all other Powers vested by this Constitution in the Government of the United States, or in any Department or Officer thereof.

Federal legislation is mandatory primary authority. In some areas, the power conferred to Congress is exclusive. Therefore, regardless of whether Congress acts, it is the only governmental body that can act in these areas. Congressional power preempts these areas, and the states may not legislate on them.

EXAMPLE

Article I, Section 8, Clause 4, gives Congress the power to establish "uniform Laws on the subject of Bankruptcies throughout the United States." Congress, acting through its necessary and proper clause, enacted the Bankruptcy Code. The United States Bankruptcy Code is mandatory primary authority and must be followed by all states. The power to establish bankruptcy laws is also exclusive, so the states are preempted from the field. Therefore, if either State A or State B chooses to enact bankruptcy legislation, that legislation will be unconstitutional.

The holding and rationale of a United States Supreme Court opinion is mandatory primary authority.

EXAMPLE

When enacting the Bankruptcy Reform Act of 1978, Congress conferred Article III judicial power on bankruptcy court judges who were not given the life tenure and protection against salary decreases required for **Article III judges.** The lack of life tenure and protection against salary decreases meant that the judges were really only **Article I judges.** The United States Supreme Court, in *Northern Pipeline Construction Co. v. Marathon Pipe Line Co.,* 458 U.S. 50 (1982), held that this section of the Act violated Article III of the Constitution.

Article I judges could not be given the broad judicial power authorized by the Act. Congress was thus forced to restructure the bankruptcy court system to make it constitutional. Congress could either give the judges Article III status and continue the broad designation of power or give the judges Article I status and reduce their power. In either event, Congress was obligated to comply with the holding and rationale of the Supreme Court because the Court had mandatory primary authority over this issue.

State legislation is mandatory primary authority for transactions covered by state statute.

EXAMPLE

When the state of New Jersey enacted its version of the **Uniform Commercial Code (UCC),** it adopted the language of section 9–312(4) as written by the drafters, the American Law Institute and the National Conference of Commissioners on Uniform State Laws. Section 9–312(4) reads

> (4) A **purchase money security interest** in **collateral** other than **inventory** has priority over a conflicting **security interest** in the same collateral or its **proceeds** if the purchase money security interest is **perfected** at the time the debtor receives possession of the collateral or within ten days thereafter.

When the state of Florida enacted its version of the Uniform Commercial Code, it revised the language of section 9–312(4) to increase the number of days to perfect from 10 to 15.

The state of New Jersey's version of UCC § 9–312(4) is mandatory primary authority for transactions that are governed by it. The state of Florida's version of UCC § 9–312(4) is mandatory primary authority for transactions that are governed by it. Therefore, if the transaction is governed by New Jersey law, the secured party with a purchase money security interest in **equipment** must perfect within 10 days from the time the debtor receives possession of the collateral to have priority over conflicting security interests in the same collateral. If the transaction is governed by Florida law, the secured party with a purchase money security interest in equipment must perfect within 15 days from the time the debtor receives possession of the collateral to have priority over conflicting security interests in the same collateral.

PROBLEM 2.1   The Atlas Health Club of Princeton, New Jersey, has $1,000,000 in equipment, which is debt free. Atlas borrowed $300,000 from People's Bank to remodel the health club. Atlas gave People's Bank a security interest in all of its present and after-acquired equipment. (The security interest gave People's Bank the right to repossess all of Atlas's equipment if Atlas did not re-pay according to the terms of the **security agreement.**) To perfect this security interest in Atlas's equipment, People's Bank filed a **financing statement** with the Office of the Secretary of State. (A filed financing statement gave notice to third parties that People's Bank had a security interest in the equipment.)

After the club was remodeled, Atlas purchased $300,000 in new weight-room equipment from the Ace Equipment Company of Princeton, New Jersey. Rather than pay in cash, Atlas gave Ace a security interest in this new equipment. Atlas promised to pay Ace in 12 installments over the next 12 months. (The security interest gave Ace the right to repossess this equipment if Atlas did not pay. The security interest was a purchase money security interest because the seller was financing the sale.) Twelve days after Atlas received possession of the new equipment, Ace filed its financing statement. (A filed financing statement gave notice to third parties that Ace had a security interest in the equipment.)

> Atlas failed to pay either People's Bank or Ace on its obligations. Assume that if the equipment is repossessed and sold, it will not bring enough money to satisfy both obligations. Does People's Bank or Ace have priority as to the equipment Atlas purchased from Ace? See UCC §§ 9–312(4), (5)(a).

The holding and rationale of a United States bankruptcy court, a United States district court, or a United States circuit court opinion interpreting a *federal statute* is mandatory primary authority for transactions within the jurisdictional boundaries of the decision making court. It need not be followed by all courts nationwide, as a United States Supreme Court opinion must be followed.

EXAMPLE
In 1985, the United States Circuit Court for the Eleventh Circuit held that Chapter 11 is available to individuals who are not engaged in business. *In re Moog,* 774 F.2d 1073 (11th Cir. 1985). One year later, the Eighth Circuit held that Chapter 11 is not available to individuals who are not engaged in business. *Wamsganz v. Boatmen's Bank of De Soto,* 804 F.2d 503 (8th Cir. 1986). The Eleventh Circuit decision, even though primary authority, need not be followed in the Eighth Circuit because it is not mandatory authority beyond the jurisdictional boundaries of the Eleventh Circuit, which is the decision-making court.

In 1991, the United States Supreme Court held that an individual debtor not engaged in business is eligible to reorganize under Chapter 11. *Toibb v. Radloff,* 501 U.S. 157 (1991). This decision is mandatory primary authority and must be followed by all United States courts.

The holding and rationale of a United States bankruptcy court, district court, or circuit court or a state court opinion interpreting a *state statute* is mandatory primary authority for transactions within the jurisdictional boundaries of the decision making court. It need not be followed by courts beyond the decision making court's jurisdictional boundaries.

EXAMPLE
The Grand Old Theatre, located in Rhode Island, purchased theater seats from the Plush Furniture Company for $200,000. Plush, also located in Rhode Island, orally agreed to finance the sale if Grand would give Plush a security interest in the seats. Grand signed a **promissory note** for $200,000 and a financing statement but did not sign a written security agreement.

After paying $50,000, Grand defaulted on the note and filed for bankruptcy under Chapter 7 (liquidation). Both the trustee in bankruptcy and Plush claimed the theater seats. The trustee claimed that Plush was unsecured because it did not have a security agreement signed by the debtor, Grand Old Theatre, as required by UCC § 9–203(1)(a). Plush claimed that it was secured because the financing statement coupled with the promissory note satisfied the written security agreement requirement of UCC § 9–203(1)(a).

Rhode Island's version of UCC § 9–203(1)(a) provides that

> (1) . . . a security interest is not enforceable against the debtor or third parties with respect to the collateral and does not attach unless:
> (a) . . . the debtor has signed a security agreement which contains a description of the collateral . . . .

A "security agreement" is defined in UCC § 9–105(1)(l) as meaning "an agreement which creates or provides for a security interest."

In *American Card Co. v. H.M.H. Co.,* 196 A.2d 150 (R.I. 1963), the Rhode Island Supreme Court held that a financing statement could not operate as a security agreement because there was no language granting a security interest to a creditor. Implicit in UCC § 9–203 is the "creation" language of UCC § 9–105. Therefore, because *American Card* is mandatory primary authority in Rhode Island, the Bankruptcy Court for the United States District Court for the District of Rhode Island was required to follow *American Card* and hold Plush unsecured.

If Grand and Plush were both located in Maine, the answer would have been different. The Supreme Court of Maine, in *Casco Bank & Trust Co. v. Cloutier,* 398 A.2d 1224 (Me. 1979), held that a financing statement coupled with a promissory note could constitute the security agreement required by UCC § 9–203(1). Implicit in the *Casco Bank* opinion was that express "creation" language was not required for a security agreement to exist. Therefore, if the case had been before the Bankruptcy Court for the United States District Court for the District of Maine, Plush would have been secured. Because Plush filed a financing statement to become a perfected secured party (rather than remaining an unperfected secured party), Plush would have had priority over the trustee in bankruptcy (a **lien creditor**). The negative inference is derived from UCC § 9–301(1)(b).

PROBLEM 2.2   Assume that Grand and Plush are located in Gary, Indiana. Indiana has enacted sections 9–105(1)(l) and 9–203(1) of the UCC without variance from the official text. Assume that this is a case of first impression before the United States Bankruptcy Court for Indiana. Also assume that no other court having jurisdiction over cases arising in Gary, Indiana, has ruled on the issue of whether a financing statement coupled with a promissory note would satisfy the writing requirement under 9–203(1).

Should Plush or the trustee in bankruptcy prevail as to the seats? Is either *American Card* or *Casco Bank* primary authority? Is either mandatory primary authority in Indiana? Could either be persuasive primary authority in Indiana?

Judicial decisions from one federal court need not be followed in another federal court on the same level (i.e., two bankruptcy courts or two district courts), even though both courts are in the same circuit.

PROBLEM 2.3   Create an example to demonstrate the principle outlined in the previous paragraph. Use the Ninth Circuit as your circuit. This circuit includes the states of Alaska, Arizona, California, Hawaii, Idaho, Montana, Nevada, Oregon, and Washington, as well as Guam and the Northern Mariana Islands.

Primary authority in the field of bankruptcy (statutes, rules, and cases) will be covered in Sections 1, 2, and 3, respectively, of this chapter. Secondary authority (legislative history, treatises, periodicals, and form books and how they can be used in understanding the law of bankruptcy) will be covered in Section 4.

SECTION 1
THE BANKRUPTCY CODE

The Bankruptcy Reform Act of 1978, Public Law 95–598, is known as the Bankruptcy Code, or just the Code. Public Law 95–598, in its original form, can be found in the United States Statutes at Large. The designation "public law" distinguishes this bill from a "private law." A **public law** affects the nation as a whole or deals with individuals as a class and relates to public matters. A **private law** benefits only a specific individual or class of individuals and does not relate to public matters. The numbers before the dash (in this case, "95") refer to the number of the Congress. This bill came out of the 95th Congress. The numbers after the dash (in this case, "598") mean that this was the 598th bill passed by this Congress. Because the bills are arranged in the United States Statutes at Large in chronological order, rather than by subject, an amendment to this bill might not be found near 95–598.

The public laws found in the Statutes at Large are incorporated into the **United States Code** (U.S.C.). The United States Code is updated annually with cumulative supplements. It is printed and sold by the U.S. Government Printing Office and is the official edition of federal statutes. U.S.C. is organized by title and section. The citation "11 U.S.C. § 301" would mean section 301 (not page 301) of Title 11 (not volume 11) of the United States Code.

Since the U.S. Government Printing Office was slow to publish U.S.C., West Publishing Company created the series United States Code Annotated. This series, abbreviated U.S.C.A., is also organized by title and section. A statute cited as 11 U.S.C. § 301 would appear in the United States Code Annotated as 11 U.S.C.A. § 301. United States Code Annotated has several features not found in the United States Code. For example, if a Code section has been cited and discussed in a court opinion, an annotation of that opinion is included following the Code section discussed. Lawyers Co-operative Publishing Co./Bancroft Whitney Co. publishes the United States Code Service (U.S.C.S.), which is similar to U.S.C.A. United States Code Annotated will also reference American Law Reports and other Lawyers Co-operative/Bancroft Whitney publications.

Although 11 U.S.C. (the codification of bankruptcy law) and 28 U.S.C. (the provisions relating to the structure and jurisdiction of bankruptcy courts) are the substantive and procedural laws of bankruptcy, not a great deal of the "how to do it" procedural law is contained in either title of the Code. Instead, Congress decided to leave procedural matters primarily as a part of the rule making function of the United States Supreme Court. The bankruptcy rules are discussed in Section 2 of this chapter.

The provisions in 28 U.S.C. relating to bankruptcy have undergone considerable change since the enactment of the Bankruptcy Reform Act of 1978. Title 28 provisions relate to the jurisdiction of the bankruptcy court, **venue** of cases and proceedings under Title 11, removal of cases to the bankruptcy court, the structure of the court, and the appointment of bankruptcy judges. Matters pertaining to appeals in bankruptcy cases and the regulation of the United States trustees are also found in Title 28 provisions.

As pointed out in Chapter One, the drafters wrote the Code using only odd-numbered chapters: 1, 3, 5, 7, 9, 11, 13, 15. The even numbers were reserved for later additions to the Code. Chapter 15, which pertains to the pilot program for U.S. trustees, was repealed on October 27, 1986, thereby reducing the number of chapters from 1 through 15 to 1 through 13. Although Chapter 15 was repealed, the United States trustee concept was not discarded but was made a permanent part of bankruptcy law applicable to most bankruptcy courts. Pub. L. 99–554. The United States trustee chapter was not included in the 1986 version of the Bankruptcy Code (i.e., 11 U.S.C.) but became Chapter 39 of Title 28 of the United States Code (i.e., 28 U.S.C.).

Public Law 99–554 also includes the Family Farmer Bankruptcy Act of 1986. This added Chapter 12, entitled "Adjustment of Debts of a Family Farmer with Regular Annual Income," to the Code. Chapter 12 was tailored for family farmers whose needs are not met by Chapter 11 or Chapter 13. The current Code chapters are

Chapter 1   General Provisions
Chapter 3   Case Administration
Chapter 5   Creditors, Debtor, and the Estate
Chapter 7   Liquidation
Chapter 9   Adjustment of Debts of a Municipality
Chapter 11   Reorganization
Chapter 12   Adjustment of Debts of a Family Farmer with Regular Annual
               Income
Chapter 13   Adjustment of Debts of an Individual with Regular Income

The chapters of the Code, are readily divided into two groups. Chapter 1, Chapter 3, and Chapter 5 are the universal chapters. Chapter 7, Chapter 9, Chapter 11, Chapter 12, and Chapter 13 are the operative chapters.

If the section number has three digits, the first digit designates the chapter. If the section number has four digits, the first two digits designate the chapter.

EXAMPLES
Section 101 is in Chapter 1.
Section 547 is in Chapter 5.
Section 1107 is in Chapter 11.

PROBLEM 2.4   In which chapter of the Bankruptcy Code is each of the following sections found?

Section 1324
Section 324
Section 1112
Section 501

A. THE UNIVERSAL CHAPTERS

The universal chapters of the Code (1, 3, and 5) contain important definitional and administrative provisions that generally apply to all operative chapters of the Code. Only a few of the sections of Chapter 3 and Chapter 5, however, apply to Chapter 9. 11 U.S.C.A. §§ 103(e), 901.

EXAMPLE
Jane Dillon filed for bankruptcy under Chapter 7 of the Code. The provisions of Chapter 7, rather than the provisions of Chapter 9, 11, 12, or 13, will apply to Jane's case. The provisions of the universal chapters (1, 3, and 5) will also apply to Jane's case.

Richard Ramirez filed for reorganization under Chapter 11 of the Code. The provisions of Chapter 11, rather than the provisions of Chapter 7, 9, 12, or 13, will apply to Richard's case. The provisions of the universal chapters (1, 3, and 5) will also apply to Richard's case.

1. CHAPTER 1—GENERAL PROVISIONS

The Bankruptcy Code contains its own set of definitions, and they are found in Chapter 1. If a term used in the Bankruptcy Code is defined in the Bankruptcy Code, then the Bankruptcy Code definition applies and any non-Bankruptcy Code definition is inapplicable.

EXAMPLE

The Bankruptcy Code defines **debtor** as a "person or municipality concerning which a case under this title has been commenced." 11 U.S.C.A. § 101(13). Article 9 of the Uniform Commercial Code defines **debtor** as "the person who owes payment or other performance of the obligation secured, whether or not he owns or has rights in the collateral, and includes the seller of **accounts** or **chattel paper.** Where the debtor and the owner of the collateral are not the same person, the term 'debtor' means the owner of the collateral in any provision of the Article dealing with the collateral, the obligor in any provision dealing with the obligation, and may include both where the context so requires." UCC § 9–105(1)(d).

If the case is a bankruptcy case, the Bankruptcy Code definition of debtor will apply, rather than the UCC definition.

PROBLEM 2.5   Compare the Bankruptcy Code definition of "security interest" with the Uniform Commercial Code definition; i.e., compare 11 U.S.C.A. § 101(51) with UCC § 1–201(37). Does each cover real estate mortgages?

Section 101 of Chapter 1 provides an extensive list of definitions. The definitions found in section 101 apply to *all* other Bankruptcy Code sections, whether the section is found in Chapter 1 or in Chapter 3, 5, 7, 9, 11, 12, or 13. The terms defined in section 101 are arranged alphabetically.

PROBLEM 2.6   How does the Bankruptcy Code define the term "creditor"?

PROBLEM 2.7   Are the following "entities" under the Bankruptcy Code?

1. a relative who lent the debtor money
2. a partnership that sold the debtor goods on credit
3. a corporation that sold the debtor goods on credit
4. an estate that sold the debtor heirlooms on credit
5. a trust fund that owed the debtor wages for services
6. a school district that owed the debtor money for services
7. the United States trustee

A term found in a Bankruptcy Code section may itself contain terms that need to be defined. In this case, the process of using the Code to define the term continues until all the terms are defined.

EXAMPLE

A debtor under Chapter 7 may convert the case from Chapter 7 to another chapter.

(a) The debtor may convert a case under this chapter to a case under chapter 11, 12, or 13 of this title at any time, if the case has not been converted under section 1112, 1208, or 1307 of this title. Any waiver of the right to convert a case under this subsection is unenforceable. 11 U.S.C.A. § 706(a).

The term "debtor" is defined in 11 U.S.C.A. § 101(13) as

> [a] person or municipality concerning which a case under this title has been commenced.

The term "person" in section 101(13) is defined in section 101(41) to include

> individual, partnership, and corporation, but does not include governmental unit, except that a governmental unit that—
> (A) acquires an asset from a person—
> (i) as a result of the operation of a loan guarantee agreement; or
> (ii) as receiver or liquidating agent of a person;
> (B) is a guarantor of a pension benefit payable by or on behalf of the debtor or an affiliate of the debtor; or
> (C) is the legal or beneficial owner of an asset of—
> (i) an employee pension benefit plan that is a governmental plan, as defined in section 414(d) of the Internal Revenue Code of 1986; or
> (ii) an eligible deferred compensation plan, as defined in section 457(b) of the Internal Revenue Code of 1986;
> shall be considered, for purposes of section 1102 of this title, to be a person with respect to such asset or such benefit.

The term "governmental unit" is defined in section 101(27) to mean

> United States; State; Commonwealth; District; Territory; municipality; foreign state; department, agency, or instrumentality of the United States (but not a United States trustee while serving as a trustee in a case under this title), a State, a Commonwealth, a District, a Territory, a municipality, or a foreign state; or other foreign or domestic government.

PROBLEM 2.8   Which terms in the following section, 11 U.S.C.A. § 545, statutory liens, are defined in section 101?

> The trustee may avoid the fixing of a statutory lien on property of the debtor to the extent that such lien—
>
> (1) first becomes effective against the debtor—
>   (A) when a case under this title concerning the debtor is commenced;
>   (B) when an insolvency proceeding other than under this title concerning the debtor is commenced;
>   (C) when a custodian is appointed or authorized to take or takes possession;
>   (D) when the debtor becomes insolvent;
>   (E) when the debtor's financial condition fails to meet a specified standard; or
>   (F) at the time of an execution against property of the debtor levied at the instance of an entity other than the holder of such statutory lien;
> (2) is not perfected or enforceable at the time of the commencement of the case against a bona fide purchaser that purchases such property at the time of the commencement of the case, whether or not such a purchaser exists;
> (3) is for rent; or
> (4) is a lien of distress for rent.

It should be noted that not all Code definitions are found in section 101. Various chapters and subchapters of the Code also contain definitions. If, however, a definition is contained in an operative chapter rather than in Chapter 1, the definition will apply only to the chapter in which it is found and not to all other chapters.

EXAMPLE

Section 741 defines nine terms for use in Subchapter III (Stockbroker Liquidation) of Chapter 7:

1. Commission
2. Customer
3. Customer name security
4. Customer property
5. Margin payment
6. Net equity
7. Securities contract
8. Settlement payment
9. SIPC

Section 1101 defines two terms for use in Chapter 11 (Reorganization):

1. Debtor in possession
2. Substantial consummation

Not all terms are defined in the Code. When this occurs, a definition can sometimes be gleaned from the term's usage in the Code, from case law, or from common usage in the bankruptcy court.

PROBLEM 2.9   Is the term "party [or parties] in interest" defined in the Code? Does **party in interest** include the trustee, examiners, U.S. trustee, indenture trustee, creditors, and equity security holders? Are other entities of the U.S. government or state government, who do not hold a claim or have regulatory duties, parties in interest? See 11 U.S.C.A. § 102(1).

In addition to the general definitions provided in Chapter 1, a few other highlights are worth a brief mention. Chapter 1 defines the concept of "after notice and a hearing."

> The concept is central to the bill and to the separation of the administrative and judicial functions of bankruptcy judges. The phrase means after such notice as is appropriate in the particular circumstances (to be prescribed by either the Rules of Bankruptcy Procedure or by the court in individual circumstances that the Rules do not cover. In many cases, the Rules provide for combined notice of several proceedings), and such opportunity for a hearing as is appropriate in the particular circumstances. Thus, a hearing will not be necessary in every instance. If there is no objection to the proposed action, the action may go ahead without court action. This is a significant change from present law [the Bankruptcy Act of 1898], which requires the affirmative approval of the bankruptcy judge for almost every action. The change will permit the bankruptcy judge to stay removed from the administration of the bankruptcy or reorganization case, and to become involved only when there is a dispute about a proposed action, that is, only when there is an objection. The phrase "such opportunity for a hearing as is appropriate in the particular circumstances" is designed to permit the Rules and the courts to expedite or dispose with hearings when speed is essential. 11 U.S.C.A. § 102, Notes of Committee on the Judiciary, Senate Report No. 95–989.

Chapter 1 describes who may be a debtor and under which chapters a particular debtor may file a petition. 11 U.S.C.A. § 109. Chapter 1 also sets forth which chapters are applicable to a particular case under Title 11. 11 U.S.C.A. § 103.

2. CHAPTER 3—CASE ADMINISTRATION

Chapter 3 is a very important chapter of Title 11 in terms of the progress of a case through the bankruptcy court. Chapter 3 is divided into four subchapters:

Subchapter I   Commencement of a Case
Subchapter II   Officers
Subchapter III   Administration
Subchapter IV   Administrative Powers

Subchapter I (Commencement of a Case) provides for the voluntary or involuntary commencement of a case. 11 U.S.C.A. §§ 301, 303. It also authorizes an individual debtor to file a joint case with his or her spouse. 11 U.S.C.A. § 302. The court has the power to dismiss a case or to suspend all proceedings in a case. 11 U.S.C.A. § 305.

Subchapter II (Officers) covers the eligibility and qualifications of a trustee in bankruptcy, the role and capacity of the trustee, and provisions relating to compensation of trustees and professional persons employed in the administration of bankruptcy estates. 11 U.S.C.A. §§ 321–331.

Subchapter III (Administration) focuses on such topics as the meeting of creditors and equity security holders (commonly known as "the 341 meeting"), notice, examination of the debtor, self-incrimination and immunity, effect of conversion, effect of dismissal, and the closing and reopening of the case. 11 U.S.C.A. §§ 341–350.

Subchapter IV (Administrative Powers) imposes an **automatic stay** on actions against the debtor or his or her estate and authorizes the trustee to use, sell, or lease collateral in the debtor's business and to obtain credit. 11 U.S.C.A. §§ 362–364. Utilities are prohibited from altering, refraining, or discontinuing service because of nonpayment of a bill or because the debtor has filed a petition in bankruptcy. 11 U.S.C.A. § 366. If the entity affected is not afforded **adequate protection,** relief from the automatic stay will be granted or the trustee's proposed use, sale, lease, or borrowing against collateral will be prohibited. 11 U.S.C.A. § 361. Adequate protection may include cash payments, additional collateral, or replacement collateral. The trustee may assume or reject any **executory contract** or **unexpired lease** of the debtor. 11 U.S.C.A. § 365.

3. CHAPTER 5—CREDITORS, DEBTOR, AND THE ESTATE

Chapter 5 is divided into three subchapters:

Subchapter I   Creditors and Claims
Subchapter II   Debtor's Duties and Benefits
Subchapter III   The Estate

Subchapter I (Creditors and Claims) regulates the filing of **proofs of claim** or **proofs of interest,** the allowance of claims or interests, the allowance of administrative expenses, the determination of secured status, and priorities. 11 U.S.C.A. §§ 501–510. The section entitled "Determination of Secured Status" is generally regarded as one of the most important sections of Chapter 5. 11 U.S.C.A. § 506. The "Priorities" section sets forth which expenses and claims have priority and in what order. 11 U.S.C.A. § 507.

Subchapter II (Debtor's Duties and Benefits) describes the debtor's duties, provides the debtor with a choice between state and federal exemptions (unless the debtor's state has opted out of the federal exemptions), and states the effect of discharge. 11 U.S.C.A. §§ 521–524. The Code prevents discriminatory treatment of debtors. 11 U.S.C.A. § 525. This is the codification of the "fresh-start" policy, which allows the debtor to begin a new fiscal life.

The discharge provisions (11 U.S.C.A. §§ 523, 524) are of critical importance and must be read in conjunction with related provisions in the operative chapters. In Chapter 7, they are read in conjunction with section 727 (discharge); in Chapter

9, with section 944 (effect of confirmation); in Chapter 11, with section 1141 (effect of confirmation); in Chapter 12, with section 1228 (discharge); and in Chapter 13, with section 1328 (discharge).

Subchapter III (The Estate) focuses on what the **estate** consists of and on how it is collected by the trustee. 11 U.S.C.A. §§ 541, 543. Under this subchapter, the trustee has the power to avoid certain transfers, the fixing of a statutory lien, and preferences. 11 U.S.C.A. §§ 544–549. This authority furnishes the trustee with powerful means by which to collect the **property of the estate** for distribution to creditors or to preserve the property of the estate so the plan for reorganization can be successful. The trustee also has the power to **abandon property of the estate** if it is burdensome or of inconsequential value and benefit to the estate. 11 U.S.C.A. § 554.

B. THE OPERATIVE CHAPTERS

The Code has five operative chapters—Chapters 7, 9, 11, 12, and 13:

Chapter 7	Liquidation
Chapter 9	Adjustment of Debts of a Municipality
Chapter 11	Reorganization
Chapter 12	Adjustment of Debts of a Family Farmer with Regular Annual Income
Chapter 13	Adjustment of Debts of an Individual with Regular Income

Each operative chapter generally relates only to cases being administered under that particular chapter. Some Chapter 11 sections, however, apply to Chapter 9, and some Chapter 7 sections apply to Chapter 11. 11 U.S.C.A. §§ 103(b)–(i), 901, 1106.

1. CHAPTER 7—LIQUIDATION

Of the five operative chapters, only one—Chapter 7—deals with **liquidation,** the distribution of the debtor's estate to his or her creditors, as its only option. The other four operative chapters—Chapters 9, 11, 12, and 13—deal with restructuring the debt.

Liquidation under Chapter 7 is available to all persons who may be debtors under this chapter, whether they are individuals, partnerships, or corporations. Railroads, insurance companies, and certain banking institutions may not be debtors under Chapter 7. A debtor need not be insolvent to take advantage of Chapter 7 liquidation. 11 U.S.C.A. § 109(b).

Chapter 7 deals specifically with the liquidation bankruptcy in which a trustee gathers up the debtor's assets, sells them, and generally makes a one-time distribution to creditors. In some cases, there may be more than one distribution. Chapter 7 cases constitute the bulk of original bankruptcy filings. In addition to the cases originally filed as liquidation cases, many Chapter 11 and Chapter 13 filings will eventually convert to Chapter 7 filings. The Chapter 12 debtor may also convert to Chapter 7. 11 U.S.C.A. § 1208(a).

Two particularly significant sections in Chapter 7 are sections 707 and 727. Section 707 provides for dismissal of a case for dilatory tactics, nonpayment of fees, and substantial abuse of Chapter 7. The presumption, however, is in favor of the debtor. Section 727 (discharge) is the *raison d'être* of a bankruptcy filing. In order for a debtor to obtain a discharge, he or she must meet the Chapter 7 criteria for discharge as read in conjunction with the exceptions to discharge found in Chapter 5. 11 U.S.C.A. §§ 523, 727.

2. CHAPTER 9—ADJUSTMENT OF DEBTS OF A MUNICIPALITY

Chapter 9 is the least used operative chapter of the Code because the debtor must be a municipality to qualify for this chapter. If a paralegal is employed by an attorney representing either the debtor or the creditor in a municipal bankruptcy, sections 103 and 901 would be the point of embarkation. These sections list which sections in Chapters 1, 3, 5, and 11 will apply to a Chapter 9 case. 11 U.S.C.A. §§ 103, 901.

3. CHAPTER 11—REORGANIZATION

Chapter 11—the only chapter entitled "Reorganization" (although Chapters 9, 12, and 13 also involve restructuring of debt)—begins with the definition of **debtor in possession.** In the practice of law, debtor in possession is often abbreviated as: **DIP** and pronounced as initials: D I P.

Chapter 11 is the chapter of choice for many businesses, large and small, filing for relief under the Code. This chapter has just become an even more practical choice for the **small business**, given the new "fast track" provision in the Code. 11 U.S.C.A. § 1121(e). The **order for relief** in a Chapter 11 case offers a respite from the demands of creditors and affords an opportunity for the beleaguered business to resolve its difficulties. The ability to remain in operation enables the DIP to preserve ongoing relationships with both suppliers and customers as well as to keep employees on the job. 11 U.S.C.A. § 1108. The assets of some debtors may be liquidated, however, under a Chapter 11 liquidation plan. 11 U.S.C.A. § 1141(d)(3)(A).

4. CHAPTER 12—ADJUSTMENT OF DEBTS OF A FAMILY FARMER WITH REGULAR ANNUAL INCOME

Chapter 12 applies only to a special category of debtor. For Chapter 12 to apply, the debtor must be a **family farmer** with **regular annual income.** The definition of "family farmer," found in section 101(18), is long and complicated.

> (18) "family farmer" means—
>> (A) individual or individual and spouse engaged in a farming operation whose aggregate debts do not exceed $1,500,000 and not less than 80 percent of whose aggregate noncontingent, liquidated debts (excluding a debt for the principal residence of such individual or such individual and spouse unless such debt arises out of a farming operation), on the date the case is filed, arise out of a farming operation owned or operated by such individual or such individual and spouse, and such individual or such individual and spouse receive from such farming operation more than 50 percent of such individual's or such individual and spouse's gross income for the taxable year preceding the taxable year in which the case concerning such individual or such individual and spouse was filed; or
>> (B) corporation or partnership in which more than 50 percent of the outstanding stock or equity is held by one family, or by one family and the relatives of the members of such family, and such family or such relatives conduct the farming operation; and
>>> (i) more than 80 percent of the value of its assets consist of assets related to the farming operation;
>>> (ii) its aggregate debts do not exceed $1,500,000 and not less than 80 percent of its aggregate noncontingent, liquidated debts (excluding a debt for one dwelling which is owned by such corporation or partnership and which a shareholder or partner maintains as a principal residence, unless such debt arises out of a farming operation), on the date the case is filed, arise out of the farming operation owned or operated by such corporation or such partnership; and
>>> (iii) if such corporation issues stock, such stock is not publicly traded.

PROBLEM 2.10   Farmer Brown wants to file for bankruptcy under Chapter 12. Her aggregate debt totals $1,345,000. Of that debt, 85 percent arises from a farming operation. Of her gross income for the taxable year last year, 60 percent was derived from farming. Is Farmer Brown a "family farmer" and therefore eligible for Chapter 12?

5. CHAPTER 13—ADJUSTMENT OF DEBTS OF AN INDIVIDUAL WITH REGULAR INCOME

Chapter 13, like Chapter 12, applies only to a special category of debtor. For Chapter 13 to apply, the debtor must be an individual with regular income. Therefore, corporations and partnerships are not eligible for protection under Chapter 13. It is important to note that only a debtor may file a Chapter 13 petition. This means that creditors cannot force a debtor into bankruptcy under Chapter 13.

PROBLEM 2.11   Michael Gelt has never worked at a paying job. He lives on the regular income from a trust set up for his benefit by his grandmother. Michael has expensive tastes and is in debt for clothing, airfare, hotels, and restaurants. Is Michael eligible to file a petition under Chapter 13?

In a Chapter 13 case, the debtor retains possession of property of the estate. 11 U.S.C.A. § 1306(b). This is in contrast to a Chapter 7 case, in which the trustee is required to "collect and reduce to money the property of the estate." 11 U.S.C.A. § 704. This means that creditors in a Chapter 7 case will be paid by the trustee after he or she has collected and sold the property of the estate, but creditors in a Chapter 13 case will be paid by the trustee with money earned by the debtor after the filing of the petition.

SECTION 2
THE FEDERAL RULES OF BANKRUPTCY PROCEDURE AND OFFICIAL FORMS

The provision of the judiciary code relating to rules of the bankruptcy courts is found at 28 U.S.C.A. § 2075. This provision gives the United States Supreme Court the power to prescribe by general rules the forms of process, writs, pleadings and motions, and the practice and procedure in cases under Title 11. This provision requires that such rules shall not abridge, enlarge, or modify any substantive right; accordingly, the bankruptcy rules may relate only to procedural law and not to substantive law. Rules prescribed by the United States Supreme Court under this section generally take effect 90 days after they have been reported to Congress by the chief justice.

A. THE FEDERAL RULES OF BANKRUPTCY PROCEDURE AND OFFICIAL FORMS

The early predecessors of the Federal Rules of Bankruptcy Procedure were the general orders in bankruptcy adopted by the United States Supreme Court in 1898 pursuant to the authority of section 30 of the Bankruptcy Act, which was enacted in the same year. The general orders themselves provided for a set of official forms. The Federal Rules of Civil Procedure also had limited applicability.

Under the rule making authority of 28 U.S.C.A. § 2075, the Supreme Court, commencing in 1973, issued Rules of Bankruptcy Procedure for general application in the bankruptcy courts. New rules were necessitated by the passage of the Bankruptcy Reform Act of 1978. New rules of practice and procedure applicable to the bankruptcy courts were adopted and became effective August 1, 1983, and were known as the Rules of Bankruptcy Procedure. Further changes were necessitated by the ruling of the Supreme Court in *Northern Pipeline Construction Co. v. Marathon Pipe Line Co.,* 458 U.S. 50 (1982). These rules were submitted to Congress by the Supreme Court on March 30, 1987, and became effective August 1, 1987.

On August 1, 1991, the Federal Rules of Bankruptcy Procedure replaced the Bankruptcy Rules. Although the new rules did not radically change the substance of many of the old rules, the new rules updated the rules to correspond with the 1986 Amendments to the Bankruptcy Code and integrated the former U.S. Trustee Rules and former Interim Chapter 12 Rules into the new rules.

The Federal Rules of Bankruptcy Procedure is subdivided into nine parts:

Part I	Commencement of Case; Proceedings Relating to Petition and Order for Relief
Part II	Officers and Administration; Notices; Meetings; Examinations; Elections; Attorneys and Accountants
Part III	Claims and Distribution to Creditors and Equity Interest Holders; Plans
Part IV	The Debtor: Duties and Benefits
Part V	Courts and Clerks
Part VI	Collection and Liquidation of the Estate
Part VII	Adversary Proceedings
Part VIII	Appeals to District Court or Bankruptcy Appellate Panel
Part IX	General Provisions

Part I of the Federal Rules of Bankruptcy Procedure deals with the commencement of cases and with proceedings related to the petition and order for relief in both voluntary and involuntary cases. Part I also contains the rules governing proceedings initiated by such involuntary petitions.

Part II sets forth the rules pertaining to the court's officers and administration, together with notices, meetings, examinations, and elections of trustees. Part II also treats the important subject of the appointment and employment of attorneys and accountants for trustees and debtors in possession.

Part III handles the claims and distribution to creditors and equity interest holders. Part III also covers the filing and confirmation of plans in Chapter 9, 11, and 13 cases.

Part IV considers the duties of the debtor and the important benefits to the debtor, including the right to the defense of the automatic stay, claim of exemptions, proceedings dealing with the determination of dischargeability of a debt, and proceedings relating to discharge and reaffirmation hearings.

Part V provides for the operation of the court and the court clerk's office. Part V also covers record keeping, the handling of funds of bankruptcy estates, and the closing and reopening of cases. Rule 5011 deals with the matter of withdrawal of reference of a case or proceeding and abstention of the bankruptcy court from hearing a proceeding.

Part VI governs the collection and liquidation of the estate and covers such things as disbursement of money of the estate; the use, sale, or lease of property; and use of auctioneers and appraisers. Part VI also deals with the important matters of assumption, rejection and assignment of executory contracts, and abandonment or other disposition of property, together with redemption of property from a lien.

Part VII, which governs adversary proceedings, basically tracks the Federal Rules of Civil Procedure. Some Part VII rules apply to contested matters.

Part VIII provides for appeals of decisions of the bankruptcy courts to the district court or bankruptcy appellate panels.

Part IX is a collection of general provisions, including definitions and regulations of notices. Rule 9014 sets the procedures for contested matters.

Appended to the Federal Rules of Bankruptcy Procedure is a set of 19 official forms. These forms include the schedules and statement of affairs that are filed as an important part of the commencement of each bankruptcy case. Their detailed format should prove very helpful to the paralegal. Commercially prepared forms are available from a number of sources nationally and may also be available locally. For the student who would like to see some forms at this point, Chapter 7 forms are found in Chapter Five of this text.

The Bankruptcy Code, Federal Rules of Bankruptcy Procedure, and official forms are printed by several publishers in paperback format and are updated annually. An example is *Bankruptcy Code, Rules and Forms* by West Publishing Company. Several bankruptcy filing programs are available for the computer user, including

WEST'S ® BANKRUPTCY PRACTICE SYSTEMS: CHAPTERS SEVEN ● ELEVEN ● TWELVE ● THIRTEEN

The U.S. Government Printing Office reproduces some forms for the bankruptcy practitioner. They are available from the office of the clerk of the bankruptcy court. Many are standard required forms and are available from commercial sources as well. The office of the clerk of the bankruptcy court will also have copies of local court rules and various printed handouts related to filing requirements. The handouts may include such things as a sample of the acceptable format for the label matrix.

A major development is West's CD-ROM Bankruptcy Library. This computer database contains bankruptcy cases (1979 to date); the *Bankruptcy Annotated Code, Rules, and Forms; West's® Bankruptcy Digest; Cowans Bankruptcy Law and Practice;* Epstein, Nickles, and White, *Bankruptcy; Bankruptcy Bibliography;* and Russell, *Bankruptcy Evidence Manual.*

B. THE LOCAL RULES

District courts and bankruptcy courts write their own rules to supplement the Bankruptcy Code and the Federal Rules of Bankruptcy Procedure. Both sets of court rules must be consulted in bankruptcy matters.

1. DISTRICT COURT RULES

Many district courts have adopted local rules concerning bankruptcy cases and proceedings. These rules deal with the reference of cases and proceedings and the withdrawal of such references. These district court rules also deal with review of bankruptcy court decisions and appeals of the decisions of bankruptcy judges. Copies of the local district court rules may be obtained from the office of the clerk of the United States district court.

2. BANKRUPTCY COURT RULES

Each bankruptcy court has adopted a set of local rules. The rules adopted by the bankruptcy court must not be inconsistent with the bankruptcy rules emanating from either the district court or the United States Supreme Court. Copies of the local bankruptcy court rules may be obtained from the office of the clerk of the bankruptcy court.

BANKRUPTCY LAW CASES

Although a few state court cases find their way into the law of bankruptcy, most cases are from the federal courts. As Exhibit 2.1 illustrates, the federal court structure for bankruptcy has four tiers: United States Bankruptcy Court, United States District Court, United States Court of Appeals, United States Supreme Court.

A petition in bankruptcy is initiated in a United States bankruptcy court. Each of the 93 federal districts has a United States bankruptcy court. After litigation of an issue in bankruptcy court, the judge may decide to write an opinion. The judge will decide whether the opinion will be published or will remain unpublished. These decisions appear in the *Bankruptcy Reporter,* published by West Publishing Co. and cited B.R. or Bankr.; *Bankruptcy Court Decisions*, published by CRR Publishing Co. and cited B.C.D. or Bankr.Ct.Dec. (CCR); *Collier's Bankruptcy Cases*, published by Matthew Bender and cited C.B.C.2d or Collier Bankr.Cas.2d (MB); and *Bankruptcy Law Reporter,* published by Commerce Clearing House and cited Bankr.L.Rep. (CCH).

If, however, a bankruptcy proceeding only involves rights created by the Constitution, by state law, or even by common law (as distinguished from congressionally created rights), the proceeding must be initiated in a United States district court rather than in a United States bankruptcy court. The district court judge may decide to write an opinion and that opinion may be published or may remain un-

EXHIBIT 2.1
Federal Court Structure for Bankruptcy

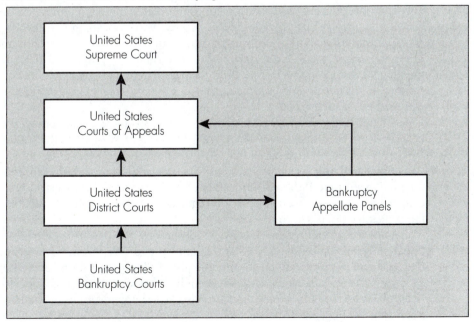

published. If published, these opinions appear in the *Federal Supplement,* published by West Publishing Co. and cited F.Supp., as well as in the *Bankruptcy Reporter, Bankruptcy Court Decisions, Collier's Bankruptcy Cases,* and *Bankruptcy Law Reporter.*

If an issue is appealed from the bankruptcy court, it will be appealed to the United States district court. The issue may be referred to a **bankruptcy appellate panel** if one has been appointed by the judicial council of a circuit. This panel is made up of three bankruptcy judges from districts within the circuit. A judge is not allowed to hear an appeal originating within that judge's own district. Consent of all the parties is necessary for a case to be heard by an appellate panel.

Appellate panels have not been established in many circuits. The number of panels are expected to increase under amended 28 U.S.C.A. § 158(b). The language has been changed from "may establish" to "shall establish," with exceptions made for "insufficient judicial resources" or "undue delay or increased cost to parties." Appellate panels are a practical solution only in heavily populated areas in which there are three sitting judges in close proximity. Not only would it be difficult to form an appellate panel in a less populated circuit, it would most likely be unnecessary because the number of appeals would be small. The exceptions were made to provide for these less populated circuits.

If an issue is appealed from the district court, it will be appealed to a United States circuit court. The 93 districts are allocated among 12 circuits. The opinions from the circuits are printed in the *Federal Reporter,* published by West Publishing Co. and cited F.2d. They may also be found in the *Bankruptcy Reporter, Bankruptcy Court Decisions, Collier's Bankruptcy Cases,* and *Bankruptcy Law Reporter.*

More and more bankruptcy cases are finding their way to the United States Supreme Court. The Supreme Court, the highest court, is a court of limited jurisdiction. Those bankruptcy cases that get to the Supreme Court do so by appeal or *certiorari.* The opinions of the Supreme Court are published in *United States Reports,* official edition and cited U.S.; *United States Supreme Court Reports,* Lawyers' Edition, published by Lawyers Co-operative Publishing Co./Bancroft Whitney Co. and cited L.Ed.2d; *Supreme Court Reporter,* published by West Publishing Co. and cited S.Ct.; *United States Law Week,* published by the Bureau of National Affairs and cited U.S.L.W.; and *United States Supreme Court Bulletin,* published by Commerce Clearing House and cited S.Ct.Bull. (CCH). They may also be found in the *Bankruptcy Reporter, Bankruptcy Court Decisions, Collier's Bankruptcy Cases,* and *Bankruptcy Law Reporter.*

In addition to the standard hard copy, opinions from all the federal courts can be found in the databases of WESTLAW, LEXIS, and West's CD-ROM Bankruptcy Library. Some unreported cases may also be located in these databases.

Shepardizing is an essential part of any legal research. Once an appropriate case has been found, the current status of that case must be investigated. Has the case been appealed, overruled, or distinguished? Are there other cases that follow the principles discussed in this case?

Shepard's Bankruptcy Citations, published by McGraw-Hill, provides this up-to-date information on the history and treatment of a case through a system of elaborate abbreviations. An explanation of the use of *Shepard's* is found at the beginning of each volume. Also included are citations of law reviews and *American Law Reports. Shepard's Bankruptcy Citations* also lists statute citations to the bankruptcy provisions of the United States Code.

SECTION 4
SECONDARY AUTHORITY

In the field of bankruptcy, secondary authority provides an insight into the Bankruptcy Code and how it is or ought to be applied to specific problems. Secondary authority may give a paralegal the drafters' intent when the Code was drafted, a lead to cases interpreting and applying specific provisions of the Code, or a legal scholar's interpretations and applications of specific provisions of the Code. The following is a brief introduction to some of the secondary sources that may aid a paralegal in his or her research.

A. LEGISLATIVE HISTORY

The legislative history concerning the Bankruptcy Code begins with the Commission Report, continues with the congressional hearings, and concludes with the House and Senate reports and statements concerning compromise as reported in the *Congressional Record*. Great care should be exercised when using legislative history because the legislative process itself is one of evolution. The legislation ultimately enacted and signed into law may differ greatly from the proposed legislation. The ultimate legislation may have been changed so the legislative history is no longer relevant. These changes may be obvious or subtle. Also, legislative history, even when relevant, is only secondary authority. The legislation itself is the primary, mandatory authority. A court may decide that Congress did not say what it intended to say.

B. DIGESTS

As discussed earlier in this chapter, past cases may be helpful in determining how a court will interpret and apply the Bankruptcy Code and other federal and state statutes. The following digests, published by West Publishing Co., are helpful in the bankruptcy field:

- *Federal Practice Digest* 3d
- *Federal Practice Digest* 4th
- *West's Bankruptcy Digest*

These digests abstract a one-sentence explanation of a topic in a case and provide the name and citation of the case. To find appropriate cases, the descriptive word index is used to identify a West digest topic and key number. Once an appropriate topic and key number are found, the West digests can be used to locate cases on that subject.

C. LOOSE-LEAF SERVICES

Loose-leaf services help keep legal professionals updated in a specialized area. Recent developments in a given field are updated weekly, biweekly, or monthly, and information is provided on recent cases, statutes, regulations, and current developments in the law. Loose-leaf services cover all jurisdictions and often report relevant lower court decisions that are not available in other case reports.

Loose-leaf services vary in format. Some have a "how-to-use" section, which is usually located at the beginning of the first volume. This section will explain what the treatise contains, how the particular treatise is organized, and how the needed information can be found. If a loose-leaf service does not contain a how-to-use section, the index or index volume can provide similar information.

Some well-known bankruptcy loose-leaf services are

- *Bankruptcy Law Reporter* (Commerce Clearing House)
- *Bankruptcy Service,* Lawyers' Edition (Clark Boardman Callaghan)
- *Collier on Bankruptcy* (15th ed., Matthew Bender)
- Murphy, *Creditors' Rights in Bankruptcy* (Shepard's/McGraw-Hill)
- Norton, *Bankruptcy Law and Practice* (2d ed., Clark Boardman Callaghan)

D. TREATISES

A treatise is a book by a legal expert that covers a particular legal subject in depth. Treatises are useful as a starting point for background research and as a way of later refining the point of research. Published as a single volume or as a multiple-volume series, treatises offer interpretation and analysis of the law pertaining to a particular subject, as well as the author's opinion on how the law should be interpreted and applied. The authors often cite helpful cases and other sources.

Some well known bankruptcy treatises are

- Anderson, *Chapter 11 Reorganizations* (Shepard's/McGraw-Hill 1983)
- Bienenstock, *Bankruptcy Reorganization* (Practicing Law Institute 1987)
- Cowans, *Bankruptcy Law and Practice* (6th ed., West Publishing Co.)
- Drake, *Bankruptcy Practice for the General Practitioner* (Shephard's/McGraw-Hill 1980)
- Jackson, *The Logic and Limits of Bankruptcy Law* (Harvard University Press 1986)
- Lopucki, *Strategies for Creditors in Bankruptcy Proceedings* (2d ed., Little, Brown 1991)

Most of these treatises have some form of periodic supplementation.

E. LEGAL PERIODICALS

Legal periodicals include law school publications (the law reviews and law journals), bar association publications, special subject periodicals, and legal newspapers. Law reviews publish leading articles written by law professors, judges, and practitioners, and student written articles, notes, and comments. Law reviews are an excellent source of information concerning a specific topic.

A number of state, county, and local bar associations publish periodicals. Some bar association publications publish articles that are often more practice oriented than the articles that appear in the law reviews.

Subject journals focus on one area of law. *American Bankruptcy Law Journal* (Am.Bankr.L.J.) is a subject journal published in the field of bankruptcy.

Legal articles can be located through the following sources:

- Index to Legal Periodicals and Books (I.L.P.)
- WILSONDISC
- Current Law Index
- Legal Resource Index
- LegalTrac

Index to Legal Periodicals and Books, published by H. W. Wilson Co., is a printed index issued monthly (except for September). with quarterly, annual, and multi-year cumulations. It contains an author/subject index, a table of cases commented upon, a table of statutes commented upon, and a book review index.

The Index to Legal Periodicals database is also available in a CD-ROM format through the H. W. Wilson Company's WILSONDISC system. The I.L.P. on WILSONDISC is distributed monthly on a cumulative disc. The I.L.P. database is also available on LEXIS, WESTLAW, and WILSONLINE.

Current Law Index (C.L.I.), published by the Information Access Company in cooperation with the American Association of Law Libraries, is a printed index issued monthly, with quarterly and annual cumulations. It contains a subject index, an author/title index, a table of cases, and a table of statutes.

Legal Resource Index (L.R.I.), also published by Information Access Company in cooperation with the American Association of Law Libraries, contains all of the titles in the Current Law Index. Legal Resource Index also indexes legal newspapers as well as law related articles in the popular press.

The L.R.I. database is also available in a CD-ROM format called LegalTrac through the Information Access Company's InfoTrac system. LegalTrac is distributed monthly on a cumulative disc. The L.R.I. database is also found on WESTLAW, LEXIS, DIALOG, and Bibliographic Retrieval Service (B.R.S.). In addition, a microfilm version of L.R.I. can be read on a specially designed, automated microfilm reader.

F. AMERICAN LAW REPORTS

American Law Reports, published by Lawyers Co-operative Publishing Co./ Bancroft Whitney Co., is currently in its Fifth Series (A.L.R. 5th) (1992–date). A companion set, *American Law Reports, Federal* (A.L.R.Fed.) (1969–date), covers federal statutes and cases. A.L.R.5th does not replace the prior four series. A.L.R. annotations are extensive and provide a rich source of case decisions on a topic. Cases are cited from all jurisdictions; both majority and minority viewpoints are given. Each annotation cross-references other Lawyers Co-operative/Bancroft Whitney publications that contain discussions on the subject. Later volumes also reference publications of other publishers. A.L.R. is supplemented so that annotations remain current.

An A.L.R. annotation can be found through the multi-volume Index to Annotations, which covers A.L.R.2d, A.L.R.3d, A.L.R.4th, A.L.R.5th, and A.L.R.Fed. Each volume has a cumulative pocket supplement inside its back cover. These volumes also contain an annotation history table and a table of the laws, rules, and regulations. A.L.R. annotations may also be found through *Shepard's* and the *American Jurisprudence* series.

G. LEGAL ENCYCLOPEDIAS

The legal encyclopedias, *American Jurisprudence 2d*, published by Lawyers Co-operative Publishing Co./Bancroft Whitney Co. and cited Am.Jur.2d, *Corpus Juris Secundum,* published by West Publishing Co., and cited C.J.S., are organized alphabetically and contain discussions on a large variety of legal subjects. These encyclopedias have a table of contents for each topic as well as a multi-volume index for the complete set.

Am.Jur.2d does not attempt to cite all reported cases but only selected decisions. It cites relevant A.L.R. annotations.

C.J.S. attempts to cite all reported cases. It also refers to relevant West digest topics and key numbers, thus facilitating access to the American Digest System.

Basic Terms and Phrases

Abandoned property of the estate
Accounts
Adequate protection
Article I judge
Article III judge
Automatic stay
Bankruptcy appellate panel
Chattel paper
Collateral
Debtor
Debtor in possession (DIP)
Equipment
Estate
Executory contract
Family farmer
Financing statement
Inventory
Lien creditor
Liquidation
Mandatory authority
Order for relief
Party in interest

Perfected security interest
Persuasive authority
Primary authority
Priority
Private law
Proceeds
Promissory note
Proof of claim
Proof of interest
Property of the estate
Public law
Purchase money security interest
Regular annual income
Secondary authority
Security agreement
Security interest
Shepardizing
Small business
Unexpired lease
Uniform Commercial Code (UCC)
United States Code (U.S.C.)
Venue

THREE

The Cast of Characters and Their Roles in the Bankruptcy Process

The bankruptcy process vitally influences the lives of great numbers of people. In addition to debtors and creditors, the bankruptcy process annually affects the employment of thousands of people, involves billions of dollars in assets, and, to a great extent, concerns the public interest. The debtors range from individuals to giant corporations. The bankruptcy process has been used by a number of major publicly held companies, including Continental Airlines, Eastern Airlines, Greyhound Lines, Inc., Johns-Manville, LTV, Texaco, TWA, and Wang.

The bankruptcy process can be characterized as a stage upon which a large cast of characters play out their respective roles. The Bankruptcy Reform Act of 1978, with its subsequent amendments, provides a script for the performance. It attempts to balance the interests among these various actors and to provide the mechanism through which each can pursue his or her own interests.

The cast of characters in the bankruptcy process can be classified into the following basic groups:

1. the debtor, the debtor's attorney, and the paralegal;
2. the bankruptcy petition preparer;
3. creditors and other parties in interest;
4. the Administrative Office of the United States Courts;
5. the bankruptcy judge and staff;
6. the office of the clerk of the bankruptcy court; and
7. the United States trustee, private trustees, and examiners.

SECTION 1
THE DEBTOR, THE DEBTOR'S ATTORNEY, AND THE PARALEGAL

The central player, the debtor, is supported by his or her attorney and the attorney's paralegal.

A. THE DEBTOR

The bankruptcy process naturally focuses on the debtor. The Bankruptcy Reform Act of 1978 selected the terminology "debtor," rather than "bankrupt," in part to remove some of the stigma from the filing of a bankruptcy case.

The Bankruptcy Reform Act of 1978 defines "debtor" as a "person or municipality concerning which a case under this title has been commenced." 11 U.S.C.A. § 101(13). The definition of "debtor" uses both the terms "person" and "municipality," since they are mutually exclusive. "Person" includes "individual, partnership, and corporation, but does not include governmental unit." 11 U.S.C.A. § 101(41). A "municipality" is a "political subdivision or public agency or instrumentality of a State." 11 U.S.C.A. § 101(40). Thus, by definition, a "person" would not include a "municipality" and a "municipality" would not include a "person."

The Code specifies who is eligible to be a debtor under bankruptcy law. 11 U.S.C.A. § 109. All persons may become debtors under the Code with three limitations. First, the person seeking to become a debtor must be a person who resides or has a domicile, a place of business, or property in the United States. 11 U.S.C.A. § 109(a).

PROBLEM 3.1   Stephanie Simpson, a reporter for a major newspaper, has been assigned for the past three years to London. Other than the condo she owns in New York City, all of her property is with her in London. Over the past few years, Stephanie has spent faster than she has earned, and she now finds herself unable to keep up with her creditors.

Is Stephanie eligible to be a debtor under the Code? Does it matter whether Stephanie is a citizen of the United States?

PROBLEM 3.2   The facts are the same as in Problem 3.1 except that Stephanie sold her condo in New York City six months ago. Is she eligible to be a debtor under the Code?

Second, an individual or family farmer may not be a debtor under the Code if he or she has been a debtor in a case pending under the Code at any time in the preceding 180 days if: (1) the case was dismissed by the court for willful failure of the debtor to abide by orders of the court or to appear before the court in proper prosecution of the case; or (2) if the debtor requested and obtained the voluntary dismissal of the case following the filing of a request for relief from the automatic stay. 11 U.S.C.A. § 109(g).

PROBLEM 3.3   On June 1, Clarence Collier filed a petition for bankruptcy under Chapter 7. On June 15, First National Bank filed a motion for relief from the automatic stay. On June 20, Clarence filed a motion requesting dismissal of his case. The case was dismissed on July 1.

Could Clarence file a new petition in bankruptcy under Chapter 7 on November 15, November 28, or December 15? Rule 9006 may provide some assistance on whether the date of the filing of the first petition should count toward the 180 days.

Third, a person generally cannot become a debtor if he or she has been a debtor and has received a discharge within the past six years. 11 U.S.C.A. §§ 727(a)(8), (9).

PROBLEM 3.4   John Graham, a freelance photographer, was seriously injured in an automobile accident in November 1990. Due to his injuries, he was unable to work during the holiday season and therefore suffered substantial financial setbacks. In February 1991, John filed a petition in bankruptcy under Chapter 7. He received a discharge in early April 1991.

Since that time, John has regained his health and opened a small photography studio. The studio prospered until downsizing by a major employer caused heavy unemployment in the city in 1996. Since family portraits were considered by many to be a luxury rather than a necessity, John's business dried up. By the fall of 1996, John was unable to pay his bills.

Can John file a petition in bankruptcy and receive a discharge under Chapter 7?

PROBLEM 3.5   In June 1992, Alice married Bob Greene and they opened a small candy store. Because neither knew anything about business, they soon were in deep financial trouble. In February 1993, Alice and Bob filed a joint petition in bankruptcy under Chapter 7. They received their discharge in late March.

The stress of the business failure and bankruptcy created a rift in the marriage, and Alice and Bob were divorced in November 1993.

In 1994, Alice married Jim Pilgrim. All went well until Jim became seriously ill two years later and was forced to take an extended leave of absence from his job. Alice quit her job to take care of Jim. Their money soon ran out and they were unable to meet their payments on their house and cars. A number of Jim's medical bills remain unpaid.

Are Jim and Alice eligible to file a joint petition in bankruptcy under Chapter 7?

If an entity is not a person, then it may still qualify as a debtor if it is a municipality. 11 U.S.C.A. § 109(c).

PROBLEM 3.6   The city of Springfield has become unable to pay its creditors. Is the city of Springfield eligible to be a debtor under the Code?

In addition to defining in general terms who may be a debtor under the Code, the Code defines who may be a debtor under each of the operative chapters of the Code. 11 U.S.C.A. §§ 109(b)–(f). The Bankruptcy Reform Act of 1994 makes two amendments to 11 U.S.C.A. § 109. Under 11 U.S.C.A. § 109(b)(2), a small business investment company licensed by the Small Business Administration may not be a debtor under Chapter 7, which also renders it ineligible to be a debtor under any chapter of the Code. Under 11 U.S.C.A. § 109(c), to be eligible to be a debtor, a municipality must be "specifically authorized" in its capacity as a municipality or by name, by state law, or by a person so empowered. This is a change from the former requirement of "generally authorized." The selection of the appropriate operative chapter will be discussed in Chapter Four.

B. THE DEBTOR'S ATTORNEY

The attorney who represents the debtor in bankruptcy may be representing an established client he or she has represented in other matters, a client referred by another attorney, a client referred by a lawyer referral service, a client who learned about this attorney through a former client, or, if the attorney advertises as a bankruptcy practitioner, a client who has seen an advertisement. If the debtor is an established client, the attorney may be aware of the client's financial problems and the two of them may start to consider bankruptcy as an option weeks before the filing of the petition. The attorney who practices bankruptcy law extensively will probably receive a number of referrals from other attorneys who do not practice bankruptcy law. A client who has gone through bankruptcy and is satisfied with an attorney's handling of the case will often speak favorably to family, friends, and neighbors, leading them to seek out this attorney if they encounter financial difficulties. Advertising in the bankruptcy area appears to be successful. The attorney who advertises will probably acquire a number of clients in this manner.

Every client who goes to an attorney with financial problems will not file bankruptcy. One of the attorney's services will be to determine whether alternatives to bankruptcy are viable for a particular client and so advise the client. Presuming there is no viable alternative, the attorney, after so advising the client, will begin the process of gathering information from the client for preparation of the bankruptcy filing. The attorney will supervise the paralegal in the preparation of pleadings, file any necessary motions, and represent the client at the meeting of creditors and at any bankruptcy court or appellate court proceedings in the case.

The length of time in which an attorney is involved in a bankruptcy case varies. A routine Chapter 7 case will be quickly finished, but a complex Chapter 11 case may take several years.

The attorney's compensation is regulated by the Code. 11 U.S.C.A. § 329.

C. THE PARALEGAL

The paralegal's role in aiding the attorney will depend on the law firm, the training and experience of the paralegal, and the type of client involved. Bankruptcy practice is handled by a number of different types of firms:

1. A small firm could consist of one attorney who may or may not specialize in bankruptcy, one paralegal, and one secretary.
2. A larger firm could consist of several attorneys who may or may not specialize in bankruptcy, several paralegals, and several secretaries.
3. A very large firm may have a bankruptcy department with a number of paralegals and secretaries.

Naturally, a paralegal who has studied bankruptcy and has extensive experience will be given more responsibility than one who is new to the bankruptcy area. The needs of a Chapter 7 debtor with few assets will be quite different from those of a large corporate client. The attorney charged with handling the case must determine the role of the paralegal and closely supervise his or her activities in every case, regardless of the size of the case or its relative importance to the firm.

A paralegal in the bankruptcy field performs a number of activities that relate to the practice of law but does not advise clients or represent clients in judicial proceedings. Paralegal activities include, but are not limited to, client interviews, investigation, legal research, and document drafting. Not all paralegals will perform all these activities. The activities performed will depend on the supervising attorney. The relationship between attorney and paralegal is constantly evolving. As the relationship grows, the range of activities the attorney assigns to the paralegal becomes broader and more complex. The following discussion touches only on some of the activities to which a paralegal could be assigned. Other activities exist as well.

At the initial interview, the paralegal may meet with the client to review an extensive questionnaire on the debtor's assets and liabilities and to help the debtor create a plan for acquiring the information necessary to complete the questionnaire. At subsequent interviews, the paralegal will review and organize the information gathered by the debtor and identify additional information needed to complete the various schedules, lists, and statements.

In addition to working with the debtor to develop the information necessary to complete the documents to be filed, the paralegal will investigate the completeness and accuracy of the information gathered by the debtor. The amounts of various debts must be confirmed, and the paralegal must determine whether these debts are secured or unsecured. Record offices should be checked for UCC filings and real estate recordings. Tax offices should be checked for unpaid taxes and whether unpaid taxes have led to tax liens. The location of the debtor's property should be determined.

The paralegal will open a bankruptcy file and prepare the inventories of the debtor's assets and liabilities. Ultimately, these inventories will become a part of Official Form No. 6 (Schedules). As part of this process, the paralegal begins the identification and classification of property that the debtor will claim as exempt. This information will be incorporated into Official Form No. 6, Schedule C (Property Claimed as Exempt). The paralegal may be responsible for arranging to have some assets appraised to establish their value.

As the information gathering stage continues, the paralegal plays an important role in maintaining contact with the debtor, asking the debtor for more information, and keeping the debtor current on the status of the case. The paralegal performs a liaison role, communicating with the client for the attorney and with the attorney for the client.

After the essential information has been gathered and verified, the paralegal begins drafting the documents needed to file the case. The first document is the **voluntary petition** in bankruptcy, Official Form No. 1. Depending on which chapter the case is being filed under, a number of schedules, lists, and statements must be completed as well. After these documents have been prepared in rough draft form, the paralegal supervises the clerical staff that finalizes the documents. The attorney reviews the final documents with the paralegal for accuracy and completeness.

The paralegal files the necessary documents at the office of the clerk of the bankruptcy court and works with the clerk's office personnel and the judge's staff on behalf of the supervising attorney for the case.

The paralegal will do legal research on specific issues raised by the attorney. This research could be required before the petition and schedules are filed, or it could be necessary for a motion or complaint that the debtor's attorney may file during the progress of the case through the court. If the bankruptcy judge's decision on a motion or a complaint is appealed, the paralegal could play an important role in the research and preparation of the appellate brief.

The paralegal may work with the trustee in bankruptcy, if a trustee has been appointed for the case, answering many of the trustee's questions about the debtor's assets and liabilities. The paralegal often coordinates calendar dates to ensure that the debtor and the attorney will be present at the meeting of creditors and at other conferences and hearings. The paralegal also monitors the case so that important deadlines are met.

The duties of a paralegal can extend beyond a given case to the function of keeping the attorney current on recent developments in the bankruptcy field. The paralegal may also be responsible for developing new office procedures to streamline the processing of bankruptcy cases, including devising a new calendar system, reorganizing work flow, determining better use of existing equipment, or purchasing more sophisticated hardware and software.

SECTION 2
THE BANKRUPTCY PETITION PREPARER

The cast of characters in the bankruptcy process has been expanded to include the **bankruptcy petition preparer.** New 11 U.S.C.A. § 110(a), added by the Bankruptcy Reform Act of 1994, defines a bankruptcy petition preparer as a "person, other than an attorney or an employee of an attorney, who prepares for compensation a document for filing." According to the legislative history, this section was added to Chapter 1 to create standards and penalties for what have been termed non-lawyer bankruptcy mills.

The petition preparer may perform typing services only and may not attempt to provide legal advice or legal service to the debtor. The bankruptcy petition preparer must:

1. print his or her name and address on any document for filing;
2. place an identifying number (social security number) on any document for filing;
3. furnish the debtor a copy of the document for filing at the time it is presented for the debtor's signature;
4. not execute a document on behalf of the debtor;
5. not use the word "legal" or any similar term in advertisements; and
6. not collect or receive any payment from the debtor or from anyone else on behalf of the debtor for filing fees.

The bankruptcy petition preparer who fails to comply with these requirements may be fined not more than $500 for each violation.

The petition preparer shall file, within 10 days after the petition is filed, a declaration disclosing any fee from the debtor or on behalf of the debtor received within 12 months prior to the filing, as well as any unpaid fee charged to the debtor. Any fee found to be excessive by the court will be disallowed and turned over to the bankruptcy trustee. The individual debtor will be allowed to exempt the funds recovered. 11 U.S.C.A. § 522(b).

The penalties become even steeper if a case is dismissed because of the preparer's failure to file papers, negligence, or intentional disregard. On the motion of a debtor, trustee, or creditor, the petition preparer shall be ordered to pay

1. the debtor's actual damages;
2. $2,000 or double the amount, whichever is greater, paid by the debtor to the preparer;
3. reasonable attorney's fees and costs.

An extra $1,000 shall be ordered paid if the movant is a trustee or creditor.

The petition preparer may be enjoined from preparing petitions for violation of the provisions of 11 U.S.C.A. § 110. The petition preparer may even face imprisonment of not more than one year or a fine, or both, for a knowing attempt to disregard the Bankruptcy Code or Federal Rules of Bankruptcy Procedure, which results in the dismissal of the bankruptcy case or related proceeding. 18 U.S.C.A. § 156.

The paralegal, as an employee of an attorney, will not be affected by 11 U.S.C.A. § 110 because he or she does not fit the definition of a bankruptcy petition preparer. A paralegal works for an attorney and under the supervision of that attorney. Any person with paralegal training who chooses to prepare bankruptcy petitions outside employment by, and supervision of, an attorney is subject to the standards and penalties set forth in the Code.

SECTION 3
THE CREDITORS AND OTHER PARTIES IN INTEREST

Creditors hold three basic types of claims: **priority, secured,** and **unsecured. Priority claims** include claims by employees for employee compensation, claims for alimony, maintenance, or support, claims by the Internal Revenue Service, and claims by the state tax commission. **Secured claims** are secured by real estate, fixtures, or personal property. The real estate, fixtures, or personal property that secures a claim is known as **collateral** and may be taken (repossessed) by the creditor if the debtor does not fulfill his or her obligation to pay the debt. **Unsecured claims** are not secured by collateral.

Creditors are **parties in interest.** Other parties in interest include equity security holders, indenture trustees, statutory lienholders, lessors, and governmental regulatory authorities. The United States trustee and private trustees, also parties in interest, are discussed in Section 7 of this chapter.

A. CREDITORS

Creditors include creditors holding secured claims, creditors holding priority claims, and creditors holding unsecured claims. The emphasis is on the claim and not on the creditor. Therefore, reference is to a creditor holding a secured claim, rather than to a secured creditor.

1. CREDITORS HOLDING SECURED CLAIMS

Creditors holding secured claims may have a security interest in real property, personal property, or fixtures. A real estate **mortgagee** has an interest in real estate that secures payment or performance of an obligation. If the **mortgagor** defaults as to his or her obligation, the mortgagee can repossess the real estate. (See Exhibit 3.1.)

> **PROBLEM 3.7**   Franklin and Sylvia Richardson purchased a house from Anthony and Gloria Woodberry for $175,000. The Richardsons paid the Woodberrys by withdrawing $17,500 from their savings account and borrowing $157,500 from the Gotham Savings and Loan Association. The Richardsons gave Gotham Savings a mortgage on the house.
>
> Who is the mortgagor and who is the mortgagee? What is the collateral for the mortgage?
>
> Three years after the sale, the Richardsons found themselves in financial difficulties and ceased paying Gotham Savings on the mortgage. Gotham Savings repossessed the house and sold it.
>
> If Gotham sells the house for more than the mortgage balance, who receives the surplus? If Gotham sells the house for less than the mortgage balance, do the Richardsons still owe Gotham the difference? Is the difference a secured or an unsecured claim?

Fixtures are goods that become so related to the real estate that an interest in them arises under state real estate law. UCC § 9–313(1)(a). Therefore, whether something is a fixture depends on state law. Fixture claimants may claim through their interest in the real estate. Thus, the mortgagor may, in a real estate mortgage, give the mortgagee more than just an interest in the real estate. The mortgagor may also give the mortgagee an interest in fixtures.

EXHIBIT 3.1
Real Estate Mortgage Transaction

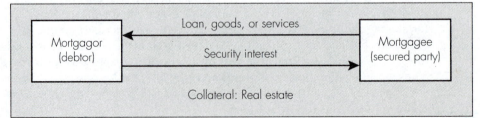

EXAMPLE
John and Martha Wright borrowed $100,000 from Credit Union to purchase a house. The Wrights gave Credit Union a mortgage on their house and the "fixtures therein." Credit Union's fixture claimant status derives from its interest in the real estate.

A **secured party** under Article 9 of the Uniform Commercial Code is "a lender, seller or other person in whose favor there is a security interest. . . ." UCC § 9–105(1)(m). A **security interest** is "an interest in personal property or fixtures which secures payment or performance of an obligation." UCC § 1–201(37). The person "who owes payment or other performance of the obligation secured" is known as the "debtor." UCC § 9–105(1)(d). The "collateral" is the property that is subject to the security interest. UCC § 9–105(1)(c). The agreement that "creates or provides for a security interest" is known as the "security agreement." UCC § 9–105(1)(l). The term "security agreement" replaces all previously used terms, such as *pledge, assignment, chattel mortgage, chattel trust, trust deed, factor's lien, equipment trust, conditional sale, trust receipt,* and other lien or title retention contract intended as security. UCC § 9–102(2). (See Exhibit 3.2.)

PROBLEM 3.8   Ronald purchased a winter coat from Baldwin's Men's Shop for $500. Ronald charged the coat on his Baldwin's credit card. Since buying the coat, Ronald has lost his job and cannot pay for the coat.

At the time of the purchase, did Ronald give Baldwin's a security interest in the coat, making Baldwin's a secured party? Now that Ronald is in default as to the purchase price, can Baldwin's repossess the coat?

PROBLEM 3.9   Ronald purchased a winter coat for his girlfriend, Janet, from Ms. Smythe's Fine Fashions for $1,000. Ronald charged the coat on his Ms. Smythe's credit card and gave Ms. Smythe's a security interest in the coat. Ronald took the coat home and hung it in a closet until he could give it to Janet for her birthday. After he bought the coat but before he could give it to Janet, Ronald lost his job and now cannot pay for the coat.

Since Ronald is in default as to the purchase price, can Ms. Smythe's repossess the coat from him?

PROBLEM 3.10   Assume the same facts as in Problem 3.9, except that Ronald gave the coat to Janet for her birthday before he lost his job and defaulted on his obligation to pay.

Now that Ronald is in default as to the purchase price, can Ms. Smythe's repossess the coat from Janet? Does it make any difference whether the secured party seeks to repossess from the debtor or from someone to whom the debtor has given the collateral? See UCC §§ 9–306(2), 9–307(1), (2).

EXHIBIT 3.2
Secured Transaction

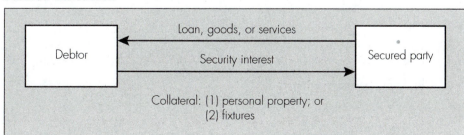

As previously stated, fixtures are goods that become so related to the real estate that an interest in them arises under state real estate law. UCC § 9–313(1)(a). Therefore, whether something is a fixture depends on state law. Fixture claimants may claim through their interest in the real estate. Fixture claimants may also be personal property claimants and claim through their interest in goods, not through an interest in real estate. Thus, a debtor may, in a UCC Article 9 security agreement, give a party an interest in goods that are fixtures or are to become fixtures. The secured party then has a security interest in fixtures.

EXAMPLE

John and Martha Wright borrowed $100,000 from Credit Union to purchase a house. The Wrights gave Credit Union a mortgage on their house and the "fixtures therein." Credit Union's fixture claimant status derives from its interest in the real estate.

John and Martha borrowed $2,000 from First Bank to purchase a new furnace for their house. The Wrights gave First Bank a security interest in the furnace. Under state law, the furnace, once installed, became a fixture. First Bank's fixture claimant status derives from its interest in the goods that became fixtures.

PROBLEM 3.11   John and Martha Wright purchased a new patio door from Quality Patio Doors, Inc. Quality financed the sale, and the Wrights gave Quality a security interest in the patio door. The Wrights installed the door in their house. How is Quality's fixture claimant status established?

The term "secured party" also includes "a person to whom accounts or chattel paper have been sold." UCC § 9–105(1)(m). The "seller of accounts or chattel paper" is also known as the "debtor." UCC § 9–105(1)(d). The collateral is the accounts or chattel paper that have been sold. UCC § 9–105(1)(c). (See Exhibit 3.3.)

The following two examples illustrate accounts and chattel paper, respectively, as collateral.

EXAMPLE

The Big Apple Office Supply Company sells office equipment and supplies on a cash and credit basis. Many large customers charge their purchases and are billed at the end of the month. If a bill is not paid in full within 30 days, a 1.5 percent finance charge is added on the next month's statement. Such obligations to pay are known as "accounts" or "accounts receivable."

The Big Apple was in need of cash, so it sold its accounts to First Bank. Even though First Bank is the buyer of the accounts, the UCC defines First Bank as a party holding a security interest in the accounts.

EXHIBIT 3.3
Sale of Accounts or Chattel Paper

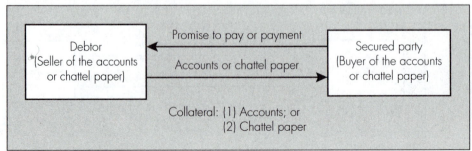

EXAMPLE

The Southpark Office Machine Company sold a photocopy machine on credit to the Newtown Pharmacy. Rather than just take Newtown's promise to pay, Southpark had Newtown sign a security agreement giving Southpark a security interest in the photocopy machine. The security agreement also contained Newtown's promise to pay.

Southpark sold Newtown's security agreement to Friendly Finance. Even though Friendly Finance is the buyer of the security agreement, the UCC defines Friendly as a party holding a security interest in Newtown's security agreement. Newtown's security agreement is chattel paper because it is a writing which evidences both a monetary obligation and a security interest in specific goods. The monetary obligation is Newtown's promise to pay. The security interest in specific goods is the security interest in the photocopy machine.

2. CREDITORS HOLDING PRIORITY CLAIMS

Creditors holding priority claims are listed in 11 U.S.C.A. §§ 507(a)(1)–(9). **Administrative expenses** permitted by the Code are priority claims. 11 U.S.C.A. § 507(a)(1). Employees with unsecured wage, salary, or commission claims hold priority claims up to $4,000 for each individual if their claims are "earned by an individual within 90 days before the date of the filing of the petition or the date of the cessation of the debtor's business, whichever occurs first." These claims may include vacation, severance, or sick leave pay. 11 U.S.C.A. § 507(a)(3).

PROBLEM 3.12   Mary Malone was the personal administrative assistant to the president of Quality Office Supply Co., a wholesale and retail office supply company. Mary's salary was $4,500 per month. For the four months before Quality filed for bankruptcy under Chapter 7, Mary had been receiving $2,300 per month.

Does Mary hold a priority claim and, if so, for how much?

Employees with unsecured claims for unpaid contributions to employee benefit plans hold priority claims if the contributions arose "from services rendered within 180 days before the date of the filing of the petition or the date of the cessation of the debtor's business, whichever occurs first." For each plan, the amount is limited to $4,000 times the number of employees covered by the plan less the aggregate amount paid to each employee as a priority claim for wages, salaries, or commissions, plus the aggregate amount paid by the estate on behalf of these employees to any other employee benefit plan. These claims are not paid directly to the employee but rather to the benefit plan. 11 U.S.C.A. § 507(a)(4).

PROBLEM 3.13   Prior to its petition in bankruptcy, Quality Office Supply had 50 employees, including Mary Malone. During each of the seven months prior to the filing of the petition, Quality failed to contribute $750 per month for each employee to the employee benefit plan. Each of 20 employees was entitled to a priority claim for unpaid wages of $700. Twenty employees were entitled to a priority claim for unpaid wages of $1,500 each. Ten employees were entitled to a priority claim for unpaid wages of $4,000 each. The estate has not paid any other employee benefit plan on behalf of Quality's employees.

Does Mary hold a priority claim for unpaid contributions to her employee benefit plan? If so, for how much?

Does the plan itself hold a priority claim for unpaid contributions to the employee benefit plan? If so, for how much?

Another group of priority claims includes claims by farmers who have unsecured claims against grain storage facilities for grain or the proceeds of grain and United States fishermen who have unsecured claims against fish produce storage or processing facilities. Each claimant is limited to a $4,000 priority claim. 11 U.S.C.A. § 507(a)(5).

Consumers who have made an unsecured money deposit in connection with the purchase, lease, or rental of property that was not delivered or for the purchase of services that were never provided are another group of priority claimants. Each consumer is limited to a priority claim of $1,800. 11 U.S.C.A. § 507(a)(6).

> **PROBLEM 3.14**   Cindy Shephard began her Christmas shopping in July. She selected a number of items from People's Department Store and had them put on layaway. At the time of purchase, Cindy paid $200 of the total bill of $2,900. On the first of each month, Cindy sent People's a check for $200. On November 15, People's filed a petition for bankruptcy under Chapter 7.
>
>   Does Cindy hold a priority claim? If so, for how much?

Allowed claims of debts owed to a spouse, former spouse, or child of the debtor for alimony, maintenance, or support have been added as the seventh priority in the list of priority claims. 11 U.S.C.A. § 507(a)(7). Official Form No. 10 (Proof of Claim) has been amended to add this priority.

Certain tax claims are the eighth priority claims. The Internal Revenue Service (IRS) may hold a priority claim for income taxes for the three tax years immediately preceding the filing of a petition in bankruptcy. 11 U.S.C.A. § 507(a)(8)(A). The IRS, therefore, will receive notice of the order for relief in any case filed under any chapter of the Bankruptcy Code. In addition to notice of the order for relief, the IRS will receive copies of notices mailed to all creditors in all chapters. These notices are mailed to the district director of Internal Revenue for the district in which the case has been filed. Fed. R. Bank. P. 2002(j).

State tax commissions potentially have an interest in any bankruptcy case and will receive notice of the order for relief in all cases. 11 U.S.C.A. § 342, Historical and Revision Notes.

Property taxes assessed before the filing of a petition in bankruptcy and last payable without penalty after one year before the date of the filing of the petition are priority claims. 11 U.S.C.A. § 507(a)(8)(B). If the debtor is an employer, taxes required to be collected or withheld and for which the debtor is liable and employment taxes on wages, salary, or commissions are among the priority claims. 11 U.S.C.A. §§ 507(a)(8)(C), (D).

The S & L priority is the eighth category of unsecured priority claims. 11 U.S.C.A. § 507(a)(9).

3. CREDITORS HOLDING UNSECURED CLAIMS

All of the debtor's creditors who have no special interest in property of the debtor's estate hold unsecured claims. **Creditors holding unsecured claims** have loaned the debtor money, performed services for the debtor, or sold the debtor merchandise *without* demanding collateral to secure the debtor's promise to pay.

EXAMPLE
Allison Smiley borrowed $1,000 from Friendly Finance. Friendly did not require collateral to secure Allison's promise to pay. Friendly Finance is a creditor holding an unsecured claim until Allison pays in full. Friendly has an unsecured claim if Allison files a petition in bankruptcy.

EXAMPLE

Allison Smiley purchased a VCR from Neighborhood Electronics for $600. Neighborhood did not take a security interest in the VCR. Allison paid $150 down and agreed to pay the balance in three equal installments, each spaced one month apart. Once the VCR is delivered to Allison, Neighborhood's interest in the VCR ceases. Until Allison pays in full, Neighborhood holds an unsecured claim.

Also included in the category of creditors with unsecured claims are those parties with secured claims who are owed more than the collateral is worth. These parties hold unsecured claims for the amounts for which they are **undercollateralized.** 11 U.S.C.A. § 506(a).

EXAMPLE

Anna Holmes purchased a TV from Quality Electronics for $700. She paid $50 down and promised to pay $50 each month for 13 months. Anna gave Quality a security interest in the TV.

Because the TV is now used, it has a resale value of $400. Quality has a secured claim for $400 and an unsecured claim for $250.

Although the creditors holding unsecured claims do not have collateral to back up payment of their claims, they play an active role in the administration of the estate. There is an ongoing struggle between the creditors holding priority and secured claims on the one hand and creditors holding unsecured claims on the other. In a liquidation, creditors holding unsecured claims, through the trustee, are trying to enhance their position by enlarging the bankruptcy estate that all creditors must share. The creditors holding unsecured claims gain when the trustee successfully challenges a creditor claiming secured claim status.

In a reorganization case, creditors holding unsecured claims are the members of the creditors' committee. They have a right to participate in the formulation of the reorganization plan and may collect and file acceptances or rejections of a plan with the court.

The United States government may hold an unsecured claim. In any case in which a debt for something other than taxes is owed to the United States, copies of notices required to be sent to all creditors must be mailed to the United States attorney for the district in which the case is pending. Copies of these notices must also be mailed to the particular department, agency, or instrumentality of the United States to which the debt is owed. Fed. R. Bank. P. 2002(j)(4).

B. OTHER PARTIES IN INTEREST

Creditors are not the only parties in interest. Also included in this category are equity security holders, indenture trustees, statutory lienholders, lessors, and governmental regulatory authorities.

1. EQUITY SECURITY HOLDERS

An **equity security holder** is one who holds an equity security of the debtor.

"[E]quity security" means—
(A) share in a corporation, whether or not transferable or denominated "stock," or similar security;
(B) interest of a limited partner in a limited partnership; or
(C) warrant or right, other than a right to convert, to purchase, sell, or subscribe to a share, security, or interest of a kind specified in subparagraph (A) or (B) of this paragraph. 11 U.S.C.A. § 101(16).

EXAMPLE
Daniel Drummond owns 100 shares of common stock in the Timber Toothpick Co. Timber filed for bankruptcy under Chapter 7. Drummond is an equity security holder.

PROBLEM 3.15   Ted, Alice, Bob, and Carol formed a partnership for the sale of hot tubs. Under the partnership, Ted and Alice were to manage the business. Bob and Carol were silent partners. They contributed most of the money for start-up costs. The partnership agreement provided that all profits would be divided equally among the four.

Within six months, the business failed and the partnership filed for bankruptcy under Chapter 7.

Are Ted, Alice, Bob, and Carol equity security holders?

If papers filed in a case disclose a stock interest of the United States, copies of notices required for all creditors must be mailed to the Secretary of the Treasury in Washington, D.C. If the United States is a creditor or equity security holder in a Chapter 11 case, the Secretary of the Treasury, acting on behalf of the United States, may accept or reject the reorganization plan. 11 U.S.C.A. § 1126(a).

2. INDENTURE TRUSTEES

An **indenture trustee** is a "trustee under an indenture." 11 U.S.C.A. § 101(29). An "indenture" is a "mortgage, deed of trust, or indenture, under which there is outstanding a security . . . constituting a claim against the debtor, a claim secured by a lien on any of the debtor's property, or an equity security of the debtor." 11 U.S.C.A. § 101(28). To qualify as an indenture under this Bankruptcy Code definition, the mortgage, deed of trust, or indenture must have outstanding a security other than a voting trust certificate.

3. STATUTORY LIENHOLDERS

When a person in the ordinary course of his or her business furnishes services or materials with respect to real estate, state statute or case law may give this person a lien on the real estate. This person is called a **statutory lienholder.** See 11 U.S.C.A. § 101(53).

EXAMPLE
Quality Roofing Co. put a new roof on Sally Mead's home. Sally agreed to pay for the roof over a period of one year. Under state statute, a person who repairs another's real estate is entitled to file a lien on the real estate in the office of real estate records. The lien gives Quality an interest in Sally's real estate for the price of the services until the lien is satisfied.

When a person in the ordinary course of his or her business furnishes services or materials with respect to the debtor's goods, state statute or case law may give this person a lien on the goods in his or her possession. See 11 U.S.C.A. § 101(53).

EXAMPLE
Phil was involved in an automobile accident, and his car sustained $1,500 in damage. Adam's Garage repaired Phil's automobile, but Phil was unable to pay the bill. Under state law, Adam's Garage may be able to retain possession of the automobile and to impose a mechanic's lien on Phil's automobile until Phil pays.

4. LESSORS

The buyer acquires an ownership interest in any personal or real property purchased. Unless the seller retains a mortgage or security interest in the property, the seller loses his or her interest in the property. If the property is purchased on credit and the buyer defaults in his or her payments, the seller who does not have a security interest in the property has no recourse against the property and must pursue remedies for breach of contract.

Rather than purchasing property, the "buyer" may only wish to acquire the use of the property for a period of time. This transaction is known as a **lease.** The lessee acquires the exclusive right to use the property for the lease term. On completion of the lease term, the property is returned to the lessor, unless a new arrangement is made. (See Exhibit 3.4.)

EXAMPLE

Sally and Jonathan MacMillion signed an agreement with Sleepy Hollow for the rental of a two bedroom apartment for $350 a month for a period of one year. This transaction is a lease. Sally and Jonathan are the lessees, and Sleepy Hollow is the lessor. The subject of the lease is real estate (the apartment).

EXAMPLE

When Bill Bailey was building a patio in his backyard, he rented a portable cement mixer from E-Z Rentals for a month. This transaction is a lease. Bill Bailey is the lessee, and E-Z Rentals is the lessor. The subject of the lease is personal property (the cement mixer).

At times, the distinction between a lease and a security agreement is not clear. If the transaction is a lease, the goods will be the property of the estate for only the lease term or until the lease has been breached. At the end of the lease term or after the lease has been breached, the lessor will be entitled to the goods leased. If, however, the transaction is not a lease but is actually a security agreement, the "lessor" will not be entitled to the goods, which will remain property of the estate. The UCC addresses this problem when it defines a security interest. UCC § 1–201(37).

A debtor in bankruptcy may be either a lessee or lessor. If the debtor is the lessee, then another party will claim to be the lessor of property that the debtor has in his or her possession at the time of filing the petition in bankruptcy. If the debtor is the lessor, then the debtor will have an ownership interest in property in the possession of another at the time of filing the petition in bankruptcy.

EXHIBIT 3.4
Lease Transaction

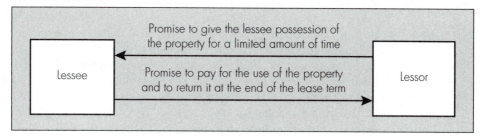

EXAMPLE

On January 1, Raymond rented a computer from ABC Computer Company for one year. On May 1, Raymond filed a petition in bankruptcy under Chapter 7. Raymond's bankruptcy estate includes a lease interest in the computer for the balance of the lease term. ABC has an ownership interest in the computer and has a right to its return at the end of the lease period.

EXAMPLE

On January 1, Raymond leased his typewriter to Oscar for one year. On May 1, Raymond filed a petition in bankruptcy under Chapter 7. Oscar has a lease interest in the typewriter for the balance of the lease term. Raymond's bankruptcy estate includes an ownership interest in the typewriter and has a right to its return at the end of the lease period.

5. GOVERNMENTAL REGULATORY AUTHORITIES

In addition to the various types of creditors who are owed money by a debtor filing a bankruptcy case, other interested parties in both the federal government and the state government may have regulatory responsibilities in connection with the debtor. If a debtor in a case is subject to regulation, the agency with jurisdiction will also receive notice. 11 U.S.C.A. § 342, Historical and Revision Notes. Government involvement may be quite important to the outcome of a case. For example, any rate change provided for in a reorganization plan must be approved by the regulatory commission with jurisdiction in order for the plan to be confirmed. 11 U.S.C.A. § 1129(a)(6).

The Securities Investor Protection Corporation (SIPC) and the Securities and Exchange Commission (SEC) both have an interest in stockbroker liquidation cases filed under Subchapter III of Chapter 7 of the Bankruptcy Code. The bankruptcy court clerk is required to give notice of the order for relief in such cases to the SIPC and the SEC. 11 U.S.C.A. § 743. In all Chapter 11 cases, copies of notices required to be mailed to all creditors must be mailed to the SEC. If the SEC has filed a notice of appearance in the case, these notices must be mailed to the SEC in Washington, D.C., as well as any other place the commission designates in writing filed with the court. If a notice of appearance has not been filed, a request in writing to receive notices in the case may be filed with the court.

The SEC may raise, appear, and be heard on any issue in a Chapter 11 case but may not appeal from any judgment, order, or decree entered in the case. 11 U.S.C.A. § 1109(a).

The SIPC may, in effect, "take over" a stockbroker liquidation case because the automatic stay provided for by 11 U.S.C.A. § 362 does not prevent the SIPC from filing an application for a protective decree under the Securities Investor Protection Act of 1970. This protective decree suspends all proceedings, except as provided by 11 U.S.C.A. § 362(b), until the SIPC has completed its action in the case. This may even mean total liquidation of the debtor by the SIPC, after which the bankruptcy case is dismissed. 11 U.S.C.A. § 742.

The state securities commission will have an interest in stockbroker liquidation cases on the state level, just as the SEC and the SIPC have an interest on the federal level.

The Commodity Futures Trading Commission has an interest in commodity broker liquidation cases filed under Subchapter IV of Chapter 7 of the Bankruptcy Code. The bankruptcy court clerk is required to give notice of the order for relief to the commission, and the commission may raise, appear, and be heard on any issue in a commodity broker liquidation case. 11 U.S.C.A. § 762. Copies of all notices required to be mailed to all creditors must be mailed to the Commodity Futures Trading Commission in a commodity broker case. Fed. R. Bank. P. 2002(j).

SECTION 4
THE ADMINISTRATIVE OFFICE OF THE UNITED STATES COURTS

Although the public has no relationship with the Administrati
States Courts, this office plays a critical role in the bankrupt.,
only the bankruptcy judge and the clerk of the bankruptcy court have a re....
with the Administrative Office (AO). The AO controls the size of the staff at the
clerk's office, the salaries (to some extent), the quarters for the court and the clerk's
office, and the rank of each employee. The AO provides the bankruptcy courts with
statistics and forms and examines the operations of each court and clerk's office. The
AO also serves as a resource on technical issues for bankruptcy courts throughout
the nation.

SECTION 5
THE BANKRUPTCY JUDGE AND STAFF

Considering the number of cases filed in each jurisdiction every year, each bankruptcy judge is supported by a relatively small staff, which includes the judge's law
clerk or law clerks, the judge's secretary, and the court reporter.

A. THE BANKRUPTCY JUDGE

The bankruptcy judges in each judicial district are a unit of the United States district
court. This unit is known as the bankruptcy court for that district. 28 U.S.C.A. § 151.
Bankruptcy judges are appointed by the United States circuit court of appeals after
recommendations of the Judicial Conference of the United States are considered. The
chief judge of any such court of appeals shall make the appointment of a bankruptcy
judge if a majority of the judges of that court cannot agree on the appointment. 28
U.S.C.A. § 152(a)(3).

The official duty stations of bankruptcy judges and the places of holding court
are determined by the Judicial Conference after recommendations of the director of
the Administrative Office of the United States Courts are considered. The recommendations of the director are formulated by consultation with the judicial council
of the circuit involved. This chain of consultation and recommendation ensures that
the needs of the circuit are determined by the circuit rather than by an individual or
group far removed from the situation. 28 U.S.C.A. § 152(b)(1). If the business of the
court necessitates holding court in places within the judicial district other than the
official duty station, a bankruptcy judge may hold court at such places. 28 U.S.C.A.
§ 152(c). A bankruptcy judge may also be designated to serve in any district adjacent
to or near the district for which he or she has been appointed. Such designation requires approval of the Judicial Conference and of the judicial councils involved. 28
U.S.C.A. § 152(d). A bankruptcy judge may even be transferred temporarily to serve
in any judicial district. Such a transfer requires approval of the judicial councils of
the circuits involved. 28 U.S.C.A. § 155(a).

The term of appointment for a bankruptcy judge is 14 years. 28 U.S.C.A. §
152(a)(1). A bankruptcy judge serves on a full-time basis and "may not engage in the
practice of law or any other practice, business, occupation or employment" that

would be "inconsistent with the expeditious, proper and impartial performance" of the judge's duties. 28 U.S.C.A. §§ 153(a), (b).

Persons appointed as bankruptcy judges are required to take the following oath or affirmation before performance of judicial duties:

> I, _____ _____, do solemnly swear (or affirm) that I will administer justice without respect to persons, and do equal right to the poor and to the rich, and that I will faithfully and impartially discharge and perform all the duties incumbent upon me as _____ according to the best of my abilities and understanding, agreeably to the Constitution and laws of the United States. So help me God.

In a bankruptcy court where more than one judge presides, the division of cases and other matters among the judges will be determined by rules promulgated by majority vote of the court.

The district court judges designate one judge to serve as chief judge of the bankruptcy court in a bankruptcy court having more than one judge. The chief judge of the district court will make the designation if the majority of the judges of the district court cannot agree.

A bankruptcy judge may be removed during the term of appointment only by the judicial council of the circuit in which the judge's official duty station is located. Removal requires concurrence in the order of removal by a majority of all the judges of the judicial council. A bankruptcy judge must be furnished a full specification of charges and must have an opportunity to be heard on the charges. Grounds for removal are incompetence, misconduct, neglect of duty, or physical or mental disability. 28 U.S.C.A. § 153(e).

If a judge dies or becomes disabled after an action has been tried and is unable to perform the duties required by the court at that point, any other judge who regularly sits in that court or is assigned to that court may perform these duties. This second judge has discretion to grant a new trial if this judge feels incapable of performing the necessary duties because he or she did not preside at the original trial or for any other reason. Fed. R. Bank. P. 9028; Fed. R. Civ. P. 63.

A retired bankruptcy judge may consent to be recalled to serve in any judicial district. The judicial council of the circuit within which the district is located would recall the judge. 11 U.S.C.A. § 155(b).

B. THE JUDGE'S LAW CLERK

The law clerk in a bankruptcy court has the same duties as a law clerk in any other court. His or her main duty is to research questions raised before the court in disputed matters. Presentation to the judge of the results of this research in an easily assimilated form is another important part of the law clerk's job. The law clerk may also play a role in scheduling court appearances.

C. THE JUDGE'S SECRETARY

The judge's secretary performs the usual duties of any secretary, such as screening telephone calls and performing word processing, but the secretarial function most likely to be of interest to the paralegal is that of keeping the judge's calendar. The coordination of the judge's in-court and out-of-court schedules is vital to a smoothly run court. It will be helpful to the paralegal to become acquainted with the judge's secretary.

D. THE COURT REPORTER

A court reporter will make a verbatim record of any proceeding in which he or she is utilized. A certified copy of the transcript of a proceeding must be filed by the court reporter with the bankruptcy court clerk. Fed. R. Bank. P. 5007(a).

SECTION 6

THE OFFICE OF THE CLERK OF THE BANKRUPTCY COURT

The office of the clerk of the bankruptcy court is comprised of the clerk and the deputy clerks. The clerk's office is the administrative center for bankruptcy cases. Cases are not only filed in this office but are also physically maintained here. Any activity that takes place in a case will be recorded in this office.

A. THE BANKRUPTCY COURT CLERK

The bankruptcy court clerk is the official custodian of the records and dockets of the court. 28 U.S.C.A. § 156(e). Records to be kept by the clerk are enumerated under Fed. R. Bank. P. 5003. A bankruptcy docket is to be kept in each and every case under the Code. Each judgment, order, and activity in the case is entered and dated on the docket. A claims register is not kept in all cases but is necessary if it appears that a distribution may be made to creditors holding unsecured claims. This claims register consists of a list of claims filed in such a case.

The clerk must keep "a correct copy of every final judgment or order affecting title to or lien on real property or for the recovery of money or property." Fed. R. Bank. P. 5003(c). On request of the prevailing party, a correct copy of every such judgment or order must be kept and indexed with the civil judgments of the district court. The court may also direct any other order to be kept. The form and manner of such copies are prescribed by the director of the Administrative Office of the United States Courts. The clerk must keep an index of all cases and a separate index of adversary proceedings in a manner also prescribed by the director of the Administrative Office. A search of these indices and certification of whether a case or proceeding has been filed in the court or transferred to the court or whether a discharge has been entered must be made by the clerk upon request. Fed. R. Bank. P. 5003(d). The director of the Administrative Office may require the clerk to keep other books and records in addition to those listed here. Fed. R. Bank. P. 5003(e).

The clerk is accountable for all fees, costs, and other monies collected and makes returns of these monies to the director of the Administrative Office of the United States Courts and the director of the Executive Office for United States Trustees. 28 U.S.C.A. § 156(f).

Rule 5001(a) provides that "[t]he courts shall be deemed always open for the purpose of filing any pleading or other proper paper, issuing and returning process, and filing, making, or entering motions, orders and rules." Rule 5001(c), however, sets forth regular hours for the clerk's office: "The clerk's office with the clerk or a deputy in attendance shall be open during business hours on all days except Saturdays, Sundays and the legal holidays listed in Rule 9006(a)." There have been instances in which a bankruptcy petition has been accepted for filing after regular hours by the bankruptcy court judge at his or her residence. The clerk might also accept such filings.

The clerk is charged with issuing "a certified copy of the record of any proceeding in a case under the Code or of any paper filed with the clerk on payment of any prescribed fee." Fed. R. Bank. P. 5006. Fees for certification and for copying are fixed by the Judicial Conference. 28 U.S.C.A. § 1930(b).

As this summary of the clerk's duties and responsibilities indicates, the bankruptcy court clerk occupies an administrative position of great importance to the smooth operation of the court.

B. THE DEPUTY CLERKS

Deputy clerks are appointed by the clerk of the bankruptcy court subject to the approval of the court. 28 U.S.C.A. § 156(b). They may be removed from office in the same manner.

The duties of the deputy clerks are many and varied, ranging from the typing and filing inherent in any clerical position to answering inquiries from attorneys, paralegals, secretaries, debtors, and creditors by telephone or in the clerk's office. The deputy clerks are the front line soldiers in the bankruptcy court and, as such, are the members of the court personnel that paralegals most often encounter. Deputy clerks process the cases that paralegals bring in to file or explain why a particular document does not meet filing requirements. Well trained, experienced deputy clerks are of inestimable aid to the paralegal.

The record keeping required by the clerk of the court under Rule 5003 is performed by the various deputy clerks under the clerk's supervision. Thus, the docket sheets will be more familiar to the particular deputy who maintains them whereas a question regarding claims will probably be answered by the deputy in charge of the claims registers.

There may or may not be a supervisor of deputies who can help with questions beyond the knowledge or authority of the deputies. If there is no supervisor or if the supervisor is unable to assist the paralegal, the clerk will be called.

From the beginning of the paralegal's career, a good working relationship should be established with all members of the clerk's office. A professional manner on the part of the paralegal ensures that he or she will receive all the services that the clerk's staff is trained to provide.

SECTION 7
THE UNITED STATES TRUSTEES, PRIVATE TRUSTEES, AND EXAMINERS

The two basic categories of trustees are United States trustees and private trustees. United States trustees are appointed by the Attorney General of the United States. Private trustees include members of the trustee panel, standing trustees for Chapter 12 and Chapter 13 cases, and other trustees, such as those who serve in Chapter 11 cases. The category of other trustees includes those who have been serving in a case before the order for relief or those who are appointed or elected to serve in a case after the order for relief. The U.S. trustee appoints private trustees. Creditors in Chapter 7 cases may, however, elect a trustee to replace the interim trustee appointed by the U.S. trustee from the trustee panel. (See Exhibit 3.5.)

EXHIBIT 3.5
United States Trustees and Private Trustees

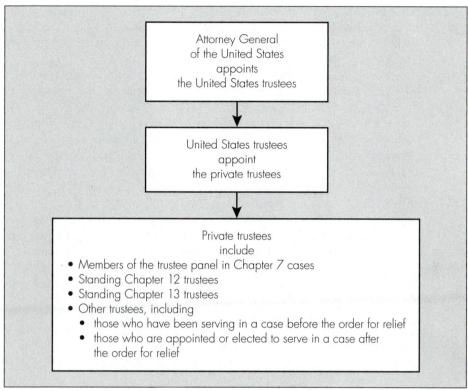

A. THE UNITED STATES TRUSTEES

Prior to the Bankruptcy Reform Act, some kind of supervision over trustees in the private trustee system was felt to be needed. The lack of such supervision was at the heart of one of the more substantive problems of the old system. The United States Trustee Pilot Program began on October 1, 1979, under former Chapter 15, when the Code went into effect in 18 judicial districts under the supervision of the United States Attorney General. The program was structured to follow the United States attorney system, so that **United States trustees** could serve in the same federal judicial districts as United States attorneys. It was contemplated in the Bankruptcy Reform Act that the system would be applied in all judicial districts if it was successful in the original 18 districts. Unless continued by Congress, the system would meet its end on April 1, 1984, according to its own **sunset provisions.** The Bankruptcy Amendments Act of 1984 extended the pilot program until September 30, 1986. This Act was followed by the Bankruptcy Judges, United States Trustees, and Family Farmer Bankruptcy Act of 1986, which not only expanded the pilot program from the original 18 judicial districts to the entire nation but also made it a permanent part of bankruptcy law.

The United States trustee system was created by statute. 28 U.S.C.A. §§ 581–589a. According to section 581, the attorney general appoints one United States trustee for each of the 21 regions composed of one or more federal judicial districts.

The United States Code provides that a United States trustee will be appointed for a term of five years and shall continue to serve until a successor is appointed and qualifies. 28 U.S.C.A. § 581(b). The United States trustee serves at the pleasure of the attorney general. The United States Code states that such trustee shall be appointed by the attorney general and provides for removal of trustees by the attorney general. 28 U.S.C.A. §§ 581(a), (c).

The duties of the United States trustee are set forth in the United States Code. 28 U.S.C.A. § 586. These duties include the establishment, maintenance, and supervision of a panel of private trustees to serve in Chapter 7 cases. The United States trustee may also be required to serve as trustee in certain cases. The United States trustee monitors applications for compensation and reimbursement and may file comments with the court regarding such applications. Plans filed in Chapters 11, 12, and 13 are monitored as are disclosure statements in Chapter 11 cases. Creditors' committees in Chapter 11 cases are appointed and supervised by the United States trustee. The United States trustee is to prevent undue delays in bankruptcy cases by monitoring the progress of cases and taking action whenever deemed necessary.

The United States trustee has been made a party in interest under the Code. 11 U.S.C.A. § 307. The Federal Rules of Bankruptcy Procedure require that he or she receive notice of practically all matters in every bankruptcy case. Fed. R. Bank. P. 2000(k), 9034. The United States trustee has the exclusive right to move for dismissal of a voluntary Chapter 7 case when the debtor fails to file a list of creditors, a schedule of assets and liabilities, a schedule of current income and current expenditures, and a statement of the debtor's financial affairs within 15 days or such period as the court has fixed for filing. 11 U.S.C.A. § 707(a)(3). The United States trustee may object to the discharge of a debtor and may request revocation of a discharge already granted. 11 U.S.C.A. §§ 727(c)(1), (d).

B. PRIVATE TRUSTEES

Some **private trustees** are members of the trustee panel who receive appointments to serve as **interim trustees** in Chapter 7 cases and continue to serve as trustees in those cases. Others are not panel members and serve only in cases in which they were serving as trustees immediately before the order for relief. **Standing trustees** who serve in Chapter 12 or Chapter 13 cases are also private trustees. Still other private trustees are members of the legal and business communities who are appointed to serve in Chapter 11 cases that require their particular expertise. Their service is on an irregular basis.

1. THE TRUSTEE PANEL

The **trustee panel,** a panel of private trustees that serves in Chapter 7 cases, is established, maintained, and supervised by the United States trustee. 28 U.S.C.A. § 586(a)(1).

a. Eligibility to Serve as a Trustee   To be eligible for the trustee panel, a prospective panel member must be eligible to serve as a trustee. The Chapter 7 trustee panel member may be an individual who is competent to perform the duties of a trustee and who resides or has an office either in the judicial district in which the case is pending or in an adjacent district. 11 U.S.C.A. § 321(a)(1). The Chapter 7 trustee panel member may also be a corporation, rather than an individual, if authorized by the corporation charter or bylaws to act as a trustee. The corporation must have an of-

fice either in the judicial district in which the case is pending or in an adjacent district. 11 U.S.C.A. § 321(a)(2).

b. Selection and Qualification   It is the duty of the United States trustee to appoint "a disinterested person" that is a panel trustee as interim trustee promptly after the order for relief in all Chapter 7 cases. A "disinterested person" is defined by the Code. 11 U.S.C.A. § 101(14). The interim trustee almost always continues as trustee for a particular case after the meeting of creditors, generally called the 341 meeting, because it is provided for by section 341 of the Code. 11 U.S.C.A. § 341. Election of a trustee by creditors is possible under the Code, but it rarely occurs. 11 U.S.C.A. § 702(b). The interim trustee continues to serve as trustee if no election takes place. 11 U.S.C.A. § 702(d). The elected trustee need not be a member of the trustee panel. If no member of the panel is willing to serve as interim trustee in a case, the U.S. trustee may serve in this capacity.

A panel trustee may also be appointed as interim trustee in a Chapter 7 involuntary case *before* the order for relief has been entered. The court may order the U.S. trustee, on request of a party in interest and after notice to the debtor and a hearing, to appoint an interium trustee to preserve the property of the estate or to prevent loss to the estate. 11 U.S.C.A. § 303(g).

After a person has been selected to serve as trustee in any case, the clerk must immediately notify this person about how to qualify. A person selected to serve in a case as interim trustee or trustee must qualify within five days after selection and before beginning official duties by filing a bond in favor of the United States. The bond is a faithful performance bond, which covers the honesty of the trustee while the duties required in a case are performed. The trustee has no personal liability for forfeiture of the debtor. 11 U.S.C.A. § 322(c).

A trustee serving as a member of the panel may be authorized by the U.S. trustee to file a blanket bond with the court. A blanket bond is a bond that covers the trustee in most cases. In cases in which assets exceed the blanket coverage, it will be necessary for the trustee to increase the bond. A trustee with a blanket bond selected to serve in a Chapter 7 or Chapter 13 case shall be deemed to have accepted service in the case unless the court has been notified in writing of rejection within five days after the trustee's receipt of notification of selection. A person without a blanket bond must notify the court in writing of acceptance within five days after receipt of notice of selection. Otherwise, this person shall be deemed to have rejected the office of trustee in this particular case. Fed. R. Bank. P. 2008.

The duties of a Chapter 7 trustee are enumerated in 11 U.S.C.A. § 704.

> The trustee shall—
>> (1) collect and reduce to money the property of the estate for which such trustee serves, and close such estate as expeditiously as is compatible with the best interests of parties in interest;
>> (2) be accountable for all property received;
>> (3) ensure that the debtor shall perform his intention as specified in section 521(2)(B) of this title;
>> (4) investigate the financial affairs of the debtor;
>> (5) if a purpose would be served, examine proofs of claims and object to the allowance of any claim that is improper;
>> (6) if advisable, oppose the discharge of the debtor;
>> (7) unless the court orders otherwise, furnish such information concerning the estate and the estate's administration as is requested by a party in interest;

(8) if the business of the debtor is authorized to be operated, file with the court, with the United States trustee, and with any government unit charged with responsibility for collection or determination of any tax arising out of such operation, periodic reports and summaries of the operation of such business, including a statement of receipts and disbursements, and such other information as the United States trustee or the court requires; and

(9) make a final report and file a final account of the administration of the estate with the court and with the United States trustee.

2. STANDING TRUSTEES

A standing trustee is one appointed by the U.S. trustee to serve in any case filed under Chapter 12 or Chapter 13. 11 U.S.C.A. §§ 1202(a), 1302(a).

The duties of a Chapter 12 trustee are enumerated in 11 U.S.C.A. § 1202(b).

(b) The trustee shall—
(1) perform the duties specified in sections 704(2), 704(3), 704(5), 704(6), 704(7) and 704(9) of this title;
(2) perform the duties specified in sections 1106(a)(3) and 1106(a)(4) of this title if the court, for cause and on request of a party in interest, the trustee, or the United States trustee, so orders;
(3) appear and be heard at any hearing that concerns—
(A) the value of property subject to a lien;
(B) confirmation of a plan;
(C) modification of the plan after confirmation; or
(D) the sale of property of the estate;
(4) ensure that the debtor commences making timely payments required by a confirmed plan; and
(5) if the debtor ceases to be a debtor in possession, perform the duties specified in sections 704(8), 1106(a)(1), 1106(a)(2), 1106(a)(6), 1106(a)(7), and 1203.

The duties of a Chapter 13 trustee are enumerated in 11 U.S.C.A. §§ 1302(b) and (c).

(b) The trustee shall—
(1) perform the duties specified in sections 704(2), 704(3), 704(4), 704(5), 704(6), 704(7), and 704(9) of this title;
(2) appear and be heard at any hearing that concerns—
(A) the value of property subject to a lien;
(B) confirmation of a plan; or
(C) modification of the plan after confirmation;
(3) dispose of, under regulations issued by the Director of the Administrative Office of the United States Courts, moneys received or to be received in a case under chapter XIII of the Bankruptcy Act; and
(4) advise, other than on legal matters, and assist the debtor in performance under the plan; and
(5) ensure that the debtor commences making timely payments under section 1326 of this title.
(c) If the debtor is engaged in business, then in addition to the duties specified in subsection (b) of this section, the trustee shall perform the duties specified in sections 1106(a)(3) and 1106(a)(4) of this title.

The U.S. trustee is not required to appoint a standing trustee for Chapter 12 and Chapter 13 cases. A disinterested person may be appointed, or the U.S. trustee may serve if necessary. 11 U.S.C.A. §§ 1202(a), 1302(a).

3. OTHER TRUSTEES

A private trustee, other than a panel trustee, is only called upon to serve as an interim trustee in a Chapter 7 case in which this person has been serving as trustee in the case immediately before the order for relief in Chapter 7. 11 U.S.C.A. § 701(a)(1). This generally occurs when a case is converted from Chapter 11 to Chapter 7.

Private trustees who are not members of the panel are more likely to serve in Chapter 11 cases. Chapter 11 reorganizations sometimes require expertise in a particular area to preserve an ongoing business and successfully reorganize it when the debtor in possession is unable to do so.

C. EXAMINERS

After notice and a hearing, an **examiner** may be appointed by the court upon request of a party in interest or the United States trustee. Such an appointment occurs only in a Chapter 11 case in which no trustee has been appointed and in which no plan has been confirmed. An examiner is charged with conducting an investigation of the debtor. This investigation includes allegations of fraud, dishonesty, incompetence, mismanagement, or irregularity in the management of the affairs of the debtor.

An examiner is appointed only if it is in the interests of creditors, equity security holders (if any), and other interests of the estate or if the debtor's fixed, liquidated unsecured debts exceed $5,000,000. Debts owed to an insider and debts for goods, services, or taxes are not included in the $5,000,000. As Chapter 11 cases have increased in number and size, there has been a corresponding increase in the appointment of examiners. 11 U.S.C.A. § 1104(c).

BASIC TERMS AND PHRASES

Accounts
Accounts receivable
Administrative expenses
Bankruptcy petition preparer
Chattel paper
Collateral
Creditor holding a priority claim
Creditor holding a secured claim
Creditor holding an unsecured claim
Equity security holder
Examiner
Fixtures
Indenture trustee
Interim trustee
Mortgagee

Mortgagor
Parties in interest
Priority claim
Private trustee
Secured claim
Secured party
Security interest
Standing trustee
Statutory lienholder
Sunset provision
Trustee panel
Undercollateralized
United States trustee
Unsecured claim
Voluntary petition

FOUR

THE CLIENT INTERVIEW, EVALUATING THE CLIENT'S OPTIONS, ADVISING THE CLIENT OF THE OPTIONS, AND DRAFTING

CHAPTER OUTLINE

Not all clients are debtors; some may be creditors. This chapter discusses both the debtor-client and the creditor-client. Once it becomes apparent whether the client is a debtor or a creditor, the attorney will evaluate the client's options, advise the client of the options, and draft the necessary documents with the aid of his or her paralegal.

SECTION 1
THE DEBTOR-CLIENT

Every attorney has his or her own method of interviewing, counseling, and drafting. Some attorneys do not interview the debtor until the debtor has completed a questionnaire (which may be done with the aid of a paralegal) and has provided substantial financial information. When the attorney first meets the debtor, it is to advise the debtor whether to pursue a bankruptcy or nonbankruptcy solution. If bankruptcy is recommended, the attorney advises the debtor under which chapter the case should be filed and proceeds to draft the various documents required for filing. Other attorneys conduct an initial interview with the debtor to solicit basic information about the debtor and the debtor's financial problems, a second meeting to advise the debtor whether to pursue a bankruptcy or nonbankruptcy solution and to instruct the debtor in terms of what information the debtor should gather, a third meeting to initiate the drafting process, and additional meetings to complete the drafting in more complicated cases.

In this chapter, the interviewing, counseling, and drafting phases of the process will be viewed as four distinct steps:

1. an initial interview, during which the attorney or paralegal gathers information from the debtor and gives the debtor basic information concerning the process;
2. the analysis, in which the attorney evaluates the information gathered and formulates a course of action;
3. a counseling session, during which the attorney reviews with the debtor the information received and makes a recommendation, gains the debtor's assent to the recommendation, secures commitment to the fee, and gathers more information; and
4. the meeting(s) to draft the documents.

These steps may be telescoped when appropriate. At the initial interview, it may be obvious that the advice will be to file bankruptcy and the debtor is prepared to proceed immediately. In such cases, the drafting of the documents may begin at this interview.

Sometimes the filing of the petition in bankruptcy is an emergency because essential property will be lost if the petition is not filed immediately. This type of situation requires that drafting of at least the petition, clerk's notice (in the case of an individual consumer debtor), statement of attorney's compensation, and matrix be done at the initial interview. The schedules and statement of financial affairs are then filed within 15 days of the petition.

EXAMPLE
The day before a foreclosure sale, Andrew Augustine visited an attorney for the first time to discuss bankruptcy. Shortly into the interview, it became clear to the attorney that

Augustine's only option was to file a Chapter 11 or Chapter 13 petition to forestall the foreclosure sale. The attorney filed the petition prior to the foreclosure sale to avoid having to revoke the foreclosure sale.

Although one debtor, such as Mr. Augustine, will see an attorney for the first time just prior to foreclosure, another may have made long term advance plans to file bankruptcy in the event that all other efforts fail to prevent foreclosure.

EXAMPLE

PRINCE ALBERT POLO CLUB FILES BANKRUPTCY
FORECLOSURE SALE AVOIDED

The Prince Albert Polo Club, Inc., paid $9 million to build the Prince Albert Race Track. The track operated for one racing season and then was idled due to financial and regulatory problems.

The Club negotiated with Friendly Bank, the Club's largest creditor, to forestall a foreclosure sale. After negotiations failed and only one hour before Friendly Bank's foreclosure sale, the Club filed a Chapter 11 bankruptcy petition, thus protecting the track from the foreclosure sale. At the time of the filing, the Club listed $8.5 million in assets and $7.1 million in liabilities. Had the Club not filed for the Bankruptcy Court's protection, the Club would have lost the opportunity to operate the track.

In an emergency situation, the law provides for the filing of a barebones case as long as the schedules and statement of financial affairs are filed within 15 days of the petition. Although good practice mandates filing all of the documents at the time the petition is filed, situations do exist that require filing the petition, clerk's notice (in the case of an individual consumer debtor), statement of attorney's compensation, and matrix without the supporting documents. Unless it is necessary to file the petition to preserve assets of the estate, filing should be delayed by a few days so that all the forms may be prepared and submitted at one time.

Some attorneys routinely file the barebones petition package and take 15 days to file the remaining documents. When such a pattern occurs, the judges begin to look at the attorneys who do this in a little different light than those attorneys who generally file all of the documents when the petition is filed. Although the statutes permit 15 days for filing the remainder of the documents, judges and the clerk's office do not like this type of practice because it places an additional burden on the clerk's office. The rule of thumb should be to file all of the documents at one time unless an emergency exists.

A. THE INITIAL INTERVIEW

During the initial interview the attorney or paralegal elicits information from the debtor and gives the debtor basic information. The attorney is seeking information to determine whether to recommend a nonbankruptcy or bankruptcy solution and if bankruptcy is the solution, under which chapter of the Bankruptcy Code the case should be filed. The debtor, of course, is seeking a viable solution to his or her financial difficulties.

One of the most important things the attorney or paralegal does at the initial interview is to put the debtor at ease. This will be the first contact with the legal world for many debtors. Many are apprehensive not only about their financial situation but may also be even more apprehensive about being in an attorney's office. Some will be embarrassed about discussing their finances and the causes of their financial dilemma. The attorney or paralegal who is sensitive to these matters will be able to allay the debtor's fears and get the necessary information in a more timely manner. The attorney or paralegal should always explain to the debtor what is needed and why it is needed in terms the debtor can understand. Although many debtors intentionally withhold vital information, others do so because they fail to understand what is required. The success of the recommended solution for a particular debtor's problems will hinge upon full knowledge of the debtor's situation. The groundwork for this success is laid at the initial interview.

The attorney and paralegal should formulate their own interview materials. If an office is computerized, the questionnaire can be maintained in the database, ready to print when the need arises. Experience will suggest additions and modifications in the format.

When assembling information for the initial interview, the official bankruptcy forms, which are a part of the Federal Rules of Bankruptcy Procedure, are helpful because they suggest much of the needed information. At almost every point in the initial interview, the placing of one item of information on the questionnaire will suggest the need for other information. The following information discusses some main points for an interview questionnaire.

IDENTITY OF THE DEBTOR

Who is the debtor? Complete information is necessary regarding the identity of the debtor and related entities. A debtor may be an individual, a partnership, a small corporation, or a large corporation.

If an individual debtor is married, the name of the debtor's spouse and information about him or her similar to that gathered about the debtor will be important. A married debtor immediately raises the question of the necessity or the desirability of filing on behalf of both the debtor and the debtor's spouse. If the filing is for an individual and his or her spouse, the case is filed as a joint case. 11 U.S.C.A. § 302. No other combination of entities may file a joint case.

The name of an individual is incomplete for bankruptcy purposes unless the full first, middle, and last names are given. "Jr." and "III" must be included when applicable. Also, all other names used by the debtor or his or her spouse during the previous six years are essential.

With regard to the precise and exact identification of the entity to be involved in the bankruptcy case, the debtor must be apprised that if an individual case is filed, all of that debtor's individually owned enterprises will be affected and cannot be divided so that only the personal debts or only the debts of one particular enterprise go into the bankruptcy case. The person who owns more than one individual proprietorship business will find that all of his or her debts (both business and personal) and all of his or her assets (both business and personal) will be affected by an individual bankruptcy filing.

EXAMPLE
A debtor may say something like "Joe's Grocery & Market is doing just fine and I don't want to put that business in bankruptcy. It is Joe's Service Station that has caused me all this trouble and I want to file for that business only." The debtor will discover, however, that the grocery store must be included in the bankruptcy filing.

If a filing is contemplated on behalf of either a partnership or a corporation, the attorney's and paralegal's job becomes more complex and further information concerning the identity of such an entity will be required. In many cases, it is necessary to file either an individual or a joint case and then to simultaneously file the case of a corporation owned by such individual or individual and spouse, because both will have financial problems. An attorney must exercise care in conferring with and representing both the owners of a corporation and the corporation itself in a Chapter 11 case. The attorney for the debtor in possession must be approved by the court in a Chapter 11 case, and it is required that an attorney not represent conflicting interests. The courts hold that while there is no disqualifying conflict of interest as such in the dual representation of a corporate Chapter 11 debtor and its stockholders, there may be a conflict of interest in representing both entities as Chapter 11 debtors.

Chapter 11 has always worked well for large corporations. The large corporate debtor has greater financial strength. Many of the issues raised against the small corporate debtor, with the exception of collateral control, will not be raised against the large corporate debtor, even if the plan does not work out and the corporation is liquidated under Chapter 11. The new **small business** Chapter 11 Reform Act provision should allow Chapter 11 to work as well now for small corporations as it has for large ones in the past.

Although bankruptcy for businesses was once thought of as an absolute last alternative, bankruptcy under Chapter 11 is increasingly becoming simply another tool to be considered in the financial restructuring of a troubled enterprise. Bankruptcy under Chapter 11 played an important role in the restructuring of the airline industry as a result of financial problems caused by deregulation.

While Chapter 7 is available, it will generally not be used for a large corporation, because the officers of large corporations do not think in terms of liquidation. They think in terms of staying in business in a restructured form.

With regard to a corporation, it is necessary to immediately see the documents under which the corporation was created and to know that the corporation is in good standing according to the laws of the jurisdiction under which it was created.

Partnerships come in two forms: the partnership and the limited partnership. The **partnership** is often created in an informal manner, possibly with a handshake. It can be created without documentation. Thus, a threshold question could be whether a partnership even exists. "A partnership is an association of two or more persons to carry on as co-owners a business for profit." Uniform Partnership Act § 6. All partners are jointly and severally liable for all debts and obligations of the partnership.

A **limited partnership** is a partnership with at least one general partner and one limited partner. Limited partners may contribute cash or other property to the partnership, but they may not contribute services. A limited partnership provides limited liability to investors in the partnership. Limited partners are not bound by the obligations of the partnership. Limited partners are not liable to creditors unless the limited partners share in or have taken control of the business. A general partner in a limited partnership is liable to creditors.

Whether a limited partnership exists is not difficult to ascertain. Limited partnerships are strictly a matter of statute. Most states have enacted the Uniform Limited Partnership Act.

What are the bankruptcy ramifications of filing as a partnership versus filing as an individual? If the case is filed as a partnership, the partnership entity is the debtor and not the individuals who make up the partnership. Therefore, the case is filed in the name of the partnership rather than in the names of the partners. The debts are the partnership debts, not individual debts.

Sometimes it is necessary to file for individuals along with the bankruptcy filing of a partnership owned by them. In the case of the filing of a partnership bankruptcy, it is necessary to establish the precise identity of the partnership and to refer carefully to the documents under which the partnership was created. The names of each of the general and limited partners and the respective interest of each in the partnership are required information. The attorney and paralegal must, of course, be dealing with either the controlling parties or parties who have the right, under the bankruptcy law, to file the bankruptcy case on behalf of the partnership.

Filing for a small corporation may also require filing for the persons closely connected to the corporation. Such persons may have guaranteed corporate debts and would not be protected from creditors under the automatic stay that applies only to the debts of the corporation. The same careful analysis required for the individuals constituting a partnership must be done for individuals operating a corporation.

DEBTOR'S ADDRESS

Where is the debtor currently living? A permanent mailing address, if the debtor has one, that will be good for some time into the future is required. Does the debtor plan to move in the near future? Some debtors will be in the process of moving out of a foreclosed house or mobile home. It is important to know how long the debtor has lived at that address to determine venue.

Where is the debtor's place of business? The location of the debtor is more than just an address. It is impossible to even determine the venue of a case without information about the legal residence and place of business of a debtor. Once venue has been determined, it may be desirable or even necessary to refer the case to counsel in another district. Perhaps the case will be filed in a district other than the one in which the debtor contemplates the case will be filed. All of this must be explained to the debtor after a thorough analysis has taken place and a decision has been made concerning where to file the case based upon the location, or situs information. If a debtor is a wage earner and has a fixed residence address, it is a simple matter to note the address of the debtor for bankruptcy filing information. In some instances, however, a partnership or a corporation will have several places of business, or its primary property will be in a district other than the place where its main office is located. There will be instances where more than one place is "a proper venue," and the court of the district in which the case is filed may transfer the case to another district for the convenience of the parties. On occasion, this will allow a debtor to do some degree of "forum shopping." The case *In re Ginco* deals with a petition to change venue.

In re Ginco, Inc.
United States Bankruptcy Court, District of New Mexico, 1986.
70 B.R. 2.

MEMORANDUM OPINION
Mark B. McFeeley,
Bankruptcy Judge

This matter came before the Court on creditor Colorado National Bank's (CNB) Motion to Dismiss or in the Alternative for Change of Venue to the United States Bankruptcy Court for the District of Colorado.

The debtor, Ginco, Inc. (Ginco) is a Nevada corporation with its principal place of business and principal corporate offices located in Denver, Colorado. On November 29, 1985, Ginco filed a chapter 7 bankruptcy petition in the District of New Mexico. On December 9, 1985, CNB moved to dismiss or in the alternative for change of venue. The motion was objected to by International State Bank, but not the debtor.

Peripheral to this bankruptcy proceeding is a diversity cause of action in the United States District Court for the District of New Mexico between two of Ginco's creditors the movant here and the objector thereto. Decision in the District Court is deferred pending this Court's ruling on CNB's motion. This Court's ruling should have no effect, in this Court's opinion, on the pending motion for change of venue in the District Court proceeding.

Permissive change of venue is authorized in 28 U.S.C. § 1475 "in the interest of justice and for the convenience of the parties." The bankruptcy rules reiterate these requirements.

> If a petition is filed in a proper district, on timely motion of a party in interest, and after hearing on notice to the petitioners and to other persons as directed by the court, the case may be transferred to any other district if the Court determines that the transfer is for the convenience of the parties and witnesses in the interest of justice.

Federal Bankruptcy Rule 1014(a)(1).

The terms "in the interest of justice" and "for the convenience of the parties" were standardized in *In re Commonwealth Oil Refining Co.,* 596 F.2d 1239 (5th Cir.1979). This Court has adhered to the five factors established by the Court in *Commonwealth. In re Ocheltree,* 71 B.R. 1 (Bankr.D.N.M. 1983), *In re Cash and Carry Tool Supply Co., Inc.,* 22 B.R. 281 (Bankr.D.N.M.1982); as well as in the decisions of other courts. *C.f., Landmark Capital Company v. North Central Development Company (In re Land-mark Capital Company),* 8 B.C.D. 1160, 20 B.R. 220 (C.D.,S.D.N.Y.1982); *In re Almeida,* 37 B.R. 186 (Bkrtcy.E.D.Pa.1984).

The five factors are:

1) Proximity of creditors of every kind to the court;
2) Proximity of the debtor to the Court;
3) Proximity of witnesses necessary to the administration of the estate;
4) Location of assets; and,

5) Economic administration of the estate. *In re Commonwealth Oil Refining, supra,* at 1247.

The party moving for the transfer has the burden of proving that the transfer would be in the interest of justice and for the convenience of the parties and in so doing he must overcome the presumption that the debtor is entitled to file and maintain his case in the venue in which he filed it. *In re Walter,* 12 B.C.D. 1057, 47 B.R. 240 (Bkrtcy. M.D.Fla. 1985).

In the instant case the Court finds the following:

A.   Proximity of Creditors to the Court

Ninety-eight percent of Ginco's taxes are owed to the State of Colorado; while two percent are owed to the State of New Mexico. Of the seven secured creditors listed with addresses (10 total), five are in Colorado and hold over 40% of the debt owed by Ginco. The two largest secured creditors are the movant, CNB, and the objector, International State Bank (ISB), to the motion under consideration. ISB is located in Raton, New Mexico, which is closer to Denver than to Albuquerque (220 miles v. 235 miles by interstate highway). Three Hundred Sixty-Eight creditors are listed by the debtor as holding unsecured claims. Of those listed with addresses 41% (151) are in Colorado and 5% (21) are in New Mexico. Schedules A1, A2 and A3 from debtor's Statement of Financial Affairs.

B.   Proximity of the Debtor to the Court

Ginco's principal place of business is in Denver, Colorado where its corporate headquarters are located. All general ledgers and accounts receivable ledgers are in Denver, Colorado in the possession of the movant. All Ginco's banking records are maintained at CNB offices in Denver.

C.   Proximity of Witnesses Necessary to the Administration of the Estate

The president of the debtor corporation is C.R. Grinder. Mr. and Mrs. Grinder are

Ginco's major stockholders and reside in Colorado. The movant states in his brief that all present and former employees knowledgeable about Ginco's books and accounting reside in Denver. The former president of ISB, Richard Berg, who authorized and executed the agreement pertinent to the ISB-CNB adversary proceeding, currently is the president of another bank located in Lakewood, Colorado, a suburb of Denver. The ISB officer who was in charge of Ginco's account, John Tate, is presently employed by a bank in Durango, Colorado. Ginco's attorney, Mr. Slivka, whose firm prepared the UCC form at issue between ISB and CNB is in Denver. The information as to the location of witnesses is uncontroverted by ISB. The named individuals are subject to the subpoena power of a Colorado court.

D.   Location of Assets

Ginco's successor business is located in Denver and has almost all Ginco's inventory and equipment. Other assets include accounts receivable and these records are in the possession of CNB in Denver; bank deposits in New Mexico; and an unliquidated debt owing to the debtor which is currently in litigation in the United States District Court for the District of Colorado.

E.   Economic Administration of the Estate

The debtor, the debtor's majority stockholders, the records relevant to the debtor's past and present financial status and the witnesses are located in Colorado. Consequently, it would be more advantageous in terms of convenience and economies for this case to be heard in a Colorado forum.

We also note that witnesses and records from Raton, New Mexico, must travel an almost equal distance to whichever forum hears the case.

Upon application of the requirements delineated in *Commonwealth, supra,* to the facts of the instant case, we conclude that the movant has met his burden and proved that the interest of justice and the convenience of the parties are best served by transferring this case to the United States Bankruptcy Court for the District of Colorado.

This opinion shall constitute findings of fact and conclusions of law. Bankruptcy Rule 7052.

An appropriate order shall enter.

DEBTOR'S EMPLOYMENT SITUATION

What is the debtor's situation? How long has the debtor been employed on his or her present job, and how stable does the job situation look? If the debtor is unemployed, a petition in bankruptcy may not be appropriate, no matter what the debt is. The unemployed individual is not eligible to file a Chapter 13 case which requires regular income. Even if the debts currently owed were to be discharged under a Chapter 7 case, more debts would be swiftly amassed that the debtor would not be able to pay. If the debtor is a wage earner, the attorney needs to obtain information to evaluate whether the debtor is a candidate for a Chapter 13.

What are the debtor's attitudes about Chapter 7 and Chapter 13, if he or she is an individual wage earner? Sometimes the debtor has a choice. Sometimes, the debtor's attitude determines which chapter will be selected. Would the debtor rather dump the whole mess or fight with it for three years? The attorney may conclude that the debtor is just not able to make a Chapter 13, because he or she does not have the staying power to carry through with the plan, or that the debt structure would be too much to meet under a Chapter 13 plan. The debt structure might be such that the debtor would have to struggle to pay off 5 percent.

CAUSES FOR THE DEBTOR'S FINANCIAL DIFFICULTIES

What caused the debtor to be in this financial condition? Although debtors very often cite an inappropriate reason for their bankruptcy, it is still necessary to have the debtor discuss the cause of his or her financial problems. Many debtors will be very anxious to reveal these matters at the earliest possible opportunity. Of course, a single triggering catastrophe, such as a long continuing illness or a lengthy period of unemployment, may reveal the fundamental cause of the financial problem. Many debtors, especially in small businesses, may be unaware of or may not want to admit the real cause of the financial problems and will simply say that they had a "cash flow" problem. The hallmark of consumer debtor and small business bankruptcies is the lack of money, but this may not be the fundamental cause. The real cause will be discovered as the debtor's case proceeds.

What are the stated causes for the debtor's financial predicament? It has been customary to attribute the causes of bankruptcy to various factors, such as economic conditions, the inability to manage financial affairs, or some catastrophe beyond the control of the future debtor in bankruptcy.

What are the real causes of the debtor's financial predicament? The answers to this question will have some bearing on the selection of a nonbankruptcy or bankruptcy solution.

A major difficulty in dealing with the causes of bankruptcy is that the party most immediately involved, the debtor in bankruptcy, very often does not state the ultimate cause of bankruptcy filing and may cite some more immediate situation. A consumer debtor may very well believe that the cause of the bankruptcy filing is a garnishment against his or her paycheck, but the objective observer sees that the actual cause behind the bankruptcy filing and the garnishment itself was the unwise use of credit. The debtor might have gone along indefinitely juggling his or her debts on a salary inadequate to cover living expenses and pay all debts, but the garnishment forced a different solution to the problem.

> **PROBLEM 4.1**   Judy Rogers earns $250 a week as a secretary. After taxes, social security withholding, and insurance, Judy takes home $700 a month. Each month she pays $200 for rent, $200 for car payments, and $250 for living expenses.
>
> Last year Judy was involved in an automobile accident (which was her fault) and spent several weeks in the hospital. Although her medical insurance covered most of her hospital and medical bills, she still owed the hospital $1,000 and the doctor $1,500. For the past year, Judy has been sending $25 a month to the hospital and $25 to the doctor.
>
> The hospital became dissatisfied with Judy's low payments and obtained a judgment against her. The hospital then had the court enter a garnishment decree for $100 a month from Judy's wages. Because of the garnishment, Judy now has only $600 a month in take-home pay and no longer has enough money to pay $200 for rent, $200 for car payments, $250 for living expenses, and $25 toward her doctor's bill.
>
> What caused Judy's current problem, and what are Judy's options? Evaluate each option.

A small business owner is very often apt to describe the cause of bankruptcy as a "cash flow" problem when the real cause of the bankruptcy filing may very well be lack of sufficient business because of poor management or improper selection of a business site.

PROBLEM 4.2   Tom's Hamburger Stand has been in business for 15 years. A year ago, a national fast-food chain opened a restaurant within a block of Tom's. Naturally, the fast-food restaurant diverted customers from the hamburger stand. During the past six months, Tom's has been unable to generate enough money to pay all of its bills.

What caused Tom's current problem, and what are the options? Evaluate each option.

When dealing with the intake of a bankruptcy case, the attorney and the paralegal must ferret out both the immediate and ultimate causes of the bankruptcy. The results of this investigation will enhance the possibility of selecting the proper alternative to follow either in taking some nonbankruptcy course of action or, if filing a bankruptcy case, in selecting the chapter of the Bankruptcy Code under which the case should be filed. Determining the causes of bankruptcy is also important in that if the proper cause is ascertained, investigation of the actual facts of the case will be facilitated. The attorney and the paralegal will know precisely what to look for to avoid any surprises and to prepare thoroughly before the case is filed in bankruptcy court.

In dealing with consumer bankruptcies, the bankruptcy population must be compared with the nonbankruptcy population. This could very well lead to the conclusion that one theory is simply, "Some do, some don't." An examination of indebtedness and other factors might reveal that many indebted persons do not file bankruptcy. Their economic conditions may actually be much worse than many of those who do file bankruptcy. Many people who do file bankruptcy might have found an acceptable alternative but have, in fact, taken what they regard to be the easy way out. Although recent amendments have attempted to deal with the "easy way out" filing, this problem still does exist.

There are a number of generally accepted reasons for bankruptcy filings. One of the basic causes, especially of business bankruptcies, is economic conditions on a national or a regional level. A general recession on a national level can be an ultimate cause of bankruptcy filings, and an increase in the number of bankruptcy filings can be expected in such times. On a regional level, a particular area of the country that is especially impacted by a recession or that is in a regional recession (for example, states with economies that depend heavily on the oil industry) can expect an increase in bankruptcy filings. Such economic conditions can be given as causes of bankruptcy filings because they do, of course, lead to higher unemployment and business failures.

A reason often cited for bankruptcy filings, particularly by persons other than the debtor in the case, is the lack of ability to manage either personal or business finances. In dealing with this cause, the attorney or the paralegal must be particularly careful to note which party is giving information. A creditor often cites lack of management ability as a reason or cause of bankruptcy, but the debtor who goes into bankruptcy seldom mentions this as a factor.

Illnesses of debtors and catastrophic losses are related because either will deplete the debtors' assets. Prolonged illness, especially involving persons without health insurance, is a common cause of bankruptcy filing, as is the occurrence of some catastrophic casualty for which the debtor has no insurance protection.

Sustained periods of unemployment by the debtor often result in a bankruptcy filing. Few people have the necessary financial cushion to meet even ordinary living expenses while unemployed, particularly if they have no source of regular income such as unemployment insurance.

Some comments should be made about the question of whether or not the enactment of the Bankruptcy Reform Act of 1978 caused an increase in the number of bankruptcy filings. There is a difference of opinion on this subject, and a person's outlook is probably going to be influenced by his or her position as a creditor or a debtor in the bankruptcy process.

The Bankruptcy Reform Act of 1978 received substantial publicity directed both to the public and to attorneys. This information may have generated more awareness of bankruptcy as an option in the would-be debtor and in the attorney counseling a client having financial difficulties. Economic conditions since the effective date of the new law have probably had as important an impact as the law itself although, admittedly, it would be difficult to separate out these factors. Consumer debt has risen to an unprecedented level in the last several years. As it continues to rise, neither debtors nor creditors seem able to say no to further indebtedness.

Another factor that has made an answer to the question of the cause of the increase in bankruptcies more difficult is that the effective date of the new law coincided with the beginning of heavy advertising by attorneys. This increased advertising in the bankruptcy area by attorneys may have actually created additional demand for legal services in debt situations. Advertising appears to be especially effective in the bankruptcy area of the law. Many debtors have never used the services of an attorney. Their creditors may be pressing them for payment when they notice an advertisement for bankruptcy services on television or in the TV section of their local newspaper. The debtor who is accustomed to using the yellow pages of the telephone directory for various types of services may seek legal help there when he or she faces garnishment or foreclosure.

> **PROBLEM 4.3**   Check the yellow pages of your local telephone directory and the TV section of your local newspaper. Find several advertisements concerning bankruptcy services and other services offered by attorneys. Compare attorney advertising in the area of bankruptcy with attorney advertising in other areas.

GENERAL NATURE OF THE DEBTOR'S FINANCIAL CONDITION

What is the debtor's financial condition? The general nature of the debtor's financial situation should be ascertained at the first opportunity. An outline of the debtor's primary assets, together with their collective value, and a rather close estimate of the debtor's total debts should be made.

If the debtor is an individual, then in addition to assets and liabilities, a complete overview of the debtor's current income and expenses is necessary. This overview should include the estimated average monthly income of the debtor and his or her spouse, if married, and the estimated average current monthly expenses of the debtor and his or her family.

The debts should be categorized as secured (noting the property by which they are secured) and as unsecured. Eventually, it will be necessary to make a precise check of assets against liabilities for liens and encumbrances, but it will be satisfactory initially to get the overall picture. The general trend of the debtor's financial situation over the past several years should be examined. This investigation may be hampered by the fact that the debtor has not kept accurate financial records, particularly if the debtor is not engaged in business. Even the debtor engaged in a small business often has inadequate records.

At this point it is not necessary to look for insolvency. In a voluntary bankruptcy situation under any chapter under the present law, insolvency is not a prerequisite to the filing of a bankruptcy petition. In fact, in many cases, the debtor's estimation of the value of assets will far exceed the amount of liabilities.

The attorney must know (the debtor should always inform the attorney immediately) of any impending threat to the debtor's assets or financial situation. It is not unusual for an attorney to receive a panicky telephone call from a debtor just before noon on Thursday advising that help is needed because a foreclosure is to take place on the debtor's principal residence or on his or her business assets on Friday morning (the next day) at 10:00 A.M.

IDENTIFICATION AND LOCATION OF THE DEBTOR'S ASSETS

What are the debtor's assets, and where are they located? The location of the debtor's assets not only affects venue but also is of vital concern for administration of the estate.

IDENTIFICATION AND LOCATION OF THE CREDITORS

The attorney or the paralegal should carefully review the creditor lists for proper and complete addresses (including zip codes) and question the debtor about any address that does not appear to be valid. The debtor should provide account numbers for all creditors who use them. Each creditor must be properly identified by the correct name of the entity involved, and the debtor should give some information regarding the type of business conducted by each creditor.

One point of critical importance is that the client should be responsible for listing all debts and assets in his or her own handwriting. The debt owed to an unlisted creditor, who has not received notice of the bankruptcy filing, will not be discharged. An attorney or a paralegal who takes such information orally is running an unnecessary risk.

All creditors must be listed regardless of whether the *debtor believes that the debt will be satisfied by other means*. If the debt ultimately is not satisfied by other means and the creditor has not received notice of the bankruptcy, the debt will not be discharged.

EXAMPLE

Jim Olson, a building contractor, entered into a contract to build an office building for the Utopia Fitness Center. Olson contracted with a number of suppliers. After the building was completed, Olson was not paid by the fitness center. Olson, in turn, did not pay his suppliers. This compounded Olson's financial problems, which were already numerous. Olson sought legal assistance.

When Olson was completing his questionnaire for the initial interview, he left out a number of debts that he had incurred with various suppliers. He rationalized that these debts would be taken care of by the court because the suppliers had filed liens against the real estate.

When the real estate was liquidated, the proceeds were inadequate to satisfy the debts of all of the suppliers. Those debts not satisfied were not discharged by the bankruptcy proceeding.

All creditors must be listed, regardless of what the *debtor plans to do about a particular debt*. If a creditor has not received notice of the bankruptcy, the debt will not be discharged.

EXAMPLE

Agnes Milbrook borrowed $500 from her sister Flo. When Agnes completed her questionnaire, she left out her debt to Flo on the ground that she intended to pay Flo after she received her discharge in bankruptcy. Regardless of Agnes's intentions, her debt to Flo should have been listed on the questionnaire.

All creditors must be listed, regardless of what the *creditor plans to do about a particular debt*. If a creditor has not received notice of the bankruptcy, the debt will not be discharged.

EXAMPLE
Simon Smith borrowed $2,000 from his mother. When Smith developed financial problems, his mother told him to forget the debt. Unknown to Smith's mother, Smith filed for bankruptcy. Believing that his mother had forgiven the debt, he did not list this debt on his schedules. Shortly after the bankruptcy, his mother died and her executor attempted to collect the debt. Regardless of whether Smith's mother told him to forget the debt, the debt should have been listed on the questionnaire.

STATUS OF THE CREDITORS AS TO COLLATERAL AND RELATIVE PRIORITIES
Who are the creditors, and how much is each creditor owed? The priority claimants must be identified. These include employees with wage claims or unpaid benefit plans and government taxing authorities owed taxes. Secured or unsecured creditors must also be distinguished. The amount of each debt must be determined. Some debtors can give the attorney or the paralegal accurate and up-to-date information on their creditors and loans; others have little or no information to provide.

It is important that the attorney and the paralegal for the debtor obtain the best information available concerning the identification and location of the collateral. Information on the status of that collateral—whether it is still owned by the debtor or it has been totally expended or utilized in the operation of the business—should be obtained. A major concern is whether the creditor holding a secured claim has properly perfected a security interest. This will have a great effect on the ability of the debtor to reaffirm a debt in many cases and of course will affect the debtor's right to effectively claim and fully utilize an exemption.

DEBTOR'S ATTEMPTS TO EFFECT A NONBANKRUPTCY SOLUTION
What has the debtor done to attempt to effect a **workout?** Has the debtor talked to his or her creditors? If so, what is the status of these discussions or what resulted from them? What is the name of the creditor or the creditor's representative with whom the debtor has been dealing, and what is his or her telephone number and address? Some debtors never try to deal with any creditors at all. Some are trying to deal with every creditor. Some are dealing successfully with some of their creditors and unsuccessfully with the others. Some debtors are dealing with their secured creditors and ignoring their unsecured creditors; others are dealing with their unsecured creditors and ignoring their secured creditors.

IDENTIFICATION OF PENDING LAWSUITS
Is the debtor the subject of a pending lawsuit or lawsuits? What is the status of this suit or suits? Some lawsuits may be on the verge of a judgment. Upon judgment, the prevailing party may seek garnishment, which should be avoided if possible. A number of debtors do not recognize a lawsuit when they see it. A debtor may mistake a summons for a letter or a collection letter for a summons or complaint. The attorney must see all letters and documents regarding financial matters pertaining to the debtor.

DETERMINATION OF WHETHER THE DEBTS ARE THE DEBTOR'S DEBTS
Whose debts are they? Are the debts the debtor's or those of another party? If the debtors are husband and wife, the debts may be only the husband's or only the

wife's. If the debtor is a partner in a partnership, the debts may be partnership debts and not personal debts. If the debtor is the president of a closely held corporation, the debts may be corporate debts and not individual debts, or individual debts and not corporate debts.

DEBTOR'S EXPECTATIONS

What are the debtor's expectations and goals? What does the debtor expect to get out of his or her meeting with an attorney or a paralegal, and where is the debtor ultimately going financially?

What are the debtor's attitudes about nonbankruptcy and bankruptcy, and what would need to be done to effect a successful nonbankruptcy solution? Some debtors will not do what is necessary to achieve a successful nonbankruptcy solution. For example, some debtors who could avoid bankruptcy by executing a deed in lieu of foreclosure to the holder of the mortgage on their house, will refuse to use this procedure.

FEES

A full discussion of fees and how they will be paid should take place at the initial interview. Many attorneys do not charge the debtor for the first interview. This gives the attorney flexibility in his or her decision to take or not take the case. It also gives the debtor the opportunity to go elsewhere. The attorney will discuss what fees would be if the case is not to be taken through bankruptcy or if the case is to be taken through bankruptcy. If the case is not to be taken through bankruptcy, the attorney may charge an hourly fee. If the case is to be taken through bankruptcy, the attorney may charge a minimum fee for the routine filing, the lien avoidances, reaffirmations, and the basic walk through. Services beyond these basics may be billed at an hourly rate. Such services would include the defense of an adversary proceeding to deny a discharge or to determine the dischargeability of a debt or litigation concerning exemptions. The discussion of fees should be followed by a written contract for services, which would be a part of the next interview when the decision on how to proceed is recommended.

Although it is not possible to make a hard and fast rule about whether the debtor should pay the fees in advance, the attorney may try to get everything paid up front. Some attorneys are not willing to take a bankruptcy case without full payment in advance. Others may be willing to permit the debtor to pay as the case progresses. Most attorneys understand that many debtors will not pay the attorney's fees after the case is finished. Fees under this arrangement are hard to collect. The biggest problem is that many debtors are very optimistic about what this bankruptcy will do for them. They very quickly find out that just making bare living expenses from a paycheck is difficult and that little will be left over to pay an attorney. For this reason, it is best to get the fees in advance. (Fees for Chapter 13 cases may not be paid in advance.) Most debtors will somehow come up with the money for fees. If they do not have it, they will find it. If fees are on credit, many debtors will never find the money to pay the fees for services rendered.

The attorney should remember to

1. discuss the amount of fees at the first interview;
2. set out the fee arrangement in writing;
3. know where the money for fees is coming from; and
4. get paid before the case is filed, if at all possible and if permitted by the Code.

The questionnaire in Appendix A organizes these general themes into a concrete list. The questionnaire is designed for both the debtor engaged in business and the debtor not engaged in business.

PROBLEM 4.4   Melinda and Curtis Henderson have been married for three years. This is the second marriage for each. Previously, Melinda was married to Robert Graham and Curtis was married to Stephanie Pratt. Melinda often goes by the nickname "Mel." Curtis is Curtis Quackenbush Henderson III.

The Hendersons have lived at 6552 Thunderbird Lane for the past 18 months. Prior to that time, Melinda was a member of the armed services and was stationed at Fort Leonard Wood in Missouri. She retired from active duty 18 months ago.

Curtis is a computer programmer. He operates his own business under the name "Henderson Enterprises." He employs several part-time programmers who work out of their own homes. Curtis's business is also located at home.

Both Melinda and Curtis brought debts into their marriage. Melinda owed Ford Motor Credit Corporation, Frontier Federal Savings and Loan Association, Philip Rodriquez Contractors, Sears, United Bank, Tri-Cities Natural Gas Company, and Dr. Raymond Nelson. The last two of these debts were paid off during the past year.

Curtis owed Manufacturers Hanover Trust, Omega Cable Television, Newtown Hospital, First Bank, and Peoples' Credit Union. Although Curtis has paid down some of these debts, he still owes on all of them except the cable television company.

All of Melinda's debts are unsecured except the one to Ford Motor Credit Corporation. All of Curtis's debts are unsecured except the one to Manufacturers Hanover Trust.

Since their marriage, Curtis and Melinda have purchased their home and have given the Sunset Savings and Loan Association a mortgage on the property. Their mortgage payment is $650 a month. They have also purchased furniture from Century Furniture Company and have given Century a security interest in the furniture purchased.

Several months ago, Melinda went to work for Alpha Insurance Company as an insurance agent. Her gross pay is $1,800 a month. After deductions, Melinda's net pay is $1,100 a month. This is a new career for Melinda. She had planned to be career military but was discharged from the military for medical reasons (a work-related injury).

Although Melinda receives a small pension from the government ($600 a month) and her salary from Alpha Insurance and Curtis earns a modest amount from his business ($1,000 a month), they have not been able to pay their debts. Because Melinda had planned to be career military, the Hendersons had not saved while Melinda was in the service and had only a few dollars in the bank when Melinda was injured. That account was soon spent.

Although the medical benefits from the government pay for most of Melinda's continuing medical expenses, some expenses are not covered. These expenses plus the expenses due to relocation have placed the Hendersons in their current unstable financial situation.

Curtis has a daughter, Deborah, by his previous marriage. She is ten and lives with her mother. Under the divorce decree, Curtis is obligated to pay $250 a month in child support. He also is obligated to pay his former wife $400 a month in alimony. He has not paid either for the past four months.

The Hendersons have calculated that their monthly expenses include

Real estate taxes	$150
Electricity	120
Gas	75
Water	25
Telephone	31
Cable TV	21
Home maintenance	80
Sales tax	25
Automobile insurance	42
Life insurance	42
Automobile payments	400
Food	400
Clothing	200
Medical	75
Dental	20
Medicines	15
Newspapers	7
Laundry and cleaning	30
Charitable contributions	25
Frontier Federal Savings and Loan Association	125
Philip Rodriquez Contractors	80
Sears Roebuck	110
United Bank	60
Manufacturers Hanover Trust	60
Newtown Hospital	40
First Bank	75
Peoples' Credit Union	15
Century Furniture Company	175

When the Hendersons were in Missouri, Curtis was involved in a partnership with another computer programmer. The relationship lasted about two years. The partnership was unsuccessful financially.

Based on this information, begin to complete the questionnaire in Appendix A. As you progress through the questionnaire, you will discover that you have incomplete information. Make a list of additional information you will need from the Hendersons.

B. ANALYSIS: NONBANKRUPTCY OR BANKRUPTCY, AND IF BANKRUPTCY, WHICH CHAPTER?

The analysis step is the point at which the attorney evaluates the information gathered and formulates a course of action. The attorney must recommend to the client whether or not to file. If the recommendation is to file, then the attorney must inform the client under which chapters of the Bankruptcy Code the case could be filed. The attorney must also help the client to evaluate the choices so that the appropriate chapter can be selected. This responsibility is substantial and cannot be taken lightly for at least two reasons. First, a debtor taken through a Chapter 7 liquidation will suffer the loss of all nonexempt assets. 11 U.S.C.A. §§ 522, 541. The attorney must evaluate whether this loss may be avoidable and, if so, determine what strategy could be used to avoid it. Second, a debtor can receive a discharge in a Chapter 7 bankruptcy case only once every six years. 11 U.S.C.A. § 727(a)(9). The attorney must determine whether the filing of a bankruptcy petition at this time is premature and would make bankruptcy unavailable if the debtor has a greater need to file at a later date.

The information obtained at the initial interview must be sufficient to enable the attorney to determine what, if any, action is necessary. If the attorney decides that some action is needed, the next step is to determine whether such action will involve bankruptcy relief or perhaps some other course of action. At times, the attorney may only need to calm the debtor and discuss nonbankruptcy strategies.

1. ALTERNATIVES TO A BANKRUPTCY FILING

After the interview, the attorney and the debtor should carefully consider alternatives to proceeding in the bankruptcy court. Nonbankruptcy alternatives will probably be less expensive and better received by the creditors. Furthermore, nonbankruptcy solutions do not carry the stigma of a bankruptcy filing. All debtors should not be taken through bankruptcy.

If the case is a consumer case and the matter is inappropriate for a bankruptcy remedy, the attorney might not handle the case at all. In a consumer situation, it is often more practical to refer the client to a credit counseling center for assistance. On the other hand, the business client will generally be facing a situation that requires an attorney's involvement.

Private nonbankruptcy alternatives available to the debtor are negotiation with creditors, consolidation loans, credit counseling, assignments for the benefit of creditors, and defending an action brought on a debt.

a. Negotiation   Negotiation may involve discussion and agreement between the debtor and a creditor whereby the creditor agrees to terms different from those originally agreed to with the debtor. Such relief may be feasible and will not require the protection of the bankruptcy court. As a result of negotiation, the debtor may receive an extension of time in which to pay the debt, a reduction in the amount of the debt, or a combination of the two. Negotiation depends on the cooperation of the creditor. For negotiation to be successful, the debtor must be able to make some payment toward the debt.

The negotiated agreement is governed by contract law. The debtor must promise to perform an act or omission in exchange for the creditor's promise to perform an act or omission. The creditor's promise is the consideration for the debtor's promise. Also, the creditor must promise to perform an act or omission in exchange for the debtor's promise to perform an act or omission. The debtor's promise is the consideration for the creditor's promise. If the debtor promises to pay the creditor what the debtor already has a duty to pay the creditor, the debtor's promise will not be consideration for the creditor's promise to accept less than what the debtor owes or to accept what the debtor owes over a longer period. The creditor is only seeking what the debtor already had a preexisting duty to do. The creditor's promise lacks consideration, and it cannot be either an offer or an acceptance. Without either an offer or an acceptance, there can be no contract.

EXAMPLE

Patsie Wilburn borrowed $1,500 from her sister Tina and promised to pay $100 a month until the loan was repaid. After Patsie became delinquent in her payments, she renegotiated the contract to reduce her payments to $75 a month.

In the original contract, the offer was Tina's promise to loan Patsie $1,500 in exchange for Patsie's promise to repay $1,500 in $100 a month installments. Patsie accepted Tina's offer by promising to pay $1,500 in installments of $100 a month in exchange for Tina's promise to loan her $1,500. Patsie's promise to repay $1,500 in monthly installments of $100 was the consideration that Tina requested for her promise to loan Patsie $1,500. Tina's promise to loan $1,500 was the consideration that Patsie requested for her promise to repay $1,500 in monthly installments of $100. Because there was consideration for both Patsie's promise and Tina's promise, there was an offer and an acceptance and thus a contract.

Patsie renegotiated the contract to reduce the monthly payments from $100 to $75. After Patsie made three $75 payments, Tina demanded that she begin paying $100 a month. When Patsie refused, Tina brought action for breach of contract, claiming that the renegotiated contract was not a contract because it lacked consideration for her promise to take less per month. When Patsie promised to pay in $75 a month installments, she promised to do what she had a preexisting duty to do (albeit less). The renegotiation is not a contract, and the original contract is enforceable.

If Patsie seeks to renegotiate her contract with Tina, she needs to offer Tina something other than what she is already obligated to do. For example, she could offer to pay interest.

EXAMPLE

Belinda Richards owns a small business in partnership with her twin sister, Delinda. Belinda borrowed $30,000 from United Bank for improvements for her business and gave United a security interest in her present and after-acquired inventory. At the time the loan was made, United Bank did not ask Belinda whether she owned the business as an individual or as a partner in a partnership. United Bank attempted to perfect by filing a financing statement under the name of Belinda Richards rather than under the name of the partnership, Richards Cosmetics.

In recent months Richards Cosmetics has been losing money. If the partnership files for bankruptcy, United Bank will be treated as an unsecured creditor because it does not have a perfected security interest. It will join the pool of other unsecured creditors and will probably receive only a small payoff when the assets are liquidated. If Belinda could effect a workout with United Bank to avoid having the partnership file for bankruptcy, the bank might gain a larger payoff and the partnership could continue in business.

If the attorney determines that the debtor has nonexempt property that he or she cannot afford to jeopardize, a solution might be available to utilize the nonexempt property to keep the debtor out of bankruptcy.

EXAMPLE

Charlene Brown, age 30, owes $10,000 in medical bills from a prolonged illness. Her doctors and hospital have become impatient and have refused to wait for payment. They have threatened to sue. Charlene wants to file a Chapter 7.

Charlene has accumulated $5,000 in a 401(k). If she files for bankruptcy under Chapter 7, the 401(k) is nonexempt property and would be distributed among her creditors. She would also have the stigma of bankruptcy if she files a Chapter 7.

Charlene could save her 401(k) if a nonbankruptcy solution could be arranged. If Charlene could use the 401(k) as collateral for a $4,000 loan and if she could negotiate a settlement with her doctors and hospital to pay 40 cents on the dollar, she could pay them off. She could then repay the $4,000 loan over a period of time. After paying the loan, Charlene would still have her 401(k) for retirement.

If a negotiated agreement involves a debtor and two or more creditors, it is an extension or a composition, or both. If the debtor and the creditors agree to permit the debtor additional time to pay the debt, the agreement is called an **extension.** If the debtor and the creditors agree to permit the debtor to satisfy the debt by paying less than the full amount, the agreement is called a **composition.**

The consideration problem present in a negotiation between a debtor and one creditor (preexisting duty) may not exist in an extension or a composition. The fact that only two parties were in the original transaction but three or more parties are in the new transaction permits promises to be made between parties who were not parties in the original contract and thus eliminates the preexisting duty problem.

An extension allows a debtor additional time to pay his or her debts. Creditors will usually agree to an extension if it is justified. They base their decision on the past payment record of the debtor and on the debtor's future prospects. Extensions offer an advantage to both creditors and debtor; the creditors get all the money owed to them and the debtor stays out of bankruptcy court. The problems with an extension are that all creditors may not agree to it and that the debts may be so large that it is not feasible for the debtor to pay them.

EXAMPLE

Arnold Everett borrowed $5,000 against each of his three credit cards. When he was unable to pay his minimum monthly payments, he negotiated an agreement with two of the credit card companies. Under the agreement, Arnold returned the credit cards to the issuers (and thereby accrued no new charges) and promised to pay half of his minimum monthly payments until each balance was reduced to zero. The unpaid balance would continue to accrue interest at the normal rate.

After Arnold sent the three credit card companies half of their minimum monthly payment, the company that did not participate in the extension sued Arnold for breach of contract. Because this company was not a party to the extension, it was not bound by the contract.

In a composition the creditors agree to accept a reduced amount in satisfaction of the debts. It may be necessary to deal with only one or a few of the creditors. A remedy may be worked out with multiple creditors on a collective basis if they are all willing to work together, perhaps under the leadership of one of the creditors or one of the creditors with the assistance of the debtor's attorney. A composition is especially beneficial to the debtor because it discharges a portion of the debt without having to go through bankruptcy proceedings. Composition, however, should not be considered unless the debtor has the money to pay off the reduced debt immediately or is prepared to file for bankruptcy and has made the creditor aware of this. If the debtor files for bankruptcy, the creditor may receive nothing, so the threat of bankruptcy on the part of the debtor may make the creditor more amenable to a composition agreement. A composition poses the same problem that an extension does: some creditors may not agree to it. For a creditor to agree to a composition, he or she has to be assured of receipt of the promised payment from the debtor or at least receipt of more than if a bankruptcy claim was filed. Compositions are used by businesses more often than by individuals and are often arranged by workout departments in many banks. Some law firms have gained considerable expertise in nonjudicial workouts.

EXAMPLE

John and Alice Washington owned the majority interest in a partnership in a restaurant. The restaurant was profitable, but John and Alice had problems with their personal expenses. The monthly mortgage payments on their house coupled with debts from living beyond their means raised serious problems with personal, rather than business, debts.

If John and Alice filed bankruptcy, their partnership interest in the restaurant would be an asset of the estate and would be distributed to creditors. If John and Alice did not file bankruptcy, they could try to effectuate a workout on a piecemeal basis.

John and Alice restructured their business by selling a further interest in the partnership to one of their partners. This raised money to pay their creditors. John and Alice sought a composition with their creditors to satisfy their unsecured debts. They also conveyed their house by deed in lieu of foreclosure to the bank that held the mortgage. This got them out from under the monthly mortgage payments that they were unable to maintain. This solution gave John and Alice the relief they needed from their debts and did not jeopardize their interest in the restaurant.

At times, it may be beneficial for the debtor to give up a part of his or her property that would be nonexempt in bankruptcy in return for being able to keep the remainder.

EXAMPLE
James and Rachael McArthur own a number of heirlooms that were left to Rachael by her grandmother when she died. Their value is $100,000. Rachael has a deep attachment to this property. The McArthurs owe unsecured creditors $150,000.

The McArthurs know that Rachael's heirlooms are nonexempt and would become an asset of the estate for distribution among creditors if they file for bankruptcy under Chapter 7. If the McArthurs could arrange a composition with their creditors for 50 cents on the dollar, then Rachael could select the heirlooms she wants to keep and sell the remainder to raise $75,000 to pay the creditors.

If the debtor has only nondischargeable debts, then a negotiated settlement, rather than bankruptcy, may be the more appropriate solution to the debtor's problem.

EXAMPLE
Aaron Stevenson recently graduated from college and went to work for a radio station as a disc jockey. During college, Aaron accumulated $50,000 in college loans. The student loans are nondischargeable. Therefore, bankruptcy under Chapter 7 will not provide him with the relief that he seeks. Aaron negotiates to pay the loans off over a longer period of time.

b. Consolidation Loan   A **consolidation loan** allows a debtor to obtain one loan large enough to pay off all of his or her debts. The monthly payment on the consolidation loan is less than the total of the monthly payments on the many small debts. The consolidation loan may require the debtor to pay a higher interest rate than the debtor was previously paying and to pay the debt over a longer period. Consolidation loans may be secured by the debtor's property.

EXAMPLE
Ethel and Fred Kurtz had $15,000 in debts that were divided among seven creditors. All were unsecured. Each month the payments on these debts totaled $1,000. The Kurtzes obtained a consolidation loan to repay all of their creditors. The consolidation loan encumbered all of their property and required the Kurtzes to pay $750 a month.

A debtor considering a consolidation loan must be aware of the actual cost of the loan, especially the finance charges and interest rates. There can be a big difference in the cost of the loan, depending on whether interest is charged only on the unpaid balance or on the total amount to be paid in a fixed number of installments. It is always advisable for a debtor to consult an attorney about any consolidation loan to prevent problems such as usury, which may cost the debtor a great deal more in the long run than the original debts.

If the consolidation loan is secured by collateral, it is important that the debtor thoroughly understand the security agreement. A consolidation loan security agreement may cover exempt and nonexempt property. In the event a debtor must file bankruptcy after having tried a consolidation loan, he or she may lose both exempt and nonexempt property. In bankruptcy, the debtor will keep exempt property and has an option to keep some nonexempt property through reaffirmation agreements.

EXAMPLE

After several months, the Kurtzes found that the $750 monthly payment on the consolidation loan exceeded their ability to pay and they defaulted on the consolidation loan. Since the loan was secured, the lender repossessed all of the Kurtzes' property.

Had the Kurtzes filed bankruptcy under Chapter 7, rather than obtaining a consolidation loan, they would have been able to retain their house and car as well as other exempt and some nonexempt property.

c. Credit Counseling   Some debtors should go to **credit counseling** rather than file for bankruptcy. If a Chapter 7 bankruptcy is filed on their behalf and their financial problems are temporarily solved, the debtors will not be able to discharge their debts under Chapter 7 again for another six years. In the event of a catastrophic situation such as unemployment, an uninsured loss, or large medical bills prior to the expiration of the six year period, debtors have no bankruptcy solution unless they fit within Chapter 13, and Chapter 13 solves only a limited number of cases.

Many debtors owe a relatively small amount of debt but have financial problems because of their spending habits. Such debtors need education and should be referred to credit counseling. If the educational process is ignored, these debtors will continue to have financial problems. Credit Counseling Centers are licensed and bonded. They analyze the debtor's obligations and negotiate with creditors for the repayment of the debtor's bills on a schedule the agency feels the debtor can manage. These agencies do not lend money. They only distribute the debtor's money to the debtor's creditors. Creditor participation is totally voluntary. Credit Counseling Centers offer no protection to the debtor if the creditor decides to initiate a suit for the debtor's default.

Providing credit counseling services for a fee is illegal in the majority of states, but nonfee services are located in many states as a community service. Credit Counseling Centers are often supported by community charity campaigns such as United Way and by the nominal fee charged the creditor.

EXAMPLE

Terry Kelly earns $15,000 a year as a legal secretary. He has outstanding unsecured debts of $5,000. If he files for bankruptcy under Chapter 7, his $5,000 in debts will be discharged. He will, however, preclude himself from filing another Chapter 7 petition for six years. During that period he could lose his job, have an accident on his motorcycle, or accumulate medical bills far beyond his ability to pay. If he loses his job, he cannot consider Chapter 13 because he will have no regular income to support a Chapter 13 plan. Therefore, arranging the payment of his debts through a Credit Counseling Center will preserve Terry's opportunity to file a Chapter 7 case in the future if the need arises.

d. Assignments for the Benefit of Creditors   **Assignments for the benefit of creditors** involve the transfer of the debtor's assets to a third party to ensure the payment of the debtor's obligations. Assignments for the benefit of creditors are used almost exclusively by business debtors. In an assignment for the benefit of creditors, a business debtor liquidates its assets and distributes the proceeds to its creditors. In the case of an ongoing business, particularly the small retail establishment, perhaps the key creditor, either a wholesaler or a lender, can assist in finding a buyer who believes that a turnaround is possible under new management. The liquidation is carried out by an assignee appointed by the creditor. The assignee acts as a trustee and is regulated by the principles of trust law.

Advantages of an assignment for the benefit of creditors include the time and money saved over the cost of bankruptcy and the fact that higher prices are often obtained in this type of liquidation than might be realized in a bankruptcy liquidation, thereby enabling the creditors to realize a higher return on their claims. An assignment for the benefit of creditors is covered by state statute in the majority of states and is a voluntary act on the part of the debtor.

e. Defending a State Court Action   Another situation in which a nonbankruptcy solution, rather than a bankruptcy solution, may be chosen involves a nondischargeable debt. If the debtor has been sued in a state court on such a debt, then the debtor must choose whether to continue to defend the state court action or to file a petition in the bankruptcy court, which will stay the action in the state court.

> **EXAMPLE**
>
> Alistair Jenson, the debtor, is being sued in state court for fraud in the procurement of a loan. Alistair is faced with a choice of whether he wants to defend this case in the state court or to file a petition in bankruptcy to defend the nondischargeability issue (based on fraud in the procurement of a loan) in the bankruptcy court.
>
> Alistair may be better off staying in state court and concentrating on defending the fraud charge. The focus in the state court will be the elements of fraud. There will be no concern for the nondischargeability issue, which is the bankruptcy court issue. If Alistair wins the case in state court, there will be no judgment against him for fraud. If he loses in state court, he can file a petition in bankruptcy and still have the opportunity to defend the nondischargeability issue. If Alistair wins the nondischargeability issue, the debt will be discharged and he will have his exempt property.

At times, a debtor may arrange a nonbankruptcy solution without the aid of an attorney. The nonbankruptcy solution may defeat the fresh start that bankruptcy affords a debtor.

> **EXAMPLE**
>
> Pierre LaPointe owns a small French restaurant. He owes a number of unsecured creditors $50,000 and the federal and state governments $50,000 in taxes (including FICA). Pierre has about $50,000 in assets. Without seeking legal advice, Pierre pays his unsecured creditors. Later, when the tax collectors threaten action, Pierre seeks legal advice regarding the filing of a Chapter 7 to discharge his tax obligations.
>
> Unfortunately, Pierre has approached the solution backwards. His debts to his unsecured creditors are dischargeable debts, but his debts to the two governments are nondischargeable debts. If Pierre files for bankruptcy now, he will still owe the taxes. Had he paid the taxes but not paid the unsecured creditors, the latter debts would be dischargeable in bankruptcy and he would no longer owe these creditors.

2. BANKRUPTCY CHOICES

If it is decided that the debtor should file for bankruptcy, the attorney must work with the debtor to decide if the bankruptcy filing will be as an individual, a partnership, or a corporation, or possibly as an individual and a partnership or as an individual and a corporation. A choice must also be made regarding which bankruptcy chapter will best suit the debtor's needs.

The married debtor has a choice between filing as an individual or filing a joint petition with his or her spouse. The decision is made on the basis of who owes the debts. Do both spouses owe the debts or does only one owe the debts? Does one spouse have separate property that is not subject to the other's debts? Attorneys occasionally erroneously assume that both spouses owe the debts. It is important to investigate who owes the debts before the decision is made to file an individual or a joint petition.

EXAMPLE

After John and Alice were married, Alice moved into John's house. Alice owned her own business, a consignment shop, and kept her own records. John owned his own business, a print shop, and kept his own records. Both maintained their own business and personal charge accounts and checking accounts.

Alice overextended her credit on both the consignment shop and her personal charge accounts. John's business is thriving and he is able to pay both his business and personal debts.

If John and Alice decide on bankruptcy, Alice should file as an individual because all of the problem debts are hers. The case should not be filed as a joint petition because John's credit is not overextended. If a joint petition is filed, John's assets will be used to pay Alice's creditors.

Section 109 may be treated as the "scope" provision for each of the operative chapters of the Bankruptcy Code. 11 U.S.C.A. § 109. The different operative chapters (7, 9, 11, 12, and 13) apply to different classifications of debtors. Exhibit 4.1 presents an overview of who may be a debtor under which operative chapter.

The operative chapters follow two distinct drafting patterns. Chapters 7 and 11 apply to all debtors, subject to express exclusions. Chapters 9, 12, and 13 apply only to specifically enumerated debtors.

a. Chapter 7—Liquidation ("Straight" Bankruptcy)   A Chapter 7 case should generally be filed only as a last resort. It should not be filed until absolutely necessary or until it is definitely ready for filing. The proper approach to a Chapter 7 filing is to be deliberate. There should be no rush jobs unless it is truly an emergency and there is no other course. Therefore, in preparing to file a Chapter 7, the attorney should answer the following questions:

1. What kind of a client is involved?
2. How ready is the client for the bankruptcy case?
3. How much interviewing is needed to satisfy the attorney and the paralegal that they have all the necessary information?

Section 109(b) defines eligibility for liquidation under Chapter 7. All persons are eligible except railroads, insurance companies, and certain banking institutions.

> (b) A person may be a debtor under chapter 7 of this title only if such person is not—
>   (1) a railroad;
>   (2) a domestic insurance company, bank, savings bank, cooperative bank, savings and loan association, building and loan association, homestead association, a small business investment company licensed by the Small Business Administration under subsection (c) or (d) of section 301 of the Small Business Investment Act of 1958, credit union, or industrial bank or similar institution which is an insured bank as defined in section 3(h) of the Federal Deposit Insurance Act; or

EXHIBIT 4.1
Debtors and Operative Chapters of the Code

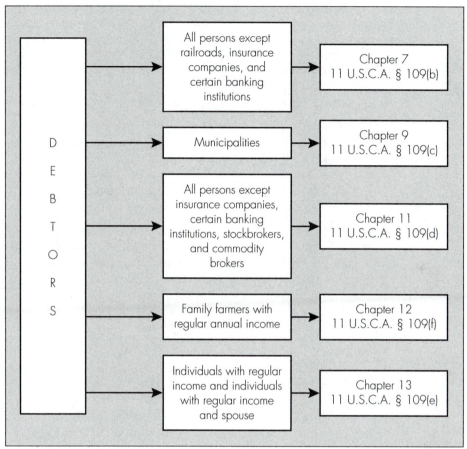

(3) a foreign insurance company, bank, savings bank, cooperative bank, savings and loan association, building and loan association, homestead association, or credit union, engaged in such business in the United States.

Banking institutions and insurance companies engaged in business in the United States are excluded from liquidation under the bankruptcy laws because they are covered for insolvency and receivership purposes under other state and federal legislation. When a foreign bank or insurance company is not engaged in the banking or insurance business in the United States, these regulatory laws are inapplicable and the bankruptcy laws are the only laws available for administration of any assets found in the United States.

PROBLEM 4.5 The Lone Star Railroad Company has been in financial difficulties for several years. The company would like to cease doing business and divide its assets among its many creditors. Unfortunately, the assets are insufficient to satisfy all the creditors.

Can Lone Star file for bankruptcy under Chapter 7 of the Code?

PROBLEM 4.6 Over the past several years, the Gotham Teachers Credit Union has loaned substantial sums of money to oil well speculators without obtaining adequate security. The glut of oil on the world market led to substantially lower oil prices and to default on a number of these loans. This placed the credit union in financial difficulty.

Can Gotham Teachers Credit Union file for bankruptcy under Chapter 7 of the Code?

PROBLEM 4.7   Charles Smithfield, a fifth grade teacher, was unable to pay his bills as they came due. Can Charles file for bankruptcy under Chapter 7 of the Code?

PROBLEM 4.8   Wilma and Walter O'Connor retired several years ago. Wilma had been a nurse at St. Francis Hospital and Walter had been a police officer. Both had small pensions and social security benefits. Walter, who had been a heavy smoker, developed lung cancer. Although Walter pulled through surgery and chemotherapy, his medical bills surpassed his insurance coverage.

Can Wilma and Walter file for bankruptcy under Chapter 7 of the Code? If they can file, should they file a joint petition?

PROBLEM 4.9   John and Martha Babbitt own a 160-acre farm. For the past three years, the Babbitts have had to contend with natural disasters. Three years ago, their crops were partially destroyed by locusts. Two years ago, their crops were parched by a drought. Last year, their yield was low due to the floods. Although John and Martha have planted this year, their creditors are demanding payment and the bank is threatening to foreclose on the farm.

Can John and Martha file for bankruptcy under Chapter 7 of the Code?

PROBLEM 4.10   Mary Valesquez and Cynthia Webster formed a partnership for the purpose of operating an interior decorating shop. Mary and Cynthia found it difficult to pay their creditors, and after the first year in business, the shop closed.

Can Mary and Cynthia file for bankruptcy under Chapter 7 of the Code? If they can file, should they file as a partnership or as individuals? Can they file a joint petition?

PROBLEM 4.11   The Waterfront Fish Market was incorporated under the laws of Delaware. For many years the market was able to show a small profit. About a year ago, a new fish market opened nearby and the Waterfront Fish Market lost some of its customers. For the past several months, the market has been unable to pay its creditors.

Can the Waterfront Fish Market file for bankruptcy under Chapter 7 of the Code?

PROBLEM 4.12   Since the federal government deregulated the airlines, Blue Sky Airlines, a major commercial passenger carrier, has been losing money. The airlines has cut back on its routes and has sold some of its equipment.

Can Blue Sky Airlines file for bankruptcy under Chapter 7 of the Code?

b. Chapter 9—Municipalities   Chapter 9 is a specialized chapter for municipalities only. A municipality seeking relief under Chapter 9 must be specifically authorized to be a debtor under Chapter 9 by state law or authorized by a governmental officer or organization empowered by state law to authorize such entity to be a debtor under Chapter 9. The municipality must be insolvent (unable to meet its debts as they mature) and must meet the other requirements of 11 U.S.C.A. § 109(c). Because Chapter 9 has limited application, it will not be covered here. A short discussion of Chapter 9 can be found in Appendix C.

c. Chapter 11—Reorganization Persons who may be debtors under Chapter 7, with the exception of stockbrokers or commodity brokers, may be debtors under Chapter 11. Although the courts were divided over whether the debtor needed a business objective or a business purpose to file under Chapter 11, the issue was resolved by the United States Supreme Court in 1991, when it held that an individual debtor not engaged in business was eligible to reorganize under Chapter 11. *Toibb v. Radloff,* 501 U.S. 157 (1991).

Stockbrokers and commodity brokers are eligible for relief only under specially tailored provisions found in Chapter 7. 11 U.S.C.A. §§ 741–752 (stockbroker liquidation) and 11 U.S.C.A. §§ 761–766 (commodity broker liquidation). Railroads, excluded under Chapter 7, may be debtors under special provisions in Chapter 11. 11 U.S.C.A. §§ 1161–1174 (railroad reorganization). Insurance companies and certain banking institutions—debtors expressly excluded from Chapter 7—are also excluded from Chapter 11 because, unlike railroads, they are not expressly included in Chapter 11. 11 U.S.C.A. § 109(d).

> (d) Only a person that may be a debtor under chapter 7 of this title, except a stockbroker or a commodity broker, and a railroad may be a debtor under chapter 11 of this title.

PROBLEM 4.13 Can the Lone Star Railroad Company in Problem 4.5 file for bankruptcy under Chapter 11 of the Code?

PROBLEM 4.14 Can the Gotham Teachers Credit Union in Problem 4.6 file for bankruptcy under Chapter 11 of the Code?

PROBLEM 4.15 Can Charles Smithfield in Problem 4.7 file for bankruptcy under Chapter 11 of the Code?

PROBLEM 4.16 Can Wilma and Walter O'Connor in Problem 4.8 file for bankruptcy under Chapter 11 of the Code? If they can file, should they file a joint petition?

PROBLEM 4.17 Can John and Martha Babbitt in Problem 4.9 file for bankruptcy under Chapter 11 of the Code?

PROBLEM 4.18 Can Mary Valesquez and Cynthia Webster in Problem 4.10 file for bankruptcy under Chapter 11 of the Code? If they can file, should they file as a partnership or as individuals? Can they file a joint petition?

PROBLEM 4.19 Can the Waterfront Fish Market in Problem 4.11 file for bankruptcy under Chapter 11 of the Code?

PROBLEM 4.20 Can Blue Sky Airlines in Problem 4.12 file for bankruptcy under Chapter 11 of the Code?

d. Chapter 12—Adjustment of Debts of a Family Farmer with Regular Annual Income
The new Chapter 12 is available only to family farmers, as defined in section 101(18) of the Code, who have regular annual income. Section 101 of the Bankruptcy Code defines **family farmer with regular annual income**.

> (19) "family farmer with regular annual income" means family farmer whose annual income is sufficiently stable and regular to enable such family farmer to make payments under a plan under chapter 12 of this title. 11 U.S.C.A. § 101(19).

Because this definition is worded in terms of a family farmer with regular annual income, it becomes necessary to consult the definition of **family farmer** which is also found in section 101.

(18) "family farmer" means—

    (A) individual or individual and spouse engaged in a farming operation whose aggregate debts do not exceed $1,500,000 and not less than 80 percent of whose aggregate noncontingent, liquidated debts (excluding a debt for the principal residence of such individual or such individual and spouse unless such debt arises out of a farming operation), on the date the case is filed, arise out of a farming operation owned or operated by such individual or such individual and spouse, and such individual or such individual and spouse receive from such farming operation more than 50 percent of such individual's or such individual and spouse's gross income for the taxable year preceding the taxable year in which the case concerning such individual or such individual and spouse was filed; or

    (B) corporation or partnership in which more than 50 percent of the outstanding stock or equity is held by one family, or by one family and the relatives of the members of such family, and such family or such relatives conduct the farming operation; and

        (i) more than 80 percent of the value of its assets consists of assets related to the farming operation;

        (ii) its aggregate debts do not exceed $1,500,000 and not less than 80 percent of its aggregate noncontingent, liquidated debts (excluding a debt for one dwelling which is owned by such corporation or partnership and which a shareholder or partner maintains as a principal residence, unless such debt arises out of a farming operation), on the date the case is filed, arise out of the farming operation owned or operated by such corporation or such partnership; and

        (iii) if such corporation issues stock, such stock is not publicly traded. 11 U.S.C.A. § 101(18).

Since the definition of family farmer includes the term **farming operation,** it becomes necessary to consider the definition of farming operation. This term is also defined in section 101.

(21) "farming operation" includes farming, tillage of the soil, dairy farming, ranching, production or raising of crops, poultry, or livestock, and production of poultry or livestock products in an unmanufactured state. 11 U.S.C.A. § 101(21).

PROBLEM 4.21   Can the Lone Star Railroad Company in Problem 4.5 file for bankruptcy under Chapter 12 of the Code?

PROBLEM 4.22   Can the Gotham Teachers Credit Union in Problem 4.6 file for bankruptcy under Chapter 12 of the Code?

PROBLEM 4.23   Can Charles Smithfield in Problem 4.7 file for bankruptcy under Chapter 12 of the Code?

PROBLEM 4.24   Can Wilma and Walter O'Connor in Problem 4.8 file for bankruptcy under Chapter 12 of the Code? If they can file, should they file a joint petition?

PROBLEM 4.25   Can John and Martha Babbitt in Problem 4.9 file for bankruptcy under Chapter 12 of the Code?

PROBLEM 4.26   Can Mary Valesquez and Cynthia Webster in Problem 4.10 file for bankruptcy under Chapter 12 of the Code? If they can file, should they file as a partnership or as individuals? Can they file a joint petition?

PROBLEM 4.27   Can the Waterfront Fish Market in Problem 4.11 file for bankruptcy under Chapter 12 of the Code?

PROBLEM 4.28   Can Blue Sky Airlines in Problem 4.12 file for bankruptcy under Chapter 12 of the Code?

e. Chapter 13—Adjustment of Debts of an Individual with Regular Income   Chapter 13 is available only to individuals with regular income who owe debts of less than $250,000 unsecured and $750,000 secured.

> (e) Only an individual with regular income that owes, on the date of the filing of the petition, noncontingent, liquidated, unsecured debts of less than $250,000 and noncontingent, liquidated, secured debts of less than $750,000, or an individual with regular income and such individual's spouse, except a stockbroker or a commodity broker, that owe, on the date of the filing of the petition, noncontingent, liquidated, unsecured debts that aggregate less than $250,000 and noncontingent, liquidated, secured debts of less than $750,000 may be a debtor under chapter 13 of this title. 11 U.S.C.A. § 109(e).

PROBLEM 4.29   Can the Lone Star Railroad Company in Problem 4.5 file for bankruptcy under Chapter 13 of the Code?

PROBLEM 4.30   Can the Gotham Teachers Credit Union in Problem 4.6 file for bankruptcy under Chapter 13 of the Code?

PROBLEM 4.31   Can Charles Smithfield in Problem 4.7 file for bankruptcy under Chapter 13 of the Code?

PROBLEM 4.32   Can Wilma and Walter O'Connor in Problem 4.8 file for bankruptcy under Chapter 13 of the Code? If they can file, should they file a joint petition?

PROBLEM 4.33   Can John and Martha Babbitt in Problem 4.9 file for bankruptcy under Chapter 13 of the Code?

PROBLEM 4.34   Can Mary Valesquez and Cynthia Webster in Problem 4.10 file for bankruptcy under Chapter 13 of the Code? If they can file, should they file as a partnership or as individuals? Can they file a joint petition?

PROBLEM 4.35   Can the Waterfront Fish Market in Problem 4.11 file for bankruptcy under Chapter 13 of the Code?

PROBLEM 4.36   Can Blue Sky Airlines in Problem 4.12 file for bankruptcy under Chapter 13 of the Code?

3. SELECTING THE APPROPRIATE TYPE OF BANKRUPTCY FILING
After the attorney or the paralegal has interviewed the debtor and obtained all pertinent information and the decision has been made to file a petition in bankruptcy, it is necessary to determine which bankruptcy chapter fits the needs of the debtor.

The Bankruptcy Code defines who may be a debtor under each of the operative chapters. 11 U.S.C.A. §§ 109(b)–(f). It is, of course, to be expected that the drafters of the Bankruptcy Code would seek to provide a process within the scope of the Code in which all types of entities could seek relief. Certain entities, however, are excluded entirely from eligibility under the Bankruptcy Code and others are restricted as to the chapter under which they may file. For example, a small business may wish to continue to operate but find Chapter 11 burdensome and too expensive. An individual engaged in business might file under Chapter 13, but the small partnership or corporation is ineligible for this chapter. The addition of the **fast track provision** in 11 U.S.C.A. § 1121 for small businesses (as defined in 11 U.S.C.A. § 101(51C)) should make Chapter 11 a workable alternative in such cases.

At one extreme are the very large corporate cases which should obviously be filed under Chapter 11. At the other extreme are the cases involving debtors with very little disposable income and a great many debts which should obviously be filed under Chapter 7. In between these two extremes lie the cases in which the debtor has options and in which most mistakes are made.

Under the facts in some situations, a bankruptcy case can be filed under only one of the operative chapters.

EXAMPLE

For the last five years, the Red, White, and Blue Railroad's expenses have exceeded its revenues. The railroad, unable to increase its revenues, began to trim its schedules. Due to long term contracts, the railroad was unable to substantially reduce either the benefits paid employees or the number of employees. The railroad may only file for bankruptcy under Subchapter IV of Chapter 11.

Given a different set of facts, a bankruptcy case could be filed under any of the four operative chapters of the Code.

EXAMPLE

John and Cora Jackson live on a family farm of 160 acres. Cora works full-time for the U.S. Postal Service as a rural mail carrier. The Jacksons owe $13,000 in unsecured debts and $245,000 in secured debts. Their farm income last year was $28,000. Cora earned $26,000 from her job.

　　The Jacksons could file to liquidate under Chapter 7, to reorganize under Chapter 11, or to adjust their debts under Chapters 12 or 13.

As Exhibit 4.2 indicates, pairing the four operative chapters yields six combinations. This section will explore these six possible pairings and the factors that should be considered in the selection of one chapter over another.

EXHIBIT 4.2
Pairings of Operative Chapters of the Code

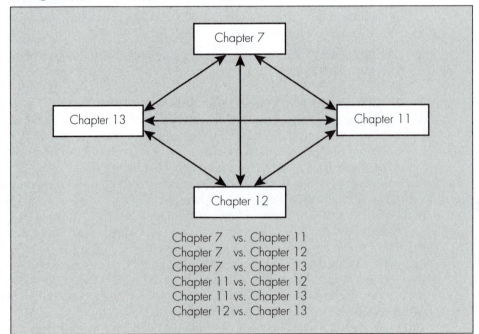

Chapter 7　vs. Chapter 11
Chapter 7　vs. Chapter 12
Chapter 7　vs. Chapter 13
Chapter 11 vs. Chapter 12
Chapter 11 vs. Chapter 13
Chapter 12 vs. Chapter 13

a. Chapter 7 vs. Chapter 11   The following factors are important when evaluating whether to file a Chapter 7 or a Chapter 11 petition.

Does the Debtor Have a Choice between Chapter 7 and Chapter 11?   The ultimate choice for the debtor between filing Chapter 7 or Chapter 11 probably hinges on whether he or she really wants to continue his or her business. The desire to continue business operations may be based on either a practical assessment of reorganization possibilities or an emotional tie to the business. If the debtor wishes to continue the business, for whatever reason, the choice will have to be Chapter 11.

As a general rule any person is eligible to be a debtor under both Chapter 7 and Chapter 11. Several exceptions do exist. A stockbroker or a commodity broker, excluded from Chapter 11, may be a debtor under specially tailored provisions found in Chapter 7. A railroad, excluded from Chapter 7, may be a debtor only under special provisions in Chapter 11. Insurance companies and certain banking institutions, debtors expressly excluded from Chapter 7, are also excluded from Chapter 11. (See Exhibit 4.3.)

The scope section for Chapter 11 does not mandate a business objective or purpose.

> (d) Only a person that may be a debtor under chapter 7 of this title, except a stockbroker or a commodity broker, and a railroad may be a debtor under chapter 11 of this title. 11 U.S.C.A. § 109(d).

This section establishes the outer limits for Chapter 11. A person must qualify as a debtor under Chapter 7 to qualify as a debtor under Chapter 11 unless expressly included within Chapter 11.

Is the Debtor Eligible for a Discharge?   The primary objective of a debtor is to obtain a **discharge** of his or her debts. The individual debtor is eligible for a discharge under both Chapter 7 and Chapter 11. An individual filing under Chapter 11 is not eligible for the discharge of debts that he or she cannot discharge under Chapter 7. A corporation or partnership is not eligible for a discharge under Chapter 7 but is eligible for a discharge under Chapter 11 through **confirmation of a plan.** A confirmed **Chapter 11 plan** will discharge all debts of a corporation except those to be repaid under the plan.

> (3) The confirmation of a plan does not discharge a debtor if—
>> (A) the plan provides for the liquidation of all or substantially all of the property of the estate;
>> (B) the debtor does not engage in business after consummation of the plan; and
>> (C) the debtor would be denied a discharge under section 727(a) of this title if the case were a case under chapter 7 of this title. 11 U.S.C.A. § 1141(d)(3).

EXHIBIT 4.3
Debtors Eligible to File under Chapter 7, Chapter 11, or Both

Chapter 7	Chapters 7 and 11	Chapter 11
All persons except railroads, insurance companies, and certain banking institutions	All persons except stockbrokers, commodity brokers, railroads, insurance companies, and certain banking institutions	All persons except stockbrokers, commodity brokers, insurance companies, and certain banking institutions

The corporate business entity is eliminated (rather than having its debts discharged) by liquidation to prevent trafficking in corporate shells. If this entity rises phoenix-like from its ashes, it will still be held liable for its debts.

The courts will stringently follow 11 U.S.C.A. § 727 to determine whether the debtor is entitled to a discharge under Chapter 7. The denial of a discharge is a serious matter. A Chapter 7 debtor automatically receives a discharge unless a party in interest objects. The following case, *In re Sowell,* illustrates a set of circumstances that led to the denial of a discharge.

In re Sowell
United States Bankruptcy Court, Middle District of Florida, 1988.
92 B.R. 944.

FINDINGS OF FACT AND CONCLUSIONS OF LAW
George L. Proctor, Bankruptcy Judge

This adversary proceeding is before the Court upon the complaint objecting to defendants' discharge pursuant to 11 U.S.C. § 727(a)(3) and (4). The complaint alleges that the defendants purposely failed to preserve books, records, documents and other papers from which their financial condition could be ascertained, and secondly, that the defendants transferred, removed, destroyed, or concealed property of the estate with the intention of hindering, delaying and defrauding creditors.

A trial of this adversary proceeding was held August 4, 1988, and upon the evidence presented, the Court enters the following Findings of Fact and Conclusions of Law:

FINDINGS OF FACT

1. The defendants at time of filing were engaged in a single-family farming operation. The gross profits derived from the operation of this business exceeded $300,000 in each of the years 1984, 1985, and 1986. Seventy-five to eighty-five percent of these proceeds were generated from the sale of fern to regular customers along a specified truck route, while the remaining fifteen to twenty-five percent of proceeds were derived from the shipment of fern to out-of-town buyers.

2. On May 27, 1986, the defendants filed a petition for relief under Chapter 7 of the Bankruptcy Code. As part of the bankruptcy process, debtors are required to "schedule" or list all cash on hand and money in bank accounts. The defendants in this instance reported $23 cash on hand for Mr. Sowell, $18 for Mrs. Sowell, and $25 in a joint bank account at Barnett Bank.

The bankruptcy schedules also ask the debtors to list all liquidated debts owing to them. The defendants represented that there were none. On June 2, 1987, however, this portion of the schedules was amended to add four parties owing debts of $1,116.25.

3. On July 18, 1986, a meeting of creditors pursuant to 11 U.S.C. § 341 was conducted. At that meeting, Mr. Sowell stated that he had ceased doing business under the name J.F. Sowell and was now conducting business under the trade name M & K Greens. He further stated that he no longer received any income from the former business. However, defendant, James F. Sowell, admitted that he had continued to receive payment on J.F. Sowell's accounts receivable after the name change had been effectuated.

4. On December 8, 1986, the Court entered an order requiring the defendants to produce a customer list for J.F. Sowell for 1985 and 1986. The list of 42 names prepared by the defendants does not include 12 regular customers on the truck route and 18 regular shipping customers. The omitted names include several of the Sowell's largest customers, including Nix's, Tommy's, Rosedale, Rainbow Growers, Fairmont Wholesale, and Charleston Florist.

5. In September of 1985, the defendants completed a personal financial statement listing accounts receivable of $26,014.30 owing for a 30 to 60 day period as opposed to $1,116.25 in accounts receivable on July 18, 1986. The defendants' only explanation for the $24,898.05 difference in accounts receivable between September, 1985, and the petition date was that greater effort had been made to collect the accounts. However, the bank records for the earlier time period contradict defendants' testimony and reflect greater amounts being deposited than for the same period in 1986.

6. At the trial, the defendants produced the weekly "route books" of J.F. Sowell for January through May 19, 1986, and M & K Greens for May 26, 1986, through December, 1986. The books are numbered sequentially 1 through 50 but do not include the books numbered 6, 12 and 18. The missing books correspond to the weeks prior to and including Valentine's Day, Easter and Mother's Day. The defendants testified at trial that these three holidays are the most profitable weeks for the sale of fern.

    Testimony reveals that the books contained the only accurate records of the weekly sales of fern to customers on the truck route and the amounts paid or carried as an account receivable during this crucial time period. Mr. Sowell then stated that the books had been inadvertently destroyed through no fault of his own.

7. To estimate the amount of accounts receivable for the truck route at the date of the petition requires a comparison of the bank deposit slips and the route books for the truck route. The missing route books make it difficult, if not impossible, to determine the exact amount of sales for the busiest weeks of the year. However, the defendants' certified public accountant, James Dreggers, testified that he spent several weeks reviewing the documents and was able to conclude that the value of the accounts receivable due and owing at the time of the petition exceeded $8,000. These accounts receivable were not listed in either the initial schedules or the amendments.

8. Not only did the debtors understate the true value of their accounts receivables, they also failed to adequately explain the flow of funds in and out of various bank accounts. For instance, the records of Vista Bank reflect that the defendants made deposits to their bank account totalling $6,637.08 immediately prior to the petition date and an additional $27,954.25 shortly thereafter. When asked about these funds, the defendants could not satisfactorily explain the whereabouts of the $6,637.08 or the source of the $27,954.25.

CONCLUSIONS OF LAW

1. The granting or denial of a discharge in bankruptcy is governed by 11 U.S.C. § 727 which provides that an individual debtor is entitled to a discharge unless the debtor has engaged in certain fraudulent or improper acts.

    Sections 727(a)(3) and (4) provide in relevant part:

    (a) The court shall grant the debtor a discharge, unless—
        (3) the debtor has concealed, destroyed, mutilated, falsified, or failed to keep or preserve any recorded information, including books, documents, records, and papers, from which the debtor's

financial condition or business transactions might be ascertained, unless such act or failure to act was justified under all the circumstances of the case;

(4) the debtor knowingly and fraudulently, in or in connection with the case—

(A) made a false oath or account;

The purpose of the bankruptcy discharge is to give the honest debtor a fresh start in life. In exchange for that privilege, the bankruptcy laws require that the debtors accurately and truthfully present themselves before the Court. *Matter of Garman,* 643 F.2d 1252 (7th Cir.1980). Where, as here, the debtors have repeatedly tried to hinder, delay, and defraud creditors through non-disclosure or concealment of their assets, the privilege of the "fresh start" should be denied.

2. Ordinarily, the failure to disclose assets of insignificant value will not support a denial of a debtor's discharge. *Matter of Galbraith,* 17 B.R. 302, 305 (Bkrptcy.M.D.Fla.1982). Where, however, the debtor has failed to schedule assets of significant value, the presumption is that the assets were omitted purposely with fraudulent intent. *In re Topping,* 84 B.R. 840, 842 (Bkrptcy.M.D.Fla.1988); *In re Collins,* 19 B.R. 874 (Bkrptcy.M.D.Fla.1982).

In the present case, the defendants have failed to disclose nearly $8,000 in accounts receivables, $6,637.08 on deposit with Vista Bank, and the source of nearly $27,000 deposited to that same account shortly after the petition had been filed. Given the nature of these omissions, the size of the bankruptcy estate, and the unsatisfactory explanations offered at trial, the Court concludes that these assets were intentionally left off the bankruptcy schedules. Under § 727(a)(3), the discharge of the defendants should be denied.

3. A separate allegation in this adversary proceeding is that the defendants failed

to maintain adequate business records. Although a full accounting of every business transaction is not required, there should be some written records, orderly made and preserved, from which the present and past financial condition of the debtor may be ascertained with substantial completeness and accuracy. *See e.g., In re Goff,* 495 F.2d 199, 201 (5th Cir.1974).

The defendants suggest that, as farmers, they should be given special consideration in regard to their record keeping practices. The Court does not agree. While a farmer or wage earner dealing primarily in cash ought not routinely be denied a discharge for failure to keep accurate records, a higher standard is imposed upon debtors actively engaged in credit transactions. Where, as here, the credit sales of the debtors make up a substantial portion of the gross profits, there should be a more accurate set of business records.

In the present case, the only business records which the defendants have produced are the deposit slips relating to the Barnett Bank business account and the weekly sales invoices associated with the "truck route." There are no records regarding credit sales or shipments made to out-of-town customers. Furthermore, an examination of the deposit slips shows that only the amount deposited in the defendants' business account is accounted for, not the actual amount paid in cash or charged as a credit during these three weeks. These records are far from accurate and the destruction of the three route books for the weeks surrounding Valentine's Day, Easter and Mother's Day has made it almost impossible to reconstruct the actual sales which occurred during the most productive weeks of the year. Under § 727(a)(3), this is sufficient cause for denying the defendants' discharge.

4. In addition to the above factors, the Court finds that the defendants have, on more than one occasion, made a false oath or account in connection with their case. For instance, the defendants failed to comply with the order directing them to produce a list of their customers by turning over only a partial list. On another occasion, July 18, 1986, they gave false testimony under oath regarding the source and location of cash assets. This is not to mention the fact that the defendants supplied misleading information in their bankruptcy schedules which, in and of itself, will support a finding of false oath or account in connection with this case.

5. It is evident that throughout this case the defendants have not cooperated with creditors. They have failed to adequately disclose their assets, they have concealed important information, and they have destroyed vital information necessary to a proper creditor investigation. The defendants have also failed to obey the lawful orders of this Court by disregarding orders such as the one entered December 8, 1986, directing them to produce certain documents. This is not the type of conduct which the Court will sanction. Accordingly, the Court will, upon separate order, deny the defendants' discharge pursuant to 11 U.S.C. §§ 727(a)(3) and (4).

Does the Debtor Have a Problem with the Dischargeability of a Debt?   The **dischargeability** of a debt concerns whether or not that particular debt will be discharged. If the debtor is entitled to a discharge of his or her debts, the debtor's second hurdle is whether he or she will be discharged from all debts or only from some. The discharge in bankruptcy has the effect of discharging only those debts that are dischargeable under the Code, and the court has the power to make determinations that certain debts are not dischargeable. 11 U.S.C.A. § 523. It is, of course, important for a debtor to know, or to have a good estimate of, the debts that can be discharged in the bankruptcy case and the debts that cannot be discharged. Particularly troublesome in consumer debtor cases are those claims that are often asserted by creditors to be nondischargeable because the merchandise, services, or a loan of money was obtained under false pretenses or by fraud. Claims based on fraud or defalcation while acting in a fiduciary capacity and claims for willful and malicious injury by the debtor to another entity or to the property of another entity are encountered occasionally.

The same nondischargeability problems follow the individual debtor in a Chapter 11 that he or she would face in a Chapter 7. Dischargeability is, therefore, not a factor in a choice between Chapter 7 and Chapter 11.

Is Liquidation Inevitable?   A number of small businesses are prolonged by filing under Chapter 11 when they should have filed under Chapter 7. The results obtained in such cases do not warrant the time and money spent on a Chapter 11 because creditors wind up with less than they would have received under Chapter 7.

Large cases involving corporate debtors will be filed under Chapter 11 for the purpose of reorganization, even though they may ultimately be liquidated under Chapter 11. Such cases are the exceptions to the general rule that Chapter 11 is for reorganization and requires a reorganization plan. It is possible to liquidate in Chapter 11 under a liquidating plan using Chapter 11 provisions and 11 U.S.C.A. § 363. Some districts even permit liquidation under Chapter 11 without a plan. If liquidation is inevitable, it is important to try to control who will liquidate. There is always the possibility that the debtor in possession in a Chapter 11 will do the liquidation. It would be advantageous to handle it in this manner because the debtor will have special incentive to go beyond what a trustee would do to obtain more money for the liquidation of the debtor's business.

Can the Debtor Meet the Expense of a Chapter 11 and Formulate a Viable Plan?   The filing of a Chapter 11 has always been an expensive and cumbersome process for the smaller business and was often a mistake. Small businesses often filed under Chapter 11 in a last gasp effort to keep the business going when there was no realistic hope of reorganization. Some small businesses merely wanted to keep operating until a buyer was found in the hope that the sale would provide the debtor with new assets that could be used to pay existing creditors. This strategy nearly always failed, and the business almost always liquidated. As noted earlier, the addition of the fast track provision in 11 U.S.C.A. § 1121 for small businesses (as defined in 11 U.S.C.A. § 101(51C)) should make Chapter 11 a workable alternative in such cases.

Because Chapter 7 is liquidation, it does not involve a reorganization plan. Chapter 11 is reorganization and does require a reorganization plan. 11 U.S.C.A. § 1106. The concept of cramdown of the plan in a Chapter 11 case is an important factor for the debtor to consider. **Cramdown** is the confirmation of a plan over the objections of creditors holding secured claims. What the debtor is concerned about in a Chapter 11 cramdown is the secured creditors. The plan must meet the **best interests of creditors test** (i.e., the creditors would receive no less than what they would receive in a Chapter 7). This is combined with a **fair and equitable test** (i.e., unless the creditors agree otherwise, that going down the line of priorities, the creditors on the bottom receive nothing unless the group immediately above is paid in full). Cramdown, the best interests of creditors test, and the fair and equitable test, as they relate to a Chapter 11 case, will be discussed in Chapter Eight of this text.

b. Chapter 7 vs. Chapter 12   The following factors are important when evaluating whether to file a Chapter 7 or a Chapter 12 petition.

Does the Debtor Have a Choice between Chapter 7 and Chapter 12?   While Chapter 7 encompasses almost all debtors (any person is eligible to be a debtor under Chapter 7 with the exception of railroads, insurance companies, and certain banking institutions), Chapter 12 is available only to family farmers who have a regular annual income, that is, family farmers whose annual income is sufficiently stable and regular to enable them to make payments under a Chapter 12 plan. (See Exhibit 4.4.) The term "family farmer" is further restricted because not all persons involved in farming operations are defined as family farmers under the Bankruptcy Code. For an individual or an individual and spouse to be considered a family farmer, the aggregate debts must not exceed $1,500,000; at least 80 percent of the aggregate noncontingent, liquidated debts must arise out of the debtor's farming operation; and more than 50 percent of the debtor's gross income for the preceding taxable year must have been received from the farming operation. For a partnership or a corporation to be considered a family farmer, more than 50 percent of the partnership or the outstanding stock must be held by one family conducting the farming operation; more than 80 percent of the value of the partnership or the corporate assets must consist of assets relating to the farming operation; the aggregate debts must not exceed $1,500,000; and not less than 80 percent of its aggregate noncontingent, liquidated debts must arise out of the farming operation. If the entity is a corporation that issued stock, the stock must not be publicly traded.

EXHIBIT 4.4
Debtors Eligible to File under Chapter 7, Chapter 12, or Both

Chapter 7	Chapters 7 and 12	Chapter 12
All persons except railroads, insurance companies, and certain banking institutions	Family farmer	Family farmer

Is the Debtor Eligible for a Discharge under Chapter 7 or Chapter 12, and Is There a Difference between the Discharges in Chapter 7 and Chapter 12?   If the debtor has been discharged under Chapter 7 in the past six years or has debts that are nondischargeable under Chapter 7, a Chapter 12 filing can offer relief. The Chapter 12 discharge is a broad one that discharges many of the debts that are not discharged in a Chapter 7 case. There is also a hardship discharge available to the family farmer who is unable to complete a plan. This type of discharge is narrower than the normal Chapter 12 discharge and is similar to the Chapter 7 discharge. Thus, even if the debtor is ineligible for a Chapter 7 discharge and is unable to pay out the Chapter 12 plan, he or she may still be eligible for a discharge if the requisite conditions are met. 11 U.S.C.A. § 1228(b).

Is Liquidation Inevitable?   Does the family farmer have land that he or she hopes to save and is it realistic to try to do so? This is often the heart of the question for the family farmer. If the decision is to try to hold on to the farm and not liquidate, then Chapter 7 is eliminated as an option. There may be a highly charged emotional component in this decision. The land in question may have been in the family for generations and long ago ceased to be merely a piece of property. Many family farmers will hold on to their land even if it means the sacrifice of almost everything else they own.

If it appears that liquidation is inevitable, perhaps the family farmer may be able to keep going under a Chapter 12 until a buyer is found for the farm. It is conceivable, although unlikely, that the farming operations could continue long enough for the farm to be sold and the family farmer to realize a small net gain from the transaction.

Can the Debtor Formulate a Viable Plan?   Because Chapter 7 is liquidation, it does not involve a reorganization plan. Chapter 12, however, is a type of reorganization and does require a plan for the adjustment of debts. 11 U.S.C.A. § 1221.

Cramdown under Chapter 12 is a simple cramdown without application of the fair and equitable doctrine. Because the fair and equitable test does not apply in a Chapter 12, the debtor can retain everything and need only meet the best interests of creditors test. This may leave the unsecured creditors with nothing. Cramdown and the best interests of creditors test, as they relate to a Chapter 12 case, will be discussed in Chapter Seven of this text.

c. Chapter 7 vs. Chapter 13   The following factors are important when evaluating whether to file a Chapter 7 or a Chapter 13 petition.

Does the Debtor Have a Choice between Chapter 7 and Chapter 13?   While Chapter 7 encompasses almost all debtors (any person is eligible to be a debtor under

Chapter 7 with the exception of railroads, insurance companies, and certain banking institutions), but Chapter 13 is available only to an individual (or individual and spouse) with regular income who owes unsecured debts that aggregate less than $250,000 and secured debts that aggregate less than $750,000. Stockbrokers and commodity brokers are excluded. (See Exhibit 4.5.)

Does the Debtor Have a Problem with the Dischargeability of a Debt under Chapter 7?   Depending on the status of the law in a particular jurisdiction, it may be possible to scale down a nondischargeable debt by filing under Chapter 13. The discharge in a Chapter 13 case allows for discharge of debts that might otherwise be nondischargeable in a Chapter 7. If this view is accepted in a particular jurisdiction, it may allow a debtor to discharge a nondischargeable debt for something less than 100 cents on the dollar. In some jurisdictions, the filing of a Chapter 13 under these circumstances is deemed to be a filing in bad faith and the case will be dismissed.

> **PROBLEM 4.37**   Dana Jones, an individual, has a number of debts, one of which is a loan she obtained to pay college tuition. Should Dana file under Chapter 7 or Chapter 13? Consult 11 U.S.C.A. §§ 1328(a)(2) and 523(a)(8) to aid Dana Jones in her choice.

Is Liquidation Inevitable?   A small business can be kept in operation under a Chapter 13 until a buyer is found, rather than closing it prematurely under Chapter 7. The price received for the business will add to the property of the estate, which will be in the best interests of both the debtor and the creditors.

> **PROBLEM 4.38**   Mom's & Pop's, a small grocery store, is in a good location and has been a going concern for a number of years. The proprietors' daughter-in-law, who had the best business sense in the family, divorced Pop, Jr., and left town two years ago. Due to poor management, Mom's & Pop's is now in financial difficulty.
>   Should Mom's & Pop's file under Chapter 7 or Chapter 13?

Is there any hope for turning the business around with more advertising or better management? Does the business have a history of success that might enable the current owners to sell it? Is the business in what is generally regarded as a good location?

EXHIBIT 4.5
Debtors Eligible to File under Chapter 7, Chapter 13, or Both

Chapter 7	Chapters 7 and 13	Chapter 13
All persons except railroads, insurance companies, and certain banking institutions	Individual or individual and spouse with regular income who owes less than $250,000 unsecured and $750,000 secured*	Individual or individual and spouse with regular income who owes less than $250,000 unsecured and $750,000 secured

*The attitude of the court and the U.S. trustee in the district in which the debtor is filing is important because they may not view Chapters 7 and 13 as alternatives but may dismiss a Chapter 7 filed by a debtor who is eligible for a Chapter 13 and who has enough disposable income to pay out a Chapter 13 plan.

PROBLEM 4.39   Lozers', a restaurant and club owned by John and Jean Lozer, is located on Route 66, once a major route from Chicago to Los Angeles. With the advent of the interstate highway system, a new tollway was built parallel to Route 66. Once Lozers' attracted a substantial number of customers from Route 66 traffic; now the restaurant receives no customers from the interstate because it is impossible to exit the interstate near Lozers'. Therefore, Lozers' must now be supported by local patrons.

In spite of generally good management, heavy advertising, and various promotional efforts, the business is no longer profitable. The Lozers have tried, without success, to sell the business. The poor location is apparently impossible to overcome, and the debts continue to mount up. The Lozers currently owe $178,000 in unsecured debts and $720,000 in secured debts.

Should the Lozers go ahead and file a Chapter 7 now, or should they try to hang on to the business under a Chapter 13?

Can the Debtor Formulate a Viable Plan?   Because Chapter 7 is liquidation, it does not involve a payment plan. Chapter 13, however, is adjustment of debt under a plan. The contents of a Chapter 13 plan are very similar to the contents of a Chapter 12 plan. Compare 11 U.S.C.A. § 1222 with 11 U.S.C.A. § 1322.

Only the debtor is allowed to file a Chapter 13 plan. The creditors have no input. This gives the debtor control over formulation of the plan.

The debtor must comply with all the provisions of Chapter 13 to get a plan confirmed. The debtor must pay all fees and must pay the creditors as much as they would receive under Chapter 7.

A separate requirement for confirmation of a Chapter 13 plan is that a plan be proposed in good faith. 11 U.S.C.A. § 1325(a)(3). A Chapter 13 case would be dismissed for bad faith in some districts if the plan provides for the discharge of a debt that is nondischargeable under Chapter 7. In other districts, it would not be considered bad faith. For the view that the plan seeking to discharge an otherwise nondischargeable debt in a Chapter 13 case does not preclude a finding of good faith, see *In re Slade,* 8 B.C.D. 558 (Bankr. 9th Cir. 1981). For the contrary view holding such plans to be in bad faith, see *In re Seely,* 6 B.C.D. 1003 (Bankr.E.D.Va.1980).

EXAMPLE

Sarah Jane Stuart, a divorced woman with a 15-year-old daughter at home, works for the ABC Packing Company as a secretary. She earns a gross salary of $1,500 a month with a take-home paycheck of $1,281. Sarah also receives $300 a month for child support from her former husband. She rents an apartment. She owns an automobile, which is financed, and some household furnishings and her wearing apparel. Everything she owns is exempt property under the applicable law of the state where she resides. The daughter has continuing medical problems because of arthritis, but most of these medical expenses are covered by insurance. Sarah is finding it extremely difficult to meet her financial obligations and is considering filing bankruptcy. Her attorney has advised her to file under Chapter 13.

The statement of income and expenditures reflects monthly expenses of $1,203, giving Sarah $378 a month as **disposable income** in accordance with the required calculation method. (See Fed. R. Bank. P. 1007(b)(1). This refers to Official Form No. 6, Schedules I and J. See also 11 U.S.C.A. § 1325(b)(2) defining "disposable income." Note the requirement for inclusion of the support payment as a part of income.) The living expense items on the income and expense statement are based on what the debtor will be paying over the plan period. Certain items that may have been installment payments will be paid over the plan period; these items are part of the plan, not part of the income and expenditures statements.

The district in which Sarah will file her Chapter 13 case requires that installment payments for automobiles be made through the plan and through the trustee. Basically, the debtor in a Chapter 13 case must pay disposable income for 36 months to the trustee. See 11 U.S.C.A. § 1325(b)(1)(B). The $378 a month will, for the first 24 months, be applied to the payment of administrative costs (including the trustee's fees of 10 percent and the balance of the fee owed to the attorney), to the $280 monthly car payment, and then to other creditors. The car will be paid off in 24 months, at which point the entire payment to the trustee will be applied to the administrative costs and other creditors. The only secured creditor is First Bank for the car payment. There are unsecured debts of $9,417. The car is worth a little more than the debt against it and Sarah will propose in the plan to make the payments as scheduled in her original loan agreement. If the car were worth an amount less than the loan amount, the loan could be restructured in the Chapter 13 plan. Up to this point the case is a routine situation without a substantial problem.

This particular debtor, however, does have a problem. While Sarah's situation might point to the filing of a Chapter 13 case without this problem, the fact that she has a debt that may not be dischargeable under Chapter 7 makes filing under Chapter 13 even more desirable. About one year ago, Sarah and her former husband borrowed money from Friendly Finance Company, a consumer finance company, for the purpose (according to the loan application) of buying furniture for their home. An invoice was rendered by a local furniture company and was taken with the loan application to the Friendly Finance office. The furniture was to be collateral for the loan. Everything was signed and the money was received from Friendly Finance, but the furniture was never purchased.

If Sarah files a Chapter 7 case, Friendly Finance would probably sue her by filing a complaint in the bankruptcy court claiming a nondischargeable debt on account of obtaining money by false pretenses. 11 U.S.C.A. § 523(a)(2)(A). This indebtedness is for $3,000, and the possibility of defending against a nondischargeability claim does not appear to be good. The effect of a Chapter 7 case would be that Sarah would not be paying the other unsecured creditors, people whom she would really like to pay. She would have to discharge those debts in order to be able to pay the cost of defending the nondischargeability case. The $3,000 debt would very likely be declared nondischargeable, and Sarah would ultimately have to pay it. Chapter 13 would permit her to pay less than 100 percent on her debt and the broad Chapter 13 discharge would allow her to discharge a debt that would be nondischargeable in a Chapter 7.

Assuming a plan based on these considerations, the unsecured creditors, including Friendly Finance, would receive about 50 cents on the dollar, the automobile would be paid off in two years, and the problem of the nondischargeable debt would be solved. Thus, in this case, it would appear to be a good strategic move to recommend a Chapter 13 filing.

The percentage needed to be paid on an unsecured debt, both in the case in which the debts are all fairly dischargeable and in the case in which part may be nondischargeable, will probably depend on the particular district or even the attitude of each bankruptcy judge within the district. The majority of the cases, however, do not require any particular percentage, and the Code requires only that the debtor's disposable income be committed for three years.

In a Chapter 13, it is unnecessary to cramdown unsecured creditors because they have no vote. Cramdown in a Chapter 13 applies only to secured creditors. If the creditor does not accept the settlement, the debtor must surrender the property securing the claim to the creditor. If the value of the secured property does not fully cover the claim, there will be a deficiency. The deficiency becomes an unsecured claim. The attorney for the debtor may want to obtain a full release from the creditor when the property is surrendered. This should be provided for in the plan. The full release in the plan eliminates the deficiency claim. If the debtor cannot get a release upon surrender of the property, then the plan must provide that the creditor will retain the unsecured claim.

Cramdown under Chapter 13 is a simple cramdown without application of the fair and equitable doctrine. The debtor can retain everything and only meet the best interests of creditors test. This may leave the unsecured creditors with nothing. Cramdown and the fair and equitable doctrine, as they relate to a Chapter 13 case, will be discussed in Chapter Six of this text.

Does the Debtor Have the Ability to Pay Out a Chapter 13 Plan?   The debtor's ability to pay out a Chapter 13 plan will involve personal motivation and disposable income. The debtor's personal motivation encompasses a number of factors. One debtor may be motivated to pay off his or her debts because of a desire to maintain personal integrity or because of social pressures exerted by family or friends. One important factor may be the debtor's obligations to family members or friends who are cosigners on some of the debts owed. On the other hand, another debtor may simply not care about what others think if he or she files a Chapter 7 bankruptcy petition. This type of debtor may also have no qualms about leaving cosigners holding the bag. Paying creditors may not be high on this debtor's list of priorities either.

The highly motivated debtor may be able to pay off creditors in a Chapter 13 with no more disposable income than the poorly motivated debtor who would simply not have the discipline to do so. The most highly motivated debtor, however, cannot successfully pay out a Chapter 13 plan without adequate disposable income. Thus, if the debtor lacks either adequate disposable income or the necessary motivation to pay out a Chapter 13 plan, a Chapter 7 filing is in order.

Will the Court or the U.S. Trustee Limit the Debtor's Selection of Chapter 7 if Chapter 13 Is Available?   The 1984 amendments that contain what are called the "consumer amendments," particularly the "Chapter 13 enhancement" provisions, encourage people to file Chapter 13 and, in some cases, put pressure on them to do so. The Chapter 13 amendments regarding disposable income, dismissal for substantial abuse, and the disclosure of Chapter 13 by the clerk and the debtor's attorney are definitely related.

The required income and expense statement, an important element in the "Chapter 13 enhancement" provisions, is a centerpiece in consumer bankruptcy cases. It is a central element of the decision to file under Chapter 7 or under Chapter 13. If it is followed as Congress intended it to be followed, the effect will be to cause some people to file Chapter 13 even when they do not want to. If an income and expense statement is filed that shows an excess of income over necessary expenses, that excess constitutes what Chapter 13 refers to as disposable income. In some courts, these income and expense statements are monitored and show-cause orders for dismissal under 707(b) are issued for the cases with statements showing disposable income. This action, of course, will cause a case to be dismissed if it is not converted to Chapter 13 by the debtor.

d. Chapter 11 vs. Chapter 12   The following factors are important when evaluating whether to file a Chapter 11 or a Chapter 12 petition.

Does the Debtor Have a Choice between Chapter 11 and Chapter 12?   While Chapter 11 encompasses almost all debtors (it includes all persons who may be a debtor under Chapter 7 with the exception of stockbrokers and commodity brokers but with the inclusion of railroads), Chapter 12 is available only to family farmers who have a regular annual income that is sufficiently stable to enable them to make payments under a Chapter 12 plan. (See Exhibit 4.6.) The term "family farmer" is further restricted because not all persons involved in farming operations are defined as family farmers under the Bankruptcy Code. For an individual or an individual and spouse to be considered a family farmer, the aggregate debts must not exceed $1,500,000; at least 80 percent of the aggregate noncontingent, liquidated debts must arise out of the debtor's farming operation; and more than 50 percent of the debtor's gross income for the preceding taxable year must have been received from the farming operation. For a partnership or a corporation to be considered a family farmer, more than 50 percent of the partnership or the outstanding stock must be held by one family conducting the farming operation; more than 80 percent of the value of the partnership or the corporate assets must consist of assets relating to the farming operation; the aggregate debts must not exceed $1,500,000; and not less than 80 percent of its aggregate noncontingent, liquidated debts must arise out of the farming operation. If the entity is a corporation that issued stock, the stock must not be publicly traded.

Can the Debtor Formulate a Viable Plan?   Both Chapter 11 and Chapter 12 require a plan. The Chapter 11 plan is a reorganization plan. 11 U.S.C.A. § 1123. The Chapter 12 plan is for the adjustment of debts. 11 U.S.C.A. § 1222.

Does the Procedure Make a Difference to the Debtor?   One big advantage for the family farmer in filing a Chapter 12 as opposed to a Chapter 11 is the fact that creditors have no input on the plan and do not vote on it. Another factor favoring Chapter 12 over Chapter 11 is the adequate protection requirement for secured creditors. Adequate protection in Chapter 11 cases generally requires large cash payments. Chapter 12 provides that the family farmer may pay the secured creditor the customary rent for use of farmland. This usually does not represent as large a sum of money as the regular payments would be. This may be the most important provision in Chapter 12 and will influence the choice of the chapter under which a family farmer will file.

Cramdown under Chapter 12 is a simple cramdown without application of the fair and equitable doctrine. Because the fair and equitable test does not apply in a Chapter 12, the debtor needs only to meet the best interests of creditors test in order to retain everything. This may leave the unsecured creditors with nothing.

Is Codebtor Protection Important to the Debtor?   Chapter 12 provides the **codebtor protection** that is lacking under Chapter 11. This will often be an important consideration for the family farmer because of the long-standing tradition in farming families of family members cosigning loans for each other.

EXHIBIT 4.6
Debtors Eligible to File under Chapter 11, Chapter 12, or Both

Chapter 11	Chapters 11 and 12	Chapter 12
All persons except insurance companies, certain banking institutions, stockbrokers, and commodity brokers	Family farmer	Family farmer

e. Chapter 11 vs. Chapter 13   The following factors are important when evaluating whether to file a Chapter 11 or a Chapter 13 petition.

Does the Debtor Have a Choice between Chapter 11 and Chapter 13?   While Chapter 11 encompasses almost all debtors (it includes all persons who may be a debtor under Chapter 7, with the exception of stockholders and commodity brokers but with the inclusion of railroads), but Chapter 13 is available only to an individual (or an individual and spouse) with regular income who owe(s) unsecured debts that aggregate less than $250,000 and secured debts that aggregate less than $750,000. (See Exhibit 4.7.)

Is Codebtor Protection Important?   The debtor who is eligible for both Chapter 11 and Chapter 13 and whose friends or relatives have cosigned loans, can obtain codebtor protection for these cosigners by filing Chapter 13. This automatic stay of action against codebtors is not provided for under Chapter 11.

Does the Procedure Make a Difference?   If a small business shows promise of being able to reorganize and can meet the filing criteria for Chapter 13, it may be a better choice than Chapter 11 because the debtor has more control under Chapter 13. For example, only the debtor may file a Chapter 13 plan, and there is no voting on the plan by creditors. In almost every small Chapter 11, the debtor is in greater jeopardy than the debtor in a large Chapter 11. The debtor in a small Chapter 11 will almost always find that the secured creditors will ask to have the stay modified so they can repossess the collateral. The court will set adequate protection payments. One of the key fights in a Chapter 11 will be for control of collateral. If the debtor in possession keeps the property and uses it, the question becomes what the debtor will have to pay the creditor to use the collateral and under what terms.

The smaller debtors are in so much greater jeopardy because they have less financial strength. The creditors may ask for cash collateral orders, appointment of a trustee, conversion to Chapter 7, or dismissal of the case. Many small corporations filing a Chapter 11 in the past did not make it through a plan and wound up liquidating under Chapter 11 or converting to Chapter 7. The new "small business" Chapter 11, as defined in 11 U.S.C.A. § 101(51C), should give the small corporation a fighting chance to reorganize under Chapter 11. The option to elect the small business Chapter 11 may prove a valuable alternative for the debtor who cannot meet the filing criteria of Chapter 13.

Cramdown under Chapter 13 is a simple cramdown without application of the fair and equitable doctrine. Because the fair and equitable test does not apply in a

EXHIBIT 4.7
Debtors Eligible to File under Chapter 11, Chapter 13, or Both

Chapter 11	Chapters 11 and 13	Chapter 13
All persons except stockbrokers, commodity brokers, insurance companies, and certain banking institutions	Individual or individual and spouse with regular income who owes less than $250,000 unsecured and $750,000 secured	Individual or individual and spouse with regular income who owes less than $250,000 unsecured and $750,000 secured

Chapter 13, the debtor needs only to meet the best interests of creditors test in order to retain everything. This may leave the unsecured creditors with nothing.

f. Chapter 12 vs. Chapter 13   The following factors are important when evaluating whether to file a Chapter 12 or a Chapter 13 petition.

Does the Debtor Have a Choice between Chapter 12 and Chapter 13?   Chapter 12 is available only to family farmers who have regular annual income, that is, family farmers whose annual income is sufficiently stable and regular to enable them to make payments under a Chapter 12 plan. Not all farming operations are defined as "family farmers" under the Bankruptcy Code. For an individual or an individual and spouse to be considered a family farmer, the aggregate debts must not exceed $1,500,000; at least 80 percent of the aggregate noncontingent, liquidated debts must arise out of the debtor's farming operation; and more than 50 percent of the debtor's gross income for the preceding taxable year must have been received from the farming operation. For a partnership or corporation to be considered a family farmer, more than 50 percent of the partnership or the outstanding stock must be held by one family conducting the farming operation; more than 80 percent of the value of the partnership or corporate assets must consist of assets relating to the farming operation; the aggregate debts must not exceed $1,500,000; and not less than 80 percent of its aggregate noncontingent, liquidated debts must arise out of the farming operation. If the entity is a corporation that issued stock, the stock must not be publicly traded.

Chapter 13 is available only to an individual (or an individual and spouse) with regular income who owe(s) unsecured debts that aggregate less than $250,000 and secured debts that aggregate less than $750,000. Stockbrokers and commodity brokers are excluded. (See Exhibit 4.8.)

> **PROBLEM 4.40**   Fran and Fred Barnhart have unsecured debts of $7,000 and secured debts of $280,000. They own a small farm on which they grow summer vegetables for sale to a large wholesale produce company. They also harvest a pecan crop every fall for sale to the same company. Fred is employed 30 hours a week by a nursery as a master gardener.
>
> Are the Barnharts eligible to file under Chapter 12, Chapter 13, or both?

Does the Procedure Make a Difference?   Cramdown under Chapter 12 and under Chapter 13 is identical. It is a simple cramdown without application of the fair and equitable doctrine. Because the fair and equitable test does not apply in either a Chapter 12 or a Chapter 13, the debtor need only meet the best interests of creditors

EXHIBIT 4.8
Debtors Eligible to File under Chapter 12, Chapter 13, or Both

Chapter 12	Chapters 12 and 13	Chapter 13
Family farmer	Family farmer who is an individual or individual and spouse with regular income who owes less than $250,000 unsecured and $750,000 secured	Individual or individual and spouse with regular income who owes less than $250,000 unsecured and $750,000 secured

test in order to retain everything. This may leave the unsecured creditors with nothing.

Is Codebtor Protection Important?   The codebtor stay applies to both Chapter 12 (11 U.S.C.A. § 1201) and Chapter 13 (11 U.S.C.A. § 1301), so it has no bearing on a choice between the two chapters.

C. THE COUNSELING SESSION

The attorney will review the information received, give his or her recommendation, and gain the debtor's assent to the recommendation during the counseling session. This is also the time to gather more information if necessary. Often, the attorney will not begin to draft the bankruptcy documents at this point. Instead, he or she will request that the debtor come in three or four more times before the drafting. This is done to determine that the client is ready to file bankruptcy—that he or she knows it is the last resort and inevitable. Several meetings will also provide enough information for the attorney and the paralegal to prepare everything that is needed for filing.

Substantial discussion may be necessary before filing a case to determine that a debtor who wants to retain an item of property will be able to do so from the standpoint of exemption and encumbrance. Retention will depend on the debtor's ability to pay for the item and to make a reaffirmation, as well as on whether he or she is in arrears. It will also depend on who has a security interest in the item and if the security interest is perfected. In other words, is the debtor really going to be able to keep a particular item of property? Does the debtor understand what can be kept and what cannot be kept and the conditions for each item? If there is any question involved, does the debtor understand how that question can be resolved and that it may go for or against the debtor? There should be no surprises.

After the attorney and the debtor discuss the various solutions available to the debtor, fees should be discussed again. This discussion should culminate in a written document to avoid any misunderstanding. If a decision to file bankruptcy has been made, the Administrative Office's form for disclosure of attorney's compensation will provide the necessary information. The document should be signed by the debtor and can be used as the written contract for services. If an alternative other than bankruptcy has been selected, the attorney will need to draft his or her own contract.

D. DRAFTING OF BANKRUPTCY FORMS

The attorney or the paralegal is ready for drafting when a clear understanding has been reached regarding the property of the debtor. A simple case may be drafted in an hour and a little more difficult one in two hours; a complex case may be drafted over several days. Even a simpler case may take longer to complete if there is not enough information and the debtor must be contacted to provide it. A paralegal trained in this field could sit down with the information and draft a total filing set. Some attorneys do it that way and some do not. One attorney may want to do all the drafting, while another may turn over part or all of the drafting to a paralegal.

The debtor should be present when the forms are drafted to avoid errors in the final form. The drafting should go smoothly if a questionnaire has been used. The drafting of the necessary forms in a Chapter 7 case will be discussed in detail, line by line, in Chapter Five of this text.

SECTION 2
THE CREDITOR-CLIENT

The attorney representing the creditor-client may be operating in a nonbankruptcy situation, a voluntary bankruptcy situation, or an involuntary bankruptcy situation. In a nonbankruptcy situation, the creditor may work with the debtor toward a solution to the problem through the use of a private alternative to bankruptcy or through a state court alternative such as garnishment of wages. If the debtor files a voluntary bankruptcy petition, the attorney for the creditor may, among other things, attend the meeting of creditors and file a proof of claim. If the debtor does not file a voluntary bankruptcy petition, the creditor-client and his or her attorney may decide it is necessary to file an involuntary bankruptcy petition against the debtor to protect the creditor's interests.

A. THE CAUSES OF THE CREDITOR'S DISTRESS

The creditor is distressed because he or she is losing present dollars. These are the dollars currently loaned to the debtor. The creditor also may be losing future dollars if the debtor has been a regular customer and their relationship has suddenly been jeopardized or terminated by the insolvency or bankruptcy of the debtor.

Creditors who are regulated by state or federal agencies face periodic audits. Those who are faced with regulatory examinations are concerned because they may have made a very bad loan to begin with and the examiner may express concern. This may lead to additional regulatory scrutiny, sanctions, and loss of control over the institution.

A loss may be large enough to jeopardize a small institution's capital and its own financial stability. A loss of half a million dollars may throw the small lending institution into insolvency.

A director or officer of a lending institution will be concerned about impairment of his or her own financial position. An officer or director often is a stockholder or has options and other valuable rights, and his or her whole future will be jeopardized by a large loss.

Credit problems certainly add administrative costs through attorney fees to creditors. They also cost substantial staff time, especially if the debtor wants to do a workout and the creditors want to do a part of the work themselves. Costs will be involved if the creditors want to follow the workout and analyze it closely as it progresses. Creditors may become apprehensive enough to neglect other work that they should be doing.

Creditor problems may have a bad psychological effect on the creditor's staff. Lending officers may become skittish when making loans and may pass up good opportunities because they have been burned in the past.

B. THE INITIAL INTERVIEW

The initial interview with the creditor-client may be very different from that with the debtor-client. The creditor-client often has a long-standing relationship with an attorney, and the steps necessary for the debtor-client may not be necessary for the creditor-client. Many times the creditor does not need to meet with his or her attorney. All that needs to be done is for the attorney to receive necessary papers and instructions specific to the case at hand. The attorney will generally know what to do, how to do it, and when to do it in representing a long-standing client. Certain basic information will, of course, be necessary for representation of the creditor-client. This information may be obtained by mail, telephone or facsimile in many cases. At least one meeting will be necessary in others. The attorney and the paralegal should make sure they are furnished all necessary information by the creditor. Some creditor-clients will know exactly what information the attorney needs and will provide this information without the necessity of a formal request by the attorney or the paralegal. Other clients will have the information but may not provide it to the attorney or the paralegal except on request.

The attorney may have an arrangement in advance with the creditor on how much to bill for services if the creditor is a regular client. If no prior fee arrangement has been made with the creditor, it will be necessary for the attorney to get an agreement in writing at the beginning of his or her representation of the creditor. Often attorneys doing collections will provide the services on a flat rate basis, a percentage of collection basis, a straight hourly fee, or a combination. Generally banks, credit unions, and savings and loan associations will pay fees on an hourly basis.

For a sample interview questionnaire for the creditor-client, see Appendix B.

C. ANALYSIS: IF THE DEBTOR HAS FILED BANKRUPTCY

This subsection sets forth the steps an attorney should take on behalf of a creditor-client if the debtor has filed bankruptcy. What must first be determined is whether the debtor has filed a Chapter 7, 11, 12, or 13 case.

1. IF THE DEBTOR HAS FILED A CHAPTER 7 CASE

If the debtor has filed a Chapter 7 case, the attorney for the creditor should

1. review the debtor's statement of financial affairs and schedules;
2. determine the value of the collateral;
3. file a proof of claim;
4. go after any co-obligors or guarantors on the creditor's claim against the debtor (unless they also have filed bankruptcy);
5. decide if client or attorney, or both, should attend the meeting of creditors;
6. report to the trustee any evidence or even suspicions that the debtor is concealing or disposing of assets;
7. check with the trustee to see if he or she plans to take action to avoid a preferential transfer;
8. check out the possibility of objecting to the debtor's discharge or to the dischargeability of the creditor's claim; and
9. if the debt is secured, try to get a reaffirmation agreement; or
10. if the debt is secured, have the automatic stay modified to reclaim secured property of the creditor or get the property abandoned.

Although Chapter 7 creditors' committees are provided for in the Code (11 U.S.C.A. § 705(a)), they are generally not viable because the creditors holding unsecured claims will almost always be wiped out in these cases. Anything that is worthwhile will be taken by a creditor holding a secured claim or will be the subject of a priority claim that will not be dischargeable. The creditors holding unsecured claims will finish in second place.

2. IF THE DEBTOR HAS FILED A CHAPTER 11 CASE

If the debtor has filed a Chapter 11 case, the attorney for the creditor-client should consider:

1. whether to file a motion for modification of the stay or what should constitute adequate protection;
2. how to determine the value of the collateral;
3. whether to oppose a motion for use of cash collateral or to put conditions on the use of cash collateral;
4. the extent to which the case should be pursued on a win or lose basis or whether some compromise should be instituted (and on what terms);
5. under what terms a disclosure statement will be approved;
6. how to vote on the confirmation of a plan;
7. what should be negotiated in the plan to achieve better terms for the creditor's claim;
8. whether motions should be filed to dismiss a Chapter 11, to appoint a trustee, or to convert the case to Chapter 7 and when such motions should be filed;
9. whether to move to change the venue, where the venue should be changed to, and how much should be invested in such a motion;
10. whether the creditor should seek a liquidation under Chapter 11;
11. whether a trustee should be appointed in a Chapter 11 rather than converting to a Chapter 7;
12. whether the client is eligible for the creditors' committee and, if so, whether the client should serve on the committee; and
13. whether there are any co-obligors or guarantors on the creditor's claim against the debtor (unless they also have filed bankruptcy).

If the debtor is in a Chapter 11, getting secured property may be time consuming and expensive. It may take years and thousands of dollars to finally pull real estate or a large asset out of a bankruptcy. Often an attorney can look at a situation and realize that the Chapter 11 will be a failure. For a year or so, the debtor in possession may keep the case alive, then the adequate protection payments are not met, and finally the creditor gets the asset back (which he or she did not want in the first place).

From the smaller to the larger cases, one of the main issues is usually collateral control. Several concerns are apparent in a lender/borrower situation that involves a security interest:

1. Who gets to keep the collateral?
2. Under what terms does the debtor get to use the collateral?
3. What does the debtor have to pay to continue to use the collateral?
4. What will it cost the creditor to get the collateral?
5. What condition will the collateral be in when the creditor gets it, and what will its value be?
6. How quickly can the collateral be offered for sale?

Under the Bankruptcy Code, creditors holding unsecured claims have substantial clout in Chapter 11 cases. They have the right to elect a trustee, the right to choose a creditors' committee, and the right to have the creditors' committee operate with representation of counsel and with hired professionals. Although the creditors' committee is uncompensated, the attorney for the creditors' committee will be paid. The creditors holding unsecured claims have an opportunity to provide input, which may give them some protection in a Chapter 11.

3. IF THE DEBTOR HAS FILED A CHAPTER 12 CASE

If the debtor has filed a Chapter 12 case, the attorney for the creditor should:

1. make sure the client understands the automatic stay against both the debtor and the codebtor;
2. determine if the debtor has possession of the creditor's collateral and, if so, the condition and value of the collateral;
3. file a proof of claim;
4. determine whether adequate protection exists when the debtor moves for the use of the creditor's cash collateral; and
5. object to confirmation of the plan if the interests of the creditors holding unsecured claims are not sufficiently protected. This objection could be based on the inability of the debtor to meet the terms of the plan or on the fact that all the money available for the plan has not been included.

4. IF THE DEBTOR HAS FILED A CHAPTER 13 CASE

If the debtor has filed a Chapter 13 case, the attorney for the creditor should:

1. check to see whether the creditor's claim is a dischargeable debt under Chapter 13 and, if so, consider a motion to convert to Chapter 7 if the debt would be nondischargeable under Chapter 7;
2. file a proof of claim;
3. examine the debtor's plan to see if the payments are a reasonable amount;
4. make sure the creditor-client understands the automatic stay against both the debtor and the codebtor;
5. check whether the amount to be paid to the creditors holding unsecured claims under the plan is not less than the amount these creditors would receive under Chapter 7; and
6. determine that the plan provides that all the debtor's projected disposable income be made available under the plan.

D. ANALYSIS: ALTERNATIVES IF THE DEBTOR HAS NOT FILED BANKRUPTCY

The creditor may pursue a number of alternatives if the debtor has not filed a voluntary bankruptcy petition. The creditor may pursue private alternatives by working directly with the debtor. State court remedies are also available to the creditor. In particular, the creditor holding a secured claim has several options in state court. If none of the private or state court alternatives work for the creditor, it is possible to file an involuntary bankruptcy petition against the debtor in some instances.

1. PRIVATE ALTERNATIVE

A creditor can work individually with the debtor to solve the creditor's problems and to help the debtor's position or, if more than one creditor is involved, a creditor can try to get all the creditors to work together to find a remedy. A creditor is required to act in good faith toward the debtor and may be subject to bad faith claims. A creditor must also closely monitor the security and resources of the debtor without becoming so involved with the debtor's situation that the creditor becomes liable to other creditors. The creditor should consider the following when making a decision about working with the debtor:

1. Does the debtor have reason to think that the relationship between the debtor and the creditor will continue?

2. Has the debtor been given adequate notice that the obligation has been called in to allow time to work something out?

3. Should an attorney be consulted concerning the creditor's proper course of action?

If a creditor does decide to work with the debtor, the creditor has the options of totally forgiving the debt or providing temporary relief until the debtor resolves his or her problems. Because few creditors are likely to forgive a debt, that leaves the option of providing temporary relief. Temporary relief involves negotiations, extensions, and compositions, all of which have been discussed under the debtor's remedies.

2. STATE COURT ALTERNATIVES

Legal remedies vary depending on whether the creditor holds an unsecured or secured claim and whether the remedy is a prejudgment or postjudgment remedy. A creditor holding an unsecured claim has few remedies available. Usually, a creditor holding an unsecured claim can only file a claim, obtain a judgment, and then execute the judgment against the property of the debtor. The majority of states permit prejudgment garnishment and attachment of a debtor's property when a creditor files suit, so that the property is secured if the creditor prevails on the claim. Caution should be exercised, however, in order to comply strictly with statutes that protect the debtor's due process rights.

a. Prejudgment Garnishment   **Garnishment** is the taking of the debtor's property, in the control of a third party, to satisfy the debtor's obligation to the creditor. Property garnished is usually in the form of bank accounts or wages of the debtor. A creditor may have to post a bond when garnishment proceedings are initiated. Garnishment of wages is not allowed in all states. A creditor may be liable to a debtor if the debtor prevails on a claim of wrongful garnishment.

b. Attachment   **Attachment** is the process of taking another person's property as the result of a judicial order. The sheriff is sent out to seize the property. The property is then sold at a public sale. Attachment can be used to secure any judgment that may be rendered in the future against the debtor. Attachment proceedings are governed by state statute and vary from state to state. Federal courts follow the applicable state statute.

Attachment is not always available and can only be used in certain situations listed in the statutes. Attachment can generally be used when the creditor cannot reach the debtor because he or she cannot be found or is residing in another state; when the creditor can claim fraud or other extenuating circumstances; or when the debtor is preparing to conceal or assign the property to defraud the creditor. Most statutes require that a bond be posted in the event the creditor does not prevail against the debtor. Some statutes also require notice and a hearing be given the debtor before property is seized.

To obtain an attachment, the creditor usually has to file a complaint. After the complaint is filed, the creditor must file an affidavit, bond, and writ of attachment. If an order of attachment is obtained, it is given to the county sheriff who will seize the property.

Attachment has several advantages. It keeps the debtor from transferring or disposing of the property. If the debtor is in default to other creditors, the attachment serves as a priority lien over the other creditors. Attachment gives the creditor an advantage over the debtor. Seizure of the debtor's property may result in the debtor paying off the obligation.

Attachment has disadvantages as well. It can be expensive. A bond is required and fees must be paid to the attorney and the sheriff. If a creditor does not obtain judgment against the debtor, the creditor is liable to the debtor for any damages the debtor incurs as a result of the loss of property. If a debtor files for bankruptcy within 90 days of the attachment, the attachment is invalid. A debtor may post a bond that results in termination of the attachment.

c. Receivership   A **receivership** is an equitable remedy whereby a receiver is appointed to protect the debtor's assets and to satisfy the claims of creditors. Receivership is usually a postjudgment remedy and therefore is only a last resort in prejudgment situations. All other remedies must be exhausted before receivership is allowed. The powers of the receiver are given by the court or by statute. The receiver has possession of the debtor's property but does not have title. In a prejudgment receivership, a receiver does little more than hold the property pending outcome of the judgment. Receivership does not give a creditor any advantage over other creditors; any existing liens on the property are still valid.

d. UCC § 2–702   Section 2–702 of the Uniform Commercial Code allows an additional remedy to a creditor holding an unsecured claim who is a seller of goods. A seller of goods to an insolvent buyer may refuse to deliver goods unless paid in cash and may also stop delivery of goods that have already been shipped. If the insolvent buyer has already received the goods, the seller can reclaim the goods on demand if demand is made within 10 days of receipt. The 10-day limit does not apply if the seller was led to believe the buyer was solvent by a written statement to that effect made by the buyer within three months previous to delivery.

A creditor holding a secured claim has all the remedies available to a creditor holding an unsecured claim, plus some additional remedies: replevin, self-help repossession, disposition of the collateral, and retention of the collateral.

e. Replevin   **Replevin** is an action similar to attachment but is limited to personal property to which the creditor has title or a lien. In an action of replevin, the sheriff seizes the applicable piece of property and gives it to the creditor until title to the property is decided. The debtor may countermand this action with a delivery bond.

f. Self-Help Repossession   **Self-help repossession** is governed by UCC § 9–503, which allows the creditor to take possession of collateral upon default of the debtor. A limitation on self-help repossession is that it cannot be done if it will breach the peace. This is a problem area because the UCC does not define what constitutes a breach of the peace.

The creditor can either sell or retain the repossessed collateral. When repossessing collateral, the creditor must be careful to take only the property that is collateral, must avoid any damage to the property, and should have a witness to the repossession in case problems arise later.

One of the immediate problems a creditor faces is the administration of repossessed collateral. Repossession often is a last resort because lending institutions do not really want to own oil wells or fleets of automobiles and trucks. Mobile home dealers do not want to own lots filled with used mobile homes. The lender may be frustrated by repossession because he or she may not want to take collateral back.

One solution for the creditor is to write off bad debts and take a corresponding loss on taxes. Internal Revenue Code § 166 allows a bad debt to be written off when it is uncollectible. The loan then changes from an asset to an expense on the balance sheet which lowers the year-to-date earnings of the creditor.

g. Disposition of Collateral   A creditor who decides to dispose of collateral of which he or she has obtained possession is governed by UCC § 9–504. Section 9–504 allows a creditor to sell the collateral at a public or private sale provided notice of the sale is given to the debtor. Notice must be given within a reasonable time so that the debtor has time to remedy the situation or participate in the sale. Sale of collateral has the effect of discharging the security interest or lien of the creditor.

h. Retention of Collateral   UCC § 9–505 authorizes a creditor to keep the collateral and, by doing so, to discharge the debt. Retention usually occurs when the value of the collateral is greater than the debt or when it may be difficult to sell the collateral. Written notice must be provided by the creditor to the debtor that the creditor intends to keep the collateral and that the debtor's obligation is discharged. Other requirements apply to whether the collateral involves consumer goods and whether the debtor has paid a certain percentage of the obligation.

i. Cognovit Judgment   One other prejudgment creditor remedy that deserves mention is the cognovit judgment (judgment by confession). In a **cognovit judgment**, the debtor and the creditor agree at the time the debtor-creditor relationship is created that if the debtor defaults, the creditor can obtain a judgment without any notice to the debtor or a hearing. Upon default, the creditor's attorney makes a court appearance to confess judgment against the debtor for any unpaid obligation and for fees and charges. Because the debtor has probably not received service of process, the debtor will not be prepared to contest the creditor's confession of judgment.

Although the cognovit judgment has survived (although not unscathed) constitutional attack, most states have either eliminated the cognovit judgment or have severely restricted its application. See *D. H. Overmyer Co. v. Frick Co.,* 405 U.S. 174 (1972); *Swarb v. Lennox,* 405 U.S. 191 (1972).

> **PROBLEM 4.41**   Check the current status of the cognovit judgment (judgment by confession) in your state. Check both statute and case law.

j. Judgment Lien   A **judgment lien** is a statutory measure providing that a judgment entered against a debtor becomes a lien on the debtor's property. A judgment lien is general. It does not relate to a specific piece of property but to all the property of the debtor, including any property obtained after the judgment lien is created. The judgment lien does not solve all the creditor's problems. It merely gives the creditor the right to levy on the debtor's property. Most states have a statute of limitations on judgment liens that dissolves the lien if the creditor does not act within a specified time.

k. Execution Lien   **Execution liens** are regulated by statute and provide for a writ of execution, which allows the creditor to seize the debtor's property and have it sold to satisfy the creditor's judgment against the debtor. An execution lien can usually be applied to both real and personal property. The writ of execution is carried out by the county sheriff rather than by the creditor. Problems with writs of execution are the possibility of liability for improper seizure and the possibility that the debtor's property was purchased by a third party before seizure but after the writ of execution was given. Execution liens are subject to a statute of limitations.

l. Execution Sale   An **execution sale** is the actual sale of the debtor's property to satisfy the creditor's lien or judgment. Proceeds from an execution sale go to satisfy the creditor first. Anything left over goes to the debtor. Execution sales are governed by statute and differ from a judicial sale in that they do not deal with specific property. Any property of the debtor can be sold under an execution sale.

m. Creditor's Bill   A **creditor's bill** is an equitable remedy allowing for a lien to be instituted against nonexempt property that is alienable or assignable under state law. A creditor's bill can be used as a bankruptcy alternative allowing all the debtor's creditors to join together. If a creditor's bill is for the benefit of only one creditor, then that creditor has priority over others. A creditor's bill allows for court discovery of a debtor's property. After discovery an injunction is issued against the debtor to prevent transfer of the property, and a receiver may also be appointed. Since the creditor's bill is an equitable remedy, it cannot be used if a legal remedy is available.

n. Supplementary Proceedings   **Supplementary proceedings** are proceedings supplementary to execution. They are used as a discovery mechanism for the debtor's property in the event an execution has not been satisfied. Supplementary proceedings are similar to a creditor's bill because they provide for discovery, injunction, receivership, and sale of property. Supplementary proceedings are not available when a third party has an interest in the debtor's property.

o. Postjudgment Garnishment   **Postjudgment garnishment** is similar to prejudgment garnishment, which was discussed earlier.

p. Fraudulent Conveyance   A **fraudulent conveyance** is one in which a debtor transfers his or her interest in property to friends or relatives to avoid the creditor's claims but still uses the property. Under the Uniform Fraudulent Conveyances Act, a creditor can recover property if he or she can prove it was fraudulently conveyed.

q. Consensual Lien   A **consensual lien** is an agreement entered into by the creditor and the debtor that gives the creditor a lien on specific property of the debtor, such as a car or a house. A consensual lien conveys added rights to a creditor, including foreclosure and priority over other creditors. Consensual liens in personal property and fixtures are governed by Article 9 of the Uniform Commercial Code. Consensual liens in real property, known as real estate mortgages, are governed by the real property laws of the state. A real estate mortgage can also include an interest in fixtures.

r. Equitable Lien   An **equitable lien** is given when a consensual lien was intended but never created or when failure to give the lien would result in unjust enrichment. Under an equitable lien, the property of the debtor can be sold to satisfy the creditor's claim.

In addition to the remedies just listed, state and federal statutes have instituted a number of other liens that may provide a benefit to a debtor or a creditor. Examples of these liens are materialmen's and mechanic's liens, tax liens, employee's liens, and landlord's liens.

3. INVOLUNTARY BANKRUPTCY CHOICES

The filing of an involuntary petition should be carefully considered as a last resort for the creditor seeking a solution to problems with a debtor engaged in business.

There are limitations regarding which debtors may be filed against.

> (a) An involuntary case may be commenced only under chapter 7 or 11 of this title, and only against a person, except a farmer, family farmer, or a corporation that is not a moneyed business, or commercial corporation, that may be a debtor under the chapter under which such case is commenced. 11 U.S.C.A. § 303(a).

In addition to the limitation on the types of debtors who may be filed against, there can be substantial penalties for the creditor if the involuntary case is dismissed.

> (i) If the court dismisses a petition under this section other than on consent of all petitioners and the debtor, and if the debtor does not waive the right to judgment under this subsection, the court may grant judgment—
>
> > (1) against the petitioners and in favor of the debtor for—
> >
> > > (A) costs; or
> > > (B) a reasonable attorney's fee; or
> >
> > (2) against any petitioner that filed the petition in bad faith, for—
> >
> > > (A) any damages proximately caused by such filing; or
> > > (B) punitive damages. 11 U.S.C.A. § 303(i).

Even though the debtor may file a voluntary petition in bankruptcy if he or she knows the creditor is considering filing an involuntary petition, the creditor must be careful not to threaten the debtor. This could prove costly to the creditor, especially if the involuntary petition is dismissed.

Except for the gap between the filing date and the order for relief, an involuntary case will proceed in the same manner as a voluntary case. The involuntary filing creates an estate and invokes the automatic stay. This protects the creditor not only by preventing the debtor from disposing of the assets but also by preventing other creditors from seizing the assets. It also protects the debtor by keeping the creditors at arm's length.

Only about 1 percent of all bankruptcies filed are involuntary cases. For this reason, the coverage of involuntary cases will not be extensive in this text.

a. Involuntary Chapter 7—Liquidation ("Straight" Bankruptcy)   The involuntary Chapter 7 may be filed by creditors who really want to see the debtor in Chapter 11 but do not want to pay the filing fee for a Chapter 11. The Chapter 7 also is filed against the debtor who appears to the petitioning creditors to have no prospect for reorganization. The creditors in this type of case just want to see the debtor liquidated before all assets are dissipated. This may be their only hope of collecting anything on what is owed them.

If a case is filed as an involuntary Chapter 7, the debtor engaged in business will be provided with the incentive to move to convert to a Chapter 11 to keep the business operating and the debtor in possession and control of the assets.

b. Involuntary Chapter 11—Reorganization   Creditors usually file an involuntary Chapter 11 petition against a debtor when they have evidence of either dishonesty or incompetence in the operation of the debtor's business. By filing an involuntary Chapter 11 reorganization petition, the creditors may be able to maintain the debtor's assets in a more valuable state for creditors. Property may be deteriorating or disappearing through seizure by other creditors, or the debtor may be concealing or transferring property to avoid paying creditors. In this type of situation, the petitioning creditors should move to have a trustee appointed. The incompetent or dishonest debtor should not remain in control of the assets to the extent allowed the debtor in possession under a Chapter 11.

E. THE COUNSELING SESSION

A second meeting may be necessary in some cases. At this session, the attorney will counsel the creditor-client and draft the necessary documents.

1. COUNSELING THE CREDITOR-CLIENT

If a second meeting is necessary, the attorney will review the information received from the creditor-client, discuss the available alternatives, make a recommendation concerning how to proceed to protect the creditor's interests, and gain the assent of the creditor to proceed.

The attorney and the paralegal should keep creditor-clients fully informed at each step of the process. Creditor-clients should be allowed to participate to the extent that they are able and want to participate. Their direct participation at hearings, depositions, meetings, and conferences should be encouraged. The attorney and the paralegal should get direct and, at times, written approval from the client before taking any substantial steps. This permits the client to consent to or disagree with the strategy suggested by the attorney at each juncture of the process. Creditor-clients will often be knowledgeable about the bankruptcy process and have their own thoughts on how the attorney should proceed. If several choices exist, the creditor-client should be consulted and his or her consent should be secured.

The creditor-client can be an excellent resource in matters such as obtaining an expert witness and should be utilized by the attorney and the paralegal.

If necessary, fee arrangements should be finalized and the contract for services should be signed at the second meeting.

2. DRAFTING BANKRUPTCY FORMS

To avoid errors, the creditor should be present when the forms are drafted. The drafting of the necessary forms in a Chapter 7 case will be discussed in Chapter Five of this text.

SECTION 3
THE DEBTOR-CLIENT IN AN INVOLUNTARY BANKRUPTCY

Representing the debtor-client in an involuntary bankruptcy can be very much the same as representing the debtor in a voluntary bankruptcy if he or she concedes. At this point an order for relief will be entered and the attorney and the paralegal will proceed with the preparation of the necessary forms. If, however, the debtor decides to defend against the involuntary filing, the work of the attorney and the paralegal will be substantially different.

A. THE INITIAL INTERVIEW

In the initial interview with the debtor-client against whom an involuntary bankruptcy petition has been filed, the attorney and the paralegal will attempt to obtain as much pertinent information as possible. The attorney may also explain the options available to the debtor. What the debtor needs to do may be obvious at this point, or the course of action may require further analysis by the attorney.

There should always be a discussion of fees at the first interview. Involuntary cases will probably be handled on an hourly fee basis, unless the debtor concedes to the involuntary filing. If the case has been filed in Chapter 7 and remains in Chapter 7 or is converted to Chapter 13, the attorney often charges a standard fee for these bankruptcy chapters. A written contract should be prepared setting forth the fee agreement.

B. ANALYSIS

The attorney representing the debtor-client in an involuntary bankruptcy will have three basic options to consider:

1. the debtor may concede and remain in the bankruptcy chapter initiated by the creditors;

2. the debtor may concede and convert to another chapter; or

3. the debtor may assert the various defenses available.

An involuntary filing will generally involve a business debtor. The filing will be Chapter 7 or Chapter 11. If the filing began as a Chapter 11, the debtor will be more likely to concede and remain in that chapter. A Chapter 11 reorganization is no longer considered a fatal blow to a business by many in the business community. It is being used routinely and voluntarily by many corporations to buy the time necessary to turn a bad situation around.

Many times creditors will file an involuntary case as a Chapter 7 to avoid the hefty Chapter 11 filing fee. If the debtor concedes and converts to Chapter 11, he or she must pay the difference. Some debtors who realize they have little hope of reorganization will concede and remain in the Chapter 7. A debtor engaged in a small business can either convert to Chapter 13 to avoid the cumbersome procedures of the traditional Chapter 11 or utilize the fast track procedures established by the new small business Chapter 11.

The debtor who is totally opposed to bankruptcy in any form or who believes the involuntary filing is unwarranted may choose to defend. The debtor's first line of defense is to ask the bankruptcy court to abstain from exercising jurisdiction. 11 U.S.C.A. § 305. The debtor may assert that the court lacks jurisdiction or venue. If that does not work, the debtor can attack the merits of the petition, asserting that debts are being paid or that no custodian has been appointed. The debtor may question the claims of the petitioning creditors. Perhaps the amount owed is not as much as is required by the Code or some of the claims are contingent. 11 U.S.C.A. § 303(b). The debtor may attempt to get an indemnity bond furnished by the petitioning creditors before the case is allowed to go forward. The purpose of such a bond would be to protect the debtor against losses that might be incurred because of the involuntary filing.

C. THE COUNSELING SESSION

During the counseling session, the attorney will explain fully the options available to the debtor, make a recommendation on which option will best preserve the debtor's assets, and gain the assent of the debtor to proceed. If more information was needed following the initial interview, the paralegal will have obtained it.

If the contract for fees was not signed at the first interview, it should be handled at this time.

BASIC TERMS AND PHRASES

Assignments for the benefit of creditors
Attachment
Best interests of creditors test
Chapter 11 plan
Codebtor protection
Cognovit judgment
Composition
Confirmation of a plan
Consensual lien
Consolidation loan
Cramdown
Credit counseling
Creditor's bill
Discharge
Dischargeability of a debt
Disposable income
Equitable lien
Execution lien
Execution sale
Extension

Fair and equitable test
Family farmer
Family farmer with regular annual
    income
Farming operation
Fast track provision
Fraudulent conveyance
Garnishment
Judicial lien
Limited partnership
Negotiation
Partnership
Postjudgment garnishment
Receivership
Replevin
Self-help repossession
Small business
Supplementary proceedings
Workout

FIVE

THE VOLUNTARY CHAPTER 7 BANKRUPTCY (LIQUIDATION OR "STRAIGHT" BANKRUPTCY)

This chapter is devoted exclusively to voluntary Chapter 7 bankruptcy, commonly known as **liquidation** or **"straight" bankruptcy.** A Chapter 7 case is developed in chronological order, beginning with the filing of the petition and concluding with the closing of the case.

This chapter discusses the filing of the petition and the significance of the filing, the order for relief, the creation of the estate (and what the estate encompasses), and the automatic stay, which protects the estate from dismemberment and the debtor from collection procedures. This chapter also covers the appointment of the interim trustee, along with the power of the trustee to abandon property of the estate; to assume or reject executory contracts; to avoid certain transfers of property of the estate as voidable preferences, fraudulent transfers, or postpetition transfers; and to avoid certain claimed security interests as unperfected. Proofs of claim and proofs of interest are explained. This chapter discusses the difference between contested matters and adversary proceedings and the motions and complaints used for each. The bankruptcy court's order and the clerk's notice to the trustee, all creditors, indenture trustees, and the U.S. trustee of the bankruptcy filing, the meeting of creditors, and the various important dates in the case are examined. The creditors' meeting, commonly known as the "341 meeting," is described.

If the debtor is an individual, a discharge and reaffirmation hearing may be held. Corporations and partnerships are not discharged from their debts under Chapter 7. The discharge and reaffirmation hearing is described. Although an individual debtor may receive a discharge from his or her debts, the property of the estate could be distributed without a discharge. Conversely, an individual debtor with no assets could receive a discharge even though there is no property of the estate to distribute. If property of the estate exists, the question of distribution comes into play.

The trustee's final accounting, approval of the trustee's final accounting, discharge of the trustee, and closing of the case, as well as further action on the case after it is closed, are also covered in this chapter.

For those readers who like information presented in chart form, a "road map" for the Chapter 7 bankruptcy case follows. Exhibit 5.1 provides a quick overview of the textual material. It is also useful as a checklist for taking a Chapter 7 case through the bankruptcy court from filing through closing and beyond closing, if that should ever become necessary. As readers progress through this chapter, periodic reference to this "road map" may be helpful.

EXHIBIT 5.1
Chapter 7 Liquidation (Voluntary Petition)

Filing the Petition

The debtor files with the bankruptcy court clerk's office:

1. Filing fee and administrative fee
2. Voluntary Petition (including Exhibit B, if the debtor is an individual whose debts are primarily consumer debts)
3. Clerk's notice (if an individual consumer debtor), if required by the court
4. Corporate resolution authorizing the filing of the Chapter 7 petition (if the debtor is a corporation)
5. Disclosure of attorney's compensation statement or disclosure of compensation statement by a non-attorney bankruptcy petition preparer
6. Matrix (serves as the list of creditors)
7. Schedules
   a. Summary of Schedules
   b. Schedule A: Real Property
   c. Schedule B: Personal Property
   d. Schedule C: Property Claimed as Exempt
   e. Schedule D: Creditors Holding Secured Claims
   f. Schedule E: Creditors Holding Unsecured Priority Claims
   g. Schedule F: Creditors Holding Unsecured Nonpriority Claims
   h. Schedule G: Executory Contracts and Unexpired Leases
   i. Schedule H: Codebtors
   j. Schedule I: Current Income of Individual Debtor(s)
   k. Schedule J: Current Expenditures of Individual Debtor(s)
   l. Schedule of Income and Expenditures of a Partnership or a Corporation
   m. Declaration Concerning Debtor's Schedules, signed by the debtor(s)
8. Statement of Financial Affairs

If the petition is accompanied by the matrix, the debtor has up to 15 days to file 7 and 8.

9. An individual debtor with consumer debts secured by property of the estate must file a statement of intention within 30 days after the date of filing the petition or by the date of the meeting of creditors, whichever is earlier.

Prior to the time the case is closed, the debtor may amend the petition, lists, schedules, and statements. The debtor has a duty to supplement the schedules for certain property acquired after the petition has been filed.

Upon filing of the petition, which constitutes an order for relief, an estate is created and the automatic stay goes into effect, protecting the estate from dismemberment and the debtor from collection procedures.

Promptly after the petition is filed, an interim trustee is appointed by the U.S. trustee.

EXHIBIT 5.1
Continued

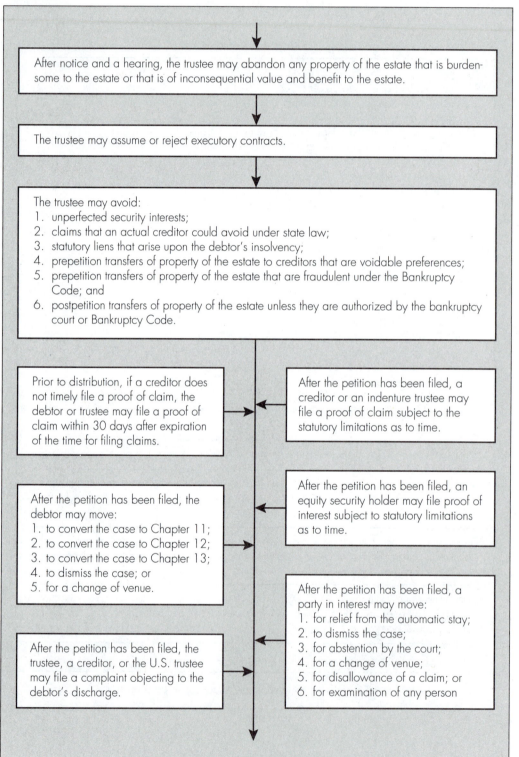

After notice and a hearing, the trustee may abandon any property of the estate that is burdensome to the estate or that is of inconsequential value and benefit to the estate.

The trustee may assume or reject executory contracts.

The trustee may avoid:
1. unperfected security interests;
2. claims that an actual creditor could avoid under state law;
3. statutory liens that arise upon the debtor's insolvency;
4. prepetition transfers of property of the estate to creditors that are voidable preferences;
5. prepetition transfers of property of the estate that are fraudulent under the Bankruptcy Code; and
6. postpetition transfers of property of the estate unless they are authorized by the bankruptcy court or Bankruptcy Code.

Prior to distribution, if a creditor does not timely file a proof of claim, the debtor or trustee may file a proof of claim within 30 days after expiration of the time for filing claims.

After the petition has been filed, a creditor or an indenture trustee may file a proof of claim subject to the statutory limitations as to time.

After the petition has been filed, the debtor may move:
1. to convert the case to Chapter 11;
2. to convert the case to Chapter 12;
3. to convert the case to Chapter 13;
4. to dismiss the case; or
5. for a change of venue.

After the petition has been filed, an equity security holder may file proof of interest subject to statutory limitations as to time.

After the petition has been filed, the trustee, a creditor, or the U.S. trustee may file a complaint objecting to the debtor's discharge.

After the petition has been filed, a party in interest may move:
1. for relief from the automatic stay;
2. to dismiss the case;
3. for abstention by the court;
4. for a change of venue;
5. for disallowance of a claim; or
6. for examination of any person

EXHIBIT 5.1
Continued

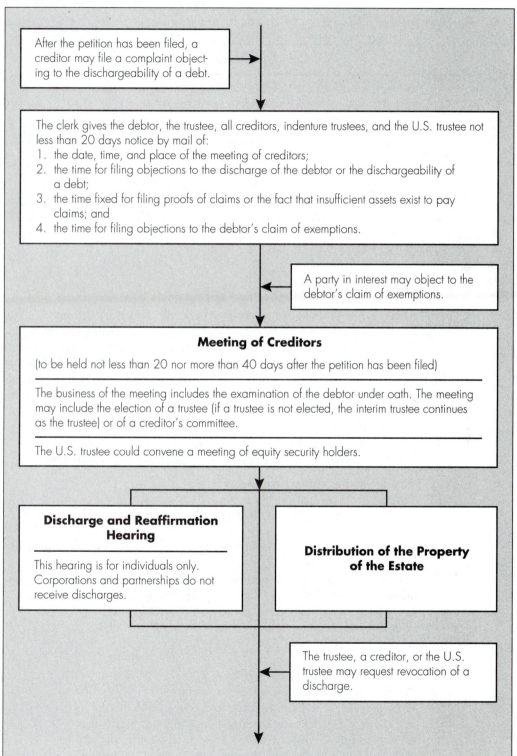

After the petition has been filed, a creditor may file a complaint objecting to the dischargeability of a debt.

The clerk gives the debtor, the trustee, all creditors, indenture trustees, and the U.S. trustee not less than 20 days notice by mail of:
1. the date, time, and place of the meeting of creditors;
2. the time for filing objections to the discharge of the debtor or the dischargeability of a debt;
3. the time fixed for filing proofs of claims or the fact that insufficient assets exist to pay claims; and
4. the time for filing objections to the debtor's claim of exemptions.

A party in interest may object to the debtor's claim of exemptions.

Meeting of Creditors

(to be held not less than 20 nor more than 40 days after the petition has been filed)

The business of the meeting includes the examination of the debtor under oath. The meeting may include the election of a trustee (if a trustee is not elected, the interim trustee continues as the trustee) or of a creditor's committee.

The U.S. trustee could convene a meeting of equity security holders.

Discharge and Reaffirmation Hearing

This hearing is for individuals only. Corporations and partnerships do not receive discharges.

Distribution of the Property of the Estate

The trustee, a creditor, or the U.S. trustee may request revocation of a discharge.

EXHIBIT 5.1
Continued

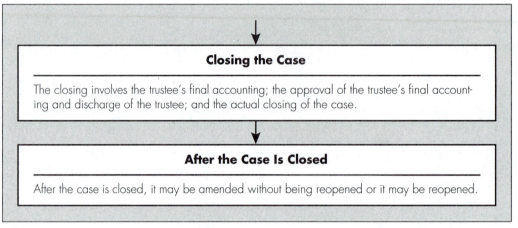

Closing the Case

The closing involves the trustee's final accounting; the approval of the trustee's final accounting and discharge of the trustee; and the actual closing of the case.

After the Case Is Closed

After the case is closed, it may be amended without being reopened or it may be reopened.

SECTION 1
THE FILING OF THE PETITION

Once the client has been properly interviewed and the necessary information has been gathered, the preparation of the petition and supporting documents can begin. The preparation for filing must be done carefully, and all documents must be completed in accordance with the Bankruptcy Code, the Federal Rules of Bankruptcy Procedure, and local court rules. Even if the case appears to be a walk-through, it is best not to regard any bankruptcy case as simple or routine. If difficulties with the court, the office of the court clerk, the trustee in bankruptcy assigned to this case, the creditors, and the office of the U.S. trustee are to be avoided, the appropriate forms must be properly completed.

In a voluntary Chapter 7, the debtor must file a number of documents:

1. Filing fee and administrative fee;
2. Voluntary Petition (Official Form No. 1);
3. The clerk's notice if the debtor is an individual consumer debtor and if reqired by the court;
4. Corporate resolution authorizing the filing of a Chapter 7 petition (if the debtor is a corporation);
5. Disclosure of attorney's compensation statement or disclosure of compensation statement by a non-attorney bankruptcy petition preparer;
6. Matrix (the matrix also serves as the list of creditors);
7. Schedules (Official Form No. 6)
    a. Summary of Schedules
    b. Schedule A: Real Property
    c. Schedule B: Personal Property
    d. Schedule C: Property Claimed as Exempt
    e. Schedule D: Creditors Holding Secured Claims
    f. Schedule E: Creditors Holding Unsecured Priority Claims
    g. Schedule F: Creditors Holding Unsecured Nonpriority Claims
    h. Schedule G: Executory Contracts and Unexpired Leases
    i. Schedule H: Codebtors
    j. Schedule I: Current Income of Individual Debtor(s)

k. Schedule J: Current Expenditures of Individual Debtor(s)

l. Schedule of Income and Expenditures of a Partnership or a Corporation

m. Declaration Concerning Debtor's Schedules, signed by the debtor(s);

8. Statement of financial affairs (Official Form No. 7);

9. Statement of intention (Official Form No. 8) (if the debtor is an individual debtor with consumer debts).

Good practice mandates that the petition, matrix, schedules, and statements be filed at one time. If, however, the petition is accompanied by the matrix (the list of all creditors), the debtor has up to 15 days after the date of filing to file the schedules and the statement of financial affairs. Fed. R. Bank. P. 1007(c). If an individual debtor has consumer debts that are secured by property of the estate, the debtor has 30 days after the filing of a petition or until the meeting of creditors, whichever is earlier, or until the time set by the court for cause, which is between the 30 days and the meeting of creditors, to file a statement of his or her intention to redeem or reaffirm debts secured by property of the estate. 11 U.S.C.A. § 521(2)(A). These grace periods should be used only in emergency situations and should not be a common practice.

The documents filed for a Chapter 7 case are filed with the clerk of the bankruptcy court. Fed. R. Bank. P. 1002(a). They are to be printed on one side of the paper only, and each page is to be prepunched with two holes at the top, leaving sufficient top margin so that neither the caption nor the text is destroyed or obscured. This requirement is designed to facilitate both the securing of the documents in the case file and the review of the file by those interested.

The filing consists of handing the documents, the filing fee, and the administrative fee to a deputy clerk in the office of the clerk. The deputy clerk places the appropriate stamps on the petition to indicate the court, date, and time.

A. THE DEBTOR'S PETITION (OFFICIAL FORM NO. 1)

The **debtor's petition** to commence a voluntary Chapter 7 must substantially conform to Official Form No. 1. Fed. R. Bank. P. 1002(a). This form is found in any printed set of bankruptcy forms and computer bankruptcy filing programs. By filing the voluntary petition, the debtor actually initiates the case. (See Exhibit 5.2.)

The petition may be filed by a person who may be a debtor under Chapter 7, such as an individual debtor or joint debtors. 11 U.S.C.A. §§ 301, 302. Only an individual debtor and his or her spouse may be joint debtors. 11 U.S.C.A. § 302(a). Unmarried couples cannot file a joint case. The joint case permits a husband and wife, who hold most of their property jointly and who are liable on their debts jointly, to consolidate their estates and thus benefit both themselves and their creditors by reducing administrative costs. The joint case also reduces the cost of filing to one filing fee.

The petition (Official Form No. 1)—a two page form—should not be confused with the entire filing package. The filing package is usually stapled together and includes the schedules and the statement of financial affairs. In practice, it is customary to refer to the package as "the petition," even though technically only the two-page Official Form No. 1 is the petition.

Official Form No. 1 has been revised to create space for a new requirement. The Bankruptcy Reform Act of 1994 requires that a **bankruptcy petition preparer** (a person other than an attorney or employee of an attorney) who prepares a document to be filed in a bankruptcy case must, in addition to signing the document, include his or her name, address, and social security number. 11 U.S.C.A. § 110.

EXHIBIT 5.2
Official Form No. 1 (The Debtor's Petition)

FORM B1
(12/94)

FORM 1. VOLUNTARY PETITION

A United States Bankruptcy Court District of _____	VOLUNTARY PETITION

IN RE (Name of debtor - if individual, enter Last, First, Middle) B	NAME OF JOINT DEBTOR (Spouse)(Last, First, Middle) B

ALL OTHER NAMES used by the debtor in the last 6 years (Include married, maiden, and trade names) C	ALL OTHER NAMES used by the joint debtor in the last 6 years (Include married, maiden, and trade names) C

SOC.SEC./TAX I.D. NO. (If more than one, state all) D	SOC.SEC./TAX I.D. NO. (If more than one, state all) D

STREET ADDRESS OF DEBTOR (No. and street, city, state, and zip code)	STREET ADDRESS OF JOINT DEBTOR (No. and street, city, state, and zip code)
COUNTY OF RESIDENCE OR PRINCIPAL PLACE OF BUSINESS	COUNTY OF RESIDENCE OR PRINCIPAL PLACE OF BUSINESS

MAILING ADDRESS OF DEBTOR (If different from street address)	MAILING ADDRESS OF JOINT DEBTOR (If different from street address)

LOCATION OF PRINCIPAL ASSETS OF BUSINESS DEBTOR (If different from addresses listed above)	VENUE (Check one box)
	☐ Debtor has been domiciled or has had a residence, principal place of business, or principal assets in this District for 180 days immediately preceding the date of this petition or for a longer part of such 180 days than in any other District. ☐ There is a bankruptcy case concerning debtor's affiliate, general partner, or partnership pending in this District. E

INFORMATION REGARDING DEBTOR (Check applicable boxes)

TYPE OF DEBTOR (Check one box) F
- ☐ Individual
- ☐ Joint (Husband and Wife)
- ☐ Partnership
- ☐ Other_____
- ☐ Corporation Publicly Held
- ☐ Corporation Not Publicly Held
- ☐ Municipality

NATURE OF DEBT (Check one box) G
- ☐ Non-Business/Consumer
- ☐ Business - Complete A & B below

A. TYPE OF BUSINESS (Check one box)
- ☐ Farming
- ☐ Professional
- ☐ Retail/Wholesale
- ☐ Railroad
- ☐ Transportation
- ☐ Manufacturing/Mining
- ☐ Stockbroker
- ☐ Commodity Broker
- ☐ Construction
- ☐ Real Estate
- ☐ Other Business

B. BRIEFLY DESCRIBE NATURE OF BUSINESS H

CHAPTER OR SECTION OF BANKRUPTCY CODE UNDER WHICH THE PETITION IS FILED (Check one box) I
- ☐ Chapter 7
- ☐ Chapter 9
- ☐ Chapter 11
- ☐ Chapter 12
- ☐ Chapter 13
- ☐ Sec. 304 - Case Ancillary to Foreign Proceeding

SMALL BUSINESS (Chapter 11 only)
- ☐ Debtor is a small business as defined in U.S.C. § 101
- ☐ Debtor is and elects to be considered a small business under 11 U.S.C. §1121(e) (Optional)

FILING FEE (Check one box) J
- ☐ Filing fee attached
- ☐ Filing fee to be paid in installments. (Applicable to individuals only.) Must attach signed application for the court's consideration certifying that the debtor is unable to pay fee except in installments. Rule 1006(b). See Official Form No. 3.

NAME AND ADDRESS OF LAW FIRM OR ATTORNEY K

L

Telephone No.

NAME(S) OF ATTORNEY(S) DESIGNATED TO REPRESENT DEBTOR

M

STATISTICAL/ADMINISTRATIVE INFORMATION (28 U.S.C.A. § 604) (Estimates only)(Check applicable boxes)	☐ Debtor is not represented by an attorney. Telephone No. of Debtor not represented by an attorney: N

☐ Debtor estimates that funds will be available for distribution to unsecured creditors.
☐ Debtor estimates that, after any exempt property is excluded and administrative expenses paid, there will be no funds available for distribution to unsecured creditors.

THIS SPACE FOR COURT USE ONLY

ESTIMATED NUMBER OF CREDITORS

1-15	16-49	50-99	100-199	200-999	1000-over	
☐	☐	☐	☐	☐	☐	O

ESTIMATED ASSETS (In thousands of dollars)

Under 50	50-99	100-499	500-999	1000-9999	10,000-99,999	100,000-over	
☐	☐	☐	☐	☐	☐	☐	P

ESTIMATED LIABILITIES (In thousands of dollars)

Under 50	50-99	100-499	500-999	1000-9999	10,000-99,999	100,000-over	
☐	☐	☐	☐	☐	☐	☐	Q

EST. NO. OF EMPLOYEES - CH. 11 & 12 ONLY

0	1-19	20-99	100-999	1000-over
☐	☐	☐	☐	☐

EST. NO. OF EQUITY SECURITY HOLDERS - CH. 11 & 12 ONLY

0	1-19	20-99	100-499	500-over
☐	☐	☐	☐	☐

EXHIBIT 5.2
Continued

FORM B1 - Cont.
(12/94)

Name of Debtor _____ **R** _____

Case No. _____ **S** _____

FILING OF PLAN

For Chapter 9,11,12, and 13 cases only. Check appropriate box.

☐ A copy of debtor's proposed plan dated _____ is attached.

☐ Debtor intends to file a plan within the time allowed by statute, rule or order of the court.

T   PRIOR BANKRUPTCY CASE FILED WITHIN LAST 6 YEARS (If more than one, attach additional sheet)

Location Where Filed **U**	Case Number	Date Filed

PENDING BANKRUPTCY CASE FILED BY ANY SPOUSE, PARTNER, OR AFFILIATE OF THE DEBTOR (If more than one, attach additional sheet)

Name of Debtor	Case Number **V**	Date
Relationship	District	Judge

REQUEST FOR RELIEF

Debtor is eligible for and requests relief in accordance with the chapter of title 11, United States Code Annotated specified in this petition.

SIGNATURES

ATTORNEY

X _____ **W** _____

Signature   Date

INDIVIDUAL/JOINT DEBTOR(S)	CORPORATE OR PARTNERSHIP DEBTOR
I declare under penalty of perjury that the information provided in this petition is true and correct.	I declare under penalty of perjury that the information provided in this petition is true and correct and that I have been authorized to file this petition on behalf of the debtor.
X _____ **X** _____ Signature of Debtor	X _____ **Y** _____ Signature of Authorized Individual
Date _____ **Z** _____	_____ Print or Type Name of Authorized Individual
X _____ Signature of Joint Debtor	_____ Title of Individual Authorized by Debtor to File this Petition **Z**
Date _____	Date If debtor is a corporation filing under chapter 11, Exhibit "A" is attached and made part of this petition.

TO BE COMPLETED BY INDIVIDUAL CHAPTER 7 DEBTOR WITH PRIMARILY CONSUMER DEBTS (See P.L. 98-353 § 322)	CERTIFICATION AND SIGNATURE OF NON-ATTORNEY BANKRUPTCY PETITION PREPARER (See 11 U.S.C. § 110)
I am aware that I may proceed under chapter 7, 11, or 12, or 13 of title 11, United States Code Annotated, understand the relief available under each such chapter, and choose to proceed under chapter 7 of such title.	I certify that I am a bankruptcy petition preparer as defined in 11 U.S.C. § 110, that I prepared this document for compensation, and that I have provided the debtor with a copy of this document. **CC**
If I am represented by an attorney, Exhibit B has been completed.	Printed or Typed Name of Bankruptcy Petition Preparer
X _____ **AA** _____ Signature of Debtor Date	Social Security Number
X _____ Signature of Joint Debtor Date	Address Tel. No.: Names and Social Security numbers of all other individuals who prepared or assisted in preparing this document:
EXHIBIT "B" (To be completed by attorney for individual chapter 7 debtor(s) with primarily consumer debts.)	
I, the attorney for the debtor(s) named in the foregoing petition, declare that I have informed the debtor(s) that (he,she, or they) may proceed under chapter 7,11, 12, or 13 of title 11, United States Code Annotated, and have explained the relief available under such chapter.	If more than one person prepared this document, attach additional signed sheets conforming to the appropriate Official Form for each person. X _____ Signature of Bankruptcy Petition Preparer
X _____ **BB** _____ Signature of Attorney Date	A bankruptcy petition preparer's failure to comply with the provisions of title 11 and the Federal Rules of Bankruptcy Procedure may result in fines or imprisonment or both. 11 U.S.C. §110; 18 U.S.C. § 156.

Instructions for Completing Official Form No. 1 (The Debtor's Petition)

A   Complete the name of the bankruptcy court in which the petition is filed.

Examples: For a state that has more than one federal district, indicate the district and the state: United States Bankruptcy Court for the Northern District of Oklahoma.

For a state that has only one federal district, indicate only the state: United States Bankruptcy Court for the District of Vermont.

B   Complete the name of the debtor.

Examples: For an individual debtor . . .

If the debtor is an individual, the debtor's name must appear in the following order: last name, first name, middle name. The complete middle name in full, rather than an initial, must be used:
Jones, James Wesley
Brown, John William, Jr.
Delany, Donald Douglas III

If the debtor does not have a middle name, so indicate by NMN:
Mead, Joan (NMN)

If the debtor has four names, include all four:
Taft, John William Howard

If the debtor uses a hyphenated name, use the hyphenated name:
Holland-Smyth, Mary Agnes

If the debtor is a medical doctor or a dentist, M.D. and D.D.S. are optional:
Brown, John William, M.D., or Brown, John William
Walsh, Jane Sampson, D.D.S., or Walsh, Jane Sampson

If the debtor is an attorney or has a doctorate degree, do not include Esq. or Ph.D.

Examples: For a partnership debtor . . .

Use the name of the partnership and not the names of the partners:
Mary and Joe's Dinette
The Rainbow Inn
John Winkler & Associates
Roy Frazier & Daughter

Examples: For a corporate debtor . . .

Use the official name of the corporation and not its trade name:
The Whitehouse Restaurant, Inc.
Ricky Pratt & Son, Co., Inc.
Ms. Judy's School of Dance, Inc.

C   List all other names used by the debtor(s) during the six years prior to the filing of the petition. Include maiden names, married names, aka's (also known as), fka's (formerly known as), and dba's (doing business as). If more space is needed, type the names on a separate page as an addendum to the petition. At the top of each addendum page, include the debtor's full name as it appears on the petition, the case number, the chapter under which the case was filed, and the title of the document.

Examples: For an individual debtor . . .

If the debtor is an unmarried woman filing as an individual and she has used two additional names during the previous six years:
Joan Ann Mead, aka Sue Lynn Mead, Jean Ann Mead

If the debtor is an unmarried woman filing as an individual and she has been married and divorced during the previous six years:
Joan Ann Mead, fka Joan Mead Reynolds

If the debtor is an unmarried woman filing as an individual and she has been married and divorced twice during the previous six years:
Joan Ann Mead, fka Joan Mead Reynolds, Joan Mead Washburn

If the debtor is a married woman filing as an individual and she was married during the previous six years:
Joan Mead Reynolds, fka Joan Ann Mead

If the debtor is a transsexual and was a man during the previous six years:
Roberta Ann Mead, fka Robert Albert Mead

If the debtor has a business:
Joan Ann Mead, dba Honest Joan's Loan, Gun and Pawn Shoppe

Examples: For a partnership debtor . . .

If the partnership is known by a trade name or has changed names within the past six years:
Mary and Joe's Dinette, aka M & J's Dinette, fka The Route 66 Dinette
The Rainbow Inn, aka The Rainbow Club, fka Eric's Bar and Grill
John Winkler & Associates, aka The Fireworks Man, fka John Winkler
Roy Frazier & Daughters, aka Frazier's Doughnut Delight, fka Roy Frazier & Daughter

Examples: For a corporate debtor . . .

If the corporation is known by a trade name or has changed names within the past six years:
The Whitehouse Restaurant, Inc., aka Mel's Place, fka Mel's Restaurant
Ricky Pratt & Son, Co., Inc., aka The Quality Fur Salon
Ms. Judy's School of Dance, Inc., fka East Ridge School of Dance

D   List the debtor's social security number and employer's tax identification number, if one is applicable.

Federal law requires every employer to have an employer's tax identification number, which is secured from the Social Security Administration (Form SS-4). This number is generally two digits followed by seven digits (73-5467821). If the debtor should have an employer's tax identification number but does not, the answer should be "none."

The debtor's social security number or employer's tax ID number (employer's taxpayer identification number) will be used to assure accurate identification and recording of the debtor's case, to assure that papers pertaining to the debtor's case will be filed under the appropriate case, and to facilitate the sending of accurate notice to debtors.

The employer's tax ID number must be included if the debtor is a corporation, partnership, or individual who is doing business.

E   Check one box. The information in these boxes establishes whether the petition has been filed in a bankruptcy court that has jurisdiction.

F   The petition may be filed by a person who may be a debtor under Chapter 7, such as an individual debtor or joint debtors. 11 U.S.C.A. §§ 301, 302. Only an individual debtor and his or her spouse may be joint debtors. 11 U.S.C.A. § 302(a). Unmarried couples cannot file a joint case. The joint case permits a husband and a wife, who hold most of their property jointly and who are liable on their debts jointly, to consolidate their estates and thus benefit both themselves and their creditors by reducing the cost of administration. The joint case also reduces the cost of filing to one filing fee.

G   If the debtor is an individual whose debts are primarily consumer debt, select the Non-Business/Consumer category.

If the debtor is a business enterprise or if most of the debts of an individual arose from the operation of a business or self-employment, "Business" should be selected. If the Business category is selected, answer questions A and B.

H   Examples of the nature of business are

Antique Dealer	Massage Parlor
Appliance Sales and Service (Retail)	Modeling School
Architect	Oil Producer
Attorney at Law	Paint Store
Automobile Repair	Pest Control Service
Bookkeeper	Physician
Carpet Sales (Retail)	Printing Shop
Clothing Sales (Retail)	Rancher
Computer Dealer	Restaurant
Dentist	Roofing Contractor
Employment Agency	Shoe Store (Retail)
Florist (Retail)	Tanning Salon
Furniture Dealer (Retail)	Tropical Fish Sales (Retail)
Grocer (Retail)	Trucking Company
Health Club	Used Book Store
Heating Contractor	Yogurt Shop
Home Builder	Zipper Repairs
Insurance Agency	

I   Select Chapter 7.

J   Payment of the filing fee in installments is applicable only to individual debtor(s). If the filing fee is to be paid in installments, Official Form No. 3 must be completed and attached to the petition. In Official Form No. 3, the debtor's application to the court, the debtor must certify that he or she is unable to pay the filing fee except in installments. Fed. R. Bank. P. 1006(b).

K   If the attorney is a member of a law firm, use the law firm's name.

Example: Savage, O'Donnell, Scott, McNulty, Affeldt, and Genges, rather than Warren L. McConnico

If the attorney is a solo practitioner, use the attorney's name.

Example: John T. Mortimer

If the debtor has no attorney and is filing pro se, write "none" under "name of law firm or attorney."

L   Include the area code.

Example: (918) 599-9000

M   Include the name of the attorney and his or her bar membership number.

Example: Warren L. McConnico, #5907

If the debtor has no attorney and is filing pro se, write "none" under "name(s) of attorney(s) designated to represent debtor."

N   If the debtor has no attorney, the box is checked. If the debtor is represented by an attorney, the box is left blank.

O   This estimate should correspond to the information appearing in the debtor's schedules. See Schedules D, E, and F. The estimate should be the debtor's best estimate and need not be exact.

P   This estimate should correspond to the information appearing in the debtor's schedules. See Schedules A, B, and C. The estimate should be the debtor's best estimate and need not be exact.

Q   This estimate should correspond to the information appearing in the debtor's schedules. See Schedules D, E, and F. The estimate should be the debtor's best estimate and need not be exact.

R   The name of the debtor should be the full name of the debtor (last name, first name, full middle name) as it appears on the first page of Official Form No. 1.

S   The case number is provided by the clerk of the bankruptcy court when the petition is filed. Since the petition has not been filed at this time, a case number does not exist. The line should be left blank.

T   These questions are answered only if the debtor has filed a prior bankruptcy case within the last six years. If there was more than one bankruptcy case filed by the debtor during the past six years, attach an additional page and provide the requested information.

   The client should be questioned about prior bankruptcies. The client may have previously filed a petition in bankruptcy without understanding what he or she did.

   The paralegal or the attorney must understand where and when the debtor has filed prior bankruptcy petitions. Therefore, the information is available if it subsequently becomes necessary to look up the prior bankruptcies. Sometimes, in prior bankruptcies, it is important to know what happened and when it happened. Debtors may be in error about what type of case the prior bankruptcy was, or may lose track of the actual date of a prior bankruptcy and be in error by several years, or may be in error as to the disposition of the previous bankruptcy.

U   These questions are answered only if there is a pending bankruptcy case filed by any spouse, partner, or affiliate of the debtor. If there is more than one pending case, attach an additional page and provide the requested information.

   If there is a related bankruptcy case, complete the name of the debtor as it appears on that petition (last name, first name, full middle name).

   Because entities may be interlocked in one way or another and various bankruptcy petitions may be filed in relation to the various entities, all related bankruptcy cases must be referenced, one to another. The court may ultimately consider joint administration or consolidation.

V   The case number is the number assigned to the case by the deputy clerk.

W   The signature of the debtor's attorney and the date signed are entered here. If the debtor is not represented by an attorney, then this line is left blank.

X   After the petition has been completed, the debtor must sign the petition. The debtor must sign his or her name in the following order: first name, middle name, last name. The debtor must sign his or her complete middle name in full, rather than use an initial, regardless of the fact that the debtor normally signs an initial in place of his or her middle name. If the debtor has been known by more than one name, the debtor must sign the first name that appears in "B." This is the name under which the case is docketed.

   If a joint petition is filed, both debtors must sign their full names as they appear in "B." The debtors must sign their complete middle names in full.

Y   If the petition is filed by a partnership, one of the partners of the partnership must sign on behalf of the partnership.

   Example: The Mellon Shop, by James Earl Quackenbush, partner

   If the petition is filed by a corporation, an authorized officer of the corporation must sign on behalf of the corporation and his or her corporate position must be indicated.

   Example: The Snidley Gas and Oil Exploration Corporation, by Elmer J. Snidley, Jr., President

Z   After the petition is signed by the debtor(s), the date on which the debtor(s) signed the petition is added by the debtor(s). The date must include the month, day, and year.

   Examples: July 1, 1997
          7/1/97
          1 July 1997

AA   This is a statement by an individual Chapter 7 debtor, whose debts are primarily consumer debts, that the debtor has been informed that he or she may proceed under Chapter 7, 11, 12, or 13 and has chosen to proceed under Chapter 7. The debtor must sign and date, signing his or her name as it appears on the first page of the petition. If the petition is being filed by joint debtors, both must sign and date this statement.

If an individual debtor, whose debts are primarily consumer debts, is filing the petition without an attorney, AA can be disregarded.

BB   To complete Exhibit "B," the debtor's attorney must declare that he or she has informed the debtor that the debtor could proceed under Chapter 7, 11, 12, or 13 and has explained the relief available under each chapter. The signature of the debtor's attorney must correspond to the attorney's name as it appears on page one of the petition. The attorney must also indicate the date of his or her signature.

CC   This section applies to the "non-attorney bankruptcy preparer," who is defined in 11 U.S.C.A. § 110(a)(1) as "a person, other than an attorney or an employee of an attorney, who prepares for compensation a document for filing." This section should be left blank.

PROBLEM 5.1   The following case will be filed in the United States bankruptcy court in the district in which you reside. The date is the current date.

The debtors are Pamela Lynn Laughlin and Michael Douglas Richards, husband and wife. Pamela Laughlin is a veterinarian and works for the Highland Animal Clinic, which is located in your city. Michael Richards is a university professor and teaches history at the state university in your city. Pamela Laughlin earned her Doctor of Veterinary Medicine degree from the University of Kansas. Michael Richards earned his Ph.D. from Stanford.

This is the second marriage for both. Pamela Laughlin was previously married to Carl Moore, Jr. She has a four-year-old daughter, Irene, from that marriage. Michael Richards has an 18-year-old son, Michael Douglas Richards, Jr., from his previous marriage. Michael, Jr., is currently a freshman at a state university in your state.

Pamela Laughlin has used her maiden name as her professional name throughout her career. She always signs her name "Dr. Pamela L. Laughlin," although she at times is known socially as Pamela Richards. She has never used her full middle name.

Pamela Laughlin's Social Security number is 445-74-2787. Michael Richards' Social Security number is 403-54-1227. Because both are employees, neither has an employer's identification number.

The Richards live at 8129 Silver Meadow Circle in your city, county, and state. They have lived at this address since they were married. Prior to that time, Pamela lived at 542 Evergreen Lane in your city, county, and state. She had lived at that address for only the year between her previous marriage and her marriage to Michael Richards. During her previous marriage, Pamela Laughlin lived at 3120 East Avenue in your city, county, and state.

You and your professor are members of a major law firm in your city, and you both specialize in bankruptcy law. You have interviewed Pamela Laughlin and Michael Richards, and the above information appears on their questionnaire. After discussing this case with you, your professor has decided that Laughlin and Richards should file a Chapter 7 petition and has recommended this to the clients; they have concurred. It is now your responsibility to complete the petition (Official Form No. 1) and Exhibit "B," if appropriate. Complete these forms for your professor's review and for Pamela Laughlin's and Michael Richards' signatures.

B. THE FILING FEE

Every petition must be accompanied by the **filing fee,** except when the payment of the filing fee is in installments. Fed. R. Bank. P. 1006(a). The filing fee must be paid in full before the debtor can pay an attorney or any other person for services in connection with the case. Fed. R. Bank. P. 1006(b)(3). The filing fee for a voluntary Chapter 7 is found in 28 U.S.C.A. § 1930(a)(1). The fees are paid in cash, by check, or with a money order. The checks and money orders are drawn to the order of "United States Bankruptcy Court" or to the order of the specific United States bankruptcy court in which the case is filed.

EXAMPLES
United States Bankruptcy Court
U.S. Bankruptcy Court
United States Bankruptcy Court
for the Southern District of New York

Paying the filing fee in installments, while rare, is permissible.

(b)   Payment of Filing Fee in Installments.
(1) Application for Permission to Pay Filing Fee in Installments. A voluntary petition by an individual shall be accepted for filing if accompanied by the debtor's signed application stating that the debtor is unable to pay the filing fee except in installments. The application shall state the proposed terms of the installment payments and that the applicant has neither paid any money nor transferred any property to an attorney for services in connection with the case.

(2) Action on Application. Prior to the meeting of creditors, the court may order the filing fee paid to the clerk or grant leave to pay in installments and fix the number, amount and dates of payment. The number of installments shall not exceed four, and the final installment shall be payable not later than 120 days after filing the petition. For cause shown, the court may extend the time of any installment, provided the last installment is paid not later than 180 days after filing the petition. Fed. R. Bank P. 1006(b).

The application and order to pay the filing fee in installments is Official Form No. 3. (See Exhibit 5.3.) Although Official Form No. 3 is designed for an individual debtor, it may be revised for use by individual debtors filing a joint petition by changing the term "debtor" to "debtors" and by making other appropriate changes.

EXHIBIT 5.3
Official Form No. 3 (Payment of Filing Fee in Installments)

FORM B3
(12/94)

United States Bankruptcy Court
District of _____ **A**

In re _____ **B** Case No. _____ **C**
Debtor Chapter _____

APPLICATION TO PAY FILING FEES IN INSTALLMENTS

In accordance with Fed. R. Bankr. P. 1006, application is made for permission to pay the filing fee on the following terms:

$ _____ **D** with the filing of the petition, and the balance of

$ _____ in _____ installments, as follows:

$ _____ on or before _____

$ _____ on or before _____

$ _____ on or before _____

$ _____ on or before _____

I certify that I am unable to pay the filing fee except in installments. I further certify that I have not paid any money or transferred any property to an attorney or any other person for services in connection with this case or in connection with any other pending bankruptcy case and that I will not make any payment or transfer any property for services in connection with the case until the filing fee is paid in full.

Date _____ **E** _____
Applicant

_____
Attorney for Applicant

CERTIFICATION AND SIGNATURE OF NON-ATTORNEY BANKRUPTCY PETITION PREPARER (See 11 U.S.C. § 110)

I certify that I am a bankruptcy petition preparer as defined in 11 U.S.C. §110, that I prepared this document for compensation, and that I have provided the debtor with a copy of this document.

_____ **F** _____
Printed or Typed Name of Bankruptcy Petition Preparer Social Security No.

_____
Address
Names and Social Security numbers of all other individuals who prepared or assisted in preparing this doucment:

If more than one person prepared this document, attach additional signed sheets conforming to the appropriate Official form for each person.

X _____ _____
Signature of Bankruptcy Petition Preparer Date

A bankruptcy petition preparer's failure to comply with the provisions of title 11 and the Federal rules of Bankruptcy Procedure may result in fines or imprisonment or both. 11 U.S.C. §110, 18 U.S.C. §156.

ORDER

IT IS ORDERED that the debtor pay the filing fee in installments on the terms set forth in the foregoing application.

IT IS FURTHER ORDERED that until the filing fee is paid in full the debtor shall not pay, and no person shall accept, any money for services in connection with his case, and the debtor shall not relinquish and no person shall accept, any property as payment for services in connection with this case.

BY THE COURT

Date _____ _____
United States Bankruptcy Judge

Instructions for Completing Official Form No. 3 (Payment of Filing Fee in Installments)

A Complete the name of the court in which the petition is filed. See Official Form No. 1.

B Complete the name of the debtor as it appears on the bankruptcy petition.

C   Complete the case number by inserting the bankruptcy case number assigned by the court at the time the petition is filed.

D   Complete the payment schedule. The number of installments cannot exceed four and the final installment must be paid no later than 120 days after the filing of the petition. Before completing the payment schedule, a paralegal should check with his or her local bankruptcy court clerk's office for information concerning the amount that must be paid when the petition is filed and the amount that must be paid in each installment.

The court, for cause, can extend the time for paying the last installment from 120 to 180 days after the filing of the petition.

E   Complete the date, signature, and address of the debtor(s). The name(s) of the debtor(s) and address must correspond to the name(s) and address found on the petition (and on this form under "B"). The debtor must sign his or her name in the following order: first name, middle name, last name. The debtor must sign his or her complete middle name, rather than use an initial, regardless of the fact that the debtor normally signs an initial in place of his or her middle name.
The date should be the date signed by the debtor(s) and need not be the date the petition is filed.

F   This section applies to the "non-attorney bankruptcy petition preparer," who is defined in 11 U.S.C.A. § 110(a)(1) as "a person, other than an attorney or an employee of an attorney, who prepares for compensation a document for filing." This section should be left blank.

PROBLEM 5.2   Using the information in Problem 5.1 and the following information, decide whether Pamela Laughlin and Michael Richards should apply to pay their filing fee in installments. If you decide that they should so apply, complete Official Form No. 3—Application to Pay Filing Fees in Installments.

Pamela Laughlin and Michael Richards have little cash on hand. Pamela expects to be paid at the end of the month. Michael could borrow the filing fee from his father, although he would be embarrassed to do so. They could reduce some expenses by driving only one car and canceling the insurance on the other car, which is also due this month. This would also save about $50 a month on gasoline and about $50 a month on maintenance.

C. THE CLERK'S NOTICE

If the debtor is an individual and the debts are primarily consumer debts, then the **clerk's notice** must be completed if required by the court. Exhibit "B" in the petition (Official Form No. 1) is a statement by the debtor's attorney that he or she has informed the debtor that he or she may proceed under Chapter 7, 11, 12, or 13 of Title 11 of the Bankruptcy Code and has explained the relief available under each such chapter to the debtor. The Bankruptcy Code, however, in 11 U.S.C.A. § 342(b), requires the clerk to give written notice to the debtor as to each operative chapter of the Bankruptcy Code under which the debtor could proceed and makes no mention of the debtor's attorney giving the notice. In practice, B 201, although not an official form, was issued by the Administrative Office of the United States Courts for use in compliance with 11 U.S.C.A. § 342. The clerk of the bankruptcy court now gives B 201 to the debtor's attorney, who in turn explains the various chapters of the Bankruptcy Code to the debtor and obtains the debtor's signature on the bottom of the form. B 201 is then filed along with the petition.

The following forms are the notice to the individual consumer debtor and the affirmation by the debtor that he or she has been notified. (See Exhibit 5.4.)

EXHIBIT 5.4
Clerk's Notice to Individual Consumer Debtor(s)

B 201
(Rev. 11/95)

United States Bankruptcy Court

NOTICE TO INDIVIDUAL CONSUMER DEBTOR

The purpose of this notice is to acquaint you with the four chapters of the federal Bankruptcy Code under which you may file a bankruptcy petition. The bankruptcy law is complicated and not easily described. Therefore, you should seek the advice of an attorney to learn of your rights and responsibilities under the law should you decide to file a petition with the court. Court employees are prohibited from giving you legal advice.

Chapter 7: Liquidation ($130 filing fee plus $30 administrative fee plus $15 trustee surcharge)

1. Chapter 7 is designed for debtors in financial difficulty who do not have the ability to pay their existing debts.

2. Under chapter 7 a trustee takes possession of all your property. You may claim certain of your property as exempt under governing law. The trustee then liquidates the property and uses the proceeds to pay your creditors according to priorities of the Bankruptcy Code.

3. The purpose of filing a chapter 7 case is to obtain a discharge of your existing debts. If, however, you are found to have committed certain kinds of improper conduct described in the Bankruptcy Code, your discharge may be denied by the court, and the purpose for which you filed the bankruptcy petition will be defeated.

4. Even if you receive a discharge, there are some debts that are not discharged under the law. Therefore, you may still be responsible for such debts as certain taxes and student loans, alimony and support payments, criminal restitution, and debts for death or personal injury caused by driving while intoxicated from alcohol or drugs.

5. Under certain circumstances you may keep property that you have purchased subject to valid security interest. Your attorney can explain the options that are available to you.

Chapter 13: Repayment of All or Part of the Debts of an Individual with Regular Income ($130 filing fee plus $30 administrative fee)

1. Chapter 13 is designed for individuals with regular income who are temporarily unable to pay their debts but would like to pay them in installments over a period of time. You are only eligible for chapter 13 if your debts do not exceed certain dollar amounts set forth in the Bankruptcy Code.

2. Under chapter 13 you must file a plan with the court to repay your creditors all or part of the money that you owe them, using your future earnings. Usually, the period allowed by the court to repay your debts is three years, but no more than five years. Your plan must be approved by the court before it can take effect.

3. Under chapter 13, unlike chapter 7, you may keep all your property, both exempt and non-exempt, as long as you continue to make payments under the plan.

4. After completion of payments under your plan, your debts are discharged except alimony and support payments, student loans, certain debts including criminal fines and restitution and debts for death or personal injury caused by driving while intoxicated from alcohol or drugs, and long term secured obligations.

Chapter 11: Reorganization ($800 filing fee)

Chapter 11 is designed primarily for the reorganization of a business but is also available to consumer debtors. Its provisions are quite complicated, and any decision by an individual to file a chapter 11 petition should be reviewed with an attorney.

Chapter 12: Family farmer ($200 filing fee)

Chapter 12 is designed to permit family farmers to repay their debts over a period of time from future earnings and is in many ways similar to chapter 13. The eligibility requirements are restrictive, limiting its use to those whose income arises primarily from a family-owned farm.

I, the debtor, affirm that I have read this notice.

A

_____   _____   _____
Date   Signature of Debtor   Case Number
                              WHITE—DEBTOR COPY   PINK— COURT COPY

Instructions for Completing the Clerk's Notice to Individual Consumer Debtor(s)

A   Complete the date and signature of the debtor(s). The name(s) of the debtor(s) must correspond to the name(s) found on the petition. The debtor must sign his or her name in the following order: first name, middle name, last name. The debtor must sign his or her complete middle name, rather than use an initial, regardless of the fact that the debtor normally signs an initial in place of his or her middle name. If the debtor has been known under more than one name, the debtor must sign the name under which the case is docketed.

The date should be the date signed by the debtor(s) and need not be the date the petition is filed.

PROBLEM 5.3   Using the information in Problem 5.1, complete the Notice to Individual Consumer Debtor(s) form.

D. CORPORATE RESOLUTION AUTHORIZING FILING OF CHAPTER 7

The corporate resolution gives the person filing the Chapter 7 case authority to file the case and to engage and reimburse any attorney or accountant whose services are necessary in the case. The corporate resolution must be consistent with the corporate charter and state law. (See Exhibit 5.5.)

EXHIBIT 5.5
Corporate Resolution Authorizing Filing of a Chapter 7 Petition

---

```
                RESOLUTION OF THE BOARD OF DIRECTORS
                        OF [DEBTOR'S NAME]

            Special Meeting of [SPECIAL MEETING DATE]

     The Board of Directors met at this special meeting to
discuss the financial condition of the corporation.  After
discussion a motion was made and seconded to adopt the
following resolution:
     Whereas the affairs of the business of this corporation
have not been successfully conducted for several months,
     Be it therefore resolved that this corporation file its
voluntary Petition for relief under Chapter  of Title 11 of
the United States Code in the United States Bankruptcy Court
and
     Be it further resolved that [PETITION AUTHORITY]  is
hereby authorized to prepare the necessary Petition for
relief and by that person's single signature execute all
necessary documents and bind this corporation thereby and
     Be it further resolved that [REPRESENTATIVE AUTHORITY]
is hereby authorized to engage the services of any attorney
or accountant or both as shall appear necessary to assist in
this matter and to reimburse any attorney or accountant so
engaged out of the assets of the corporation.
     The motion was adopted by a vote of [VOTES FOR]  to
[VOTES AGAINST]  .
     There being no further business to come before this
meeting, a motion to adjourn was made and seconded and the
meeting was adjourned.




                         _____
                         Chair




                         _____
                         Secretary to the Board of Directors

Affix the corporate seal
```

E. DISCLOSURE OF ATTORNEY'S COMPENSATION STATEMENT

The Code requires any attorney representing a debtor in a case under the Bankruptcy Code to file with the court a statement of the compensation paid or agreed to be paid for services connected with the bankruptcy case and the source of the compensation. 11 U.S.C.A. § 329. This **disclosure of attorney's compensation statement** must be completed regardless of whether the attorney applies to the court for compensation. The Federal Rules of Bankruptcy Procedure also require the debtor's attorney to transmit the statement of compensation to the United States trustee. Fed. R. Bank. P. 2016(b). (See Exhibit 5.6.)

This reporting requirement serves two functions:

1. It permits the court to determine whether the compensation exceeds the reasonable value of the services rendered. 11 U.S.C.A. § 329. See also 28 U.S.C.A. § 586(a)(3)(A). If the court determines that the compensation exceeds the reasonable value of the services rendered, it may deny compensation to the attorney, cancel the agreement to pay compensation, or order the return of compensation paid. 11 U.S.C.A. § 329(b); 28 U.S.C.A. § 586(a)(3)(A).

2. The disclosure permits the court to determine whether the attorney has made an agreement to share compensation. The Code prohibits the debtor's attorney from sharing or agreeing to share with another person any compensation or reimbursement received by either the attorney for the debtor or the other person. This prohibits fee splitting among attorneys, other professionals, or trustees. The debtor's attorney is, however, permitted to share compensation with partners or associates in his or her professional association, partnership, or corporation. 11 U.S.C.A. § 504.

The disclosure of attorney's compensation statement must be filed with the court and transmitted to the United States trustee within 15 days after the petition has been filed or by another date set by the court. Fed. R. Bank. P. 2016(b).

Because the statement specifies the services the attorney will provide the client and the compensation the client will provide the attorney, it can also serve as the written contract between attorney and client. A copy of the statement should be signed by the client for the attorney's records. The client could also be provided a copy for his or her records.

EXHIBIT 5.6
Disclosure of Attorney's Compensation Statement

B 203
(1/88)

United States Bankruptcy Court

_____ District of _____ **A** _____

In re

Bankruptcy Case No. _____ **C** _____

Debtor _____ **B** _____   Chapter _____ **D** _____

DISCLOSURE OF COMPENSATION OF ATTORNEY FOR DEBTOR

1. Pursuant to 11 U.S.C. § 329(a) and Bankruptcy Rule 2016(b), I certify that I am the attorney for the above-named debtor(s) and that compensation paid to me within one year before the filing of the petition in bankruptcy, or agreed to be paid to me, for services rendered or to be rendered on behalf of the debtor(s) in contemplation of or in connection with the bankruptcy case is as follows:

For legal services, I have agreed to accept . . . . $_____ **E** _____

Prior to the filing of this statement I have received . . . . $_____

Balance Due . . . . $_____

2. The source of the compensation paid to me was:

  ☐ Debtor   ☐ Other (specify)   **F**

3. The source of compensation to be paid to me is:

  ☐ Debtor   ☐ Other (specify)   **G**

4. ☐ I have not agreed to share the above-disclosed compensation with any other person unless they are members and associates of my law firm.   **H**

  ☐ I have agreed to share the above-disclosed compensation with a person or persons who are not members or associates of my law firm. A copy of the agreement, together with a list of the names of the people sharing in the compensation, is attached.

5. In return for the above-disclosed fee, I have agreed to render legal service for all aspects of the bankruptcy case, including: **I**

  a. Analysis of the debtor's financial situation, and rendering advice to the debtor in determining whether to file a petition in bankruptcy;

  b. Preparation and filing of any petition, schedules, statement of affairs and plan which may be required;

  c. Representation of the debtor at the meeting of creditors and confirmation hearing, and any adjourned hearings thereof;

EXHIBIT 5.6
Continued

DISCLOSURE OF COMPENSATION OF ATTORNEY FOR DEBTOR (Continued)

d. Representation of the debtor in adversary proceedings and other contested bankruptcy matters;

e. [Other provisions as needed]

6. By agreement with the debtor(s), the above-disclosed fee does not include the following services:

J

CERTIFICATION

I certify that the foregoing is a complete statement of any agreement or arrangement for payment to me for representation of the debtor(s) in this bankruptcy proceeding.

_____   _____

Date   **K**

                                         Signature of Attorney

                                         _____

                                         Name of law firm

Instructions for Completing the Disclosure of Attorney's Compensation Statement

The disclosure of attorney's compensation statement is completed and signed by the debtor's attorney. Although the statement is self-explanatory, the following tips may be helpful.

A   Complete the name of the court in which the petition is filed. See Official Form No. 1.

B   Complete the name of the debtor as it appears on the bankruptcy petition.

C   Complete the case number by inserting the bankruptcy case number assigned by the court at the time the petition was filed. Since the petition has not been filed at this time, there will not be an assigned number so case number should be left blank.

D   Insert "Chapter 7."

E   State the dollar amount of the agreed upon legal fees, the dollar amount that the attorney has already received, and the balance due.

If a fixed fee will be charged for the basic filing and an hourly fee will be charged for enumerated services, so indicate.

If more than one attorney or one or more paralegals will be working on the case, itemize the hourly rates for each attorney or paralegal.

Example: a) Attorney $ _____/hour
            b) Attorney $ _____/hour
            c) Paralegal $ _____/hour

The amount to be deducted from the total fee is not only the amount received prior to the completion of the disclosure of compensation statement but also the amount that will be received prior to the filing of the disclosure statement. Therefore, include any fee that will be paid prior to the filing of the petition.

F   Check the box to indicate the source of the compensation already paid. If the source is "Other," specify the source. If the source is from the debtor and others, indicate both sources.

G   Check the box to indicate the source of the compensation to be paid in the future. If the source is "Other," specify the source. If the source is from the debtor and others, indicate both sources.

H   Check whether the attorney has agreed or has not agreed to share the compensation with a person other than a member or associate of his or her law firm. If the attorney has agreed to share the compensation with such a person, a copy of the agreement and the names of those who will share in the compensation must be attached. Remember to label those attachments with the name of the debtor, last name first, and the debtor's social security number.

I   Write "NA" by any services listed in question 5 that will not be provided. Especially note 5(d), "Representation of the debtor in adversary proceedings and other contested bankruptcy matters." Leaving these services in as a part of the fixed fee may be damaging to an attorney if the attorney is later required to represent the client at no extra charge at such matters as an objection to discharge or an objection to dischargeability. Defending an objection to discharge could cost several thousand dollars and the attorney would not want to include these services in his or her fixed fee. Complete question 5(e) in detail. Specify other services to be rendered. Use additional pages, if necessary, and attach them to this form.

Example: e.   1.   negotiation and preparation of reaffirmation agreements;
                  2.   preparation and filing of pleadings and representation of the debtor in all proceedings relating to:
                        a) the use of cash collateral;
                        b) the modification or enforcement of the automatic stay;
                        c) the rejection, assumption, assignment of executory contracts;
                  3.   representation of the debtor in motions as necessary and proper to avoid liens pursuant to 11 U.S.C.A. §§ 522(f), 506(d); and

      4. representation of the debtor at any reaffirmation or discharge hearing

If no other services, then state "none" or "NA."

J   Complete question 6 in detail. Specify services that will not be rendered. Use additional pages, if necessary, and attach them to this form.

    Example: 6. Notwithstanding 5(d) above:

        a. representation of the debtor in adversary proceedings and other contested bankruptcy matters (e.g., contest of exemption claims, objection to discharge or dischargeability of a claim, redemption of real or personal property, and motions to dismiss);

        b. representation of the debtor in any state court matter;

        c. representation of the debtor in any criminal matter; and

        d. examination of any person pursuant to Federal Rules of Bankruptcy Procedure 2004

K   This section is self-explanatory. The address and telephone number of the attorney or the firm should not be included.

PROBLEM 5.4   Using the information in Problem 5.1 and in Problem 5.2, complete the disclosure of attorney's compensation statement.

F. THE MATRIX (THE LIST OF CREDITORS)

The debtor is required to file with the petition a list containing the name and address of each creditor. 11 U.S.C.A. § 521(1); Fed. R. Bank. P. 1007(a)(1). This list gives the clerk's office information necessary for the mailing of the notice of the meeting of creditors and the order for relief.

    The **list of creditors** is presented to the court in matrix form. The **matrix** is no more than a typed list of the names and addresses of creditors and other parties in interest. In some districts the matrix is typed in three vertical columns. The spacing of the names and addresses is critical because the typed matrix is processed in a photocopy machine and the information is reproduced on mailing labels. The labels are transferred by deputy clerks to the various notices that are sent by the office of the clerk of the court.

    Exhibit 5.7 depicts the matrix master and a sample matrix page. The master and matrix are standard stationery size ($8\frac{1}{2} \times 11$ inches). *This is an example of a master and matrix; it is important for a paralegal to consult local court rules because each district may have its own variations.*

EXHIBIT 5.7
Matrix Master and Sample Matrix Page (reduced from $8\frac{1}{2} \times 11$ inches)

	Place a sheet of typing paper over the matrix master, and type the names and addresses of creditors and other parties in interest within the lines.	

Instructions for Preparing the Matrix

- Place a white sheet of paper in front of the matrix master. Type the names and addresses of the creditors and other parties in interest within the bordered area. The first name on the list should be the debtor's. The second name should be the debtor's attorney.
- The names and addresses of the creditors and other parties in interest will be found on the schedules.
- The typed names should include each creditor's name and address, including zip code.
- The debtor(s) should read the completed list carefully and verify its accuracy.

PROBLEM 5.5   Using the information in Problem 5.1 and in Problem 5.7, prepare a matrix for Pamela Laughlin and Michael Richards.

For the past several years, the bankruptcy courts have been phasing in computer systems that automate some of the routine work previously performed by deputy clerks. Some courts are using Bankruptcy Court Automation Project (BANCAP); others are using NIBS (National Integrated Bankruptcy System). In each system, an optical character reader (OCR) reads typewritten lists of creditors and transfers this information to a computer database. From this database, the office of the clerk of the bankruptcy court generates its notices electronically, thereby eliminating the process of transferring the matrix to mailing labels and sticking the labels on envelopes.

Since the OCR can only read certain fonts and pitches, a petition may not be accepted by the office of the clerk of the court if it does not comply with the following format for the matrix. (See Exhibit 5.8.) Therefore, prior to preparing the matrix, a paralegal should check with the office of the clerk of the court to ascertain the format required by that office.

EXHIBIT 5.8
Examples of Creditors' List

Courier 10 Pitch

```
First City Nat'l Bank
of Beaumont
P.O. Box 3391
Beaumont, TX   77704

Flex Northwest
1540 NW 46th Street
Seattle, WA   98372

Glander International
Lake Success Plaza
One Hollow Lane
Lake Success, NY   11042
```

Letter Gothic

```
City of Unalaska
P.O. Box 89
Unalaska, AK   99685

Classified Directory
615 Main Street
P.O. Box 2230
Niagara Falls, NY   14302

Coast Engine and
Equipment Corporation
401 Alexander Building
Suite 580
Tacoma, WA   98421
```

Prestige Elite

```
Metromedia Video Productions
1224 Murray Avenue
San Luis Obispo, CA   93401

Multitronics Animations
3837 Stone Way North
Studio 7
Baltimore, MD   20459

Eastman Kodak
Special Films Division
8742 Kodak Avenue
Rochester, NY   20948
```

Instructions for Preparing the Matrix (Revised Format)

- Lists must be typed in one of the following standard typefaces or print styles:

  Courier 10 pitch
  Prestige Elite
  Letter Gothic

- Lists should be typed on a single page in a single column, rather than in three columns.
  The addresses must be in a single column because the optical character reader scans the material automatically from left to right, line by line. If on the current matrices being submitted to the court, the first column has an address with three lines, the second column has an address with four lines, and the third column has an address with five lines, the optical character reader will see the blank line after the first address and not read any further. Thus, single-column addresses must be fed into the OCR.

- Lists must be typed so that no letters are closer than 1/2 inch from any edge of the paper.

- Each name/address must consist of no more than five total lines, with at least *one blank line* between each of the name/address blocks.

- Each line must be 40 characters or less in length.

- DO NOT include the following people (who were formerly required on the matrices).

      Debtor
      Joint Debtor
      Attorney for the Debtor(s)

  They will be retrieved automatically by the computer for noticing.

Things to Avoid

Although the court is using sophisticated equipment and software to ensure accuracy in creditor list reading, certain problems can still occur. (See Exhibit 5.9.) By following these guidelines, you will help the court to avoid delays or additional effort in mailing notices.

The following problems can prevent your lists from being read by the optical scanner, requiring you to resubmit your creditors' list in an acceptable form.

Avoid:

- Extra marks on the list, such as letterhead, dates, coffee stains, handwritten marks.

- Nonstandard paper, such as onion skin, half-sized paper, or colored (such as yellow) paper.

- Poor quality type caused by submitting a photocopy.

- Unreadable typeface or print styles, such as proportionally spaced fonts, dot-matrix printing, or exotic fonts (e.g., Olde English or script). Use only Courier 10 pitch, Prestige Elite, or Letter Gothic.

- Misaligned lists are caused by removing the paper from the typewriter before completing the list or inserting the paper into the typewriter crookedly.

- Incorrect typewriter settings. Make certain that your typewriter is set for 10 pitch if you are using a 10-pitch type style.

- Stray marks. Do not type lines, debtor name, page numbers, or anything else on the front of a creditors' list. Any identifying marks you choose to add can be typed on the back of the list.

- Type in uppercase and lowercase, as you would in a letter.

- Incorrect last line. The zip code must be on the last line. Nine digit zip codes should be typed with a hyphen separating the two groups of digits. Do NOT type attention lines or account numbers on the last line; put these on the second line of the name/address, if needed. (The zip code must be at the end for the zip code sorting equipment to find it.)

- Fabric ribbons. They produce letters that are too blurred to be properly scanned.

EXHIBIT 5.9

Errors to Avoid in Preparing the Matrix for an Optical Scanner

Debtor: Allnet Svcs.

PAGE TITLES
If you want to type titles or other identification on lists, type it on the back of list, never on the front.

ALL UPPERCASE
Use uppercase and lower-case (capitals and small letters), as if you were typing a letter.

BOLD TYPE
Do not use boldface setting on your typewriter or word processor.

WRONG FONT
You may use Courier 10 Pitch, Prestige Elite, or Letter Gothic. No other font is acceptable.

WRONG PITCH
If you use a 10-pitch font, make sure typewriter is set to 10 pitch.

HANDWRITING
Handwriting is not scannable and will interfere with the reading of the rest of list.

Stephen R. Miller III
Coal Building
1092 17th Street, NW
Baltimore, MD 20207

MULTI-TRONICS ANIMATIONS
3837 STRONG WAY NORTH
SUITE 10
BALTIMORE, MD 20938
OR
107-D CASTLE BUILDING
NORTH PARKWAY BLVD.
HOUSTON, TX 10938

Arctic Expeditions
Incorporated
536 East 48th Ave.
Anchorage, AK 99505

Gow Fire Protection, Inc.
459 North 98th Street
Hoquiam, WA 98550
ATTN: Steve Jamison

Larry Miller, Jr.
Landover Food & Bev.
Suite 12B
Burg, MD 24039 5182

Coopers & Lybrand
Box 3605
Los Altos, CA 94022

TOO CLOSE TO EDGE
You must keep all typing at least 1/2 inch from any edge: top, bottom, or side.

TOO LONG
A name/address block must be 5 lines of 40 characters or less each.

FABRIC RIBBON
Use an office-quality film ribbon to ensure proper scanning.

ATTENTION LINE
If you must type an attention line or account number for a creditor, put it on the second line of the address, not at the end.

9-DIGIT ZIP CODE
Separate the two groups of digits with a hyphen, not a space.

STRAY MARKS
No lines, symbols, letterhead, or other non-address data should appear on creditors' list.

PAGE NUMBER ———————➤ -17-
Do not number pages or type anything but creditors on the list.

PROBLEM 5.6   Using the facts in Problem 5.5, prepare a matrix for the optical scanner. Use one of the three appropriate typefaces or print styles. Also prepare a Verification of Matrix form. (See Exhibit 5.10.)

EXHIBIT 5.10
Verification of Matrix

UNITED STATES BANKRUPTCY COURT
EASTERN DISTRICT OF OKLAHOMA

In re: JOHN DOE and JANE J. DOE,

Case No. _____
Chapter _____

Debtors.

VERIFICATION OF CREDITOR MATRIX

The above named Debtor(s) hereby verifies that the attached list of creditors is true and correct to the best of his/her knowledge.

Date:_____   _____
                                     Debtor

                                     _____
                                     Joint Debtor

G. SCHEDULES (OFFICIAL FORM NO. 6)

The **Summary of Schedules** (Official Form No. 6) is a listing of all of the debtor's real and personal property, claimed exemptions, creditors, executory contracts and unexpired leases, codebtors, and the current income and current expenditures for an individual debtor or husband and wife filing a joint petition. (See Exhibit 5.11.) The Schedules A–J form the heart of the Chapter 7 bankruptcy filing. The debtor is required to sign an unsworn declaration under penalty of perjury to the Summary and Schedules. The form for the unsworn declaration appears at the end of Official Form No. 6.

EXHIBIT 5.11
Official Form No. 6 (Summary of Schedules)

FORM B6 - Cont.
(6/90)

United States Bankruptcy Court

_____ District of _____

In re _____ Case No. _____
Debtor   (If known)

SUMMARY OF SCHEDULES

Indicate as to each schedule whether that schedule is attached and state the number of pages in each. Report the totals from Schedules A, B, D, E, F, I, and J in the boxes provided. Add the amounts from Schedules A and B to determine the total amount of the debtor's assets. Add the amounts from Schedules D, E, and F to determine the total amount of the debtor's liabilities.

NAME OF SCHEDULE	ATTACHED (YES/NO)	NO. OF SHEETS	AMOUNTS SCHEDULED		
			ASSETS	LIABILITIES	OTHER
A. Real Property			$		
B. Personal Property			$		
C. Property Claimed As Exempt					
D. Creditors Holding Secured Claims				$	
E. Creditors Holding Unsecured Priority Claims				$	
F. Creditors Holding Unsecured Nonpriority Claims				$	
G. Executory Contracts and Unexpired Leases					
H. Codebtors					
I. Current Income of Individual Debtor(s)					$
J. Current Expenses of Individual Debtor(s)					$
Total Number of Sheets In ALL Schedules					
Total Assets			$		
Total Liabilities				$	

© 1991 WEST PUBLISHING COMPANY

Schedule A is the listing of all real property with the exception of interests in executory contracts and unexpired leases. This schedule shows the current market value of the debtor's interest with no deductions for secured claims or exemptions. Section 521(3) of the Bankruptcy Code requires the debtor to cooperate with the trustee. This cooperation may take the form of furnishing documents required by the trustee to enable the trustee to perform his or her duties in effective administration of the bankruptcy estate. The description of property, for example, might be inaccurate on the schedules, leading the trustee to ask for a copy of the deed to the property in question.

Schedule B is the listing of all personal property with the exception of interests in executory contracts and unexpired leases. The debtor is required to cooperate with requests made by the trustee for copies of documents relating to the debtor's personal property in order to facilitate administration of the estate.

Schedule C is a listing of the property that the debtor claims as exempt.

Schedules D, E, and F classify the creditors into creditors holding secured claims (Schedule D), creditors holding unsecured priority claims (Schedule E), and creditors holding unsecured nonpriority claims (Schedule F). Schedules D, E, and F are designed so that claims need to be listed only once.

Schedule G is a listing of executory contracts and unexpired leases.

Schedule H is a listing of the codebtors.

Schedules I (Current Income) and J (Current Expenditures) are applicable only to an individual debtor or to a husband and wife filing a joint petition.

Although the Summary of Schedules appears before Schedules A–J, it is compiled from the totals that are generated on all the other schedules.

1. SCHEDULE A: REAL PROPERTY

Schedule A (see Exhibit 5.12) is used to report all of the debtor's interests in real property except executory contracts and unexpired leases, which are to be listed in Schedule G.

Schedule A requires five items of information for each item of real property:

1. a description and location of all real property in which the debtor has an interest (the interest may be present or future, legal or equitable, entire or partial);
2. the nature of the debtor's interest;
3. if the debtor is married, an indication of who owns the property (husband, wife, joint, or community);
4. the current market value of the debtor's interest in the property without deducting for secured claims or exemptions; and
5. the amount of any secured claim on that property.

Requiring the married debtor to indicate who owns the property is designed to minimize the potential for concealment of assets. The trustee can request copies of any documents concerning the debtor's property necessary to the administration of the estate.

EXHIBIT 5.12
Official Form No. 6, Schedule A (Real Property)

FORM B6A
(10/89)

In re _____,   Case No. _____
                    Debtor   (If known)

SCHEDULE A – REAL PROPERTY

Except as directed below, list all real property in which the debtor has any legal, equitable, or future interest, including all property owned as a co-tenant, community property, or in which the debtor has a life estate. Include any property in which the debtor holds rights and powers exercisable for the debtor's own benefit. If the debtor is married, state whether husband, wife, or both own the property by placing an "H," "W," "J," or "C" in the column labeled "Husband, Wife, Joint, or Community." If the debtor holds no interest in real property, write "None" under "Description and Location of Property."

Do not include interests in executory contracts and unexpired leases on this schedule. List them in Schedule G–Executory Contracts and Unexpired Leases.

If an entity claims to have a lien or hold a secured interest in any property, state the amount of the secured claim. See Schedule D. If no entity claims to hold a secured interest in the property, write "None" in the column labeled "Amount of Secured Claim."

If the debtor is an individual or if a joint petition is filed, state the amount of any exemption claimed in the property only in Schedule C–Property Claimed as Exempt.

DESCRIPTION AND LOCATION OF PROPERTY	NATURE OF DEBTOR'S INTEREST IN PROPERTY	HUSBAND,WIFE,JOINT, OR COMMUNITY	CURRENT MARKET VALUE OF DEBTOR'S INTEREST IN PROPERTY WITHOUT DEDUCTING ANY SECURED CLAIM OR EXEMPTION	AMOUNT OF SECURED CLAIM
A **B**	**C**	**D**	**E**	**F**

© 1991 WEST PUBLISHING COMPANY

Total $ **G**

(Report also on Summary of Schedules)

Instructions for Completing Official Form No. 6, Schedule A (Real Property)

A List by legal description (e.g., lot number, block number, addition, city, county, and state) all real property in which the debtor has a legal, equitable, or future interest.

Example: Lot 2, Block 2, Brookwood Addition
Tulsa, Tulsa County, Oklahoma

Do not include interests in executory contracts (e.g., one-year lease on residential or business property) and unexpired leases. They will be listed in Schedule G.

List any property in which the debtor holds rights and powers exercisable for the debtor's own benefit.

If the debtor does not hold any interest in real property, state "none."

B In addition to the legal description, provide the mailing address (street, city, state, zip code) for all real property.

Example: 3214 Beaver Creek Lane
Northbrook, IL 62105

C State the nature of the debtor's interest in the property.

Examples: fee simple
option to purchase
life estate

D If the debtor is married, state whether the property is owned by the husband, wife, jointly, or as community property. Use the initials H, W, J, and C. If the debtor is not married, leave this column blank.

E State the current market value of the debtor's interest in the property. Do not deduct any secured claim or exemption.

Example:	current market value	$40,000
	secured claim	$20,000
	exemption	$ 8,000

List $40,000, the current market value.

Appraisals are not required for the schedules. The current market value for scheduling purposes is established by the debtor's best judgment. The debtor may use whatever source he or she wishes.

F If the real property has a secured claim, state the amount of that claim.

The amount of the indebtedness against the real property cannot exceed the current market value of the property. 11 U.S.C.A. § 506(a).

Example:	current market value	$40,000
	amount of the indebtedness	$50,000

List $40,000 as the current market value.

G Total the amounts of all interests of real property. Report the total on the Summary of Schedules.

PROBLEM 5.7   Using the information in Problem 5.1 and the following information, complete Schedule A of Official Form No. 6 for Pamela Laughlin and Michael Richards.

Pamela Laughlin is a salaried employee. Her salary is $72,000 a year. Dr. Laughlin's monthly check is reduced by FICA and payroll taxes of $1,800 a month.

She pays $240 a year for her state license and $210 for professional books and journals.

Twice a year Dr. Laughlin receives royalties on a book. The royalty checks average $400 each.

Michael Richards earns $24,000 a year at the university. He is paid on a 12-month basis. Dr. Richards' monthly check is reduced by FICA and payroll taxes by $600 a month.

Dr. Richards pays his first wife, Sarah Jane, $200 in alimony a month. She has not remarried although she has a boyfriend with whom she shares an apartment.

The Silver Meadow Circle house was purchased for $150,000. At the time of purchase, Dr. Laughlin and Dr. Richards paid $15,000 and took a $135,000 mortgage from People's Savings and Loan Association. Their mortgage payment is $1,950 a month. This includes home insurance ($175), interest payments ($1,125), and real estate taxes ($275). Because the house is aging, maintenance has increased. Last year they spent $1,300 on routine repairs. They still owe the Jiffy Plumbing Company $600 and the Rockwell Construction Company $500.

The house has an electric air conditioning system, and electricity has averaged $150 a month. The house is heated by natural gas, and the gas bill averages $225 a month. The water bill is generally about $25 a month. The telephone usually averages about $50 a month.

The Richards family usually spends about $325 a week on food. This includes about $125 in groceries and $200 for lunches and dinners at restaurants. The Richards family also spends about $500 a month on clothing.

Because of their busy schedules, Pamela and Michael send the laundry out on a weekly basis. This costs about $35 a week. Dry cleaning averages about $20 a week.

The Richards receive home delivery of their local newspaper, which costs $7.50 a month.

Most medical and dental bills are covered by insurance. Although insurance covers most of the prescribed medications, the insured must pay $2 per prescription. All members of the family suffer from allergies and take prescribed medications for this condition. The monthly medical bills average $40, which includes the deductible.

Both Dr. Laughlin and Dr. Richards have BMWs. Each car was purchased for $25,000 from Southside Motors last year. Southside has a security interest in both vehicles and $15,000 remains to be paid on each vehicle. The payments are $400 a month on each vehicle. Total automobile and transportation costs average $230 a month.

Irene attends a private preschool program. This costs $1,820 a year in tuition. Because the preschool program is only for half a day, Dr. Laughlin has made arrangements for a child care center to pick up Irene at the preschool program and care for her for the remainder of the day. The child care center charges $65 a week.

Michael, Jr., attends the state university. His tuition, room, and board cost $4,800 for the year.

Dr. Laughlin and Dr. Richards have pledged $45 a month to their church for the building fund. They have not made a payment during the last three months.

Dr. Laughlin owns a small rental house in her own name in Cleveland. It normally rents for $300 a month and is currently occupied by her sister. Her sister has not been paying rent. The house is valued at $65,000. The house has a $40,000 mortgage with Erie Bank and monthly payments are $535.

Dr. Laughlin also owns several shares of stock in a municipal baseball team. Generally, during a good season, the stock pays $70 in dividends.

Dr. Laughlin has $3,000 in U.S. Savings Bonds that have matured but have not been cashed in. They are in the family safe deposit box at First Bank. The annual rental for the safe deposit box costs the family $60.

Dr. Laughlin received $400 a month in alimony when she was divorced, but those payments have ceased since she remarried. She receives $500 a month from Carl for child support for Irene. Irene spends the summer with her father, and the airfare for this trip usually costs about $1,000. Dr. Laughlin pays this airfare.

Dr. Laughlin often earns from $100 to $500 as a guest lecturer. Generally, she may be invited to lecture two or three times a month.

Dr. Richards pays $700 a year for professional books and journals.

Dr. Richards has $800 in a checking account at Second Bank that has earned $25 interest this past year.

Dr. Laughlin and Dr. Richards own a small cottage on a lake, about 50 miles from the city. They purchased the property for $60,000 and have a $50,000 mortgage on it. Their monthly payments are $650, which includes insurance ($80), taxes ($90), and interest ($380). Midtown Bank holds the mortgage. The bank has not been paid for four months.

Dr. Laughlin pays a cleaning service $50 a week to clean the house. Dr. Richards pays a yard service $45 a week to mow the grass, rake leaves, and tend to the flower gardens.

Over the years, both Dr. Laughlin and Dr. Richards have overcharged on their credit cards. Dr. Laughlin owes VISA® $2,500, Discover Card® $2,000, and American Express® $3,500. Each charges 1.5 percent interest each month on the unpaid balance. Dr. Richards owes MasterCard® $3,200, which also charges 1.5 percent interest each month. They have not paid any of these credit cards for the last three months.

The final outstanding obligation is to Thrifty Credit Union. This involves an educational loan made to Pamela Laughlin while she was attending veterinary school. The outstanding balance is $35,000. The interest rate is 12 percent a year. Monthly payments are scheduled at $400. Thrifty has not been paid for the past six months.

2. SCHEDULE B: PERSONAL PROPERTY

Schedule B (see Exhibit 5.13) is used to report all of the debtor's interests in personal property except executory contracts and unexpired leases, which are to be listed in Schedule G.

Schedule B categorizes personal property into 33 types of property. Three items of information are required for each type of personal property that the debtor owns:

1. a description and location of the various items of property;
2. if the debtor is married, an indication of who owns the property; and
3. the current market value of the debtor's interest in the property, without deducting for secured claims or exemptions.

EXHIBIT 5.13
Official Form No. 6, Schedule B (Personal Property)

FORM B6B
(10/89)

In re _____.   Case No. _____
                        Debtor   (If known)

SCHEDULE B – PERSONAL PROPERTY

Except as directed below, list all personal property of the debtor of whatever kind. If the debtor has no property in one or more of the categories, place an "X" in the appropriate position in the column labeled "None." If additional space is needed in any category, attach a separate sheet properly identified with the case name, case number, and the number of the category. If the debtor is married, state whether husband, wife, or both own the property by placing an "H," "W," "J," or "C" in the column labeled "Husband, Wife, Joint, or Community." If the debtor is an individual or a joint petition is filed, state the amount of any exemptions claimed only in Schedule C– Property Claimed as Exempt.

Do not list interests in executory contracts and unexpired leases on this schedule. List them in Schedule G– Executory Contracts and Unexpired Leases.

If the property is being held for the debtor by someone else, state that person's name and address under "Description and Location of Property."

TYPE OF PROPERTY	NONE	DESCRIPTION AND LOCATION OF PROPERTY	HUSBAND, WIFE, JOINT OR COMMUNITY	CURRENT MARKET VALUE OF DEBTOR'S INTEREST IN PROPERTY, WITHOUT DEDUCTING ANY SECURED CLAIM OR EXEMPTION
1. Cash on hand.		A		
2. Checking, savings or other financial accounts, certificates of deposit, or shares in banks, savings and loan, thrift, building and loan, and homestead associations, or credit unions, brokerage houses, or cooperatives.		B		
3. Security deposits with public utilities, telephone companies, landlords, and others.		C		
4. Household goods and furnishings, including audio, video, and computer equipment.		D		
5. Books, pictures and other art objects, antiques, stamp, coin, record, tape, compact disc, and other collections or collectibles.		E		

EXHIBIT 5.13
Continued

FORM B6B -
Cont.
(10/89)

In re _____   Case No. _____
                    Debtor   (If known)

SCHEDULE B – PERSONAL PROPERTY
(Continuation Sheet)

TYPE OF PROPERTY	NONE	DESCRIPTION AND LOCATION OF PROPERTY	HUSBAND,WIFE,JOINT, OR COMMUNITY	CURRENT MARKET VALUE OF DEBTOR'S INTEREST IN PROPERTY, WITHOUT DEDUCTING ANY SECURED CLAIM OR EXEMPTION
6. Wearing apparel.		**F**		
7. Furs and jewelry.		**G**		
8. Firearms and sports, photographic and other hobby equipment.		**H**		
9. Interests in insurance policies. Name insurance company of each policy and itemize surrender or refund value of each.		**I**		
10. Annuities. Itemize and name each issuer.		**J**		
11. Interests in IRA, ERISA, Keogh, or other pension or profit sharing plans. Itemize.		**K**		
12. Stock and interests in incorporated and unincorporated businesses. Itemize.		**L**		

EXHIBIT 5.13
Continued

FORM B6B -
Cont.
(10/89)

In re _____   Case No. _____
                              Debtor   (If known)

SCHEDULE B – PERSONAL PROPERTY
(Continuation Sheet)

TYPE OF PROPERTY	NONE	DESCRIPTION AND LOCATION OF PROPERTY	HUSBAND, WIFE, JOINT, OR COMMUNITY	CURRENT MARKET VALUE OF DEBTOR'S INTEREST IN PROPERTY, WITHOUT DEDUCTING ANY SECURED CLAIM OR EXEMPTION
13. Interests in partnerships or joint ventures. Itemize.		**M**		
14. Government and corporate bonds and other negotiable and non-negotiable instruments.		**N**		
15. Accounts receivable.		**O**		
16. Alimony, maintenance, support, and property settlements to which the debtor is or may be entitled. Give particulars.		**P**		
17. Other liquidated debts owing debtor including tax refunds. Give particulars.		**Q**		
18. Equitable or future interests, life estates, and rights or powers exercisable for the benefit of the debtor other than those listed in Schedule of Real Property.		**R**		
19. Contingent and non-contingent interests in estate of a decedent, death benefit plan, life insurance policy, or trust.		**S**		

© 1991 WEST PUBLISHING COMPANY

EXHIBIT 5.13
Continued

FORM B6B -
Cont.
(10/89)

In re _____   Case No. _____
                        Debtor   (If known)

SCHEDULE B – PERSONAL PROPERTY
(Continuation Sheet)

TYPE OF PROPERTY	NONE	DESCRIPTION AND LOCATION OF PROPERTY	HUSBAND, WIFE, JOINT, OR COMMUNITY	CURRENT MARKET VALUE OF DEBTOR'S INTEREST IN PROPERTY, WITHOUT DEDUCTING ANY SECURED CLAIM OR EXEMPTION
20. Other contingent and unliquidated claims of every nature, including tax refunds, counterclaims of the debtor, and rights to setoff claims. Give estimated value of each.		T		
21. Patents, copyrights, and other intellectual property. Give particulars.		U		
22. Licenses, franchises, and other general intangibles. Give particulars.		V		
23. Automobiles, trucks, trailers, and other vehicles and accessories.		W		
24. Boats, motors, and accessories.		X		
25. Aircraft and accessories.		Y		
26. Office equipment, furnishings, and supplies.		Z		

EXHIBIT 5.13
Continued

FORM B6B -
Cont.
(10/89)

In re _____   Case No. _____
                    Debtor   (If known)

SCHEDULE B – PERSONAL PROPERTY
(Continuation Sheet)

TYPE OF PROPERTY	NONE	DESCRIPTION AND LOCATION OF PROPERTY	HUSBAND, WIFE, JOINT, OR COMMUNITY	CURRENT MARKET VALUE OF DEBTOR'S INTEREST IN PROPERTY, WITHOUT DEDUCTING ANY SECURED CLAIM OR EXEMPTION
27. Machinery, fixtures, equipment and supplies used in business.		AA		
28. Inventory.		BB		
29. Animals.		CC		
30. Crops - growing or harvested. Give particulars.		DD		
31. Farming equipment and implements.		EE		
32. Farm supplies, chemicals, and feed.		FF		
33. Other personal property of any kind not already listed. Itemize.		GG		

© 1991 WEST PUBLISHING COMPANY   _____ continuation sheets attached   Total $ **HH**

(Include amounts from any continuation sheets attached. Report total also on Summary of Schedules.)

EXHIBIT 5.13
Continued

FORM B6B -
Cont.
(10/89)

In re _____   Case No. _____
                 Debtor   (If known)

SCHEDULE B – PERSONAL PROPERTY
(Continuation Sheet)

TYPE OF PROPERTY	NONE	DESCRIPTION AND LOCATION OF PROPERTY	HUSBAND, WIFE, JOINT, OR COMMUNITY	CURRENT MARKET VALUE OF DEBTOR'S INTEREST IN PROPERTY, WITHOUT DEDUCTING ANY SECURED CLAIM OR EXEMPTION

© 1991 WEST PUBLISHING COMPANY

_____ continuation sheets attached   Total | $

(Include amounts from any continuation sheets attached. Report total also on Summary of Schedules.)

Instructions for Completing Official Form No. 6, Schedule B (Personal Property)

If the debtor does not hold any interest in a type of personal property, state "none" for that type.

A   Cash on hand
Example: currency and coin

If the cash is kept at a business location, state the address (including the zip code) of the business.

If the cash is kept at a private residence, state the address (including the zip code) of the residence.

If property is being held for the debtor by someone else, state that person's name and address.

State the current market value of the debtor's interest in the cash on hand, without deducting any secured claim or exemption. The amount of any exemption will be claimed in Schedule C—Property Claimed as Exempt.

B   Checking, savings or other financial accounts, certificates of deposit, or shares in banks, savings and loan, thrift, building and loan, and homestead associations, or credit unions, brokerage houses, or cooperatives

Examples: checking account
Account No. 343721-6
Pioneer National Bank

savings account
Account No. 44510-7
Peoples State Bank

State the address (including zip code) of the financial institution.

The current market value of shares of stock can be ascertained from a stockbroker or ticker tape.

The amount of any exemption will be claimed in Schedule C—Property Claimed as Exempt.

C   Security deposits with public utilities, telephone companies, landlords, and others
State the entity holding the security deposit.

Example: Public Service Co.

State the address (including the zip code) of the entity holding the security deposit.

D   Household goods and furnishings, including audio, video, and computer equipment
Examples: general household goods
IBM PS2/50 computer

State the address (including zip code) of the residence where the household goods and furnishings are generally located.

Current market value is the debtor's best estimate. The amount of any exemption will be claimed in Schedule C—Property Claimed as Exempt.

E   Books, pictures and other art objects, antiques, stamp, coin, record, tape, compact disc, and other collections or collectibles
Examples: books
records
paintings
stamp collection
butterfly collection

State the address (including zip code) of the residence where the books, pictures, and other collections or collectibles are generally located.

The current market value is the debtor's best estimate. The amount of any exemption will be claimed in Schedule C—Property Claimed as Exempt.

F   Wearing apparel

Example: personal clothing

State the address (including zip code) of the residence where the wearing apparel is generally located.

The current market value is the debtor's best estimate. The amount of any exemption will be claimed in Schedule C—Property Claimed as Exempt.

G   Furs and jewelry

Examples: mink coat
Rolex watch

If furs are in storage, state the address (including zip code) of the furrier or other entity where the furs are stored.

If jewelry is in a safe deposit box, state the address (including zip code) of the institution where the box is located.

State the address (including zip code) of the residence where the furs or jewelry are generally located.

The current market value is the debtor's best estimate. The amount of any exemption will be claimed in Schedule C—Property Claimed as Exempt.

H   Firearms and sports, photographic, and other equipment

Examples: 357 Magnum
sports equipment

State the address (including zip code) of the residence where the equipment is generally located.

The current market value is the debtor's best estimate. The amount of any exemption will be claimed in Schedule C—Property Claimed as Exempt.

I   Interests in insurance policies

For each policy that has a surrender or refund value, describe the type of insurance and name the insurance company.

List only the insurance policies that have a cash value. Do not list term insurance.

Examples: cash surrender value
life insurance on life of debtor
with Met Life issued 1–10–54

refund of premium from auto insurance
on vehicle that will be sold
State Farm

State the address (including zip code) where the policies are generally kept (e.g., home, safe deposit box, office).

A statement in writing of the cash surrender value or refund due on the premiums should be obtained from the agent servicing each policy. The amount of any exemption will be claimed in Schedule C—Property Claimed as Exempt.

J   Annuities

Itemize and name each issuer.

List all annuities, whether or not the debtor is currently receiving payments.

Example: retirement annuity
Florida Teachers Retirement Fund

State the address (including zip code) where the certificate is generally kept (e.g., home, safe deposit box, office).

Use the current value of the fund as of the date of the filing of the petition. The amount of any exemption will be claimed in Schedule C—Property Claimed as Exempt.

K   Interests in IRA, ERISA, Keogh, or other pension or profit-sharing plans

List each interest separately.

Example: IRA
            Friendly Federal Savings

State the address (including zip code) where the institution is located.

The current market value is the balance in the plan. The amount of any exemption will be claimed in Schedule C—Property Claimed as Exempt.

L   Stock and interests in incorporated and unincorporated businesses

List each holding separately.

Example: 15 common shares of General Toaster

State the address (including zip code) where the stock certificates are kept.

The current market value is the debtor's best estimate as determined by the sources available to the debtor.

M   Interests in partnerships or joint ventures

List each interest separately.

Example: $\frac{1}{4}$ limited partnership interest in Omni Toy Company

If the debtor has a document, then state the address where the document is kept. If the debtor has no document, then state the address (including zip code) of the entity.

The current market value is the debtor's best estimate as determined by the sources available to the debtor.

N   Government and corporate bonds and other negotiable and non-negotiable instruments

Examples: T-Bill matures 7–1–98, discount 8.32
             checks
             note from J. Smith

State the address (including zip code) where the certificate is kept.

The current market value is determined by the market on which they are commonly traded. The amount of any exemption will be claimed in Schedule C—Property Claimed as Exempt.

O   Accounts receivable

Include the name of the account debtor and when the account first became due.

Example: Accounts Receivable
            Mary L. Wentworth
            due 12/5/95

State the address (including zip code) of the account debtor.

The current market value is the amount due.

P   Alimony, maintenance, support, and property settlements to which the debtor is or may be entitled

Include what the obligation is based on, the name of the person who owes the obligation, the recipient of the obligation, the court issuing the decree, and the date of the decree.

Example: alimony due from Jack Williamson (former spouse)
            for Jackie Williamson
            Cherokee County Court
            Idabelle, NC
            12/24/94

State the address (including zip code) of the person who owes the obligation.

The current market value is either the total amount due or the amount of the monthly payments and the length of time over which they are to be paid, depending on the arrangement. The amount of any exemption will be claimed in Schedule C—Property Claimed as Exempt.

Q   Other liquidated debts owing debtor, including tax refunds

    Examples: Federal Tax refund on 1040 for 1996
                    due from U.S. Treasury

                    State Tax refund for 1996
                    due from Oklahoma Tax Commission

                    Ad valorem tax refund for 1996
                    due from Beaver County Treasurer

State the address (including zip code) of the person or entity who owes the obligation.

The current market value is the amount due. The amount of any exemption will be claimed in Schedule C—Property Claimed as Exempt.

R   Equitable or future interests, life estates, and rights or powers exercisable for the benefit of the debtor other than those listed in Schedule A—Real Property

    Example: life estate
                  Walker Trust Fund

State the address (including zip code) of the trustee, if one exists.

The current market value is the debtor's best judgment. The amount of any exemption will be claimed in Schedule C—Property Claimed as Exempt.

S   Contingent and noncontingent interests in estate of a decedent, death benefit plan, life insurance policy, or trust

    Example: TIAA/CREF
                  contingent interest in annuity
                  of Agnes Adams, deceased

State the address (including zip code) of the person who will administer the estate or trust.

The current market value is the face value shown on the document. The amount of any exemption will be claimed in Schedule C—Property Claimed as Exempt.

T   Other contingent and unliquidated claims of every nature, including tax refunds, counterclaims of the debtor, and rights to setoff claims

    Examples: Jones v. Smyth
                    action for damages
                    for breach of contract

                    Jones v. Everton Press
                    workers' compensation claim

State the address (including zip code) of the defendant.

The current market value is the debtor's best estimate of what the claims are worth. The amount of any exemption will be claimed in Schedule C—Property Claimed as Exempt.

U   Patents, copyrights, and other intellectual property

    Examples: patent on submersible pump
                    U.S. Patent #10,239,341
                    (copy of U.S. Patent in debtor's possession)

                    Patent Application Serial #876,923
                    filed 1/4/95
                    (copy of patent application in debtor's possession)

1,325,004 for the trademark "Wong's Wok"
(copy of trademark registration in debtor's possession)

Copyright G 104,995—copyright for
"Exploring Outer Space"
(copy of copyright certificate attached)

State the address (including zip code) where the documentation is generally kept.

The current market value is the debtor's best estimate of what the property interest is worth.

V   Licenses, franchises, and other general intangibles

Example: franchise for MacDougal's Restaurant

State the address (including zip code) where the documentation is generally kept.

The current market value is the debtor's best estimate based on whatever sources are available.

W   Automobiles, trucks, trailers, and other vehicles and accessories

Include serial number if the vehicle has one.

Examples: 1976 Ford Mustang II
6F02Y122713

1985 Mercury Cougar
IMEBP92F6FH656643

1986 Kawasaki Voyager XII

1978 29-ft. Elandan II Winnebago

State the address (including zip code) where the vehicle is generally parked.

The current market value is the debtor's best estimate, which may be determined from bluebook or other sources (including the debtor's opinion). The amount of any exemption will be claimed in Schedule C—Property Claimed as Exempt.

X   Boats, motors, and accessories

Examples: Sea Bass Boat
Johnson 75 hp motor
Dilly Trailer

State the address (including zip code) where the boats, motors, and accessories are generally kept (e.g., home, marina, storage facility).

The current market value is the debtor's best estimate, which may be determined from bluebook or other sources (including the debtor's opinion). The amount of any exemption will be claimed in Schedule C—Property Claimed as Exempt.

Y   Aircraft and accessories

Example: 1971 Cessna TT

State the address (including zip code) where the aircraft and accessories are generally hangared.

The current market value is the debtor's best estimate, which may be determined from various sources, including the debtor's opinion.

Z   Office equipment, furnishings, and supplies

Examples: desk
IBM Selectric typewriter
IBM PS2/50

State the address (including zip code) of the office where the equipment, furnishings, and supplies can be found.

The current market value is the debtor's best estimate. The amount of any exemption will be claimed in Schedule C—Property Claimed as Exempt.

AA   Machinery, fixtures, equipment, and supplies used in business

   Examples: cement mixer
                     compressor
                     2 bags cement

State the address (including zip code) of the business where the machinery, fixtures, equipment, and supplies can be found.

The current market value is the debtor's best estimate. The amount of any exemption will be claimed in Schedule C—Property Claimed as Exempt.

BB   Inventory

   Example: stock of groceries

State the address (including zip code) where the inventory is physically located (e.g., factory, warehouse).

For the current market value, use cost basis or accrual method, depending on the accounting method used in the Schedule of Current Income and Current Expenditures for a Partnership or Corporation.

CC   Animals

   Examples: 93 head Holstein milk cows
                     100 chickens
                     registered German Shepherd (female)
                     Myna bird

State the address (including zip code) where the animals are physically located.

If a market exists, use the established market for the current market value. If no established market exists, use the debtor's best estimate. The amount of any exemption will be claimed in Schedule C—Property Claimed as Exempt.

DD   Crops—growing or harvested

   Example: 180 acres of cotton in the field

State the address (including zip code) where the crops are physically located.

The current market value is the debtor's best estimate, which may be based on an established market, if one exists. The amount of any exemption will be claimed in Schedule C—Property Claimed as Exempt.

EE   Farming equipment and implements

   Examples: Case tractor
                     Deere plow

State the address (including zip code) where the farming equipment or implements are physically located.

The current market value is the debtor's best estimate. The amount of any exemption will be claimed in Schedule C—Property Claimed as Exempt.

FF   Farm supplies, chemicals, and feed

   Example: 80 gal. of Malathion

State the address (including zip code) where the farm supplies, chemicals, and feed are physically located.

For the current market value, use cost basis or accrual method, depending on the accounting method used in the Schedule of Current Income and Current Expenditures for a Partnership or Corporation. The amount of any exemption will be claimed in Schedule C—Property Claimed as Exempt.

GG   Other personal property of any kind not already listed

The amount of any exemption will be claimed in Schedule C—Property Claimed as Exempt.

HH   Total the amounts of all items of personal property. Report the total on the Summary of Schedules.

PROBLEM 5.8   Using the information in Problem 5.1 and Problem 5.7 complete Schedule B of Official Form No. 6 for Pamela Laughlin and Michael Richards.

3. SCHEDULE C: PROPERTY CLAIMED AS EXEMPT

The Code requires the debtor to file a list of property that he or she claims as exempt property from the property of the estate. 11 U.S.C.A. § 522 (1); Fed. R. Bank. P. 4003(a). If a debtor fails to file a list to claim the exemptions, then a dependent of the debtor ("dependent," by definition, includes the spouse of the debtor, whether or not the spouse is actually dependent) may file the list of property. Absent an objection to the list by a party in interest, the property claimed on the list as exempt is exempt. Rule 1007(c) requires the schedules to be filed within 15 days after the order for relief, unless the court extends the time.

Schedule C of Official Form No. 6 (see Exhibit 5.14) is a list of property claimed as exempt. Local court rules may affect the exact method for claiming exempt property including the time and place for claiming exemptions and the manner of indicating what property is claimed as exempt. Whether a debtor may claim specific items of real and personal property as exempt will be explored in detail later in this chapter.

To claim an exemption, the debtor must provide the following information:

1. a description of property;
2. the statute creating the exemption;
3. the value claimed as exempt; and
4. the current market value of the property without the deduction of the exemption.

The current market value of the property without the deduction of the exemption should correspond to the current market value as indicated in Schedules A and B.

EXHIBIT 5.14
Official Form No. 6, Schedule C (Property Claimed as Exempt)

FORM B6C
(6/90)

In re _____　　Case No. _____
　　　　　　　　　　　　Debtor　　　　　　　　　　　　　　　　　　　　　　　　(If known)

SCHEDULE C – PROPERTY CLAIMED AS EXEMPT

Debtor elects the exemption to which debtor is entitled under

(Check one box)

A

☐ 11 U.S.C.A. § 522(b)(1)　Exemptions provided in 11 U.S.C.A. § 522(d). Note: These exemptions are available only in certain states.

☐ 11 U.S.C.A. § 522(b)(2)　Exemptions available under applicable nonbankruptcy federal laws, state or local law where the debtor's domicile has been located for the 180 days immediately preceding the filing of the petition, or for a longer portion of the 180-day period than in any other place, and the debtor's interest as a tenant by the entirety or joint tenant to the extent the interest is exempt from process under applicable nonbankruptcy law.

DESCRIPTION OF PROPERTY	SPECIFY LAW PROVIDING EACH EXEMPTION	VALUE OF CLAIMED EXEMPTION	CURRENT MARKET VALUE OF PROPERTY WITHOUT DEDUCTING EXEMPTIONS
B	**C**	**D**	**E**

© 1991 WEST PUBLISHING COMPANY

Instructions for Completing Official Form No. 6, Schedule C (Property Claimed as Exempt)

A   The debtor must elect either the federal exemptions or the state exemptions. Whether this choice exists will depend on whether the debtor's state has opted out of the federal exemptions. Thirty-seven states have chosen to "opt out" of the federal bankruptcy exemption alternative. Opting out will be discussed in detail later in this chapter. If the debtor's state has opted out of the federal bankruptcy exemptions, check the box for 11 U.S.C.A. § 522(b)(2). If the debtor's state has not opted out of the federal bankruptcy exemptions but the debtor has elected to claim state exemptions, also check the box for 11 U.S.C.A. § 522(b)(2).

If the debtor's state has not opted out of the federal bankruptcy exemptions and the debtor has elected the federal bankruptcy exemptions, then check the box for 11 U.S.C.A. § 522(b)(1).

By checking the first box, the debtor has chosen the federal bankruptcy exemptions. By checking the second box, the debtor has chosen the state exemptions and the federal nonbankruptcy exemptions.

B   Since the property claimed as exempt has already been listed and described either on Schedule A—Real Property or on Schedule B—Personal Property, the same description should be entered on Schedule C.

List the property in the order in which it appears on Schedule A and Schedule B.

C   Specify the law that provides the exemption.

Examples: OK Stat. Ann. tit. 31, § 2 (1981)
        11 U.S.C.A. § 522(d)(3)
        42 U.S.C.A. § 407

D   State the value of the claimed exemption.

For statutes carrying value limitations, use the value limitation, unless the statutory exemption exceeds the market value of the property. In that event, only the market value of the property can be claimed as the exemption.

Example: "The debtor's interest, not to exceed $2,400 in value, in one motor vehicle." 11 U.S.C.A. § 522(d)(2).

For statutes not carrying value limitations, use the current market value of the property.

Example: "Any unmatured life insurance contract owned by the debtor, other than a credit life insurance contract." 11 U.S.C.A. § 522(d)(7).

E   State the current market value of the property without deducting the exemption.

The current market value should correspond to the current market value given for the property when it was listed on either Schedule A or Schedule B.

Example: If the current market value reported on Schedule B is $40,000 and the exemption is $8,000, report $40,000.

> **PROBLEM 5.9**   Using the information in Problem 5.1 and Problem 5.7, complete Schedule C of Official Form No. 6 for Pamela Laughlin and Michael Richards.
>
> Check to see if your state has opted out of the federal exemptions before you begin this problem.

4. SCHEDULE D: CREDITORS HOLDING SECURED CLAIMS

Official Form No. 6, Schedule D (see Exhibit 5.15) lists all entities holding claims secured by property of the debtor as of the date of the filing of the petition. Included are judgment liens, garnishments, statutory liens, mortgages, deeds of trust, and other security interests.

Schedule D requires the following information for each **creditor holding a secured claim:**

1. the creditor's name, mailing address (including zip code), and account number, if any;
2. whether a codebtor exists (other than a spouse in a joint case) who is liable on a claim;
3. if the debtor is married, whether the property is held by the husband, wife, jointly, or as community property;
4. the date when the claim was incurred by the debtor, the nature of the lien, and a description and the market value of the property subject to the lien;
5. an indication if the claim is contingent, unliquidated, or disputed;
6. the amount of the claim without deducting the value of the collateral; and
7. the amount of the unsecured portion of the claim, if any.

EXHIBIT 5.15
Official Form No. 6, Schedule D (Creditors Holding Secured Claims)

FORM B6D
(6/90)

In re _____   Case No. _____
                    Debtor   (If known)

SCHEDULE D – CREDITORS HOLDING SECURED CLAIMS

State the name, mailing address, including zip code, and account number, if any, of all entities holding claims by property of the debtor as of the date of filing of the petition. List creditors holding all types of secured interests such as judgment liens, garnishments, statutory liens, mortgages, deeds of trust, and other security interests. List creditors in alphabetical order to the extent practicable. If all secured creditors will not fit on this page, use the continuation sheet provided.

If any entity other than a spouse in a joint case may be jointly liable on a claim, place an "X" in the column labeled "Codebtor," include the entity on the appropriate schedule of creditors, and complete Schedule H—Codebtors. If a joint petition is filed, state whether husband, wife, both of them, or the marital community may be liable on each claim by placing an "H," "W," "J," or "C" in the column labeled "Husband, Wife, Joint, or Community."

If the claim is contingent, place an "X" in the column labeled "Contingent." If the claim is unliquidated, place an "X" in the column labeled "Unliquidated." If the claim is disputed, place an "X" in the column labeled "Disputed." (You may need to place an "X" in more than one of these three columns.)

Report the total of all claims listed on this schedule in the box labeled "Total" on the last sheet of the completed schedule. Report this total also on the Summary of Schedules.

A ☐ Check this box if debtor has no creditors holding secured claims to report on this Schedule D.

CREDITOR'S NAME AND MAILING ADDRESS INCLUDING ZIP CODE	CODEBTOR	HUSBAND, WIFE, JOINT, OR COMMUNITY	DATE CLAIM WAS INCURRED, NATURE OF LIEN, AND DESCRIPTION AND MARKET VALUE OF PROPERTY SUBJECT TO LIEN	CONTINGENT	UNLIQUIDATED	DISPUTED	AMOUNT OF CLAIM WITHOUT DEDUCTING VALUE OF COLLATERAL	UNSECURED PORTION, IF ANY
ACCOUNT NO. **B**	**C**	**D**	**E** **F** **G**		**H**		**I**	**J**
			VALUE $					
ACCOUNT NO.								
			VALUE $					
ACCOUNT NO.								
			VALUE $					
ACCOUNT NO.								
			VALUE $					

Subtotal (Total of this page) $ _____

Total (Use only on last page) $ **K**

(Report total also on Summary of Schedules)

_____ continuation sheets attached

Instructions for Completing Official Form No. 6, Schedule D (Creditors Holding Secured Claims)

A   Does the debtor have creditors holding secured claims to report on Schedule D?

The following are secured claims that must be listed on Schedule D:

judgment lien
garnishment
statutory lien
mortgage
deed of trust
UCC article 9 security interest
any other security interest

A creditor's claim should be listed only once even if the claim is secured in part. The remainder of the claim should be treated as a general unsecured claim. A partially secured claim should be listed on Schedule D. The unsecured portion of the claim should *not* be listed on Schedule F.

If the debtor has no creditors holding secured claims, then this box should be checked and the total, "–0–," should be entered on the Summary of Schedules. This completes Schedule D.

B   Creditor's account number, name, and mailing address

Creditors should be listed in alphabetical order to the extent practicable.

If the account number is unknown, state "unknown." If the claim does not have an account number, state "none."

If the creditor is represented by a collection agency or an attorney, list the name of the collection agency or the attorney. Indicate that the collection agency or the attorney is the representative for the creditor. The collection agency or the attorney should be listed among the creditors in alphabetical order.

If the creditor is represented by a collection agency or an attorney, state the mailing address of the collection agency or the attorney.

C   Codebtors (other than a spouse in a joint petition)

If any entity, other than a spouse in a joint petition, may be jointly liable on the claim, indicate "yes" by placing an " × " in the Codebtor column. If no entities are jointly liable on the claim, leave the Codebtor column blank. If there is a codebtor, then complete Schedule H—Codebtors.

D   When a joint petition is filed, the debtors must indicate who is liable on each claim by the first letter of the designation:

Example: husband   H
wife   W
jointly   J
marital community   C

If the petition is not joint, leave this column blank.

E   The nature of the lien

Examples: judgment lien
garnishment
mechanic's lien
real estate mortgage
deed of trust
UCC article 9 security interest

F   A description of the property subject to the lien

Examples: *judgment lien:* List every item of property of the judgment debtor that is subject to the lien. Use the description from Schedule A or Schedule B.

garnishment: State the source of the judgment debtor's wages:
Ajax Manufacturing Co. wages garnished from debtor's employer.

mechanic's lien: Describe the property that is subject to the lien. Use the description from Schedule B.

real estate mortgage: Use the legal description as it appears in Schedule A, rather than the mailing address:

> 2d mortgage on homestead
> Lot 2, Block 2, Brookwood Addition
> Tulsa, Tulsa County, OK

deed of trust: Describe the property that is subject to the deed of trust. Use the description from Schedule A or Schedule B.

UCC article 9 security interest: Describe the collateral that is subject to the security interest. Use the description from Schedule B.

G   The market value of the property subject to the lien

For the market value of the property of the debtor that is subject to the lien, use the current market value stated in Schedule A or Schedule B.

The market value of the property subject to the lien should be the amount of the lien but should not exceed either the value of the property or the value of the property subject to the lien.

Examples: If the property has a market value of $125,000 with a lien of $100,000, the market value of the property subject to the lien is $100,000.

If the property has a market value of $125,000 with a lien of $100,000, and the debtor can claim a $50,000 exemption, the market value of the property subject to the lien is $75,000.

If the property has a market value of $75,000 with a lien of $100,000, the market value of property subject to the lien is $75,000.

If the property has a market value of $75,000 with a lien of $100,000, and the debtor can claim a $50,000 exemption, the market value of the property subject to the lien is $25,000.

For garnishment, use the amount of the judgment but no more than the amount subject to garnishment under the law.

H   Indicate whether the claim is contingent, unliquidated or disputed. Since a claim may qualify under more than one category (i.e., a claim may be contingent and unliquidated, contingent and disputed, unliquidated and disputed, or contingent, unliquidated and disputed), indicate each category.

1.   *Contingent:*   A **contingent claim** is dependent on some future event that may or may not take place.

Example: Before Janice's mother filed for bankruptcy under Chapter 7, Janice borrowed $1,000 from First Bank and signed a promissory note. Before First Bank would loan Janice the money, the Bank required Janice to have her mother sign a security agreement giving the bank a security interest in a diamond bracelet. The security agreement provided that if Janice did not pay the note when due, Janice's mother would either pay Janice's obligation or permit the bank to repossess the bracelet. First Bank's claim against Janice's mother is a contingent claim.

If the claim is contingent, place an " $\times$ " in the Contingent column. If the claim is not contingent, leave the Contingent column blank.

2.   *Unliquidated:*   An **unliquidated claim** is a claim the amount of which is uncertain.

Example: The Flower Market hired the Metro Agency to design an advertising campaign. The compensation was set as "a reasonable fee." Metro designed the campaign but has not sent a bill to the Flower Market. The Metro Agency borrowed $10,000 from Gotham Bank and gave Gotham a security interest in its accounts receivable, including the Flower Market's promise to pay "a reasonable fee." Subsequently, the Metro Agency filed a petition in bankruptcy under Chapter 7. Gotham's claim as to the Flower Market account receivable is unliquidated.

If the claim is unliquidated, place an "×" in the column labeled "Unliquidated."

If the claim is not unliquidated, leave the Unliquidated column blank.

3. *Disputed:*   A **disputed claim** is a claim contested by the debtor.

Example: Ethel and Roland Charles, husband and wife, owned a tractor. Roland borrowed $5,000 from People's Bank and gave People's a security interest in the tractor. When signing the security agreement, Roland signed his own name and Ethel's name. When Roland died, Ethel inherited Roland's interest in the tractor. Ethel refused to pay the loan, claiming that her signature was a forgery. Ethel filed for bankruptcy under Chapter 7. The bank's claim as to the tractor is disputed.

If the claim is disputed, place an "×" in the column labeled "Disputed." If the claim is not disputed, leave the Disputed column blank.

I   State the amount of the claim secured by property of the debtor without deducting the value of the collateral.

The claim secured by property of the debtor (the lien) is the amount of the claim not to exceed the value of the property.

$100,000   market value of the property
60,000   first mortgage holder
70,000   second mortgage holder
20,000   third mortgage holder

The first mortgage holder has a secured claim of $60,000. The second mortgage holder has a secured claim of $40,000. The third mortgage holder has no secured claim. See 11 U.S.C.A. § 506(a).

If the creditor is represented by a collection agency or an attorney, the amount of the claim secured by property of the debtor will be zero.

J   State the amount of the unsecured portion of the claim, if any.

The claim secured by the property of the debtor (the lien) is the amount of the claim not to exceed the value of the property.

$100,000   market value of the property
60,000   first mortgage holder
70,000   second mortgage holder
20,000   third mortgage holder

The first mortgage holder has no unsecured claim. The second mortgage holder has an unsecured claim of $30,000. The third mortgage holder has an unsecured claim of $20,000. See 11 U.S.C.A. § 506(a).

K   Total the amount of the claims without deducting the value of the collateral. Report the total on the Summary of Schedules.

PROBLEM 5.10   Using the information in Problem 5.1 and Problem 5.7, complete Schedule D of Official Form No. 6 for Pamela Laughlin and Michael Richards.

5. SCHEDULE E: CREDITORS HOLDING UNSECURED PRIORITY CLAIMS

The categories of creditors having priority status in a voluntary Chapter 7 case are listed in the Bankruptcy Code. See 11 U.S.C.A. §§ 507(a)(3)–(9). Official Form No. 6,

Schedule E (see Exhibit 5.16) summarizes these categories and requires the debtor to indicate claims for each category.

A claim that is entitled to priority in whole or in part should be listed on Schedule E only. Whether the claim is listed on Schedule E will not determine the rights among the parties or how the property will ultimately be distributed. Each claimant will appear on the matrix and will have an opportunity to litigate its claim.

Schedule E requires the following information for each **creditor holding an unsecured priority claim:**

1. the creditor's name, mailing address (including zip code), and account number, if any;
2. whether a codebtor exists (other than a spouse in a joint case) who is liable on a claim;
3. if the debtor is married, whether the property is held by the husband, wife, jointly, or as community property;
4. the date when the claim was incurred and the consideration for the claim;
5. an indication if the claim is contingent, unliquidated, or disputed;
6. the total amount of the claim; and
7. the amount entitled to priority.

Requests for information concerning judgments and negotiable instruments have been deleted from the schedules. Such requests are left to the trustee's inquiries.

EXHIBIT 5.16
Official Form No. 6, Schedule E (Creditors Holding Unsecured Priority Claims)

FORM B6E
(12/94)

In re _____   Case No. _____
                    Debtor   (If known)

SCHEDULE E – CREDITORS HOLDING UNSECURED PRIORITY CLAIMS

A complete list of claims entitled to priority, listed separately by type of priority, is to be set forth on the sheets provided. Only holders of unsecured claims entitled to priority should be listed in this schedule. In the boxes provided on the attached sheets, state the name and mailing address, including zip code, and account number if any, of all entities holding priority claims against the debtor or the property of the debtor, as of the date of the filing of this petition.

If any entity other than a spouse in a joint case may be jointly liable on a claim, place an "X" in the column labeled "Codebtor," include the entity on the appropriate schedule of creditors, and complete Schedule H–Codebtors. If a joint petition is filed, state whether husband, wife, both of them, or the marital community may be liable on each claim by placing an "H," "W," "J," or "C" in the column labeled "Husband, Wife, Joint, or Community."

If the claim is contingent, place an "X" in the column labeled "Contingent." If the claim is unliquidated, place an "X" in the column labeled "Unliquidated." If the claim is disputed, place an "X" in the column labeled "Disputed." (You may need to place an "X" in more than one of these three columns.)

Report the total of claims listed on each sheet in the box labeled, "Subtotal" on each sheet. Report the total of all claims listed on this Schedule E in the box labeled "Total" on the last sheet of the completed schedule. Repeat this total also on the Summary of Schedules.

☐   Check this box if debtor has no creditors holding unsecured priority claims to report on this Schedule E.   **A**

TYPES OF PRIORITY CLAIMS   (Check the appropriate box(es) below if claims in that category are listed on the attached sheets)   **B**

☐   **Extensions of credit in an involuntary case**

Claims arising in the ordinary course of the debtor's business or financial affairs after the commencement of the case but before the earlier of the appointment of a trustee or the order for relief. 11 U.S.C. § 507(a)(2).

☐   **Wages, salaries, and commissions**

Wages, salaries, and commissions, including vacation, severance, and sick leave pay owing to employees and commissions owing to qualifying independent sales representatives , up to maximum of $4000* per employee, earned within 90 days immediately preceding the filing of the original petition, or the cessation of business, whichever occurred first, to the extent provided in 11 U.S.C. § 507(a)(3).

☐   **Contributions to employee benefit plans**

Money owed to employee benefit plans for services rendered within 180 days immediately preceding the filing of theoriginal petition, or the cessation of business, whichever occurred first, to the extent provided in 11 U.S.C. § 507(a)(4).

☐   **Certain farmers and fishermen**

Claims of certain farmers and fishermen, up to a maximum of $4000* per farmer or fisherman, against the debtor, as provided in 11 U.S.C.. § 507(a)(5).

☐   **Deposits by individuals**

Claims of individuals up to $1800* for deposits for the purchase, lease, or rental of property or services for personal, family, or household use, that were not delivered or provided. 11 U.S.C. § 507(a)(6).

☐   **Alimony, Maintenance, or Support**

Claims of a spouse, former spouse, or child of the debtor for alimony, maintenance, or support, to the extent provided in 11 U.S.C. § 507(a)(7).

☐   **Taxes and Certain Other Debts Owed to Governmental Units**

Taxes, customs duties, and penalties owing to federal, state, and local governmental units as set forth in 11 U.S.C. § 507(a)(8).

☐   **Commitments to Maintain the Capital of an Insured Depository Institution**

Claims based on a commitment to the FDIC, RTC, Directory of the Office of Thrift Supervision, Comptroller of the Currency, or Board of Governors of the Federal Reserve System, or their predecessors or successors, to maintain the capital of an insured depository institution. 11 U.S.C. § 507(a)(9).

* Amounts are subject to adjustment on April 1, 1998, and every three years thereafter with respect to cases commenced on or after the date of adjustment

_____   continuation sheets attached

EXHIBIT 5.16
Continued

FORM B6—Cont.
(12/94)

In re _____,   Case No. _____
            Debtor   (If known)

SCHEDULE E—CREDITORS HOLDING UNSECURED PRIORITY CLAIMS
(Continuation Sheet)

_____
TYPE OF PRIORITY

CREDITOR'S NAME AND MAILING ADDRESS INCLUDING ZIP CODE	CODEBTOR	HUSBAND, WIFE, JOINT, OR COMMUNITY	DATE CLAIM WAS INCURRED AND CONSIDERATION FOR CLAIM	CONTINGENT	UNLIQUIDATED	DISPUTED	TOTAL AMOUNT OF CLAIM	AMOUNT ENTITLED TO PRIORITY
ACCOUNT NO. **C**								
ACCOUNT NO.								
ACCOUNT NO.								
ACCOUNT NO.								
ACCOUNT NO.								

Sheet no. _____ of _____ sheets attached to Schedule of Creditors
Holding Priority Claims

Subtotal ▶ $ _____
(Total of this page)
Total ▶ $ _____   **D**
(Use only on last page of the completed Schedule E.)
(Report total also on Summary of Schedules)

Instructions for Completing Official Form No. 6, Schedule E (Creditors Holding Unsecured Priority Claims)

A   If, after answering "no" to the questions in "B" (i.e., Does the debtor have a creditor holding an unsecured priority claim?), there is no claim to report on Schedule E, then this box should be checked and "–0–" entered on the Summary of Schedules. This completes Schedule E.

The first type of priority claim listed in Schedule E applies only to an insolvency case. There will be no creditors in this category for the voluntary Chapter 7 case. Therefore, either state "none" or leave the box blank.

B   A creditor holding an unsecured priority claim in a voluntary Chapter 7 case may be classified under one of seven categories.

1.   Does the debtor have a creditor holding an unsecured claim for wages, salaries, and commissions?

This claim is for wages, salaries, and commissions, including vacation, severance, and sick-leave pay owing to employees, up to a maximum of $4,000 per employee, earned within 90 days immediately preceding the filing of the original petition, or the cessation of business, whichever occurred first, to the extent provided in 11 U.S.C.A. § 507(a)(3).

If there is no creditor in this category, either state "none" or leave the box blank.

2.   Does the debtor have a creditor holding an unsecured claim for contributions to employee benefit plans?

This claim arises due to money owed to employee benefit plans for services rendered within 180 days immediately preceding the filing of the original petition, or the cessation of business, whichever occurred first, to the extent provided in 11 U.S.C.A. § 507(a)(4).

Example: retirement funds

If there is no creditor in this category, either state "none" or leave the box blank.

3.   Does the debtor have a creditor holding an unsecured claim of certain farmers and fishermen?

This claim arises from unsecured claims of certain farmers and fishermen, up to a maximum of $4,000 per farmer or fisherman, against the debtor, as provided in 11 U.S.C.A. § 507(a)(5).

Examples: A farmer has left grain with a grain elevator, and the elevator files for bankruptcy before paying for the grain.

A fisherman has left a fish catch with a cannery, and the cannery files for bankruptcy before paying for the catch.

If there is no creditor in this category, either state "none" or leave the box blank.

4.   Does the debtor have a creditor holding an unsecured claim of an individual arising from deposits?

These claims are unsecured claims of individuals up to a maximum of $1,800 for deposits for the purchase, lease, or rental of property or services for personal, family, or household use, that were not delivered or provided. 11 U.S.C.A. § 507(a)(6).

Examples: layaways
         deposits for concert tickets

If there is no creditor in this category, either state "none" or leave the box blank.

5.   Does the debtor have a creditor holding an unsecured claim for alimony, maintenance, or support for a spouse, former spouse, or child of the debtor?

These claims arise in connection with a separation agreement, divorce decree, or other order of the court. 11 U.S.C.A. § 507(a)(7).

If there is no creditor in this category, either state "none" or leave the box blank.

6. Does the debtor have a creditor holding an unsecured claim of governmental units for taxes and certain other debts owed?

These claims arise from taxes, customs duties, and penalties owing to federal, state, and local governmental units as set forth in 11 U.S.C.A. § 507(a)(8).

Examples: income tax
           payroll tax
           social security tax
           excise tax
           sales tax
           corporate tax

If there is no creditor in this category, either state "none" or leave the box blank.

7. Does the debtor have a creditor holding an unsecured claim based on a commitment to an authority to maintain the capital of an insured depository institution?

These unsecured claims are based on any commitment by the debtor to the Federal Deposit Insurance Corporation (FDIC), the Resolution Trust Corporation (RTC), the Director of the Office of Thrift Supervision, the Comptroller of the Currency, or the Board of Governors of the Federal Reserve System, or their predecessors or successors, to maintain the capital of an insured depository institution. 11 U.S.C.A. § 507(a)(9).

If there is no creditor in this category, either state "none" or leave the box blank.

If the debtor has answered one or more of the above questions "yes," then each type of priority must be listed on a separate "continuation sheet." (Note the "Type of Priority" line in the upper right portion of the Schedule E form.)

C For each claim, provide the following information.

1. Creditor's account number, name, and mailing address. Creditors should be listed in alphabetical order to the extent practicable. A creditor's claim should be listed only once, even if the claim is entitled only in part to priority under 11 U.S.C.A. § 507(a), with the remainder of the claim to be treated as a general unsecured claim. A claim entitled only in part to priority should be listed on Schedule E. The portion of the claim not entitled to priority should not be listed on Schedule F.

Example: For an unsecured claim for contributions to an employee benefit plan, the nature of the claim would be "retirement fund" and the name of the creditor would be the name of the fund itself.

If the account number is unknown, state "unknown." If the claim does not have an account number, state "none."

2. If there is a codebtor other than a spouse in a joint case (i.e., an entity jointly liable on the claim), place an "×" in the column labeled "Codebtor." If there are no entities jointly liable on the claim, leave the Codebtor column blank.

If there is a codebtor, then complete Schedule H—Codebtors.

3. If a joint petition is filed, indicate whether the debt is owed by the husband (H), wife (W), jointly (J), or as community property (C). If the petition is not joint, leave this column blank.

When a joint petition is filed, the debtors must indicate who is liable on each claim.

4. Provide the following information:

a. the date the claim was incurred by the debtor

b. the consideration for the claim
    Examples: wages
                  vacation pay
                  severance pay
                  sick leave

5. Indicate whether the claim is contingent, unliquidated, or disputed.

   a. *Contingent:* A claim is contingent if it is dependent on some future event that may or may not take place.

   Example: A wage claim to which the debtor is a guarantor.

   If the claim is contingent place an "×" in the Contingent column. If the claim is not contingent, leave the Contingent column blank.

   b. *Unliquidated:* A claim is unliquidated if the amount of the claim is uncertain.

   If the claim is unliquidated, place an "×" in the column labeled "Unliquidated." If the claim is not unliquidated, leave the Unliquidated column blank.

   Example: A tax claim is unliquidated if, at the time of bankruptcy, it is uncertain as to the amount due.

   c. *Disputed:* A claim by a creditor is disputed when the debtor contests the claim.

   If the claim is disputed, place an "×" in the column labeled "Disputed." If the claim is not disputed, leave the Disputed column blank.

6. State the total amount of the claim.

7. State the amount entitled to priority.

D Total the amount of the claims. Report the total on the Summary of Schedules.

PROBLEM 5.11   Using the information in Problem 5.1 and Problem 5.7, complete Schedule E for Pamela Laughlin and Michael Richards.

6. SCHEDULE F: CREDITORS HOLDING UNSECURED NONPRIORITY CLAIMS

Schedule F (see Exhibit 5.17) is for **creditors holding unsecured nonpriority claims.** If a claim is partially secured or entitled in part to priority, it should be listed on Schedule D or Schedule E, respectively, and not on Schedule F.

Schedule F requires the following information for each creditor holding an unsecured nonpriority claim:

1. the creditor's name, mailing address (including zip code), and account number, if any;
2. whether a codebtor exists (other than a spouse in a joint case) who is liable on a claim;
3. if the debtor is married, whether the debt is owed by the husband, wife, jointly, or as community property;
4. the date when the claim was incurred by the debtor, the consideration for the claim, and whether the claim is subject to a setoff;
5. an indication if the claim is contingent, unliquidated, or disputed; and
6. the total amount of the claim.

EXHIBIT 5.17
Official Form No. 6, Schedule F (Creditors Holding Unsecured Nonpriority Claims)

FORM B6F
(10/89)

In re _____,   Case No. _____
                              Debtor   (If known)

SCHEDULE F – CREDITORS HOLDING UNSECURED NONPRIORITY CLAIMS

State the name, mailing address, including zip code, and account number, if any, of all entities holding unsecured claims without priority against the debtor or the property of the debtor, as of the date of filing of the petition. Do not include claims listed in schedules D and E. If all creditors will not fit on this page, use the continuation sheet provided.

If any entity other than a spouse in a joint case may be jointly liable on a claim, place an "X" in the column labeled "Codebtor," include the entity on the appropriate schedule of creditors, and complete Schedule H–Codebtors. If a joint petition is filed, state whether husband, wife, both of them, or the marital community may be liable on each claim by placing an "H," "W," "J," or "C" in the column labeled "Husband, Wife, Joint or Community."

If the claim is contingent, place an "X" in the column labeled "Contingent." If the claim is unliquidated, place an "X" in the column labeled "Unliquidated." If the claim is disputed, place an "X" in the column labeled "Disputed." (You may need to place an "X" in more than one of these three columns.)

Report total of all claims listed on this schedule in the box labeled "Total" on the last sheet of the completed schedule. Report this total also on the Summary of Schedules.

A ☐ Check this box if debtor has no creditors holding unsecured nonpriority claims to report on this Schedule F.

CREDITOR'S NAME AND MAILING ADDRESS INCLUDING ZIP CODE	CODEBTOR	HUSBAND,WIFE,JOINT, OR COMMUNITY	DATE CLAIM WAS INCURRED AND CONSIDERATION FOR CLAIM, IF CLAIM IS SUBJECT TO SETOFF, SO STATE	CONTINGENT	UNLIQUIDATED	DISPUTED	AMOUNT OF CLAIM
ACCOUNT NO. **B**	**C**	**D**	**E**	**F**			**G**
ACCOUNT NO. 							
ACCOUNT NO. 							
ACCOUNT NO. 							

_____ continuation sheets attached

Subtotal $ _____
Total $ _____   **H**

© 1991 WEST PUBLISHING COMPANY

(Report total also on Summary of Schedules)

Instructions for Completing Official Form No. 6, Schedule F (Creditors Holding Unsecured Nonpriority Claims)

A A creditor's claim should be listed only once even if the claim is secured in part. The remainder of the claim should be treated as a general unsecured claim. A partially secured claim should be listed on Schedule D. A claim entitled to priority in part under 11 U.S.C.A. § 507(a) should be listed on Schedule E. The unsecured portion of either claim should not be listed on Schedule F.

If the debtor has no creditors holding unsecured nonpriority claims, then this box should be checked and "–0–" should be entered on the Summary of Schedules. This completes Schedule F.

B Creditor's account number, name, and mailing address

Creditors should be listed in alphabetical order to the extent practicable.

If the account number is unknown, state "unknown." If the claim does not have an account number, state "none."

If the creditor is represented by a collection agency or an attorney, list the name of the collection agency or the attorney. Indicate that the collection agency or the attorney is the representative for the creditor. The collection agency or the attorney should be listed among the creditors in alphabetical order.

If the creditor is represented by a collection agency or an attorney, state the mailing address of the collection agency or the attorney.

C Codebtors (other than a spouse in a joint petition)

If any entity, other than a spouse in a joint petition, may be jointly liable on the claim, indicate "yes" by placing an " × " in the Codebtor column. If no entities are jointly liable on the claim, leave the Codebtor column blank. If there is a codebtor, then complete Schedule H—Codebtors.

D When a joint petition is filed, the debtors must indicate who is liable on each claim by the first letter of the designation:

Examples: husband   H
             wife   W
             jointly   J
             marital community   C

If the petition is not joint, then leave this column blank.

E Provide the following information:

1. The date the claim was incurred by the debtor

2. The consideration for the claim

Examples: services
             merchandise
             loan

3. If the claim is subject to a setoff, state "Claim is subject to a setoff."

A **setoff** is the crediting of one claim against another without an actual exchange of money between the parties.

Example: Agnes owes her doctor $100 for medical services. Her doctor owes Agnes $80 for bookkeeping. The $80 claim can be credited against the $100 claim.

F Indicate whether the claim is contingent, unliquidated, or disputed. Since a claim may qualify under more than one category (i.e., a claim may be contingent and unliquidated, contingent and disputed, unliquidated and disputed, or contingent, unliquidated and disputed), indicate each category.

1. *Contingent:*   A claim is contingent if it is dependent on some future event that may or may not take place.

   Example: Janice borrowed $1,000 from First Bank and signed a promissory note. Before First Bank would loan Janice the money, the Bank required Janice to have her mother sign the promissory note as an accommodation maker. Janice's mother signed as co–maker with the notation "collection guaranteed." By adding "collection guaranteed," Janice's mother promised that if the note is not paid by Janice when due, she will pay the note, but only after First Bank has reduced its claim against Janice to judgment and execution on the judgment has been returned unsatisfied, or after Janice has become insolvent or it is otherwise apparent that it is useless to proceed against her. First Bank's claim against Janice's mother is a contingent claim.

   If the claim is contingent, place an "×" in the Contingent column. If the claim is not contingent, leave the Contingent column blank.

2. *Unliquidated:*   A claim is unliquidated if the amount of the claim is uncertain.

   Example: The Flower Market hired the Metro Agency to design an advertising campaign. The compensation was set as "a reasonable fee." Metro designed the campaign and presented its bill for $5,000. Flower Market refused to pay the bill, claiming that it should be $2,000. Because the contract stated that the fee would be a "reasonable fee," Metro's claim is unliquidated.

   If the claim is unliquidated, place an "×" in the column labeled "Unliquidated." If the claim is not unliquidated, leave the Unliquidated column blank.

3. *Disputed:*   A claim by a creditor is disputed if the debtor contests the claim.

   Example: Alexander Wiggins and Vanessa Gray were involved in an automobile accident. Both Alexander and Vanessa claim to have had the right of way, and neither admits to being at fault. Each claim is disputed.

   If the claim is disputed, place an "×" in the column labeled "Disputed." If the claim is not disputed, leave the Disputed column blank.

G State the amount of the claim.

The amount of a contingent or unliquidated claim is the debtor's best estimate, considering all of the factors involved, of what will be due on the claim.

The amount of the claim, if disputed, is the debtor's best estimate of what the claimant may recover.

If the claim is not contingent, unliquidated, or disputed, the amount of the claim is the debtor's best estimate of how much is owed on the debt.

The debtor's best estimate may be zero. The amount listed will be the amount discharged.

If the creditor is represented by a collection agency or an attorney, the amount of the claim should be listed as zero with the representative's name since the amount of the claim has been listed with the creditor's name.

H Total the amount of the claims. Report the total on the Summary of Schedules.

> **PROBLEM 5.12**   Using the information in Problem 5.1 and Problem 5.7, complete Schedule F for Pamela Laughlin and Michael Richards.

7. SCHEDULE G: EXECUTORY CONTRACTS AND UNEXPIRED LEASES

Rule 1007(b)(1) requires the debtor to file a schedule of **executory contracts** and **unexpired leases,** unless the court orders otherwise. In bankruptcy, a contract is executory if it remains unexecuted on both sides (i.e., not fully performed on either side). If the contract is executory, both parties to the contract continue to have a duty to perform. A contract is nonexecutory when one or both parties have fully performed their contractual duties.

EXAMPLE

Mary enters into a brokerage arrangement with Neighborhood Realtors for the sale of her house. During the term of the brokerage contract and before the house is sold, Mary files for bankruptcy under Chapter 7. Since both Mary and Neighborhood Realtors have duties under the contract, the contract is still an executory contract.

EXAMPLE

Jorge's leases a store in Greenacres Shopping Center for 36 months. Six months into the lease period, Jorge's files a petition for bankruptcy. The lease is unexpired because there are 30 months still remaining on the lease period. The lease is also an executory contract since both parties continue to have duties.

EXAMPLE

Ted and Carol enter into a timeshare arrangement for a Florida condo with six other families. When Ted and Carol file for bankruptcy, their timeshare interest in the condo is an executory contract.

Schedule G—Executory Contracts and Unexpired Leases (see Exhibit 5.18), provides the vehicle for listing contracts that have performance remaining by both contracting parties as of the date of the filing of the petition in bankruptcy. Schedule G also requires a listing of all unexpired leases of real or personal property, including timeshare interests.

Schedule G requires the following information:

1. the names and the mailing addresses (including zip codes) of the other parties to the executory contract or unexpired lease; and

2. a description of the executory contract or unexpired lease, and the nature of the debtor's interest.

EXHIBIT 5.18
Official Form No. 6, Schedule G (Executory Contracts and Unexpired Leases)

FORM B6G
(10/89)

In re _____   Case No. _____
                    Debtor   (If known)

SCHEDULE G – EXECUTORY CONTRACTS AND UNEXPIRED LEASES

Describe all executory contracts of any nature and all unexpired leases of real or personal property. Include any timeshare interests.

State nature of debtor's interest in contract, i.e., "Purchaser," "Agent," etc. State whether debtor is the lessor or lessee of a lease.

Provide the names and complete mailing addresses of all other parties to each lease or contract described.

NOTE: A party listed on this schedule will not receive notice of the filing of this case unless the party is also scheduled in the appropriate schedule of creditors.

A ☐ Check this box if debtor has no executory contracts or unexpired leases.

NAME AND MAILING ADDRESS, INCLUDING ZIP CODE , OF OTHER PARTIES TO LEASE OR CONTRACT	DESCRIPTION OF CONTRACT OR LEASE AND NATURE OF DEBTOR'S INTEREST. STATE WHETHER LEASE IS FOR NONRESIDENTIAL REAL PROPERTY. STATE CONTRACT NUMBER OF ANY GOVERNMENT CONTRACT
B	**C**

© 1991 WEST PUBLISHING COMPANY

Instructions for Completing Official Form No. 6, Schedule G (Executory Contracts and Unexpired Leases)

A If the debtor has no executory contracts or unexpired leases, then check this box. This completes Schedule G.

B State the names and the mailing addresses (including zip codes) of other parties to the executory contract or unexpired lease.

C For each executory contract and unexpired lease, provide the following information:

   1. Description of the contract or lease

   Examples: dance lessons
                6 lessons

                exterminator
                4 months

                apartment lease
                9 months

                office lease
                35 months

                equipment lease
                48 months

   If an executory contract does not have a set term, but is month to month, then list one month.

   2. The nature of the debtor's interest

   Examples: executory contract
                    purchaser
                    agent
                    broker

                unexpired lease
                    lessor
                    lessee

   3. If the lease is for nonresidential real property, state "nonresidential real property."

   4. If a government contract is involved, state the contract number.

   PROBLEM 5.13   Using the information in Problem 5.1 and Problem 5.7, complete Schedule G for Pamela Laughlin and Michael Richards.

8. SCHEDULE H: CODEBTORS

Schedule H (see Exhibit 5.19) must be completed when a codebtor is indicated in Schedule D—Creditors Holding Secured Claims, Schedule E—Creditors Holding Unsecured Priority Claims, or Schedule F—Creditors Holding Unsecured Nonpriority Claims.

Schedule H is designed to provide the trustee and the creditors with information about codebtors who are nondebtors in this case. A **codebtor** is a person or entity also liable on any debt listed by the debtor in the schedules of creditors. Since a spouse in a **joint case** is a debtor, a spouse in a joint case will not be listed in Schedule H. Codebtors include guarantors and cosigners.

In a **community property state,** a married debtor not filing a joint case should report the name and the address of the nondebtor spouse on this schedule. All names used by the nondebtor spouse during the six years immediately preceding the commencement of this case should be included.

Schedule H requires the following information:

   1. the name and address of the codebtor; and

   2. the name and address of the creditor.

EXHIBIT 5.19
Official Form No. 6, Schedule H (Codebtors)

FORM B6H
(6/90)

In re _____ ,   Case No. _____
                        Debtor   (If known)

SCHEDULE H – CODEBTORS

Provide the information requested concerning any person or entity, other than a spouse in a joint case, that is also liable on any debts listed by debtor in the schedules of creditors. Include all guarantors and co-signers. In community property states, a married debtor not filing a joint case should report the name and address of the nondebtor spouse on this schedule. Include all names used by the nondebtor spouse during the six years immediately preceding the commencement of this case.

A ☐ Check this box if debtor has no codebtors.

NAME AND ADDRESS OF CODEBTOR	NAME AND ADDRESS OF CREDITOR
B	**C**

© 1991 WEST PUBLISHING COMPANY

Instructions for Completing Official Form No. 6, Schedule H (Codebtors)

A A codebtor is a person or entity also liable on any debt listed by the debtor in the schedules of creditors. All codebtors indicated on Schedules D, E, and F must be listed on Schedule H.

In a joint case: A spouse in a joint case will not be listed in Schedule H.

Example: Gerald and Sydney, husband and wife, have filed a joint petition for bankruptcy under Chapter 7. Neither Sydney nor Gerald is a codebtor for the purposes of Schedule H.

For an individual not filing a joint case: A married debtor not filing a joint case should report the name and the address of the nondebtor spouse on Schedule H if that person is also liable on the debt.

Example: Gerald and Sydney are husband and wife. Sydney files as an individual for bankruptcy under Chapter 7. Gerald is a codebtor on their home mortgage and is therefore a codebtor for the purposes of Schedule H.

If the debtor has no codebtors, then check this box. This completes Schedule H.

B State the name and the complete mailing address (including zip code) of the codebtor.

List all the names used by the nondebtor spouse during the six years immediately preceding the commencement of this case.

C State the name and the complete mailing address (including zip code) of the creditor.

> **PROBLEM 5.14**   Using the information in Problem 5.1 and Problem 5.7, complete Schedule H for Pamela Laughlin and Michael Richards.

9. SCHEDULE I: CURRENT INCOME OF INDIVIDUAL DEBTOR(S)

Official Form No. 6, Schedule I (see Exhibit 5.20), is a comprehensive statement of the total **current monthly income of an individual debtor** or a husband and wife filing a joint petition. Schedule I is designed only for an individual debtor or for a husband and wife filing a joint petition. Schedule I is keyed to the bankruptcy court's power to dismiss a case if substantial abuse of Chapter 7 is determined to exist in a case. 11 U.S.C.A. § 707(b).

EXHIBIT 5.20
Official Form No. 6, Schedule I (Current Income of Individual Debtor(s))

FORM B6I
(6/90)

In re _____,   Case No. _____
                    Debtor   (If known)

SCHEDULE I – CURRENT INCOME OF INDIVIDUAL DEBTOR(S)

The column labeled "Spouse" must be completed in all cases filed by joint debtors and by a married debtor in a chapter 12 or 13 case whether or not a joint petition is filed, unless the spouses are separated and a joint petition is not filed.

Debtor's Marital Status:	DEPENDENTS OF DEBTOR AND SPOUSE		
A	NAMES **B**	AGE	RELATIONSHIP

EMPLOYMENT:	DEBTOR	SPOUSE
Occupation		
Name of Employer **C**		
How long employed		
Address of Employer		

Income: (Estimate of average monthly income)   DEBTOR   SPOUSE
Current monthly gross wages, salary, and commissions **D**
 (pro rate if not paid monthly) $ _____ $ _____
Estimated monthly overtime $ _____ $ _____

SUBTOTAL $ _____ $ _____

LESS PAYROLL DEDUCTIONS
 a. Payroll taxes and social security $ _____ $ _____
 b. Insurance $ _____ $ _____
 c. Union dues $ _____ $ _____
 d. Other (Specify _____) $ _____ $ _____

  SUBTOTAL OF PAYROLL DEDUCTIONS $ _____ $ _____

TOTAL NET MONTHLY TAKE HOME PAY $ _____ $ _____

Regular income from operation of business or profession or farm $ _____ $ _____
(attach detailed statement)

Income from real property $ _____ $ _____

Interest and dividends $ _____ $ _____

Alimony, maintenance or support payments payable to the debtor for the
debtor's use or that of dependents listed above. $ _____ $ _____

Social security or other government assistance
(Specify) _____ $ _____ $ _____

Pension or retirement income $ _____ $ _____
Other monthly income _____ $ _____ $ _____
(Specify) _____ $ _____ $ _____

       _____ $ _____ $ _____

TOTAL MONTHLY INCOME $ _____ $ _____

TOTAL COMBINED MONTHLY INCOME $_____   (Report also on Summary of Schedules)

Describe any increase or decrease of more than 10% in any of the above categories anticipated to occur within the year
following the filing of this document: **E**

Instructions for Completing Official Form No. 6, Schedule I (Current Income of Individual Debtor(s))

All questions on Schedule I must be answered. If a question seeks descriptive information that does not apply to the debtor, indicate "not applicable." If a question seeks numerical information and the debtor's response is zero, indicate "–0–."

A Indicate the debtor's marital status.

Examples: married
            single
            divorced
            widowed
            separated

B State the full names of the debtor's dependents—first name, middle name (no middle initial), last name—including the debtor's spouse. Give the age of each and the relationship (son, daughter, stepson, granddaughter, mother).

Examples: Agatha Anne Wilson   spouse   43
            Mary Jo Wilson   daughter   16
            Billy Joe Short   stepson   15
            Anna Wilson Smith   mother   82

C If the debtor is currently employed outside the home, state the debtor's occupation and the name of the debtor's employer. State how long the debtor has been employed with this employer and the employer's address. If the debtor has recently changed jobs, list the current employment.

If the debtor is currently self-employed, state the debtor's occupation, the name of the debtor's business, how long the debtor has been self-employed in that business, and the address of the debtor's place of business, including zip code.

Example: florist
           Fred's Floral Arrangements
           3 years
           86 East Fourth Avenue
           Oklahoma City, OK 73149

If the debtor is not currently employed outside the home, state the debtor's status in lieu of an occupation.

Examples: homemaker
            retired
            unemployed
            medical leave
            disabled

If the debtor is married, complete this information for the debtor's spouse, regardless of whether the debtor is filing as an individual or with the spouse in a joint petition.

D The schedule of current income has a double column for current income, one for the debtor and the other for the debtor's spouse. If the debtor is married, complete an income statement for the debtor and for the debtor's spouse, even if the debtor contemplates filing as an individual rather than with his or her spouse in a joint petition.

Note that these figures represent the debtor's estimated average monthly income. If income fluctuates over several months or over the year, average the income for the months of that period.

If the debtor ceased employment several months ago and currently has no take-home pay, the current income should be shown rather than what the debtor earned while employed.

Remember that this form will be used to determine whether the debtor has disposable income sufficient to support a Chapter 13 plan. This may determine whether the debtor should file a Chapter 13 rather than a Chapter 7.

The following information lists and explains possible sources of income.

1. Gross monthly take-home pay
   a. Current monthly gross wages, salary, and commissions

      If the debtor is paid by tips, the amount should be the actual amount the debtor receives in tips and not an arbitrary number set by the government for tax withholding purposes.

      Include bonuses, prizes, and awards if they occur on a regular basis. Omit bonuses, prizes, and awards if their incidence is unpredictable and may or may not occur again.

      If the debtor is a commission salesperson, deduct all of the debtor's business expenses: e.g., hotels and motels, mileage or gasoline, other expenses for operating his or her business vehicle, installment payments on the vehicle (or some calculation for replacement), and auto insurance. Therefore, the take-home pay of a commission salesperson will be similar to a debtor with a paycheck after taxes. If the debtor's expenses are not taken off here, the income statement will be distorted. The debtor's food expense will not be deducted under "other" because the debtor would need to eat whether or not he or she was on the road.
   b. Estimated monthly overtime
2. Payroll deductions

   The debtor's take-home pay is calculated by taking the debtor's gross pay and subtracting all deductions. The deductions include
   a. payroll taxes and social security
   b. insurance
   c. union dues

   For many debtors, gross wages and take-home pay can be calculated directly from the debtor's pay stub. Care should be taken, however, when dealing with deductions on pay stubs for installment loans and garnishments. For example, installment payments may be directly deducted for automobile payments made to a credit union. This amount should be added back into gross wages and take-home pay and should appear as an expense under Schedule J—Current Expenditures of Individual Debtor(s).
3. Regular income from the operation of a business, profession, or farm

   Indicate the net income, rather than the gross income, for operating a business, profession, or farm. To arrive at regular income, subtract all business expenses.
4. Income from real property
5. Interest and dividends
6. Alimony, maintenance, or support payments

   Include
   a. Payments payable to the debtor for the debtor's use
   b. Payments payable to the debtor for the support of another, such as child support.

      The name, age, and relationship of the person for whose benefit the payments are made should be listed at the beginning of this schedule.
7. Social Security or other government assistance (specify the type of assistance)

   Examples: Supplemental Security Income (SSI)
                    food stamps
8. Pension or retirement income
9. Other monthly income

   Examples: income from personal property
                    other investment income
                    royalties

E Within the year following the filing of this document, does the debtor anticipate an increase or a decrease of more than 10 percent in any of the above categories?

State, in an addendum, whatever it is that will affect income the debtor knows about. This could include seasonal layoffs or seasonal overtime, if the debtor could reasonably forecast that the event will occur. Describe the change and its impact on current income.

Example: Debtor is expecting a baby in July and anticipates taking three months of unpaid maternity leave. Therefore, the debtor's total net monthly take-home pay will be reduced to zero for that period.

Also, the debtor anticipates receiving additional income on other than a monthly basis in the next year (such as an income tax refund), use an addendum to describe the nature of the income, when it is expected, and the amount.

10. SCHEDULE J: CURRENT EXPENDITURES OF INDIVIDUAL DEBTOR(S)

Official Form No. 6, Schedule J (see Exhibit 5.21), is a comprehensive list of the total **current monthly expenditures of the debtor** and the debtor's family. Schedule J is designed for use by an individual debtor or a husband and wife filing a joint petition. It is keyed to the bankruptcy court's power to dismiss a case if substantial abuse of Chapter 7 is determined to exist in a case. 11 U.S.C.A. § 707(b).

EXHIBIT 5.21
Official Form No. 6, Schedule J (Current Expenditures of Individual Debtor(s))

FORM B6J
(6/90)

In re _____ ,   Case No. _____
                    Debtor   (If known)

SCHEDULE J – CURRENT EXPENDITURES OF INDIVIDUAL DEBTORS

A

Complete this schedule by estimating the average monthly expenses of the debtor and the debtor's family. Pro rate any payments made bi-weekly, quarterly, semi-annually, or annually to show monthly rate.

B ☐ Check this box if a joint petition is filed and debtor's spouse maintains a separate household. Complete a separate schedule of expenditures labeled "Spouse."

C

Rent or home mortgage payment (include lot rented for mobile home) $ _____
Are real estate taxes included?   Yes _____   No _____
Is property insurance included?   Yes _____   No _____
Utilities Electricity and heating fuel $ _____
       Water and sewer $ _____
       Telephone $ _____
       Other _____ $ _____
Home Maintenance (Repairs and upkeep) $ _____
Food $ _____
Clothing $ _____
Laundry and dry cleaning $ _____
Medical and dental expenses $ _____
Transportation (not including car payments) $ _____
Recreation, clubs and entertainment, newspapers, magazines, etc. $ _____
Charitable contributions $ _____
Insurance (not deducted from wages or included in home mortgage payments)
       Homeowner's or renter's $ _____
       Life $ _____
       Health $ _____
       Auto $ _____
       Other _____ $ _____
Taxes (not deducted from wages or included in home mortgage payments)
(Specify) _____ $ _____
Installment payments (In chapter 12 and 13 cases, do not list payments to be included in the plan)
       Auto $ _____
       Other _____ $ _____
       Other _____ $ _____
Alimony, maintenance and support paid to others $ _____
Payments for support of additional dependents not living at your home $ _____
Regular expenses from operation of business, profession, or farm (attached detailed statement) $ _____
Other_____ $ _____

TOTAL MONTHLY EXPENSES (Report also on Summary of Schedules) $ _____

(FOR CHAPTER 12 AND 13 DEBTORS ONLY)
Provide the information requested below, including whether plan payments are to be made bi-weekly, monthly, annually, or at some other regular interval.
A. Total projected monthly income $ _____
B. Total projected monthly expenses $ _____
C. Excess income (A minus B) $ _____
D. Total amount to be paid into plan each _____ $ _____
                                        (interval)

© 1991 WEST PUBLISHING COMPANY

Instructions for Completing Official Form No. 6, Schedule J (Current Expenditures of Individual Debtor(s))

All questions on Schedule J must be answered. If a question seeks descriptive information but does not apply to the debtor, indicate "not applicable." If a question seeks numerical information and the debtor's response is zero, indicate "–0–."

A Complete the expenses statement, giving estimated average current monthly expenses of the debtor and the debtor's family. LIST ONLY EXPENSES THAT THE DEBTOR WOULD BE PAYING IF HE OR SHE WERE TO RECEIVE A DISCHARGE UNDER CHAPTER 7. Therefore, do not list expenses based on debts that will be discharged.

Example: At the time of completing the current expenditures schedule, the Alexanders own two automobiles, a Buick and a Ford. The Alexanders intend to reaffirm their obligation on the Ford but not on the Buick. Therefore, the Buick will be repossessed. The payments on the Buick should not appear as an expense because if the Alexanders were to receive a discharge under Chapter 7, that debt would be discharged and they would make no further payments.

B If the debtor and his or her spouse maintain separate households, the debtor must check the box and complete a separate schedule of expenditures for his or her spouse. Label the spouse's schedule of expenditures "Spouse."

C The expenses are the total family expenses and not the expenses of an individual debtor. Therefore, it is critical to show the expenses of the debtor and the expenses of the debtor's spouse, whether the case will be filed as an individual or a joint case. The following information lists and explains types of expenses.

1. Rent or home mortgage payment

a. Home mortgage payment

b. Rent, if debtor does not own a home

c. Condominium fees

d. Lot rental for mobile home

If real estate taxes are included under rent or home mortgage payments, they cannot be included as current expenditures under the heading of taxes.

If property insurance is included under rent or home mortgage payments, it cannot be included as current expenditures under the heading of insurance.

If mortgage insurance is included under rent or home mortgage payments, it cannot be included as current expenditures under the heading of insurance.

2. Utilities

a. Electricity

b. Heating fuel (e.g., coal, gas, oil)

c. Water

d. Sewer

e. Telephone

f. Other

Examples: trash and garbage removal
cable TV

3. Home maintenance (repairs and upkeep)

Include installment payments for home repairs, such as a new roof, fence, driveway, or foundation restoration. The payments could be made to the contractor or to a lending institution.

Also estimate home maintenance expenses for a one-year period and divide by 12.

4. Food

Include: groceries
restaurants
school lunches

If the debtor has a dependent not living at home, the food for that dependent could be included here or under the category "Payments for support of additional dependents not living at your home."

Include the food for a salesperson on commission here, since this amount was not deducted from take-home pay under income on the income statement.

5. Clothing

Include uniforms

6. Laundry and dry cleaning

7. Medical and dental expenses

Include medicines

Include only the amount not covered by insurance

8. Transportation (not including car payments)

Do not include installment payments on automobiles, trucks, and other vehicles used for transportation. They will be included under "Installment payments."

Include: gasoline
maintenance
taxi fares (including tips)
bus fares
train fares
air fares

9. Recreation, clubs and entertainment, newspapers, magazines

Include: admission fees for movies and sporting events
home video rentals
night clubs
health clubs (e.g., exercise club memberships, tennis clubs, swim clubs)
country club membership
lodge and fraternal order memberships

10. Charitable contributions

Include: churches
Salvation Army
Red Cross
CARE
Goodwill Industries
United Way
Boy Scouts
Girl Scouts of the U.S.A.
Boys Club of America
veterans' and certain cultural groups
nonprofit schools and hospitals
public parks and recreational facilities

11. Insurance (not deducted from wages or included in home mortgage payments)

a. Homeowner's or renter's insurance

b. Life insurance

c. Health insurance

d. Auto insurance

If the debtor is a salesperson on commission and has deducted automobile insurance from his or her gross wages, salary, or commission on the income statement, that automobile insurance should not be shown here.

e. Other insurance (specify the type of insurance)

Under "Other insurance" include home mortgage insurance.

12. Taxes (not deducted from wages or not included in home mortgage payments)

The taxes must be specified.

Include: real estate taxes
            sales tax
            excise taxes

13. Installment payments

Installment payments must be specified.

Include: automobiles
            trucks
            recreational vehicles
            boats
            airplanes
            consumer goods (e.g., refrigerator, washer, dryer, freezer, TV, VCR,
            computer equipment, typewriter, stereo, exercise machine, bicycle,
            clothing, jewelry)

If the debtor is a salesperson on commission who has deducted installment payments on a business vehicle in his or her income statement, then installment payments on that vehicle should *not* be shown here. That has already been taken into account.

14. Alimony, maintenance, and support paid to others

List the name, age, and relationship to the debtor of each recipient of payments.

15. Payments for support of additional dependents not living at your home

If the debtor is supporting a child living away at school, include tuition, room, board, laundry, books and supplies, vehicle costs, transportation, and additional spending money. The name of the child should be listed as a dependent in the family status section of Schedule I—Current Income.

Also include other payments for support of dependents not living at home and not at school.

If the debtor is supporting a parent who is not living with the debtor, include payments made by the debtor on a regular basis. This would include any money sent by the debtor to his or her parent or paid to a nursing facility on a monthly basis. The name of the parent should be listed as a dependent in the family status section of Schedule I—Current Income.

16. Regular expenses from operation of business, profession, or farm

To claim these expenses, a detailed statement of these expenses must be included.

17. Other

Specify the expenses.

Include: child-care expenses
            education costs not previously claimed (e.g., tuition, school books)

PROBLEM 5.15   Using the information in Problem 5.1 and Problem 5.7, complete Official Form No. 6, Schedules I and J, for Pamela Laughlin and Michael Richards.

11. THE SCHEDULE OF CURRENT INCOME AND CURRENT EXPENDITURES OF A PARTNERSHIP OR CORPORATION

When the Bankruptcy Code mandates that the debtor must file a schedule of current income and current expenditures, the mandate is not limited to individual debtors. See 11 U.S.C.A. § 521(1); Fed. R. Bank. P. 1007(b)(1). The mandate also applies to partnership and corporate debtors. Official Form No. 6, Schedule J, however, applies only to an individual debtor or to a husband and wife filing a joint petition. No official form has been drafted for the partnership or corporate debtor. In practice, partnership and corporate debtors file a schedule of current income and current expenditures, unless waived by the court.

Since no official form has been created, the schedule filed with the court need only be in substantial compliance with the rules. An illustration of a Schedule of Current Income and Current Expenditures of a Partnership or Corporation appears in Exhibit 5.22. A debtor may choose to file a more elaborate schedule, i.e., one with printouts and attachments.

EXHIBIT 5.22
Schedule of Current Income and Current Expenditures of a Partnership or Corporation

---

IN THE UNITED STATES BANKRUPTCY COURT FOR THE
_____ DISTRICT OF _____

In re _____ ,
              Debtor   Case No. _____

                                                        Chapter _____

SCHEDULE OF CURRENT INCOME AND CURRENT EXPENDITURES
OF A PARTNERSHIP OR CORPORATION

1. The debtor's accounting records are kept on a cash basis ___**A**___ or accrual method
   _____ .

   Complete question 2 if the debtor's accounting records are kept on a cash basis or question 3 if the debtor's accounting records are kept on an accrual method.

2. Cash basis: Summarize the debtor's cash flow for a period ending no more than 30 days prior to the commencement of this case. The summary period shall be not less than 90 nor more than 120 days in duration.

   a. Beginning date _____
   b. Ending date _____   **B**
   c. Cash balance at the beginning date $ _____
   d. Cash receipts during this period $ _____
   e. Cash disbursements during this period $ _____
   f. Cash balance at the ending date $ _____

3. Accrual method: Summarize the debtor's revenue and expenses on an accrual method for a period ending no more than 30 days prior to the commencement of this case. The summary period shall be not less than 90 or more than 120 days in duration.

   a. Beginning date _____
   b. Ending date _____   **C**
   c. Revenue during this period $ _____
   d. Expenses during this period $ _____
   e. Net gain or (loss) during this period $ _____

4. Attach a copy of the most recent financial statement (audited or unaudited) which has been prepared by or for the debtor.
                                                                         D

Instructions for Completing the Schedule of Current Income and Current Expenditures of a Partnership or Corporation

A Check whether the debtor's accounting records are kept on a cash basis or accrual method.

Records kept on a cash basis will report revenues and expenses in the year in which the revenues were received or the expenses were paid. Under the cash basis, revenues are not allocated to the year in which they were earned nor are expenses allocated to the year in which they relate. Records kept on an accrual method will allocate revenues to the year in which they were earned and allocate expenses to the year in which they relate. Under the accrual method, revenues are not necessarily allocated to the year in which they were received unless that also was the year in which they were earned. Likewise, expenses are not necessarily allocated to the year in which they were incurred unless that also was the year in which they were paid.

Example: The Sunshine Bake Shoppe supplies the New York Delicatessen with all of its bakery products. Rather than require cash as each daily delivery is made, Sunshine sends the delicatessen a bill at the first of each week for bakery products delivered the previous week. Payment is due by the following Friday. Under this system, bakery products delivered during the last week of a month are paid for in the following month. Bakery products delivered during the last week of the year are paid for in the following year.

Under the cash basis of accounting, the date Sunshine receives payment is the date the revenue is indicated on Sunshine's ledger. For products delivered during the last week of the year, the payment would not appear until the following year.

Under an accrual method of accounting, the date the income is earned is the date the revenue is indicated on Sunshine's ledger. For products delivered during the last week of the year, income would be shown for that week even though the actual payment will not be received until the following year.

B Cash basis: Complete this question if the debtor's accounting records are kept on a cash basis. If the debtor's accounting records are kept on an accrual method, indicate "not applicable."

Summarize the debtor's cash flow during a 90- to 120-day period, the end date being no more than 30 days before the commencement of the case.

Complete questions (a)–(f) concerning the debtor's cash flow.

a. Beginning date

Example: If the case will be filed on July 15, the last day of the period can be no earlier than June 16. The period should begin no sooner than 90 days and no later than 120 days before the end date. Therefore, if the end date is selected as June 30, the period should begin between March 3 and April 2.

b. Ending date

c. Cash balance at the beginning date

The cash balance at the beginning date can be found in the debtor's financial statement.

d. Cash receipts during this period

The cash receipts during this period can be calculated by adding the various entries found in the debtor's accounting records.

If the debtor has not kept accurate records of cash receipts, a best estimate should be used. If accurate records have not been kept, a creditor may object to discharge based on the debtor's failure to explain satisfactorily any loss of assets or deficiency of assets to meet the debtor's liability or based on the debtor's failure to keep books or records. 11 U.S.C.A. §§ 727(a)(3), (5).

   e. State the cash disbursements during this period

   The cash disbursements during this period can be calculated by adding the various entries found in the debtor's accounting records.

   If the debtor has not kept accurate records of disbursements, a best estimate should be used. If accurate records have not been kept, a creditor may object to discharge based on the debtor's failure to explain satisfactorily any loss of assets or deficiency of assets to meet the debtor's liability or based on the debtor's failure to keep books or records. 11 U.S.C.A. §§ 727(a)(3), (5).

   f. State the cash balance at the ending date

   The cash balance at the ending date can be found in the debtor's financial statement.

C Accrual method: Complete this question if the debtor's accounting records are kept on an accrual method. If the debtor's accounting records are kept on a cash basis, indicate "not applicable."

Summarize the debtor's revenue and expenses on an accrual method during a 90- to 120-day period, the end date being no more than 30 days before the commencement of the case.

Complete questions (a)–(e) concerning the debtor's cash flow.

   a. Beginning date

   The beginning date can be determined by identifying the end date for the summary period (which must be not more than 30 days from the commencement of the case) and counting back from that date no more than 120 or less than 90 days.

   b. Ending date

   The summary period cannot end more than 30 days prior to the commencement of this case and must be not less than 90 or more than 120 days in duration.

   c. Revenue during this period

   This information can be found in the debtor's financial statement.

   d. Expenses during this period

   This information can be found in the debtor's financial statement.

   e. Net gain or (loss) during this period

   This information can be found in the debtor's financial statement.

D Attach a copy of the debtor's most recent financial statement. Indicate in the top left corner the name of the debtor (as it appears on the petition) and the debtor's employer's tax identification number. Although either an audited or unaudited financial statement is acceptable, an audited statement should be submitted if available.

12. DECLARATION CONCERNING DEBTOR'S SCHEDULES

The **Declaration Concerning Debtor's Schedules** (see Exhibit 5.23) is the signature page for the schedules. The declaration has three parts: one for the individual debtor, one for the nonattorney bankruptcy petition preparer, and one for a corporation or partnership. The Declaration Concerning Debtor's Schedules follows the requirement set forth in 28 U.S.C.A. § 1746.

EXHIBIT 5.23
Declaration Concerning Debtor's Schedules

FORM B6 - Cont.
(12/94)

In re _____   Case No. _____
　　　　　　　　　　　　Debtor　　　　　　　　　　　　　　　　　　　　　　　(If known)

DECLARATION CONCERNING DEBTOR'S SCHEDULES

DECLARATION UNDER PENALTY OF PERJURY BY INDIVIDUAL DEBTOR

I declare under penalty of perjury that I have read the foregoing summary and schedules, consisting of _____**A**_____
sheets, and that they are true and correct to the best of my knowledge, information, and belief.　　(Total shown on summary page plus 1)

Date _____**B**____   Signature _____
　　　　　　　　　　　　　　　　　　　　　　　　　　　　　　　　　Debtor

Date_____   Signature _____
　　　　　　　　　　　　　　　　　　　　　　　　　　　　　　(Joint Debtor, if any)
　　　　　　　　　　　　　　　　　　　　　　　　　　(If joint case, both spouses must sign)

CERTIFICATION AND SIGNATURE OF NON-ATTORNEY BANKRUPTCY PETITION PREPARER (See 11 U.S.C. § 110)

I certify that I am a bankruptcy petition preparer as defined in 11 U.S.C. §110, that I prepared this document for compensation, and that I have provided the debtor with a copy of this document.

_____
Printed or Typed Name of Bankruptcy Petition Preparer　　　　　Social Security No.

_____
Address

Names and Social Security numbers of all other individuals who prepared or assisted in preparing this document:

If more than one person prepared this document, attach additional signed sheets conforming to the appropriate Official form for each person.

X_____　　　　　_____
Signature of Bankruptcy Petition Preparer　　　　　　　　　　　　　　Date

A bankruptcy petition preparer's failure to comply with the provisions of title 11 and the Federal Rules of Bankruptcy Procedure may result in fines or imprisonment or both. 11 U.S.C. §110, 18 U.S.C. §156.

DECLARATION UNDER PENALTY OF PERJURY ON BEHALF OF CORPORATION OR PARTNERSHIP

I, the _____**C**_____(the president or other officer or an authorized agent of the corporation or a member or
an authorized agent of the partnership) of the _____**D**_____ (corporation or partnership) named as debtor in
this case, declare under penalty of perjury that I have read the foregoing summary and schedules, consisting of _____**E**_____
sheets, and that they are true and correct to the best of my knowledge, information, and belief.　　(Total shown on summary page plus 1)

Date_____   Signature _____**G**_____

　　　　　　　　　　　　　　　　　F _____
　　　　　　　　　　　　　　　　　　　　(Print or type name of individual signing on behalf of debtor)

(An individual signing on behalf of a partnership or corporation must indicate position or relationship to debtor.)

Penalty for making a false statement or concealing property. Fine of up to $500,000 or imprisonment for up to 5 years or both. 18 U.S.C.A. §§ 152 and 3571.

Instructions for Completing the Declaration Concerning Debtor's Schedules

If the debtor is an individual or a husband and wife filing a joint petition:

A Enter the total number of pages. This is the number of pages as shown on the summary page plus one.

B Before the debtor signs his or her name, each entry on the schedules should be carefully reviewed with the debtor. The declaration should then be read to the debtor. If the debtor assents, the debtor should sign his or her full name (as it appears on the petition) and date the declaration. The date is the date the debtor signs the declaration and not the date the petition is filed. If a joint petition is being filed, these steps should be taken for both debtors.

If the debtor is a partnership or a corporation:

C State the title of the person signing the declaration or in what capacity the declarant is signing.

   Examples: If a corporation, use "President."
                    If a partnership, use "Partner."

D State the name of the entity filing the petition. State the name as it appears on the petition.

E Enter the total number of pages. This is the number of pages as shown on the summary page plus one.

F Type or print the name of the individual who will be signing on behalf of the partnership or corporation. The name typed or printed should be the same as it will appear in the signature.

G Before the individual signing on behalf of the partnership or corporation signs his or her name, each entry on the schedules should be carefully reviewed with that individual. The declaration should then be read to that individual. If the individual assents, have him or her sign his or her name as it appears on the typed line and date the declaration. The date is the date the individual signs the declaration and not the date the petition is filed.

H. STATEMENT OF FINANCIAL AFFAIRS

The debtor's statement of financial affairs, Official Form No. 7 (see Exhibit 5.24), must be completed by all debtors. Spouses filing a joint petition may file a single statement on which the information for both spouses is combined. An individual debtor in business as a sole proprietor, partner, family farmer, or self-employed professional must provide the information requested on this statement concerning all business activities as well as the debtor's personal affairs.

Questions 1–15 must be completed by all debtors. Debtors that are or have been "in business" also must complete Questions 16–21. A debtor is "in business" for the purpose of this form if the debtor is

   1. a corporation
   2. a partnership
   3. an individual who is or has been within the two years immediately preceding the filing of this bankruptcy case
      a. an officer, director, managing executive, or person in control of a corporation
      b. a partner, other than a limited partner, of a partnership
      c. a sole proprietor or self-employed

Prior to completing the statement of financial affairs, it is of critical importance for the paralegal or the attorney to understand what the debtor means by being in business. What is important is not the debtor's perception of whether he or she was in business but whether the debtor fits within the definition of "in business" as stated in Official Form No. 7. In some cases, the question may be whether the debtor is a sole proprietor or otherwise self-employed (and therefore in business) or an employee (and therefore not in business).

In *In re Montoya,* a doctor of medicine specializing in neurological surgery claimed to be an employee of a professional association rather than an independent contractor. Prior to the filing of his petition for bankruptcy, Dr. Montoya, who had been a shareholder in a neurological association, which is a professional association (P.A.), sold his interest in the professional association at fair market value, to the remaining shareholders. After the transfer, Dr. Montoya retained no ownership interest in the P.A. or in its accounts. After the sale, Dr. Montoya, however, remained as an associate with the P.A. under a document entitled "Employment Agreement." The bankruptcy court, in the following excerpt, was faced with the issue of whether Dr. Montoya was paid wages as an employee or compensation as an independent contractor.

In re Montoya
United States Bankruptcy Court, Middle District of Florida, 1987.
77 B.R. 926, 928–30.

To determine whether a person is an employee or an independent contractor, the facts of each case must be taken into account. Rather than categorizing a person as an employee or an independent contractor solely on the basis of his job title, case law has looked to factors for determining a person's employment relationship. *Refco, Inc. v. Sarmiento,* 487 So.2d 75 (3d DCA, Fla. 1986). These factors were addressed in the case of *In re Moriarty. Supra.* The *Moriarty* court looked at: The existence of an employment contract; who was to furnish tools and supplies; the right to control progress of the employee's work; the method of payment; and whether the work performed is part of the regular business of the employer. *Id.* at 74. In *Moriarty,* the debtor was a real estate agent whose compensation was based solely on commissions, whose progress of work was not subject to control by the real estate company and whose expenses were not reimbursed by the company. The court held that the debtor was an independent contractor rather than an employee. *Id.* As set forth below, the relevant factors when applied to the facts of this case establishes that the Debtor is an employee . . . .

The first factor is the existence of an employment contract itself. A contract is the best possible evidence of whether the contracting parties intended to form an employee-employer relationship or merely engage the services of an independent contractor. *Ware v. Money-Plan Intern, Inc.,* 467 So.2d 1072 (2d DCA, Fla.1985). In this case the Debtor entered into an Employment Agreement with the P.A. which is quite comprehensive. The P.A. provides the Debtor with facilities, equipment and supplies and pays for his professional liability insurance, occupational license fees and many other expenses which would typically only be paid by an employer in an employee-employer relationship. The Employment Agreement gives the P.A. authority to establish policies and procedures to be followed in treating patients and to determine which patients the Debtor may treat. Additionally, the agreement establishes a fixed salary for the Debtor. The agreement itself is strong evidence the parties intended to create an employee-employer relationship.

The next applicable indicia addressed by the *Moriarty* court is the obligation to furnish necessary tools and supplies. Typically, an independent contractor furnishes his/her own tools and supplies whereas an employer generally furnishes any necessary tools and supplies for employees. In this case, the P.A. is responsible for providing medical facilities, offices, equipment, utilities, supplies and drugs which are necessary for the Debtor to use in the course of his employment. Additionally, the P.A. is responsible for providing all necessary support personnel. The Debtor is not required to purchase any supplies nor employ any other personnel. Thus, the P.A.'s obligation to furnish necessary tools and supplies is further evidence that an employee-employer relationship was created.

The next factor, and perhaps the most important factor, in determining whether a person is an employee or an independent contractor is the right to control the progress of the work. Typically an employer has a right to control the progress of an employee's work but does not have the right to control the progress of an independent contractor's work. As evidenced by the Employment Agreement in this case, the P.A. has the exclusive authority to establish the professional policies and procedures for treating patients. Through these policies and procedures the P.A. has the right to control the means by which the Debtor may treat his patients. If the Debtor is subject to control as to the means used in treating his patients, he is an employee. *D.O. Creasman Electronics, Inc. v. State Department of Labor,* 458 So.2d 894 (2d DCA, Fla.1984). Additionally, the Employ-

ment Agreement gives the P.A. the right to determine what patients the Debtor may treat. The Trustee has argued that the P.A. has not actually controlled or interfered with the Debtor's treatment of the P.A. patients. However, as stated by the Florida Supreme Court in *National Surety Corporation v. Windham,* 74 So. 2d 549 (Fla.1954) "[i]t is the *right* of control, not actual control or actual interference with the work, which is significant in distinguishing between an independent contractor and a servant." The court held that the "right to control depends upon the terms of the contract of employment." *Id.* at 550. In this case, the Employment Agreement granted the P.A. the right to control the work of the Debtor regardless of whether the P.A. ever chooses to exercise that right. Thus, the P.A.'s right to control is an additional indicator of the existence of an employee-employer relationship.

Turning next to the method of payment, the Debtor's compensation typifies that of an employee rather than that of an independent contractor. An employee is typically paid by time, whether it be by salary or by hourly rate, whereas an independent contractor is typically paid by the job. In the instant case, the Debtor is paid a straight salary by the P.A. His salary remains constant regardless of how much money the P.A. is paid for his services or whether the P.A. incurs profits or losses. Thus, the Debtor's wages are indicative of that of an employee.

The final factor addressed by the *Moriarty* court is whether the work is part of the regular business of the employer. In the instant case, the P.A. is a professional association comprised of physicians engaged in the practice of medicine. The P.A.'s sole enterprise is that of providing medical services. Therefore, the Debtor satisfies this test as an employee.

. . . .

PROBLEM 5.16   J&B Produce Company, a nonregulated carrier of farm produce, transports produce by truck from the West Coast to the East Coast of the United States exclusively for Riteway Enterprises, a produce transportation broker. J&B uses trucks it owns, trucks it leases, and trucks owned by drivers who haul for J&B. J&B instructs its drivers on the times and places to report to work, to pick up the cargo, and to deliver it. J&B, rather than the drivers, often selects assistant drivers for the trips.

On the return trips, J&B often leases its trucks to other carriers and compensates the drivers. If J&B does not lease its trucks on the return trips, the drivers may contract to haul produce from the East Coast to the West Coast, as long as it does not interfere with J&B's schedules. J&B secures the necessary carrier permits and vehicle licenses from the states through which the trucks pass in transporting the cargo. Upon Riteway's request, J&B directs the drivers to telephone Riteway twice a day to report the location of J&B's trucks.

J&B pays for the liability insurance and operating expenses of the trucks and requires the drivers to report mechanical breakdowns and other problems with the trucks, to obtain approval for repairs costing more than $25, and to maintain an accounting of the gas and oil expenses. The drivers are permitted to select their own routes, driving times, and speeds. The drivers are paid by the trip rather than by the hour.

Based on the factors raised by the court in *In re Montoya,* are the drivers employees of J&B or self-employed?

Official Form No. 7, the **Statement of Financial Affairs** (see Exhibit 5.24), contains questions concerning the source of the debtor's income; payments to creditors; lawsuits, executions, garnishments, and attachments; transfers of property prior to the filing of the petition in bankruptcy; casualty or gambling losses; the location of safe deposit boxes; setoffs; property of others held by the debtor; and previous addresses of the debtor. In addition to these questions, a debtor "in business" must provide information concerning the books, records, and financial statements of the business; the last two inventories; current and former partners, officers, directors, and shareholders; and withdrawals from a partnership or distributions by a corporation.

After the statement of financial affairs has been completed, the debtor (in the case of an individual debtor) or the debtors (in the case of a husband and wife filing a joint petition) must complete the unsworn declaration. The debtor must declare under penalty of perjury that he or she has read the answers contained in the statement of financial affairs and any attachments and that they are true and correct. For a partnership or a corporation, the person with authority to represent the debtor must declare under penalty of perjury that he or she has read the answers contained in the statement of financial affairs and any attachments and that they are true and correct to the best of his or her knowledge.

EXHIBIT 5.24
Official Form No. 7 (Statement of Financial Affairs)

FORM 7
(11/94)

UNITED STATES BANKRUPTCY COURT

_____ **District of** _____

In Re: _____   Case No. _____
                    Debtor   (If known)

STATEMENT OF FINANCIAL AFFAIRS

This statement is to be completed by every debtor. Spouses filing a joint petition may file a single statement on which the information for both spouses is combined. If the case is filed under chapter 12 or chapter 13, a married debtor must furnish information for both spouses whether or not a joint petition is filed, unless the spouses are separated and a joint petition is not filed. An individual debtor engaged in business as a sole proprietor, partner, family farmer, or self-employed professional, should provide the information requested on this statement concerning all such activities as well as the individual's personal affairs.

Questions 1 - 15 are to be completed by all debtors. Debtors that are or have been in business, as defined below, also must complete Questions 16 - 21. If the answer to any question is "None," or the question is not applicable, mark the box labeled "None." If additional space is needed for the answer to any question, use and attach a separate sheet properly identified with the case name, case number (if known), and the number of the question.

DEFINITIONS

"In business." A debtor is "in business" for the purpose of this form if the debtor is a corporation or partnership. An individual debtor is "in business" for the purpose of this form if the debtor is or has been, within the two years immediately preceding the filing of this bankruptcy case, any of the following: an officer, director, managing executive, or person in control of a corporation; a partner, other than a limited partner, of a partnership; a sole proprietor; or self-employed.

"Insider." The term "insider" includes but is not limited to: relatives of the debtor; general partners of the debtor and their relatives; corporations of which the debtor is an officer, director, or person in control; officers, directors, and any person in control of a corporate debtor and their relatives; affiliates of the debtor and insiders of such affiliates; any managing agent of the debtor. 11 U.S.C. § 101(30).

A   1.   Income from employment or operation of business

None   State the gross amount of income the debtor has received from employment, trade, or
☐   profession, or from operation of the debtor's business from the beginning of this calendar year to the
            date this case was commenced. State also the gross amounts received during the two years
            immediately preceding this calendar year. (A debtor that maintains, or has maintained, financial
            records on the basis of a fiscal rather than a calendar year may report fiscal year income. Identify the
            beginning and ending dates of the debtor's fiscal year.) If a joint petition is filed, state income for each
            spouse separately. (Married debtors filing under chapter 12 or chapter 13 must state income of both
            spouses whether or not a joint petition is filed, unless the spouses are separated and a joint petition is
            not filed.)

PARTY	METHOD	START	END	AMOUNT	SOURCE (if more than one)

EXHIBIT 5.24
Continued

B   2.   Income other than from employment or operation of business

None   State the amount of income received by the debtor other than from employment, trade,
☐   profession, or operation of the debtor's business during the two years immediately preceding the
        commencement of this case. Give particulars. If a joint petition is filed, state income for each spouse
        separately. (Married debtors filing under chapter 12 or chapter 13 must state income for each spouse
        whether or not a joint petition is filed, unless the spouses are separated and a joint petition is not filed.)

PARTY   AMOUNT   SOURCE

_____

C   3.   Payments to creditors

None   a.   List all payments on loans, installment purchases of goods or services, and other debts,
☐   aggregating more than $600 to any creditor, made within 90 days immediately preceding the
        commencement of this case. (Married debtors filing under chapter 12 or chapter 13 must include
        payments by either or both spouses whether or not a joint petition is filed, unless the spouses are
        separated and a joint petition is not filed.)

NAME AND ADDRESS OF CREDITOR	DATES OF PAYMENTS	AMOUNT PAID	AMOUNT STILL OWING

_____

None   b.   List all payments made within one year immediately preceding the commencement of this case
☐   to or for the benefit of creditors who are or were insiders. (Married debtors filing under chapter 12 or
        chapter 13 must include payments by either or both spouses whether or not a joint petition is filed,
        unless the spouses are separated and a joint petition is not filed.)

NAME AND ADDRESS OF CREDITOR AND RELATIONSHIP TO DEBTOR	DATE OF PAYMENT	AMOUNT PAID	AMOUNT STILL OWING

_____

D   4.   Suits and administrative proceedings, executions, garnishments and attachments

None   a.   List all suits and administrative proceedings to which the debtor is or was a party within one year immediately
☐   of this bankruptcy case. (Married debtors filing under chapter 12 or chapter 13 must include
        information concerning either or both spouses whether or not a joint petition is filed, unless the
        spouses are separated and a joint petition is not filed.)

CAPTION OF SUIT AND CASE NUMBER	NATURE OF PROCEEDING	COURT OR AGENCY AND LOCATION	STATUS OR DISPOSITION

_____

EXHIBIT 5.24
Continued

None b.   Describe all property that has been attached, garnished or seized under any legal or equitable
☐   process within one year immediately preceding the commencement of this case. (Married debtors
       filing under chapter 12 or chapter 13 must include information concerning property of either or both
       spouses whether or not a joint petition is filed, unless the spouses are separated and a joint petition is
       not filed.)

NAME AND ADDRESS
OF PERSON FOR WHOSE   DESCRIPTION AND VALUE
BENEFIT PROPERTY WAS SEIZED   DATE OF SEIZURE   OF PROPERTY

_____

E   5.   Repossessions, foreclosures and returns

None   List all property that has been repossessed by a creditor, sold at a foreclosure sale, transferred
☐   through a deed in lieu of foreclosure or returned to the seller, within one year immediately preceding
       the commencement of this case. (Married debtors filing under chapter 12 or chapter 13 must include
       information concerning property of either or both spouses whether or not a joint petition is filed, unless
       the spouses are separated and a joint petition is not filed.)

                                   DATE OF
                                   REPOSSESSION,
                                   FORECLOSURE
NAME AND ADDRESS   SALE, TRANSFER   DESCRIPTION AND VALUE
OF CREDITOR OR SELLER   OR RETURN   OF PROPERTY

_____

F   6.   Assignments and receiverships

None a.   Describe any assignment of property for the benefit of creditors made within 120 days immediately
☐   preceding the commencement of this case. (Married debtors filing under chapter 12 or chapter 13 must
       include any assignment by either or both spouses whether or not a joint petition is filed, unless the
       spouses are separated and a joint petition is not filed.)

                                   DATE OF   TERMS OF ASSIGNMENT
NAME AND ADDRESS OF ASSIGNEE   ASSIGNMENT   OR SETTLEMENT

_____

None b.   List all property which has been in the hands of a custodian, receiver, or court-appointed official
☐   within one year immediately preceding the commencement of this case. (Married debtors filing under
       chapter 12 or chapter 13 must include information concerning property of either or both spouses whether
       or not a joint petition is filed, unless the spouses are separated and a joint petition is not filed.)

                                   NAME AND LOCATION
                                   OF COURT   DESCRIPTION
NAME AND ADDRESS   CASE TITLE   AND VALUE
OF CUSTODIAN   & NUMBER   DATE OF ORDER   OF PROPERTY

_____

EXHIBIT 5.24
Continued

G   7.   Gifts

None
☐   List all gifts or charitable contributions made within one year immediately preceding the commencement of this case except ordinary and usual gifts to family members aggregating less than $200 in value per individual family member and charitable contributions aggregating less than $100 per recipient. (Married debtors filing under chapter 12 or chapter 13 must include gifts or contributions by either or both spouses whether or not a joint petition is filed, unless the spouses are separated and a joint petition is not filed.)

NAME AND ADDRESS OF PERSON OR ORGANIZATION	RELATIONSHIP TO DEBTOR, IF ANY	DATE OF GIFT	DESCRIPTION AND VALUE OF GIFT

H   8.   Losses

None
☐   List all losses from fire, theft, other casualty or gambling within one year immediately preceding the commencement of this case or since the commencement of this case. (Married debtors filing under chapter 12 or chapter 13 must include losses by either or both spouses whether or not a joint petition is filed, unless the spouses are separated and a joint petition is not filed.)

DESCRIPTION AND VALUE OF PROPERTY	DESCRIPTION OF CIRCUMSTANCES AND, IF LOSS WAS COVERED IN WHOLE OR IN PART BY INSURANCE, GIVE PARTICULARS	DATE OF LOSS

I   9.   Payments related to debt counseling or bankruptcy

None
☐   List all payments made or property transferred by or on behalf of the debtor to any persons, including attorneys, for consultation concerning debt consolidation, relief under the bankruptcy law or preparation of a petition in bankruptcy within one year immediately preceding the commencement of this case.

NAME AND ADDRESS OF PAYEE	DATE OF PAYMENT, NAME OF PAYOR IF OTHER THAN DEBTOR	AMOUNT OF MONEY OR DESCRIPTION AND VALUE OF PROPERTY

J   10.   Other transfers

None
☐   List all other property, other than property transferred in the ordinary course of the business or financial affairs of the debtor, transferred either absolutely or as security within one year immediately preceding the commencement of this case. (Married debtors filing under chapter 12 or chapter 13 must include transfers by either or both spouses whether or not a joint petition is filed, unless the spouses are separated and a joint petition is not filed.)

NAME AND ADDRESS OF TRANSFEREE, RELATIONSHIP TO DEBTOR	DATE	DESCRIBE PROPERTY TRANSFERRED AND VALUE RECEIVED

EXHIBIT 5.24
Continued

K   11. Closed financial accounts

None   List all financial accounts and instruments held in the name of the debtor or for the benefit of the
☐   debtor which were closed, sold, or otherwise transferred within one year immediately preceding the
commencement of this case. Include checking, savings, or other financial accounts, certificates of
deposit, or other instruments; shares and share accounts held in banks, credit unions, pension funds,
cooperatives, associations, brokerage houses and other financial institutions. (Married debtors filing
under chapter 12 or chapter 13 must include information concerning accounts or instruments held by or
for either or both spouses whether or not a joint petition is filed, unless the spouses are separated and a
joint petition is not filed.)

NAME AND ADDRESS OF INSTITUTION	TYPE AND NUMBER OF ACCOUNT AND AMOUNT OF FINAL BALANCE	AMOUNT AND DATE OF SALE OR CLOSING

L   12. Safe deposit boxes

None   List each safe deposit or other box or depository in which the debtor has or had securities, cash, or
☐   other valuables within one year immediately preceding the commencement of this case. (Married
debtors filing under chapter 12 or chapter 13 must include boxes or depositories of either or both
spouses whether or not a joint petition is filed, unless the spouses are separated and a joint petition is
not filed.)

NAME AND ADDRESS OF BANK OR OTHER DEPOSITORY	DESCRIPTION OF CONTENTS	DATE OF TRANSFER OR SURRENDER, IF ANY	NAMES AND ADDRESSES OF THOSE WITH ACCESS TO BOX OR DEPOSITORY

M   13. Setoffs

None   List all setoffs made by any creditor, including a bank, against a debt or deposit of the debtor
☐   within 90 days preceding the commencement of this case. (Married debtors filing under chapter 12 or
chapter 13 must include information concerning either or both spouses whether or not a joint petition is
filed, unless the spouses are separated and a joint petition is not filed.)

NAME AND ADDRESS OF CREDITOR	DATE OF SETOFF	AMOUNT OF SETOFF

N   14. Property held for another person

None   List all property owned by another person that the debtor holds or controls.
☐

NAME AND ADDRESS OF OWNER	DESCRIPTION AND VALUE OF PROPERTY	LOCATION OF PROPERTY

EXHIBIT 5.24
Continued

O   15. Prior address of debtor

None
☐   If the debtor has moved within the two years immediately preceding the commencement of this
       case, list all premises which the debtor occupied during that period and vacated prior to the
       commencement of this case. If a joint petition is filed, report also any separate address of either
       spouse.

ADDRESS   NAME USED   DATES OF OCCUPANCY

P
       The following questions are to be completed by every debtor that is a corporation or partnership and by
any individual debtor who is or has been, within the two years immediately preceding the commencement of
this case, any of the following: an officer, director, managing executive, or owner of more than 5 percent of
the voting securities of a corporation; a partner, other than a limited partner, of a partnership; a sole proprietor
or otherwise self-employed.

       *(An individual or joint debtor should complete this portion of the statement only if the debtor is or has been
in business, as defined above, within the two years immediately preceding the commencement of this case.)*

Q   16. Nature, location and name of business

None a.   If the debtor is an individual, list the names and addresses of all businesses in which the debtor was
☐   an officer, director, partner, or managing executive of a corporation, partnership, sole proprietorship, or
           was a self-employed professional within the two years immediately preceding the commencement of
           this case, or in which the debtor owned 5 percent or more of the voting or equity securities within the two
           years immediately preceding the commencement of this case.

      b.   If the debtor is a partnership, list the names and addresses of all businesses in which the debtor was
           a partner or owned 5 percent or more of the voting securities, within the two years immediately
           preceding the commencement of this case.

      c.   If the debtor is a corporation, list the names and addresses of all businesses in which the debtor was
           a partner or owned 5 percent or more of the voting securities within the two years immediately
           preceding the commencement of this case.

			BEGINNING AND ENDING DATES
NAME	ADDRESS	NATURE OF BUSINESS	OF OPERATION

R   17. Books, records and financial statements

None a.   List all bookkeepers and accountants who within the six years immediately preceding the filing of
☐   this bankruptcy case kept or supervised the keeping of books of account and records of the debtor.

NAME AND ADDRESS   DATES SERVICES RENDERED

None b.   List all firms or individuals who within the two years immediately preceding the filing of this
☐   bankruptcy case have audited the books of account and records, or prepared a financial statement of
           the debtor.

NAME   ADDRESS   DATES SERVICES RENDERED

EXHIBIT 5.24
Continued

None   c.   List all firms or individuals who at the time of the commencement of this case were in possession of
☐   the books of account and records of the debtor. If any of the books of account and records are not
          available, explain.

NAME   ADDRESS   EXPLAIN IF NOT AVAILABLE

None   d.   List all financial institutions, creditors and other parties, including mercantile and trade agencies, to
☐   whom a financial statement was issued within the two years immediately preceding the
          commencement of this case by the debtor.

NAME AND ADDRESS   DATE ISSUED

S   18.   Inventories

None   a.   List the dates of the last two inventories taken of your property, the name of the person who
☐   supervised the taking of each inventory, and the dollar amount and basis of each inventory.

                                                                DOLLAR AMOUNT OF INVENTORY
DATE OF INVENTORY   INVENTORY SUPERVISOR   (Specify cost, market or other basis)

None   b.   List the name and address of the person having possession of the records of each of the two
☐   inventories reported in a., above.

                          NAME AND ADDRESS OF CUSTODIAN
DATE OF INVENTORY   OF INVENTORY RECORDS

T   19.   Current Partners, Officers, Directors and Shareholders

None   a.   If the debtor is a partnership, list the nature and percentage of partnership interest of each member
☐   of the partnership.

NAME AND ADDRESS   NATURE OF INTEREST   PERCENTAGE OF INTEREST

None   b.   If the debtor is a corporation, list all officers and directors of the corporation, and each stockholder
☐   who directly or indirectly owns, controls, or holds 5 percent or more of the voting securities of the
          corporation.

                                                                NATURE AND PERCENTAGE
NAME AND ADDRESS   TITLE   OF STOCK OWNERSHIP

EXHIBIT 5.24
Continued

U   20. Former partners, officers, directors and shareholders

None   a.   If the debtor is a partnership, list each member who withdrew from the partnership within one
☐   year immediately preceding the commencement of this case.

NAME   ADDRESS   DATE OF WITHDRAWAL

_____

None   b.   If the debtor is a corporation, list all officers, or directors whose relationship with the corporation
☐   terminated within one year immediately preceding the commencement of this case.

NAME AND ADDRESS   TITLE   DATE OF TERMINATION

_____

V   21. Withdrawals from a partnership or distributions by a corporation

None   If the debtor is a partnership or corporation, list all withdrawals or distributions credited or given
☐   to an insider, including compensation in any form, bonuses, loans, stock redemptions, options exercised
and any other perquisite during one year immediately preceding the commencement of this case.

NAME & ADDRESS   AMOUNT OF MONEY
OF RECIPIENT,   DATE AND PURPOSE   OR DESCRIPTION
RELATIONSHIP TO DEBTOR   OF WITHDRAWAL   AND VALUE OF PROPERTY

_____

EXHIBIT 5.24
Continued

W Complete the unsworn declaration.

[If completed by an individual or individual and spouse]

I declare under penalty of perjury that I have read the answers contained in the foregoing statement of financial affairs and any attachments thereto and that they are true and correct.

Date _____   Signature _____
                                   of Debtor

Date _____   Signature _____
                                   of Joint Debtor
                                   (if any)

CERTIFICATION AND SIGNATURE OF NON-ATTORNEY BANKRUPTCY PETITION PREPARER (See 11 U.S.C. § 110)

I certify that I am a bankruptcy petition preparer as defined in 11 U.S.C. § 110, that I prepared this document for compensation, and that I have provided the debtor with a copy of this document.

_____   _____
Printed or Typed Name of Bankruptcy Petition Preparer   Social Security No.

_____
Address

Names and Social Security numbers of all other individuals who prepared or assisted in preparing this document:

If more than one person prepared this document, attach additional signed sheets conforming to the appropriate Official Form for each person.

X_____   _____
Signature of Bankruptcy Petition Preparer   Date

A bankruptcy petition preparer's failure to comply with the provisions of title 11 and the Federal Rules of Bankruptcy Procedure may result in fines or imprisonment or both. 11 U.S.C. § 110; 18 U.S.C. § 156.

[If completed on behalf of a partnership or corporation]

I declare under penalty of perjury that I have read the answers contained in the foregoing statement of financial affairs and any attachments thereto and that they are true and correct to the best of my knowledge, information and belief.

Date _____   Signature _____

                                   _____
                                   Print Name and Title

[An individual signing on behalf of a partnership or corporation must indicate position or relationship to debtor.]
_____ continuation sheets attached

Penalty for making a false statement: Fine of up to $500,000 or imprisonment
for up to 5 years, or both. 18 U.S.C. § 152 and 3571

Instructions for Completing Official Form No. 7 (Statement of Financial Affairs)

The questions on Official Form No. 7 track the questions on the debtor-client questionnaire. (See Appendix A.) The debtor's answers to the questionnaire should be used as an aid in filling out this statement of financial affairs. The paralegal or the attorney should proceed through the questions on the statement of financial affairs very carefully with the debtor-client, using the previously prepared questionnaire as a starting point. The debtor's answers on the questionnaire are often incomplete and may suggest further questions that the paralegal or the attorney must follow up with the debtor.

A Income from employment or operation of business

See client's answers to Debtor-Client Questionnaire, Part VII, Question 1.

From the beginning of this calendar year to the date this case was commenced, state the gross amount of income the debtor has received from employment, trade, or profession or from operation of the debtor's business. Also state the sources of this income.

If the debtor's financial records are maintained on a fiscal-year basis, report fiscal-year rather than calendar-year income. Identify the beginning and ending dates of the debtor's fiscal year.

For the two years immediately preceding this calendar or fiscal year, state the gross amounts received from employment, trade, or profession, or from operation of the debtor's business. Also state the sources of this income.

If a husband and wife have filed a joint petition, state the income for each spouse separately.

If the debtor has had no income from employment or the operation of a business during either of these periods, check the "none" box for question 1.

B   Income other than from employment or operation of business

See client's answers to Debtor-Client Questionnaire, Part VII, Question 2.

For the two years immediately preceding the commencement of this case, state the amount of income received by the debtor other than from employment, trade, profession, or operation of the debtor's business. Also state the sources of this income.

If a joint petition is filed, state the amount of income and its sources for each spouse separately.

If the debtor has had no other income during this period, check the "none" box for question 2.

C   Payments to creditors

See client's answers to Debtor-Client Questionnaire, Part VII, Question 3.

a. Payments made within 90 days

For the 90 days immediately preceding the commencement of this case, list all payments of loans, installment purchases of goods or services, and other debts aggregating more than $600 to any creditor.

For each creditor, include the following:

(1) the name and address of the creditor
(2) the dates of payments
(3) the amount paid
(4) the amount still owing

If the debtor has made no payment during this period, check the "none" box for question 3.a.

This question relates to the 90-day preference. See 11 U.S.C.A. § 547.

b. Payments made within one year to insiders

For the one-year period immediately preceding the commencement of this case, list all payments made to or for the benefit of creditors who are or were insiders. For each creditor, include the name and address of the creditor and the relationship to the debtor, the date of payment, the amount paid, and the amount still owing.

If the debtor has made no payment during this period to an insider, check the "none" box for question 3.b.

The term "insider" includes but is not limited to
1) relatives of the debtor;
2) general partners of the debtor and their relatives;
3) corporations of which the debtor is an officer, director, or person in control;
4) officers, directors, and any person in control of a corporate debtor and their relatives;
5) affiliates of the debtor and insiders of such affiliates; and
6) any managing agent of the debtor. 11 U.S.C.A. § 101(31).

This question relates to the one-year preference period for payments to an insider. See 11 U.S.C.A. § 547.

D Suits and administrative proceedings, executions, garnishments, and attachments

See client's answers to Debtor-Client Questionnaire, Part VII, Question 4.

a. Lawsuits

For the one-year period immediately preceding the filing of this bankruptcy case, list all suits to which the debtor is or was a party. Include the following information:
1) the caption of the lawsuit and the case number
2) the nature of the lawsuit
3) the court in which the lawsuit was filed and court's location
4) the current status or disposition of the lawsuit
Repeat until all lawsuits have been listed.

The paralegal or the attorney may need to conduct a personal investigation regarding lawsuits against the debtor. This information must be accurate. Some debtors do not understand why they have been summoned and the significance of the summons.

If the debtor has not been a party to a lawsuit during this period, check the "none" box for question 4.a.

b. Attachments, seizures, and garnishments

For the one-year period immediately preceding the commencement of this case, provide the following information as to property attached, seized, or garnished under any legal or equitable process:
1) the name of the person for whose benefit the property was attached or seized
2) the address of the person for whose benefit the property was attached or seized
3) the date of attachment or seizure
4) a description of the property
5) the value of the property
Repeat until all attachments, seizures, and garnishments have been listed.

If a garnishment, execution, or attachment is underway which would constitute a judicial lien, it may be subject to avoidance by the debtor to the extent that the lien impairs an exemption to which the debtor would be entitled under 11 U.S.C.A. § 522(b). 11 U.S.C.A. § 522(f).

If the debtor has not had property attached, seized, or garnished during this period, check the "none" box for question 4.b.

E Repossessions, foreclosures, and returns

See client's answers to Debtor-Client Questionnaire, Part VII, Question 5.

For the one-year period immediately preceding the commencement of this case, provide the following information for each repossession, foreclosure, or return:
1) the name of the creditor or seller
2) the address of the creditor or seller
3) the date of repossession, foreclosure sale, transfer, or return
4) a description of the property
5) the value of the property

If there has been no repossession, foreclosure, or return during this period, check the "none" box for question 5.

F Assignments and receiverships

See client's answers to Debtor-Client Questionnaire, Part VII, Question 6.

a. Assignments

For the 120 days immediately preceding the commencement of this case, provide the following information for each assignment of property for the benefit of creditors:
1) the name of the assignee
2) the assignee's address
3) the date of the assignment
4) the terms of the assignment or settlement

If there has been no assignment of property for the benefit of creditors during this period, check the "none" box for question 6.a.

b. Receiverships

For the one-year period immediately preceding the commencement of this case, provide the following information for any property which has been in the hands of a custodian, receiver, or court-appointed official:

(1) the name of the custodian
(2) the address of the custodian
(3) the name of the court
(4) the location of the court
(5) the case title
(6) the case number
(7) the date of the order
(8) a description of the property
(9) the value of the property

If there has been no property in the hands of a custodian, receiver, or court-appointed official during this period, check the "none" box for question 6.b.

G Gifts

See client's answers to Debtor-Client Questionnaire, Part VII, Question 7.

For the one-year period immediately preceding the commencement of this case, provide the following information for all gifts or charitable contributions, except ordinary and usual gifts made to family members aggregating less than $200 in value per individual family member and charitable contributions aggregating less than $100 per recipient:

1) the name of the person or organization receiving the gift
2) the address of the person or organization receiving the gift
3) the relationship of the recipient to the debtor, if any
4) the date of the gift
5) a description of the gift
6) the value of the gift

If no such gifts were made, check the "none" box for question 7.

Question 7 relates to preferences (11 U.S.C.A. § 547), fraudulent transfers (11 U.S.C.A. § 548), and voidable transfers under the Uniform Fraudulent Conveyances Act, the Uniform Fraudulent Transfer Act, and other state laws. 11 U.S.C.A. § 544(b).

H Losses

See client's answers to Debtor-Client Questionnaire, Part VII, Question 8.

For the one-year period immediately preceding the commencement of this case or since the commencement of this case, provide the following information for all losses from fire, theft, other casualty, or gambling:

1) a description of the property
2) the value of the property
3) a description of the circumstances surrounding the loss
4) if the loss was covered in whole or in part by insurance, the particulars of the insurance coverage
5) the date of the loss

If the debtor suffered no losses from fire, theft, other casualty, or gambling during this period, check the "none" box for question 8.

I Payments related to debt counseling or bankruptcy

See client's answers to Debtor-Client Questionnaire, Part VII, Question 9.

a. Payments

For the one-year period immediately preceding the commencement of this case, provide the following information for all payments made by or on behalf of the debtor to any person, including attorneys, for consultation concerning debt consolidation, relief under the bankruptcy law, or preparation of a petition in bankruptcy:

1) the name of the payee
2) the address of the payee
3) the date of the payment
4) the name of the payor, if other than the debtor
5) the amount of money paid

b. Transfers

For the one-year period immediately preceding the commencement of this case, provide the following information for all property transferred by or on behalf of the debtor to any person, including attorneys, for consultation concerning debt consolidation, relief under the bankruptcy law, or preparation of a petition in bankruptcy:

1) the name of the transferee
2) the address of the transferee
3) the date of the transfer
4) the name of the transferor, if other than the debtor
5) a description and the value of the property transferred

If no payments were made or no property was transferred during this period, check the "none" box for question 9.

J   Other transfers

See client's answers to Debtor-Client Questionnaire, Part VII, Question 10.

For the one-year period immediately preceding the commencement of this case, provide the following information for all other property, other than property transferred in the ordinary course of the business or financial affairs of the debtor, transferred either absolutely or as security:

1) the name of the transferee
2) the address of the transferee
3) the relationship of the transferee to the debtor
4) the date of the transfer
5) a description of the property transferred
6) the value received for the property

These questions relate to fraudulent transfers (11 U.S.C.A. § 548), and voidable transfers under applicable law (11 U.S.C.A § 544(b)).

The debtor may not fully comprehend what constitutes a transfer. Some debtors do not understand that a sale is a transfer. They may believe that only gifts are transfers.

Some debtors believe that only a sale is a transfer. Therefore, a debtor may not have stated that she gave a car to her son because the car was not sold but was given as a gift.

Some debtors believe that only the transfer of property that is collateral for a security interest is a transfer of property. Therefore, a debtor may not have stated that she gave a car to her son because the car was hers when she gave it to him.

Some debtors believe that transfer of property refers only to real property. Therefore, a debtor may not have stated that he gave a car to his daughter because it was not real property.

If no other property was transferred absolutely or as security within this period, other than property transferred in the ordinary course of the business or financial affairs of the debtor, check the "none" box for question 10.

K   Close financial accounts

See client's answers to Debtor-Client Questionnaire, Part VII, Question 11.

For the one-year period immediately preceding the commencement of this case, provide the following information for all financial accounts and instruments (including checking accounts, savings accounts, other financial accounts, certificates of deposit, shares and

share accounts held in banks, credit unions, pension funds, cooperatives, associations, brokerage houses, and other financial institutions) held in the name of the debtor or for the benefit of the debtor which were closed, sold, or otherwise transferred:
1) the name of the institution
2) the address of the institution
3) the name under which the account was carried
4) the type of account and the account number
5) the amount of the final balance
6) the amount and the date of the sale or closing

If no financial accounts or instruments were closed, sold, or otherwise transferred during this period, check the "none" box for question 11.

L Safe deposit boxes

See client's answers to Debtor-Client Questionnaire, Part VII, Question 12.

For the one-year period immediately preceding the commencement of this case, list each safe deposit box or other box or depository in which the debtor has or had securities, cash, or other valuables. For each box or depository, provide the following information:
1) the name of the bank or other depository
2) the address of the bank or other depository
3) the name of every person who had the right of access to the box or depository
4) the address of every person who had the right of access to the box or depository
5) a brief description of the contents
6) if the box or other depository has been transferred, state the transfer date
7) if the box or other depository has been surrendered, state the date of surrender

If the debtor did not have a safe deposit box or other box or depository which has or had securities, cash, or other valuables during this period, check the "none" box for question 12.

M Setoffs

See client's answers to Debtor-Client Questionnaire, Part VII, Question 13.

For the 90 days preceding the commencement of the case, list all setoffs made by any creditor, including a bank, against a debtor or a deposit of the debtor. If there has been such a setoff, provide the following information:
1) the name of the creditor
2) the address of the creditor
3) the date of the setoff
4) the amount of the debt owed to the creditor
5) the amount of the setoff.

See 11 U.S.C.A. § 553 for the right of setoff.

If no setoffs were made during this period, check the "none" box for question 13.

N Property held for another person

See client's answers to Debtor-Client Questionnaire, Part VII, Question 14.

List all property owned by another person that the debtor holds or controls. For each item of property held or controlled by the debtor, provide the following information:
1) the name of the owner
2) the address of the owner
3) the description of the property
4) the value of the property
5) the location of the property

If the debtor does not hold or control any property owned by another person, check the "none" box for question 14.

O Prior address of debtor

See client's answers to Debtor-Client Questionnaire, Part VII, Question 15.

If the debtor has moved within the two years immediately preceding the commencement of this case, list all premises which the debtor occupied during that period and vacated prior to the commencement of this case. For each such address of the debtor, provide the following information:

1) the former address
2) the name under which the premises were occupied
3) the dates of occupancy

If a joint petition, also state any separate address of the debtor's spouse during this period. For each separate address of the debtor's spouse, provide the following information:

1) the former address
2) the name under which the premises were occupied
3) the dates of occupancy

If the debtor or, in the case of a joint petition, the debtor and his or her spouse have not moved within this period, or the debtor's spouse has not had a separate address, check the "none" box for question 15.

P Complete questions 16–21 if the answer to any one of the following questions is "yes."

1) Is the debtor a corporation?
2) Is the debtor a partnership?
3) Is the debtor an individual debtor who is or has been, within the two years immediately preceding the commencement of this case, any of the following?
    a) an officer, director, managing executive, or owner of more than 5 percent of the voting securities of a corporation
    b) a partner, other than a limited partner, of a partnership
    c) a sole proprietor or otherwise self-employed

If the debtor has answered "no" to all three questions, check the "none" boxes for questions 16–21.

The Statement of Financial Affairs is now complete except for the unsworn declaration which follows question 21.

Q Nature, location, and name of business

See client's answers to Debtor-Client Questionnaire, Part VII, Question 16.

a. Answer this question if the debtor is filing as an individual. If question 16.a. does not apply to the debtor, check the "none" box.

1) For the two years immediately preceding the commencement of this case, list all businesses in which the debtor was an
    a) officer
    b) director
    c) partner
    d) managing executive of a
        (1) corporation
        (2) partnership
        (3) sole proprietorship

2) For the two years immediately preceding the commencement of this case, list all businesses in which the debtor was a self-employed professional.

3) For the two years immediately preceding the commencement of this case, list all businesses in which the debtor owned 5 percent or more of the voting or equity securities.

For each operation, provide the following information:

1) the name
2) the address
3) the nature of the business
4) the beginning date of operation
5) the ending date of operation

If the debtor has nothing to report for question 16.a., check the "none" box.

b. Answer this question if the debtor is filing as a partnership. If question 16.b. does not apply to the debtor, check the "none" box.

For the two years immediately preceding the commencement of this case, list all businesses in which the debtor was
1) a partner
2) owned 5 percent or more of the voting securities

For each business, provide the following information:
1) the name
2) the address
3) the nature of the business
4) the beginning date of operation
5) the ending date of operation

If the debtor has nothing to report for question 16.b., check the "none" box.

c. Answer this question if the debtor is filing as a corporation. If question 16.c. does not apply to the debtor, check the "none" box.

For the two years immediately preceding the commencement of this case, list all businesses in which the debtor was
1) a partner
2) owned 5 percent or more of the voting securities

For each business, provide the following information:
1) the name
2) the address
3) the nature of the business
4) the beginning date of operation
5) the ending date of operation

If the debtor has nothing to report for question 16.c., check the "none" box.

R Books, records, and financial statements

See client's answers to Debtor-Client Questionnaire, Part VII, Question 17.

a. Bookkeepers and accountants

For the six years immediately preceding the filing of this bankruptcy case, list all bookkeepers and accountants who kept or supervised the keeping of the debtor's account books and records. For any such bookkeeper or accountant, provide the following information:
1) the name of the bookkeeper or accountant
2) the address of the bookkeeper or accountant
3) the dates the services were rendered

If there were no bookkeepers or accountants who kept or supervised the keeping of the debtor's books of account and records during this period, check the "none" box for question 17.a.

b. Audits and preparation of financial statements

For the two years immediately preceding the filing of this bankruptcy case, list the firms or individuals who audited the books of account and records or prepared a financial statement of the debtor. For any such services, provide the following information:
1) the name of the firm or individual
2) the address of the firm or individual
3) the dates the services were rendered

If no firm or individual audited the debtor's books of account and records or prepared a financial statement of the debtor, check "none" for question 17.b.

c. Possession of books and records

Provide the following information concerning the firms or individuals who currently have possession of the debtor's books of account or records:

1) the name of the firm or individual who currently has possession of the debtor's books of account or records
2) the address of the firm or individual

If any of these books or records are unavailable, explain the circumstances surrounding the unavailability of these books or records. See 11 U.S.C.A. § 727(a)(3) concerning the relationship between the failure to preserve books and records and discharge of the debtor.

If no firm or individual was in possession of the debtor's books of account or records at the time of the commencement of this case, check the "none" box for question 17.c.

d. Financial statements

List all financial institutions, creditors and other parties (including mercantile and trade agencies) to whom a financial statement was issued within the two years immediately preceding the commencement of this case by the debtor. For each, provide the following information:
1) the name of the person receiving the written financial statement
2) the address of the person receiving the written financial statement
3) the date the financial statement was issued

If no financial statement was issued during this period, check the "none" box for question 17.d.

S Inventories

See client's answers to Debtor-Client Questionnaire, Part VII, Question 18.

a. The last two inventories

For the last two inventories of the debtor's property, provide the following information:
1) the date the inventory of the debtor's property was taken
2) whether the inventory was the last or second to last taken
3) the name of the person who took, or under whose supervision, the inventory was taken
4) the dollar amount of the inventory
5) whether the inventory was taken at cost, market, or other basis

If an inventory of the debtor's property has not been taken, check the "none" box for question 18.a.

b. Custodian of the inventory records

State the following information concerning the custodian of the inventory records for the last two inventories:
1) the name of the custodian of the records
2) the address of the custodian of the records

If an inventory has not been taken or if no one has possession of the records of the inventory, check the "none" box for question 18.b.

T Current partners, officers, directors, and shareholders

See client's answers to Debtor-Client Questionnaire, Part VII, Question 19.

a. Answer this question if the debtor is filing as a partnership. If this question is not applicable to the debtor, check the "none" box for question 19.a.

For each member of the partnership, provide the following information:
1) the name of the partner
2) the address of the partner
3) the nature of the partner's interest
4) the percentage of the partnership interest

b. Answer this question if the debtor is filing as a corporation. If this question is not applicable to the debtor, check the "none" box for question 19.b.

For each officer or director of the corporation and each stockholder who directly or indirectly owns, controls, or holds 5 percent or more of the voting securities of the corporation, provide the following information:

   1) the name of the officer, director, or stockholder
   2) the address of the officer, director, or stockholder
   3) the title of the party
   4) the nature of stock ownership
   5) the percentage of stock ownership

U Former partners, officers, directors, and shareholders

See client's answers to Debtor-Client Questionnaire, Part VII, Question 20.

a. Answer this question if the debtor is filing as a partnership. If this question is not applicable to the debtor, check the "none" box for question 20.a.

For each member of the partnership who withdrew from the partnership within one year immediately preceding the commencement of this case, provide the following information:
1) the name of the former partner
2) the address of the former partner
3) the date of withdrawal from the partnership

If no member withdrew from the partnership within one year immediately preceding the commencement of this case, check the "none" box for question 20.a.

b. Answer this question if the debtor is filing as a corporation. If this question is not applicable to the debtor, check the "none" box for question 20.b.

For each officer or director of the corporation whose relationship with the corporation terminated within one year immediately preceding the commencement of this case, provide the following information:
1) the name of the officer or director
2) the address of the officer or director
3) the title of the officer or director
4) the date of termination of the relationship with the corporation

If no officer's or director's relationship with the corporation terminated within one year immediately preceding the commencement of this case, check the "none" box for question 20.b.

V Withdrawals from a partnership or distributions by a corporation

See client's answers to Debtor-Client Questionnaire, Part VII, Question 21.

Answer this question if the debtor is filing as a partnership or as a corporation. If the debtor is an individual who must answer questions 16–21 and therefore question 21 is not applicable, check the "none" box for question 21.

For the one-year period immediately preceding the commencement of the case, list all withdrawals or distributions credited or given to an insider (including compensation in any form, bonuses, loans, stock redemptions, options exercised, or any other perquisite). For each insider recipient, provide the following information:
1) the name of the recipient
2) the address of the recipient
3) the recipient's relationship to the debtor
4) the date of the withdrawal
5) the purpose of the withdrawal
6) the amount of money withdrawn or a description of and the value of the property distributed

Question 21 relates to preferences, 11 U.S.C.A. § 547.

If there were no withdrawals or distributions credited or given to an insider during this period, check the "none" box for question 21.

The Statement of Financial Affairs is now complete except for the unsworn declaration.

W Complete the unsworn declaration

a. If the debtor is an individual or a husband and wife filing a joint petition, complete the first unsworn declaration. Review the completed Statement of Financial Affairs with the debtor or with the joint debtors if a husband and wife are filing a joint petition. Read the declaration to the debtor(s) prior to the signing. After the unsworn declaration has been signed, have the declarant(s) date the declaration with the date the declaration was signed (not the date the petition or statement will be filed or was filed).

b. If the debtor is a partnership or a corporation, the party signing on behalf of the partnership or the corporation must complete the second unsworn declaration. Type or print the name and title of the party signing on behalf of the debtor. Review the completed Statement of Financial Affairs with the party who will sign on behalf of the debtor. Read the declaration to the party signing prior to his or her signing. After the unsworn declaration has been signed, have the declarant date the declaration with the date the declaration was signed (not the date the petition or statement will be filed or was filed).

PROBLEM 5.17   Using the information in Problem 5.1 and Problem 5.7, complete the Statement of Financial Affairs for Dr. Laughlin and Dr. Richards.

I. STATEMENT OF INTENTION IF THE DEBTOR IS AN INDIVIDUAL WITH CONSUMER DEBTS

An individual debtor whose schedule of assets and liabilities includes consumer debts secured by property of the estate must file with the bankruptcy court clerk a **statement of intention** with respect to the retention or surrender of the property. (See Exhibit 5.25.) If this property is claimed as exempt, the debtor must state whether he or she intends to redeem the property or to reaffirm debts secured by the property. 11 U.S.C.A. § 521(2)(A).

On or before the filing of the statement, a copy must be served on the trustee and named creditors. Fed. R. Bank. P. 1107(b)(2). The debtor must carry out his or her intention with respect to the property in question within 45 days after filing the statement of intention. The court, for cause, may (within the 45-day period) allow additional time for the debtor to perform his or her intention. 11 U.S.C.A. § 521(2)(B).

The debtor may amend his or her statement of intention at any time before the expiration of the 45-day period (or longer period allowed by the court) for carrying out his or her intention. If the debtor wishes to amend the statement of intention, he or she must give notice of the amendment to the trustee and to any party affected by the amendment. Fed. R. Bank. P. 1009(b).

The debtor who seeks to amend his or her statement of intention may be saved from a harsh application of the 45-day limitation (or longer time limitation at the court's discretion) of Fed. R. Bank. P. 1009(b).

> The debtor shall—
>
> . . .
>
> (2) if an individual debtor's schedule of assets and liabilities includes consumer debts which are secured by property of the estate—
>
> . . .
>
> > (C) nothing in subparagraphs (A) and (B) of this paragraph shall alter the debtor's or the trustee's rights with regard to such property under this title; . . . . 11 U.S.C.A. § 521(2)(C).

The Statement of Intention Official Form No. 8—need only be completed by an individual debtor or by individual debtors (husband and wife) filing a joint petition. In the case of individual debtors filing a joint petition:

1. if the property and debts of the debtors are the same, each debtor must sign Official Form 8;

2. if the debts of the debtors are separate, each debtor must use a separate Official Form 8.

EXHIBIT 5.25
Official Form No. 8 (Chapter 7 Individual Debtor's Statement of Intention)

FORM B8
(11/94)

United States Bankruptcy Court
District of _____

In re _____   Case No. _____
                    Debtor   Chapter _____ Seven _____

CHAPTER 7 INDIVIDUAL DEBTOR'S STATEMENT OF INTENTION

1. I, the debtor, have filed a schedule of assets and liabilities which includes consumer debts secured by property of the estate.
2. My intention with respect to the property of the estate which secures those consumer debts is as follows:

   a. Property to Be Surrendered.

   Description of Property   Creditor's Name

   1. _____   **A**   _____

   2. _____   _____

   3. _____   _____

   b. Property to Be Retained. [Check applicable statement of debtor's intention concerning reaffirmation, redemption, or lien avoidance.]

Description of property	Creditor's name	Debt will be reaffirmed pursuant to § 524(c)	Property is claimed as exempt and will be redeemed pursuant to § 722	Lien will be avoided pursuant to § 522(f) and property will be claimed as exempt
1.	**B**		**C**	
2.				
3.				
4.				
5.				

3. I understand that § 521(2)(B) of the Bankruptcy Code requires that I perform the above stated intention within 45 days of the filing of this statement with the court, or within such additional time as the court, for cause, within such 45-day period fixes.

Date: _____   **D**   _____
                                             Signature of Debtor

Date: _____   _____
                                             Signature of Joint Debtor

CERTIFICATION AND SIGNATURE OF NON-ATTORNEY BANKRUPTCY PETITION PREPARER (See 11 U.S.C. § 110)

I certify that I am a bankruptcy petition preparer as defined in 11 U.S.C. §110, that I prepared this document for compensation, and that I have provided the debtor with a copy of this document.

_____   _____
Printed or Typed Name of Bankruptcy Petition Preparer   Social Security No.

_____
Address

Names and Social Security numbers of all other individuals who prepared or assisted in preparing this document:

If more than one person prepared this document, attach additional signed sheets conforming to the appropriate Official form for each person.

X_____   _____
Signature of Bankruptcy Petition Preparer   Date

A bankruptcy petition preparer's failure to comply with the provisions of title 11 and the Federal Rules of Bankruptcy Procedure may result in fines or imprisonment or both. 11 U.S.C. §110, 18 U.S.C. §156.

© 1995 WEST PUBLISHING COMPANY

Instructions for Completing Official Form No. 8 (Chapter 7 Individual Debtor's Statement of Intention)

A Describe the property to be surrendered. Use the description as it appears in Schedule A or Schedule B. State the creditor's name as it appears in Schedule A or Schedule B.

B Describe the property to be retained. Use the description as it appears in Schedule A or Schedule B. State the creditor's name as it appears in Schedule A or Schedule B.

C Select the applicable statement of the debtor's intention by placing a check mark under the selected statement:

1. the debt will be reaffirmed pursuant to 11 U.S.C.A. § 524(c);

2. the Property is claimed as exempt and will be redeemed pursuant to 11 U.S.C.A. § 722;

3. the lien will be avoided pursuant to 11 U.S.C.A. § 522(f) and property will be claimed as exempt.

D The debtor signs his or her name as it appears on the petition. The debtor also dates the statement of intention.

> **PROBLEM 5.18**   Complete the statement of intention for Dr. Laughlin and Dr. Richards using the information found in Problem 5.1 and Problem 5.7.

J. DEBTOR'S DUTY TO SUPPLEMENT THE SCHEDULES

The commencement of the case under Chapter 7 creates the estate, which consists of all property owned by the debtor as of the date of the filing of the petition. The Code provides that in some instances, although the frequency of occurrence is small, property acquired by the debtor after the filing of the petition may also become property of the estate.

> (a) The commencement of a case under section 301, 302, or 303 of this title creates an estate. Such estate is comprised of all the following property, wherever located and by whomever held:
>
> . . .
>
> (5) Any interest in property that would have been property of the estate if such interest had been an interest of the debtor on the date of the filing of the petition, and that the debtor acquires or becomes entitled to acquire within 180 days after such date—
>
> (A) by bequest, devise, or inheritance;
>
> (B) as a result of a property settlement agreement with the debtor's spouse, or of an interlocutory or final divorce decree; or
>
> (C) as a beneficiary of a life insurance policy or of a death benefit plan. 11 U.S.C.A. § 541(a)(5).

If the debtor acquires this property after the schedule of assets has been filed, the debtor must file a supplemental schedule listing the after-acquired property. This supplemental schedule must be filed "within 10 days after the information comes to the debtor's knowledge or within such further time as the court may allow . . . . If any of the property required to be reported under this subdivision is claimed by the debtor as exempt, the debtor shall claim the exemptions in the supplemental schedule." Fed. R. Bank. P. 1007(h).

The debtor's duty to file a supplemental schedule continues even though the case has been closed if the debtor's duty to file arose before the case was closed, and the case was closed before the duty was or could be performed. Fed. R. Bank. P. 1007(h).

K. DEBTOR'S RIGHT TO AMEND THE PETITION, LISTS, SCHEDULES, AND STATEMENTS

A problem more common than after-acquired property involves errors in the documents filed. The errors may involve property or obligations that existed at the time of filing the petition that should have been listed on the various lists, schedules, or statements. The debtor may have forgotten about certain assets or debts or may have misunderstood the attorney's or the paralegal's instructions about what should be included in the lists, schedules, or statements. The attorney or the paralegal may have misunderstood the debtor when the lists, schedules, and statements were being prepared.

The Federal Rules of Bankruptcy Procedure authorize the debtor to amend.

> A voluntary petition, list, schedule, or statement may be amended by the debtor as a matter of course at any time before the case is closed. The debtor shall give notice of the amendment to the trustee and to any entity affected thereby. Fed. R. Bank. P. 1009(a).

After the notice has been given, if parties affected by the amendment do not challenge the debtor's right to make the amendment or do not bring a motion for disallowance of a claimed exemption, the petition, lists, schedules, or statements will stand as amended. If, however, the amendment would prejudice a party in interest, the court may refuse to let the debtor amend.

SECTION 2

The Significance of Filing a Petition

Once the petition for bankruptcy has been filed and the bankruptcy estate is created, the debtor's interest in the property ceases. Therefore, if the debtor dies while the case is pending, only property exempted from the bankruptcy estate, abandoned by the trustee, or acquired after commencement of the case (and not included as property of the estate) will be available to the representative of the debtor's probate estate. The bankruptcy proceeding will continue as it relates to the property of the bankruptcy estate. 11 U.S.C.A. § 541.

> **PROBLEM 5.19**   On March 1, Donald Duncan filed a petition under Chapter 7 of the Bankruptcy Code. Two months later, Donald died intestate, leaving a wife and two children.
>
> Will the property of Donald's bankruptcy estate be divided among his creditors or among his widow and children?

In a Chapter 7 case, the trustee in bankruptcy collects and sells the "property of the estate." 11 U.S.C.A. § 704. The trustee then distributes the proceeds from the sale among the creditors. 11 U.S.C.A. § 726. The larger the estate, the more the debtor gives up and the more the trustee sells. The more the trustee sells, the more there is to divide among the creditors. The debtor may be discharged from his or her outstanding obligations and receive a "fresh start" *during* this process of "reallocation of wealth."

A. THE ORDER FOR RELIEF

The commencement of a voluntary case under Chapter 7 by a single debtor or by joint debtors (i.e., the filing of the petition with the bankruptcy court) constitutes an

order for relief under Chapter 7. 11 U.S.C.A. §§ 301, 302. The clerk will affix a filing stamp showing the date and time filed and the court in which the petition was filed. The petition is stamped with a case number at this time.

B. THE ESTATE IS CREATED

Upon the filing of a bankruptcy petition, an **estate in bankruptcy** is automatically created. 11 U.S.C.A. § 541(a). This estate includes all legal and equitable interests of the debtor, with minor exceptions. 11 U.S.C.A. §§ 541(b), (c)(2). The debtor may claim certain property of the estate as exempt. This exempt property is then removed from the bankruptcy estate. Other items of property of the estate may be abandoned by the trustee in bankruptcy. The remaining assets of the estate will be subject to administration by the bankruptcy trustee for the benefit of creditors. (See Exhibit 5.26.)

EXHIBIT 5.26
Creating the Estate

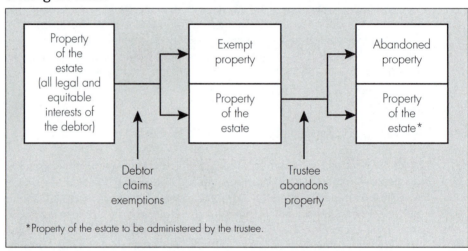

*Property of the estate to be administered by the trustee.

1. PROPERTY OF THE ESTATE

Property is generally defined as those things capable of being the subject of ownership. Ownership is the right of a person to possess and use a thing to the exclusion of others.

Property is generally classified as being either real or personal. Real property is land and those things that are permanently affixed to land. Personal property is all property not classified as real property and may be tangible or intangible.

EXAMPLE
Jane wrote a song and went through the copyright process. Jane owns both the physical paper on which the song is written and the copyright. The paper on which the song is written is tangible property. The copyright is intangible property.

PROBLEM 5.20   Craig, a building contractor, remodeled Matthew's house. On completion of the work, Craig presented Matthew with a bill for $2,500. Is this account receivable tangible or intangible property?

An interest in property may be a present or a future interest. A present interest entitles the owner to an immediate right to possess the property. A future interest entitles the owner to a right to possess the property at some future time.

EXAMPLE
William promised his sister Alice that if she would promise to live in his house and care for him for the remainder of his life, he would give her the house in fee simple. If Alice promises William, a contract is formed. Alice has a future interest in William's house. Alice may not claim William's house until William dies.

PROBLEM 5.21   Martha has three daughters named Amanda, Beth, and Carrie. Each would like to use Martha's beach house in Hawaii. Each daughter has a large family and does not want to share the beach house with her sisters. Martha decided that she would allow each daughter to use the beach house for four months during the year. The dates were allocated by lot. Amanda drew January through April. Beth drew May through August. Carrie drew September through December.

The date is today's date. Who has a present interest and who has a future interest? Assume that this arrangement is to continue for five years.

EXAMPLE
Catherine owns Greenacre which she has leased to Donald for 10 years. Both Catherine and Donald have an interest in Greenacre. Catherine has a fee simple interest subject to Donald's 10-year lease. Donald's 10-year lease interest is a present possessory interest. Catherine has a present ownership interest. Catherine's right to possession is a future interest.

An interest in property may be entire or concurrent. Concurrent owners share ownership of the same interest in property.

EXAMPLE
Charles and Agnes, husband and wife, purchased Blackacre "as joint tenants and not as tenants in common, together with the right of survivorship." During their lives, both Charles and Agnes own Blackacre. If Charles dies first, Agnes is freed from Charles's claim and continues in her full ownership capacity. During the lives of the joint tenants, their interests in Blackacre are concurrent.

The property of a bankruptcy estate may include both real and personal property. Although federal bankruptcy law provides a system for dealing with property interests, it does not define the nature of the debtor's interest in property. To determine whether the debtor has an interest in property, the paralegal or the attorney must look at nonbankruptcy law which is primarily state law.

The "property of the estate" includes all legal or equitable interests of the debtor in property held by the debtor at the time of the filing of the petition. Section 541(a) itemizes what is included as "property of the estate" and is very inclusive.

(a) The commencement of a case under section 301, 302, or 303 of this title creates an estate. Such estate is comprised of all the following property, wherever located and by whomever held:
   (1) Except as provided in subsections (b) and (c)(2) of this section, all legal or equitable interests of the debtor in property as of the commencement of the case.

(2) All interests of the debtor and the debtor's spouse in community property as of the commencement of the case that is—

(A) under the sole, equal, or joint management and control of the debtor; or

(B) liable for an allowable claim against the debtor, or for both an allowable claim against the debtor and an allowable claim against the debtor's spouse, to the extent that such interest is so liable.

(3) Any interest in property that the trustee recovers under section 329(b), 363(n), 543, 550, 553, or 723 of this title.

(4) Any interest in property preserved for the benefit of or ordered transferred to the estate under section 510(c) or 551 of this title.

(5) Any interest in property that would have been property of the estate if such interest had been an interest of the debtor on the date of the filing of the petition, and that the debtor acquires or becomes entitled to acquire within 180 days after such date—

(A) by bequest, devise, or inheritance;

(B) as a result of a property settlement agreement with the debtor's spouse, or of an interlocutory or final divorce decree; or

(C) as a beneficiary of a life insurance policy or of a death benefit plan.

(6) Proceeds, product, offspring, rents, or profits of or from property of the estate, except such as are earnings from services performed by an individual debtor after the commencement of the case.

(7) Any interest in property that the estate acquires after the commencement of the case.

(b) Property of the estate does not include—

(1) any power that the debtor may exercise solely for the benefit of an entity other than the debtor;

(2) any interest of the debtor as a lessee under a lease of nonresidential real property that has terminated at the expiration of the stated term of such lease before the commencement of the case under this title, and ceases to include any interest of the debtor as a lessee under a lease of nonresidential real property that has terminated at the expiration of the stated term of such lease during the case;

(3) any eligibility of the debtor to participate in programs authorized under the Higher Education Act of 1965 (20 U.S.C. 1001 et seq.; 42 U.S.C. 2751 et seq.), or any accreditation status or State licensure of the debtor as an educational institution;

(4) any interest of the debtor in liquid or gaseous hydrocarbons to the extent that—

(A) (i) the debtor has transferred or has agreed to transfer such interest pursuant to a farmout agreement or any written agreement directly related to a farmout agreement; and

(ii) but for the operation of this paragraph, the estate could include the interest referred to in clause (i) only by virtue of section 365 or 544(a)(3) of this title; or

(B) (i) the debtor has transferred such interest pursuant to a written conveyance of a production payment to an entity that does not participate in the operation of the property from which such production payment is transferred; and

(ii) but for the operation of this paragraph, the estate could include the interest referred to in clause (i) only by virtue of section 542 of this title;

Paragraph (4) shall not be construed to exclude from the estate any consideration the debtor retains, receives, or is entitled to receive for transferring an interest in liquid or gaseous hydrocarbons pursuant to a farmout agreement; or

(5) any interest in cash or cash equivalents that constitute proceeds of a sale by the debtor of a money order that is made—

(A) on or after the date that is 14 days prior to the date on which the petition if filed; and

(B) under an agreement with a money order issuer that prohibits the commingling of such proceeds with property of the debtor (notwithstanding that, contrary to the agreement, the proceeds may have been commingled with property of the debtor), unless the money order issuer had not taken action, prior to the filing of the petition, to require compliance with the prohibition.

(c) (1) Except as provided in paragraph (2) of this subsection, an interest of the debtor in property becomes property of the estate under subsection (a)(1), (a)(2), or (a)(5) of this section notwithstanding any provision in an agreement, transfer instrument, or applicable nonbankruptcy law—

(A) that restricts or conditions transfer of such interest by the debtor; or

(B) that is conditioned on the insolvency or financial condition of the debtor, on the commencement of a case under this title, or on the appointment of or taking possession by a trustee in a case under this title or a custodian before such commencement and that effects or gives an option to effect a forfeiture, modification, or termination of the debtor's interest in property.

(2) A restriction on the transfer of a beneficial interest of the debtor in a trust that is enforceable under applicable nonbankruptcy law is enforceable in a case under this title.

(d) Property in which the debtor holds, as of the commencement of the case, only legal title and not an equitable interest, such as a mortgage secured by real property, or an interest in such a mortgage, sold by the debtor but as to which the debtor retains legal title to service or supervise the servicing of such mortgage or interest, becomes property of the estate under subsection (a)(1) or (2) of this section only to the extent of the debtor's legal title to such property, but not to the extent of any equitable interest in such property that the debtor does not hold. 11 U.S.C.A. § 541.

Only six very limited classes of property do not become property of the estate. The first is "any power that the debtor may exercise solely for the benefit of an entity other than the debtor." 11 U.S.C.A. § 541(b)(1).

PROBLEM 5.22   Brenda Cherry filed a petition for bankruptcy under Chapter 7 listing as one of her assets the premises located at 5035 Green Street, Philadelphia, Pennsylvania. The title to this property, however, was in the name of Brenda Cherry as "Executrix of the Estate of Virginia Cherry, deceased."

Is this realty the property of Brenda Cherry's estate?

The second is "any interest of the debtor as a lessee under a lease of nonresidential real property that has terminated at the expiration of the stated term of such lease before the commencement of the case." 11 U.S.C.A. § 541(b)(2). Because the property of the estate will be liquidated, this limitation seldom occurs in a Chapter 7 case.

The third is "any eligibility of the debtor to participate in programs authorized under the Higher Education Act of 1965 (20 U.S.C. § 1001; 42 U.S.C. § 2751), or any accreditation status or State licensure of the debtor as an educational institution." 11 U.S.C.A. § 541(b)(3).

The fourth is "any interest of the debtor in liquid or gaseous hydrocarbons" within the limitations set forth in the section. 11 U.S.C.A. § 541(a)(4).

The fifth is "any interest in cash or cash equivalents that constitute proceeds of a sale by the debtor of a money order that is made" under certain circumstances. 11 U.S.C.A. § 541(a)(5).

The sixth is "[a] restriction on the transfer of a beneficial interest of the debtor in a trust that is enforceable under applicable nonbankruptcy law." 11 U.S.C.A. § 541(c)(2).

EXAMPLE

When Horace Hemphill died testate, he left his entire estate to his only child, Maxwell. Because Horace was concerned that Maxwell would squander his inheritance, Horace did not give his estate to Maxwell outright but created a spendthrift trust instead. Under the terms of the trust, the trustee would determine how much money Maxwell should receive from the interest and principal and when he should receive it.

Shortly after Horace's death, Maxwell filed a petition in bankruptcy. Under 11 U.S.C.A. § 541(c)(2), the spendthrift trust was not property of the estate. The restriction on the transfer of Maxwell's interest in the trust, which was enforceable under state law was also enforceable under bankruptcy law. The spendthrift trust therefore continues even though Maxwell has filed a petition in bankruptcy.

2. LOCATION OF PROPERTY

The United States bankruptcy court in which a bankruptcy case is filed has exclusive jurisdiction over the property of the debtor, regardless of where the property is located.

> (e) The district court in which a case under title 11 is commenced or is pending shall have exclusive jurisdiction of all of the property, wherever located, of the debtor as of the commencement of such case, and of property of the estate. 28 U.S.C.A. § 1334(e).

EXAMPLE

Darla Ravenswood, whose domicile is Nashville, Tennessee, filed a petition in bankruptcy in the United States Bankruptcy Court for the Middle District of Tennessee. Darla owns property in Nashville and Chattanooga, Tennessee, and in Florida, California, and New York. Nashville and Chattanooga are located in the Middle and Eastern Districts of Tennessee, respectively. The United States Bankruptcy Court for the Middle District of Tennessee has exclusive jurisdiction over Darla's property, regardless of whether it is located in the Middle or Eastern Districts of Tennessee or in Florida, California, or New York.

PROBLEM 5.23   Delores Montague, whose domicile is Denver, Colorado, has property in Denver and in Melbourne, Australia. Delores files her petition in bankruptcy in the United States Bankruptcy Court for the District of Colorado.

Is Delores's property in Melbourne property of the estate?

Does the United States Bankruptcy Court for the District of Colorado have jurisdiction over Delores's property in Melbourne?

3. PROPERTY ACQUIRED AFTER FILING THE PETITION

In addition to the property in which the debtor owns an interest at the time of the filing of the bankruptcy petition, the estate of the debtor includes

> (5) Any interest in property that would have been property of the estate if such interest had been an interest of the debtor on the date of the filing of the petition, and that the debtor acquires or becomes entitled to acquire within 180 days after such date—
>
> (A) by bequest, devise, or inheritance;
>
> (B) as a result of a property settlement agreement with the debtor's spouse, or of an interlocutory or final divorce decree; or
>
> (C) as a beneficiary of a life insurance policy or of a death benefit plan. 11 U.S.C.A. § 541(a)(5).

Federal Rules of Bankruptcy Procedure 1007(h) implements 11 U.S.C.A. § 541(a)(5) by requiring the debtor to file a supplemental schedule.

(h) Interests Acquired or Arising After Petition. If, as provided by § 541(a)(5) of the Code, the debtor acquires or becomes entitled to acquire any interest in property, the debtor shall within 10 days after the information comes to the debtor's knowledge or within such further time the court may allow, file a supplemental schedule in the chapter 7 liquidation case . . . . If any of the property required to be reported under this subdivision is claimed by the debtor as exempt, the debtor shall claim the exemptions in the supplemental schedule. The duty to file a supplemental schedule in accordance with this subdivision continues notwithstanding the closing of the case . . . .

EXAMPLE

On June 1, the debtor files for bankruptcy under Chapter 7. On July 1, the debtor's father dies and leaves his son $100,000 in his will.

Because the debtor acquired his interest in the $100,000 by devise within 180 days of his filing the bankruptcy petition, the $100,000 becomes property of the estate and the debtor is required to file a supplemental schedule. 11 U.S.C.A. § 541(a)(5)(A); Fed. R. Bank. P. 1007(h).

EXAMPLE

On February 1, the debtor and his spouse were divorced. The divorce decree provides that the debtor and his former spouse will equally divide the proceeds from the sale of their home. On June 1, the debtor filed for bankruptcy under Chapter 7. On July 1, the house was sold for $150,000.

Because the debtor acquired his interest in the $75,000 as a result of the property settlement agreement within 180 days of his filing the bankruptcy petition, the $75,000 becomes property of the estate and the debtor is required to file a supplemental schedule. 11 U.S.C.A. § 541(a)(5)(B); Fed. R. Bank. P. 1007(h).

EXAMPLE

On June 1, the debtor filed for bankruptcy under Chapter 7. On August 1, the debtor's mother died and named him as the sole beneficiary under her $40,000 life insurance policy.

Because the debtor acquired his interest in the $40,000 as a result of being the beneficiary of his mother's life insurance policy and this interest arose within 180 days of his filing the bankruptcy petition, the $40,000 becomes property of the estate and the debtor is required to file a supplemental schedule. 11 U.S.C.A. § 541(a)(5)(C); Fed. R. Bank. P. 1007(h).

Consistent with the idea of a fresh start, earnings from services performed by an individual debtor after the commencement of the case are excluded from the bankruptcy estate.

(a) The commencement of a case under section 301, 302, or 303 of this title creates an estate. Such estate is comprised of all the following property, wherever located and by whomever held:

. . . .

(6) Proceeds, product, offspring, rents, or profits of or from property of the estate, except such as are earnings from services performed by an individual debtor after the commencement of the case. 11 U.S.C.A. § 541(a)(6).

EXAMPLE

Dawn Darling, a professional singer, filed a petition in bankruptcy on Friday, January 16. During February, Dawn worked at the Pink Kitty Kat Lounge and earned $6,000. These earnings are excluded from the bankruptcy estate.

PROBLEM 5.24   Dawn's previous job began on Friday, January 2, and ended on Thursday, January 29. She earned $6,000 which was paid in one lump sum when she completed her last performance on January 29.

Are all or some of these earnings excluded from the bankruptcy estate?

4. CONTRACTUAL PROVISIONS LIMITING TRANSFERABILITY OF PROPERTY

At times a contract may attempt to place a restriction on the transferability of property if a bankruptcy petition is filed. According to the terms of the contract, the debtor's property interest in the contract is forfeited upon the filing of the bankruptcy petition.

EXAMPLE

An illustration of the type of provisions often found in franchise agreements follows:

> Unless the Company promptly after discovery of the relevant facts notifies Franchisee to the contrary in writing, the Franchise will immediately terminate without notice (or at the earliest time permitted by applicable law) if
>
> (1) Franchisee becomes insolvent or is unable to pay its debts as they become due, Franchisee is adjudicated bankrupt, or files a petition or pleading under the federal bankruptcy law or under any other state or federal bankruptcy or insolvency laws, or an involuntary petition is filed with respect to Franchisee under any such laws and is not dismissed within 60 days after it is filed, or a permanent or temporary receiver or trustee for the Company or all or substantially all of Franchisee's property is appointed by any court, or any such appointment is acquiesced in, consented to, or not opposed through legal action, by Franchisee, or Franchisee makes a general assignment for the benefit of creditors or makes a written statement to the effect that Franchisee is unable to pay its debts as they become due, or a levy, execution, or attachment remains on all or a substantial part of the Company or of Franchisee's assets for 30 days, or Franchisee fails, within 60 days of the entry of a final judgment against Franchisee in any amount exceeding $50,000, to discharge, vacate or reverse the judgment, or to stay execution of it, or if appealed, to discharge the judgment within 30 days after a final adverse decision in the appeal.

EXAMPLE

Debbie Foy owns and operates Sunshine Burgers, a fast-food restaurant, under a franchise agreement with the parent company, Sunshine Burgers, Inc. The franchise agreement contains a provision rendering the agreement nontransferable and voiding the franchise in the event Debbie files a bankruptcy petition or a bankruptcy petition is filed against Debbie.

The purpose for this restriction is to prevent third parties from dictating what property will or will not go into a bankruptcy estate and thereby be subject to bankruptcy protection and administration. Section 541 curtails the effectiveness of such a restriction on the transferability of property and voids the effect of any forfeiture provided for in this clause.

> (c)(1) . . . an interest of the debtor in property becomes property of the estate . . . notwithstanding any provision in an agreement . . .
>> (B) that is conditioned on the insolvency or financial condition of the debtor, on the commencement of a case under this title, or on the appointment of or taking possession by a trustee in a case under this title or a custodian before such commencement and that effects or gives an option to effect a forfeiture, modification, or termination of the debtor's interest in property. 11 U.S.C.A. § 541(c)(1)(B).

Section 541(c)(1)(B), in effect, eliminates the clause restricting the transferability of the property from the contract. The remainder of the contract is then enforceable.

PROBLEM 5.25   If Debbie Foy files a petition in bankruptcy, does her fast-food restaurant franchise become property of the estate?

5. POSSESSION AND CONTROL OF PROPERTY OF THE ESTATE

The Bankruptcy Code defines property of the estate without regard to possession. 11 U.S.C.A. § 541. It is, of course, essential that the trustee obtain possession and control of the property of the estate in order to properly administer the estate in liquidation cases. The trustee has the right to proceed in the bankruptcy case to recover the property of the estate from persons other than custodians. 11 U.S.C.A. § 542. In the event any property of the estate is in the possession of a custodian, the trustee has the right to recover that property as well. 11 U.S.C.A. § 543.

C. EXEMPTIONS

At the time of the filing of the petition in bankruptcy, the debtor's bankruptcy estate includes all the debtor's property, whether nonexempt or exempt. 11 U.S.C.A. § 541. The debtor, however, is permitted to exempt certain property from the property of the estate. 11 U.S.C.A. § 522. By permitting exemptions, the Bankruptcy Code enables the debtor to keep those assets needed for a fresh start. "Exempt property" refers to property protected from seizure by either a creditor or the trustee in bankruptcy.

1. EXEMPTIONS UNDER THE BANKRUPTCY CODE: STATE VS. FEDERAL EXEMPTIONS

The Bankruptcy Act of 1898 provided that the bankrupt was entitled to those exemptions authorized under the state law of his or her domicile and under nonbankruptcy federal law. There were no exemptions under the Bankruptcy Act itself. The policy supporting this scheme of exemptions drew substantial criticism, primarily on the basis that it had a tendency to render the bankruptcy law itself nonuniform and, in effect, gave a different meaning to "fresh start" depending on the domicile of the debtor. The lawmakers and writers felt that the policy of bankruptcy law as it related to a fresh start was rendered ineffective in those states with inadequate exemption laws. One proposal put forward in connection with the debates on the Bankruptcy Reform Act of 1978 urged a preemptive federal exemption law. The scheme of the old law, however, had substantial support. The legislation finally adopted in the Bankruptcy Code was a compromise.

The provision adopted relating to the debtor's exemptions, 11 U.S.C.A. § 522, gave the debtor a choice between the state exemption laws and the federal nonbankruptcy exemption laws on the one hand and a "laundry list" of federal bankruptcy exemptions on the other. A listing of some of the nonbankruptcy exemptions is found in the Historical and Revision Notes following 11 U.S.C.A. § 522.

All debtors, however, would not ultimately receive this choice. One important qualification in 11 U.S.C.A. § 522 permits individual states to "opt out" of the federal bankruptcy exemption alternative of 11 U.S.C.A. § 522(d). Any state legislature could, by the terms of 11 U.S.C.A. § 522(b)(1), forbid election of the exemptions available under 11 U.S.C.A. § 522(d) by its citizens.

EXAMPLE

The following Wyoming provision illustrates the statutory language one state used to "opt out."

> In accordance with section 522(b)(2) of the Bankruptcy Reform Act of 1978, 11 U.S.C. § 522(b)(1) [11 U.S.C. § 522(b)(2)], the exemptions from property of the estate in bankruptcy provided in 11 U.S.C. § 522(d) are not authorized in cases where Wyoming law is applicable on the date of the filing of the petition and the debtor's domicile has been located in Wyoming for the one hundred eighty (180) days immediately preceding the date of the filing of the petition or for a longer portion of the one hundred eighty (180) day period than in any other place. Wyoming Stat. Ann. 1–20–109 (1987 Cum. Supp.).

Thirty-seven states have chosen to opt out of the federal bankruptcy exemption alternative:

Alabama	Kansas	North Carolina
Alaska	Kentucky	North Dakota
Arizona	Louisiana	Ohio
Arkansas	Maine	Oklahoma
California	Maryland	Oregon
Colorado	Mississippi	South Carolina
Delaware	Missouri	South Dakota
Florida	Montana	Tennessee
Georgia	Nebraska	Utah
Idaho	Nevada	Virginia
Illinois	New Hampshire	West Virginia
Indiana	New York	Wyoming
Iowa		

In those states that have opted out, the debtor must depend on the generosity of the exemptions of the debtor's state of domicile and the federal nonbankruptcy exemptions.

EXAMPLE

Oklahoma and Missouri have opted out of federal bankruptcy exemptions. Under Oklahoma law, if the homestead is outside a city or town, the debtor may exempt a homestead of up to 160 acres, regardless of value. If, however, the homestead is inside a city or town, the debtor may exempt a homestead of up to 1 acre as long as the value of the homestead does not exceed $5,000, but in no event could the homestead be reduced to less than 1/4 acre, regardless of value. Okla. Stat. Ann. tit. 31, § 2 (West 1991). Under Missouri law, the debtor may exempt a homestead with an $8,000 value limitation. Vernon's Ann. Mo. Stat. § 513.475 (Supp. 1995).

If a husband and a wife file a joint case in a state that has *not* opted out of the federal bankruptcy exemptions (11 U.S.C.A. § 522(d)), both must elect the same option. A wife may not elect to exempt property under 522(d) if her husband elects to exempt property under the state exemptions, or vice versa. If the debtors cannot agree on the option to be elected, they will be deemed to have elected the federal bankruptcy exemptions. 11 U.S.C.A. § 522(b).

PROBLEM 5.26   Danielle and Donald Dailey of Santa Fe, New Mexico, filed a joint petition for bankruptcy under Chapter 7 of the Bankruptcy Code. New Mexico has not opted out of the federal bankruptcy exemptions. The debtors may elect to exempt property under 522(d) or under the New Mexico exemption laws. Danielle and Donald cannot agree on which set of exemptions to claim. Danielle wants to claim the federal bankruptcy exemptions while Donald wants to claim the New Mexico exemptions. If the parties cannot agree on which set of exemptions to elect, which exemptions will apply?

Could Danielle and Donald elect some exemptions from the New Mexico exemptions and some from 522(d)?

Would your answer to the original question be different if Danielle and Donald Dailey were domiciled in Omaha, Nebraska, rather than in Santa Fe, New Mexico?

If the federal bankruptcy exemptions apply, the term "dependent" used throughout section 522 is defined in 11 U.S.C.A. § 522(a)(1) as including the debtor's spouse, whether or not he or she is actually dependent. Also, the term "value" used throughout section 522 is defined in 11 U.S.C.A. § 522(a)(2) to mean the fair market value. The "value" is assessed as of the date the property becomes property of the estate, whether it is at the time the petition is filed or at a later date.

PROBLEM 5.27 Dorothy and Dennis Taylor have filed a joint petition in bankruptcy under Chapter 7. Their estate consists of the following items:

1. A homestead valued at $85,000 that has a $55,000 mortgage
2. A lake house valued at $65,000
3. Three motor vehicles (Dorothy's car valued at $7,000; Dennis's car valued at $4,000; and Dennis's truck valued at $3,500, which he uses for business)
4. A pet dog named Alphie valued at $400
5. Household items valued at $14,000
6. Clothing valued at $15,000
7. Dennis's trombone valued at $625
8. Dorothy's drums valued at $1,250
9. Household furniture valued at $15,000
10. Refrigerator valued at $250
11. Office furniture valued at $10,000
12. A diamond ring valued at $5,000
13. One man's and one woman's watch valued at $300 each
14. Tools of the trade valued at $2,500
15. $50,000 life insurance policy on Dorothy's life with loan value of $1,200
16. Dorothy's hearing aid valued at $350
17. Dennis's monthly check of $600 from his profit-sharing plan
18. Dorothy's personal injury claim against Ace Cleaners, Inc., which arose out of an automobile accident involving an Ace employee (claim includes compensatory damages as well as damages for pain and suffering)

Can Dorothy and Dennis claim any of these items and, if so, how much of each, under their 522(d) exemptions?

Property may be exempt even if it is subject to a lien or security interest, but only the unencumbered portion of the property can be counted as the "value" of the property for purposes of exemption. (This is significant only if the debtor is dealing with a value-type exemption and not an item-type exemption; e.g., $3,000 vs. 1/4 acre.)

EXAMPLE

Denny Vernon has filed a petition in bankruptcy under Chapter 7. Her residence, valued at $100,000, has a $95,000 mortgage. Under 522(d)(1), Denny is entitled to only $5,000 of the $15,000 exemption on her residence, the difference between its value and the mortgage.

PROBLEM 5.28 If the mortgage in the previous Example is only $75,000, how much is Denny's exemption under 522(d)(1)?

If a state has not opted out of the federal exemptions provided in 11 U.S.C.A. § 522(d) of the Bankruptcy Code, the debtor may choose these exemptions or the other federal law exemptions he or she is entitled to (exemptions found in U.S.C.A. sections other than 11 U.S.C.A. § 522(d) of the Bankruptcy Code) and the exemptions permitted under the laws of the state of his or her domicile. If the state has opted out of the federal Bankruptcy Code exemptions provided in 11 U.S.C.A. § 522(d), then this debtor has no choice and is entitled to only the other federal law exemptions and the exemptions permitted under the laws of the state of his or her domicile. (See Exhibit 5.27.)

EXHIBIT 5.27
Opting Out of Federal Bankruptcy Exemptions

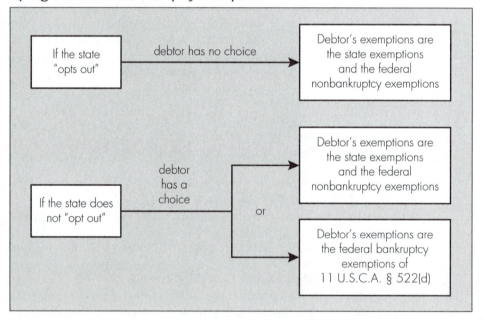

In August 1976, the Commissioners on Uniform State Laws promulgated the Uniform Exemptions Act. Only one state, Alaska, has enacted this act. Alaska Stat. 09.38.010–09.38.510.

PROBLEM 5.29 Compare the exemptions available in your state with the exemptions provided by 11 U.S.C.A. § 522(d). What are the similarities and the differences?

Although exempt property is protected from most prepetition claims, it is not shielded from all such claims. Under 11 U.S.C.A. § 522(c), exempt property is not protected from tax claims; valid liens; alimony, maintenance, or support claims that are excepted from discharge; and claims that are based on a commitment of the debtor to maintain the capital of an insured depository institution.

EXAMPLE

Charles Lincoln has a prepetition divorce decree that contains provisions for child support. Several months after the decree was entered, Charles filed a petition for bankruptcy under Chapter 7. His postpetition wages, which would normally be exempt, are not exempt as to the collection of the child support.

The Bankruptcy Code protects the debtor's exemptions by permitting the debtor to avoid certain liens on exempt property. The debtor may avoid a judicial lien on any property to the extent that the property could have been exempted in the absence of the lien.

> (f)(1) Notwithstanding any waiver of exemptions, but subject to paragraph (3), the debtor may avoid the fixing of a lien on an interest of the debtor in property to the extent that such lien impairs an exemption to which the debtor would have been entitled under subsection (b) of this section, if such lien is—
> (A) a judicial lien . . . . 11 U.S.C.A. § 522(f)(1)(A).

Under the Bankruptcy Reform Act of 1994, the debtor may no longer avoid a judicial lien impairing an exemption for alimony, maintenance, or support secured by the lien. 11 U.S.C.A. § 522(f)(1)(A). "Lien" means charge against or interest in property to secure payment of a debt or performance of an obligation. 11 U.S.C.A. § 101(37). "Judicial lien" means lien obtained by judgment, levy, sequestration, or other legal or equitable process or proceeding. 11 U.S.C.A. § 101(36).

> **PROBLEM 5.30**   Frank Farragut sued Shirley Yancy in state court for breach of contract and recovered a judgment. Farragut recorded the judgment in the land records in the county clerk's office. The judgment now appears against Yancy's homestead.
> After learning about the recordation, Yancy can quiet title in state court because the recording of the judgment is not technically a lien against the homestead.
> If Yancy files a petition in bankruptcy under Chapter 7, can she avoid the judgment under 11 U.S.C.A. § 522(f)(1)?

The debtor also may avoid a nonpossessory, nonpurchase money security interest in certain household and personal goods.

> (f)(1) Notwithstanding any waiver of exemptions, but subject to paragraph (3), the debtor may avoid the fixing of a lien on an interest of the debtor in property to the extent that such lien impairs an exemption to which the debtor would have been entitled under subsection (b) of this section, if such lien is—
> . . .
> (B) a nonpossessory, nonpurchase money security interest in any—
>   (i) household furnishings, household goods, wearing apparel, appliances, books, animals, crops, musical instruments, or jewelry that are held primarily for the personal, family, or household use of the debtor or a dependent of the debtor;
>   (ii) implements, professional books, or tools, of the trade of the debtor or the trade of a dependent of the debtor; or
>   (iii) professionally prescribed health aids for the debtor or a dependent of the debtor. 11 U.S.C.A. § 522(f)(1)(B).

A security interest is a purchase money security interest when it complies with the definition of "purchase money security interest" in the Uniform Commercial Code.

A security interest is a "purchase money security interest" to the extent that it is
(a) taken or retained by the seller of the collateral to secure all or part of its price; or
(b) taken by a person who by making advances or incurring an obligation gives value to enable the debtor to acquire rights in or the use of collateral if such value is in fact so used. UCC § 9–107.

EXAMPLE

John and Agnes Anderson purchased a four-piece living room suite on credit from the Blue Sky Furniture Company. The Andersons gave Blue Sky a security interest in the living room suite. Blue Sky has a purchase money security interest in the living room suite under UCC § 9–107(a) because the seller (Blue Sky) took a security interest in the living room suite to secure at least a part of its purchase price.

EXAMPLE

John and Agnes Anderson purchased a four-piece living room suite from the Blue Sky Furniture Company. In order to finance the purchase, the Andersons obtained a loan from Friendly Finance Company. The Andersons gave Friendly Finance a security interest in the living room suite. Friendly Finance has a purchase money security interest in the living room suite under UCC § 9–107(b) because Friendly, by making the advance (the loan), has given the Andersons the money to enable them to purchase the living room suite from Blue Sky.

EXAMPLE

Allison Brown purchased a boat, motor, and trailer on credit from Speedway Boat Company. Allison gave Speedway a security interest in the boat, motor, and trailer. After making monthly payments for 24 months, Allison paid off her debt to Speedway.

Three months later, Allison borrowed $10,000 from the People's Credit Union and gave the credit union a security interest in the boat, motor, and trailer. The credit union's security interest is nonpurchase money (the credit union did not finance the purchase) and nonpossessory (Allison retains possession of the collateral).

PROBLEM 5.31   Gerald Red Corn is employed by a major airlines as a mechanic. Gerald borrowed $2,000 from Elk City Finance and gave as security his toolbox (valued at $2,500).

If Gerald files a petition in bankruptcy under Chapter 7, can he avoid this security interest?

Courts are divided on whether 522(f) applies if a state has opted out. For those who find it necessary to pursue this issue, the case of *In re Nehring*, 84 B.R. 571 (Bankr. S.D. Iowa 1988), may be of interest.

A related section provides that an individual debtor may redeem tangible personal property intended primarily for personal, family, or household use from a lien securing a dischargeable consumer debt if the personal property was exempted under section 522 or abandoned under section 554. 11 U.S.C.A. § 722. The debtor must pay the lienholder the amount of the allowed secured claim.

> An individual debtor may, whether or not the debtor has waived the right to redeem under this section, redeem tangible personal property intended primarily for personal, family, or household use, from a lien securing a dischargeable consumer debt, if such property is exempted under section 522 of this title or has been abandoned under sec-

tion 554 of this title, by paying the holder of such lien the amount of the allowed secured claim of such holder that is secured by such lien. 11 U.S.C.A. § 722.

In this instance the claim of the lienholder must be evaluated under 11 U.S.C.A. §
506(a) and the allowed amount of the secured claim determined. The property may
then be redeemed by the debtor for the amount of the claim. The courts almost uni-
versally require this redemption to be done in a single, lump sum cash payment.
Accordingly, it is not possible for the debtor to use a combination of reaffirmation
and redemption to retain a single piece of property.

EXAMPLE
David Henry owns an old Cadillac worth $2,000. The Cadillac is subject to a $2,800 security interest (the lien) held by Friendly Finance. If David files his petition in bankruptcy
under Chapter 7 in a state that has not opted out and he chooses the 522(d) exemptions, he is permitted a $2,400 exemption in his car. 11 U.S.C.A. § 522(d)(2). Under the
redemption provision of section 722, David can pay $2,000 to Friendly Finance, the
holder of the security interest, and redeem the entire Cadillac. The balance of the
$2,800 debt ($800) will be an unsecured claim.

2. CONVERTING NONEXEMPT PROPERTY TO EXEMPT PROPERTY
Because the Bankruptcy Code permits the debtor to claim exemptions in order to retain assets necessary for a fresh start and because the property that can be claimed
as exempt must be in an enumerated category, it is to the debtor's advantage to have
as many assets as possible in exempt property categories prior to the filing of the
petition in bankruptcy. The Bankruptcy Code is silent on the issue of whether a
debtor can **convert nonexempt property to exempt property** prior to bankruptcy. The courts, however, have permitted the debtor to convert nonexempt property into exempt property if the conversion occurs before the filing of a bankruptcy
petition. This practice, which permits the debtor to make full use of the exemptions
to which he or she is entitled under the law, is not considered fraudulent per se. See
11 U.S.C.A. § 522, Historical and Revision Notes.

> **PROBLEM 5.32**   Louis Bennasar's 1996 Ford was recently repossessed by the
> finance company because he could not make his payments. Louis traded his
> boat, motor, and boat trailer for a 1988 Ford, valued at $1,000, for needed trans-
> portation. This was an even trade since the boat, motor, and boat trailer were
> valued at $1,000. At the time of the trade, the boat, motor, and boat trailer were
> clear of any security interest.
>
> A week later, Louis filed for bankruptcy under Chapter 7. Is this an ac-
> ceptable practice?

Courts may restrict the debtor's right to convert nonexempt property to exempt
property on the eve of bankruptcy. The debtor may not convert nonexempt property into exempt property if the nonexempt property was procured through fraudulent conduct or if the debtor has abused or taken unreasonable advantage of his or
her ability to convert nonexempt property into exempt property.

In *In re Elliott,* Elliott, a produce broker, purchased large quantities of lettuce
on credit (an open account). Rather than pay the lettuce supplier, Elliott used money
that had been accumulating in an account (this money was not derived from Elliott's
sale of the lettuce) to pay off the mortgage on his house.

In re Elliott
United States Bankruptcy Court, Middle District of Florida, 1987.
79 B.R. 944.

FINDINGS OF FACT AND CONCLUSIONS OF LAW
George L. Proctor,
Bankruptcy Judge

This cause was tried before the Court on August 3, 1987, on a creditor's objection to Debtor's claim of exemptions. After hearing the arguments of counsel and reviewing the supporting evidence, the Court makes the following Findings of Fact and Conclusions of Law.

FINDINGS OF FACT

1. The Debtor was until mid-1985 a sole proprietor engaged in the business of buying and selling agricultural commodities as a produce broker.

2. In September of 1983, Debtor and his non-filing spouse, as tenants by the entirety, purchased certain real property located in Seminole County, Florida, which was encumbered with a mortgage for $162,000. The real property has remained their homestead at all times material to this decision.

3. Between May 22, 1984, and September 14, 1984, Debtor purchased several large quantities of lettuce on open account from Bud Antle, Inc. (hereinafter known as "Antle"). The history of the credit sales are more fully set forth in the account ledger (Debtor's Exhibit 1). Debtor paid Antle the approximate sum of $15,500 on the account, leaving a balance due of $49,167.05.

4. On September 20, 1984, the Debtor deposited $162,412 in his account. This money was derived from sales of produce not connected with Antle.

5. On September 21, 1984, Debtor withdrew $162,000 from the account and paid off the mortgage on his house. See Antle's Exhibits 2 and 3.

6. While Antle accuses the Debtor of stockpiling the monies he received to accumulate $162,412, the bank statement for the month shows that it was not uncommon for the Debtor to make large deposits. For instance, $27,149 was deposited ten days before the $162,412 deposit, $38,571.24 one day before, $53,371 four days later, and $27,033 three days thereafter. Debtor continued in business for another nine months until he lost his license to broker produce.

7. At the time Debtor withdrew the money and paid off the mortgage, he had a large amount of accounts receivable. However, he later encountered difficulties in collecting many receivables even though he pursued them to judgment. Debtor testified that he was solvent at the time of the payment of his mortgage.

8. When Debtor defaulted on the account, Antle filed a suit on October 16, 1984, with the Department of Agriculture under the Produce Agricultural Commodity Act, hereinafter known as "PACA." Antle did not allege fraud in that complaint. Judgment was rendered in favor of Antle.

9. The judgment was not paid, and the Department of Agriculture revoked the broker's license sometime in mid-1985.

10. Debtor claimed his home as exempt under Article X, Section 4, of the Florida Constitution and has at all times maintained this as his principal place of residence with his wife.

CONCLUSIONS OF LAW

1. The issue is not whether Debtor is entitled to claim this particular property as his homestead under Article X, Section 4, of the Florida Constitution. Rather, the matter before this Court is whether the Debtor should be denied this exemption under 11 U.S.C. § 522 to the extent he used business assets to pay off the mortgage on his home.

2. It is generally recognized that a Debtor is entitled to convert non-exempt property into exempt property up until the filing of the bankruptcy petition. It is further recognized that this practice is not fraudulent per se. *See In re Ford,* 3 B.R. 559 (Bkrptcy.D.Md. 1980). However, when the conversion is intended to defeat the interests of creditors, such exemptions may be denied to the extent of any fraudulent conduct.

3. In order to prevail in this objection, Antle must prove that the conversion of business assets into exempt assets was undertaken with the intent to hinder, delay, or defraud creditors. Antle has argued that the delay in depositing the funds derived from the sale of produce, the immediate withdrawal of funds after depositing the checks, the procurement of a cashier's check from the proceeds, and the conversion of non-exempt business assets to exempt personal assets, all done at a time when the debtor was insolvent, establishes the necessary intent to deny this Debtor the full extent of his homestead exemption.

   However, this Court finds that the evidence presented by Antle is insufficient to establish a fraudulent intent in regards to this transfer. As noted, it is not fraudulent per se for a debtor to convert non-exempt property to exempt property prior to the filing of the petition. Additionally, there was no evidence that the satisfaction of the mortgage was done in secrecy or otherwise concealed by the Debtor.

4. The most important factor is that the transfer occurred some two and one-half years before the bankruptcy rather than on the "eve of bankruptcy" as was the case in this Court's decision of *In re Collins,* 19 B.R. 874 (Bkrptcy.M.D.Fla. 1982).

5. Antle has failed to establish that the Debtor was insolvent when the transfer occurred. While Antle has shown that the Debtor's credibility is questionable, this Court choses to accept the Debtor's testimony that he believed he was solvent when the transfer occurred. Indeed, the Debtor's own schedules indicate that he had accounts receivable in the amount of $750,000 and unsecured debts of $582,000 when the petition was filed.

6. Other factors weighing in favor of the debtor is the fact that he remained in business some nine months after the transfer and continued to make deposits and withdrawals in the account. It was not until he lost his broker's license that he ceased his business operation.

7. Based upon the foregoing, Antle's objection to exemption will be denied. This decision is without prejudice to Antle's adversary proceeding objecting to discharge of debtor based upon fraudulent transfers.

   A separate order overruling Antle's objection to Debtor's exemptions will be entered.

3. WAIVER OF EXEMPTIONS AND WAIVER OF AVOIDING POWERS

Federal Rules of Bankruptcy Procedure 4003(b) provides that

> The trustee or any creditor may file objections to the list of property claimed as exempt within 30 days after the conclusion of the meeting of creditors held pursuant to Rule 2003(a) or the filing of any amendment to the list or supplemental schedules unless, within such period, further time is granted by the court. Copies of the objections shall be delivered or mailed to the trustee and to the person filing the list and the attorney for such person.

If the debtor waives his or her right to claim an exemption, the property that would have been exempt will remain property of the estate. The Bankruptcy Code, however, protects the debtor from making a waiver in favor of a creditor who holds an unsecured claim by making such a waiver unenforceable.

> (e) A waiver of an exemption executed in favor of a creditor that holds an unsecured claim against the debtor is unenforceable in a case under this title with respect to such claim against property that the debtor may exempt under subsection (b) of this section. 11 U.S.C.A. § 522(e), sentence 1.

The debtor may be asked to waive his or her power to avoid certain liens and nonpurchase money security interests in certain household and personal goods or to exempt property that the trustee recovered under one of the trustee's **avoidance powers.** The Bankruptcy Code, however, protects the debtor from making a waiver of this power by making such a waiver unenforceable.

> A waiver by the debtor of a power under subsection (f) or (h) of this section to avoid a transfer, under subsection (g) or (i) of this section to exempt property, or under subsection (i) of this section to recover property or to preserve a transfer, is unenforceable in a case under this title. 11 U.S.C.A. § 522(e), sentence 2.

The Bankruptcy Code attempts to protect the debtor from improvident waiver of exemptions in certain consumer goods by giving the debtor the power to avoid nonpossessory, nonpurchase money security interests in these consumer goods and by making any attempted waiver unenforceable. See 11 U.S.C.A. §§ 522(e), (f).

EXAMPLE

Sarah Estrada borrowed $1,000 from Friendly Finance and gave Friendly a security interest in her TV, VCR, and compact disc player. When Sarah defaulted on her loan, Friendly threatened to repossess unless Sarah would sign a waiver of her exemptions as to these items if she subsequently filed for bankruptcy under Chapter 7. To replace these items would cost Sarah $1,800. If Friendly Finance repossessed these items and resold them, the items would bring $500.

This practice would give Friendly an unconscionable advantage over Sarah because Friendly's security interest in the goods would be much more valuable as leverage to coerce Sarah into repaying the loan. If Sarah files for bankruptcy under Chapter 7, she may avoid Friendly's lien because the waiver is unenforceable. 11 U.S.C.A. §§ 522(e), (f).

D. THE AUTOMATIC STAY

Immediately upon the filing of the case, the property of the estate comes under the protection of the **automatic stay.** 11 U.S.C.A. § 362(a).

> The automatic stay is one of the fundamental debtor protections provided by the bankruptcy laws. It gives the debtor a breathing spell from his creditors. It stops all collection efforts, all harassment, and all foreclosure actions. It permits the debtor to attempt

a repayment or reorganization plan, or simply to be relieved of the financial pressures that drove him into bankruptcy. 11 U.S.C.A. § 362, Notes of Committee on the Judiciary, Senate Report No. 95-989.

The automatic stay is broad and inclusive. It protects both the debtor and the property of the estate.

(a) Except as provided in subsection (b) of this section, a petition filed under section 301, 302, or 303 of this title . . . operates as a stay, applicable to all entities, of—

(1) the commencement or continuation, including the issuance or employment of process, of a judicial, administrative, or other action or proceeding against the debtor that was or could have been commenced before the commencement of the case under this title, or to recover a claim against the debtor that arose before the commencement of the case under this title;

(2) the enforcement, against the debtor or against property of the estate, of a judgment obtained before the commencement of the case under this title;

(3) any act to obtain possession of property of the estate or of property from the estate or to exercise control over property of the estate;

(4) any act to create, perfect, or enforce any lien against property of the estate;

(5) any act to create, perfect, or enforce against property of the debtor any lien to the extent that such lien secures a claim that arose before the commencement of the case under this title;

(6) any act to collect, assess, or recover a claim against the debtor that arose before the commencement of the case under this title;

(7) the setoff of any debt owing to the debtor that arose before the commencement of the case under this title against any claim against the debtor; and

(8) the commencement or continuation of a proceeding before the United States Tax Court concerning the debtor. 11 U.S.C.A. § 362(a).

EXAMPLE
On February 1, Ricardo Garcia was involved in an automobile accident while on his way to work. He was rendered unconscious by the impact and was taken to the emergency room at St. Mary's Hospital by paramedics. Dr. Ross provided medical services and billed Garcia $750. Garcia paid $150 and promised to pay the balance as soon as he could. The hospital sent Garcia a bill for $1,200, which he did not pay. The hospital then sued Garcia in small claims court and recovered a judgment for $1,200 plus attorney fees.

Shortly after the accident, Garcia purchased a new Mercury Cougar from Green Country Ford & Mercury for $17,000. Garcia paid $2,000 down and financed the car with People's Credit Union. The payments were $600 a month for 36 months. Garcia gave People's Credit Union a purchase money security interest in the car. After making the first monthly payment, Garcia ceased paying.

On March 1, Garcia purchased a computer for his office from EXCEL Computer Store. Garcia gave EXCEL a purchase money security interest in the computer.

On March 5, Garcia hired the Bayshore Roofing Company to put a new roof on his house. The cost of the roof was $6,000. Garcia paid $2,500 and promised to pay $500 a month. Bayshore had a mechanic's and materialmen's lien put on the house. Garcia made only the April payment.

On March 15, Garcia went to Dr. Campbell, a dentist, for a root canal. Garcia paid $50 of the $225 bill. Dr. Campbell referred the bill to the Persistent Collection Agency. On April 1, the collection agency began its weekly telephone calls to Garcia.

On June 1, Garcia filed for bankruptcy under Chapter 7. Upon the filing of the petition, the automatic stay went into effect. After receiving notice of Garcia's bankruptcy, EXCEL discovered that it had not filed a financing statement to perfect its security interest in the computer. The IRS was scheduled to file its petition against Garcia in United States Tax Court on June 4 for failure to pay his previous year's income tax.

The stay prohibits

1. Dr. Ross from filing suit against Garcia for the balance owed for his services (11 U.S.C.A. § 362(a)(1));
2. St. Mary's Hospital from enforcing the judgment by garnishing Garcia's wages (11 U.S.C.A. § 362(a)(2));
3. People's Credit Union from filing a replevin action to recover the car (11 U.S.C.A. § 362(a)(3));
4. EXCEL from filing a financing statement to perfect its security interest in the computer (11 U.S.C.A. § 362(a)(4));
5. Bayshore Roofing Company from enforcing its lien (11 U.S.C.A. § 362(a)(5));
6. the Persistent Collection Agency from telephoning Garcia concerning Dr. Campbell's bill (11 U.S.C.A. § 362(a)(6));
7. People's Credit Union from setting off its claim against Garcia's balance in his checking account (11 U.S.C.A. § 362(a)(7)); and
8. the IRS from commencing an action against Garcia for nonpayment of his past year's income tax (11 U.S.C.A. § 362(a)(8)).

Exceptions to the automatic stay do exist.

(b) The filing of a petition under section 301 . . . does not operate as a stay—
    (1) under subsection (a) of this section, of the commencement or continuation of a criminal action or proceeding against the debtor;
    (2) under subsection (a) of this section—
        (A) of the commencement or continuation of an action or proceeding for—
            (i) the establishment of paternity; or
            (ii) the establishment or modification of an order for alimony, maintenance, or support; or
        (B) of the collection of alimony, maintenance, or support from property that is not property of the estate;
    (3) under subsection (a) of this section, of any act to perfect, or to maintain or continue the perfection of, an interest in property to the extent that the trustee's rights and powers are subject to such perfection under section 546(b) of this title or to the extent that such act is accomplished within the period provided under section 547(e)(2)(A) of this title;

    . . .

    (9) under subsection (a), of—
        (A) an audit by a governmental unit to determine tax liability;
        (B) the issuance to the debtor by a governmental unit of a notice of tax deficiency;
        (C) a demand for tax returns; or
        (D) the making of an assessment for any tax and issuance of a notice and demand for payment of such an assessment (but any tax lien that would otherwise attach to property of the estate by reason of such an assessment shall not take effect unless such tax is a debt of the debtor that will not be discharged in the case and such property or its proceeds are transferred out of the estate to, or otherwise revested in, the debtor). 11 U.S.C.A. § 362(b).

Knowingly violating the automatic stay is contempt and could be punishable by the bankruptcy court.

EXAMPLE

Willy Walton was a tenant at the Silver Dollar Apartments. When Willy fell two months behind in his rent, the landlord procured a judgment in small claims court. The landlord then proceeded to tell Willy, "I don't care whether you file bankruptcy or not. I have a judgment, and I'm going to collect it." Upon hearing this, Willy filed a petition in bankruptcy under Chapter 7.

Before receiving notice of Willy's petition in bankruptcy, the landlord filed a forcible entry and detainer and had a summons served on Willy to evict him. The landlord's action would be a nullity but would not lead to contempt proceedings in the bankruptcy court.

The debtor may also seek damages and attorneys' fees against the creditor for violation of the automatic stay. The Code provides that the debtor may make such recovery.

(h) An individual injured by any willful violation of a stay provided by this section shall recover actual damages, including costs and attorneys' fees, and, in appropriate circumstances, may recover punitive damages. 11 U.S.C.A. § 362(h).

EXAMPLE
After receiving notice of Willy's petition in bankruptcy, the landlord, in violation of the stay, garnished Willy's bank account. The landlord's actions were an intentional and willful violation of the stay. The bankruptcy judge could assess actual damages, including attorneys' fees and costs, and punitive damages to the landlord.

In *Soiett v. United States Veterans' Administration,* the debtor, an employee of the Veterans Administration (V.A.), received advanced sick leave and advanced annual leave while under a doctor's care for emotional and physical exhaustion resulting from stress. After receiving notice of the debtor's petition in bankruptcy and the commencement of the automatic stay, the V.A. notified the debtor that her final net paycheck, earned postpetition, was being applied to its claim for the advanced leave. The debtor sought to recover damages for contempt against the V.A. for violating the automatic stay.

Soiett v. United States Veterans' Administration
United States Bankruptcy Court, District of Maine, 1988.
92 B.R. 563.

MEMORANDUM OF OPINION
James A. Goodman,
Bankruptcy Judge
This matter is before the court on a complaint by the chapter 7 debtor seeking to recover a set-off and damages for contempt against the United States Veterans' Administration ("the V.A.") for violating the provisions of 11 U.S.C. § 362(a)[7] and § 524(a)(2). The issue is a core matter pursuant to 28 U.S.C. § 157.

Plaintiff filed a motion for judgment on the pleadings and this Court has treated such motion as one for summary judgment. Bankruptcy Rule 7012; Fed.R.Civ.P. 12(c); Fed.R.Civ.P. 56. The parties have submitted an agreed statement of facts and briefs.

The Court finds the following facts. Debtor ("plaintiff") was an employee of the V.A. During her employment and in accordance with 5 U.S.C. § 6307, plaintiff received advanced sick leave and advanced annual leave from June 3, 1985 through October 17, 1985 while under a doctor's care for emotional and physical exhaustion due to stress. Plaintiff had accrued a debit to her account of 149.75 hours of sick leave and due to a clerical error was accidently advanced 4.5 hours of annual leave prior to the filing of her chapter 7 on September 12, 1986.

After the V.A. received notice of the plaintiff's petition and commencement of the automatic stay, the V.A. nonetheles notified plaintiff by letter that she was indebted to the V.A. for $1,523.50* and her final net paycheck, earned postpetition, in the amount of $579.40 was being "applied to" the claim.

This Court finds that both the advanced sick leave and advanced annual leave were debts at the time the petition was filed and are dischargable pursuant to 11 U.S.C. § 727. Additionally, this Court finds the V.A. willfully violated the automatic stay provisions and holds the V.A. in contempt.

A "debt" is defined as a liability on a claim. 11 U.S.C. § 101(11). Section 101(4) defines "claim" as:

(a) a right to payment, whether or not such right is reduced to judgment, liquidated, unliquidated, fixed, contingent, matured, unmatured, disputed, undisputed, legal, equitable, secured or unsecured; or

(b) a right to equitable remedy for breach of performance if such breach gives rise to a right to payment, whether or not such right to an equitable remedy is reduced to judgment, fixed, contingent, matured, unmatured, disputed, undisputed, secured or unsecured;

Plaintiff's advanced sick leave debit was partially set off prior to her filing bankruptcy but was also reduced by the V.A. by set-off against debtor's postpetition earnings. The advanced annual leave error discovered prior to, but set off after the plaintiff filed bankruptcy, was also reduced in this manner.

It is the V.A.'s contention that set-off is the only means available to recover an employee's advanced sick leave and annual leave obligations and such contingent obligations are not debts and are not dischargeable. This Court disagrees. The definition of a debt is amply broad to include

obligations that are fixed, contingent, matured and unmatured. *Id.*

The V.A. asserts that it "has not waived its sovereign immunity" for the attorneys' fees, contempt finding or punitive damages sought by plaintiff. The V.A. has failed to cite any authority supporting its position that a "governmental unit" must waive its sovereign immunity before the Court can hold it in civil contempt and award costs and punitive damages. This Court is satisfied by the facts before it that the V.A. had adequate notice of the debtor's insolvency and that it took action to collect a debit when it was stayed from doing so. There is ample authority to hold the V.A. in contempt for its active violation of the automatic stay and to impose sanctions.

An award of costs, fees and punitive damages to a debtor for a creditor's willing violation of the automatic stay is expressly allowed pursuant to 11 U.S.C. § 362(h); § 105(a); and 28 U.S.C. § 2412(a), (b) (allowing awards of costs and fees against the United States and its agencies in civil actions). A finding of contempt is appropriate where a creditor knowingly violates a bankruptcy court order. *In re Haddad,* 68 B.R. 944, 953 (Bankr.D.Mass.1987); *Fidelity Mortgage Investors v. Camelia Builders, Inc.,* 550 F.2d 47, 51 (2d Cir.1976).

The V.A. had notice that the plaintiff filed a chapter 7 petition on September 12, 1986. On February 2, 1987 the V.A. sent a letter to the plaintiff informing her that she continued to be indebted to the V.A. for advanced sick leave and advanced health benefits, and made demand for the payment of those sums. On February 18, 1987 plaintiff's counsel wrote to the V.A. demanding that the V.A. cease any further attempt to collect the debt, refund any amounts deducted from her paycheck post-filing, reimburse her for any sick or annual leave improperly set off, and provide an accounting.

The record in this case shows the V.A. continued to violate the automatic stay. Had the V.A. any legal basis for collecting a pre-filing debt against a post-filing asset of the debtor, it could have and should have peti-

---

*Plaintiff had been removed from employment for alleged wrongdoing on January 5, 1987 but was subsequently reinstated.

tioned the Court for relief from the stay to proceed on its claim. *In Re Pody,* 42 B.R. 570, 573 (N.D.Ala.1984). The Court finds that the V.A.'s continuing conduct, however, was at a bare minimum contemptuous. The Court therefore holds the V.A. in civil contempt.

The Court has considered all the evidence and arguments of counsel, regardless of whether or not they are specifically referred to in this Opinion.

The foregoing shall constitute findings of fact and conclusions of law pursuant to Bankruptcy Rule 7052.

This Court shall hold an additional hearing to determine the exact amount of the improper set-off, costs, attorneys' fees and punitive damages, if any. An appropriate judgment consistent with this Opinion shall be entered.

If not modified by order of the court, the automatic stay will remain in effect until the property subject to the stay is no longer property of the estate. 11 U.S.C.A. § 362(c)(1).

EXAMPLE
The debtor's car is encumbered for $1,500 although its value is only $1,000. The debtor files a petition in bankruptcy under Chapter 7. If the debtor's trustee abandons the car, it will no longer be property of the estate. The stay no longer applies to the car.

The automatic stay will remain in effect as to any other act subject to the stay until the time the case is closed or dismissed, or a discharge is granted or denied, whichever is the earliest. 11 U.S.C.A. § 362(c)(2).

EXAMPLE
The debtor files for bankruptcy under Chapter 7 on June 1, and the automatic stay goes into effect. On June 25, the bankruptcy court sustains a creditor's complaint objecting to discharge. The denial of a discharge vacates the automatic stay. All the creditors now may attempt collection from the debtor's resources.

SECTION 3
THE APPOINTMENT AND POWERS OF AN INTERIM TRUSTEE

It is the duty of the United States trustee to appoint a panel trustee as **interim trustee** promptly after the order for relief in all Chapter 7 cases. 11 U.S.C.A. § 701(a)(1). If no panel member is willing to serve as interim trustee in a case, the U.S. trustee may serve in this capacity. A private trustee, who is not a panel trustee, will only be called upon to serve as an interim trustee in a Chapter 7 case in which this person has been serving as trustee in the case immediately before the order for relief. This will only occur in a Chapter 11 case that has been converted to a Chapter 7.

The trustee's powers include the power to abandon property of the estate, to assume or reject executory contracts, to seek the disallowance of a creditor's claim as a secured claim, to avoid prepetition transfers that are voidable preferences or fraudulent, and to avoid certain postpetition transfers.

A. ABANDON PROPERTY OF THE ESTATE

Property of the estate that has not been claimed by the debtor as exempt may be abandoned by the trustee in bankruptcy (after notice and a hearing) if the property is either burdensome to the estate or of inconsequential value and benefit to the estate. 11 U.S.C.A. § 554(a). When the property is abandoned by the trustee, it ceases to be property of the estate.

Property that is burdensome to the estate is property that will cost more to administer than its value or that is encumbered by a lien securing a debt for more than the value of the property plus the exemption amount.

> **PROBLEM 5.33**   Mary Lou Williamson filed a petition for bankruptcy under Chapter 7. Mary Lou owned a Doberman. Mary Lou did not claim the Doberman as exempt.
>
> Should the trustee abandon the Doberman?

Property of inconsequential value and benefit to the estate is property that is of insufficient value to justify administration by the trustee.

> **EXAMPLE**
> At the time of filing her petition in bankruptcy under Chapter 7, Georgia O'Riley, a single parent with a teen-age daughter, had two cars—a Thunderbird valued at $4,000 and an old Honda valued at $300.
>
> Georgia owed Red Bud Valley Bank $3,000 on the Thunderbird, and she had given Red Bud Valley a security interest in that vehicle. The security interest appeared on the Thunderbird's certificate of title. Georgia reaffirmed her $3,000 obligation to Red Bud Valley and claimed the remaining $1,000 equity in the Thunderbird as exempt.
>
> The trustee estimated that it would cost her $350 to administer the Honda as property of the estate. Because the estimated cost to administer this car exceeded its value, the Honda was burdensome to the estate.
>
> Even if the Honda had been valued at $375, so its value exceeded the cost to administer by $25, it would have been of inconsequential value and benefit to the estate.
>
> In either case, the trustee may abandon the Honda as property of the estate.

> **PROBLEM 5.34**   During the spring, Georgia O'Riley purchased a sailboat from Surf & Sail for $7,500. She gave Surf & Sail $2,000 and a security interest in the sailboat. Surf & Sail perfected its security interest.
>
> Georgia used the boat during the summer, did not make another payment, and filed for bankruptcy under Chapter 7 on October 1. The value of the sailboat on October 1 had decreased to $5,000.
>
> May the trustee abandon the sailboat?
>
> If the trustee does abandon the sailboat, is the sailboat property of the estate?

In the event the trustee neglects or declines to take the initiative on the matter of abandonment, a party in interest may request the court to order the trustee to abandon any property of the estate that is either burdensome to the estate or of inconsequential value and benefit to the estate. The court, after notice and a hearing, may order the trustee to abandon the property. 11 U.S.C.A. § 554(b).

> **EXAMPLE**
> Using the facts in Problem 5.34, assume that the trustee declined to abandon the sailboat and that Surf & Sail moved the bankruptcy court to modify the stay and order the trustee to abandon the sailboat. After notice and a hearing, the court may order the trustee to abandon. Once abandoned, the sailboat is no longer property of the bankruptcy estate and Surf & Sail could then repossess it.

If property is scheduled by the debtor and not otherwise administered at the time of the closing of a case, such property is deemed abandoned. 11 U.S.C.A. § 554(c).

EXAMPLE
At the time of filing her petition in bankruptcy under Chapter 7, Georgia O'Riley owned a motorcycle valued at $250. The motorcycle was listed on her schedule of assets. The trustee took no action concerning the motorcycle, and the case was closed.
    The motorcycle is considered abandoned, and Georgia does not lose her ownership interest.

PROBLEM 5.35   When completing her schedule of assets, Georgia O'Riley listed her home computer, TV, VCR, jewelry, and saxophone. She used her exemptions to claim other items of consumer goods but did not claim any of these items. After the estate was administered and the case was closed, Georgia still had possession of these items. What is the status of these items?

Property of the estate that is not duly scheduled by the debtor in accordance with 11 U.S.C.A. § 521(1) and that is not abandoned or otherwise dealt with in the administration remains property of the estate even after the closing of the case. 11 U.S.C.A. § 554(d).

PROBLEM 5.36   Now assume that when Georgia completed her schedule of assets, she did not list her home computer, TV, VCR, jewelry, and saxophone. After the estate was administered and the case was closed, Georgia still had possession of these items. What is the status of these items?

The procedure for abandonment is provided in Rule 6007.

(a) **Notice of Proposed Abandonment or Disposition; Objections.** Unless otherwise directed by the court, the trustee or debtor in possession shall give notice of a proposed abandonment or disposition of property to the United States trustee, all creditors, indenture trustees and committees elected pursuant to § 705 . . . of the Code. A party in interest may file and serve an objection within 15 days of the mailing of the notice, or within the time fixed by the court. If a timely objection is made, the court shall set a hearing on notice to the United States trustee and to other entities as the court may direct.
(b) **Motion by Party in Interest.** A party in interest may file and serve a motion requiring the trustee or debtor in possession to abandon property of the estate.

Because the rule prescribes that this procedure is to be followed "unless otherwise directed by the court," the court could enter a separate order providing for limitations on the noticing in order to shorten the time or to limit the parties to be given notice.

B. ASSUME OR REJECT EXECUTORY CONTRACTS

The provisions relating to executory contracts provide for the orderly adjustment of contractual rights that existed prior to the bankruptcy and give the trustee an opportunity to shed some of the contractual obligations of the debtor that may be too burdensome to allow the debtor a fresh start. The executory contract provisions are employed primarily in reorganization cases, but do arise occasionally in Chapter 7 cases.

EXAMPLE
Charles Bell had a contract to perform services for the United States Army. Prior to the beginning of performance of this contract, Charles filed for bankruptcy under Chapter

7. Charles listed his contract with the army on his schedules. He then asked the trustee to reject the executory contract, which the trustee did. Charles then renegotiated the contract with the army because he still wanted to perform the contract and the army still needed his services. Although the executory contract was an asset of the estate, it was of no value to the estate. Therefore, the trustee's rejection of the contract did not decrease the net worth of the estate. The renegotiated contract, which was made after the filing of the petition in bankruptcy, was not property of the estate.

C. AVOIDING TRANSFERS

The avoidance powers given to the trustee are in support of the idea of equitable distribution, which means equal distribution or prorated distribution among the unsecured creditors. For an equitable distribution to occur, it is necessary to curb the tendency that creditors have to attempt to dismember the assets of an ailing entity prior to the filing of bankruptcy. The trustee may have to actually bring property back into the estate for the purpose of distribution if the property was seized by one creditor prior to the bankruptcy filing.

This policy of equitable distribution is supported by powers that the trustee has to avoid certain transfers. These avoidance powers apply to unperfected security interests, claims that an actual creditor could avoid under state law, statutory liens arising on the debtor's insolvency, prepetition transfers of property of the estate to creditors that are voidable preferences, prepetition transfers of property of the estate that are fraudulent under the Bankruptcy Code, and certain postpetition transfers of property of the estate unless they are authorized by the bankruptcy court or the Bankruptcy Code.

The Bankruptcy Reform Act of 1994 imposes a two-year statute of limitations, running from the date of the order for relief, on the trustee's avoidance powers. 11 U.S.C.A. § 546(a)(1)(A). A trustee elected or appointed before expiration of the two-year period specified in subparagraph (A) has only one year to begin an avoidance action or proceeding. 11 U.S.C.A. § 546(a)(1)(B).

1. AVOIDING UNPERFECTED SECURITY INTERESTS

The trustee has the rights of a hypothetical lien creditor as of the date of bankruptcy. 11 U.S.C.A. § 544(a). This power given under section 544(a) is known as the "strong-arm power" and enables the trustee to set aside unperfected security interests and certain other transfers that would be invalid against a creditor who levied under state law before the filing of a bankruptcy petition.

This strong-arm power operates in the following manner. The Uniform Commercial Code parallels 544(a) of the Bankruptcy Code and provides that a trustee in bankruptcy is a lien creditor for UCC purposes. UCC § 9–301(3). As a lien creditor under the UCC, the trustee has priority as to the collateral over a creditor holding an unperfected security interest. UCC § 9–301(1)(b).

EXAMPLE

Royal Cleaners purchased an automatic shirt-folding machine from United Laundry Equipment Company. United took a security interest in the machine but did not file a financing statement. United's security interest was therefore unperfected.

Royal filed a petition in bankruptcy under Chapter 7. Royal's trustee is a hypothetical lien creditor under 544(a) of the Bankruptcy Code and 9–301(3) of the Uniform Commercial Code. UCC § 9–301(1)(b) gives Royal's trustee priority over United's unperfected security interest in the machine.

Therefore, it is incumbent on the trustee to challenge claims asserted as perfected security interests. If the trustee can prevail in the challenge, the claim will be reduced to unsecured and the property will remain property of the estate. It will be liquidated, and the proceeds will be distributed in the administration of the estate.

In *In re Landry,* Landry purchased a Honda Accord and gave the Shawmut Bank a security interest in the vehicle. Landry registered her Accord in New Hampshire and listed Shawmut Bank as the lienholder on the application for a certificate of title. The bank appeared on the New Hampshire certificate when it was issued by New Hampshire. Landry moved to Massachusetts and applied for a Massachusetts certificate of title. The bank was listed as a lienholder on the application, although the date of the lien was left blank. Massachusetts issued the certificate but did not list the bank as a lienholder. Landry then filed a petition in bankruptcy under Chapter 7. The bank moved to lift the automatic stay so it could repossess the Accord. The trustee for the bankruptcy estate objected on the ground that the bank's security interest was unperfected as of the time of the filing of the bankruptcy petition.

In re Landry
United States Bankruptcy Court, District of Massachusetts, 1994.
165 B.R. 738.

MEMORANDUM DECISION REGARDING MOTION TO LIFT AUTOMATIC STAY AND REQUEST FOR AUTHORIZATION TO REPOSSESS COLLATERAL
William C. Hallman,
Bankruptcy Judge

Debtor purchased a 1992 Honda Accord on August 22, 1992, and entered into a motor vehicle installment agreement with Shawmut Bank, N.A. (the "Bank"). On September 15, 1992, she registered the motor vehicle in New Hampshire and listed the Bank as the lienholder on the application for a title certificate. The record is not clear as to whether the Bank appeared on the New Hampshire certificate as issued, but I will assume that it did.

Debtor later moved to Massachusetts, and on March 4, 1993, applied for a new title in Massachusetts. The Massachusetts application form requires the lien holder's name and address and the date of the lien. While the Bank was listed as the lienholder of record on the application, the space for the date of the lien was left blank.

On March 26, 1993, Massachusetts issued a certificate of title which listed no lienholder.

On December 7, 1993, Debtor filed a voluntary petition under Chapter 7 of the Code. On January 13, 1994, the Bank filed the present motion.

The trustee filed an objection asserting that the Bank's security interest in the motor vehicle was unperfected as the Bank was not listed on the Massachusetts certificate of title. After hearing, I took the matter under advisement.

This memorandum decision constitutes my findings of fact and conclusions of law.

DISCUSSION

A trustee in bankruptcy has, as of the commencement of the case, the status of a hypothetical judicial lien creditor and is empowered to avoid any transfer of property of the debtor that could be avoided by such a creditor. *Fruehauf Corp. v. M.G. Sherman (In re Gringeri Bros. Transportation Co., Inc.),* 14 B.R. 396, 399 (Bankr.D.Mass.1981). Once the trustee has assumed the status of a hypothetical lien creditor, state law is used to determine whether a security interest in a motor vehicle has been perfected against the trustee. *Id. See also In re Cushman Bakery,* 526 F.2d 23, 27–28 (1st Cir.1975), *cert. denied,* 425 U.S. 937, 96 S. Ct. 1670, 48 L.Ed.2d 178 (1976); *Robinson v. Howard Bank (In re Kors, Inc.),* 819 F.2d 19, 22–23 (2d Cir.1987).

In Massachusetts, the perfection of a security interest in a motor vehicle is governed by M.G.L. c. 106, the Uniform Commercial Code ("UCC"), and by M.G.L. c. 90D, the Motor Vehicle Certificate of Title Act ("Chapter 90D"). UCC § 9–302(3) and (4) provide:

> "(3) The filing of a financing statement otherwise required by this Article is not necessary or effective to perfect a security interest in property subject to—
> "(b) chapter ninety D; . . . or
> "(c) a certificate of title statute of another jurisdiction under the law of which indication of a security interest on the certificate is required as a condition of perfection (subsection (2) of section 9–103).
> "(4) Compliance with a statute . . . described in subsection (3) is equivalent to the filing of a financing statement under this Article, and a security interest in property subject to the statute . . . can be perfected only by compliance therewith except as provided in section 9–103 on multiple state transactions. Duration and renewal of perfection of a security interest perfected by compliance with the statute . . . are governed by the provisions of the statute . . .; in other respects the security interest is subject to this Article."

Chapter 90D tells us that

> "A security interest in a vehicle for which a certificate of title is issued under this chapter is perfected by the delivery to the registrar of the existing certificate of title, if any, an application for a certificate of title containing the name and address of the lienholder *and the date of his security agreement* and the required fee. It is perfected as of the time of its creation if the delivery is completed within ten days thereafter, otherwise, as of the time of the delivery." Mass.Gen.L. c. 90D, § 21 [*emphasis added*].

The Bank argues that its security interest in the motor vehicle is duly perfected because it delivered to the Massachusetts registrar an application for title containing "all of the necessary information." The Trustee contends that perfection did not occur because the Massachusetts certificate of title did not list the Bank as a lienholder.

On its face § 21 of Chapter 90D supports the Bank's position that delivery of an application for a certificate of title listing the required information and accompanied by the required fee is sufficient to perfect a lien, notwithstanding that the certificate of title thereafter issued failed to list the lienholder. However, the date of the lien was not listed on the application involved here as required by the statute.

The Supreme Judicial court made the decision even more certain against the Bank when it decided in *City of Boston v. Rockland Trust Co.* that §§ 21, 22, and 26 of Chapter 90D combine to require something more and that "the exclusive method of perfecting a security interest in a motor vehicle is through notation of the lien on a valid certificate of title." 391 Mass. 48, 51, 460 N.E.2d 1269, 1271 (1984). *See also General Motors Acceptance Corp. v. Waligora,* 24 B.R. 905, 907 (W.D.N.Y.1982).

One last point should be mentioned. The vehicle in issue here originated in New Hampshire. Pursuant to § 21 of Chapter 90D "[t]he validity and perfection of a security interest in a vehicle subject to such security interest when the vehicle is brought into the commonwealth is to be determined in accordance with the rules in [UCC § 9–103] . . . ." Section 9–103(2)(b) provides:

> "Except as otherwise provided in this subsection, perfection and the effect of perfection or nonperfection of the security interest are governed by the law . . . of the jurisdiction issuing the certificate until four months after the goods are removed from that jurisdiction and thereafter until the goods are registered in another jurisdiction, but in any event not beyond surrender of the certificate. After the expiration of that period, the goods are not covered by the certificate of title within the meaning of this section."

In the instant case, even assuming as I have perfection of the Bank's security interest by notation on the New Hampshire certificate of title, I find that the Bank's perfection has lapsed. The pleadings establish that Massachusetts issued the certificate of title on March 26, 1993. Even if the Debtor did not remove the vehicle from New Hampshire to Massachusetts until the date of filing of the application for a certificate of title in Massachusetts on March 4, 1993, perfection lapsed automatically in July of 1993 because there had been a change of location for over four months and reregistration occurred. *City of Boston v. Rockland Trust Co.,* 391 Mass. at 53, 460 N.E.2d at 1272 ("we conclude that the lapse of perfection occurs automatically when these two factors, i.e., change of location for over four months and reregistration, occur.").

The Bank's interest is unperfected and an order will enter denying the motion before the court.

---

2. AVOIDING CLAIMS THAT AN ACTUAL CREDITOR CAN AVOID UNDER STATE LAW

The trustee may avoid transfers that an actual creditor with a provable claim could have avoided under state law, such as the Uniform Fraudulent Transfers Act. 11 U.S.C.A. § 544(b). Section 544(b) states that the trustee has the right to avoid any prepetition transfer that is "voidable under applicable law by a creditor holding an unsecured claim that is allowable." Thus, 544(b) gives the trustee the power to avoid transfers that are voidable under state fraudulent transfer and bulk sales laws. The transaction can be set aside for the benefit of all creditors.

EXAMPLE

Mom's & Pop's Corner Store purchased its inventory from a number of suppliers on credit. After a larger competitor opened down the block, Mom's & Pop's decided to close the store. Mom's & Pop's sold its inventory to the Dollar Store without notifying its creditors. Mom's & Pop's then filed for bankruptcy under Chapter 7. Because the sale to the Dollar Store violated the state bulk sales law, the Mom's & Pop's trustee could avoid this prepetition transfer.

In *In re Damar Creative Group, Inc.,* Damar Creative Group gave Daniel Ottow, its principal shareholder, officer, and director, a $225,050 bonus. Damar then filed for bankruptcy under Chapter 7. The trustee sought to use 544(b) and the state's fraudulent transfer act to avoid the transfer.

In re Damar Creative Group, Inc.
United States District Court, Northern District of Illinois, 1995.
1995 WL 571374.

MEMORANDUM OPINION AND ORDER
James H. Alesia,
District Judge

The matter now before the court is a bankruptcy appeal. Plaintiff-appellant, David R. Herzog, the trustee in bankruptcy, appeals from an order entered by the bankruptcy court on January 20, 1995, in favor of the defendant-appellee, Daniel Ottow ("Ottow"). In that order, the bankruptcy court dismissed the bankruptcy trustee's claim under 11 U.S.C. § 544(b) because the trustee lacked standing to bring an action under that section. The bankruptcy trustee has appealed to this court. For the reasons set forth below, this court reverses the bankruptcy court's order and remands this matter for further proceedings consistent with this opinion.

I. BACKGROUND

On January 21, 1992, the debtor, Damar Creative Group, Inc. ("debtor"), filed a petition for bankruptcy under Chapter 7 of the Bankruptcy Code, 11 U.S.C. § 701 et seq. ("the Code"). Thereafter, David R. Herzog was appointed as trustee in bankruptcy. In accordance with his duties as trustee, Herzog brought a two-count complaint against the defendant, Daniel Ottow, the principal shareholder, officer, and director of the debtor.

In Count I, the trustee alleged that a $37,355 bonus that Ottow received from the debtor within one year of the filing of the bankruptcy petition was a fraudulent conveyance under Section 548 of the Code. The parties have since settled with respect to this claim. In Count II, the trustee alleged that a $225,050 bonus that Ottow received from the debtor in June 1990 was a fraudulent transfer under Section 544 of the Code.

Ottow moved to dismiss Count II on the basis that the bankruptcy trustee had no standing to bring any action under Section 544 of the Code. His argument was based on his contention that in order to have standing under Section 544(b), a bankruptcy trustee must identify a specific unsecured creditor who existed at the time of the transfer. Since the parties had already stipulated that, at the time of the transfer, no such creditor existed, Ottow moved the bankruptcy court for dismissal of Count II. The court agreed, holding that "a trustee must first establish that at the time the transaction at issue occurred there was in fact a creditor in existence who had an unsecured claim allowable against the debtor's estate." *In re Damar Creative Group, Inc.*, No. 92 B 1225 (Bankr.N.D.Ill. January 20, 1995). Accordingly, the bankruptcy court dismissed Count II.

II. DISCUSSION

No issues of fact are raised on appeal by the trustee. Therefore, this court need only perform a de novo review of the challenged conclusion of law. *Matter of Yonikus,* 996 F.2d 866, 868 (7th Cir.1993).

The trustee's action, and the result here, depends on the court's interpretation of Section 544(b) of the Code. Section 544(b) provides:

> The trustee shall avoid any transfer of an interest of the debtor in property or any obligation incurred by the debtor that is voidable under applicable law by a creditor holding an unsecured claim that is allowable under section 502 of this title or that is not allowable only under section 502(e) of this title. 11 U.S.C. § 544(b).

For purposes of standing, Section 544(b) contains only one express restriction: the trustee must be able to assert the rights of at least one of the present unsecured creditors of the estate holding a claim that is either allowable under Section 502 or not allowable only under Section 502(e). 4 COLLIER ON BANKRUPTCY 544.03 (15th ed. 1988). Once the trustee overcomes this restriction, Section 544(b) gives him the power to avoid any of the debtor's transfers or obligations that are voidable for fraud or any other reason under applicable state or federal law. *Id.* Section 544(b) does not contain any substantive provisions to determine when and under what circumstances a particular transfer or obligation may be avoided; those circumstances are set by the applicable state or federal law affording grounds for avoidance. *Id.; In re Wedtech Corp.*, 88 B.R. 619, 622–23 (Bankr.S.D.N.Y. 1988); see also *In re Lico Mfg. Co., Inc.*, 201 F.Supp. 899, 903 (D.Conn.), aff'd, 323 F.2d 871 (2d Cir.1963) (no requirement that there be a creditor at the time of the transaction in former Section 70(e), the predecessor statute to Section 544(b); only applicable requirements are those contained in the state law giving rise to the cause of action).

Here, the bankruptcy court dismissed the trustee's claim because there was no unsecured creditor of the debtor's estate who existed at the time the debtor gave Ottow his bonus. From that, it is evident that the bankruptcy court has inserted an additional prerequisite that at least one unsecured creditor with an allowable claim exist at the time of the alleged transfer in order for a trustee to have standing under Section 544(b). However, the court sees no basis in the law for such a restriction. As stated above, for purposes of standing, the trustee must point to at least one of the present unsecured creditors holding an allowable claim. The bankruptcy court did not address this requirement in its order but this court finds no reason to dispute the trustee's assertion that there are at least thirty-two present unsecured claims allowable under Section 502.

Once the bankruptcy court is assured of that, it must look to the applicable state or federal law that the trustee has asserted in order to determine the circumstances in which a particular transfer may be avoided. The court notes that in many instances, the state fraudulent conveyance laws will not allow recovery for future creditors. R. GINSBERG AND R. MARTIN, BANKRUPTCY: TEXT, STATUTES, RULES, § 902(c) at p. 9–17 (3d ed.). If that were the case here, the bankruptcy court would have had every reason to dismiss the action. However, the Illinois statute which the trustee relied on, an adoption of the Uniform Fraudulent Transfer Act, does not limit recovery to creditors whose claims arose before the transfer. 740 ILCS 160/5. The statute states, in pertinent part:

> A transfer made or obligation incurred by a debtor is fraudulent as to a creditor, whether the creditor's claim arose before or after the transfer was made or obligation was incurred, if ... 740 ILCS 160/5 (emphasis added).

Therefore, since the applicable state law imposes no requirement that at least one unsecured creditor exist at the time of the alleged fraudulent transfer, the court finds no reason to dismiss the trustee for lack of standing.

Accordingly, this court reverses the Bankruptcy Court's order of January 20, 1995, and remands this case to the Bankruptcy Court for further proceedings consistent with this opinion. In doing so, this court expresses no opinion as to whether the alleged transfer was fraudulent under the Illinois statute; we merely remand this case to the Bankruptcy Court so that it can conduct further proceedings.

CONCLUSION

For the reasons outlined above, this court reverses the Bankruptcy Court's order of January 20, 1995, and remands this case to the Bankruptcy Court for further proceedings consistent with this opinion.

3. AVOIDING STATUTORY LIENS THAT ARISE
ON THE DEBTOR'S BANKRUPTCY OR INSOLVENCY

Statutory liens that arise on the debtor's bankruptcy or insolvency can also be avoided. 11 U.S.C.A. § 545. This section prevents states from creating statutory liens that would circumvent the priority scheme of the Bankruptcy Code.

4. AVOIDING PREPETITION TRANSFERS OF PROPERTY
OF THE ESTATE TO CREDITORS THAT ARE VOIDABLE PREFERENCES

The trustee's power to avoid preferential transfers by recovering for the estate money or property transferred is of great importance. Preferential transfers are avoidable under 11 U.S.C.A. § 547. Payment of an old unsecured debt will be recoverable upon proof as follows:

1. the payment or transfer was to or for the benefit of a creditor;
2. the payment or transfer was on an account of an antecedent debt owed by the debtor before the transfer was made;
3. the transfer was made while the debtor was insolvent;
4. the payment or transfer was made within 90 days prior to the filing of a bankruptcy case or between 90 days and one year before the filing of the petition, if the creditor at the time of the transfer was an insider; and
5. the creditor received as the result of the transfer more than he or she would have received in a bankruptcy liquidation case under Chapter 7.

The debtor is presumed to have been insolvent during the 90-day period prior to filing. 11 U.S.C.A. § 547(f).

Transfers otherwise avoidable will not be avoided if made in payment of a debt incurred in the ordinary course of business or financial affairs of the debtor and of the transferee, and the transfer was made in accordance with ordinary business terms. 11 U.S.C.A. § 547(c)(2). The trustee may not avoid a transfer that was "a bona fide payment of a debt to a spouse, former spouse, or child of the debtor, for alimony to, maintenance for, or support of such spouse or child," or "in a case filed by an individual debtor whose debts are primarily consumer debts, the aggregate value of all property that constitutes or is affected by such transfer is less than $600." 11 U.S.C.A. §§ 547(c)(7), (8).

In *In re Djerf,* the debtors made several payments on their American Express account within 90 days of the date they filed for bankruptcy under Chapter 7. The trustee filed a complaint against American Express seeking to avoid the transfer as a voidable preference under 547(b).

In re Djerf
United States Bankruptcy Court, District of Minnesota, 1995.
188 B.R. 586.

ORDER
Nancy C. Dreher,
Bankruptcy Judge

The above-entitled matter came on for hearing before the undersigned on November 8, 1995, on a motion of the defendant, American Express Travel Related Services Company, Inc. ("American Express"), for dismissal of the Complaint for failure to state a claim and for improper venue pursuant to Rule 7012(b)(6) of the Federal Rules of Bankruptcy Procedure and 28 U.S.C. § 1409(b), respectively. Appearances were noted in the record.

FACTS AND POSITIONS OF THE PARTIES

The Complaint filed by the Chapter 7 Trustee, Julia A. Christians ("Trustee"), seeks to avoid and recover from the defendants pursuant to 11 U.S.C. §§ 547(b), 549, and 550(a), the value of a series of transfers made by the debtors, Gary and Lynette Djerf ("Debtors"). The Trustee alleges that within ninety days before the date of the filing of the petition, Debtors, while insolvent, transferred to the defendants the sum of $890.00 on account of an antecedent debt. The aforementioned sum was transferred prepetition on two separate occasions in the following amounts:

Date of Transfer	Amount of Transfer
4/10/95	$690.00
5/24/95	$200.00
TOTAL	$890.00

Since the transfers enabled the defendants to receive more than they would otherwise receive in a Chapter 7, the Trustee contends that the transfers are preferential within the meaning of § 547(b) of the Bankruptcy Code. The Trustee further alleges that following the commencement of the case, the Debtors transferred to the defendants an additional $200.00. The Trustee contends that this transfer was an unauthorized post-petition transfer and avoidable pursuant to § 549(a). The aggregate amount that the Trustee seeks to avoid and recover for the benefit of the estate pursuant to §§ 547(b), 549(a), and 550(a) totals $1,090.00.

American Express, a New York Corporation which is headquartered in New York, argues that under § 547(c)(8), there is no preference with respect *to any individual transfer* whose value is less than $600.00 and, correspondingly, separate transfers of less than $600.00 to a single creditor may not be aggregated or combined in order to reach the section's minimum monetary threshold. Accordingly, American Express contends that since the plain language of § 547(c)(8) requires *each* transfer to a single creditor to exceed $600.00 in order to be avoidable, the subtraction of the $200.00 prepetition transfer from the total the Trustee can legitimately seek to recover ($890.00) requires that the case be dismissed in its entirety since venue is improper under 28 U.S.C. § 1409(b), which requires a trustee seeking a monetary recovery of less than $1,000.00 to commence the action in the district in which the defendant resides. *See* 28 U.S.C. § 1409(b).

DISCUSSION

Section 547(b) of the Code enables a trustee in bankruptcy to avoid any transfer of a debtor's interest in property that is made to a creditor on account of an antecedent debt within ninety days of the commencement of the case. 11 U.S.C. § 547(b). The purpose of § 547(b) is to deter creditors from racing to the courthouse and dismembering or pressuring debtors during their slide into bankruptcy and to further the prime bankruptcy policy of equality of distribution among similarly situated creditors. H.R.Rep. No. 595, 95th Cong., 1st Sess. 177–78, *reprinted in* 1978 U.S.C.C.A.N. 5787, 5963, 6138. Section 547(c)(8), redesignated from paragraph (7) by the Bankruptcy Reform Act of 1994 and frequently referred to in bankruptcy parlance as the "small preference" exception, contains an exception to the trustee's avoiding power "if, in a case filed by an individual debtor whose debts are primarily consumer debts, the *aggregate value* of *all* property that constitutes or is affected by such *transfer* is less than $600." 11 U.S.C. § 547(c)(8) (emphasis added).

It is clear that although one of the prepetition transfers in this case was for less than $600.00, the aggregate of the two prepetition transfers exceeds the statutory minimum. The issue before the Court is whether two or more transfers made to a single creditor during the prepetition preference period may be added together or aggregated for purposes of reaching the $600.00 monetary minimum of 11 U.S.C. § 547(c)(8). Although there is authority to the contrary, *see, e.g., Wilkey v. Credit Bureau Sys., Inc. (In re Clark),* 171 B.R. 563 (Bankr. W.D.Ky.1994); *Howes v. Hannibal Clinic (In re Howes),* 165 B.R. 270 (Bankr.E.D.Mo. 1994); *Ray v. Cannon's Inc. (In re Vickery),* 63 B.R. 222 (Bankr. E.D.Tenn.1986); and the issue appears to divide those few courts which have had occasion to consider it, this court is of the view that such transfers to a single creditor can be aggregated and follows those courts which have so concluded. *See, e.g., Alarcon v. Commercial Credit Corp. (In re Alarcon),* 186 B.R. 135 (Bankr.D.N.M.1995); *In re Bunner,* 145 B.R. 266 (Bankr.C.D.Ill.1992). *See also In re Passmore,* 156 B.R. 595 (Bankr.E.D.Wis. 1993); *Lewis v. State Employees Credit Union of Maryland, Inc. (In re Lewis),* 116 B.R. 54 (Bankr.D.Md.1990); *Holdway v. Duvoisin (In re Holdway),* 83 B.R. 510 (Bankr.E.D.Tenn.1988) (cases in dicta aggregating transfers for purposes of calculating the $600.00 minimum under § 547(c)(8)).

Courts interpreting the exception embodied in § 547(c)(8) and the paucity of legislative history surrounding its addition to the Code by the Bankruptcy Amendments and Federal Judgeship Act of 1984 have generally concluded that its design is to permit a relatively small in dollar amount or a nominal prepetition transfer to a consumer creditor to withstand attack under § 547(b) notwithstanding its preferential effect. *See Johnson v. Ford Motor Credit (In re Johnson),* 53 B.R. 919, 921 & n. 4 (Bankr. N.D.Ill.1985). *See generally* Vern Countryman, *The Concept of a Voidable Preference,* 38 Vand. L.Rev. 713, 812–15 (1985). The exception often operates as an adjunct to the "ordinary course of business" exception by reducing litigation over relatively nominal payments made to creditors in the ordinary course of the financial affairs of consumer debtors which do not seriously impinge upon the goals of equality of treatment and the avoidance of undue pressure for payment or the grab-bag effect. The small preference exception can also be justified on the grounds that the expense associated with the recovery of relatively small payments from individual creditors is often disproportionate to any eventual distribution to unsecured creditors as a class. Moreover, in many cases the costs associated with defending against such a preference attack would force creditors with small claims to capitulate to a trustee's demand for payment. Therefore, in the absence of the small preference exception, the mere threat of litigation would often effectively force small consumer creditors to waive any otherwise meritorious defense to a trustee's preference attack.

American Express argues that since the plain language of § 547(c)(8) uses the term "transfer" rather than "transfers," that *each* transfer must, as a matter of law, be considered *individually,* rather than aggregated, and gauged against the $600.00 statutory minimum. Any transfer which is less than $600.00, reasons American Express, is not susceptible to avoidance and recovery as a preference and may be retained by the creditor. According to American Express, this holds true even if, for example, under an extremely unlikely scenario, a debtor makes ninety payments to a single creditor of $599.00 each during the applicable preference period as long as no single payment exceeds the $600.00 cut-off mark.[1]

The language of the statute itself and its ostensible purpose militates against the construction American Express urges and the reasoning embodied in the authority it cites, such as *In re Clark,* 171 B.R. 563 (Bankr.W.D.Ky.1994), as support for the proposition that the exception embodied in § 547(c)(8) applies to each payment or transfer separately. Section 547(c)(8) specifically addresses the "aggregate" value of "all" property that constitutes a transfer. The terms "aggregate" and "all" that Congress chose as a prerequisite to the application of an exception to otherwise preferential transfers would be essentially devoid of any meaning and rendered merely surplusage if the statute was to be construed in the fashion American Express argues is appropriate. *Accord In re Alarcon,* 186 B.R. 135, 137 (Bankr.D.N.M.1995); *In re Bunner,* 145 B.R. 266, 267 (Bankr.C.D.Ill.1992). Moreover, the rules of construction found at § 102 of the Code further support the conclusion that multiple, discrete transfers to a single creditor made during the preference period may be aggregated when determining the applicability of the small preference exception since paragraph (7) of § 102 provides that when construing the statutory provisions of Title 11, "the singular includes the plural." 11 U.S.C. § 102(7). As such, the use of term "transfer" in § 547(c)(8) includes the plural, "transfers."

As a matter of policy, a single transfer interpretation of § 547(c)(8) seems inimical to one of the goals of preference law since it could actually encourage creditors to pressure debtors who are in financial straits into paying discrete transfers of less than

$600.00 each. The Bankruptcy Code's definition of the term "transfer," found in § 101(54) and meant to include "every mode" of disposing or parting with property, is broadly defined and designed to preclude such ingenious methods of circumvention:

> "All technicality and narrowness of meaning is precluded. The word is used in its most comprehensive sense, and is intended to include every means and manner by which property can pass from the ownership and possession of another, and by which the result forbidden by the statute may be accomplished. . . ."

Katz v. First Nat'l Bank, 568 F.2d 964, 969 n. 4 (2d Cir.1977) (quoting *Pirie v. Chicago Title & Trust Co.,* 182 U.S. 438, 444, 21 S.Ct. 906, 908-09, 45 L.Ed. 1171 (1901)), *cert. denied,* 434 U.S. 1069, 98 S.Ct. 1250, 55 L.Ed. 2d 771 (1978). *Accord National Bank v. National Herkimer County Bank,* 225 U.S. 178, 184, 32 S.Ct. 633, 635, 56 L.Ed. 1042 (1912). An interpretation of § 547(c)(8) that permits the aggregation of transfers to a single creditor and operates to discourage such strategic transfers is therefore consistent with the broad definition that the term transfer is accorded in the context of avoidable preferences as well as the goals of preference law.

Accordingly, and for reasons stated, IT IS HEREBY ORDERED that the motion by American Express Travel Related Services Company, Inc., for a dismissal of the above-entitled adversary proceeding for failure to state a claim and for improper venue is DENIED.

SO ORDERED.

---

[1]Under such an example, an unsecured creditor would be entitled to shield or exempt a payment stream which totals $53,910.00 from avoidance as a preference even though the transfers in all other respects satisfy the elements of § 547(b)— hardly the relatively small amount contemplated by the framers of the small preference exception!

5. AVOIDING PREPETITION TRANSFERS OF PROPERTY OF THE ESTATE THAT ARE FRAUDULENT UNDER THE BANKRUPTCY CODE

Fraudulent transfers are avoidable under 11 U.S.C.A. § 548 without regard to the debtor's solvency or insolvency if such transfers occurred or such obligations were incurred within one year before bankruptcy when the transfer or obligation involved an actual intent to hinder, delay, or defraud creditors. Such a transfer is also avoidable if the transfer is for less than reasonably equivalent value and the debtor was insolvent or became insolvent as a result of the transaction. If the debtor had or was left with unreasonably small capital for current or contemplated business transactions or intended or believed he or she would incur debts beyond his or her other ability to pay as they became due, the trustee may avoid the transfer.

In *In re O'Connor,* Vincent O'Connor and his ex-wife, Diane, formed a corporation and transferred their respective interests in four lots to this corporation. The corporate shares were divided equally between the O'Connors. The O'Connors sold their respective shares in the corporation to Natalie and Michael Christy. Vincent O'Connor did not receive any part of the proceeds from this sale of stock. Vincent O'Connor then filed for bankruptcy under Chapter 7. The Chapter 7 trustee filed a complaint against Diane O'Connor seeking to recover Vincent O'Connor's share of the proceeds from the sale. The trustee alleged that Vincent O'Connor, the debtor, received no adequate equivalent value for the transfer of his stock, in which he had a one-half interest, and that the transfer occurred while he was insolvent. Thus, the retention of his share by his ex-wife was avoidable as a fraudulent transfer pursuant to § 548.

In re O'Connor
United States Bankruptcy Court, Middle District of Florida, 1995.
178 B.R. 872.

FINDINGS OF FACT, CONCLUSIONS OF LAW AND MEMORANDUM OPINION
Alexander L. Paskay,
Chief Judge

This is a Chapter 7 liquidation case and the matter under consideration is a claim set forth by Diane L. Jensen (Trustee) against Diane O'Connor (Ms. O'Connor) in a two-count complaint. In Count I the Trustee seeks to recover $50,000 which according to the Trustee is a voidable preference pursuant to § 547(b) of the Bankruptcy Code. The claim in Count II is based on the allegation of a fraudulent transfer and the Trustee seeks to recover the same amount pursuant to § 548(a)(2) of the Bankruptcy Code.

The facts are not in serious dispute, as they have been stipulated to by the parties

in conjunction with a previous Motion for Summary Judgment filed by the Trustee. On July 14, 1994, this Court entered an Order and denied the Motion and held that the only issue which remained for resolution was whether or not the stocks sold by the Debtor and Ms. O'Connor were, in fact, the sole property of Ms. O'Connor; therefore the Debtor was not entitled to any part of the proceeds received from the sale. The facts which are without dispute as appear from the stipulation and from testimony are as follows:

Prior to the commencement of this case, the Debtor and Ms. O'Connor were married. This marriage was dissolved by a Final Decree entered by the Circuit Court of the Twentieth Judicial Circuit in and for Charlotte County, Florida, which ratified a

Separation and Property Settlement Agreement entered into between the parties on April 29, 1986. The Final Decree, in the relevant portions, awarded full ownership to the Debtor of certain lots referred to as Lots 11 and 12 on which a pub was operated under the name of the Bull & Bear Pub. Lots 7 and 10 were adjacent and contiguous to Lots 11 and 12 were awarded to Ms. O'Connor. After the entry of the Divorce Decree, the parties reunited and lived together although they did not remarry.

Lot 7 was originally owned by Mr. and Mrs. Perry who conveyed title to the lot on April 24, 1987 to O'Connor Enterprises of Florida, Inc., a Florida corporation (O'Connor Enterprises). On July 30, 1987, O'Connor Enterprises conveyed Lot 7 to the Debtor and Ms. O'Connor, as single persons. Lot 10 was originally owned by Mr. Owens and was conveyed to O'Connor Enterprises on April 24, 1987. Again, on July 30, 1987, O'Connor Enterprises conveyed the ownership of the lot to the Debtor and Ms. O'Connor, as single persons. On December 16, 1987, the Debtor and Ms. O'Connor conveyed title to Lot 10 to O'Connor Enterprises and on the same date the title was reconveyed again to the Debtor and Ms. O'Connor. On October 7, 1991 all four lots, Lots 7, 10, 11 and 12 were transferred by the Debtor, a single man, and Ms. O'Connor, a single woman, by quit claim deed to Ms. O'Connor. There is no dispute that the Debtor received no consideration for the transfer of his interest in Lots 11 and 12.

It is without dispute that from February 26, 1990 until March 20, 1992 the Bull & Bear Pub was operated by a tenant. The Debtor and Ms. O'Connor filed a suit to remove the tenant from the property and sought damages for breach by the tenant of the lease. It is noteworthy that this action was brought in March 1992 by the Debtor and Ms. O'Connor even though by that time, by virtue of the quit claim deed executed October 7, 1991, Lots 7, 10, 11 and 12, together with the improvements, were owned only by Ms. O'Connor.

On April 8, 1992, the Debtor and Ms. O'Connor formed a corporation, known as CoCo, Inc. of Englewood (CoCo) and on April 28, 1992 the four lots were transferred to this newly formed corporation by Ms. O'Connor. All shares in CoCo were issued fifty-fifty to the Debtor and to Ms. O'Connor respectively.

It appears that on October 1, 1992, the Debtor and Ms. O'Connor sold their respective shares in CoCo to Natalie and Michael Christy, who paid $99,650 for the stock. Out of that amount, Ms. O'Connor settled the claim of a business broker and paid $12,100 to the broker and $3,035 to an attorney who represented her in the dispute with the business broker. She also loaned $5,000 to a friend, which loan was ultimately repaid with $2,500 paid to the Debtor and $2,500 to Ms. O'Connor. It is again without dispute that the Debtor did not receive any part of the proceeds obtained from the sale of the CoCo stock.

The claim for relief by the Trustee is based on three different theories. First, it is the contention of the Trustee that one-half of the proceeds obtained from the sale of the stock in CoCo rightfully belongs to the Debtor and, in turn, it is property of the estate and subject to administration by the Trustee. Second, if the appropriation of the Debtor's one-half interest in the proceeds was repayment of an alleged debt owed by the Debtor to his former wife, Ms. O'Connor, this occurred within 90 days of the commencement of the case while the Debtor was insolvent thus this transfer is avoidable by the Trustee pursuant to § 547(b) of the Code. Third, in any event, so contends the Trustee, the Debtor received no adequate equivalent value for the transfer of his stock in which the Debtor had a one-half interest and the transfer occurred while the Debtor was insolvent thus the retention of the Debtor's share is avoidable as a fraudulent transfer pursuant to § 548(a)(2)(A) of the Code.

In opposing the claims of the Trustee, Ms. O'Connor contends that notwithstanding what appears on the relevant documents, she was, in fact, the equitable owner of Lots 10 and 11 notwithstanding that the same were awarded to the Debtor in the divorce because while they were married and even after the divorce when they lived together, she saved the property by expanding large amounts of monies not only for the improvements of the property but also by making the mortgage payments in order to fend off a threatened foreclosure action which was a reality because the Debtor was seriously in default on the mortgage which encumbered Lots 10 and 11. It is contended by Ms. O'Connor that the transfer of the Lots to a newly formed corporation for which the Debtor and Ms. O'Connor received the stock was a real estate sale only and not a capital contribution.

Ms. O'Connor contends that the Debtor had no funds during the relevant time and only her funds were used to maintain and preserve the property and for this reason the proceeds from the sale of the stock were rightfully hers and never property of the Debtor, notwithstanding the fact that the CoCo stocks were issued in the name of the Debtor and Ms. O'Connor and not Ms. O'Connor only.

Concerning the third contention of the Trustee first, which is based on the fraudulent transfer theory, the following should be noted.

Section 548 of the Bankruptcy Code provides in pertinent part, as follows:

§ 548. Fraudulent transfers and obligations.
(a) The trustee may avoid any transfer of an interest of the debtor in property, or any obligation incurred by the debtor, that was made or incurred on or within one year before the date of the filing of the petition, if the debtor voluntarily or involuntarily
  (1) made such transfer or incurred such obligation with actual intent to hinder, delay, or defraud any entity to which the debtor was or became, on or after the date that such transfer was made or such obligation was incurred, indebted; or
  (2)(A) received less than a reasonably equivalent value in exchange for such transfer or obligation; and

(B)(i) was insolvent on the date that such transfer was made or such obligation was incurred, or became insolvent as a result of such transfer or obligation;

In the present instance, there is no doubt that the stock in CoCo was owned fifty percent by the Debtor and fifty percent by Ms. O'Connor. It is equally evident that the Debtor did not receive a dime from the monies paid by the Christys for the purchase of all outstanding shares in CoCo. The question then remains, however, whether the Debtor's interest in the CoCo stock was limited to bare legal title, or whether his interest was actually a cognizable ownership interest which, in turn, would entitle him to one-half of the proceeds realized from the sale. If the Debtor had an actual ownership interest, it is clear that the sale of the stock could be challenged by the Trustee as a fraudulent transfer pursuant to § 548 of the Bankruptcy Code. *In re Gillman,* 120 B.R. 219 (Bankr. M.D.Fla.1990). The facts presented in the present instance, although scarce, show that the Debtor was actively involved in the operation, maintenance and management of the property. The Debtor participated in operating the restaurant and bar on the property. Ultimately, both the Debtor and Ms. O'Connor jointly leased the pub and jointly filed a tenant eviction action when the lease was breached by the tenant. Finally, they were jointly involved in locating the Christys as a potential purchaser of the stock of the corporation and negotiated the stock purchase jointly.

Based on the foregoing, this Court is satisfied that the Debtor had more than bare legal title to the stock in the corporation, that there is no competent evidence in this record to establish that the use of the Debtor's funds obtained from the stock sale was repaying a bona fide loan to the Debtor by Ms. O'Connor. Lastly, it is clear that the Debtor received nothing in return for divesting himself of his one-half interest in the stock in question.

In sum, this Court is satisfied that the one-half of the stock in CoCo was in fact owned by the Debtor; that the Debtor received no consideration for his transfer and, lastly, this Court is satisfied that there is no competent evidence that the Debtor was in fact indebted to Ms. O'Connor. For this reason, it is unnecessary to consider whether or not this alleged repayment of a loan was or was not a voidable preference.

This Court is also satisfied that the transfer in fact was a fraudulent transfer within the meaning of § 548(a)(2)(A).

A separate final judgment shall be entered in accordance with the foregoing.

6. AVOIDING POSTPETITION TRANSFERS OF PROPERTY OF THE ESTATE UNLESS THEY ARE AUTHORIZED BY THE BANKRUPTCY CODE OR BY THE BANKRUPTCY COURT

Postpetition transfers may be avoided by the trustee unless they are authorized by the Bankruptcy Code or by the bankruptcy court. 11 U.S.C.A. § 549(a).

EXAMPLE

William Pratt filed a petition in bankruptcy under Chapter 7 on December 3. On December 4, Pratt sold his coin collection to Toni Rogers for $5,000. At the time of the filing of the petition, the coin collection was property of the estate. This postpetition transfer of property of the estate may be avoided by the trustee because it was authorized by neither the Bankruptcy Code nor the bankruptcy court.

PROBLEM 5.37   On June 1, William Pratt borrowed $10,000 from People's Bank. This loan was unsecured. On December 7, four days after filing his Chapter 7 petition, Pratt paid People's Bank $2,000.

Can Pratt's trustee recover the $2,000 from People's Bank?

The Bankruptcy Code protects some postpetition transfers of realty by the debtor from the trustee's avoidance powers. To be protected, the transfer must have occurred and be properly recorded before a copy of the bankruptcy petition is filed in the real estate records for the county where the real estate is located, and the transferee must be a good faith purchaser who has no knowledge of the bankruptcy petition and has paid present fair equivalent value. A good faith purchaser who meets all the requirements but has paid less than present fair equivalent value only has a lien on the property to the extent of present value given. 11 U.S.C.A. § 549(c).

PROBLEM 5.38   William Pratt filed a petition in bankruptcy under Chapter 7 on December 3. On December 4, Pratt sold his lakeshore home valued at $85,000 to Michelle Hodges for $85,000. She paid $10,000 down and took a $75,000 mortgage from First Bank. Hodges recorded her deed on December 5. On December 6, Pratt's petition in bankruptcy was filed in the office of the real estate records in the county where the lakeshore home was located. On December 7, Hodges learned of Pratt's bankruptcy.

Could Pratt's trustee in bankruptcy avoid the sale of the lakeshore home to Hodges?

PROBLEM 5.39   Assume the same facts as in Problem 5.38, except that Hodges paid $10,000 down and Pratt carried the mortgage.

Could Pratt's trustee in bankruptcy avoid the sale of the lakeshore home to Hodges?

SECTION 4
PROOFS OF CLAIM AND PROOFS OF INTEREST

Proofs of claim or proofs of interest filed under 11 U.S.C.A. § 501 are deemed allowed unless a party in interest objects. 11 U.S.C.A. § 502(a). A claim may be contingent, unliquidated, or disputed. A contingent claim depends on some future event that may or may not take place.

EXAMPLE
Janice borrowed $1,000 from First Bank and signed a promissory note. Before First Bank would loan Janice the money, the bank required Janice to have her mother sign the promissory note as an accommodation maker. Janice's mother signed as comaker with the notation "collection guaranteed." By adding "collection guaranteed," Janice's mother promised that if the note is not paid by Janice when due, she will pay it. Janice's mother, however, will pay the note only after First Bank has reduced its claim against Janice to judgment and execution on the judgment has been returned unsatisfied, or after Janice has become insolvent or it is otherwise apparent that it is useless to proceed against her. First Bank's claim again Janice's mother is a contingent claim.

The amount of the claim is uncertain in an unliquidated claim.

EXAMPLE
The Flower Market hired the Metro Agency to design an advertising campaign. The compensation was set as "a reasonable fee." Metro designed the campaign and presented its bill for $5,000. Flower Market refused to pay the bill, claiming that it should be $2,000. Because the contract stated that the fee would be "a reasonable fee," Metro's claim is unliquidated.

A disputed claim is a claim by a creditor that is contested by the debtor.

EXAMPLE
Alexander Wiggins and Vanessa Gray were involved in an automobile accident. Both Alexander and Vanessa claimed to have had the right of way and therefore neither admitted to being at fault. Each claim is disputed.

PROBLEM 5.40   Charles Rigby & Daughter, building contractors, contracted with Peaceful Valley Property Company to construct an apartment complex. Guaranty Surety Company issued a surety bond with Charles Rigby & Daughter as principal and Peaceful Valley as beneficiary. The bond provides that if the principal does not complete construction of the apartment complex, Guaranty will pay to complete the work.

Is Guaranty's liability contingent, unliquidated, or disputed?

A. CREDITORS' AND INDENTURE TRUSTEES' PROOFS OF CLAIM

A claim is a right to payment or a right to an equitable remedy for breach of performance if the breach gives rise to a right to payment. 11 U.S.C.A. § 101(5). Creditors (except for equity security holders) and indenture trustees file proofs of claim in a Chapter 7 case.

If a creditor does not file a proof of claim on or before the first date set for the meeting of creditors, the debtor or the trustee may file it within 30 days following the deadline. Fed. R. Bank. P. 3004. An entity that is liable with the debtor to the creditor or that has secured the creditor may also file a proof of claim if the creditor does not timely file such proof. (See Exhibit 5.28.)

EXHIBIT 5.28
Proof of Claim

B10 (Official Form 10)
(Rev. 12/94)

United States Bankruptcy Court _____ District of _____	**PROOF OF CLAIM**
In re (Name of Debtor)	Case Number

NOTE: This form should not be used to make a claim for an administrative expense arising after the commencement of the case. A "request" for payment of an administrative expense may be filed pursuant to 11 U.S.C. § 503.

Name of Creditor *(The person or other entity to whom the debtor owes money or property)* Name and Address Where Notices Should be Sent Telephone No.	☐ Check box if you are aware that any- one else has filed a proof of claim relating to your claim. Attach copy of statement giving particulars. ☐ Check box if you have never received any notices from the bankruptcy court in this case. ☐ Check box if the address differs from the address on the envelope sent to you by the court.	THIS SPACE IS FOR COURT USE ONLY

ACCOUNT OR OTHER NUMBER BY WHICH CREDITOR IDENTIFIES DEBTOR:

Check here if this claim ☐ replaces ☐ amends   a previously filed claim, dated:_____

1. BASIS FOR CLAIM

☐ Goods sold
☐ Services performed
☐ Money loaned
☐ Personal injury/wrongful death
☐ Taxes
☐ Other (Describe briefly)

☐ Retiree benefits as defined in 11 U.S.C. § 1114(a)
☐ Wages, salaries, and compensation (Fill out below)
Your social security number_____
Unpaid compensation for services performed
from_____ to _____
(date)   (date)

2. DATE DEBT WAS INCURRED

3. IF COURT, JUDGMENT, DATE OBTAINED:

4. CLASSIFICATION OF CLAIM. Under the Bankruptcy Code all claims are classified as one or more of the following: (1) Unsecured nonpriority, (2) Unsecured Priority, (3) Secured. It is possible for part of a claim to be in one category and part in another.
CHECK THE APPROPRIATE BOX OR BOXES that best describe your claim and STATE THE AMOUNT OF THE CLAIM AT TIME CASE FILED.

☐ SECURED CLAIM $ _____
Attach evidence of perfection of security interest
Brief Description of Collateral:
☐ Real Estate ☐ Motor Vehicle ☐ Other (Describe briefly)

Amount of arrearage and other charges at time case filed included in secured claim above, if any $ _____

☐ UNSECURED NONPRIORITY CLAIM $ _____
A claim is unsecured if there is no collateral or lien on property of the debtor securing the claim or to the extent that the value of such property is less than the amount of the claim.

☐ UNSECURED PRIORITY CLAIM $ _____
Specify the priority of the claim.

☐ Wages, salaries, or commissions (up to $4000),* earned not more than 90 days before filing of the bankruptcy petition or cessation of the debtor's business, whichever is earlier—11 U.S.C. § 507(a)(3)

☐ Contributions to an employee benefit plan—11 U.S.C. § 507(a)(4)

☐ Up to $1,800* of deposits toward purchase, lease, or rental of property or services for personal, family, or household use—11 U.S.C. § 507(a)(6)

☐ Alimony, maintenance, or support owed to a spouse, former spouse, or child—11 U.S.C. § 507(a)(7)

☐ Taxes or penalties of governmental units—11 U.S.C. § 507(a)(8)

☐ Other—Specify applicable paragraph of 11 U.S.C. § 507(a)_____
*Amounts are subject to adjustment on 4/1/98 and every 3 years thereafter with respect to cases commenced on or after the date of adjustment.

5. TOTAL AMOUNT OF CLAIM AT TIME CASE FILED:
$ _____ (Unsecured) $ _____ (Secured) $ _____ (Priority) $ _____ (Total)

☐ Check this box if claim includes charges in addition to the principal amount of the claim. Attach itemized statement of all additional charges.

6. CREDITS AND SETOFFS: The amount of all payments on this claim has been credited and deducted for the purpose of making this proof of claim. In filing this claim, claimant has deducted all amounts that claimant owes to debtor.

7. SUPPORTING DOCUMENTS: *Attach copies of supporting documents,* such as promissory notes, purchase orders, invoices, itemized statements of running accounts, contracts, court judgments, or evidence of security interests. If the documents are not available, explain. If the documents are voluminous, attach a summary.

8. TIME-STAMPED COPY: To receive an acknowledgement of the filing of your claim, enclose a stamped, self-addressed envelope and copy of this proof of claim.

THIS SPACE IS FOR
COURT USE ONLY

Date	Sign and print the name and title, if any, of the creditor or other person authorized to file this claim (attach copy of power of attorney, if any)

Penalty for presenting fraudulent claim: Fine of up to $500,000 or imprisonment for up to 5 years, or both. 18 U.S.C. §§ 152 and 3571.

B. EQUITY SECURITY HOLDERS' PROOFS OF INTEREST

An interest can be the interest of a limited partner in a limited partnership. A share in a corporation is also an interest. These interests are called equity securities and are held by equity security holders. Equity security holders file proofs of interest in a Chapter 7 case.

SECTION 5
MOTIONS AND COMPLAINTS AFTER THE ORDER FOR RELIEF

Disputed matters in the bankruptcy process are designated as either contested matters or adversary proceedings. A **contested matter** is initiated by a motion. An **adversary proceeding** is initiated by a complaint.

The difference between raising an issue by motion or by complaint is very striking. If the issue is raised by a complaint, it becomes the basis of a federal court lawsuit. The complaint must be filed in the bankruptcy court, a copy transmitted to the United States trustee, and the filing fee paid. The Federal Rules of Civil Procedure apply to the process for resolving the dispute, except as altered to meet the necessities of bankruptcy practice. See Fed. R. Bank. P. 7002–7087.

If an issue is raised by motion, the motion is filed with the bankruptcy court and a copy is transmitted to the United States trustee. No filing fee is paid. A motion results in a decision that is a judgment. That judgment is final for that particular issue, unless appealed.

The formalities of the adversary proceeding process and the time required to serve pleadings run counter to an expedited schedule. The motion practice, on the other hand, is better suited to an expedited schedule because it gives the bankruptcy court flexibility to fix hearing dates and other deadlines that are tailored to the case.

In bankruptcy practice, some judges allow a party to raise a disputed matter by motion, even though it should have been by complaint, if no one objects. If an objection is raised, the judge may require the disputed matter to be tried as an adversary proceeding. If a procedure for resolving a dispute should have been by complaint but was raised by motion and if the procedure was not challenged, the challenge to the procedure has been waived.

Whether an issue must be raised by motion or by complaint is governed by Federal Rules of Bankruptcy Procedure 9014 and 7001. Rule 9014, entitled "Contested Matters," begins by stating

> In a contested matter in a case under the Code not otherwise governed by these rules, relief shall be requested by motion . . . .

"[N]ot otherwise governed by these rules" refers to Rule 7001, entitled "Scope of Rules of Part VII." The Rules in Part VII deal exclusively with adversary proceedings. Rule 7001 begins with the sentence

> An adversary proceeding is governed by the rules of this Part VII.

Rule 7001 delineates those proceedings that must be brought under Part VII by a complaint and therefore are adversary proceedings:

> (1) to recover money or property, except a proceeding to compel the debtor to deliver property to the trustee, or a proceeding under § 554(b) or § 725 of the Code, Rule 2017, or Rule 6002;

(2) to determine the validity, priority, or extent of a lien or other interest in property, other than a proceeding under Rule 4003(d);

(3) to obtain approval pursuant to § 363(h) for the sale of both the interest of the estate and of a co-owner in property;

(4) to object to or revoke a discharge;

(5) to revoke an order of confirmation of a chapter 11, chapter 12, or chapter 13 plan;

(6) to determine the dischargeability of a debt;

(7) to obtain an injunction or other equitable relief;

(8) to subordinate any allowed claim or interest, except when subordination is provided in a chapter 9, 11, 12, or 13 plan;

(9) to obtain a declaratory judgment relating to any of the foregoing; or

(10) to determine a claim or cause of action removed pursuant to 28 U.S.C. § 1452.

EXAMPLE

Title 11 U.S.C.A. § 522(f) states those instances in which the debtor may avoid a lien on his or her property to the extent that the lien impairs an exemption to which the debtor would have been entitled. This section of the Code does not state whether the debtor must seek to avoid the lien by filing a complaint or by filing a motion. Federal Rules of Bankruptcy Procedure 4003(d), however, states that the debtor's proceeding to avoid the lien is by motion in accordance with Rule 9014.

EXAMPLE

The Code does not state whether relief from the automatic stay is by motion or by complaint.

(d) *On request of a party in interest* and after notice and a hearing, the court shall grant relief from the stay provided under subsection (a) of this section, such as by terminating, annulling, modifying, or conditioning such stay—

(1) for cause, including the lack of adequate protection of an interest in property of such party in interest;

(2) with respect to a stay of an act against property under subsection (a) of this section, if—

(A) the debtor does not have an equity in such property; and

(B) such property is not necessary to an effective reorganization.

(3) . . . .

11 U.S.C.A. § 362(d). (*Emphasis added.*)

Rule 4001(a), however, provides that a request for relief from an automatic stay must be made in accordance with Rule 9014, the rule authorizing motions. Therefore, requests for relief from an automatic stay do not commence with an adversary proceeding but rather with a motion.

A. MOTIONS

Motions may be made by the debtor, by a party in interest, by the United States trustee, and by the court.

1. MOTIONS BY THE DEBTOR

The Chapter 7 debtor may move to convert the case to Chapter 11, 12, or 13, to dismiss the case, or to change venue.

a. Motion to Convert to a Chapter 11, 12, or 13   Although a debtor who has filed a Chapter 7 case is authorized by the Code to convert the case to a Chapter 11, 12, or 13, this right is rarely, if ever, exercised. 11 U.S.C.A. § 706(a). The filing of a

Chapter 7 petition creates the estate and begins the process of liquidation, which depletes the assets that would be used in the Chapter 11, 12, or 13 plan. If the debtor changes his or her mind for some reason and decides to convert to another chapter, the conversion would have to take place before essential assets are liquidated to enable the debtor to prepare a viable plan.

The debtor may not elect to convert a Chapter 7 case if the case has already been converted to a liquidation proceeding from Chapter 11, 12, or 13. 11 U.S.C.A. § 706(a). Also, the debtor may not waive the right to convert. An attempted waiver would be unenforceable. 11 U.S.C.A. § 706(a). See Exhibit 5.29 for a sample motion to convert the case.

EXHIBIT 5.29
Debtor's Motion to Convert from Chapter 7 to Chapter 11, 12, or 13

UNITED STATES BANKRUPTCY COURT
_____ **DISTRICT OF** _____

In re_____,
                    Debtor   Case No. _____

                                                         Chapter 7

DEBTOR'S MOTION TO CONVERT FROM CHAPTER 7
TO CHAPTER 11, 12, or 13

_____, debtor, moves the court:
                                            1.
Debtor filed a petition under Chapter 7 of the Bankruptcy Code on
_____ , 19 _____ .
                                            2.
      Debtor is eligible for relief under Chapter _____ of the Bankruptcy Code, having not previously converted this case from a case filed under Chapter 11, 12, or 13 of the Bankruptcy Code.
                                            3.
      Debtor moves the court to convert the Chapter 7 case to a case under Chapter _____ .
                                            4.
      A copy of debtor's proposed plan:
[ ] is attached; or
[ ] will be filed pursuant to Chapter _____ of the Bankruptcy Code.
      WHEREFORE, debtor prays for an order for relief under Chapter _____ of the Bankruptcy Code.

Dated:_____ , 19_____ _____
                                                      Attorney for the Debtor

DECLARATION
      I, _____ , declare under penalty of perjury that I have read the foregoing motion, and that it is true and correct to the best of my knowledge, information, and belief.

Executed on:_____ _____
                                                   Debtor

b. Motion to Dismiss the Case   Although the Bankruptcy Code does not state that a Chapter 7 debtor may move to dismiss the case, the Rules do so provide. Compare 11 U.S.C.A. § 707 with Fed. R. Bank. P. 1017(a). If a debtor moves to dismiss the case, the debtor is required to file a list of all creditors' names and addresses within a time fixed by the court, unless a list was previously filed. Notice is sent by the office of the bankruptcy court clerk to all creditors and a hearing on the issue of dismissal is held. See Fed. R. Bank. P. 2002(a). See Exhibit 5.30 for a sample motion to dismiss the case.

EXAMPLE
On March 15, Sharon Sanders filed a petition in bankruptcy under Chapter 7. On April 1, she discovered that she would receive a $5,000 refund from the IRS as an overpayment on her last year's taxes. She also discovered that because she has filed a petition in bankruptcy, her tax refund will become property of the estate. Sanders may decide to file a motion to dismiss her case to retain the IRS refund.

PROBLEM 5.41   On July 1, Henry Hunter filed a petition in bankruptcy under Chapter 7. Shortly after filing, Hunter discovered that the security interest on his new Rolls Royce was unperfected by First Bank and that the exemption he could claim for the Rolls was limited to $3,000. Hunter had thought the security interest on the Rolls was perfected by First Bank and that he could enter a reaffirmation agreement with First Bank and thus retain the Rolls.

Hunter does not want to part with his Rolls. What should he do and why?

EXHIBIT 5.30
Debtor's Motion to Dismiss the Bankruptcy Case

UNITED STATES BANKRUPTCY COURT
_____ DISTRICT OF _____

In re_____,
          Debtor   Case No. _____
                                           Chapter 7

DEBTOR'S MOTION TO DISMISS THE BANKRUPTCY CASE

_____, debtor, moves the court:

1.

Debtor filed a petition under Chapter 7 of the Bankruptcy Code on
_____ , 19 _____ .

2.

Debtor moves the court to dismiss this case.

3.

Debtor feels that he/she can resolve his/her financial affairs with creditors without the aid of proceedings under the Bankruptcy Code and that the best interests of debtor and his/her creditors are served by dismissal of this case.

WHEREFORE, debtor prays for an order dismissing this case.

Dated:_____ , 19_____ _____
                                                 Attorney for the Debtor

DECLARATION

I, _____ , declare under penalty of perjury that I have read the foregoing motion, and that it is true and correct to the best of my knowledge, information, and belief.

Executed on:_____   _____
                                               Debtor

c. Motion for a Change of Venue   The United States district courts "have original and exclusive jurisdiction of all cases under title 11." 28 U.S.C.A. § 1334(a). This jurisdictional grant is then passed on to the bankruptcy court. "Each district court may provide that any or all cases under title 11 and any or all proceedings arising under title 11 or arising in or related to a case under title 11 shall be referred to the bankruptcy judges for the district." 28 U.S.C.A. § 157(a). When a court has jurisdiction, it has the power to decide a case. Therefore, all United States bankruptcy courts have jurisdiction over all bankruptcy cases.

Not every United States bankruptcy court, however, will have venue over a particular case. Venue is the location at which a particular case or issue in a particular case will be heard and decided. More than one United States bankruptcy court may have venue to hear a case or issue. 28 U.S.C.A. § 1408.

> Except as provided in section 1410 of this title, a case under title 11 may be commenced in the district court for the district—
>
> (1) in which the domicile, residence, principal place of business in the United States, or principal assets in the United States, of the person or entity that is the subject of such case have been located for the one hundred and eighty days immediately preceding such commencement, or for a longer portion of such one-hundred-and-eighty-day period than the domicile, residence, or principal place of business, in the United States, or principal assets in the United States, of such person were located in any other district . . . . 28 U.S.C.A. § 1408(1).

Exhibit 5.31 illustrates 28 U.S.C.A. § 1408(1).

EXHIBIT 5.31
Establishing Venue for a Bankruptcy Case

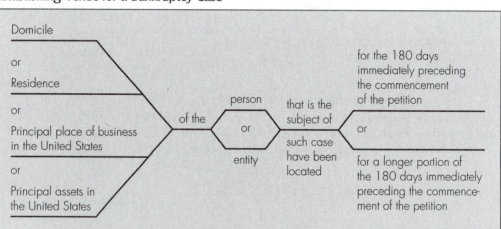

EXAMPLE
For the 180 days immediately preceding the filing of a Chapter 7 petition in bankruptcy, the debtor's domicile was in the Eastern District of Tennessee, although her principal place of business was in the Middle District of Tennessee. The debtor has the option to file her Chapter 7 petition in either the Eastern or the Middle District.

PROBLEM 5.42   For the 180 days immediately preceding the filing of a Chapter 7 petition in bankruptcy, the debtor moved twice. She resided in the Eastern District of Tennessee for the first 80 days, in the Middle District of Tennessee for the next 55 days, and in the Western District of Tennessee for the final 45 days. During this time, the debtor's principal place of business was in the Eastern District of Tennessee for the first 80 days and in the Western District of Tennessee for the last 100 days.

Which district would have venue?

Could more than one district have venue?

A debtor may move to have the court transfer the case to another district if the transfer is "in the interest of justice or for the convenience of the parties." 28 U.S.C.A. § 1412. In a bankruptcy case, the proximity of the debtor, the creditors, and witnesses to the court; the location of assets; and the economic and efficient administration of the case are factors. See *In re Old Delmar Corp.,* 45 B.R. 883 (Bankr. S.D.N.Y. 1985). See Exhibit 5.32 for a sample motion to change venue.

EXHIBIT 5.32
Debtor's Motion to Transfer the Bankruptcy Case

UNITED STATES BANKRUPTCY COURT
_____ DISTRICT OF _____

In re_____,
           Debtor   Case No. _____
                                               Chapter 7

DEBTOR'S MOTION TO TRANSFER THE CASE

_____, debtor, moves the court:
                                        1.
Debtor filed a petition under Chapter 7 of the Bankruptcy Code on
_____ , 19 _____ .
                                        2.
       Debtor moves the court to transfer the case to the United States Bankruptcy Court for the _____ District of _____.
                                        3.
       Debtor no longer has his/her residence or domicile in this district and the debtor has a substantial amount of his/her assets in the _____ District of
_____.
       WHEREFORE, debtor prays for an order transferring this case.

Dated:_____ , 19_____ _____
                                               Attorney for the Debtor

DECLARATION
       I, _____ , declare under penalty of perjury that I have read the foregoing motion, and that it is true and correct to the best of my knowledge, information, and belief.

Executed on:_____   _____
                                               Debtor

PROBLEM 5.43   The debtor lived in the Eastern District of New York up until six months before she filed a petition in bankruptcy. When she left the Eastern District of New York for the District of Kansas, she left most of her assets in the Eastern District of New York. Two weeks after filing her petition in bankruptcy under Chapter 7 in the District of Kansas, the debtor was transferred back to the Eastern District of New York.

Should the debtor's case be transferred to the Eastern District of New York?

In addition to venue of the entire bankruptcy case, individual items of litigation are subject to venue. Contrast 28 U.S.C.A. § 1408 with 28 U.S.C.A. § 1409. The debtor may move to change venue of an individual item of litigation. 28 U.S.C.A. § 1412.

d. Motion to Enforce the Automatic Stay   The automatic stay, although broad and inclusive, does not operate to stay a number of activities enumerated in 11 U.S.C.A. § 362(b). Parties in interest involved in an activity under 11 U.S.C.A. § 362(b) may move to modify the stay to clarify their rights. In practice, however, the parties in interest usually continue with their activities, and it is the debtor who will move to enforce the stay. If a motion is made, the bankruptcy court must then determine whether the activity is within the exceptions of § 362(b).

EXAMPLE
On June 1, Oscar Moorehead purchased a TV from Pappy's Appliances and paid by check. On June 7, the check was dishonored by Moorehead's bank and returned to Pappy's Appliances for lack of sufficient funds. On June 12, Moorehead filed a petition in bankruptcy under Chapter 7. On June 15, Pappy's telephoned the county district attorney to file a complaint concerning the hot check.
On June 20, the district attorney filed charges on the hot check. Moorehead filed a motion in the bankruptcy court to stay the criminal proceedings in state court.
Most bankruptcy courts will not enjoin the county district attorney from prosecuting the debtor because the automatic stay does not operate to stay the commencement of a criminal action against the debtor. 11 U.S.C.A. § 362(b)(1).

EXAMPLE
Assume the same facts as in the previous example except that on June 20 the district attorney wrote Moorehead the following letter: "If you do not pay this bad check within seven days, we will prosecute you." At the time of writing the letter, the district attorney knew that Moorehead had filed for bankruptcy. Moorehead did not respond to the letter, and the district attorney filed charges on the hot check. Moorehead filed a motion in the bankruptcy court to stay the criminal proceedings in state court.
Many bankruptcy courts will enjoin the county district attorney from prosecuting the debtor on the ground that the prosecution is being used as a collection device and not in a good faith effort to enforce the criminal laws. 11 U.S.C.A. § 362(b)(1).

2. MOTIONS BY A PARTY IN INTEREST

A party in interest may move for relief from the automatic stay, to dismiss the case, for abstention by the court, to change venue, for disallowance of a claim, or for an examination of any entity.

a. Motion for Relief from the Automatic Stay   As discussed earlier, the filing of a petition brings into effect an "order for relief" and invokes the automatic stay. 11 U.S.C.A. § 362(a). This, of course, gives complete and immediate protection to the debtor from the acts affected by the automatic stay, such as dismemberment of the estate by a party in interest.

Even if the property is subject to the automatic stay under 11 U.S.C.A. § 362(a), a party in interest may still have an off-setting right. A party in interest may move for a modification of the stay.

> (d) On request of a party in interest and after notice and a hearing, the court shall grant relief from the stay . . . such as by terminating, annulling, modifying, or conditioning such stay—
> (1) for cause, including the lack of adequate protection of an interest in property of such party in interest . . . . 11 U.S.C.A. § 362(d)(1).

Upon the filing of the case, the debtor will not discontinue the use of property, and much of the property of the debtor that becomes a part of the debtor's estate will represent collateral secured by one or more secured creditors. This property may be of substantial value, depreciating with use, and subject to possible loss or damage incurred in the use.

Much bankruptcy litigation involves a party in interest's motion to modify the automatic stay. In *In re King,* Metropolitan Mortgage and Securities Company held the first mortgage ($60,236) on real estate owned by King, the Chapter 7 debtor. In addition to Metropolitan's claim, four other entities also asserted claims against the property. Their claims totaled $70,000. The fair market value of the property was only $95,000. Metropolitan moved to modify the automatic stay so it could repossess and foreclose its security interest on the real property.

In re King
United States District Court, Northern District of Ohio, 1994.
1994 WL 328618.

MEMORANDUM OPINION AND ORDER
Richard L. Speer,
Bankruptcy Judge

This cause comes before the Court after Hearing on Creditor's Motion for Relief from Stay and Abandonment, Debtor's Objection, and Creditor's Relief from Stay Worksheet. The Court has reviewed the written arguments of Counsel, supporting affidavits, all correspondences, and written exhibits, as well as the entire record in the case. Based on that review, and for the following reasons, the Court finds that the Motion for Relief from Stay and Abandonment should be Granted.

FACTS

Metropolitan Mortgage and Securities Company, Inc. (hereafter "Creditor") holds a secured first mortgage on real estate owned by Chapter 7 Debtor, Deborah A. King (hereafter "Debtor"). The property is located at 1019 N. Byrne Road, Toledo, Ohio (hereafter "Property"). See Creditor's Exhibit "A").

The mortgage loan is in default for October, 1992, and all subsequent months, and the approximate balance due and owing on said mortgage loan account is Sixty Thousand Two Hundred Thirty-Six and 16/100 Dollars ($60,236.16). (See Creditor's Relief from Stay Worksheet). The fair market value of the Property at this time is approximately Ninety-Five Thousand and 00/100 Dollars ($95,000.00). (See Creditor's Relief from Stay Worksheet).

The Debtor may additionally claim an exemption of Five Thousand and 00/100 Dollars ($5,000.00) in the Property during a

Chapter 7 Bankruptcy by state law. Ohio Rev. Code Ann. § 2329.69(A)(1) (Anderson 1991).

According to the Schedules, the State of Ohio has a secondary priority claim in the Property of Five Thousand Two and 79/100 Dollars ($5,002.79) plus interest from March 26, 1987.

Adams-Huron Investments also has a claim by virtue of a certified judgment lien filed for record in the Lucas County Court of Common Pleas on October 6, 1989, of Five Thousand Thirty-Seven and 64/100 Dollars ($5,037.64) plus ten percent (10%) interest from September 22, 1989.

Real estate taxes are also outstanding against the Property. The total outstanding is One Thousand One Hundred Forty-Four and 33/100 Dollars ($1,144.33) plus penalty.

In addition, the Creditor raised a concern at the Hearing about a claim the Internal Revenue Service (hereafter "IRS") has or may have, by virtue of five (5) federal tax liens of approximately One Hundred Ten Thousand and 00/100 Dollars ($110,000.00). The Debtor is currently seeking abatement of the five (5) IRS claims pursuant to 26 U.S.C. § 6013 and 26 U.S.C. § 6404; however, at this time, Debtor has not been absolved of the liabilities.

The Creditor has filed a Motion under 11 U.S.C. § 362(d) for Relief from Stay and Abandonment, and the Debtor has Objected.

LAW

11 U.S.C. § 362 Automatic Stay.

(d) On request of a party in interest and after notice and a hearing, the court shall grant relief from the stay provided under subsection (a) of this section, such as by terminating, annulling, modifying, or conditioning such stay—

(1) for cause, including the lack of protection of an interest in property of such party in interest; or

(2) with respect to a stay of an act against property under subsection (a) of this section, if—

(A) the debtor does not have an equity in such property; and

(B) such property is not necessary to an effective reorganization.

(g) In any hearing under subsection (d) or (e) of this section concerning relief from the stay of any act under subsection (a) of this section—

(1) the party requesting such relief has the burden of proof on the issue of debtor's equity in the property; and

(2) the party opposing such relief has the burden of proof on all other issues.

DISCUSSION

The Creditor, who holds a secured first priority mortgage of property of Chapter 7 Debtor, has Motioned for Relief from Stay and Abandonment. The Debtor objects because she believes she has equity in the Property.

The issue before the Court involves a Relief from Stay and Abandonment. Pursuant to 11 U.S.C. § 157(b)(2)(G), core proceedings include motions to terminate, annul, or modify the automatic stay. This is a core proceeding.

By statute the Court must grant relief if a creditor shows that cause exists to lift the stay due to lack of adequate protection or if the creditor shows both that the debtor does not have equity in the property and the property is not necessary to an effective reorganization. 11 U.S.C. § 362(d). See also *In re Shriver,* 33 B.R. 176 (N.D.Ohio 1983).

The creditor has the burden of proof on the issue of a debtor's equity in the property, and the debtor has all other burdens of proof. 11 U.S.C. § 362(g).

In this case, the first test is not met by the Creditor. The Property has a fair market value of Ninety-Five Thousand and 00/100 Dollars ($95,000.00). The Creditor's secured first prioirty interest in the Property is estimated at Sixty Thousand Two Hundred Thirty-Six and 16/100 Dollars ($60,236.16). Therefore the Court finds that the Creditor does not lack adequate protection of its interest.

However, the Creditor does meet the alternative secondary test. There are four (4) definite additional claims against the Property. The Debtor has a statutory exemption of Five Thousand and 00/100 Dollars ($5,000.00). Ohio Rev. Code Ann. § 2329.69(A)(1) (Anderson 1991). The State of Ohio holds a second claim for approximately Five Thousand and 00/100 Dollars ($5,000.00). Adams-Huron Investments has an additional claim by virtue of a certified judgment lien filed for record on October 6, 1989, of Five Thousand Thirty-Seven and 64/100 Dollars ($5,037.64) plus ten percent (10%) interest from September 22, 1989. Real estate taxes are also outstanding against the Property. The total outstanding is One Thousand One Hundred Forty-Four and 33/100 Dollars ($1,144.33) plus penalty.

Combined, the five (5) interests against the Property total approximately Seventy-Five Thousand and 00/100 Dollars ($75,000.00). That leaves Twenty Thousand and 00/100 Dollars ($20,000.00) in estimated equity, subject to penalties, interest charges, and the potential sixth claim of the IRS for One Hundred Ten Thousand and 00/100 Dollars ($110,000.00).

On the issue of determining the Debtor's equity in the Property, the burden of proof lies with the Creditor. 11 U.S.C. § 362(g)(1). The Court finds that the Creditor has shown sufficient proof that Debtor does not have equity in the Property.

The Court further finds that the Property is not necessary for reorganization. If this Motion for Relief is Granted, the Property will be liquidated and all secured creditors paid. Maintaining the Property's current status does not protect any asset of the estate for potential unsecured creditors. The liquidation of this Property will not interfere with the reorganization process, and therefore preventing the liquidation of the Property is not necessary.

CONCLUSION

The Court finds that the Debtor does not have equity in the Property due to potentially six (6) priority claims or exemptions against it. The Court further finds that a continued stay under 11 U.S.C. § 362(a) is not necessary for the reorganization of the estate.

In reaching the conclusion found herein, the Court has considered all of the evidence, exhibits, and arguments of counsel, regardless of whether or not they are specifically referred to in this opinion.

Accordingly, it is

ORDERED that Creditor's Motion for Relief from Stay and Abandonment be, and is hereby GRANTED.

The modification of the automatic stay with respect to one act or item of property will not affect the applicability of the stay to other acts or other items of property.

When a party in interest files a motion to modify the automatic stay, the Code mandates that the hearing be on an accelerated calendar. 11 U.S.C.A. § 362(e).

The bankruptcy court has the power to grant a modification of the stay on the request of a party in interest without a hearing if necessary to prevent irreparable damage to that party's interest in the property. Such a modification of the stay will only be granted if the interest will suffer irreparable damage before there is an opportunity for notice and a hearing under 11 U.S.C.A. §§ 362(d) or (e). 11 U.S.C.A. § 362(f).

In any hearing concerning relief from the automatic stay, the party requesting the relief has the burden of proof on the issue of the debtor's equity in property and the party opposing the relief has the burden of proof on all other issues. 11 U.S.C.A. § 362(g).

EXAMPLE

Mark Buffington, the owner of commercial real estate, financed his purchase of the real estate with Grand Avenue Bank. The real estate mortgage was substantial in light of the value of the real estate. Shortly after purchasing the property, Buffington defaulted on his mortgage payments and filed for bankruptcy under Chapter 7. Because the commercial real estate was property of the estate, it was subject to the automatic stay.

Grand Avenue Bank filed a motion to modify the stay so it could foreclose on the property and sell it. Grand Avenue Bank claimed that there was no equity in the property because the mortgage was larger than the value of the property.

In the hearing on the motion to modify the stay, Grand Avenue Bank, the party making the motion to modify the stay, has the burden of proof on the issue of the debtor's equity in the property. Therefore, the bank will be required to demonstrate the value of the property.

If the court determines that there is in fact an equity cushion, the cushion will be deemed to be adequate protection even without mortgage payments being made.

Buffington, the party opposing the bank's motion, has the burden of proof on all other issues.

The parties may agree that the stay is not enforceable or will not be enforced with respect to certain property. The parties can also agree that certain conditions are required for the automatic stay to remain in effect. Very often these agreements are strictly informal, without a writing. See Exhibit 5.33 for a sample motion for relief from the automatic stay.

EXHIBIT 5.33
Party in Interest's Motion for Relief from the Automatic Stay

---

UNITED STATES BANKRUPTCY COURT
_____ **DISTRICT OF** _____

In re _____ ,
                    Debtor   Case No. _____
                                                        Chapter 7

           MOTION FOR RELIEF FROM AUTOMATIC STAY AND NOTICE OF INTENT TO
SEEK ABANDONMENT OF PROPERTY, OR ALTERNATIVELY SEEKING ADEQUATE
PROTECTION AND RELIEF IN SUPPORT THEREOF

           COMES NOW, _____ , [hereinafter referred
to as movant] pursuant to 11 U.S.C.A. §§ 361, 362, and 554, and moves the
court to grant it relief from the automatic stay and order abandonment of
_____ [describe the collateral], or in the alternative, to
require debtor to provide adequate protection of movant's interest in the collateral.
           In support of its motion, movant alleges:
                                                1.
           That the maker, for consideration, issued to payee a promissory note which is at-
tached, marked Exhibit A, and made a part of this motion.
                                                2.
           As a part of the same transaction, and to secure the payment of the note and the
indebtedness represented by the note, the maker created a real estate mortgage in the
following real estate in which he/she was the owner:
                          [description of the real estate]
           A copy of the mortgage, marked Exhibit B, is attached and made a part of this
motion.
                                                3.
           Movant is the current owner and holder of the note and mortgage.
                                                4.
           The note and mortgage are in default. After allowing all just credits, movant has
due on the note and mortgage the sum of $ _____ , with _____ percent interest
per annum from _____, until paid; and the further sum of $
_____ for attorney fees.
                                                5.
           The mortgage is a valid first lien against the mortgaged property, prior and su-
perior to any right, title, lien, estate, or interest of the debtor or any other party.
                                                6.
           The debtor has no equity in the mortgaged property.
                                                7.
           Movant will suffer irreparable injury, loss, and damage unless the automatic stay
is terminated so as to permit movant to commence with its foreclosure action or, in the
alternative, the debtor shall be required to provide movant with adequate protection of
its interest in the mortgaged property.

EXHIBIT 5.33
Continued

8.

The mortgaged property is burdensome to the estate or is of inconsequential value to the estate and it is therefore in the best interest of the estate and the debtor that relief from the automatic stay be granted and that the mortgaged property be abandoned so as to permit movant to proceed in state court with an action for foreclosure.

9.

Notice of the motion and a copy of Rules _____ of the Local Rules for Bankruptcy Practice and Procedure have been mailed to the trustee, the debtor, and all parties listed on the matrix filed by the debtor.

WHEREFORE, movant moves the court for an order vacating or modifying the automatic stay as provided by 11 U.S.C.A. § 362 and directing the trustee to abandon the mortgaged property as authorized by 11 U.S.C.A. § 554 as full satisfaction of the personal liability of debtor and so as to permit movant and other interested parties to enforce their liens against the mortgaged property.

_____
Movant

By: _____
Attorney for Movant

CERTIFICATE OF SERVICE

I hereby certify that I mailed a true and correct copy of this motion with postage thereon fully prepaid to: [*name and address of debtor*], [*name and address of debtor's attorney*], [*name and address of trustee*], and to all creditors on the matrix, on _____ , 19 _____ .

_____
Attorney for Movant

b. Motion to Dismiss the Case   The case may also be dismissed for cause, including unreasonable delay by the debtor that is prejudicial to creditors. 11 U.S.C.A. § 707(a)(1). All creditors, however, must be given notice as provided in Rule 2002(a). Fed. R. Bank. P. 1017(a). See Exhibit 5.34 for a sample motion to dismiss the case.

EXHIBIT 5.34
Party in Interest's Motion to Dismiss the Bankruptcy Case

UNITED STATES BANKRUPTCY COURT

_____ **DISTRICT OF** _____

In re _____ ,

                Debtor   Case No. _____

                                Chapter 7

MOTION TO DISMISS THE BANKRUPTCY CASE

_____, moving party, moves the court:

1.

Debtor filed a petition under Chapter 7 of the Bankruptcy Code
on _____ , 19 _____ .

2.

The moving party is a creditor.

3.

    The debtor's delay in _____ is unreasonable and is prej-
udicial to the moving party in that _____ .

4.

The moving party moves the court to dismiss this case.

WHEREFORE, the moving party prays for an order dismissing this case.

Dated: _____ , 19 _____ _____
                                        Attorney for the Moving Party

CERTIFICATE OF SERVICE

    I hereby certify that I mailed a true and correct copy of this motion with postage
thereon fully prepaid to: [_name and address of debtor_], [_name and address of debtor's
attorney_], [_name and address of trustee_], and to all creditors on the matrix, on
_____ , 19 _____ .

                                        _____
                                        Attorney for Movant

c. Motion for Abstention by the Court   A party in interest may move for abstention by the court. The abstention may be from hearing the case or from hearing an issue. The motion to abstain may be necessary because another tribunal may be better suited to try the matter or because another solution to the debtor's financial problems may be possible and even preferable. Abstention is mandatory in some situations and permissive in others. 28 U.S.C.A. § 1334(c); 11 U.S.C.A. § 305.

d. Motion for a Change of Venue   A party in interest may move for a change in venue of either the entire case or an issue in the case. After notice, a hearing will be conducted on whether the transfer is in the interest of justice or for the convenience of the parties. Compare 28 U.S.C.A. § 1412 with Fed. R. Bank. P. 1014(a)(1).

e. Motion for Disallowance of a Claim   A proof of claim is deemed allowed unless there is an objection by a party in interest. 11 U.S.C.A. § 502(a). The Code prescribes nine grounds on which a claim may be disallowed. 11 U.S.C.A. § 502(b). If the objection involves the determination of the validity, priority, or extent of a lien or other interest in property, a complaint rather than a motion must be used. Fed. R. Bank. P. 7001.

f. Motion for Examination of Any Entity   A party in interest may move for the examination of any entity. Fed. R. Bank. P. 2004. Attendance of a witness and production of documentary evidence may be compelled. Fed R. Bank. P. 9016. The examination may take place in the district in which the case is pending or in another district. An entity other than the debtor will receive mileage and a witness fee, of which payment for one day must be tendered before the witness is required to attend. The debtor will receive mileage only (no witness fee) for attending an examination more than 100 miles from his or her residence for the amount over 100 miles.

The scope of the examination is limited to the acts, conduct, property, liabilities, and financial condition of the debtor; to any matter that may affect the administration of the estate; or to the debtor's right to a discharge. Fed. R. Bank. P. 2004(b).

3. MOTION BY THE UNITED STATES TRUSTEE TO DISMISS THE CASE

The United States trustee may move to dismiss a case for the debtor's failure to file—within 15 days or such additional time as the court may have allowed—the schedules and statement of financial affairs. 11 U.S.C.A. § 707(a)(3).

The United States trustee also may move to dismiss a case filed by an individual debtor under Chapter 7 whose debts are primarily consumer debts. The court, after notice and a hearing, will dismiss the case if it finds that the granting of relief would be a substantial abuse of the provisions of Chapter 7. The presumption, however, is in favor of the debtor for granting the relief that he or she requested. 11 U.S.C.A. § 707(b).

In re Tindall involves a motion by the U.S. trustee to dismiss the case for substantial abuse of the provisions of Chapter 7 under 11 U.S.C.A. § 707(b). Richard Tindall was retired from the United States Air Force and his wife, Grace, was employed by Northwest Airlines. Their Schedules of Current Income and Expenditures indicate their expenses exceed their income. The U.S. Trustee, however, claimed that the debtors actually did have monthly disposable income and that they did have the ability to pay a substantial portion of their creditors.

In re Tindall
United States Bankruptcy Court, Middle District of Florida, 1994.
184 B.R. 842.

**ORDER ON UNITED STATES
TRUSTEE'S MOTION TO DISMISS
CHAPTER 7 CASE**
Paul M. Glenn,
Bankruptcy Judge

This case came on for consideration on the United States Trustee's Motion to Dismiss Chapter 7 Case Pursuant to 11 U.S.C. § 707(b). In the Motion, the U.S. Trustee requests that this Chapter 7 case be dismissed pursuant to § 707(b) because granting relief would be a substantial abuse of the provisions of Chapter 7 of the Bankruptcy Code. Richard Dean Tindall and Grace Ann Tindall (Debtors) filed a response justifying their expenses and claiming that they are unable to pay a meaningful portion of their total unsecured debt.

The facts relevant to the resolution of this Motion, as established by the record and at hearing, are as follows: Richard Dean Tindall is retired from the United States Air Force and Grace Ann Tindall is employed, and has been for 14 years, by Northwest Airlines, Inc. The husband's retirement income is stable, and although the wife's income has been reduced recently because of a company-wide expense reduction, there is no indication that her employment will terminate in the near future. On May 20, 1993, the Debtors filed a voluntary Petition for relief under Chapter 7 of the Bankruptcy Code. An examination of the Debtors' Schedules of Assets and Liabilities indicates the following: (1) there is one creditor with a secured claim totaling $81,000.00, secured by the Debtors' homestead; (2) there are no priority creditors holding claims; and (3) there are 13 general unsecured creditors holding claims in the scheduled amount of $75,961.28, all of which were incurred by credit card purchases. In their Schedules of Current Income and Expenditures, the Debtors show a combined monthly income

of $4,628.86, and total monthly expenses of $5,381.07. The reduction in the wife's income reduces the combined monthly income to $4,347.84. Accordingly, scheduled expenses exceed the Debtors' income by $1,033.23.

The U.S. Trustee alleges that the Debtors actually have monthly disposable income. It asserts that their monthly expense budget should not contain at least the following items which the Debtors have included: cash reserve for newer car—$600.00; hospital expense reserve—$100.00; and home repairs of $729.00. Without these items in the budget, the Debtors would have monthly expenditures of $3,952.07, leaving a net disposable income of $395.77. The U.S. Trustee also points out that the budget includes other items such as recreation expense of $325.78, transportation expense (not including car payments, car insurance, or the reserve for a newer car) of $542.13, which the U.S. Trustee argues are excessive considering the financial condition of the Debtors. The U.S. Trustee argues that the Debtors have the ability to pay a substantial portion of their creditors, their income is stable, and the Chapter 7 filing was not precipitated by a sudden illness or calamity. Based on these facts, the U.S. Trustee asserts that the Chapter 7 case should be dismissed.

Section 707 of the Bankruptcy Code authorizes a court to dismiss a case under Chapter 7 if the filing represents a substantial abuse of that Chapter:

> (b) After notice and a hearing, the court, on its own motion or on a motion by the United States trustee, but not at the request or suggestion of any party in interest, may dismiss a case filed by an individual debtor under this chapter whose debts are primarily consumer debts if it finds that the

granting of relief would be a substantial abuse of the provisions of this chapter. There shall be a presumption in favor of granting the relief requested by the debtor.

When evaluating possible dismissal of a Chapter 7 case under § 707(b), it is important to consider: (1) whether the debts are primarily consumer debts; and (2) whether the granting of relief would be a substantial abuse of the provisions of Chapter 7. Additionally, there is a presumption in favor of granting the relief requested by the debtor.

All of the debts in this case are consumer debts. The secured debt is a note and mortgage for the Debtors' residence, which is a consumer debt. *See In re Kelly*, 841 F.2d 908, 913 (9th Cir.1988). The thirteen scheduled items of unsecured debt are all for credit card purchases, and the Debtors do not dispute that these are consumer debts.

There are a number of bankruptcy court and circuit court cases discussing guidelines for determining substantial abuse of Chapter 7. In all of these, the ability to repay creditors is a factor which is considered. In some cases it is the exclusive factor; in others, the primary factor. This Court agrees with the reasoning in the case *In re Green,* 934 F.2d 568 (4th Cir.1991), in which the ability to repay creditors is a factor to be considered along with other factors. That case concludes that the substantial abuse determination must be made on a case by case basis, in light of the totality of the circumstances. In *Green,* the court stated at page 572:

> The 'totality of the circumstances' approach involves an evaluation of factors such as the following:
>
> 1. Whether the bankruptcy petition was filed because of sudden illness, calamity, disability, or unemployment;
> 2. Whether the debtor incurred cash advances and made consumer purchases far in excess of his ability to repay;
> 3. Whether the debtor's proposed family budget is excessive or unreasonable;

> 4. Whether the debtor's schedules and statement of current income and expenses reasonably and accurately reflect the true financial condition; and
> 5. Whether the petition was filed in good faith.

Exploring these factors, as well as the relation of the debtor's future income to his future necessary expenses, allows the court to determine more accurately whether the particular debtor's case exemplifies the real concern behind Section 707(b): abuse of the bankruptcy process by a debtor seeking to take unfair advantage of his creditors. The debtor's relative solvency may raise an inference that such a situation exists. Nevertheless, in light of the statutory presumption that a debtor's Chapter 7 petition should be granted, solvency alone is not a sufficient basis for finding that the debtor has in fact substantially abused the provisions of Chapter 7.

The Court shall utilize the factors outlined in Green to evaluate this case.

1. *Whether the bankruptcy petition was filed because of sudden illness, calamity, disability, or unemployment.* In this case, the petition was not filed because of sudden illness, calamity, disability, or unemployment. The husband testified that he pursued three failed business ventures, and the Debtor simply were not able to pay expenses. This is not like the loss of employment; there are risks inherent in business ventures which do not accompany regular employment. While the circumstances are unfortunate, there is no sudden illness, calamity, disability, or unemployment.

2. *Whether the debtor incurred cash advances and made consumer purchases far in excess of his ability to repay.* The Debtors have carefully budgeted their expenses, and their regular, stable income does not allow them to meet their projected expenses. It is apparent that the Debtors have made consumer purchases far in excess of their ability to repay.

3. *Whether the debtor's proposed family budget is excessive or unreasonable.* The Court believes that the Debtors' proposed family budget is excessive and unreasonable. The Debtors' proposed budget contains both budgeted expenses and reserves for future anticipated expenses. It includes a cash reserve for a newer car of $600.00 per month, in addition to a transportation expense of $542.00 per month (which includes a reserve of $222.00 for projected repair expenses, and a reserve of $200.00 for projected major expenses). It includes a food budget of $645.00 for two people. It includes $325.00 per month for recreation expenses (which includes a $100.00 reserve for a vacation, and $90.00 monthly for haircuts, perms, nails, etc.). Also, it includes a home maintenance expense of $1,219.00 per month, which consists of $707.00 per month for forecast actual expenses within the next 12 months, and a savings reserve of $512.00 per month for projected future costs of items which the Debtors will wish to replace at the conclusion of their estimated useful lives. While some of these are necessary items, others are items such as a television set in the master bedroom, a microwave, a VCR, and a remote control stereo. Additionally, the reserves proposed to be set aside currently are for the replacement of items which, with few exceptions, have remaining estimated useful lives of 3, 5, 7, and 10 years. By budgeting current reserves for future expenses, the Debtors are asking that their present creditors (which may have helped, directly or indirectly, obtain many of these items) remain unpaid so the Debtors will be able to obtain new items at a later time. The Court does not believe it is appropriate to require the current creditors to remain unpaid so the Debtors can reserve for many of the forecast actual expenses[1] and many of the projected future replacement expenses.[2,3]

It is not this Court's function to propose a budget for the Debtors, but it is this Court's task to evaluate whether the budget they have proposed is excessive or unreasonable. The Court believes that this proposed budget is excessive and unreasonable.[4]

4. *Whether the debtor's schedules and statement of current income and expenses reasonably and accurately reflect the true financial condition.* The Court believes that the Debtors' schedules and statement of current income and expenses accurately reflect the true financial condition. The husband is a thorough and detail-oriented person. The income is accurately stated and the expenses are carefully budgeted. If the Debtors had sufficient income to pay their current debts and fund this budget, it would be a prudent budget. While the Court believes that the schedules are accurate, it does not believe that the amounts or reserves are reasonable in the situation where the Debtors also have unsecured consumer debt totaling $75,961.28.

5. *Whether the petition was filed in good faith.* With respect to whether the petition was filed in good faith, the Court finds no expressed unscrupulous motive in the filing of the petition. The Debtors are in their early 60's, one is retired, and they are planning for the other's retirement. They are careful planners and must view this petition as a way of assuring their later comfort. While the Court is sympathetic with this motive, this does not outweigh the other factors.

Considering these factors, in view of the totality of the circumstances, this Court believes that the Motion of the United States Trustee should be granted and the petition should be dismissed pursuant to 11 U.S.C. § 707(b).

Accordingly,

IT IS ORDERED that:

1. The United States Trustee's Motion to Dismiss Chapter 7 Case is granted and this case is dismissed.

2. Dismissal will be delayed for 10 days from the entry of this Order to allow the Debtors to file a notice of voluntary conversion to Chapter 13, if they wish.

---

[1] The Court does not believe it is appropriate to require the present creditors to remain unpaid so the Debtors can reserve for many of the forecast actual expenses, such as a T.V. set in the master bedroom. Some of the other items, such as a new fence and gate, linoleum replacement and fireplace repair, appear to be cosmetic or not actually necessary.

[2] The Court does not believe it is appropriate to require the present creditors to remain unpaid so the Debtors can reserve for many of the projected future replacement expenses, such as a refrigerator which may be needed in 8 years, a sofa which may be needed in 6 years, a loveseat which may be needed in 3½ years, a sofa which may be needed in 3½ years, a washer and a dryer which may be needed in 5 years, a microwave which may be needed in 3 years as well as a stove which may be needed in 3 years, a mattress and box springs which may be needed in 5 years, a garage door opener which may be needed in 4 years, new telephones which may be needed in 3 years, a VCR for their family room which may be needed in 2 years, a new television set in their family room which may be needed in 2 years, a remote control stereo which may be needed in 4 years, a new roof which may be needed in 13 years, replacing carpet which may be needed in 3 years, and painting the interior of their house which may be needed in 3 years. These future needs, some of which are for necessary items and some of which are for luxuries, are not certain and are well in the future, and their cost should not be borne by current creditors.

[3] The Court also notes that there are two reserves for miscellaneous expenses which total $450.00 per year. While some cushion is appropriate, these reserves in combination with the numerous other reserves are excessive.

[4] The Court believes that a budget which is more in line with current, reasonably necessary expenses would enable the Debtors to pay a substantial amount of their consumer debt under a Chapter 13 plan.

---

4. MOTION BY THE COURT TO DISMISS THE CASE

The court on its own motion may, after notice and a hearing, dismiss a Chapter 7 case for cause, such as the debtor's unreasonable delay if the delay is prejudicial to creditors or the debtor's nonpayment of any fees or charges. The court may dismiss the debtor's petition, after hearing on notice to the debtor and the trustee, for failure to pay any installment of the filing fee. Within 30 days after dismissal for failure to pay the filing fee, all creditors appearing on the list of creditors and creditors who have filed claims must be given notice of the dismissal. This type of dismissal requires a hearing after notice to the debtor, the trustee, and other parties in interest as the court directs. This notice must advise the debtor of all matters that will be considered by the court at the hearing. 11 U.S.C.A. § 707(a); Fed. R. Bank. P. 1017.

The court on its own motion may also, after notice and a hearing, dismiss a Chapter 7 case filed by an individual debtor whose debts are primarily consumer debts if the court finds that the granting of relief would be a substantial abuse of the provisions of Chapter 7. 11 U.S.C.A. § 707(b).

B. COMPLAINTS

Complaints may be filed by a creditor, the trustee, and the U.S. trustee.

1. COMPLAINTS BY A CREDITOR

A creditor may file a complaint objecting to the debtor's discharge or objecting to the dischargeability of a debt.

a. Complaint Objecting to Debtor's Discharge   At any time after the order for relief but not later than 60 days following the first date set for the section 341 meeting of creditors, a creditor may file a **complaint objecting to the debtor's discharge**. 11 U.S.C.A. § 727(c)(1); Fed. R. Bank. P. 4004(a), 7001. See Exhibit 5.35 for a sample complaint objecting to the debtor's discharge.

EXHIBIT 5.35
Complaint Objecting to Debtor's Discharge

UNITED STATES BANKRUPTCY COURT
_____ DISTRICT OF _____

In re _____ ,)
                Debtor   )   Case No. _____
)
_____   ,)   Chapter _____
                Plaintiff   )
)
        v.   )
)
_____   ,)   Adv. Proc. No. _____
                Defendant   )

COMPLAINT OBJECTING TO DEBTOR'S DISCHARGE

The court has jurisdiction over this proceeding pursuant to 28 U.S.C.A. § 1334, 28 U.S.C.A. § 157, and 11 U.S.C.A. § 727. The plaintiff proceeds pursuant to Fed. R. Bank. P. 7001 and 4004.

1.

The plaintiff, _____, a creditor of _____ _____ , defendant, brings this action to object to the discharge of the defendant, all according to the following:

2.

The defendant filed a voluntary petition in bankruptcy on _____, 19____, in the United States Bankruptcy Court for the _____ District of _____ , Bankruptcy No. _____ , in which the plaintiff was listed as a creditor.

3.

The defendant is indebted to the plaintiff in the principal amount of $_____, plus interest, attorney fees, and costs, all as evidenced by the proof of claim filed in this case, marked Exhibit A, attached and incorporated in this complaint by reference.

4.

Plaintiff objects to the discharge of the defendant for the reasons stated in 11 U.S.C.A. § 727(a)(2)(A), in that the defendant, with intent to hinder, delay, or defraud the plaintiff, has transferred the following described real property within one year before the date of the filing of the bankruptcy petition and has failed to list the transfer of this real estate in his bankruptcy schedules.

The East One Hundred and Fifty (150) feet of Lots Five (5) through Ten (10), inclusive, GOLDEN MEADOWS ADDITION, City of Metropolis, State of Utopia.

The general warranty deed from the defendant to _____ , his wife, was filed with the county clerk of Metropolis County, Utopia, on _____ , 19_____ , and recorded at Book 2365, page 1269. A true and correct copy, marked Exhibit B, is attached to and incorporated in this complaint by reference.

EXHIBIT 5.35
Continued

5.

Plaintiff objects to the discharge of the defendant for the reasons stated in 11 U.S.C.A. § 727(a)(2)(A), in that the defendant, with intent to hinder, delay, or defraud the plaintiff, has transferred equipment, furniture, inventory, and accounts receivable to the _____ Church within one year of bankruptcy.

6.

Plaintiff objects to the discharge of the defendant for the reasons stated in 11 U.S.C.A. § 727(a)(5), in that the defendant has failed to explain satisfactorily any loss of the assets described above.

7.

Plaintiff objects to the discharge of the defendant for the reasons stated in 11 U.S.C.A. § 727(a)(3) in that he failed to keep or preserve any recorded information, including books, documents, records, and papers, from which his financial condition might be ascertained.

8.

Plaintiff objects to the discharge of the defendant for the reasons stated in 11 U.S.C.A. § 727(a)(4)(A) in that he knowingly and fraudulently in connection with the case made the following false oaths.

(a) He failed to list a personal account that he had at East Park State Bank within the two years immediately preceding the filing of the bankruptcy petition.

(b) He failed to list a lawsuit in which he was a party at the time of filing the bankruptcy petition.

(c) He failed to list a lawsuit in which he was a party that was terminated within the year immediately preceding the filing of the bankruptcy petition.

(d) He stated that none of his property had been garnished within the year immediately preceding the filing of the bankruptcy petition. The plaintiff garnished the defendant's property within the year immediately preceding the filing of the bankruptcy petition in Case No. CJ-90-003476, Metropolis County District Court, Utopia. A true and correct copy, marked Exhibit C, is attached to and incorporated in this complaint by reference.

(e) He failed to disclose certain gambling losses that he incurred during the year immediately preceding the filing of the bankruptcy petition.

WHEREFORE, plaintiff respectfully requests:

1.

For a determination that the defendant be denied a discharge in bankruptcy;

2.

For a judgment in favor of plaintiff against the defendant in the principal sum of $_____ , plus interest, reasonable attorney fees, and all costs of this action;

3.

For such further and additional relief as this court may deem to be just and equitable and to which the plaintiff may show himself/herself to be entitled.

_____
Name of firm

By: _____
Attorney for the Plaintiff

In the following case, *In re Cohen,* a creditor filed a complaint objecting to the debtor's discharge on five enumerated grounds. The court carefully examined each allegation in relation to the evidence the debtor presented to the court.

In re Cohen
United States Bankruptcy Court, Southern District of Florida, 1985.
47 B.R. 871.

FINDINGS OF FACT AND CONCLUSIONS OF LAW
Sidney M. Weaver,
Bankruptcy Judge

This cause came on before the Court upon an Amended Complaint Objecting to Discharge of the Debtor, and the Court, having reviewed the file, heard the testimony, examined the evidence presented, observed the candor and demeanor of the witnesses, considered the legal argument of counsel for the parties, and, being otherwise fully advised in the premises, does hereby make the following findings of fact and conclusions of law:

The Court has jurisdiction over this "core" matter, as defined in 28 U.S.C. 157.

Plaintiff objects to the Debtor's discharge under 11 U.S.C. 727(a)(2), (3), (4), and (5).

The facts are largely undisputed. Defendant is an auto mechanic by trade and has an eighth-grade formal education. Prior to his personal bankruptcy, Defendant owned real property on which he operated a truck repair business, known as T & M AUTO SERVICE, INC. ("T & M"). T & M is also a Chapter 7 Debtor, in proceedings pending in the Southern District of Florida. Defendant is the sole shareholder of T & M.

On or about October 22, 1982, Defendant entered into a somewhat complex business transaction with CARL PLATT, as Trustee. The business deal called for the sale of the property, with a lease back of the property to T & M. As a result of this transaction, Defendant was to receive cash at closing ($57,975.00), and, thereafter, payments on promissory notes ($121,175.00) and "credit units" ($162,000.00).

The Court finds, based upon the testimony presented, that Defendant received payments on account of the sale over a period of time prior to bankruptcy. While the payment checks were made to the Defendant personally, it was Defendant's regular practice to deposit the checks in the business checking account of T & M. From this account, Defendant would pay various corporate and personal obligations, including the debt owed to Plaintiff herein.

In the months following the sale, the business was robbed and vandalized in excess of 21 times. During this period, Defendant was faced with a situation wherein the bank would not immediately clear the checks deposited into the T & M account, and the Defendant began to cash his checks with his son. The cash was then deposited into the T & M account and checks were written on the available funds.

On or about May 2, 1983, a loan was arranged between Plaintiff and Defendant for $25,000.00. The loan was collateralized by Defendant's pledge of 4 promissory notes from third parties that were originally payable to Defendant. Plaintiff admits that $18,750.00 was repaid to her by the Defendant on account of the loan.

Ultimately, a fire occurred at the business premises of T & M which caused the final demise of the business. Thereafter, personal and corporate Chapter 7 Bankruptcies were filed by the Defendant herein and T & M AUTO SERVICE, INC.

The Debtor's Schedules, including the Statement of Financial Affairs, of which the Court has taken judicial notice, provide in part that the income received from the

Debtor/Defendant's trade or profession during each of the two calendar years immediately preceding the filing of the Chapter 7 was: $13,200.00 for the calendar year 1982 and reflects no income for the year 1983. The Statement further requires information on income received from other sources during each of these two years, for which the Debtor/Defendant listed income for the year of 1982 only.

Plaintiff alleges several distinct grounds in support of her objection to discharge: (1) that Defendant has failed to explain loss or deficiency of assets to meet his liabilities; (2) that Defendant's Schedules and Statement of Affairs do not fully reflect monies received prior to Bankruptcy; (3) that Defendant has concealed or failed to keep books and records; (4) that Defendant has transferred his assets to insiders; and (5) that Defendant has acted with the intent to defraud, hinder or delay creditors of the estate.

Each of these allegations shall be examined in relationship to the evidence presented to the Court.

Section 727 provides that the Court will grant a discharge to a Chapter 7 debtor unless one or more of the specific grounds for the denial of discharge is proven to exist. The House Report accompanying the Bankruptcy Reform Act has described Section 727 as "the heart of the fresh start provisions of the bankruptcy law." H.R. Rep. No. 595, 95th Cong., 1st Sess. 384 (1977), U.S. Code Cong. & Admin. News 1978, pp. 5787, 6340.

This Court observes that the Reform Bankruptcy Code offers to debtors what may well be the most extensive "fresh start" since the seven year release described in the *Old Testament*. Deuteronomy, 15:1 and 2. Traditionally, the debtor's fresh start is one of the primary purposes of bankruptcy law; consequently, exceptions to discharge must be strictly construed. *Matter of Vickers,* 577 F.2d 683, 687 (10th Cir.1978) citing to *Gleason v. Thaw,* 236 U.S. 558, 35 S.Ct. 287, 59 L.Ed. 717 (1915).

B.R. 4005 places the burden of proof upon the party objecting to discharge. This burden must be met with evidence that is clear and convincing. "It has always been fundamental that the conduct of mankind is presumed to be upright and those who allege to the contrary have the burden of strict proof as to every allegation." *In re Ashley,* 5 B.R. 262, 2 C.B.C.2d 949 (Bkrtcy. E.D.Tenn.1980).

The evidence must be such that, when considered in light of all the facts, it leads the Court to the conclusion that the debtor has violated the spirit of the bankruptcy laws and should therefore be denied the privilege of eliminating the legal obligation of his debts. Plaintiff has failed to carry the burden of proof in this case.

Plaintiff contends under 727(a)(5) that Defendant has failed to explain the loss or deficiency of assets to meet his liabilities. However, the Court finds that the Defendant's explanation of how the land sale payments were received and disbursed, including the partial repayment of Plaintiff's debt, is satisfactory.

A satisfactory explanation requires the debtor to demonstrate good faith in the conduct of his affairs and in explaining the loss of assets. 4 *Collier on Bankruptcy,* Section 727.08 (15th ed. 1983), *In re Shapiro & Ornish,* 37 F.2d 403 (D.C.Tex. 1929), aff'd, *Shapiro & Ornish v. Holliday,* 37 F.2d 407 (5th Cir.1930). In the *Shapiro* case, the Court found

> The word "satisfactorily," . . . may mean reasonable, or it may mean that the court, after having heard the excuse, the explanation, has that mental attitude which finds contentment in saying that he believes the explanation—he believes what the (debtors) say with reference to the disappearance or the shortage. . . . He no longer wonders. He is contented.

This Court adopts the *Shapiro* definition. The standard by which the explanation is measured may then be said to be one of reasonableness or credibility. *In re Wheeler,* 38 B.R. 842, 846 (E.D.Tenn.1984).

After careful review of the evidence and testimony, the Court finds that it is satisfied with the Defendant's explanation as to the disposition of his assets, and that there should be no denial of discharge under 727(a)(5).

Plaintiff next seeks to block Defendant's discharge under Section 727(a)(4). At issue is whether the Defendant's Schedules and Statement of Affairs fully reflected the monies received from the land sale.

Defendant is an unsophisticated man; he relied upon his accountant of some 20 years to assist him in answering the questions in the Statement of Affairs. The accountant was under the impression that the tax returns of the Defendant were to have been made a part of the Debtor's Schedules, and, in fact, the 1982 tax return does detail the land sale transaction proceeds.

It is well established that a debtor should be granted discharge under Section 727(a)(4) unless there is an *intentional* effort made to defraud. *In re Schnoll*, 31 B.R. 909, 912 (E.D.Wis.1983); *In re Kirst*, 37 B.R. 275 (E.D.Wis.1983). The record before this Court is devoid of any evidence which would indicate that errors in Defendant's Schedules were made with a fraudulent intent. As has been enunciated in the past by this Court,

> The basic rule in Bankruptcy Court in the Southern District of Florida is that any false oath must be made intentionally and must hinder the administration of the estate. . . . The element of fraud required to satisfy 727(a)(4) is established when statements are made "with a calculated disregard for the importance of the documents signed under penalty of perjury. . . ." *In re Wasserman*, 33 B.R. 779, 780 (S.D.Fla. 1983).

The omissions in the Defendant's Schedules do not reach a level of activity this Court would deem bad faith or fraud upon the Court and creditors of the debtor estate. Plaintiff has *not* shown any intentional design to defraud. The Court does not find that the Debtor's discharge should be denied under 727(a)(4).

The third basis for Plaintiff's objection to discharge is the allegation that the Defendant failed to keep books and records or that the Defendant has concealed his records.

The Court finds that the evidence presented does not prove that the Debtor concealed records.

On the question of failure to preserve records, Section 727(a)(3) of the Code recognizes that circumstances may occur which would justify such failure. The Court may in its discretion excuse any failure to keep or preserve records given justifiable circumstances. *In re Kirst,* Supra; *In re Kinney,* 33 B.R. 594, 9 C.B.C.2d 502 (N.D.OH 1983). In this case, it is unrefuted that robberies, vandalism and a fire occurred at the T & M Property where Defendant's personal records had been kept.

In view of the foregoing circumstances, the Court does not believe that Plaintiff has met her burden of proof to warrant denial of discharge under 727(a)(3).

In the next allegation of Plaintiff's Complaint, it is alleged that Defendant transferred his assets to family members or corporations controlled by relatives.

The Court finds the fact that the Debtor's son cashed checks does not rise to the level of proof required under Rule 4005 to impute a fraudulent intent by the Defendant.

Section 727(a)(2) provides in part that the act complained of must be done with the *intent* to hinder, delay or defraud a creditor or officer of the estate. "This intent must be an actual fraudulent intent as distinguished from constructive intent." *Colliers,* 15th Ed., Section 727.02.

The Court is satisfied with the Debtor's explanation as to why the practice of check cashing was used. It is reasonable to find that, in months preceding the Bankruptcy, the bank with whom the Defendant did business would hold checks for clearance, and that the Defendant was reluctant to issue checks against uncollected funds—hence the check cashing practice. Plaintiff has failed to prove the requisite intent and has therefore not proven all elements necessary to prevail under 727(a)(2).

Finally, Plaintiff has claimed that, under 727(a)(2), Defendant acted with the intent to defraud, hinder or delay Plaintiff, by failing to remit to Plaintiff monies received by Defendant from third parties.

After careful review of the evidence, the Court finds that Defendant used the proceeds from the land sale to pay business expenses, including periodic payments on his obligation to Plaintiff.

The Court further finds that there was no assignment of these notes to the Plaintiff, and that the agreement between Plaintiff and Defendant did not preclude Defendant from receiving payments on the third party notes.

In order to succeed in her efforts to prevent the granting of discharge, Plaintiff must prove that "... the transfer of the Debtor's property (has) been done with the intention to hinder, delay, or defraud a creditor or creditors." *In re Crane, Jr.,* 7 B.R. 859, 7 B.C.D. 36, 37 (N.D.Ala.1980). Based on the foregoing, the Court finds that no

misrepresentations were made and there is no proof that the Debtor acted with the intention of transferring, removing, destroying or concealing his property.

The Court, upon review of the testimony of the witnesses and argument presented by respective counsel, and examination of the documentary evidence, finds that the Plaintiff has not presented clear, cogent and convincing evidence that this Debtor has conducted himself in such a manner as to warrant denial of a discharge under 727(a)(2), (3), (4) or (5).

The denial of a discharge of a debtor is not a step to be taken lightly and is not justified here.

This Memorandum shall constitute Findings of Fact and Conclusions of Law. As is required by B.R. 9021, a Final Judgment pursuant to these Findings and Conclusions is being entered this date.

In *Grogan v. Garner,* 498 U.S. 279 (1991), the United States Supreme Court held that the preponderance of the evidence standard, rather than the clear and convincing evidence standard, applies to all exceptions from dischargeability of debts contained in Bankruptcy Code, 11 U.S.C.A. § 523(a), including nondischargeability for fraud provision.

b. Complaint Objecting to the Dischargeability of a Debt   At any time after the order for relief, a creditor may file a **complaint objecting to the dischargeability of a debt**. 11 U.S.C.A. § 523; Fed. R. Bank. P. 4007(a), 7001. See Exhibit 5.36 for a sample complaint objecting to the dischargeability of a debt.

EXHIBIT 5.36
Complaint Objecting to the Dischargeability of a Debt

UNITED STATES BANKRUPTCY COURT
_____ **DISTRICT OF** _____

In re _____   ,)
                    Debtor   )   Case No. _____
)
_____   ,)   Chapter _____
                    Plaintiff   )
)
               v.   )
)
_____   ,)   Adv. Proc. No. _____
                    Defendant   )

COMPLAINT OBJECTING TO THE DISCHARGEABILITY OF A DEBT

The court has jurisdiction over this proceeding pursuant to 28 U.S.C.A. § 1334, 28 U.S.C.A. § 157, and 11 U.S.C.A. § 523(c). The plaintiff proceeds pursuant to Fed R. Bank. P. 7001 and 4007(a).

1.

Plaintiff _____ is an individual residing in _____ _____ County, _____ , within the _____ District of _____ .

2.

Defendant _____ is an individual residing in _____ County, _____ , and is the debtor in the above-captioned bankruptcy case.

3.

This bankruptcy case was initiated by the defendant by filing a voluntary petition on _____ , 19 _____ .

4.

On _____ , 19 _____ , the defendant purchased _____ _____ from the plaintiff and paid the plaintiff with a check for $ _____ drawn on the First National Bank. Upon receipt of the check, plaintiff delivered the _____ to the defendant. The plaintiff presented the check for payment to First National Bank but the check was dishonored because the defendant no longer had an account with the bank. A copy of the dishonored check, marked Exhibit A, is attached to this complaint and made a part of this complaint by reference.

5.

Two weeks after the issuance of the check, the defendant filed a petition in bankruptcy under Chapter 7.

6.

When the plaintiff delivered _____ to the defendant, the defendant at no time intended to pay. By virtue of this fraud, the plaintiff's claim

EXHIBIT 5.36
Continued

against defendant for $ _____ is nondischargeable pursuant to 11 U.S.C.A.
§ 523(a)(2)(A).

WHEREFORE, the plaintiff respectfully requests:

1.

For a determination that the indebtedness owed by the defendant to the plaintiff
is nondischargeable;

2.

For a judgment in favor of the plaintiff against the defendant in the principal sum
of $ _____ , plus interest reasonable attorney fees, and all costs of this ac-
tion;

3.

For such further and additional relief as this court may deem to be just and equitable and to which the plaintiff may show himself/herself to be entitled.

_____
Name of firm

By: _____
Attorney for the Plaintiff

In the following case, *In re Keenan,* a student loan foundation brought a complaint seeking a determination whether two loans insured by the foundation were
dischargeable.

In re Keenan
United States Bankruptcy Court, District of Connecticut, 1985.
53 B.R. 913.

MEMORANDUM OF DECISION
Alan H.W. Shiff,
Bankruptcy Judge

The plaintiff, Connecticut Student Loan
Foundation,[1] brought this adversary proceeding seeking a determination, pursuant
to 11 U.S.C. § 523(a)(8),[2] that two loans insured by the plaintiff were not discharged
by this court's July 6, 1983 order of discharge on the basis that the loans became
due within five years of the debtor's petition for discharge. For the reasons set forth
below, I conclude that these loans were discharged by that order.

BACKGROUND

In August 1975 and January 1976, the defendant obtained two student loans of
$750.00 each from the Union Trust
Company, a Connecticut banking institution, to finance vocational training. These
loans were insured by the plaintiff. From
September 1975 through June 1976, the defendant attended the New Haven Academy
of Business for training as a keypunch op-
erator. Under the terms of the notes signed
by the defendant, the educational loans
were to become due on the first day of the
thirteenth month following the month in

which the defendant completed her academic program, which in this case was July 1, 1977.

On February 10, 1983, the defendant filed a petition in this court, seeking relief under Chapter 7 of the 1978 Bankruptcy Code. Thus, absent any valid suspension of the repayment period, these loans became due more than five years prior to the defendant's petition for relief and would be dischargeable. The plaintiff, however, gave the defendant two six-month deferments,[3] to wit: July 1, 1977 to January 1, 1978, granted on October 26, 1977, and January 1, 1978 to July 1, 1978, granted on August 18, 1978. Both deferments were granted to the defendant as "unemployment deferments."

The issue here is the effect of those deferments. The plaintiff claims that the student loans were not discharged because the effect of those deferments was to suspend the repayment and cause the loans to become due less than five years prior to the defendant's petition. The defendant, on the other hand, asserts that the deferments were invalid, so that the loans were in fact due more than five years prior to the petition, and that the loans are, therefore, dischargeable. Moreover, the defendant asserts that the loans should be discharged as they impose an undue hardship on the defendant and her dependents.

DISCUSSION

A.
Burden of Proof

1.
Under § 523(a)(8)(A)

Neither Code § 523 nor the Bankruptcy Rules provides an allocation of the burden of proof in dischargeability proceedings. Thus, courts are guided by the construction of the particular part of section 523 under consideration, its legislative history and the evolving body of court decisions on that subject.

Although the court in *In re Wright*, 7 B.R. 197 (Bankr.N.D.Ala.1980) was not

faced with the task of allocating the burden of proof on the five year issue in post discharge litigation under Code § 523(a)(8)(A), it did recognize that "there will be interesting questions raised involving the burden of proof depending on which party initiates the complaint." *Id.* at 200. The court then observed that "it would appear that the burden is on the creditor to show that the loan first became due before the date of filing the petition. Otherwise the loan is presumed discharged." *Id.* The court in *In re Norman*, 25 B.R. 545 (Bankr.S.D.Cal.1982), following *Wright* held:

> [T]he creditor must establish the existence of the debt, that it is owed to or insured or guaranteed by a governmental agency or a non-profit institution of higher education, and that it first became due less than five years prior to the date the bankruptcy petition was filed.

Id. at 548. *(citation omitted)*

A review of the legislative history of Code § 523(a)(8) disclosed the congressional view that, as a condition precedent to nondischargeability, the loan must have been made, insured, or guaranteed within five years of the filing of the bankruptcy petition. *See* Senate Report No. 96-230, 96th Cong., 1st Sess. 3 (1979), *reprinted in* 1979 U.S.Cong. and Admin.News 936. It therefore follows that a post discharge student loan creditor who asserts a right to payment on the basis that the debt was not discharged should have the burden of proving that the debt comes within the definition of student loans that are not discharged.

The same result may be reached from a different direction. Since a post discharge student loan creditor would be free to sue on the debt in either state or bankruptcy court, the bankruptcy court having concurrent jurisdiction on such debts, and since a student loan creditor as a plaintiff in a state court action would have the burden of proving that the debt was viable, it is not unfair to impose the same burden upon the creditor in bankruptcy court. *See In re Roberts*, 13 B.R. 832, 835 (Bankr.N.D.Ohio 1981). Moreover, this apportionment is consistent with the parties' relative access to information. A student loan creditor is in the best position to show, through the records which it is required to maintain, that a loan has in fact come due within five years of the filing of a petition. Placement of the burden upon the party in the best position to know the facts to be proven accords with considerations of fairness. *See Keyes v. School District No. 1, Denver, Colo.,* 413 U.S. 189, 210, 93 S.Ct. 2686, 2698, 37 L.Ed.2d 548 (1973); 9 Wigmore on Evidence § 2486 (3d ed. 1940).

Having concluded that the burden of proof is upon the creditor on the five year issue under Code § 523(a)(8)(A), it follows that the burden of proof is also upon the creditor on the issue involving the validity of any suspension of that five year period.

2.
Under § 523(a)(8)(B)

Bankruptcy courts are in general agreement that in student loan dischargeability litigation based upon undue hardship, the burden of proof is upon the debtor for the reason that the assertion of undue hardship is in the nature of an affirmative defense or an exception to the exception of such a debt from discharge. In *In re Norman,* 25 B.R. 545 (Banks.S.D.Ca.1982) the court quoted the reasoning of Justice Holmes on a similar question:

> By the very form of the law the debtor is discharged subject to an exception, and one who would bring himself within the exception must offer evidence to do so. [citation] But there is an *exception to the exception,* . . . and, by the same principle, if the debtor would get the benefit of that he must offer evidence to show his right.

Id. at 549, *quoting, Hill v. Smith,* 260 U.S. 592, 595, 43 S.Ct. 219, 220, 67 L.Ed. 419 (1923) (emphasis added by court in *Norman*). *See also In re Fitzgerald,* 40 B.R. 528, 529 (Bankr.E.D.Pa.1984); *In re Richardson,* 32 B.R. 5 (Bankr.S.D.Ohio1983).

This allocation is consistent with the legislative history of Code § 523(a)(8) which indicates that this "provision is intended to

be self executing and the lender or institution is not required to file a complaint to determine the nondischargeability of any student loan." S.Rep. No. 95-989, 95th Cong., 2d Sess. 79 (1978), *reprinted in* 1978 U.S. Code Cong. & Admin.News 5787, 5865. The case law and legislative history of this Code section persuade me that the burden of proof on the issue of undue hardship should be on the debtor.

B.
Dischargeability under Code § 523(a)(8)(A): Validity of Unemployment Extensions

John A. Kearns, the plaintiff's vice president, testified that at the time the second loan deferment was granted, the plaintiff had regulations which authorized unemployment deferments, but that such deferments would not apply to any period during which the loan recipient was actually employed.[4] Further, deferments would not be proper if the debtor did not request such treatment.[5]

It is apparent from the evidence that on August 18, 1978, the plaintiff granted the defendant a second retroactive unemployment deferment, effective from January 1, 1978 to July 1, 1978,[6] in reliance upon a July 5, 1978 letter[7] from the defendant. The plaintiff's reliance on that letter was misplaced. The letter stated:

> I am presently unemployed but I am seeking full time employment. Whenever I secure employment, I will notify you immediately.

The letter does not state that the defendant had been unemployed during the period from January 1, 1978 to July 1, 1978. Nor does the letter request an extension, retroactive or otherwise, of her loan.

On the contrary, the defendant denied that she sought any deferment and specifically testified that she had been fully employed during five of the six months during which the plaintiff gave her the second unemployment deferment. The deferment was therefore not valid. *Cf. In re Crumley,* 21 B.R. 170, 172 (Bankr.E.D.Tenn.1982) (student loan creditor granted deferment for 19 months, 8 months longer than requested by the debtor).

An improper deferment does not suspend the time between the date an educational loan first comes due and the filing of a petition in bankruptcy. *In re Whitbead,* 31 B.R. 381 (Bankr.S.D.Ohio1983); *In re Crumley,* 21 B.R. at 172. Since, here, the second deferment was invalid, the loans first became due more than five years before the defendant's petition was filed, and the debt arising out of those loans is therefore dischargeable.

The same result is reached upon an analysis of the first deferment. Even if the defendant was unemployed during the period from July 1, 1977 to January 1, 1978, the period of the first unemployment deferment, the applicable regulations did not authorize unemployment deferments during that period. Under the applicable regulations, deferments were allowable only for periods during which the borrower was in the Armed Forces of the United States, serving in the Peace Corps as a volunteer, or serving as a full-time volunteer under title VIII of the Economic Opportunity Act of 1964. *See* 45 C.F.R. § 177.46(f) (1978).[8]

C.

Dischargeability under Code § 523(a)(8)(B): Undue Hardship

It is a well recognized principle of construction that statutes are to be construed so that they carry out legislative intent. That is, the language of a statute should be read with the assumption that the legislative branch chose particular words to accomplish a specific purpose. *Rockefeller v. Commissioner of Internal Revenue Service,* 676 F.2d 35, 36 (2d Cir. 1982). Under the guidance of that rule, bankruptcy courts have uniformly applied Code § 523(a)(8)(B) narrowly. It is not enough that a student loan imposes a hardship upon the debtor and the debtor's dependents. Most, if not all, debtors could make such a claim in good faith. To qualify for discharge, the debt must be an "undue hardship."

As the court in *In re Brown,* 18 B.R. 219, 222 (Bankr.D.Ka.1982) observed:

> The Code does not define "undue hardship" . . . it seems universally accepted, however, that "undue hardship" contemplates unique and extraordinary circumstances. Mere financial adversity is insufficient, for that is the basis of all petitions in bankruptcy.

See also, In re Fischer, 23 B.R. 432, 433 (Bankr.W.D.Ky.1982); *In re Densmore,* 7 B.C.D. 271, 272, 8 B.R. 308 (Bankr.N.D.Cal. 1980).

The evidence in this proceeding demonstrates that the defendant supports herself and her three sons. One of the defendant's sons is unable to work because of a psychiatric disability. The defendant has endured many surgical procedures. She suffers from serious, chronic medical conditions, including hypertension, for which she cannot afford prescribed medication. The defendant's net income is well below the federal poverty guideline, and her expenses significantly exceed her monthly income. Moreover, it appears that the defendant's illnesses will continue to adversely affect her employability, and it appears highly unlikely that her monthly income will, in the foreseeable future, exceed her expenses.

Having analyzed the evidence in this proceeding, including the defendant's testimony, I am persuaded that the defendant has sustained the burden of proving that repayment of the student loans would impose an undue hardship upon her and upon her dependents, and therefore the debt arising out of the student loans is dischargeable. *Cf. In re La Chance,* 17 B.R. 1023 (Bankr. D.Me.1982) (impossible for debtor to generate enough income in foreseeable future to pay off loan and maintain debtor and dependents above poverty level); *In re Diaz,* 5 B.R. 253, 254 (Bankr.N.D.N.Y.1980) (debtor spending more money per week than she earns). *Cf. In re Dresser,* 33 B.R. 63

(Bankr.D.Me.1983) (no prospect for relief from medical symptoms adversely affecting debtor's employability); *In re Connolly,* 29 B.R. 978 (Bankr.M.D.Fla.1983).

CONCLUSION

For the foregoing reasons, the two educational loans insured by the plaintiff are dischargeable pursuant to Code § 523(a)(8)(A) and (B), they were discharged by the July 6, 1983 order of discharge, and judgment may enter accordingly.

_____

[1] A nonprofit corporation formed for the purpose of improving educational opportunities by guaranteeing loans for post-secondary education. Conn.Gen.Stat. § 10a–201. (Formerly § 10–358)

[2] Code section 523(a) provides in pertinent part:

A discharge under section 722 . . . of this title does not discharge an individual debtor from any debt—

. . .

(8) for an educational loan made, insured, or guaranteed by a governmental unit, or made under any program funded in whole or in part by a governmental unit or a nonprofit institution of higher education, unless—

(A) such loan first became due before five years (exclusive of any applicable suspension of the repayment period) before the date of the filing of the petition; or

(B) excepting such debt from discharge under this paragraph will impose an undue

hardship on the debtor and the debtor's dependents.

[3] Plaintiff's Exhibits 3 and 6 are loan extension agreements purporting to show a request by the debtor for, and the granting of, unemployment extensions. The loan extension requests were submitted by Union Trust to CSLF, the guarantor of the loans, for its approval.

[4] Tr. Mar. 15, 1985 at 73.

[5] Tr. Mar. 15, 1985 at 78.

[6] Plaintiff's Exhibit 6.

[7] Plaintiff's Exhibit 5.

[8] 45 C.F.R. § 177.46(f) reads:

(f) *Deferment.* Periodic installments of principal need not be paid, but interest shall accrue and be paid, during any period (1) in which the borrower is pursuing a full-time course of study at an eligible institution, (2) not in excess of 3 years, during which the borrower is a member of the Armed Forces of the United States, (3) not in excess of 3 years during which the borrower is in service as a volunteer under the Peace Corps Act or (4) not in excess of 3 years during which the borrower is in service as a full-time volunteer under title VIII of the Economic Opportunity Act of 1964. Where repayment of the loan is deferred, the minimum or maximum periods allowed for repayment of the loan are provided for in paragraph (e) of this section.

---

2. COMPLAINT BY THE TRUSTEE OR THE UNITED STATES TRUSTEE OBJECTING TO DEBTOR'S DISCHARGE

At any time after the order for relief but not later than 60 days following the first date set for the section 341 meeting of creditors, the trustee or the United States trustee may file a complaint objecting to the debtor's discharge. 11 U.S.C.A. § 727(c)(1); Fed. R. Bank. P. 4004(a), 7001.

3. COMPLAINT BY THE TRUSTEE TO AVOID PREPETITION AND POSTPETITION TRANSFERS

The trustee has the power to avoid prepetition transfers that involve voidable preference and fraudulent transfer by filing a complaint. 11 U.S.C.A. §§ 547, 548. The trustee may also avoid postpetition transfers not authorized by the Bankruptcy Code or by the bankruptcy court. 11 U.S.C.A. § 549(a). The trustee has the rights of a hypothetical lien creditor, which enable the trustee to set aside unperfected security interests. 11 U.S.C.A. § 544(a). These powers were discussed in Section 3 of this chapter in relation to the appointment of an interim trustee.

SECTION 6
ORDER AND NOTICE OF CHAPTER 7 BANKRUPTCY FILING, MEETING OF CREDITORS, AND FIXING OF DATES

Under the Federal Rules of Bankruptcy Procedure, the clerk, or some other person as the court may direct, is mandated to give the debtor, the trustee, all creditors, and indenture trustees notice by mail of the meeting of creditors. (See Exhibit 5.37.) The notice must be given not less than 20 days before the 341 meeting. Fed. R. Bank. P. 2002(a). If the court finds notice by mail is impracticable (perhaps due to large numbers of creditors) or if there is a need to supplement the notice, notice may be given by publication. Fed. R. Bank. P. 2002(l).

EXHIBIT 5.37

Order and Notice of Chapter 7 Bankruptcy Filing, Meeting of Creditors, and Fixing of Dates

---

FORM B9A
(Rev. 12/94)

United States Bankruptcy Court

Case Number

_____ District of _____

NOTICE OF COMMENCEMENT OF CASE UNDER CHAPTER 7 OF THE BANKRUPTCY CODE.
MEETING OF CREDITORS, AND FIXING DATES
(Individual or Joint Debtor No Asset Case)

In re (Name of Debtor)	Address of Debtor	Soc. Sec./Tax Id. Nos.
	Date Case Filed (or Converted)	
Name and Address of Attorney for Debtor	Name and Address of Trustee	
Telephone Number	Telephone Number	

☐ This is a converted case originally filed under chapter _____ on _____ (date).

DATE, TIME, AND LOCATION OF MEETING OF CREDITORS

DISCHARGE OF DEBTS

Deadline to File a Complaint Objecting to Discharge of the Debtor or toDetermine Dischargeability of Certain Types of Debts:

AT THIS TIME THERE APPEAR TO BE NO ASSETS AVAILABLE FROM WHICH PAYMENT MAY BE MADE TO UNSECURED CREDITORS. DO NOT FILE A PROOF OF CLAIM UNTIL YOU RECEIVE NOTICE TO DO SO.

COMMENCEMENT OF CASE. A petition for liquidation under chapter 7 of the Bankruptcy Code has been filed in this court by or against the person or persons named above as the debtor, and an order for relief has been entered. You will not receive notice of all documents filed in this case. All documents filed with the court, including lists of the debtor's property, debts, and property claimed as exempt are available for inspection at the office of the clerk of the bankruptcy court.

CREDITORS MAY NOT TAKE CERTAIN ACTIONS. A creditor is anyone to whom the debtor owes money or property. Under the Bankruptcy Code, the debtor is granted certain protection against creditors. Common examples of prohibited actions by creditors are contacting the debtor to demand repayment, taking action against the debtor to collect money owed to creditors or to take property of the debtor, and starting or continuing foreclosure actions, repossessions, or wage deductions. If unauthorized actions are taken by a creditor against a debtor, the court may penalize that creditor. A creditor who is considering taking action against the debtor or the property of the debtor should review 362 of the Bankruptcy Code and may wish to seek legal advice. The staff of the clerk of the bankruptcy court is not permitted to give legal advice.

MEETING OF CREDITORS. The debtor (both husband and wife in a joint case) is required to appear at the meeting of creditors on the date and at the place set forth above for the purpose of being examined under oath. Attendance by creditors at the meeting is welcomed, but not required. At the meeting, the creditors may elect a trustee other than the one named above, elect a committee of creditors, examine the debtor, and transact such other business as may properly come before the meeting. The meeting may be continued or adjourned from time to time by notice at the meeting, without further written notice to creditors.

LIQUIDATION OF THE DEBTOR'S PROPERTY. The trustee will collect the debtor's property and turn any that is not exempt into money. At this time, however, it appears from the schedules of the debtor that there are no assets from which any distribution can be paid to creditors. If at a later date it appears that there are assets from which a distribution may be paid, the creditors will be notified and given an opportunity to file claims.

EXEMPT PROPERTY. Under state and federal law, the debtor is permitted to keep certain money or property as exempt. If a creditor believes that an exemption of money or property is not authorized by law, the creditor may file an objection. An objection must be filed not later than 30 days after the conclusion of the meeting of creditors.

DISCHARGE OF DEBTS. The debtor is seeking discharge of debts. A discharge means that certain debts are made unenforceable against the debtor personally. Creditors whose claims against the debtor are discharged may never take action against the debtor to collect the discharged debts. If a creditor believes that the debtor should not receive any discharge of debts under § 727 of the Bankruptcy Code or that a debt owed to the creditor is not dischargeable under § 523(a),(2),(4), (6), or (15) of the Bankruptcy Code, timely action must be taken in the bankruptcy court by the deadline set forth above in the box labeled "Discharge of Debts." Creditors considering taking such action may wish to seek legal advice.

DO NOT FILE A PROOF OF CLAIM UNLESS YOU RECEIVE A COURT NOTICE TO DO SO

Address of the Clerk of the Bankruptcy Court	For the Court:
	Clerk of the Bankruptcy Court
	Date

SECTION 7
OBJECTIONS BY A PARTY IN INTEREST TO DEBTOR'S CLAIM OF EXEMPTIONS

Any creditor or the trustee may object to the debtor's claim of exemptions. Objections may be filed within 30 days after the meeting of creditors or after the filing of either an amendment to the list of property claimed as exempt or supplemental schedules. The court may extend this period. The Rules require the party filing an objection to either mail or deliver a copy of this objection to the trustee, the person filing the list (usually the debtor), and the attorney for that person. Fed. R. Bank. P. 4003(b).

SECTION 8
MEETING OF CREDITORS (THE SECTION 341 MEETING) AND MEETING OF EQUITY SECURITY HOLDERS

After the petition has been filed, the United States trustee must call a **meeting of creditors** and may call a **meeting of equity security holders.**

A. THE MEETING OF CREDITORS

The 341 meeting is to be held not less than 20 nor more than 40 days after the order for relief. Fed. R. Bank. P. 2003(a).

1. EXAMINATION OF THE DEBTOR

The debtor is required to appear at the meeting of creditors and to answer questions under oath. The oath will be administered by the United States trustee who will preside at the meeting. In some districts, the interim trustees appointed in Chapter 7 cases preside at the 341 meetings. The debtor may be examined by creditors, the trustee, an indenture trustee, or the United States trustee. 11 U.S.C.A. § 343. The scope of this examination is limited to the acts, conduct, property, liabilities, and financial condition of the debtor; to any matter that may affect the administration of the estate; or to the debtor's right to a discharge. Fed. R. Bank. P. 2004(b). The purpose of this examination is to aid the trustee and creditors in determining if any assets have been concealed or disposed of improperly. Grounds for objection to discharge may surface at this meeting.

The examination of the debtor by the trustee at the meeting of creditors has been expanded. The trustee is now required to examine the debtor orally to determine the debtor's awareness on several points:

1. the potential consequences of seeking a discharge in bankruptcy, including the effects on credit history;
2. the debtor's ability to file a petition under a different chapter of this title;
3. the effect of receiving a discharge of debts under this title; and
4. the effect of reaffirming a debt, including the debtor's knowledge of the provisions of section 524(d) of this title. 11 U.S.C.A. § 341(d).

Any examination under oath at the 341 meeting must be recorded verbatim by electronic recording sound equipment or by other means by the United States trustee. Fed. R. Bank. P. 2003(c).

2. ELECTION OF A TRUSTEE OR A CREDITORS' COMMITTEE

Creditors who are allowed to vote under the Code may request the election of a trustee at the 341 meeting. 11 U.S.C.A. § 702(b). A trustee elected by the creditors will serve in the case rather than having the interim trustee continue as trustee. 11 U.S.C.A. § 702(d). The creditors may recommend to the court the amount of the elected trustee's bond.

Creditors who may vote for a trustee under 11 U.S.C.A. § 702(a) may also elect a committee of creditors consisting of not fewer than three nor more than 11 creditors. Each of these creditors must hold an allowable unsecured claim. 11 U.S.C.A. § 705(a). This elected committee may consult with the trustee or the United States trustee regarding administration of the estate. The committee may submit questions affecting administration of the estate to the court or to the United States trustee and may make recommendations to the trustee or to the United States trustee regarding performance of the trustee's duties. 11 U.S.C.A. § 705(b). The presiding officer must report to the court the name and address of any person elected to be trustee or of any entity elected as a member of a creditors' committee. Fed. R. Bank. P. 2003(d).

The meeting of creditors may be adjourned from time to time without further written notice. An announcement at the meeting of the adjourned date and time is sufficient notice. Fed. R. Bank. P. 2003(e).

B. THE MEETING OF EQUITY SECURITY HOLDERS

The United States trustee may convene a meeting of any equity security holders. 11 U.S.C.A. § 341(b). The United States trustee shall fix a date for the meeting and shall preside at the meeting of equity security holders. Fed. R. Bank. P. 2003(b)(2). A meeting of equity security holders generally is not particularly beneficial in a Chapter 7 case, because Chapter 7 leads to liquidation and not to a reorganization plan. The equity security holders share in the distribution of the debtor's assets regardless of their input. The equity security holders, however, can play a role if they have the opportunity to increase the bankruptcy estate so that there will be more assets to distribute.

SECTION 9
DISCHARGE AND REAFFIRMATION HEARING

A discharge and reaffirmation hearing may or may not be held. If a hearing is held, the debtor is required to attend.

A. DISCHARGE AND REAFFIRMATION HEARING

Prior to the 1986 amendments, a **discharge and reaffirmation hearing** was held in every case involving individuals entitled to discharge under 11 U.S.C.A. § 727. Any reaffirmation agreement the debtor wished to enter into was scrutinized by the court at this hearing. In 1986, the Code was changed from "shall hold a hearing" to "the court may hold a hearing." 11 U.S.C.A. § 524(d). The debtor, however, is still required to attend the hearing if the court holds one. Most courts no longer hold a discharge hearing.

It is important to remember that Chapter 7 has two aspects: (1) the debtor seeks a fresh start; and (2) the assets of the estate are administered. Each process goes down a separate, independent track with little convergence. Although one debtor could be denied a discharge and all his or her assets could be administered and distributed, another debtor could be granted a discharge although he or she has no assets to be administered. In some situations, however, the two processes may come together. For example, if a debtor conceals assets, his or her discharge will be denied.

If the discharge has been granted and if the debtor wants to enter into a reaffirmation agreement and was not represented by an attorney during the course of negotiating the agreement

> . . . the court shall hold a hearing at which the debtor shall appear in person and at such hearing the court shall
>
> (1) inform the debtor—
>> (A) that such an agreement is not required under this title, under nonbankruptcy law, or under any agreement not made in accordance with the provisions of subsection (c) of this section; and
>> (B) of the legal effect and consequences of—
>>> (i) an agreement of the kind specified in subsection (c) of this section; and
>>> (ii) a default under such an agreement; and
>
> (2) determine whether the agreement that the debtor desires to make complies with the requirements of subsection (c)(6) of this section, if the consideration for such agreement is based in whole or in part on a consumer debt that is not secured by real property of the debtor. 11 U.S.C.A. § 524(d).

Although hearings on reaffirmation have been dispensed with in a few districts in spite of the "shall" language of 524(d), this approach seems to be one of "throwing the baby out with the bathwater." Discontinuing discharge hearings is a sensible, practical way of saving valuable court time without a risk to any of the parties. Discontinuing reaffirmation hearings deprives the debtor of the court's scrutiny of the agreement and may encourage the unscrupulous creditor to put pressure on the debtor to sign a reaffirmation agreement that would impose an undue hardship and not be in the best interest of the debtor. 11 U.S.C.A. § 524(c)(6)(A). See Exhibit 5.38 for a **reaffirmation agreement**.

EXHIBIT 5.38
Reaffirmation Agreement

FORM B 240
(1/88)

United States Bankruptcy Court

_____ **District of** _____

REAFFIRMATION AGREEMENT	
Debtor's Name	Bankruptcy Case No.

INSTRUCTIONS:

1) Write debtor's name and bankruptcy case number above.
2) Part A — Must be signed by both the debtor and the creditor.
3) Part B — Must be signed by the attorney who represents the debtor in this bankruptcy case.
4) Part C — Must be completed by the debtor if the debtor is not represented by an attorney in this bankruptcy case.
5) File the completed form by mailing or delivering to the Bankruptcy Clerk.
6) Attach written agreement, if any.

COURT USE ONLY

PART A — AGREEMENT

Creditor's Name and Address

Summary of Terms of the New Agreement
a) Principal Amount $ _____
   Interest Rate (APR) _____ %
   Monthly Payments $ _____
b) Description of Security:

Date Set for Discharge Hearing (if any)

Present Market Value $

The parties understand that this agreement is purely voluntary and that the debtor may rescind the agreement at any time prior to discharge or within 60 days after such agreement is filed with the court, whichever occurs later, by giving notice of recission to the creditor.

Date _____

Signature of Debtor _____

Signature of Creditor _____

Signature of Joint Debtor _____

PART B — ATTORNEY'S DECLARATION

This agreement represents a fully informed and voluntary agreement that does not impose an undue hardship on the debtor or any dependent of the debtor.

Date _____

Signature of Debtor's Attorney _____

PART C — MOTION FOR COURT APPROVAL OF AGREEMENT —   Complete only where debtor is not represented by an attorney.

I (we), the debtor, affirm the following to be true and correct:

1) I am not represented by an attorney in connection with this bankruptcy case.
2) My current monthly net income is $ _____
3) My current monthly expenses total $ _____, including any payment due under this agreement.
4) I believe that this agreement is in my best interest because

_____

Therefore, I ask the court for an order approving this reaffirmation agreement.

Date _____

Signature of Debtor _____

Signature of Joint Debtor _____

PART D — COURT ORDER

The Court grants the debtor's motion and approves the voluntary agreement upon the terms specified above.

Date _____

Bankruptcy Judge _____

© 1991 WEST PUBLISHING COMPANY

B. REVOCATION OF DISCHARGE

A Chapter 7 discharge may be revoked by the filing of a complaint within one year for fraud in obtaining the discharge. For any other grounds, a complaint must be filed before one year after the discharge or the date the case was closed, whichever is later. The complaint may be filed by the trustee, a creditor, or the United States trustee. 11 U.S.C.A. §§ 727(d), (e).

SECTION 10

DISTRIBUTION OF THE PROPERTY OF THE ESTATE

Distribution of the property of the estate takes place after the trustee has collected the property and reduced it to money as required by the Code. 11 U.S.C.A. § 704(1). The trustee will file a final report and proposed distribution. The office of the bankruptcy court clerk will mail the notice to all creditors and other parties in interest. After the court's review and ruling on fees and objections to claims, the trustee distributes the assets of the estate.

The order in which distribution takes place in Chapter 7 cases is set forth in 11 U.S.C.A. § 726. Section 726 refers to section 507 for priorities and to section 503(b) for administrative expenses.

A. PRIORITY CLAIMS

Priority claims include administrative expenses; wages, salaries, or commissions; contributions to employee benefit plans; consumer deposits; farmer and fishermen claims; debts owed for alimony, maintenance, or support; certain governmental tax claims; and insured depository institution claims. 11 U.S.C.A. § 507.

1. ADMINISTRATIVE EXPENSES

Administrative expenses are the actual, necessary costs of preserving and administering the estate. Trustees, examiners, professional persons employed by the estate with approval of the court, and the debtor's attorney are included in this category. 11 U.S.C.A. § 507(a)(1).

EXAMPLE
Sylvia Williams filed for bankruptcy under Chapter 7. Upon the filing of the petition, her second car, a 1993 Buick, became an asset of the bankruptcy estate. The trustee's administrative expenses for liquidating the car include the expense for picking the car up, storing it, preparing it for sale, and the auctioneer's fee for selling it.

2. WAGES, SALARIES, OR COMMISSIONS

Individuals with allowed unsecured claims for wages, salaries, or commissions, up to $4,000 for each individual, are included in this category. Vacation, severance, or sick leave pay is considered part of wages, salaries, or commissions. To be eligible for this priority, an individual must have earned what is claimed within 90 days before the filing of the petition or the date the debtor's business ceased, whichever occurred first. 11 U.S.C.A. § 507(a)(3).

EXAMPLE
On June 1, the Sun Valley Casino filed for bankruptcy under Chapter 7. For the 90 days preceding the filing of the petition, the Sun Valley employees had been paid only half

of their wages. Therefore, at the time of the filing, Jerri Jackson, an employee, had a wage claim against the estate of $5,000 for this 90-day period. Of the $5,000 wage claim, $4,000 will be a priority claim and $1,000 will be an unsecured claim.

3. CONTRIBUTIONS TO EMPLOYEE BENEFIT PLANS

Allowed unsecured claims for contributions to an employee benefit plan must arise within 180 days before the date the debtor's petition was filed or the date the debtor's business ceased, whichever occurred first. These claims are only to the extent, for each plan, of the number of employees covered by the plan multiplied by $4,000, minus the aggregate amount paid to employees under the wages, salaries, or commissions provision, plus the aggregate amount paid by the estate on behalf of these employees to any other employee benefit plan. 11 U.S.C.A. § 507(a)(4).

EXAMPLE
On June 1, the Sun Valley Casino filed for bankruptcy under Chapter 7. The casino had a collective bargaining agreement with the Western States Casino Workers Union by which Sun Valley was to contribute to the employee retirement fund administered by the union. Five hundred Sun Valley employees were covered by the plan. During the 180 days preceding the filing of the petition, although Sun Valley was obligated to contribute $2,500,000 to the fund on behalf of its employees, it did not do so.

At the time of the filing of the petition, the union had an employee benefit claim against the estate for the unpaid benefit for this 180-day period. The union's priority claim will be $4,000 times the number of employees covered by the plan (500) or $2,000,000. Because the employees did not claim retirement contributions in their priority claims for unsecured wages, and no other employee benefit plan received money from the estate on behalf of these employees, the $2,000,000 stands without deduction and is the union's priority claim for the employee benefit plan. The balance of the union's claim ($500,000) will be unsecured.

4. FARMER AND FISHERMEN CLAIMS

The allowed unsecured claims of grain farmers and United States fishermen, to the extent of $4,000 for each individual, are priority claims. This priority was designed to protect the farmer and fisherman from loss when a grain storage facility or a fish storage or processing facility files bankruptcy. 11 U.S.C.A. §§ 507(a)(5)(A), (B).

5. CONSUMER DEPOSITS

Individuals with allowed unsecured claims up to the extent of $1,800 arising from a deposit of money for consumer goods or services before the commencement of the case are included in this priority. The deposit of money could be in connection with the purchase of services that were not delivered or provided. The goods or services must have been intended for personal, family, or household use only. 11 U.S.C.A. § 507(a)(6).

EXAMPLE
During the fall, a number of customers of Cheryl's Department Store selected Christmas gifts and placed them on layaway. Over the next several months, each customer made monthly payments toward the purchase price. Three weeks before Christmas, Cheryl's filed a petition in bankruptcy under Chapter 7. Each customer is entitled to a priority claim of up to $1,800 for the money paid in connection with the purchase.

6. ALIMONY, MAINTENANCE, AND SUPPORT CLAIMS

Allowed claims for debts to a spouse, former spouse, or child of the debtor for alimony, maintenance, or support are included in this category of priority claims.

These claims arise in connection with a separation agreement, divorce decree, or other order of the court. 11 U.S.C.A. § 507(a)(7).

7. CERTAIN GOVERNMENTAL TAX CLAIMS

Allowed unsecured tax claims of governmental units for various taxes are included in this category. A tax on income or gross receipts is probably the tax most commonly owed by debtors. Other tax claims filed may be for property tax, sales tax, employee withholding such as social security and unemployment insurance, and customs duties. A penalty related to actual loss is also a priority claim, but a penalty that is punitive only is not a priority claim. 11 U.S.C.A. § 507(a)(8).

> **EXAMPLE**
> Last year Juanito's Restaurant failed to pay the United States Treasury its payroll taxes. Juanito's has filed a petition in bankruptcy under Chapter 7. The Internal Revenue Service has a priority claim for the unpaid taxes.

8. INSURED DEPOSITORY INSTITUTION CLAIMS

This so-called S&L priority has been added to the list of priority claims because of the failure of financial institutions. Allowed unsecured claims that are based on a commitment of the debtor to the Federal Deposit Insurance Corporation (FDIC), the Resolution Trust Corporation (RTC), the Director of the Office of Thrift Supervision, the Comptroller of the Currency, or the Board of Governors of the Federal Reserve System, or their predecessors or successors, to maintain the capital of an insured depository institution, are priority claims. 11 U.S.C.A. § 507(a)(9).

B. NONPRIORITY CLAIMS

After distribution to priority claimants in the order set forth in section 507, distribution is then made to the general unsecured creditors.

1. TIMELY FILED UNSUBORDINATED GENERAL UNSECURED CLAIMS AND TARDILY FILED UNSECURED CLAIMS WHERE CREDITOR DID NOT HAVE NOTICE BUT PROOF OF CLAIM FILED IN TIME TO MAKE PAYMENT

Tardily filed unsecured claims are included in the same class as timely filed unsecured claims if the tardiness in filing came about because the creditor had neither notice nor knowledge of the bankruptcy case. Proof of the claim, however, must be filed in time to permit payment of the claim.

2. OTHER TARDILY FILED UNSECURED CLAIMS

The tardily filed unsecured claim which comes about through failure of the creditor to timely act is subordinated to the timely filed and tardily filed claim due to lack of notice.

3. PENALTY-TYPE CLAIMS

A penalty-type claim, secured or unsecured, to the extent that it is not compensation for actual pecuniary loss, arising before the order for relief or the appointment of a trustee, whichever is earlier, comes fourth in distribution of the estate. This type of claim will be paid only if there are assets left after distribution that would otherwise go to the debtor when the case is closed.

4. INTEREST ON PRIORITY AND NONPRIORITY PREPETITION CLAIMS

Postpetition interest on prepetition claims, priority or nonpriority, will be paid only if a surplus of assets will be available to return to the debtor when the case is closed.

5. DEBTOR

If, when all claims have been paid, a surplus remains, it will be paid to the debtor.

SECTION 11
CLOSING THE CASE

The **closing of a case** begins with the trustee's final report and proposed distribution of the assets of the bankruptcy estate. The office of the bankruptcy clerk mails notice to all creditors and other parties in interest. After the court's review and ruling on fees and objections to claims, the trustee distributes the assets of the estate. The trustee then reports his or her post-distribution activities and requests discharge from any further duties. The trustee is discharged and the case closed.

A. TRUSTEE'S FINAL REPORT AND PROPOSED DISTRIBUTION

Exhibit 5.39 is a sample of the trustee's final report and proposed distribution.

The creditors and other parties in interest are then notified of the Trustee's Final Report and Proposed Distribution. They are given 30 days in which to file a written objection. See Exhibit 5.40 for the notice to creditors and parties in interest.

EXHIBIT 5.39
Trustee's Final Report and Proposed Distribution

IN THE UNITED STATES BANKRUPTCY COURT
FOR THE _____ DISTRICT OF _____

In re:)
)
)   Chapter 7
)
)
              Debtor (s).   )   Case No.

TRUSTEE'S FINAL REPORT
AND PROPOSED DISTRIBUTION

I. FINAL REPORT:

The petition commencing this case was filed on _____ , 19___ , and the undersigned was (appointed) (elected) trustee on _____ , 19___ . The amount of the trustee's bond is now $_____ .

The trustee certifies that the balance in his or her office account, bank account, bank account number _____ at _____ _____ , is in the amount of $_____ . This amount includes all earned interest and is subject to check for payment to creditors.

All property of the estate, except that claimed exempt by the debtor(s), without objection, or determined by the Court as exempt, has been inventoried, collected and liquidated, or abandoned.

All claims have been examined and objections have been ruled on by the Court. Applications for approval of compensation and expenses of professional persons have been ruled on by the Court. Any property not abandoned by the trustee before is now abandoned and is scheduled on the attached Proposed Distribution. (See Section II.)

1. THE VALUE OF:

    Administered property totals: $_____
    Exempt property totals: $_____
    Abandoned property totals: $_____
    (Attached hereto as Form 1)

EXHIBIT 5.39
Continued

2. The trustee adopts the schedules of the petition filed as his or her inventory.
   (YES) _____   (NO) _____
   (if "NO," inventory attached)

3. Final Account as of _____ , 19 ____ .

RECEIPTS: (Attached hereto as Form 2) $_____

DISBURSEMENTS: (Attached hereto as Form 2) $_____ .

BALANCE OF FUNDS ON HAND: $_____

ANALYSIS OF CLAIMS FILED (Attached hereto as Form 3)

PROPOSED DISTRIBUTION (See Section II, entitled "Proposed Distribution")

4. The net estate upon which the trustee's compensation was computed is
   $_____ . This does not include any exemptions paid to the debtor(s)
   or any refunds to be made to the debtor(s).

The undersigned trustee certifies under penalty of perjury that the foregoing Final Report, and attached forms, are true and correct to the best of his or her knowledge and belief. The trustee hereby requests the United States trustee to approve this Final Report and requests the Court to provide for notice and opportunity for a hearing under 11 U.S.C. §§ 502(b) and 503(b) and thereafter to make final allowance for the purposes of distribution to claims, administrative expenses, and other payments stated in this Final Report and Proposed Distribution.

WHEREFORE, the trustee requests that this Final Report and Proposed Distribution be approved by this Court.

TRUSTEE NAME: _____   DATE: _____

SIGNED: _____   ADDRESS: _____

_____

TELEPHONE: _____

EXHIBIT 5.39
Continued

Page 1

Case No.: _____
Case Name: _____

Trustee Name: _____
Dates Submitted: _____

FORM 1
INDIVIDUAL ESTATE PROPERTY RECORD AND REPORT
ASSET CASES

Ref. No.	1 Asset Description (Scheduled and Unscheduled Property)	2 Petition/ Unscheduled Values	3 Value Determined by Trustee Less Liens and Exemption	4 Property Abandoned	5 Sales/ Funds Received by the Estate	6 Asset Fully Administered/ Value of Remaining Assets (Yes or Dollar Amount of Remaining Assets)
1	Residence, Happy Rock MO	220,000.00	12,000		275,000	Yes
2	Cash on Hand	10.00	0			Yes
3	Deposits	250.00	0			Yes
4	Household Goods	1,000.00	0			Yes
5	Jewelry	2,000.00	1,360		5,000	Yes
6	1980 Cadillac	1,000.00	0	(1)		Yes
7	1990 Corvette	25,000.00	21,000		20,000	Yes
8	1986 BMW	12,000.00	1,500	(1)		Yes
9	Mach./Equipment	9,000.00	0	Yes		Yes
10	Air Compressor	1,500.00	0	(1)		Yes

* (1) Abandoned at close of case.

TOTALS _____   Value of Remaining Assets _____
(Total Dollar Amount in Column 6)

Major activities affecting case closing which are not reflected above.

Matters Pending _____   Date of Hearing or Sale _____   Other Action _____

Projected Date of Final Report _____

EXHIBIT 5.39
Continued

FORM 2

CASH RECEIPTS AND DISBURSEMENT RECORD

Page 1

Case No. _____

Case Name: _____
Taxpayer ID #: _____

Bank Name : _____

Savings Account #: _____
Checking Account #: _____
Bond Amount: _____

(indicate if blanket bond)

1	2	3	4	5	6	7	8
Trans. Date	Check or Reference Number	Paid to/ Received From	Description of Transaction	Deposit $	Disburs. $	Checking Account Balance	Savings (s) Invest. (i) Balance
7/29/90	5	ABC Jewelry	Sale of Jewelry	5,000.00		5,000.00	
7/30/90	101	J & M Buzzard	Exemption - jewelry		640.00(D)	4,360.00	
7/31/90	102	MO Western	Transfer to Savings		3,860.00(T)	500.00	3,860.00(S)
8/10/90	12	MO Sharpshooters	Sale of Guns	3,500.00		4,000.00	3,860.00(S)
8/11/90	103	ABC Bank	Lien on Guns		2,500.00	1,500.00	3,860.00(S)
8/15/90	104	Ins. Brokers	Trustee Bond		100.00	1,400.00	3,860.00(S)
8/16/90	7	Joe Cool	Sale of 90 Corv.	20,000.00		21,400.00	3,860.00(S)
8/16/90	105	XYZ Bank	Lien on 90 Corv.		3,500.00	17,900.00	3,860.00(S)
8/16/90	106	J & M Buzzard	Exemption -Corvette		500.00(D)	17,400.00	3,860.00(S)
8/16/90	107	MO Western	Transfer to Savings		16,900.00(T)	500.00	20,760.00(S)
8/31/90	—	MO Western	Interest 8/31/90	68.32		568.32	20,760.00(S)
9/3/90	14(u)	Smalltown Bank	Cert. of Deposit	10,000.00		10,568.32	20,760.00(S)
9/4/90	15(u)	Darrell Buzzard	1/2 Int. in Boat	50,000.00		60,568.32	20,760.00(S)
9/4/90	108	MO Western	Transfer to Savings		60,068.32(T)	500.00	80,828.32(S)
9/6/90	18(u)	Jackie Luft Eqpt	Preference	2,300.00		2,800.00	80,828.32(S)
9/6/90	19(u)	Goforth Mfg. Co.	Preference	5,000.00		7,800.00	80,828.32(S)
9/8/90	23(u)	Red Barn Ins. Co.	Insurance - barn	6,500.00		14,300.00	80,828.32(S)
9/15/90	1	Happy Rock Title	Sales of Residence	275,000.00		289,300.00	80,828.32(S)
9/15/90	109	Happy Rock Title	Closing Costs/Comm.	275,000.00	23,142.91	266,157.09	80,828.32(S)

EXHIBIT 5.39
Continued

Page 1

FORM 3
ANALYSIS OF CLAIMS REGISTER
DEBTOR NAME _____

CASE # _____
BAR DATE FOR CLAIMS _____
CLAIMS REVIEWED BY _____

Number	Creditor	Date of Claim	Priority (Amount)	Taxes (Amount)	Liens (Amt.)	Secured (Amt.)	Unsecured (Amt.)	Abandon (Date)	Reaffirm (Date)	Other	Contest
1	Ace Carpenter	7/20/90	2,600.00								Objection (over $2,000)
1a	Ace Carpenter	8/10/90	2,000.00								
1b	Ace Carpenter	8/10/90					600.00				
2	Ben Easymark	7/21/90	20,000.00								Objection (over $900)
2a	Ben Easymark	8/11/90	900.00								
2b	Ben Easymark	8/11/90					19,100.00				
3	Justin Taken	7/22/90	10,000.00								Objection (over $900)
3a	Justin Taken	8/12/90	900.00								
3b	Justin Taken	8/12/90					9,100.00				
4	Sue Brown	7/22/90	1,200.00								
5	Bob Jones	7/22/90	700.00								
6	IRS	7/31/90		60,000.00							
7	Joseph Jones	8/1/90	500.00								

EXHIBIT 5.39
Continued

II. PROPOSED DISTRIBUTION: (*** Pursuant to Fed. R. Bank. P. 3010, all funds less than $5.00 will be paid into the Registry fund of this Court without further order.)

A. ADMINISTRATIVE EXPENSES (U.S.C. § 507(a)(1)):

  1. Professionals (with date(s) appointed by Court order(s))

Professional (name(s) and date(s) appointed)	Amount(s) Paid (date(s) of Court order(s))
a. Trustee's Compensation	
b. Trustee's Expenses	
c. Attorney for Trustee's Compensation	
d. Attorney for Trustee's Expenses	
e. Accountant's Compensation	
f. Accountant's Expenses	
g. Appraiser's Compensation	
h. Appraiser's Expenses	
i. Attorney for Debtor's Compensation	
j. Attorney for Debtor's Expenses	
k. Attorney for Others' Compensation	
l. Attorney for Others' Expenses	
m. Auctioneer's Compensation	
n. Auctioneer's Expenses	
o. Harvester's Compensation	
p. Harvester's Expenses	
q. Real Estate Agent's Compensation	
r. Real Estate Agent's Expenses	
s. Other Professionals' Compensation (list)	
t. Other Professionals' Expenses (list)	

SUBTOTAL (Professionals) $_____

EXHIBIT 5.39
Continued

2. Other Administrative Expenses

Type	Amount of Claim	Amount to be Paid

a. Super-Priority Claims (list)

b. Court costs, filing and notice fees

c. Other (list)

SUBTOTAL (Other Administrative Expenses) $_____
TOTAL ADMINISTRATIVE EXPENSES
(Professional and Other) $_____
Note: All 507(a)(1) Fees Share Pro Rata

B. SECURED CLAIMS

Claimant	Amount of Claim	Amount to be Paid

(list)

TOTAL SECURED CLAIMS $_____

C. PRIORITY CLAIMS
   1. Wage Claims (U.S.C. § 507(a)(3))

Claimant	Claim Amount	Dividend	Employee Share Fed. W/H	Employee Share Soc. Sec.	Soc. Sec. W/H	Net

(list)

TOTALS

Net to Employees $_____
Total for IRS $_____
Total to be Paid $_____

Gross $_____
Employers FICA $_____
SUBTOTAL (Wage Claims) $_____

The trustee should issue a check payable to the Director of Internal Revenue in the appropriate amount, for each wage claimant, representing withholding for income tax, the Employee's portion of Social Security and the Employer's portion of Social Security.

EXHIBIT 5.39
Continued

2. Contributions To Employee Funds
   (U.S.C. § 507(a)(4))
   Claimant Amount of Claim   Amount to be Paid

   (list)

   SUBTOTAL (Contributions to Employee Funds) $_____

3. Tax Claims (U.S.C. § 507(a)(7))

   Type   Amount of Claim   Amount to be Paid

   a. Federal

   b. State

   c. County

   d. Employment

   e. Fuel

   f. Other (list)

   SUBTOTAL (Tax Claims) $_____

4. Other Priority Claims

   Claimant   Amount of Claim   Amount to be Paid

   (list)

   SUBTOTAL (Other Priority Claims) $_____

   TOTAL PRIORITY CLAIMS
   (Wage + Tax + Contributions + Other) $_____

D. GENERAL UNSECURED CLAIMS

Name and Address of Creditor	Amount of the Claim	% to be Paid	Amount to be Paid
_____	$_____	_____%	$_____
_____	$_____	_____%	$_____
_____	$_____	_____%	$_____
_____	$_____	_____%	$_____

EXHIBIT 5.39
Continued

	$	%	$
_____	$_____	____%	$_____
_____	$_____	____%	$_____
_____	$_____	____%	$_____
_____	$_____	____%	$_____
_____	$_____	____%	$_____
_____	$_____	____%	$_____
_____	$_____	____%	$_____
_____	$_____	____%	$_____
_____	$_____	____%	$_____
_____	$_____	____%	$_____
_____	$_____	____%	$_____
_____	$_____	____%	$_____
_____	$_____	____%	$_____
_____	$_____	____%	$_____
_____	$_____	____%	$_____
TOTAL UNSECURED CLAIMS	$_____		$_____

If additional space is needed, continue on an attached page(s). Check here if additional page(s) is attached [   ].

E. ABANDONMENT OF ESTATE PROPERTY

Unless objection is made in writing to the Clerk of the Court and request for notice and hearing requested, the trustee, pursuant to 11 U.S.C. § 554, abandons the following property:

Property	Lienholder & Address	Stored at	Value	Reason for Abandonment

TOTAL PROPOSED DISTRIBUTION
 Administrative Expenses $_____
 Secured Claims $_____
 Priority Claims $_____
 General Unsecured Claims $_____

  TOTAL $_____

EXHIBIT 5.40
Notice to Creditors and Other Parties in Interest Concerning the Trustee's Final Report and Proposed Distribution

---

IN THE UNITED STATES BANKRUPTCY COURT
FOR THE _____ DISTRICT OF _____

In re:)
)
)   Chapter 7
)
)
                        Debtor(s).   )   Case No.

NOTICE DIRECTING AFFECTED CREDITORS AND PARTIES IN INTEREST
TO SHOW CAUSE IN WRITING WITHIN 30 DAYS OF THIS NOTICE WHY
TRUSTEE'S FINAL REPORT SHOULD NOT BE APPROVED AND WHY
TRUSTEE'S PROPOSED DISTRIBUTION SHOULD NOT BE MADE

Notice is hereby given to all affected creditors that any claimant may object to any of the foregoing statements or take exception to them or offer written evidence to contradict them and may object to the proposed distribution on any grounds available to them. If there are no objections, exceptions or submissions of controverting evidence, the trustee will make distribution in accordance with the foregoing proposed distribution. It is therefore

DIRECTED that all affected creditors and parties in interest, or any of them, show cause within thirty (30) days of the mailing of this notice by filing with the court and simultaneously serving such on the trustee at the below address and on the Office of the United States trustee, _____ , _____ , a written objection setting forth the reasons why the trustee's final account should not be approved and why the trustee's distribution should not be made.

_____   _____
Date   Trustee in bankruptcy

                    Address: _____
                                          _____

B. TRUSTEE'S FINAL ACCOUNT AFTER DISTRIBUTION AND REQUEST FOR DISCHARGE

After the court rules on the objections to the trustee's final report and proposed distribution, and after any adjustments are made, the court approves the trustee's final report and proposed distribution of the assets of the bankruptcy estate. The trustee then distributes the assets of the estate and files the trustee's final account after distribution. The trustee certifies to the court and the U.S. trustee that the estate has been fully administered and requests that the court order the case be closed and the trustee be discharged from any further duties. Exhibit 5.41 is the trustee's declaration that the estate has been fully administered. Exhibit 5.42 is the trustee's final account after distribution and his or request for discharge.

EXHIBIT 5.41
Trustee's Declaration that the Estate Has Been Fully Administered

---

**IN THE UNITED STATES BANKRUPTCY COURT
FOR THE _____ DISTRICT OF _____**

In re:)
)
)   Chapter 7
)
)
              Debtor(s).   )   Case No.

DECLARATION THAT ESTATE HAS BEEN FULLY ADMINISTERED,
THAT BANK ACCOUNT HAS A ZERO BALANCE, AND THAT UNCLAIMED
FUNDS ATTRIBUTABLE TO CERTAIN CLAIMANTS HAVE BEEN
DEPOSITED IN THE REGISTRY OF THE COURT

Comes now the trustee in bankruptcy of the above styled bankruptcy estate and hereby

DECLARES that the above estate has been fully administered; and further

DECLARES that the trustee's bank account formerly maintained as an account for this case now has a zero balance; and further

DECLARES that unclaimed funds attributable to the following claimants have been deposited in the registry of the court:

Name of Claimant	Last Known Address	Amount
_____	_____	_____
_____	_____	_____
_____	_____	_____
_____	_____	_____
_____	_____	_____
_____	_____	_____

[   ] Check here if additional pages are attached

_____   _____

Date   Trustee in bankruptcy

EXHIBIT 5.42
Trustee's Final Account after Distribution and Request for Discharge

---

IN THE UNITED STATES BANKRUPTCY COURT
FOR THE _____ DISTRICT OF _____

In re:)   Chapter 7
)   Case No.
)
)   FINAL ACCOUNT AFTER
)   DISTRIBUTION AND REQUEST
                          Debtor(s).)   FOR DISCHARGE OF TRUSTEE

The undersigned trustee reports:

1. The balance on hand has been distributed in accordance with the trustee's Final Report Before Distribution as amended (if any) by Court Order except for unclaimed dividends paid to the Court Registry Fund as follows:

Creditor
(Name and Address)   Claim No.   Amount
_____   _____   _____

2. Gross receipts of $_____ from liquidation of all property of the estate has been distributed under 11 U.S.C. § 726 as follows:

$_____   a. Trustee Compensation
$_____   b. Fee for Attorney for Trustee
$_____   c. Fee for Attorney for Debtor
$_____   d. Other Professionals
$_____   e. *All* expenses, including Trustee and Court costs
$_____   f. Secured Creditors
$_____   g. Priority Creditors
$_____   h. Unsecured Creditors
$_____   i. Other Payments, *except to Debtor*
$_____   j. SUBTOTAL (sum of lines a through i)
$_____   k. Payments to Debtor
$_____   l. TOTAL DISBURSEMENTS
                                          (sum of lines j and k)

3. The final bank statement of the estate and all canceled checks evidencing the distribution have been submitted to the United States trustee.

I hereby certify to the Court and the United States trustee, that this estate has been fully administered. A Final Report has been filed and proper disbursements completed. No funds or assets of the estate remain.

EXHIBIT 5.42
Continued

Therefore, pursuant to Fed. R. Bank. P. 5009, the trustee requests that this Final Account After Distribution be accepted, and that the Court order the case closed and discharge the trustee of any further duties.

_____   _____
Date   Trustee

                                 _____
                                 Address

                                 _____

REVIEW BY UNITED STATES TRUSTEE

I have reviewed the trustee's Final Account After Distribution for Closing and Discharge.

_____   _____
Date   United States trustee

                         By: _____

C. CLOSING THE CASE

After the court issues the final decree (See Exhibit 5.43) the case file is reviewed by the office of the clerk of the bankruptcy court. After a period of time, the case file will be shipped to a central regional location for storage.

EXHIBIT 5.43
Final Decree

UNITED STATES BANKRUPTCY COURT
_____ **DISTRICT OF** _____

In re _____ ,   )
    [Set forth here all names including married,   )
    maiden, and trade names used by debtor within)
    last 6 years.]   )
                              Debtor   ) Case No. _____
)
) Chapter _____
)
Social Secutiry No(s). _____ and all   )
Employer's Tax Identification Nos. *[if any]* _____   )
_____   )

FINAL DECREE

The estate of the above named debtor has been fully administered.

IT IS ORDERED THAT:
    [name of the trustee]
    is discharged as trustee of the estate of the above named debtor and the bond is canceled;
    The Chapter 7 case of the above named debtor is closed.

_____
Date

                                    _____
                                    United States Bankruptcy Judge

---

SECTION 12

After the Case is Closed

After the case is closed, it may be amended without being reopened or it may be reopened.

A. AMENDING THE CASE WITHOUT REOPENING THE CASE

A case may be amended without being reopened to correct clerical errors in judgments, orders, and other parts of the record. Errors in the record caused by oversight or omission may also be corrected in a closed case.

B. REOPENING A CLOSED CASE

The two basic reasons for reopening a case are to administer assets or to include another creditor. A case may be reopened in the court in which it was closed.

In *In re Thompson,* after the debtor had received a discharge in a no-asset case and her case was closed, she petitioned the court to reopen her bankruptcy case and amend her schedule of liabilities to include an omitted creditor. The court stated that "The decision to reopen a case is within the sound discretion of the [bankruptcy court]."

In re Thompson

United Stated District Court, Eastern District of New York, 1993.
152 B.R. 24.

MEMORANDUM AND ORDER
Raymond J. Dearie,
District Judge

Debtor Henrietta Thompson appeals from a bankruptcy court order, dated October 6, 1992, denying her motion to reopen her no-asset Chapter 7 bankruptcy case for the purpose of adding a creditor and extending such creditor's time to object to discharge. There is no opposition to the appeal. This Court finds that the denial of the debtor's motion was an abuse of discretion. Accordingly, the order is vacated, and the matter is remanded to the bankruptcy court.

BACKGROUND

On October 15, 1991, Henrietta Thompson, the debtor, filed a Chapter 7 petition pursuant to 11 U.S.C. § 301 for release from consumer debts. The debtor's estate contained no assets. Scheduled creditors were sent notice of the commencement of the case and of the creditors meeting to be held on November 15, 1991. The deadline to file a complaint objecting to the discharge of the debtor or to determine dischargeability of a debt was set for January 14, 1992. Because no assets were available for distribution, the creditors were advised not to file proofs of claim until receiving notice to do so. The case proceeded without incident, and on March 12, 1992, the debtor was released from all dischargeable debts.

Approximately three months after the discharge, the debtor discovered that she had inadvertently failed to list FCDB Preferred Charge/Spiegel, an unsecured creditor for $1,775.52, on her schedule. FCDB Preferred Charge/Spiegel was subsequently informed that the debtor had filed for bankruptcy. On September 9, 1992, the debtor moved to reopen her case to add the omitted creditor to her schedule and extend the creditor's time to object to discharge. The motion was made on notice to the omitted creditor, its attorney, the interim trustee and the United States trustee. At the oral argument on October 6, 1992, no one appeared in opposition to the motion. The bankruptcy court denied the motion orally, concluding that "the rule in th[e] District is even if [the court] granted [the] motion and even if the creditor did not file an objection the debt would not be discharged. . . . [I]f [the court] granted [the] motion it would be futile and a waste of time." The debtor now appeals the ruling of the bankruptcy court. Again, there is no opposition.

DISCUSSION

The decision to reopen a case is within "the sound discretion of the [bankruptcy court]. *In re McNeil,* 13 B.R. 743, 745 (Bankr. S.D.N.Y.1981). Therefore, the bankruptcy court's decision not to reopen a case may be vacated only "upon a showing that the failure to reopen was an abuse of discretion." *In re Candelaria,* 121 B.R. 140, 142 (E.D.N.Y.1990) (quoting *In re Sheerin,* 21 B.R. 438, 440 (BAP 1st Cir.1982)). The bankruptcy court below incorrectly concluded that, as a matter of law, the debt to FCDB Preferred Charge/Spiegel would not be discharged even if the debtor's motion to reopen her case were granted and the creditor did not object to discharge. Therefore, it abused its discretion in denying the debtor's motion to reopen.

Under the Bankruptcy Code, an individual who files for relief under Chapter 7 is not discharged from any debt that is "neither listed nor scheduled . . . in time to permit . . . timely filing of a proof of claim."[1] 11 U.S.C.A. § 523(a)(3)(A) (1979 & Supp. 1992). If a debt is of a kind specified in paragraph (2), (4), or (6) of section 523(a),[2] an individual is not discharged from such debt unless it is listed or scheduled "in time to permit . . . timely request for a determination of dischargeability" in addition to timely filing of a proof of claim.[3] 11 U.S.C.A. § 523(a)(3)(B) (1979 & Supp.1992).

Generally, "a proof of claim shall be filed within 90 days after the first date set for the meeting of creditors." 11 U.S.C.A.Bankr. Rule 3002(c) (Supp.1992). However, in a case in which no assets are available for distribution, creditors may be notified that it is unnecessary to file proofs of claim. 11 U.S.C.A.Bankr.Rule 2002(e) (Supp.1992). If they are so notified, they must be informed of any subsequent discovery of assets from which a dividend may be paid. They may then file proofs of claim within ninety days. 11 U.S.C.A.Bankr.Rule 3002(c)(5) (Supp. 1992). Thus, in a no-asset case, section 523(a)(3)(A) does not preclude the discharge of an unscheduled debt until the expiration of the filing period following notice to the creditors of the existence of assets from which a dividend may be paid. *In re Candelaria,* 121 B.R. at 144; *see In re De Mare,* 74 B.R. 604, 605 (Bankr.N.D.N.Y. 1987); *In re Maddox,* 62 B.R. 510, 513 (Bankr.E.D.N.Y.1986); *In re Jensen,* 46 B.R. 578, 582 (Bankr.E.D.N.Y.1985); *In re Zablocki,* 36 B.R. 779, 782 (Bankr.D.Conn.

1984). Because no assets have been discovered in the estate of the debtor in this case, section 523(a)(3)(A) does not preclude the discharge of the debt to FCDB Preferred Charge/Spiegel.

Generally, a creditor contending that a debt is of a kind excepted from discharge pursuant to section 523(a)(2), (4), or (6)[4] must file a request for a determination of dischargeability within sixty days of the first date set for the meeting of creditors. 11 U.S.C.A. § 523(c) (Supp.1992) & Rule 4007(c) (Supp.1992). Under Rule 4007(c), motions to extend the time to file must be made within the sixty day period. However, the expiration of that period alone does not preclude the discharge of an unscheduled debt pursuant to section 523(a)(3)(B). To bring an unscheduled debt within section 523(a)(3)(B), the creditor must show that he had grounds for claiming the debt was of a kind specified in paragraph (2), (4), or (6) of section 523(a) in addition to showing that the debtor's omission deprived him of the opportunity to timely assert a claim of nondischargeability on such grounds. *In re Candelaria,* 121 B.R. at 144; *In re Zablocki,* 36 B.R. at 782.

Accordingly, the limitations of section 523(c) and Rule 4007(c) do not apply when the issue of exception to discharge pursuant to paragraph (2), (4), or (6) of section 523(a) arises in the context of exception to discharge pursuant to section 523(a)(3)(B). *In re Candelaria,* 121 B.R. at 144–45 (citing in accord *In re Jensen,* 46 B.R. at 583); *In re Zablocki,* 36 B.R. at 782. A creditor added to a debtor's schedule after the debtor is granted a discharge must be afforded a reasonable period of time to file a complaint to determine the dischargeability of the debt under section 523(a)(2), (4) or (6). *In re Candelaria,* 121 B.R. 140 at 145. If the creditor does not file a complaint, or if upon consideration of such complaint, the debt is determined to be dischargeable, the debt is then discharged. Thus, section 523(a)(3)(B) does not as a matter of law preclude the discharge of the debt to FCDB Preferred Charge/Spiegel.

CONCLUSION

Applicable law does not support the bankruptcy court's conclusion that granting the debtor's motion would have been futile. Accordingly, the Court finds that the bankruptcy court's refusal to reopen the debtor's case was an abuse of discretion. The order of the bankruptcy court is vacated, and the case is remanded for further proceedings consistent with this opinion.

    SO ORDERED.

---

[1] If a creditor has notice or actual knowledge of the debtor's bankruptcy case in time for such timely filing of a proof of claim, the debt need not be listed or scheduled in order to be discharged. 11 U.S.C.A. § 523(a)(3)(A) (1979 & Supp.1992).

[2] Paragraph (2) specifies debts obtained by false pretenses, a false representation, or actual fraud, and debts obtained by use of a materially false statement of financial condition. Paragraph (4) specifies debts "for fraud or defalcation while acting in a fiduciary capacity, embezzlement, or larceny." Paragraph (6) specifies debts "for willful and malicious injury by the debtor to another entity or to the property of another entity." 11 U.S.C.A. § 523(a).

[3] If a creditor has notice or actual knowledge of the debtor's bankruptcy case in time to permit a timely request for a determination of dischargeability in addition to timely filing of a proof of claim, the debt need not be listed or scheduled in order to be discharged. 11 U.S.C.A. § 523(a)(3)(B) (1979 & Supp.1992).

[4] See supra text accompanying note 2.

BASIC TERMS AND PHRASES

Abandoned property of the estate
Administrative expenses
Adversary proceeding
Assume or reject executory contracts
Automatic stay
Avoidance powers
Bankruptcy estate
Bankruptcy petition preparer
Clerk's notice
Closing of a case
Codebtor
Community property state
Complaint Objecting to the Debtor's Discharge
Complaint Objecting to the Dischargeability of a Debt
Contested matters
Contingent claim
Convert nonexempt property into exempt property
Creditor holding a secured claim
Creditor holding an unsecured nonpriority claim
Creditor holding an unsecured priority claim

Current monthly expenditures of an individual debtor
Current monthly income of an individual debtor
Debtor's petition
Declaration Concerning the Debtor's Schedules
Discharge and reaffirmation hearing
Disclosure of attorney's compensation statement
Disputed claim
Distribution of the property of the estate
Executory contract
Exemptions (federal)
Exemptions (state)
Exempt property
Filing fee
Interim trustee
Joint case
Liquidation
List of creditors
Matrix
Meeting of creditors
Meeting of equity security holders

Motion for abstention by the court
Motion for a change of venue
Motion for relief from the automatic
  stay
Motion to convert to a Chapter 11, 12,
  or 13
Motion to dismiss the case
Motion to enforce the automatic stay
Nonpriority claim
Order for relief
Priority claim

Property of the estate
Reaffirmation agreement
Schedules
Setoff
Statement of Financial Affairs
Statement of intention
"Straight" bankruptcy
Unexpired lease
Unliquidated claim
Waiver of avoiding powers
Waiver of exemptions

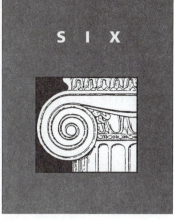

SIX

THE CHAPTER 13 BANKRUPTCY (ADJUSTMENT OF DEBTS OF AN INDIVIDUAL WITH REGULAR INCOME)

CHAPTER OUTLINE

SECTION 10
REVOCATION OF ORDER
OF CONFIRMATION

SECTION 11
DISCHARGE

SECTION 12
REVOCATION OF THE DISCHARGE

SECTION 13
CLOSING THE CASE AND AFTER
THE CASE IS CLOSED

This chapter explores the Chapter 13 bankruptcy—**adjustment of debts of an individual with regular income.** Not all debtors may file a Chapter 13 petition. A debtor may file a Chapter 13 petition only if he or she is an individual with sufficiently stable and regular income to make payments under a Chapter 13 plan, with unsecured debts of less than $250,000 and secured debts of less than $750,000. 11 U.S.C.A. § 109(e).

This chapter follows the Chapter 13 case from the filing of the petition to the closing of the case and beyond. The documents necessary for the filing of a Chapter 13 petition and the significance of filing such a petition are explored. The chapter covers the appointment of the trustee, as well as the various motions and complaints that could be filed after the order for relief. The clerk's notice and the meeting of creditors are described.

The Chapter 13 plan, filed by the debtor, is explored. The contents of a plan, the debtor's payments under the plan, and modification of the plan before confirmation are discussed. The hearing on confirmation of the plan and the concept of a Chapter 13 cramdown are examined. Modification of the plan after confirmation and revocation of an order of confirmation are investigated.

The debtor's full-compliance discharge after payments have been completed under the plan and the hardship discharge for those debtors who may be unable to complete the payments under the plan, along with revocation of a discharge, are explored.

Finally, the closing of the case and further action available after the case is closed are described.

For those who would like to follow a Chapter 13 case in diagram form, the following "road map" will prove useful. (See Exhibit 6.1.)

SECTION 1
THE FILING OF THE PETITION

The same documents necessary for the filing of the petition in a voluntary Chapter 7 case are necessary in a Chapter 13 case. A Chapter 13 filing also requires a Chapter 13 plan. The filing of a Chapter 13 case requires the following items:

1. Filing fee and administrative fee;
2. Voluntary Petition (Official Form No. 1);
3. Disclosure of attorney's compensation statement or disclosure of compensation statement by a non-attorney bankruptcy petition preparer;
4. Matrix (the list of creditors);
5. Schedules (Official Form No. 6)
   a. Summary of Schedules
   b. Schedule A: Real Property
   c. Schedule B: Personal Property
   d. Schedule C: Property Claimed as Exempt

EXHIBIT 6.1
Chapter 13 Adjustment of Debts of an Individual with Regular Income (Voluntary Petition)

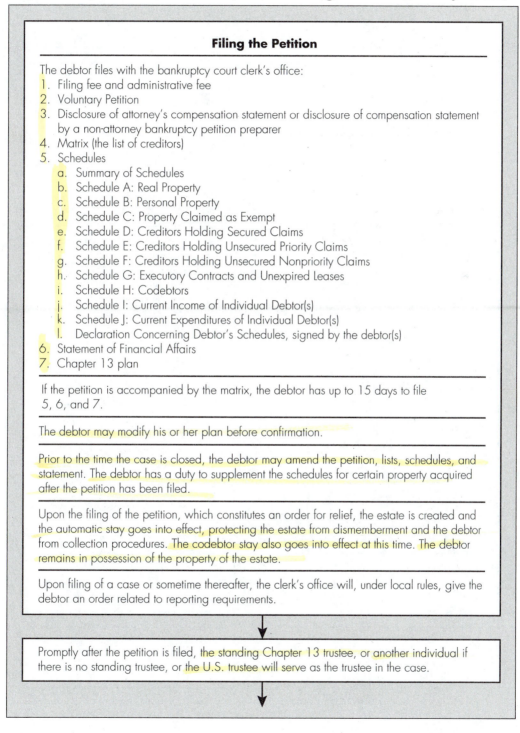

Filing the Petition

The debtor files with the bankruptcy court clerk's office:
1. Filing fee and administrative fee
2. Voluntary Petition
3. Disclosure of attorney's compensation statement or disclosure of compensation statement by a non-attorney bankruptcy petition preparer
4. Matrix (the list of creditors)
5. Schedules
   a. Summary of Schedules
   b. Schedule A: Real Property
   c. Schedule B: Personal Property
   d. Schedule C: Property Claimed as Exempt
   e. Schedule D: Creditors Holding Secured Claims
   f. Schedule E: Creditors Holding Unsecured Priority Claims
   g. Schedule F: Creditors Holding Unsecured Nonpriority Claims
   h. Schedule G: Executory Contracts and Unexpired Leases
   i. Schedule H: Codebtors
   j. Schedule I: Current Income of Individual Debtor(s)
   k. Schedule J: Current Expenditures of Individual Debtor(s)
   l. Declaration Concerning Debtor's Schedules, signed by the debtor(s)
6. Statement of Financial Affairs
7. Chapter 13 plan

If the petition is accompanied by the matrix, the debtor has up to 15 days to file 5, 6, and 7.

The debtor may modify his or her plan before confirmation.

Prior to the time the case is closed, the debtor may amend the petition, lists, schedules, and statement. The debtor has a duty to supplement the schedules for certain property acquired after the petition has been filed.

Upon the filing of the petition, which constitutes an order for relief, the estate is created and the automatic stay goes into effect, protecting the estate from dismemberment and the debtor from collection procedures. The codebtor stay also goes into effect at this time. The debtor remains in possession of the property of the estate.

Upon filing of a case or sometime thereafter, the clerk's office will, under local rules, give the debtor an order related to reporting requirements.

Promptly after the petition is filed, the standing Chapter 13 trustee, or another individual if there is no standing trustee, or the U.S. trustee will serve as the trustee in the case.

EXHIBIT 6.1
Continued

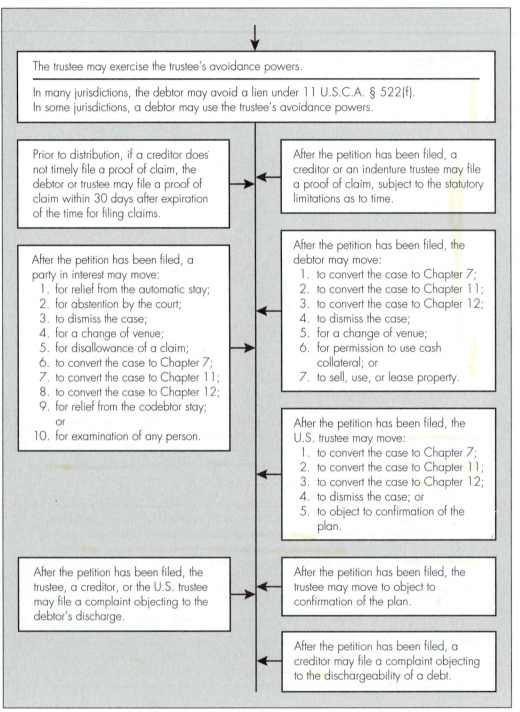

The trustee may exercise the trustee's avoidance powers.

In many jurisdictions, the debtor may avoid a lien under 11 U.S.C.A. § 522(f).
In some jurisdictions, a debtor may use the trustee's avoidance powers.

Prior to distribution, if a creditor does not timely file a proof of claim, the debtor or trustee may file a proof of claim within 30 days after expiration of the time for filing claims.

After the petition has been filed, a creditor or an indenture trustee may file a proof of claim, subject to the statutory limitations as to time.

After the petition has been filed, a party in interest may move:
1. for relief from the automatic stay;
2. for abstention by the court;
3. to dismiss the case;
4. for a change of venue;
5. for disallowance of a claim;
6. to convert the case to Chapter 7;
7. to convert the case to Chapter 11;
8. to convert the case to Chapter 12;
9. for relief from the codebtor stay; or
10. for examination of any person.

After the petition has been filed, the debtor may move:
1. to convert the case to Chapter 7;
2. to convert the case to Chapter 11;
3. to convert the case to Chapter 12;
4. to dismiss the case;
5. for a change of venue;
6. for permission to use cash collateral; or
7. to sell, use, or lease property.

After the petition has been filed, the U.S. trustee may move:
1. to convert the case to Chapter 7;
2. to convert the case to Chapter 11;
3. to convert the case to Chapter 12;
4. to dismiss the case; or
5. to object to confirmation of the plan.

After the petition has been filed, the trustee, a creditor, or the U.S. trustee may file a complaint objecting to the debtor's discharge.

After the petition has been filed, the trustee may move to object to confirmation of the plan.

After the petition has been filed, a creditor may file a complaint objecting to the dischargeability of a debt.

EXHIBIT 6.1
Continued

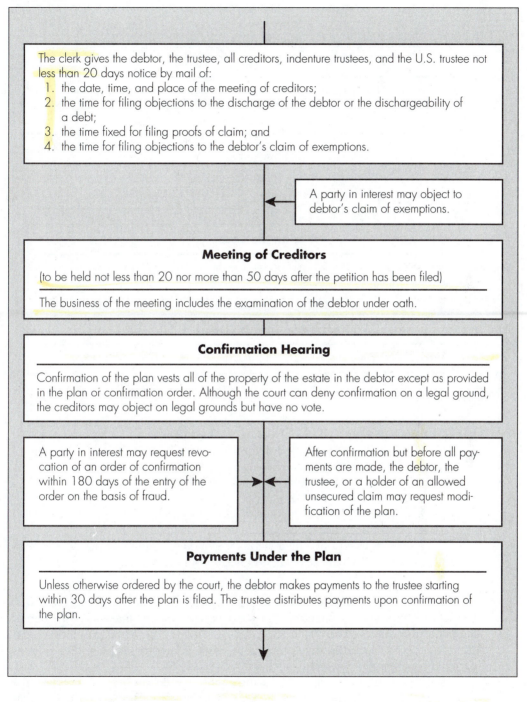

The clerk gives the debtor, the trustee, all creditors, indenture trustees, and the U.S. trustee not less than 20 days notice by mail of:
1. the date, time, and place of the meeting of creditors;
2. the time for filing objections to the discharge of the debtor or the dischargeability of a debt;
3. the time fixed for filing proofs of claim; and
4. the time for filing objections to the debtor's claim of exemptions.

A party in interest may object to debtor's claim of exemptions.

Meeting of Creditors

(to be held not less than 20 nor more than 50 days after the petition has been filed)

The business of the meeting includes the examination of the debtor under oath.

Confirmation Hearing

Confirmation of the plan vests all of the property of the estate in the debtor except as provided in the plan or confirmation order. Although the court can deny confirmation on a legal ground, the creditors may object on legal grounds but have no vote.

A party in interest may request revocation of an order of confirmation within 180 days of the entry of the order on the basis of fraud.

After confirmation but before all payments are made, the debtor, the trustee, or a holder of an allowed unsecured claim may request modification of the plan.

Payments Under the Plan

Unless otherwise ordered by the court, the debtor makes payments to the trustee starting within 30 days after the plan is filed. The trustee distributes payments upon confirmation of the plan.

EXHIBIT 6.1
Continued

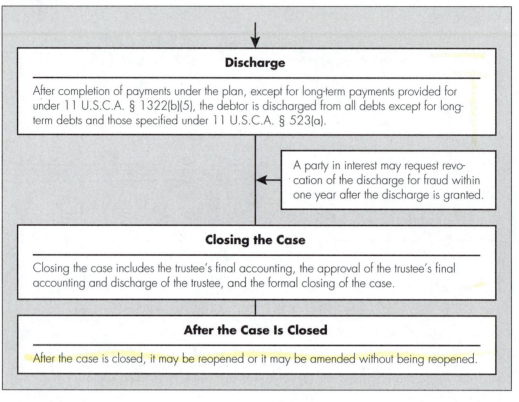

Discharge

After completion of payments under the plan, except for long-term payments provided for under 11 U.S.C.A. § 1322(b)(5), the debtor is discharged from all debts except for long-term debts and those specified under 11 U.S.C.A. § 523(a).

A party in interest may request revocation of the discharge for fraud within one year after the discharge is granted.

Closing the Case

Closing the case includes the trustee's final accounting, the approval of the trustee's final accounting and discharge of the trustee, and the formal closing of the case.

After the Case Is Closed

After the case is closed, it may be reopened or it may be amended without being reopened.

---

 e. Schedule D: Creditors Holding Secured Claims
 f. Schedule E: Creditors Holding Unsecured Priority Claims
 g. Schedule F: Creditors Holding Unsecured Nonpriority Claims
 h. Schedule G: Executory Contracts and Unexpired Leases
 i. Schedule H: Codebtors
 j. Schedule I: Current Income of Individual Debtor(s)
 k. Schedule J: Current Expenditures of Individual Debtor(s)
 l. Declaration Concerning Debtor's Schedules, signed by the debtor(s)
6. Statement of Financial Affairs (Official Form No. 7); and
7. Chapter 13 plan.

 The Bankruptcy Reform Act of 1994 provides for reasonable compensation to the debtor's attorney in a Chapter 13 case for representing the interests of the debtor in connection with the case. 11 U.S.C.A. § 303(a)(4)(B). The Act also authorizes the court to order the return of any excess to the estate if interim compensation exceeds the final compensation awarded. 11 U.S.C.A. § 330(a)(5).

 If the petition is accompanied by the matrix, the debtor has 15 days from the date of the filing of the petition to file the schedules, the statement of financial affairs, and the Chapter 13 plan. Fed. R. Bank. P. 1007, 3015.

 Prior to the time the case is closed, the debtor may amend the petition, lists, schedules, and statement previously filed. Fed. R. Bank. P. 1009. The debtor has a duty to supplement the schedules if, within 180 days after the date of filing the petition, property is acquired by bequest, devise, or inheritance or as a result of a property settlement agreement with the debtor's spouse or an interlocutory or final divorce decree. The debtor may also have acquired property as a beneficiary of a life insurance policy or a death benefit plan. 11 U.S.C.A. § 541(a)(5); Fed. R. Bank. P. 1007(h). The duty of the debtor to supplement the schedules may prove important to creditors who would otherwise be paid less or not at all. It prevents the debtor who has just been discharged of his or her debts from walking away with potentially large sums of money that could be distributed to creditors by the trustee.

SECTION 2
THE SIGNIFICANCE OF FILING A PETITION

The filing of the petition constitutes an order for relief under Chapter 13. Upon the filing of the petition, the estate is created and the automatic stay goes into effect, protecting the estate from dismemberment and the debtor from collection procedures. This prevents the more aggressive creditors from taking what is owed to them to the detriment of other creditors.

The automatic stay is the same as in a Chapter 7. There is an additional codebtor stay in Chapter 13. The **codebtor stay,** which precludes collection of all or any part of a consumer debt of the debtor from a codebtor (usually a family member), also goes into effect at this time. 11 U.S.C.A. § 1301.

EXAMPLE

After Amy Chandler graduated from college and before she began her new job as a reporter for the *Daily Bugle,* she received a trip to Europe as a graduation present from her grandfather. Amy purchased a camera from Friendly Photo Store to take pictures on the trip. She purchased the camera on credit and had her mother cosign the credit agreement.

After Amy returned home and began work for the *Daily Bugle,* her lavish living in Europe caught up with her through credit card charges not covered by grandfather's gift. Unable to fend off her creditors, Amy filed for bankruptcy under Chapter 13.

Upon the filing of the petition, the codebtor stay automatically went into effect, preventing Friendly Photo from attempting to collect for the camera from Amy's mother.

The codebtor stay does not apply if the codebtor became liable in the ordinary course of the codebtor's business or if the case is closed, dismissed, or converted to Chapter 7 or 11. 11 U.S.C.A. § 1301(a). The codebtor stay does not preclude a creditor from presenting a negotiable instrument for payment and giving notice of dishonor. 11 U.S.C.A. § 1301(b).

A creditor with a claim based on a consumer debt of the Chapter 13 debtor may seek relief from the codebtor stay if the codebtor received the consideration for the claim held by the creditor, if the Chapter 13 plan does not propose to pay the creditor his or her claim, or if the creditor's interest would be irreparably harmed by continuation of the stay. 11 U.S.C.A. § 1301(c). If the Chapter 13 plan does not propose to pay a creditor's claim and that creditor has filed a request for relief from the codebtor stay, the debtor or codebtor has 20 days to file a written objection; otherwise, the codebtor stay is terminated as to that creditor's claim. 11 U.S.C.A. § 1301(d).

After the order for relief, the various parties in interest may begin to assert their claims against the estate. A creditor or an indenture trustee may file a proof of claim subject to the time limitations found in the Rules. If a creditor does not timely file a proof of claim prior to distribution, the debtor, codebtor, or trustee may file a proof of claim within 30 days after expiration of the time for filing claims. 11 U.S.C.A. §§ 501(b), (c); Fed. R. Bank. P. 3004, 3005.

A. POSSESSION AND CONTROL OF PROPERTY OF THE ESTATE

The debtor in a Chapter 13 case remains in possession of all property of the estate except as specified and provided in the confirmed plan or order confirming a plan. 11 U.S.C.A. § 1306(b). The possession and control of property of the estate are often the controlling factors in the debtor's decision to select a Chapter 13 filing. The estate in a Chapter 13 case includes all the property specified in section 541 and all the property that the debtor acquires after the commencement of the case but before the case is closed, dismissed, or converted to a case under Chapter 7, 11, or 12, whichever occurs first. Also included in the property of the estate are earnings from services performed by the debtor after the commencement of the case but before the case is closed, dismissed, or converted to a case under Chapter 7, 11, or 12, whichever occurs first. 11 U.S.C.A. § 1306(a).

The Bankruptcy Reform Act of 1994 made an important change regarding the property of the estate in a Chapter 13 case that is converted to a case under another chapter. The property of the estate in the converted case will consist only of the property at the date of filing the Chapter 13 petition that remains in possession of or under control of the debtor on the date of conversion. This allows the debtor not only to retain the property acquired since the filing date but also to benefit from post-petition payments made on secured claims. This change provides an incentive for debtors to try Chapter 13. This change applies only if the debtor converts to another chapter in good faith. 11 U.S.C.A. § 348(f).

Three other changes made by the Reform Act regarding homestead mortgages benefit a debtor filing a Chapter 13 case:

1. The Supreme Court decision in *Rake v. Wade,* 508 U.S. 464 (1993), to impose an "interest on interest" requirement for curing mortgage arrearages has been negated by 11 U.S.C.A. § 1322(e) in agreements entered into after the October 22, 1994, effective date of the Reform Act.

2. Under revised 11 U.S.C.A. § 1322, a mortgage default may be cured until the sale of the debtor's homestead at a properly conducted foreclosure sale. This negates *Matter of Roche,* 824 F.2d 1370 (3d Cir. 1987), which extinguished the debtor's right to cure at the time of the foreclosure judgment.

3. Amended 11 U.S.C.A. § 1322 also provides that some homestead mortgages can be modified and may allow these particular mortgages to be stripped down to the value of the homestead.

B. OPERATION OF THE DEBTOR'S BUSINESS

If the debtor is engaged in business, the Code contemplates that the debtor will operate the business unless the court orders otherwise. 11 U.S.C.A. § 1304(b). The court will enter an order for periodic reports from the debtor engaged in business. Fed. R. Bank. P. 2015(c)(1). The nature of these reports will vary depending on the debtor's business and how much information is required by the court. Most courts will have a regular format for this type of report.

C. EXEMPTIONS

Exemptions are treated the same in a Chapter 13 case as in a Chapter 7 case. The listing of exemptions and the valuation of exempt property, as well as the valuation of nonexempt property, should be considered carefully. What is exempt or nonexempt, and its value, will have a definite effect on the confirmation of a plan. The value, as of the effective date of the plan, of the property to be distributed under the plan to each allowed unsecured claim cannot be less than the amount that would have been paid on such claim if the petition had been filed under Chapter 7. This is called the **best interests of creditors test.**

SECTION 3
APPOINTMENT AND DUTIES OF A CHAPTER 13 TRUSTEE

After the order for relief, the standing **Chapter 13 trustee,** or another individual if there is no standing trustee, or the U.S. trustee will serve as the trustee in the case. 11 U.S.C.A. § 1302(a). The trustee in a Chapter 13 case is accountable for all property received and must perform some of the same duties as a Chapter 7 trustee. These duties include

1. investigate the financial affairs of the debtor;
2. examine proofs of claim and object to allowance of any claim that is improper if a purpose would be served;
3. oppose the discharge of the debtor if this is advisable;
4. upon the request of a party in interest, furnish information concerning the estate and its administration unless the court orders otherwise; and
5. make a final report and file a final account with the court and the United States trustee. 11 U.S.C.A. § 1302(b)(1).

The trustee must also appear and be heard at any hearing concerning the value of property subject to a lien, the confirmation of a plan, or the modification of the plan after confirmation. The trustee may not advise the debtor on legal matters regarding the performance of the plan, but must advise and assist the debtor in other matters pertaining to performance of the plan. The trustee also has a duty to ensure that the debtor begins making timely payments as required by the Code. 11 U.S.C.A. § 1326.

Because the **trustee's avoidance powers** are spelled out in Chapter 5, a universal chapter, the trustee in a Chapter 13 case has most of the same avoidance powers granted to trustees in other types of cases. See 11 U.S.C.A. §§ 544–549. The Bankruptcy Reform Act of 1994 imposes a two-year statute of limitations on the trustee's avoidance powers that runs from the date of the order for relief. 11 U.S.C.A. § 546(a)(1)(A). A trustee elected or appointed before expiration of the two-year period specified in subparagraph (A) has only one year to begin an avoidance action or proceeding. 11 U.S.C.A. § 546(a)(1)(B).

The essential role of a Chapter 13 trustee, however, differs from the role of a Chapter 7 trustee. The primary function of a Chapter 13 trustee is to review the Chapter 13 plan, to advise the court with respect to the plan, and to act as a disbursing agent under the confirmed plan. Therefore, the Chapter 13 trustee often does not litigate actions under the avoiding powers.

The fact that the Chapter 13 trustee may choose not to exercise the trustee's avoidance power should not be taken to mean that the trustee does not have the power to avoid fraudulent and preferential transfers. In *In re Johnson,* the debtor conveyed his interest in a mobile home park several months before filing a petition in bankruptcy under Chapter 13. The transfer was fraudulent and, if it could be avoided, the value of the property could be recovered for the estate. The court discussed whether the Chapter 13 trustee had the power to avoid the transfer.

In re Johnson

United States Bankruptcy Court, District of Colorado, 1982.
26 B.R. 381.

MEMORANDUM OPINION AND ORDER
Patricia Ann Clark,
Bankruptcy Judge

This matter comes before the Court *sua sponte,* on the Court's objection to the confirmation of the Debtor's Chapter 13 Plan. A hearing on the matter was held on December 6, 1982.

The Debtor's Chapter 13 schedules reveal that on or about July 29, 1982, the Debtor, through a complicated series of real estate transactions, conveyed away all his interest in a mobile home park located in Fountain, Colorado. The Court's objection concerns the possible existence of a fraudulent transfer which may be avoidable under 11 U.S.C. § 548. If the property could be recovered for the estate under a Chapter 7 proceeding but not under a Chapter 13 proceeding, the plan would not meet the best interests test under 11 U.S.C. § 1325(a)(4) and could not be confirmed.

For the purposes of the hearing on this matter, the Debtor and the Chapter 13 trustee stipulated that the transfer was in fraud of creditors and that there was value in the Debtor's interest in the mobile home park which could be recovered for the estate. The debtor is unable to pursue the litigation but would amend his plan to allow the trustee to recover the transfer. Therefore, the only issue that remains before the Court at this time is whether the Chapter 13 trustee has the same powers as a Chapter 7 trustee to avoid a fraudulent transfer and recover the value of the property for the estate.

It is the position of the Chapter 13 trustee that she does not have these powers. The trustee's argument is based on the description of the Chapter 13 trustee's duties in 11 U.S.C. § 1302(b). This section lists several of the duties of a Chapter 7 trustee under 11 U.S.C. § 704, but omits the duty to "collect and reduce to money the property of the estate" found in 11 U.S.C. § 704(1). The trustee asserts that because of the omission of Section 704(1), she lacks the power to marshall assets of the estate, and thus has no power to exercise the avoidance powers of Chapter 5.

The Debtor's position is that the Chapter 13 trustee may avoid a fraudulent transfer under 11 U.S.C. § 548. The Debtor contends that the omission of Section 704(1) from Section 1302(b) was meant to insure that a Chapter 13 trustee's duty to collect the property of the estate is discretionary rather than mandatory. According to the Debtor, Congress intended to free the Chapter 13 trustee from pursuing property that would be of inconsequential value to the estate.

The Court concludes that the Chapter 13 trustee may exercise the power granted in 11 U.S.C. § 548 to avoid fraudulent transfers. The Court recognizes that there is an ambiguity created by the omission of the duty to collect and liquidate the property of the estate and that this may be read as inconsistent with the exercise of Chapter 5 avoidance powers by the Chapter 13 trustee. See *In re Carter,* 2 B.R. 321 (Bkrtcy.Colo.1980) wherein this ambiguity was discussed. However, the overwhelming implication of the Code read in its entirety is that the Chapter 13 trustee has the same power to avoid transfers as a trustee under Chapter 7.

The Code, in 11 U.S.C. § 103(a), provides that all of the provisions of Chapter 5 are to apply in a Chapter 13 case. Further, Section 548 itself states, without limitation, that "the trustee may" avoid certain transfers. Also, 11 U.S.C. § 546 clearly contemplates the appointment of a trustee in a Chapter 13 case in which Chapter 5 powers are utilized. Finally, Chapter 13 has no express limit on the power of the trustee to use the avoidance powers of Chapter 5. If Congress had intended to restrict the Chapter 13 trustee's use of any of the Chapter 5 avoidance powers, it could have expressly so stated.

Other courts faced with this issue have also reached the conclusion that the Chapter 13 trustee may exercise avoidance powers. In *In re Colandrea,* 17 B.R. 568 (Bkrtcy.Md.1982), the court held that the Chapter 13 trustee could avoid transfers under 11 U.S.C. § 547 and § 548. The court discussed several Code provisions, including Section 103(a), Section 548 and Section 1302(b), and stated that, "Nothing in the provisions of Chapter 13 of the Code expressly limits a Chapter 13 Trustee's powers to those set forth only in that chapter. Furthermore, the Code taken as a whole makes it evidence that a Chapter 13 Trustee possesses powers established elsewhere in the Code."

The case of *In re Walls,* 17 B.R. 701 (Bkrtcy.S.D.W.Va.1982), involved a debtor who sought to avoid an execution lien under Section 547(b). The court held that a Chapter 13 debtor could not exercise avoidance powers, but that a Chapter 13 trustee could. The court stated that the use of Chapter 5 powers was discretionary with the trustee and that the exercise of avoidance powers was consistent with the Chapter 13 trustee's duty under 11 U.S.C. § 1302(b)(3) to advise and assist the debtor in performance under the plan.

The court in *In re Reeves,* 17 B.R. 383 (Bkrtcy.W.D.La.1982), recognized that the trustee in Chapter 13 is in a "distinctly different position" than a trustee in Chapter 7. However, it decided that 11 U.S.C. § 544 did apply to a trustee in Chapter 13 because of the language in 11 U.S.C. § 103(a) and the absence of express limitations in Chapter 13 on the Chapter 13 trustee's powers.

The omission of 11 U.S.C. § 704(1) from the Chapter 13 trustee's duties cannot be read so far as to preclude the use of the Chapter 5 avoidance powers by the trustee. The most likely reason for its omission was to make it clear that the Chapter 13 trustee is not involved in the liquidation of the debtor's property. The fact that the Chapter 13 trustee does not have the *duty* to collect and liquidate the property of the estate does not limit the *power* of the trustee to avoid transactions under the provisions of Chapter 5. The powers of a trustee in Chapter 13 do not come exclusively from Section 1302(b). Without some express limitation on the Chapter 13 trustee's power, the Code must be construed as granting to the Chapter 13 trustee the avoidance powers given to all trustees in Chapter 5. However, as to all trustees, the avoidance powers are discretionary. It is left to the Chapter 13 trustee's judgment to determine when it is feasible and efficient to exercise the avoidance powers. Since the Chapter 13 trustee has the power to avoid the transfer of the Debtor's interest in the mobile home park under 11 U.S.C. § 548, a plan providing for such event would satisfy the best interests test of Section 1325(a)(4).

ORDERED that by January 10, 1983, the Debtor shall file an amended plan which provides that the Chapter 13 trustee may take all necessary action to recover the property transferred by the debtor in violation of 11 U.S.C. § 548. Such a plan will meet the best interests test of 11 U.S.C. § 1325(a)(4) and may be confirmed.

If the debtor is engaged in business, the trustee has further duties. 11 U.S.C.A. § 1302(c). These include investigating the financial condition of the debtor, the operation of the debtor's business, the desirability of continuing the business, and any other matter relevant to the case or to the formulation of a plan. 11 U.S.C.A. § 1106(a)(3). The trustee is required to file a statement on this investigation that includes any information on fraud, dishonesty, incompetence, misconduct, mismanagement, or irregularity in the management of the debtor's affairs, or any cause of action available to the estate. 11 U.S.C.A. § 1106(a)(4).

SECTION 4
MOTIONS AND COMPLAINTS AFTER THE ORDER FOR RELIEF

In most districts the debtor's plan will contain all the important issues relating to the case. The court will consider most issues at the hearing on confirmation of the plan because all of these issues will affect the plan. The Code does, however, provide for various motions and complaints that may be used to resolve issues as they arise in the case.

A. MOTIONS

After the order for relief, the *debtor* may move to convert the case from Chapter 13 to Chapter 7, 11, or 12 (11 U.S.C.A. §§ 1307(a), (e)); to dismiss the case (11 U.S.C.A. § 1307(b); Fed. R. Bank. P. 1017); for a change of venue (Fed. R. Bank. P. 1014); for permission to use cash collateral (if engaged in business) (11 U.S.C.A. § 363(c)(2)); or to sell, use, or lease property (11 U.S.C.A. § 1303; Fed. R. Bank. P. 6004(c)).

The Chapter 13 debtor may exercise 522(f) power to avoid a judicial lien on any property to the extent that the property could have been exempted in the absence of the lien and to avoid a nonpossessory, nonpurchase money security interest in certain household and personal goods. The Chapter 13 debtor may not avoid a judicial lien impairing an exemption if a debt for alimony, maintenance, or support is secured by the lien. 11 U.S.C.A. § 522(f)(1)(A).

In *In re Mulliken,* the debtor moved to avoid a lien under 11 U.S.C.A. § 522(f). The court noted that a debtor could avoid the fixing of a judicial lien on an interest of the debtor in property to the extent that such lien impairs an exemption to which the debtor would have been entitled under § 522(b). The court then investigated whether the debtor was entitled to the exemption.

The *trustee* or the *U.S. trustee* may file a motion objecting to confirmation of the plan. 11 U.S.C.A. § 1324.

In re Mulliken
United States Bankruptcy Court, District of Idaho, 1995.
1995 WL 70335.

Jim D. Pappas,
Bankruptcy Judge

Debtors William and Gayle Mulliken filed for Chapter 13 relief on December 21, 1992. Prior to the filing, Creditor David Homolka obtained a judgment against Debtor William Mulliken. Creditor recorded the judgment which created a lien in the real property of Debtors including their homestead. Idaho Code §§ 10–1110 and 55–1009. Debtors' Chapter 13 plan was confirmed by the Court on March 22, 1993, and subse-

quently modified on June 28, 1994. Debtors then filed a Motion for approval of the sale of their home. After payment of the first priority lien held by First Security Bank and closing costs, there was expected to be net proceeds of $29,220 from the sale. The Motion states that Debtors would be claiming the net proceeds as exempt and would be using $15,200 therefrom to complete their performance under the plan. The $15,200 was to be paid directly to the Trustee out of the closing. The Court entered an Order on September 29, 1994 approving the sale of Debtors' residence free and clear of liens. The Order states, however, that after payment of the first priority lien held by Creditor and closing costs, all net proceeds of the sale were to be turned over to the Chapter 13 Trustee pending further order of the Court.

Debtors have now moved to avoid the judicial lien of Creditor claiming the lien impairs their homestead exemption claim in the proceeds. Creditor objects contending that since it is Debtors' intention to use a portion of the proceeds to "pre-pay" the plan that they in effect have waived their homestead exemption claim in the proceeds.

Section 522(f)(1) of the Bankruptcy Code provides that a debtor may avoid the fixing of a judicial lien on an interest of the debtor in property to the extent that such lien impairs an exemption to which the debtor would have been entitled under Section 522(b). "Thus, under § 522(f)(1), a debtor may avoid a lien if three conditions are met: (1) there was a fixing of a lien on an interest of the debtor in property; (2) such lien impairs an exemption to which the debtor would have been entitled; and (3) such lien is a judicial lien." *In re Catli,* 999 F.2d 1405, 1406 (9th Cir.1993). Debtors bear the burden of proving that they are entitled to avoid the lien under Section 522(f)(1). *Id.* The only condition at issue in this case is whether the lien impairs an exemption to which Debtors would have been entitled.

Under subsection (b) of Section 522, Idaho has "opted-out" of the federal exemptions, and Debtors are limited to the exemptions allowed under Idaho state law. 11 U.S.C. § 522(b); Idaho Code § 11–609; *In re Land,* 94 I.B.C.R. 225, 225–26. Pursuant to Idaho Code §§ 55–1004, residents of Idaho are entitled to an exemption in a homestead. In addition, residents are also allowed an exemption, for up to one year from the date of receipt, in the proceeds from the voluntary sale of the homestead in good faith for the purpose of acquiring a new homestead. Idaho Code § 55–1008. Creditor may contest the exemption claim in connection with the Section 522(f)(1) action even though it has not made a formal

objection to the exemption claim. *In re Morgan,* 149 B.R. 147 (9th Cir. B.A.P.1993).

The purpose of the homestead provisions is to allow owners to keep their homes when they are beset by financial difficulties. *In re Fullerton,* 92 I.B.C.R. 22, 23. In other words, the homestead exemption is to protect "the property occupied as a home by the owner thereof or his or her family from attachment and execution." *In re Tomko,* 87 B.R. 372, 375 (Bankr.E.D.Pa. 1988) citing Riesenfeld, *Homestead and Bankruptcy in Colorado and Elsewhere,* 56 U.Colo.L.Rev. 175, 177 (1985). In addition, the Idaho legislature has adopted a rule that allows debtors to sell a homestead and purchase a different homestead and the new homestead will also be protected by the exemption statutes. Idaho Code § 55–1008. However, it is clear from the plain language of Idaho Code § 55–1008 that the proceeds from the voluntary sale of a home may only be claimed exempt if they are held for the "purpose of acquiring a new homestead." If the proceeds are to be used for any other purpose they may not be validly claimed as exempt.

In this case, Debtors' Motion for approval of the sale of their home requests that $15,200 of the proceeds be transferred to the Trustee to be applied to plan payments to their various creditors. As such, this portion of the proceeds will not be used for the purpose of acquiring a new homestead and therefore is not properly exempt under Idaho's homestead exemption statutes. Since Debtors are not entitled to an exemption in this portion of the proceeds, Debtors may not avoid Creditor's lien on these funds under Section 522(f)(1) because it does not impair an exemption to which Debtors would have been entitled under Section 522(b).

The remaining sale proceeds were to be turned over to Debtors after the sale. Debtors have not shown that this portion of the proceeds will be used for acquiring a new homestead and at this point they have failed to meet their burden in this regard. If within a reasonable time Debtors make an adequate showing to the Chapter 13

Trustee that the proceeds from the sale will be used to acquire a new homestead within one year from the date they receive them, Trustee may distribute the funds to Debtors. In such event, Debtors may submit an order signed by the Trustee and the lien will be avoided as to that portion of the proceeds.

Until such time the Trustee shall retain the proceeds until further order of the Court subject to Creditor's lien.

This Memorandum constitutes the Court's findings of fact and conclusions of law. F.R.B.P. 7052. Counsel for Debtors may submit an appropriate order.

A *party in interest* may move for relief from the automatic stay (11 U.S.C.A. § 362(d); Fed. R. Bank. P. 4001, 9014); for abstention by the court (11 U.S.C.A. § 305); to dismiss the case (11 U.S.C.A. § 1307(c)); for a change of venue (Fed. R. Bank. P. 1014); for disallowance of a claim (11 U.S.C.A. § 502); to convert the case to Chapter 7 or 11 (except if the debtor is a farmer) (11 U.S.C.A. §§ 1307(c)–(e)); for relief from the codebtor stay (11 U.S.C.A. § 1301(c)); or for examination of any person (Fed. R. Bank P. 2004).

The *U.S. trustee* may move to convert the case to Chapter 7 or Chapter 11 or to dismiss the case. 11 U.S.C.A. §§ 1307(c), (d). If the debtor is a farmer, the court may not convert a Chapter 13 case to Chapter 7, 11, or 12 upon the request of anyone except the debtor. 11 U.S.C.A. § 1307(e).

B. COMPLAINTS

After the order for relief, a creditor may file a complaint objecting to the dischargeability of a debt. 11 U.S.C.A. § 523; Fed R. Bank. P. 4007(a), 7001.

Proceedings brought by the *trustee* to avoid transfers are classified as adversary proceedings by Fed. R. Bank. P. 7001. This topic was discussed in Section 3 of this chapter.

Whether a Chapter 13 debtor may use the avoidance powers granted to the trustee is a question that has left the courts divided. The Chapter 13 provision that addresses the rights and powers of the Chapter 13 debtor does not address this issue. 11 U.S.C.A. § 1303. The legislative history, however, includes comments to the effect that section 1303 "does not imply that the debtor does not also possess other powers concurrently with the trustee." 124 Cong. Rec. H32,409 (Sept. 28, 1978, remarks of Rep. Edwards).

In *In re Mast,* the debtor attempted to exercise the Chapter 13 trustee's power to avoid a preferential transfer. The court discussed the division in the courts and the reasons for this division.

In re Mast
United States Bankruptcy Court, Western District of Michigan, 1987.
79 B.R. 981.

MEMORANDUM OPINION REGARDING AVOIDANCE POWERS IN CHAPTER 13 CASES
James D. Gregg,
Bankruptcy Judge

On August 5, 1987, Mary L. Mast, "Debtor," filed her Petition for Relief Under Chapter 13 of the Bankruptcy Code. 11 U.S.C. § 301; 11 U.S.C. §§ 1301–1330.[1] Brett N. Rodgers, "Trustee," was subsequently appointed by the Court to serve as the trustee in connection with the case.

On August 5, 1987, the Debtor also filed a Complaint against Borgess Medical Center, "Defendant," which seeks to avoid an involuntary transfer, pursuant to Section 547 of the Bankruptcy Code, received by the Defendant as a result of a garnishment of the Debtor's bank account which allegedly took place within 90 days of the date of the filing of the Petition. The Trustee has not joined the adversary proceeding as a party plaintiff.[2] On August 24, 1987, the Defendant filed an Answer to Complaint.

On October 16, 1987, the Debtor filed a Motion for Summary Judgment. On October 28, 1987, the Defendant filed a Cross Motion for Summary Judgment. The Defendant asserts, among other things, as a matter of law, a Chapter 13 Debtor lacks the authority to avoid a preferential transfer. At the hearings respecting the cross motions for summary judgment, both parties, through their counsel, presented argument regarding their respective legal positions. Because of the importance of the legal issues presented, the Court took the matter under advisement pending issuance of this written opinion.

Section 547(b) of the Bankruptcy Code states "the trustee may avoid" a preferential transfer by proving the requisite elements. Section 1303 of the Bankruptcy Code explicitly enumerates the rights and powers of a Chapter 13 debtor. The debtor is empowered, exclusive of the trustee, to use, sell or lease property in accordance with Sections 363(b), 363(d), 363(e), 363(f) and 363(1) of the Bankruptcy Code. If a Chapter 13 debtor is engaged in business, Section 1304 grants additional powers to the debtor to enter into ordinary business transactions under Section 363(c) and to obtain credit pursuant to Section 364 of the Bankruptcy Code.

The Court has carefully reviewed all provisions contained in Chapter 13 and there does not exist any *statutory* authority for a Chapter 13 debtor to utilize avoidance powers granted to the trustee, including those powers listed in Sections 544, 545, 547 and 548 of the Bankruptcy Code. If Congress intended to grant avoidance powers to a Chapter 13 debtor, it could have explicitly done so.[3]

There exists a split of authority regarding whether a Chapter 13 debtor may utilize a trustee's avoidance powers. After careful consideration, this Court believes those cases which hold the Chapter 13 debtor lacks the power to unilaterally set aside avoidable transfers are better reasoned and more persuasive than those cases decided to the contrary. *In re Carter,* 2 B.R. 321 (Bankr.D.Colo.1980) (Chapter 13 debtors lack § 544 "strong arm" power); *In re Walls,* 17 B.R. 701 (Bankr.S.D.W.Va.1982) (Chapter 13 debtor lacked ability to exercise power to avoid preferential transfer under § 547); *In re Driscoll,* 57 B.R. 322 (Bankr.W.D.Wis.1986) (Chapter 13 debtor may not generally utilize the trustee's Chapter 5 avoidance powers); *cf. In re Colandrea,* 17 B.R. 568 (Bankr.D.Md.1982) (Chapter 13 trustee has authority to avoid preferential transfers under § 547).

Cases decided to the contrary recognize the "realities of bankruptcy practice" to justify a strained interpretation of the

Bankruptcy Code and to conclude a Chapter 13 debtor is empowered to utilize a trustee's avoidance powers. See, e.g., *In re Ottaviano,* 68 B.R. 238, 240 (Bankr. D.Conn.1986), and the cases cited therein. As a matter of practice, a Chapter 13 debtor may easily request that the Chapter 13 trustee utilize his powers to set aside avoidable transfers.[4] If avoiding a transfer is in the interest of the estate, the trustee may unilaterally seek to avoid the transfer or consent to the debtor's possible intervention as an additional party plaintiff pursuant to Bankruptcy Rule 7024. Alternatively, the Chapter 13 Plan may propose that the debtor, on behalf of the estate, and in conjunction with the trustee, utilize avoidance powers to assure equality of distribution and no unfair discrimination among creditors. *In re Walls, supra* at 704.

The Court therefore concludes, as a matter of law, that a Chapter 13 Debtor has no independent standing to exercise the Trustee's power to avoid a preferential transfer under Section 547 of the Bankruptcy Code. The Debtor's motion for summary judgment is therefore denied. The Defendant's motion for summary judgment is granted[5] without prejudice to the Trustee to file a Complaint to avoid the alleged preferential transfer if the Trustee determines to do so in the exercise of his reasonable discretion.[6] An order shall be entered accordingly.

[1] All future references to 11 U.S.C. §§ 1301–1330 herein shall be referred to as the "Bankruptcy Code" by reference to the applicable section thereof.

[2] During argument, Debtor's counsel made an oral motion to join the Trustee as a party. The Court did not grant the motion. The Trustee was not present at the hearing and he has not consented or indicated a willingness to now be added as a party to this adversary proceeding.

[3] In Sections 1107(a) and 1203 of the Bankruptcy Code, Chapter 11 and Chapter 12 debtors are granted *all* rights and powers of a trustee, subject to any limitations or conditions which the Court may prescribe.

[4] It should be noted that when exempt property is involved, the debtor has certain avoidance powers which are independent of the trustee under Sections 522(f) and 522(h) of the Bankruptcy Code.

[5] Because the issue of standing is dispositive, the Court has not addressed the other issues raised in the Defendant's Cross Motion for Summary Judgment.

[6] In the exercise of his discretion, the Trustee may consider factors such as whether seeking to avoid a transfer will benefit the estate, whether the proposed Chapter 13 plan is confirmable absent avoidance of the transfer and the ultimate probability of success if an avoidance action is commenced.

The *debtor* may file a complaint against third parties to collect accounts receivable or to have property brought back into the estate. 11 U.S.C.A. §§ 542, 543.

SECTION 5
THE CLERK'S NOTICE

The official form for the clerk's notice in a Chapter 13 case is B9I. (See Exhibit 6.2.) The clerk must give the debtor, the trustee, all creditors, the indenture trustees, and the U.S. trustee not less than 20 days notice by mail of the date, time, and place of the meeting of creditors; the time for filing objections to the discharge of the debtor or the dischargeability of a debt; the time fixed for filing proofs of claim or the fact that insufficient assets exist for paying claims; and the time for filing objections to the debtor's claim of exemptions. This notice generally serves as the notice of the order for relief required by 11 U.S.C.A. § 342(a) and may also serve as the notice for the confirmation hearing in a Chapter 13 case. Either a copy or a summary of the plan must be included with notice of the confirmation hearing.

EXHIBIT 6.2
Notice of Commencement of Case under Chapter 13, Meeting of Creditors, and Fixing of Dates

FORM B9I (Rev. 12/94)	**United States Bankruptcy Court**	Case Number

_____ District of _____

NOTICE OF COMMENCEMENT OF CASE UNDER CHAPTER 13 OF THE BANKRUPTCY CODE.
MEETING OF CREDITORS, AND FIXING OF DATES

In re (Name of Debtor)	Address of Debtor	Soc. Sec./Tax Id. Nos.
	Date Case Filed (or Converted)	
Name and Address of Attorney for Debtor	Name and Address of Trustee	
Telephone Number	Telephone Number	

☐ This is a converted case originally filed under chapter _____ on _____ (date).

DEADLINE TO FILE A PROOF OF CLAIM

For creditors other than governmental units: For governmental units:

DATE, TIME, AND LOCATION OF MEETING OF CREDITORS

FILING OF PLAN AND DATE, TIME, AND LOCATION OF HEARING ON CONFIRMATION OF PLAN

☐ The debtor has filed a plan. The plan or a summary of the plan is enclosed. Hearing on confirmation will be held:
_____ (Date) _____ (Time) _____ (Location)

☐ The debtor has filed a plan. The plan or a summary of the plan and notice of the confirmation hearing will be sent separately.

☐ A plan has not been filed as of this date. Creditors will be given separate notice of the hearing on confirmation of the plan.

COMMENCEMENT OF CASE. An individual's debt adjustment case under chapter 13 of the Bankruptcy Code has been filed in this court by the debtor or debtors named above, and an order for relief has been entered. You will not receive notice of all documents filed in this case. All documents filed with the court, including lists of the debtor's property and debts, are available for inspection at the office of the clerk of the bankruptcy court.

CREDITORS MAY NOT TAKE CERTAIN ACTIONS. A creditor is anyone to whom the debtor owes money. Under the Bankruptcy Code, the debtor is granted certain protection against creditors. Common examples of prohibited actions by creditors are contacting the debtor to demand repayment, taking action against the debtor to collect money owed to creditors or to take property of the debtor, and starting or continuing foreclosure actions, repossessions, or wage reductions. Some protection is also given to certain codebtors of consumer debts. If unauthorized actions are taken by a creditor against a debtor, or a protected codebtor, the court may punish that creditor. A creditor who is considering taking action against the debtor or the property of the debtor, or any codebtor, should review §§ 362 and 1301 of the Bankruptcy Code and may wish to seek legal advice. The staff of the clerk of the bankruptcy court is not permitted to give legal advice.

MEETING OF CREDITORS. The debtor (both husband and wife in a joint case) is required to appear at the meeting of creditors on the date and at the place set forth above in the box labeled "Date, Time, and Location of Meeting of Creditors" for the purpose of being examined under oath. Attendance by creditors at the meeting is welcome, but not required. At the meeting, the creditors may examine the debtor and transact such other business as may properly come before the meeting. The meeting may be continued or adjourned from time by notice at the meeting, without further written notice to creditors.

PROOF OF CLAIM. Except as otherwise provided by law, in order to share in any payment from the estate, a creditor must file a proof of claim by the date set forth above in the box labeled "Deadline to File a Proof of Claim." The place to file the proof of claim, either in person or by mail, is the office of the clerk of the bankruptcy court. Proof of claim forms are available in the clerk's office of any bankruptcy court.

PURPOSE OF A CHAPTER 13 FILING. Chapter 13 of the Bankruptcy Code is designed to enable a debtor to pay debts in full or in part over a period of time pursuant to a plan. A plan is not effective unless approved by the bankruptcy court at a confirmation hearing. Creditors will be given notice in the event the case is dismissed or converted to another chapter of the Bankruptcy Code.

Address of the Clerk of the Bankruptcy Court	For the Court:
	Clerk of the Bankruptcy Court
	Date

SECTION 6
MEETING OF CREDITORS (THE SECTION 341 MEETING)

The meeting of creditors (the section 341 meeting) is held not less than 20 nor more than 50 days after the order for relief. Fed. R. Bank. P. 2003. The business of the meeting includes the examination of the debtor under oath.

It is quite common for the trustee to conduct some type of examination of the debtor, asking questions directed toward any possible indication that the plan may not be feasible. The trustee must be assured that all debts and assets have been listed. Creditors with problems will have an opportunity to talk to both the trustee and the debtor about these problems. The trustee will probably give the debtor some indication of the trustee's recommendation on the confirmation of the plan. The trustee may suggest modification of the plan in an attempt to lead the debtor and the debtor's attorney toward a confirmable plan.

SECTION 7
THE CHAPTER 13 PLAN

The debtor must file a plan showing how he or she intends to repay part or all of the allowed claims. Generally, payment will be from future earnings. Occasionally, however, there may be a surrender of collateral or transfer of a certain asset to satisfy a certain creditor. The plan must be filed not later than 15 days after the filing of the petition, although an extension may be granted by the court for cause shown. Fed. R. Bank. P. 3015. Only the debtor may file a plan in a Chapter 13 case. 11 U.S.C.A. § 1321.

A. CONTENTS OF A CHAPTER 13 PLAN

The contents of a Chapter 13 plan are delineated in the Code. 11 U.S.C.A. § 1322. Some provisions are mandatory; others are permissive. The **mandatory provisions** are noted in the Code by "shall" and the **permissive provisions** by "may." Compare 11 U.S.C.A. § 1322(a) with 11 U.S.C.A. § 1322(b).

1. MANDATORY PROVISIONS
Because Chapter 13 is designed with flexibility in mind, the Code provides only four mandatory provisions in regard to the contents of the plan.

1. A Chapter 13 plan must provide for the trustee's supervision and control of that portion of the debtor's future income necessary for the implementation of the plan. 11 U.S.C.A. § 1322(a)(1).
2. A Chapter 13 plan must provide for the full payment of all priority claims (11 U.S.C.A. § 507) unless the holder of the claim agrees to a different treatment of that claim. 11 U.S.C.A. § 1322(a)(2).
3. If the Chapter 13 plan classifies claims into classes, the plan must provide the same treatment for each claim within a particular class. 11 U.S.C.A. § 1322(a)(3).
4. The payment period under the plan may not exceed three years unless the court, for cause, approves a longer period. If a longer time period is approved, it may not exceed five years. 11 U.S.C.A. § 1322(d).

2. PERMISSIVE PROVISIONS

A Chapter 13 plan may

1. divide unsecured nonpriority claims (non-11 U.S.C.A. § 507 claims) into classes;
2. modify the rights of holders of secured and unsecured claims, except claims wholly secured by real estate mortgages;
3. cure or waive any default;
4. propose payments on unsecured claims concurrently with payments on any secured claim or any other unsecured claim; ·
5. provide for curing any default on any secured or unsecured claim on which the final payment is due after the proposed final payment under the plan;
6. provide for payment of any allowed postpetition claim;
7. assume or reject any previously unrejected executory contract, including the debtor's unexpired lease;
8. propose the payment of all or any part of any claim from property of the estate or of the debtor;
9. provide for the vesting of property of the estate; and
10. include any other provision not inconsistent with other Title 11 provisions. 11 U.S.C.A. § 1322(b).

3. A SAMPLE CHAPTER 13 PLAN

The format of a **Chapter 13 plan** may vary from district to district. Exhibit 6.3 provides a sample Chapter 13 plan.

Some jurisdictions are attempting to standardize Chapter 13 plans by creating a locally accepted format. (See Exhibit 6.4.)

EXHIBIT 6.3
A Chapter 13 Plan

IN THE UNITED STATES BANKRUPTCY COURT
FOR THE NORTHERN DISTRICT OF OKLAHOMA

In re Janet Michelle Ragsdale,
                    Debtor   Case No. _____
                                              Chapter 13
                    CHAPTER 13 PLAN

The debtor, Janet Michelle Ragsdale, proposes the following plan under 11 U.S.C.A. § 1321 and 11 U.S.C.A. § 1322.

The debtor is employed as a hotel manager at the Mayo Hotel in Tulsa, Oklahoma, in the Northern District of Oklahoma, and resides at 2106 E. 24th Court in Tulsa, Oklahoma 74105. The income of the debtor, as set forth in the Chapter 13 statement and the statement of income and expenses, would reflect a current monthly take-home pay of $1,763.25. At this time, the debtor does receive $425.00 per month in child support money from her former husband, but these payments will be discontinued in April of next year. The debtor has excluded the child support payments from her income and expense statements because of this future termination. The debtor's current monthly expenses are $1,576.00, leaving monthly disposable earnings in the amount of $187.25. From the disposable earnings, the debtor proposes to pay to the trustee the total of $6,686.45 in 36 payments: 35 payments of $185.84 and the final payment of

EXHIBIT 6.3
Continued

$182.05. The debtor has paid Counsel Warren L. McConnico a retainer fee of $410.00, together with $130.00 for filing cost, and proposes a total counsel fee of $800.00, with $390.00 to be paid through the plan out of the monies paid monthly to the trustee. The debtor has no known priority debts. The secured indebtedness is as follows:

1. $82,245.17 to Sooner Mortgage Company secured by a first real estate mortgage on the residence owned by the debtor consisting of the East 60 feet of Lot 12, Block 5, Hillcrest Addition to the City of Tulsa, Tulsa County, State of Oklahoma, known as 2106 E. 24th Court in Tulsa, Oklahoma 74105; and
2. an indebtedness in the amount of $400.00 owed to People's Credit Union and secured by a lien on a 1992 Ford Thunderbird automobile. Payments are deducted from the wages of the debtor to provide for payment in the amount of $27.00 per month.

The debtor owes $5,627.44 in unsecured indebtedness.

The debtor proposes the following treatment of claims and that the trustee will make disbursements as follows:

1. The debtor proposes to surrender all of her right, title, and interest in and to the East 60 feet of Lot 12, Block 5, Hillcrest Addition to the City of Tulsa, Tulsa County, State of Oklahoma, to Sooner Mortgage Company and proposes that the surrender of the property be deemed as full satisfaction of any and all claims of Sooner Mortgage Company against the debtor.
2. The debtor proposes, in view of the small balance of $400.00 and the amount of the payment per month of $27.00, that People's Credit Union continue to receive payments in the form of the present arrangement by payroll deduction from the wages of the debtor.
3. The debtor proposes that the trustee be paid $668.88 as trustee fee, to be paid at the rate of $18.58 a month for 36 months.
4. The debtor proposes that counsel for the debtor, Warren L. McConnico, receive $390.00 in payments through the plan at the rate of $39.00 per month for a period of 10 months.
5. The debtor proposes that the creditors holding unsecured claims be paid in full and that for the first 10 months of the plan they receive a pro rata share of $128.26 per month, for the months 11 through 35 they receive a pro rata share of $167.26 per month, and for the 36th month they receive a pro rata share of $163.34.

The debtor represents that she has presented this plan in good faith and that she has the ability to carry out the plan in accordance with its terms.

Dated: _____

Warren L. McConnico
SAVAGE, O'DONNELL, SCOTT,
McNULTY & AFFELDT
601 S. Boulder, Suite 1100
Tulsa, Oklahoma 74119
(918) 584–9000
Attorney for the Debtor

EXHIBIT 6.4
A Sample Standardized Chapter 13 Plan

IN THE UNITED STATES BANKRUPTCY COURT
FOR THE _____ DISTRICT OF _____

In re [name of the debtor]
  [spouse, if joint petition],   Case No. _____
                    Debtor (s)   Chapter 13

CHAPTER 13 PLAN

Length of plan: _____ monthly payments.
Plan Payment: Debtors to pay $ _____ per month. The Trustee shall
                             deduct the Trustee's percentage from each payment.
Commencement Date: Plan payments shall commence on or before _____
                             days after the Chapter 13 Petition of filed.

PRIORITY CLAIMS: (to be paid in full without interest)

CLAIMANT	DESCRIPTION	AMOUNT	MONTHLY PAYMENT AND HOW PAID
Attorney	Attorney Fees	$ _____	_____ @ _____ /mo.
IRS	_____ Federal Income Taxes	$ _____	_____ @ _____ /mo.

SECURED CLAIMS: (to be paid in full without interest)

CLAIMANT	TOTAL OF SCHEDULED CLAIM	COLLATERAL	VALUE (SECURED CLAIM)	INTEREST RATE	MONTHLY PAYMENT AND HOW PAID
_____	$ _____	[year, make, model]	$ _____	_____ %	___ @ _____ /mo.

NOTE: Secured creditors shall retain their liens to the extent of the value stated above. The allowed
secured claim of each creditor shall be the amount of the value stated above, with any balance of
the claim as filed being allowed as an unsecured claim, with the lien of the creditor being voided
on the unsecured portion pursuant to 11 U.S.C.A. § 506(d).

HOME MORTGAGES: (Debtor's principal residence)

CLAIMANT	DESCRIPTION	AMOUNT ALLOWED	INTEREST RATE	MONTHLY PAYMENT AND HOW PAID
_____	First Mortgage	(Regular post-petition payments directly be Deptors)		
_____	Arrearage on First Mortgage	$ _____	_____ %	_____ @ _____ /mo.
_____	Second Mortgage	(Long-term debt, regular payments through Trustee)		_____ @ _____ /mo.
_____	Arrearage on Second Mortgage	$ _____	_____ %	_____ @ _____ /mo.

EXHIBIT 6.4
Continued

PROPERTY TO BE SURRENDERED: The following property shall be surrendered to the named claimant in full satisfaction of the secured claim stated below, with the balance, if any, relegated to general unsecured status.

CLAIMANT	COLLATERAL	VALUE (SECURED CLAIM)	BALANCE TO UNSECURED

CLAIMANT	DESCRIPTION	AMOUNT	MONTHLY PAYMENT AND HOW PAID

LEIN AVOIDANCES: The Debtors shall file a separate Motion or Motions to avoid the liens or security interest of the following claimants pursuant to 11 U.S.C.A. § 522(f), and the claims of such claimants shall be relegated and treated as general unsecured claims below:

UNSECURED CLAIMS: All claims not specifically provided for above and those relegated to unsecured status above shall be paid as general unsecured claims, without interest, on a pro rata basis.

Unsecured Claims per Schedules: $_____
Claims Relegated to Unsecured Status: $_____
Total Projected Unsecured Claims: $_____
Approximate Percentage Payback to Holders
    of Unsecured Claims: _____%

OTHER PROVISIONS:
(1) All property of the estate under 11 U.S.C.A. § 1306 shall be and remain property of the estate and all stays shall remain in force and effect until conclusion of the case or other Order of the Court.
(2) All claims will be treated as set forth above unless a creditor objects prior to the confirmation hearing *and* files a claim within ninety (90) days after the first date set for the meeting of creditors called pursuant to 11 U.S.C.A. § 341(1).
(3) Creditors who fail to file a claim within the time stated in ¶ 2 above may not receive any distributions under this Plan.
(4) The provisions of Contracts with secured creditors are incorporated in this Plan except as modified by this Plan and the Order Confirming this Plan.

                [signature of the debtor's attorney]
                [typed name of debtor's attorney]
                [mailing address including zip code]
                [telephone number]

B. THE DEBTOR'S PAYMENTS UNDER THE PLAN

Starting within 30 days after the plan is filed and unless otherwise ordered by the court, the debtor begins making payments to the trustee. 11 U.S.C.A. § 1326(a)(1). The trustee retains the payments until confirmation or denial of confirmation of the plan. 11 U.S.C.A. § 1326(a)(2).

In some cases, the debtor may be unable to make even the first payment under the plan. These cases will then be converted to Chapter 7 or dismissed. 11 U.S.C.A. § 1307(c)(4).

C. MODIFICATION OF THE PLAN BEFORE CONFIRMATION

The debtor may modify his or her plan at any time before confirmation, but the plan, as modified, must meet the requirements of the Code. 11 U.S.C.A. § 1323(a). The plan, as modified, becomes the plan. A holder of a secured claim that has accepted or rejected the plan is deemed to have accepted or rejected the plan, as modified, unless the holder's rights have been changed by the modification and the holder has changed the previous acceptance or rejection.

SECTION 8
HEARING ON CONFIRMATION OF THE PLAN

After the meeting of creditors, the stage is set for the **confirmation hearing.** The paralegal should check local court rules for confirmation hearing requirements. Most courts will require the debtor to be present at the hearing on confirmation of the plan. The judge may ask the debtor's attorney to summarize the contents of the plan. The judge will also ask the trustee for comments on the plan. The trustee will advise the judge as to what the problems are and whether the plan can be confirmed. The trustee may suggest modification to make the plan confirmable. The judge may decide to continue the hearing to give the debtor an opportunity to file an amendment or a supplemental plan, or such changes may be provided for in the order of confirmation.

The trustee, a creditor, or the U.S. trustee may file an objection to confirmation of the plan. The judge, on his or her own initiative, may determine that the plan is not confirmable. 11 U.S.C.A. §§ 1324, 1325.

To be confirmed by the court, the plan must comply with the provisions of 11 U.S.C.A. § 1325. Section 1325 requires that the plan comply with Chapter 13 and other applicable provisions of the Code (11 U.S.C.A. § 1325(a)(1)); that the fees and charges required by Title 28 of the Code or by the plan be paid (11 U.S.C.A. § 1325(a)(2)); and that the plan be proposed in good faith (11 U.S.C.A. § 1325(a)(3)).

The following case *In re Curry,* demonstrates how a court has dealt with **good faith.** In *Curry,* the debtor sought to classify a voluntary charitable contribution as a reasonable living expense.

In re Curry
United States Bankruptcy Court, Southern District of Florida, 1987.
77 B.R. 969.

ORDER DENYING CONFIRMATION
Thomas C. Britton,
Chief Judge

This debtor's Chapter 13 plan provides monthly payments of $125 for three years to the trustee which amounts to 26% payment of his unsecured creditors without interest. There are 11 unsecured creditors including three disputed accounts for which no value is stated and, therefore, are not considered in the foregoing estimated distribution.

In his disclosure of his income, the debtor states that he has deducted $103 as a payroll deduction for:

"tithe to church deducted from pay."

This voluntary charitable contribution represents almost half of this debtor's disposable income after payment of his necessary living expenses.

The debtor is an ordained minister employed as a teacher by a church. The charitable contribution withheld from his salary as a voluntary payroll deduction is paid to his employer. It is not suggested that the deduction is required by the employer nor that the deduction is a device to divert income through the church to the debtor. I do not question the information set forth in the debtor's Chapter 13 statement nor the sincerity of his religious convictions. I understand that this charitable deduction, in the form of a payroll deduction, was in effect before bankruptcy.

A debtor's plan may not be confirmed unless this court finds that "the plan has been proposed in good faith." 11 U.S.C. § 1325(a)(3). I cannot make that finding in this case. Good faith requires, at least, that the debtor is willing to pay to the trustee for the benefit of his creditors all of his disposable income after provision for his neces-

sary and reasonable living expenses and a reasonable contingency. A charitable contribution, at least to the degree provided in this case, does not constitute a reasonably necessary living expense. The effect of such a deduction is to permit the debtor to require that *his creditors* contribute to his chosen charity. I do not believe that the statute contemplates such a result nor do I consider that I have discretion to permit this debtor to achieve that result.

I do not overlook the fact that there are published opinions by several of my colleagues who have reached a contrary result. Nor have I overlooked the fact that Official Form 10, authorized by B.R. 9009, provides a space to list "religious and other charitable contributions" in the debtor's budget, item 4(b)(15). The Official Forms do not override the statute. They were not approved by Congress nor by the Rules Committee. Therefore, they provide no indication of legislative intent. The Forms, though prescribed by the Judicial Conference (B.R. 9009) do not, I take it, constitute judicial precedent that religious and charitable contributions may, in effect, be imposed by a Chapter 13 debtor upon his creditors.

The Confirmation of the debtor's plan is denied. The debtor is granted leave to amend his plan to increase his monthly payment in the amount of $103, the voluntary payroll deduction presently provided for the benefit of his employer church. In all other respects, the plan meets the requirements for confirmation.

When informed of this court's conclusions and the option to amend, the debtor elected under § 1307(a) to convert this case to a Chapter 7 liquidation. By a separate order that election is recognized.

Section 1325 also requires that the payments of unsecured claims fulfill the best interests of creditors test. As mentioned earlier, under this test each unsecured claim must receive under the plan not less than it would have received had the claim been paid under Chapter 7 liquidation. 11 U.S.C.A. § 1325(a)(4). In a Chapter 13 case, it is unnecessary to cramdown unsecured creditors because they have no vote. Although unsecured creditors may object to confirmation of the plan, the plan is confirmable in regard to unsecured claims if the holders of the unsecured claims will receive an amount not less than the claims or if the plan provides that all of the debtor's projected disposable income for three years from the date the first payment is due will be applied to make payments under the plan and if it meets the best interests of creditors test. 11 U.S.C.A. § 1325(b)(1).

There are three basic ways to deal with a secured claim in a Chapter 13 plan:

1. get the holder of the secured claim to agree to accept the plan;
2. have the debtor surrender the property; or
3. cram the plan down on the creditor. 11 U.S.C.A. § 1325(a)(5).

If the holder of a secured claim does not accept the settlement stated in the plan, the debtor may surrender the property securing the claim to the creditor. If the value of the secured property does not fully cover the claim, there will be a deficiency. The deficiency becomes an unsecured claim. The attorney for the debtor may want to obtain a full release from the creditor when the property is surrendered. This can be provided for in the plan and is binding if the plan is confirmed.

If the debtor cannot get a release upon surrender of the property, then the plan must provide that the creditor will retain the unsecured claim. This last option, in which the plan provides that the holder of each secured claim may retain the lien securing the claim and receive not less than the allowed amount of the secured claim, is the **Chapter 13 cramdown.** 11 U.S.C.A. § 1325(a)(5)(B)(ii).

Cramdown under Chapter 13 is a simple cramdown without application of the **fair and equitable doctrine.** The debtor can retain everything and need only meet the best interests of creditors test. This may leave the unsecured creditors with little or nothing.

In *In re Mothershed,* International Harvester filed an objection to confirmation of the debtors' Chapter 13 plan on two grounds: (1) the plan did not propose to pay interest on the amount of the secured claim; and (2) since the plan was proposed for 60 months, its interest would not be adequately protected because its claim would become undersecured at some point during the 60 months. The *Mothershed* court explored the Code's requirements for cramdown.

In re Mothershed
United States Bankruptcy Court, Eastern District of Arkansas, 1986.
62 B.R. 113.

ORDER
James G. Mixon,
Bankruptcy Judge

On June 25, 1985, Alvie Lee Mothershed and Lavonda Jean Mothershed filed a vol-

untary petition for relief under the provisions of Chapter 13. The plan provides that it will pay two secured claims of International Harvester Credit Corporation (International Harvester) the value of the collateral or the amount of the debt, whichever is less over the life of the plan. The narrative statement of the plan values International Harvester's two pieces of collateral at $48,000.00 for a 1982 tractor and trailer and $18,000.00 for a 1979 tractor.

The testimony was that the debtors owned a 1979 International Harvester tractor. On the day the petition was filed the principal amount of the purchase money debt owed to International Harvester was $14,070.20. The contract rate of interest on the unpaid principal balance was fourteen percent per annum.

The other collateral is a 1982 International Harvester tractor and trailer. On the day the petition was filed the principal amount of the purchase money debt owed to International Harvester was $47,229.12. The contract rate of interest was fourteen percent per annum.

The parties stipulated that International Harvester holds a valid and perfected lien in both tractors and the trailer. The evidence established that International Harvester's claim as to each vehicle is fully secured.

The plan proposes sixty months of payments of $1,324.00 per month on the 1982 model tractor and trailer and $304.52 per month on the 1979 tractor. The plan does not propose to pay interest on the principal debt. The plan does not propose anything in regard to the maintenance of insurance to protect the interest of International Harvester's secured claim.

International Harvester filed an objection to confirmation. International Harvester alleged that the plan does not comply with the cramdown requirements for confirmation as contained in 11 U.S.C. § 1325(a)(5)(B)(ii) because the plan did not propose to pay interest on the allowed amount of the secured claim. This objection is sustained. If the plan proposes to pay a secured claim in installments, interest must be included in order that the secured creditor receive the present value of its secured claim. 5 *Collier on Bankruptcy* ¶ 1325.01[2][A] (15th ed. 1985); *In re Gincastro,* 48 B.R. 662 (Bkrtcy.D.R.I.1985); *Matter of Williams,* 44 B.R. 422 (Bkrtcy.N.D.Miss.1984). The applicable interest rate to determine the present value of

the secured claim is the market rate of interest at the time of confirmation. *Matter of Johnston,* 44 B.R. 66 (Bkrtcy.W.D.Mo.1984).

International Harvester also objects because the plan is proposed for sixty months. International Harvester alleges that it becomes undersecured at some point in time if the plan is to last for five years and, therefore, its interest is not adequately protected.

Under Chapter 11 a plan may be confirmed over the objection of a secured creditor if all of the requirements of 11 U.S.C. § 1129(a) and the cramdown standards of 11 U.S.C. § 1129(b)(2)(A)(i), (ii) and (iii) are met. 11 U.S.C. § 1129(b)(2)(A) provides as follows:

(A) With respect to a class of secured claims, the plan provides—
  (i)(I) that the holders of such claims retain the liens securing such claims, whether the property subject to such liens is retained by the debtor or transferred to another entity, to the extent of the allowed amount of such claims; and
  (II) that each holder of a claim of such class receive on account of such claim deferred cash payments totaling at least the allowed amount of such claim, of a value, as of the effective date of the plan, of at least the value of such holder's interest in the estate's interest in such property;
  (ii) for the sale, subject to section 363(k) of this title, of any property that is subject to the liens securing such claims, free and clear of such liens, with such liens to attach to the proceeds to such sale, and the treatment of such liens on proceeds under clause (i) or (iii) of this subparagraph; or
  (iii) for the realization by such holders of the indubitable equivalent of such claims.

Under Chapter 13 a plan may be confirmed over the dissent of a secured creditor if the requirements of 11 U.S.C. § 1325(a)(5)(B)(i) and (ii) are met. This section provides that the Court shall confirm a plan with respect to an unaccepting secured creditor if:

(B)(i) the plan provides that the holder of such claim retain the lien securing such claim; and (ii) the value, as of the effective date of the plan, of property to be distributed under the plan on account of such claim is not less than the allowed amount of such claim;

The leading treatise on bankruptcy suggests that there is no statutory requirement that the Chapter 13 plan provide adequate protection against diminution in the value of the collateral. *See 5 Collier on Bankruptcy* ¶ 1325.01[i] (15th ed. 1985). However, if the secured creditor becomes undersecured during the life of the plan, this circumstance is relevant on the issue of determining whether cause exists to extend the plan beyond the thirty-six month limit set by 11 U.S.C. § 1322(c). Since the plan must be modified to include an appropriate interest rate and since there is no evidence in the record regarding the interest rate to be selected and the amount of the payments required to pay the secured claim in full, the Court declines to address this issue at this time.

The objection to confirmation is sustained. The debtors are given twenty days in which to file a modified plan or the case will be dismissed.

IT IS SO ORDERED.

The final provision of section 1325(a) is that the debtor be able to make all payments under the plan and to comply with the plan. 11 U.S.C.A. § 1325(a)(6). The plan should be specific enough so the trustee knows exactly to whom payment should be made, how much, and when.

The confirmation of a plan binds the debtor and each creditor to the provisions of the confirmed plan, whether or not the creditor's claim is provided for by the plan and whether or not the creditor has objected to, accepted, or rejected the plan. 11 U.S.C.A. § 1327(a).

The confirmation of a plan vests all of the property of the estate in the debtor except as provided in the plan or confirmation order. The property vested in the debtor is free and clear of any claim or interest of any creditor provided for by the plan. 11 U.S.C.A. §§ 1327(b), (c). Although the court can deny confirmation on legal grounds, such as nonpayment of a fee, creditors may object on legal grounds but have no vote on the confirmation itself.

If the plan is confirmed, the trustee will distribute payments to the creditors in accordance with the plan. If the plan is not confirmed, the trustee will return the payments to the debtor, less any unpaid administrative expenses allowed under section 503(b). 11 U.S.C.A. § 1326(a)(2).

If the plan is unconfirmable, the debtor may convert the case to Chapter 7 or may request the court to dismiss the case. 11 U.S.C.A. §§ 1307(a), (b). A party in interest may also request the court to dismiss the case. 11 U.S.C.A. § 1307(c)(5).

SECTION 9
MODIFICATION OF THE PLAN AFTER CONFIRMATION

At any time after the confirmation of the plan but before the completion of payments under the plan, the debtor, the trustee, or the holder of an allowed unsecured claim may request the court to modify the plan. The plan, upon notice and opportunity for a hearing, may be modified to increase or reduce the amount of payments on claims of a particular class provided for by the plan or to extend or reduce the time for such payments. The plan may also be modified to alter the amount of the distribution to a creditor provided for by the plan to the extent necessary to take into account any payment of such claim outside the plan. 11 U.S.C.A. § 1329(a).

In *In re Arnold,* the debtor's income increased from $80,000 to $200,000 a year. At the time of confirmation, the plan called for creditors holding unsecured claims to receive 20 percent of their claims. In *Arnold,* the court explored the factors that led it to modify the plan.

In re Arnold
United States Court of Appeals, Fourth Circuit, 1989.
869 F.2d 240.

Before ERVIN, Chief Judge, and
MURNAGHAN and WILKINSON,
Circuit Judges.

Francis D. Murnaghan, Jr.
Circuit Judge

The appellant, Francis Arnold, filed for Chapter 13 bankruptcy in 1984. At the time of the confirmation hearing, Arnold reported his income as approximately $80,000 per year. In August 1985, the bankruptcy court confirmed a Chapter 13 payment plan whereby Arnold would pay $800 per month for 36 months, covering approximately 20% of the debt he owed to unsecured creditors.

On October 29, 1987, Ruth W. Weast, an unsecured creditor, moved pursuant to 11 U.S.C. § 1329 for a modification of the plan to increase the amounts Arnold would be forced to pay. By that time, Arnold's income had grown to nearly $200,000 per year. In light of Arnold's higher income, the bankruptcy court granted the motion and modified the plan to increase the monthly payment to $1,500 and to extend the payment period to 60 months.

Arnold appealed to the United States District Court for the Eastern District of Virginia, which affirmed the modification, and then to the Fourth Circuit.

Arnold is a paper products salesman whose income is dependent upon commissions. Although at the time of the confirmation Arnold predicted that his 1985 income would total approximately $80,000, it

turned out to be $102,310. In 1986, Arnold's income increased to $146,577. By December of 1987, it had increased to $199,999 per year.

Arnold contends, however, that along with the increase in income have come increased expenses. He has apparently remarried, had a new son, bought a new home, and is helping to pay the college expenses of one of his children.

INCREASE IN PAYMENTS

The Bankruptcy Court did not err in increasing Arnold's payments from $800 to $1,500 per month. The Bankruptcy Code provides in pertinent part that:

> [A]t any time after confirmation of the plan but before the completion of payments under such plan, the plan may be modified, upon request of the debtor, the trustee *or the holder of an allowed unsecured claim,* to
> (1) increase or reduce the amount of payments on claims of a particular class provided for by the plan.

11 U.S.C. § 1329(a) (emphasis added). Although § 1329(a) does not explicitly state what justifies such a modification, it is well-settled that a substantial change in the debtor's financial condition after confirmation may warrant a change in the level of payments. *See Education Assistance Corp. v. Zellner,* 827 F.2d 1222, 1226 (8th Cir.1987); *In re Fitak,* 92 B.R. 243, 248–50 (Bankr.S.D.Ohio1988), *citing* Oversight Hearings on Personal Bankruptcy Before the Subcommittee on Monopolies and

Commercial Law of the House Committee on the Judiciary, 97th Cong., 1st Sess. 181, 215–16, 221 (1981–82); *In re Gronski,* 86 B.R. 428, 432 (Bankr. E.D.Pa.1988); *In re Owens,* 82 B.R. 960, 966 (Bankr.N.D.Ill.1988); *In re Moseley,* 74 B.R. 791, 799 (Bankr.C.D.Cal.987); *In re Tschiderer,* 73 B.R. 133, 134 (Bankr. W.D.N.Y.1987). *See also,* 5 *Collier on Bankruptcy* ¶ 1329.01[b] at 1329–4 (15th ed. 1988).

Arnold has experienced a substantial increase in income since the Chapter 13 payment plan was originally confirmed. His annual income, which was projected to be $80,000 at the time of the confirmation, grew to nearly $200,000 by the time Weast sought the modification.

Arnold argues, however, that the increase in his monthly payments from $800 to $1,500 is unjustified for a number of reasons, including various public policy considerations. We address each argument:

1. Increasing the Monthly Payments Does Not Contravene Congress' Intent to Give Debtors a "Fresh Start" through Bankruptcy

Arnold correctly points out that a major goal of bankruptcy is to provide debtors a "fresh start" in life by furnishing a way to obtain relief from their debts. However, the bankruptcy's "fresh start" goal is not thwarted by increasing monthly payments in response to a substantial increase in income such as Arnold has experienced.

As Weast points out, debtors receive their "fresh start" after the discharge in bankruptcy, which does not occur until all payments under the confirmed Chapter 13 plan have been made. *See* 11 U.S.C. § 1328(a). Congress provided that Chapter 13 bankruptcy payment plans could last no longer than five years. *See* 11 U.S.C. §§ 1322(c), 1329(c). The debtor knows that after five years he is "in the clear" and has a chance for a "fresh start" in his financial life. Congress also intended, however, that the debtor repay his creditors to the extent of his capability during the Chapter 13 period. *See Deans v. O'Donnell,* 692 F.2d 968, 972 (4th Cir.1982). Certainly Congress did not intend for debtors who experience sub-

stantially improved financial conditions after confirmation to avoid paying more to their creditors. That is especially true here, where under the original Chapter 13 plan, the unsecured creditors were to receive only 20 cents on the dollar for their claims against Arnold while his income has escalated nearly 150%.

2. The Public Policy of Encouraging Productive Work Habits Does Not Preclude an Upward Readjustment in the Level of Arnold's Monthly Payments

Arnold argues that increases in income resulting from a debtor's own hard work should not be grounds for increasing the payments under a Chapter 13 plan. Arnold reasons that an increase in payments under such circumstances penalizes debtors for achieving success through hard work and will discourage such industriousness among bankrupts. That danger is especially acute here, Arnold argues, where the debtor's income depends on sales commissions which are determined by the amount of time and energy expended by the salesman. Arnold would limit increases in Chapter 13 payments to those cases in which a person's income has jumped dramatically through no real effort of his own. *E.g., In re Euerle,* 70 B.R. 72 (Bankr.D.N.H.1987) (payments readjusted upward after debtor was left an interest worth $300,000 in an estate); *In re Koonce,* 54 B.R. 643 (Bankr.D.S.C.1985) (Chapter 13 payments increased after debtor won $1,300,000 in a lottery).

Adjusting a debtor's Chapter 13 payments upward will discourage hard work far less than Arnold would have us believe. Many debtors would work hard to improve their condition even if they knew every dollar in higher pay would go to their creditors, rather than to their personal benefit, during the Chapter 13 period. The promotions or increased stature in a job or profession that result from the debtor's hard work, even if they produce no net financial gain for the debtor during the

Chapter 13 period, will produce monetary benefits for the debtor after the bankruptcy period ends.

Furthermore, some debtors, although perhaps a small, but nonetheless appreciable, minority, will welcome the opportunity to pay as much as they can afford to their creditors. Those people may feel a moral obligation to work hard to earn more money so they can repay as much of their debts as possible.

Arnold's arguments that the increased payments will discourage him from working hard ring hollow in light of the fact that, although his *monthly* gross income in December 1987 was nearly $10,000 higher than at the time of the Chapter 13 confirmation, the bankruptcy court increased his monthly payments only by $700 per month. Even with the higher Chapter 13 payments, Arnold's hard work has paid off handsomely for him.

Even if the prospect of higher Chapter 13 payments were to discourage some debtors from working to improve their income, the creditors' interests would justify increasing the level of a debtor's payments when his or her financial condition improved markedly. It is grossly unfair for a debtor, who experiences an increase in yearly income of $120,000, to refuse to share some of that with creditors who are getting no more than 20 cents on the dollar for their claims under the original Chapter 13 plan. Bankruptcy invariably involves the balancing of the interests of both the debtors and the creditors. When a debtor's financial fortunes improve, the creditors should share some of the wealth.

3. Res Judicata Does Not Bar Modification of Arnold's Monthly Payments

The doctrine of *res judicata* bars an increase in the amount of monthly payments only where there have been no unanticipated, substantial changes in the debtor's financial situation. *Fitak*, 92 B.R. at 249–50; 5 *Collier on Bankruptcy* ¶ 1329.01[b] at 1329–4 (15th ed. 1988). *See also Moseley*, 74 B.R. at 799. Here, there has been a sub-

stantial change (from $80,000 to $200,000 per year) that must be considered unanticipated. If it was anticipated, Arnold's expectations should have been disclosed to the bankruptcy court before the original 36 month, $800 per month plan was confirmed.

We adopt the objective test applied in *Fitak* to determine whether a change was unanticipated: "whether a debtor's altered financial circumstances could have been *reasonably anticipated* at the time of confirmation by the parties seeking modification." 92 B.R. at 250 (emphasis in original). Although it was reasonable to expect Arnold's income to fluctuate from year to year because it relied so heavily on sales commissions, Weast should not be expected to have anticipated a $120,000 jump in his income in only two years. *Res judicata* thus presents no bar to an upward adjustment of Arnold's monthly payment to take into account the unanticipated and substantial improvement in his financial condition.

4. Sufficient Evidence Existed to Support the Bankruptcy Court's Conclusion That Arnold Had the Ability To Pay the Extra $700 Per Month

The bankruptcy court did not abuse its discretion in increasing Arnold's payments by $700 per month. The evidence showed that his gross monthly income was almost $10,000 higher than it was at the time of confirmation.

Arnold argues, however, that his expenses had increased even faster than his income during that period. He submitted a revised financial statement at the time of the modification hearings showing that his after-tax monthly income in late 1987 was $10,068, while his total monthly expenses were $14,014. Arnold's wife, who works as a certified public accountant, purportedly contributed income that made up the monthly deficit.

Despite the purported monthly deficit, the bankruptcy court did not act unreasonably in increasing Arnold's monthly payments by $700. First, the bankruptcy court held that Arnold's wife had the capability of earning more than enough money per month to make up for the deficit in Arnold's finances. Second, the court found that many of Arnold's purported monthly expenses were unreasonably high. For example, Arnold's financial statement listed monthly expenses of $450 for clothing, $125 for gifts, and $450 for "extraordinary expenses." Most disturbing to the bankruptcy court was the $1,950 per month in improvements and upkeep on Arnold's house. Of the $1,950, $1,700 went for monthly payments on a $30,000 addition Arnold put on the house during the Chapter 13 period.

Arnold's situation is not one in which the debtor had no control over the increase in his expenses. Arnold chose to incur a relatively large expense so that he could increase the size of his home. There is no indication that Arnold could not have postponed such an expansion until his discharge in bankruptcy. Although a debtor who files for bankruptcy need not live in poverty during the payment period he should have some obligation to limit his expenses. The bankruptcy court did not abuse its discretion in forcing Arnold to share part of his new-found financial gains with his creditors.

EXTENSION OF PLAN BEYOND 36 MONTHS

The Bankruptcy Code allows a court, "for cause," to extend the Chapter 13 payment period beyond 36 months, as long as the extension does not make the total period exceed 60 months. 11 U.S.C. § 1329(c).[1] The statute does not define "cause." The courts, it seems, must determine "cause" on a case-by-case basis.

Here there was cause to extend the payment period beyond 36 months. The bankruptcy court did not discover the substantial increase in Arnold's salary until most of the original 36-month period had expired. By the time the increase in monthly payments to $1,500 became effective, only four months remained in the original 36-month

period. In order to adhere to the 36-month period and still require Arnold to pay an amount commensurate with his improved financial standing, the bankruptcy court would have found it necessary to raise Arnold's monthly payments far above $1,500. The bankruptcy court may well have concluded that it was best to spread out over several months, rather than just four, the increased amount of money Arnold would be required to pay under the Chapter 13 plan to account for his improved financial fortunes.

It might be argued, however, that the bankruptcy court abused its discretion in extending the payment period by 24 months, to a total of five years. An extension of the period by 24 months would require Arnold to pay over $13,000 more than he would have been required to pay under the original 36-month plan if his payments had been $1,500 per month from the beginning of the Chapter 13 period.[2]

Here we need not pause to consider whether the bankruptcy judge adequately exercised, albeit in a glancing way, his discretion to increase the duration of the payout period to the maximum of 60 months allowed by statute. Assuming, without deciding, that sufficient exercise of discretion did not appear from the record, nevertheless neither Arnold nor his counsel raised

---

[1] The full text of 11 U.S.C. § 1329(c) follows: A plan modified under this section may not provide for payments over a period that expires after three years after the time that the first payment under the original confirmed plan was due, unless the court, for cause, approves a longer period, but the court may not approve a period that expires after five years after such time.

---

[2] 1. To be paid under modified plan:

32 mos. × $800 =	$25,600
28 mos. × $1,500 =	42,000
	$67,600

2. Payments of $1,500 per month
   for 36 months: 36 × 1,500 = $54,000

3. Difference: $13,600

any objection in the bankruptcy court to the point now sought to be raised, and that is fatal on appeal. Arnold's excuse is that the extension of the payment period occurred at the close of proceedings, allowing insufficient time for objection. However, Arnold could have moved for reconsideration of the bankruptcy judge's decision after the extension came into being, but failed to do so.

The judgment is
AFFIRMED.

SECTION 10
REVOCATION OF ORDER OF CONFIRMATION

Upon request of a party in interest, the court may **revoke an order for confirmation** if the order was procured by fraud. The revocation must occur within 180 days after the order for confirmation and must follow notice and a hearing. 11 U.S.C.A. § 1330(a). The case in which an order for confirmation has been revoked will be converted or dismissed pursuant to Section 1307(c)(7) unless, within the time fixed by the court, the debtor proposes a modification of the plan that is confirmed by the court. 11 U.S.C.A. § 1330(b).

SECTION 11
DISCHARGE

After the payments have been completed under the plan, the court will grant the debtor a discharge of his or her debts. This is often called a **full-compliance discharge.** The debtor will not be discharged from:

1. allowed claims which were not provided for by the plan;
2. any debt for the curing of any default on any secured or unsecured claim on which the final payment is due after the proposed final payment under the plan; and
3. any debt of the kind specified in 11 U.S.C.A. § 1328(a)(2). 11 U.S.C.A.§ 1328(a).

Therefore, with the exception of alimony and child support, educational loans owing to a governmental unit or a nonprofit institution of higher education, any debts for death or personal injury caused by the debtor's operation of a motor vehicle while intoxicated, and restitution included in a sentence on the debtor's conviction of a crime, the effect of a Chapter 13 full-compliance discharge is that the debtor can be discharged from debts that would be nondischargeable under Chapter 7. The Chapter 13 full-compliance discharge is the broadest discharge available to the debtor under the Bankruptcy Code and is designed to encourage debtors to repay at least part of their debts under Chapter 13 rather than to liquidate under Chapter 7.

> **PROBLEM 6.1**   Alice borrowed $10,000 from Sunshine Federal Savings and Loan to finance her graduate education at the University of Metropolis. Alice obtained a master's degree in computer science and secured a position as a systems analyst with NCR Corporation at an annual salary of $24,000.
>
> After working for a year, Alice found herself unable to pay either her student loans or other debts that she had accumulated because of a past illness. She filed a petition in bankruptcy under Chapter 13.

Under Alice's Chapter 13 plan, she proposes to pay 35 percent of her student loan. Could Alice receive a discharge from the balance due on her student loan?

Under Alice's Chapter 13 plan, she also proposes to pay 35 percent of her other debts. Could Alice receive a discharge from the balance due on these debts?

The court may grant what is called a **hardship** or **compassionate discharge** to a debtor who has not completed payments under the plan. This type of discharge is granted only if the debtor's failure to complete the payments is due to circumstances for which the debtor should not justly be held responsible, the value of the payments made to creditors as of the effective date of the plan is not less than the amount that would have been paid on the claim if the debtor's estate had been liquidated under Chapter 7, and modification of the plan is not practicable. 11 U.S.C.A. § 1328(b).

The debtor under a hardship discharge will not be discharged from any allowed secured claims, from allowed unsecured claims that were not provided for by the plan, from any debt for the curing of any default on any secured or unsecured claim on which the final payment is due after the proposed final payment under the plan, or from any nondischargeable claims under section 523(a). 11 U.S.C.A. § 1328(c). Therefore, the effect of a hardship discharge is that the debtor will not be discharged from any secured debts or from unsecured debts that would be nondischargeable under Chapter 7.

> **PROBLEM 6.2**   If after making 60 percent of the payments of allowed unsecured claims under the plan, Alice became unable to make the payments and was entitled to a hardship discharge, would she be discharged from the balance due on these debts?

A debtor who has received either a full-compliance or a hardship discharge cannot receive a discharge in a Chapter 7 case filed within six years of the date of the Chapter 13 filing, unless payments under the Chapter 13 plan totaled 100 percent of the allowed unsecured claims, or totaled 70 percent of the allowed unsecured claims and the Chapter 13 plan was proposed by the debtor in good faith and was the debtor's best effort. 11 U.S.C.A. § 727(a)(9). A debtor who has received a discharge in a Chapter 13 case is not foreclosed from filing another Chapter 13 case or a Chapter 11 or 12 case at any time and receiving a discharge, if the debtor is otherwise eligible to file under any of these chapters and receive a discharge. 11 U.S.C.A. §§ 109, 1141, 1228, 1328.

> **PROBLEM 6.3**   Five years after the filing of her Chapter 13 case and one year after Alice's hardship discharge, she has once again become unable to pay her creditors because of medical bills from a recurrence of her previous illness.
> Is Alice eligible for a discharge under Chapter 7?
> Is Alice eligible to file a Chapter 13 case?

SECTION 12
REVOCATION OF THE DISCHARGE

A party in interest may request **revocation of the discharge** for fraud within one year after the discharge is granted if this party did not know about the fraud until after the discharge was granted. 11 U.S.C.A. § 1328(e).

SECTION 13
CLOSING THE CASE AND AFTER THE CASE IS CLOSED

Upon completion of payments under the plan and discharge of the debtor, the trustee files a final report and account, certifying that the case has been fully administered. There is a presumption that the case is fully administered unless the United States trustee or a party in interest files an objection within 30 days. If no objection is filed, the court may discharge the trustee and close the case without reviewing the final report and account. 11 U.S.C.A. § 350(a); Fed. R. Bank. P. 5009.

Even after the case is closed, it is still subject to further action. In certain situations, a case may be amended without being reopened. Clerical errors in judgments, orders, and other parts of the record or errors in the record caused by oversight or omission may be corrected. A closed case may be reopened to add a creditor or to distribute previously undistributed property of the estate. 11 U.S.C.A. § 350(b).

BASIC TERMS AND PHRASES

Adjustment of debts of an individual
    with regular income
Best interests of creditors test
Chapter 13 cramdown
Chapter 13 plan
Chapter 13 trustee
Codebtor
Confirmation hearing
Fair and equitable doctrine

Full compliance discharge
Good faith
Hardship (compassionate) discharge
Mandatory provisions
Modification of the Chapter 13 plan
Permissive provisions
Revocation of the discharge
Revocation of an order for confirmation
Trustee's avoidance powers

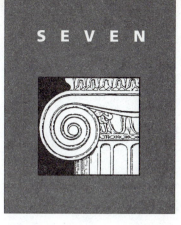

SEVEN

THE CHAPTER 12 BANKRUPTCY (ADJUSTMENT OF DEBTS OF A FAMILY FARMER WITH REGULAR ANNUAL INCOME)

CHAPTER OUTLINE

SECTION 10
REVOCATION OF ORDER OF CONFIRMATION, CONVERSION, OR DISMISSAL

SECTION 11
DISCHARGE

SECTION 12
REVOCATION OF THE DISCHARGE

SECTION 13
CLOSING THE CASE AND AFTER THE CASE IS CLOSED

This chapter explores the Chapter 12 bankruptcy—adjustment of debts of a family farmer with regular annual income. Although Chapter 7 encompasses almost all debtors (any person is eligible to be a debtor under Chapter 7, with the exception of railroads, insurance companies, and certain banking institutions), Chapter 12 is only available to family farmers who have regular annual income (11 U.S.C.A. § 109(f)), that is, family farmers whose annual income is sufficiently stable and regular to enable them to make payments under a Chapter 12 plan. 11 U.S.C.A. § 101(19).

The term **family farmer** is further restricted because not all persons involved in **farming operations** are defined as family farmers under the Bankruptcy Code. For an individual or an individual and spouse to be considered a family farmer

1. the aggregate debts must not exceed $1,500,000;
2. at least 80 percent of the aggregate noncontingent, liquidated debts must arise out of the debtor's farming operation; and
3. more than 50 percent of the debtor's gross income for the preceding taxable year must have been received from the farming operation.

For a partnership or a corporation to be considered a family farmer

1. more than 50 percent of the partnership or the outstanding stock must be held by one family conducting the farming operation;
2. more than 80 percent of the value of the partnership or the corporate assets must consist of assets related to the farming operation;
3. the aggregate debts must not exceed $1,500,000; and
4. not less than 80 percent of its aggregate noncontingent, liquidated debts must arise out of the farming operation.

If the entity is a corporation that issued stock, the stock must not be publicly traded. 11 U.S.C.A. § 101(18).

In *In re Glenn*, the debtors had a "cow and calf operation" and also sold timber off their own property and brokered their neighbors' timber. To seek protection under Chapter 12, the Glenns had to qualify as family farmers, a classification that required that they obtain more than 50 percent of their gross income from farming operations. The debtors' 1993 tax return reflected that most of their income came from the sale of timber. The court had to determine whether or not the income the Glenns earned from their timber operations constituted farm income.

In re Glenn
United States Bankruptcy Court, Eastern District of Oklahoma, 1995.
181 B.R. 105.

ORDER
Tom R. Cornish,
Bankruptcy Judge

On the 11th day of April, 1995, the creditor's, Wilburton State Bank, Motion to Dismiss and Motion for Relief from Stay came on for an evidentiary hearing in McAlester, Oklahoma.

After a review of the above-referenced pleadings, hearing testimony presented and arguments of counsel, this Court does hereby enter the following findings and conclusions in conformity with Rule 7052, Fed.R.Bankr.P., in this core proceeding:

FINDINGS OF FACT

1. The Debtors filed Chapter 7 on September 14, 1994. The case was converted to Chapter 12 on February 14, 1995. This Court previously determined that the relevant taxable year to determine Chapter 12 eligibility was calendar year 1993.

2. The Debtors' 1993 tax return reflects income as follows:

Wages	$ 9,113.00
Interest	$ 853.00
Capital gain	$23,299.00

The Debtors' capital gain was from the sale of timber. The Debtors reported a loss on their farm operation in the amount of $16,073.00. The sale of timber consisted of both selling timber off his own property or selling timber from others. Mr. Burlen Glenn testified that he purchased timber contracts from individuals, such as neighbors, and sold them to Weyerhaeuser company ("Weyerhaeuser"). Weyerhaeuser actually cut the timber. Mr. Glenn further testified that he did not cultivate or fertilize the trees. He did testify that he kept fires out of the property and managed the property.

3. Wilburton State Bank ("the Bank") filed its proof of claim in the amount of $195,038.73. As of the date of the hearing, the amount due to the Bank was $204,023.74. The Bank had a security interest in a piece of real property, all cattle and inventory, and the following equipment:

> 2 Gooseneck Trailers
> 2 Brushhogs
> Ford Tractor
> 2 Leyland Tractors
> Front End Loader
> Flatbed Trailer
> Hay Mower
> New Holland Sperry Rake
> Stock Trailer

In December, 1994, the real property was appraised at $125,000.00. At the time of one of the Bank's inspections, the Debtors had 180 head of cattle on the property, having a value of $80,400.00. The last inspection made by the Bank approximately one month ago revealed that there were 193 head of cattle on the Debtors' property. Clay Bennett, President of Wilburton State Bank, testified that he was concerned about the declining value of the cattle. However, Mr. Bennett conceded on cross-examination that the cattle market had improved over the last ten (10) months. Mr. Bennett testified that he believed the Bank's own appraisal was even too high.

4. The Trustee, Robert Hemphill, testified that the cattle were in better condition than most cattle at this time of the year. The Debtor, Mr. Glenn, testified that all of his equipment was operable.

5. The Bank has filed a Motion to Dismiss alleging that the Debtors are ineligible for Chapter 12. Additionally, the Bank seeks relief from the stay or alternatively, the Bank seeks adequate protection payments.

CONCLUSIONS OF LAW

A.   The first issue which needs to be addressed is whether the Debtors are eligible for Chapter 12 relief. Section 109(f) of the Bankruptcy Code provides that "[o]nly a family farmer with a regular annual income may be a debtor under Chapter 12 of this title." Section 101(18)(A) defines a "family farmer" as follows:

individual or individual and spouse engaged in a farming operation whose aggregate debts do not exceed $1,500,000 and not less than 80 percent of whose aggregate noncontingent, liquidated debts (excluding a debt for the principal residence of such individual or such individual and spouse unless such debt arises out of a farming operation), on the date the case is filed, arise out of a farming operation owned or operated by such individual or such individual and spouse, and such individual or individual and spouse receive from such farming operation more than 50 percent of such individual's or such individual and spouse's gross income for the taxable year preceding the taxable year in which the case concerning such individual or such individual and spouse was filed.

B. The definitions of "farmer" and "farming operation," when determining Chapter 12 eligibility, are to be liberally construed. *In re Maike,* 77 B.R. 832, 835 (Bankr. D.Kan. 1987) (*citing In re Blanton Smith Corp.,* 7 B.R. 410 (Bankr.M.D.Tenn.1980)). In *Maike,* the FDIC and Federal Land Bank of Wichita brought a motion to dismiss the bankruptcy because the debtors were not farmers. A majority of their income was derived from the breeding, raising, and sale of puppies. *Id.* at 833. The court in *Maike* framed the issue as "Does the debtors' nontraditional enterprise constitute a farming operation?" *Id.* The court in determining whether the

debtors were eligible for Chapter 12 relief noted that "while some of the more traditional farming operations are listed, other activities may be considered farming operations." *Id.* The court found:

[A] location that would be considered a farm under the traditional definition should weigh heavily in the court's decision. The enterprise at the location should next be consid ered. Functions which are strictly service oriented, and which are merely tangentially related to the breeding, maintaining and marketing of animals or the planting, maintaining and harvesting of crops, even though performed on the farm would not qualify the actor as a farmer.

Id. at 839. In *Maike,* the court found that a game farm and a kennel were considered a farming operation. *Id.*

In *In re Sugar Pine Ranch,* 100 B.R. 28 (Bankr.D.Or.1989), the court was faced with the issue of whether the Debtor qualified for Chapter 12. The court listed factors to determine Chapter 12 eligibility from various cases, as follows:

1. whether the location of the operation would be considered a traditional farm;
2. the nature of the enterprise at the location;
3. the type of the product and its eventual market, although the court should not be limited to products which are traditionally associated with farming;
4. the physical presence or absence of family members on the farm;
5. ownership of traditional farm assets;
6. whether the debtor is involved in the process of growing or developing crops or livestock;
7. whether or not the operation is subject to the inherent risks of farming.

Id. at 31 (citations omitted).

In the instant case, the Debtors have a cow and calf operation. In addition to the cow and calf operation, the Debtors have sold their own timber and brokered the timber of neighbors to Weyerhaeuser. They live in rural Southeastern Oklahoma in a traditional farm setting. The Debtors have traditional farm equipment such as tractors, a bailer, brushhogs, and trailers, as set forth in the Bank's Motion for Relief from Stay. The Debtors live and work on the farm, although Mrs. Glenn has outside employment. The Debtors' operation is subject to the inherent risks of farming. As in the *Sugar Pine* case, the timber operation is exposed to the risk of fire. A fire could potentially destroy all of the Debtors' timber for more than one year.

The Debtor, Mr. Glenn, testified that he managed the property to protect it from fire and he worked with the forestry department and other agencies. In light of the factors listed above, this Court finds that the timber operation is a farming operation. For these reasons, this Court finds that the money derived from the Debtors' timber operation constituted farm income and therefore, the Debtors qualify for Chapter 12 relief.

C. The next issue to be addressed is whether the Bank is entitled to relief from the automatic stay pursuant to § 362(d). Section 362(d) provides:

On request of a party in interest and after notice and a hearing, the court shall grant relief from the stay . . . such as by terminating, annulling, modifying, or conditioning such stay—

(1) For cause, including the lack of adequate protection of an interest in property of such party in interest;

(2) with respect to a stay of an act against property . . . if—

(A) the debtor does not have an equity in such property; and

(B) such property is not necessary to an effective reorganization.

The 100 acres in which the Bank has a security interest includes the Debtors' home. The Trustee filed an inventory listing the real property, which is mortgaged to the Bank, to be valued at $95,000, livestock at $84,900, and the equipment (less a Dodge Truck which is subject to a lien of Chrysler) in the amount of $19,700. In December, 1994, the real property was valued at $125,000. In analyzing these figures, it appears to this Court that there is a reasonable likelihood that equity does exist in this property. At the hearing, the testimony reflected that the amount of the debt was equal to the value of the land and the cattle alone. As a result, the Bank is not undersecured.

The fact that a debtor lacks equity in the property is not fatal to the protection of the automatic stay. Here, the secured claimant is adequately protected; the debtor has made progress in formulating a plan; and there is a reasonable possibility of confirmation within a reasonable time. *In re White Plains Dev. Corp.,* 140 B.R. 948 (Bankr.S.D.N.Y.1992). The court in *In re Honett,* 116 B.R. 495 (Bankr.E.D.Tex.1990) held that a mortgagee was not entitled to relief from the stay, where the Chapter 13 debtor did not have any equity in the mortgaged residence, absent a showing that the debtor would be unable to successfully propose a plan which would result in payment of the outstanding mortgage arrears. A mortgagee was not entitled to lifting of the stay where it was not clear that the debtor would be unable to effectively reorganize. *In re Century Inv. Fund VIII Ltd. Partnership,* 155 B.R. 1002 (Bankr.E.D.Wis.1989). Furthermore, the loss of the Debtors' home would be detrimental to any prospect of reorganization. *See, In re Deeter,* 53 B.R. 623, 625 (Bankr.N.D.Ind.1985).

The Debtors' Chapter 12 Plan is due on May 17, 1995. The case law has almost uniformly held that an equity cushion of 20% or more constitutes adequate protection. *In re McKillips,* 81 B.R. 454, 458 (Bankr. N.D.Ill.1987) (citations omitted). Case law has further held that an equity cushion of less than 11% is insufficient to constitute adequate protection. *Id.* However, case law is divided on whether a cushion of 12% to 20% constitutes adequate protection. *Id.* At the hearing, no evidence, other than the Trustee's inventory, was presented regarding the value of the equipment. As a result, this Court cannot accurately determine the amount of equity cushion. At the present time, the Court will not require adequate protection payments. The movant may reurge its Motion for Adequate Protection if the Debtors do not propose a feasible plan by May 17, 1995.

There was no evidence presented at trial that the Debtors would clearly not be able to reorganize. This Court is of the opinion that the Debtors should be given an opportunity to formulate a plan and work through their financial difficulties. The Motion to Modify Stay will therefore be denied with-

out prejudice to refiling if the Debtors are not able to formulate a feasible plan.

IT IS THEREFORE ORDERED that the Amended Motion to Dismiss by Wilburton State Bank is **denied.**

IT IS FURTHER ORDERED that the Motion to Modify Stay or in the Alternative Motion for Adequate Protection is hereby **denied.**

This chapter of the text follows the Chapter 12 case from the filing of the petition to the closing of the case and beyond. The documents necessary for filing a Chapter 12 petition are described, and the significance of filing such a petition is explored. The appointment of the trustee and the duties connected with the appointment are discussed. The chapter reviews the various motions and complaints that could be filed after the order for relief. The clerk's notice and the meeting of creditors are described.

The Chapter 12 plan—including a discussion of who may file a plan, the contents of a plan, the debtor's payments under the plan, and modification of the plan before confirmation—is explored. The hearing on confirmation of the plan and the concept of a Chapter 12 cramdown are examined. The modification of the plan after confirmation and the revocation of an order of confirmation are explored.

The full-compliance discharge granted after payments have been completed under the plan and the hardship discharge for those debtors who may be unable to complete the payments under the plan, along with revocation of a discharge, are discussed.

Finally, the closing of the case and further action that may take place after the case is closed are described.

Exhibit 7.1 is a "road map" for a Chapter 12 case.

SECTION 1
THE FILING OF THE PETITION

Although some of Chapter 12 has been patterned after Chapter 11, the procedural aspects of Chapters 12 and 13 are almost identical. Chapter 12 was patterned after Chapter 13 and is closer in form to Chapter 13 than to the other chapters.

The filing of the petition in a Chapter 12 case (and in a Chapter 13 case) is quite similar to the filing of the petition in a Chapter 7 case. Except for the filing of the Chapter 12 plan, the filing of a voluntary Chapter 12 bankruptcy case is substantially the same as the filing of a voluntary Chapter 7 bankruptcy case. The filing of a voluntary Chapter 12 case requires the following items:

1. Filing fee;
2. Voluntary Petition (Official Form No. 1);
3. Disclosure of attorney's compensation statement or disclosure of compensation statement by a non-attorney bankruptcy petition preparer;
4. Matrix (the list of creditors);

EXHIBIT 7.1
Chapter 12 Adjustment of Debts of a Family Farmer with Regular
Annual Income

Filing the Petition

The debtor files with the bankruptcy court clerk's office:
1. Filing fee
2. Voluntary Petition
3. Disclosure of attorney's compensation statement or disclosure of compensation statement
   by a non-attorney bankruptcy petition preparer
4. Matrix (the list of creditors)
5. Schedules
   a. Summary of Schedules
   b. Schedule A: Real Property
   c. Schedule B: Personal Property
   d. Schedule C: Property Claimed as Exempt
   e. Schedule D: Creditors Holding Secured Claims
   f. Schedule E: Creditors Holding Unsecured Priority Claims
   g. Schedule F: Creditors Holding Unsecured Nonpriority Claims
   h. Schedule G: Executory Contracts and Unexpired Leases
   i. Schedule H: Codebtors
   j. Schedule I: Current Income of Individual Debtor(s)
   k. Schedule J: Current Expenditures of Individual Debtor(s)
   l. Schedule of Income and Expenditures of a Partnership or Corporation
   m. Declaration Concerning Debtor's Schedules, signed by the debtor(s)
6. Statement of Financial Affairs

If the petition is accompanied by the matrix, the debtor has up to 15 days to file
5 and 6.

---

7. Chapter 12 plan (debtor must file a plan not later than 90 days after the filing of
   the petition)

The debtor may modify his or her plan before confirmation.

Prior to the time the case is closed, the debtor may amend the petition, lists, schedules, and
statement. The debtor has a duty to supplement the schedules for certain property acquired
after the petition has been filed.

Upon the filing of the petition, which constitutes an order for relief, the estate is created and
the automatic stay goes into effect, protecting the estate from dismemberment and the debtor
from collection procedures. The codebtor stay also goes into effect at this time. The debtor
becomes the debtor in possession.

Upon filing of a case or sometime thereafter, the clerk's office will, under local rules, give the
debtor an order related to reporting requirements.

Promptly after the petition is filed, the standing Chapter 12 trustee or another individual if
there is no standing trustee, or the U.S. trustee will serve as the trustee in the case.

EXHIBIT 7.1
Continued

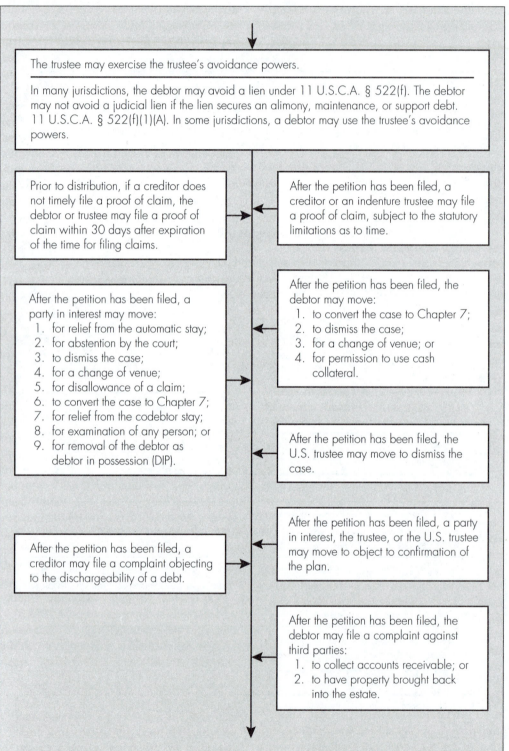

The trustee may exercise the trustee's avoidance powers.

In many jurisdictions, the debtor may avoid a lien under 11 U.S.C.A. § 522(f). The debtor may not avoid a judicial lien if the lien secures an alimony, maintenance, or support debt. 11 U.S.C.A. § 522(f)(1)(A). In some jurisdictions, a debtor may use the trustee's avoidance powers.

Prior to distribution, if a creditor does not timely file a proof of claim, the debtor or trustee may file a proof of claim within 30 days after expiration of the time for filing claims.

After the petition has been filed, a creditor or an indenture trustee may file a proof of claim, subject to the statutory limitations as to time.

After the petition has been filed, a party in interest may move:
1. for relief from the automatic stay;
2. for abstention by the court;
3. to dismiss the case;
4. for a change of venue;
5. for disallowance of a claim;
6. to convert the case to Chapter 7;
7. for relief from the codebtor stay;
8. for examination of any person; or
9. for removal of the debtor as debtor in possession (DIP).

After the petition has been filed, the debtor may move:
1. to convert the case to Chapter 7;
2. to dismiss the case;
3. for a change of venue; or
4. for permission to use cash collateral.

After the petition has been filed, the U.S. trustee may move to dismiss the case.

After the petition has been filed, a party in interest, the trustee, or the U.S. trustee may move to object to confirmation of the plan.

After the petition has been filed, a creditor may file a complaint objecting to the dischargeability of a debt.

After the petition has been filed, the debtor may file a complaint against third parties:
1. to collect accounts receivable; or
2. to have property brought back into the estate.

EXHIBIT 7.1
Continued

The clerk gives the debtor in possession, the trustee, all creditors, and indenture trustees, not less than 20 days notice by mail of:
1. the date, time, and place of the meeting of creditors;
2. the time for filing objections to the discharge of the debtor or the dischargeability of a debt;
3. the time fixed for filing proofs of claim; and
4. the time for filing objections to the debtor's claim of exemptions.

A party in interest may object to the debtor's claim of exemptions.

Meeting of Creditors

(to be held not less than 20 nor more than 35 days after the order for relief)

The business of the meeting includes the examination of the debtor under oath.

Confirmation Hearing

Confirmation of the plan vests all of the property of the estate in the debtor except as provided in the plan or confirmation order.

After confirmation but before all payments are made, the debtor, the trustee, or a holder of an allowed unsecured claim may request modification of the plan.

A party in interest may request revocation of an order of confirmation within 180 days of the entry of the order on the basis of fraud.

Payments Under the Plan

EXHIBIT 7.1
Continued

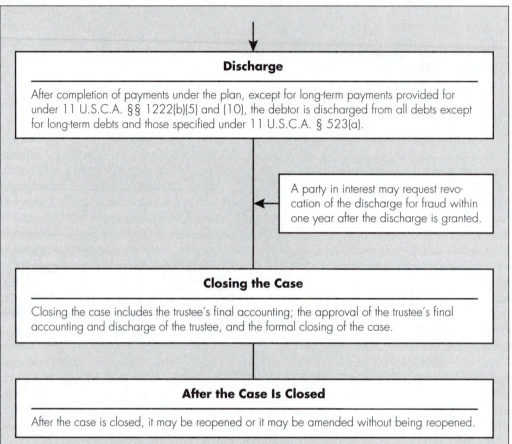

Discharge

After completion of payments under the plan, except for long-term payments provided for under 11 U.S.C.A. §§ 1222(b)(5) and (10), the debtor is discharged from all debts except for long-term debts and those specified under 11 U.S.C.A. § 523(a).

A party in interest may request revocation of the discharge for fraud within one year after the discharge is granted.

Closing the Case

Closing the case includes the trustee's final accounting; the approval of the trustee's final accounting and discharge of the trustee, and the formal closing of the case.

After the Case Is Closed

After the case is closed, it may be reopened or it may be amended without being reopened.

5. Schedules (Official Form No. 6)
   a. Summary of Schedules
   b. Schedule A: Real Property
   c. Schedule B: Personal Property
   d. Schedule C: Property Claimed as Exempt
   e. Schedule D: Creditors Holding Secured Claims
   f. Schedule E: Creditors Holding Unsecured Priority Claims
   g. Schedule F: Creditors Holding Unsecured Nonpriority Claims
   h. Schedule G: Executory Contracts and Unexpired Leases
   i. Schedule H: Codebtors
   j. Schedule I: Current Income of Individual Debtor(s)
   k. Schedule J: Current Expenditures of Individual Debtor(s)
   l. Schedule of Income and Expenditures of a Partnership or a Corporation, if applicable
   m. Declaration Concerning Debtor's Schedules, signed by the debtor(s)
6. Statement of Financial Affairs (Official Form No. 7); and
7. a Chapter 12 plan.

The Bankruptcy Reform Act of 1994 provides for reasonable compensation to the debtor's attorney in a Chapter 12 case (if the debtor is an individual) for representing the interests of the debtor in connection with the case. 11 U.S.C.A. § 330(a)(4)(B). It also authorizes the court to order the return of any excess to the estate if interim compensation exceeds the final compensation awarded. 11 U.S.C.A. § 330(a)(5).

If the petition is accompanied by the matrix, the debtor has 15 days from the filing of the petition to file the schedules and the statement of financial affairs.

Prior to the time the case is closed, the debtor may amend the petition, lists, schedules, and statement previously filed. Fed. R. Bank. P. 1009. The debtor has a duty to supplement the schedules if, within 180 days after the date of filing the petition, property is acquired by bequest, devise, or inheritance; or as a result of a property settlement agreement with the debtor's spouse or of an interlocutory or final divorce decree. The debtor may also have acquired property as a beneficiary of a life insurance policy or a death benefit plan. 11 U.S.C.A. § 541(a)(5); Fed. R. Bank. P. 1007(h). The duty of the debtor to supplement the schedules may prove important to creditors who would otherwise be paid less or not at all. It prevents the debtor who has just been discharged of his or her debts from walking away with potentially large sums of money that could be distributed to creditors by the trustee.

The Chapter 12 plan provides for payment of creditors from the debtor's future earnings. The debtor must file a Chapter 12 plan not later than 90 days after the order for relief. 11 U.S.C.A. § 1221. The period for filing a plan may be extended by the court if an extension is substantially justified. 11 U.S.C.A. § 1221. The debtor may modify his or her plan before confirmation. 11 U.S.C.A. § 1223.

SECTION 2
THE SIGNIFICANCE OF FILING A PETITION

The significance of filing a petition in a Chapter 12 is much the same as in the filing of a Chapter 7. The filing of the case constitutes an order for relief, brings the automatic stay into operation, and creates the estate. The estate in Chapter 12, however, includes both earnings and property acquired by the debtor after the filing of the petition. 11 U.S.C.A. § 1207. The debtor is entitled to exemptions, and the automatic stay goes into effect to protect the estate from dismemberment and the debtor from collection procedures. This prevents the more aggressive creditors from taking what is owed to them to the detriment of other creditors. It also gives the debtor relief from harassment by these creditors.

The **codebtor stay** goes into effect when the case is filed. 11 U.S.C.A. § 1201. Although the codebtor stay was meant to protect family members of farmers, it only protects them on consumer debts. Since the next crop must be financed before the last crop begins to pay for itself, there is a great deal of borrowing to carry on farming operations. It is common practice for members of farming families to cosign for each other's loans. Unfortunately, the codebtor stay is in large measure ineffective in Chapter 12 cases because these debts are generally not consumer debts. The codebtor stay does not apply if the codebtor became liable in the ordinary course of the codebtor's business or if the case is closed, dismissed, or converted to Chapter 7. 11 U.S.C.A. § 1201(a).

The codebtor stay does not preclude a creditor from presenting a negotiable instrument for payment and giving notice of dishonor. 11 U.S.C.A. § 1201(b). A creditor with a claim based on a consumer debt of the Chapter 12 debtor may seek relief from the codebtor stay to the extent that

1. the codebtor received the consideration for the claim held by the creditor;
2. the Chapter 12 plan does not propose to pay the creditor his or her claim; or
3. the creditor's interest would be irreparably harmed by continuation of the stay. 11 U.S.C.A. § 1201(c).

If the Chapter 12 plan does not propose to pay a creditor's claim and that creditor has filed a request for relief from the codebtor stay, the debtor or codebtor has 20 days to file a written objection; otherwise, the codebtor stay is terminated as to that creditor's claim. 11 U.S.C.A. § 1201(d).

In the case of *In re Smith,* the Smiths were farming land owned by Helen Gorham, Mrs. Smith's mother. Ms. Gorham mortgaged the farm to Wedge Bank (now Mercantile Bank) and the Smiths cosigned the note to the bank. The Smiths stopped making payments on the note and filed under Chapter 12 of the Bankruptcy Code. With the note in default, the bank filed a complaint for foreclosure against Ms. Gorham. The Smiths argued that the bank's foreclosure action violated the automatic stay as it applies to codebtors and therefore the bank should be sanctioned.

In re Smith
United States Bankruptcy Court, Central District of Illinois, 1995.
189 B.R. 11.

OPINION
Larry L. Lessen,
Bankruptcy Judge

The issue before the Court is whether a foreclosure action filed against a creditor of the Debtors violated the automatic stay of 11 U.S.C. § 362(a)(1) and (3).

The Debtors, Edward and Helen Smith, filed a petition pursuant to Chapter 12 of the Bankruptcy Code on March 21, 1995. In their schedule of Unexpired Leases, the Debtors listed a 60/40 crop share agreement with Helen Gorham. The Debtors also listed Helen Gorham as a creditor with an unsecured claim of $50,000.00. The Mercantile Bank of Illinois, formerly known as Wedge Bank, was listed as a creditor with a secured claim of $216,000.00. The security for the debt was machinery and the farm of Ms. Gorham, Mr. Smith's mother-in-law.

On July 17, 1995, Mercantile Bank of Illinois filed a Complaint for Foreclosure against Ms. Gorham. The Complaint is based on a January 15, 1992, mortgage wherein Ms. Gorham mortgaged her farm in Jersey County, Illinois, to the Mercantile Bank. Ms. Gorham is the sole owner of the farm. The Debtors are currently farming the land pursuant to their crop share agreement. The Debtors were not named in the foreclosure complaint. However, the Debtors have signed a note to the Bank as comakers, and their Chapter 12 Plan provides for full payment of the debt to Mercantile Bank. In fact, Ms. Gorham has never made payments to the Bank; the Debtors have farmed the property and made the payments to the Bank.

On August 16, 1995, the Debtors filed a Request for Sanctions which alleges that Mercantile Bank violated the automatic stay. A hearing was held on September 25, 1995, and the parties agreed that the material facts were not in dispute.

The Debtors argue that the Bank's foreclosure action violates the automatic stay of 11 U.S.C. § 362(a)(1) and (3) because it directly interferes with their Chapter 12 proceeding. They note that the Bank was aware of their tenancy and the fact that their Chapter 12 Plan proposes to pay the Bank's debt in full. The Debtors assert that the foreclosure action is an attempt to take possession of property of the bankruptcy estate in violation of the automatic stay.

The Bank responds that the foreclosure action is directed against Helen Gorham individually and not the Debtors. Ms. Gorham is equally liable with the Debtors on the debt which is the subject matter of the foreclosure action, and she is not protected by the codebtor stay of 11 U.S.C. § 1201 because the codebtor stay is limited to consumer debts. The Bank points out that while the Debtors may be tenants of Ms. Gorham, they were not made parties to the foreclosure action, and the mortgage foreclosure will be subject to the rights of the Debtors as tenants in possession.

The Debtors concede that the Bank has the right to proceed with the foreclosure action against Ms. Gorham, but the Debtors insist that the Bank erred in not first moving to lift the automatic stay. The Court agrees with the Debtors that it would have been prudent for the Bank to seek Court approval before filing the foreclosure action, but the Court finds that the failure to do so does not merit sanctions for violating the automatic stay. Ms. Gorham is not protected by the codebtor stay of § 1201, and the Bank is free to pursue its claim against Ms. Gorham. Moreover, the mortgage foreclosure does not affect the Debtors' rights under their lease with Ms. Gorham. Under the Illinois Mortgage Foreclosure Act,

> whoever takes possession can take only those rights that the mortgagor had. The Act also provides that a lease subordinate to a mortgage shall not be terminated during the pendency of a foreclosure solely by virtue of a mortgagee's entry into possession under the Act. (Ill.Rev.Stat., 1987, ch. 110, par. 15–1701(e).) . . . Since the lease is not terminated when a mortgagee takes possession, both the tenant and the mort-

gagee are bound by its terms. The mortgagee accedes only into the shoes of the mortgagor; hence, if the mortgagor would be bound by a lease, the mortgagee in possession would also be bound.

Kelley/Lehr & Associates v. O'Brien, 194 Ill.App.3d 380, 388, 141 Ill.Dec. 426, 551 N.E.2d 419 (1990). A bankruptcy court reached a similar conclusion in *In re Sauk Steel Co., Inc.,* 133 B.R. 431, 436 (Bankr. N.D.Ill.1991):

> In Illinois, neither the mortgagee's entry into possession before foreclosure, nor the appointment of a receiver, automatically terminates a junior lease. Ill.Rev.Stat. ch. 110, 15–1701 (1989). After state court entry of an order for possession against a property owner, a lessee is in exactly the same position as it was in prior to such an Order.
>
> Until a debtor is named as party-defendant, a foreclosure action does not generally affect the bankruptcy estate. *In re Comcoach Corp.,* 698 F.2d 571, 574 (2nd Cir.1983).
>
> The automatic stay prohibits actions against the debtor, the property of the debtor, and the property of the estate. 11 U.S.C. § 362(a). Since the foreclosure action in the instant case was not against the Debtor . . . there was no violation of the automatic stay.

For the foregoing reasons, the Debtors' Request for Sanctions against Mercantile Bank of Illinois is denied.

This Opinion is to serve as Findings of Fact and Conclusions of Law pursuant to Rule 7052 of the Rules of Bankruptcy Procedure.

See written Order.

ORDER

For the reasons set forth in an Opinion entered this day,

IT IS THEREFORE ORDERED that Debtors' Request for Sanctions against Mercantile Bank of Illinois be and is hereby denied.

After the order for relief, the various parties in interest may begin to assert their interests in the property of the estate. An unsecured creditor or an equity security holder must file a proof of claim or interest subject to statutory limitations as to time. Fed. R. Bank. P. 3002. If, prior to distribution, a creditor does not timely file a proof of claim, the debtor or trustee may file a proof of claim within 30 days after the expiration of the time for filing claims. Fed. R. Bank. P. 3004.

A. POSSESSION AND CONTROL OF PROPERTY OF THE ESTATE: THE DEBTOR IN POSSESSION

The Chapter 12 debtor, unlike his or her Chapter 7 counterpart, is a **debtor in possession (DIP).** The debtor will retain possession of all property of the estate (unless he or she is removed for cause such as fraud or mismanagement), except as provided in a confirmed plan or in an order confirming a plan. 11 U.S.C.A. § 1204(a). The debtor in possession may be reinstated by the court on request of a party in interest and after notice and a hearing. 11 U.S.C.A. § 1204(b).

An important change has been made regarding property of the estate in a Chapter 12 case. The Supreme Court decision in *Rake v. Wade,* 508 U.S. 464 (1993), to impose an "interest on interest" requirement for curing mortgage arrearages has been negated by 11 U.S.C.A. § 1222(d) in agreements entered into after the October 22, 1994, effective date of the Bankruptcy Reform Act of 1994.

B. OPERATION OF THE DEBTOR'S BUSINESS

The Code contemplates that the debtor will operate the business unless the court orders otherwise. 11 U.S.C.A. § 1203. The court will enter an order for periodic reports. Fed. R. Bank. P. 2015(b) and committee notes. The nature of these reports will vary depending on the debtor's situation and on how much information is required by the court. Most courts have a regular format for this type of report.

Most of the administrative powers and duties that apply to the debtor in possession in a Chapter 11 case also apply to the debtor in a Chapter 12 case. These powers and duties include providing adequate protection to creditors to preserve the automatic stay (11 U.S.C.A. § 362(d)); using, selling, or leasing property, including cash collateral (11 U.S.C.A. § 363); and obtaining credit (11 U.S.C.A. § 364), as well as the ability to assume or reject executory contracts and unexpired leases (11 U.S.C.A. § 365) and to obtain continuation of utility services (11 U.S.C.A. § 366). The important difference between a Chapter 11 debtor and a Chapter 12 debtor is that adequate protection under section 361 does not apply to a Chapter 12 case. 11 U.S.C.A. § 1205(a). When **adequate protection** is required under sections 362, 363, or 364 in a Chapter 12 case, it may be provided by

(1) requiring the trustee to make a cash payment or periodic cash payments to such entity, to the extent that the stay under section 362 of this title, use, sale, or lease under section 363 of this title, or any grant of a lien under section 364 of this title results in a decrease in the value of property securing a claim or of an entity's ownership interest in property;

(2) providing to such entity an additional or replacement lien to the extent that such stay, use, sale, lease, or grant results in a decrease in the value of property securing a claim or of an entity's ownership interest in property;

(3) paying to such entity for the use of farmland the reasonable rent customary in the community where the property is located, based upon the rental value, net income, and earning capacity of the property; or

(4) granting such other relief, other than entitling such entity to compensation allowable under section 503(b)(1) of this title as an administrative expense, as will adequately protect the value of property securing a claim or of such entity's ownership interest in property. 11 U.S.C.A. § 1205(b).

The provision for payment of the reasonable rent customary in the community as adequate protection for the use of farmland is very beneficial to the farmer. This means that only the actual value of the property must be protected. This approach to adequate protection costs the farmer far less than protecting the value of the creditor's interest in the property as required by the "indubitable equivalent" language of section 361(3).

The periodic cash payments provided for in Chapter 12 are designed to give creditors necessary protection without stripping family farmers of their chance to stay in operation. 11 U.S.C.A. § 1205(b)(1). *In re Rennich* contains a good discussion on periodic payments as adequate protection for the secured creditor without the necessity of "lost opportunity" costs. Lost opportunity is defined in the case.

In re Rennich
United States Bankruptcy Court, District of South Dakota, 1987.
70 B.R. 69.

MEMORANDUM DECISION AND ORDER
Peder K. Ecker,
Bankruptcy Judge
On December 16, 1986, Merlyn and Marlys Rennich (debtors) filed for relief under Chapter 12 of the Bankruptcy Code. According to their schedules, they operate a dairy and farming business in Harrisburg, South Dakota. Also on that date, they filed a motion for use of cash collateral.

On January 16, 1987, Federal Deposit Insurance Corporation (FDIC) filed a motion for relief from the automatic stay and determination of secured status. FDIC holds a secured interest in, among other things, certain equipment of the debtors by way of an assignment.[1] After negotiations, the FDIC and debtors entered into a cash collateral agreement which was approved by the Court at a hearing on February 6, 1987. As part of the stipulation, the debtors agreed to pay the FDIC $542 monthly to compensate for "depreciation" of its interest.

The parties also agreed to disagree and submit to the Court the issue of requiring, as part of adequate protection, interest payments for what is commonly known as lost opportunity costs. Within the context of the Eighth Circuit's holding in *In re Ahlers,* 794 F.2d 388 (8th Cir.1986), both counsel offered elaborate arguments for their positions. *See also In re Briggs Transportation Co.,* 780 F.2d 1339 (8th Cir.1985). (Bankruptcy Courts may allow lost opportunity costs in Chapter 11's.) Essentially, the debtors contend that the FDIC, as an assignee, is not entitled to lost opportunity costs as part of the "benefit of its bargain" as otherwise may be allowed under Bankruptcy Code Section 361, because, as an assignee, it never bargained with the debtors, but only the assignor. FDIC, however, insists that, as a secured creditor, through assignment or otherwise, it is entitled to lost opportunity costs.

While the Court finds both counsel's arguments interesting, it believes that the question raised is simply whether lost opportunity costs in the form of interest payments are required for retention of secured equipment as part of the concept of what is adequate protection in a case filed under Chapter 12 of the Bankruptcy Code. At the outset, the Court notes that section 1205, and not section 361, is determinative of adequate protection in a case filed under Chapter 12. 11 U.S.C. § 1205(a).[2]

The underlying basis for requiring interest payments for lost opportunity costs as part of adequate protection is the secured creditor's inability to foreclose on its interest and reinvest the proceeds because of the automatic stay provisions of the Bankruptcy Code (11 U.S.C. § 362(a)). *See id.* at 1343–51. Lost opportunity costs recovery is premised on the "indubitable equivalent" language of Bankruptcy Code Section 361(3). *See id. See also In re American Mariner Industries, Inc.,* 734 F.2d 426 (9th Cir.1984); *Grundy National Bank v. Tandem Mining Corp.,* 754 F.2d 1436 (4th Cir.1985). Unlike subsection 361(3), section 1205 does not require payment of the "indubitable equivalent" as part of adequate protection. 11 U.S.C. § 1205. Section 1205 only provides the following alternatives:

1. A creditor may receive cash payments (may be periodic) for a decrease in value of secured property resulting from automatic stay (§ 362), or use, sale, or lease of the property (§ 363), or the granting of a superior lien (§ 364).
2. A creditor may receive an additional or replacement lien for a decrease in value of secured property resulting from automatic stay (§ 362), or use, sale, or lease of the property (§ 363), or the granting of a superior lien (§ 364).
3. A creditor may receive cash payments for use of secured farmland property based upon the property's rental value, net income production, and earning capacity of the property.
4. A creditor may receive other relief, other than entitlement to compensation allowable under § 503(b)(1) [actual and necessary administrative expenses of preserving the estate], as will adequately protect the value of the secured property.

11 U.S.C. § 1205(b).[3]

From this, it necessarily follows that a debtor in a case filed under Chapter 12 of the Bankruptcy Code is not required to pay lost opportunity costs in the form of interest payments or otherwise for the retention of secured equipment to "adequately protect" the affected creditor. Under section 1205, it is enough that these debtors make the agreed periodic $542 cash payment to FDIC, thereby protecting against any decrease in value of the equipment. *See* 11 U.S.C. § 1205(b)(1).

Chapter 12's legislative history unequivocally supports this conclusion.[4] It reads as follows:

Under current law, the filing of a bankruptcy petition operates as an automatic stay against any act to create, perfect, or enforce a lien against property of the estate. The secured creditor must file a motion to have the stay lifted in order to proceed with foreclosure. The primary basis for lifting the stay is a lack of adequate protection. This term is not defined in the Bankruptcy Code, but examples of adequate protection are set out in 11 U.S.C. § 361.

The Fourth and Ninth Circuits have held that adequate protection requires the debtor to compensate the secured creditor for so-called "lost opportunity costs" in those cases where the value of the collateral is less than the amount of debt secured by the collateral. (citations omitted). The payment of lost opportunity costs requires the periodic payment of a sum of cash equal to the interest that the undercollateralized secured creditor might earn on an amount of money equal to the value of the collateral securing the debt.

Lost opportunity costs payments present serious barriers to farm reorganizations, because farmland values have dropped so dramatically in many sections of the country—making for many undercollateralized secured lenders. Family farmers are usually unable to pay lost opportunity costs. Thus, family farm reorganizations are often throttled in their infancy upon motion to lift the automatic stay.

Accordingly, section 1205 of the conference report provides a separate test for adequate protection in Chapter 12 cases. It eliminates the need of the family farmer to pay lost opportunity costs, and adds another means for providing adequate protection for farmland—paying reasonable market rent. Section 1205 eliminates the "indubitable equivalent" language of 11 U.S.C. § 361(3) and makes it clear that what needs to be protected is the value of property, not the value of the creditor's "interest" in property.

It is expected that this provision will reduce unnecessary litigation during the term of the automatic stay, and will allow the family farmer to devote proper attention to plan preparation.

Joint Explanatory Statement of the Committee of Conference, *reprinted in* 134 Cong.Rec. H8999 (daily ed. Oct. 2, 1986).

Based on this, the Court holds that a debtor in a case filed under Chapter 12 of the Bankruptcy Code is not required to pay lost opportunity costs in the form of interest payments or otherwise for the retention of secured equipment to adequately protect the affected creditor.

IT IS, THEREFORE, ORDERED that FDIC's request for lost opportunity costs in the form of interest payments is denied.

---

[1] FDIC became the assignee to the creditor bank's interest when it closed the bank and administered its assets.

[2] Section 1205(a) reads as follows:

"Section 361 does not apply in a case under this chapter."

[3] Section 1205(b) reads as follows:

(b) In a case under this chapter, when adequate protection is required under section 362, 363, or 364 of this title of an interest

of an entity in property, such adequate protection may be provided by—

(1) requiring the trustee to make a cash payment or periodic cash payments to such entity, to the extent that the stay under section 362 of this title, use, sale, or lease under section 363 of this title, or any grant of a lien under section 364 of this title results in a decrease in the value of property securing a claim or of an entity's ownership interest in property;

(2) providing to such entity an additional or replacement lien to the extent that such stay, use, sale, lease, or grant results in a decrease in the value of property securing a claim or of an entity's ownership interest in property;

(3) paying to such entity for the use of farmland the reasonable rent customary in the community where the property is located, based upon the rental value, net income, and earning capacity of the property; or

(4) granting such other relief, other than entitling such entity to compensation allowable under section 503(b)(1) of this title as an administrative expense, as will adequately protect the value of property securing a claim or of such entity's ownership interest in property.

[4] Any argument insisting that Congress only intended to preclude recovery of lost opportunity costs with respect to farmland and not equipment is without merit. The legislative history clearly reflects an intent to completely eliminate lost opportunity costs recovery. It only discusses payment of "reasonable market rent" for farmland as a plausible adequate protection alternative to that of a payment for decrease in value of that property.

C.   EXEMPTIONS

The same exemptions that can be claimed in a Chapter 7 case can be claimed in a Chapter 12 case. The listing of exemptions and the valuation of exempt property, as well as the valuation of nonexempt property, should be considered carefully. The value of nonexempt property, as of the effective date of the plan, plays a critical role in the confirmation of the plan.

SECTION 3
APPOINTMENT AND DUTIES OF A CHAPTER 12 TRUSTEE

After the order for relief, the standing **Chapter 12 trustee,** or another individual if there is no standing trustee, or the U.S. trustee will serve as the trustee in the case. 11 U.S.C.A. § 1202(a). The trustee in a Chapter 12 case is accountable for all property received and must perform some of the same duties as a Chapter 7 trustee. These duties include

1. examine proofs of claim and object to allowance of any claim that is improper if a purpose would be served;
2. oppose the discharge of the debtor if this is advisable;
3. upon the request of a party in interest, furnish information concerning the estate and its administration unless the court orders otherwise; and
4. make a final report and file a final account with the court and the United States trustee. 11 U.S.C.A. § 1202(b)(1).

The trustee in a Chapter 12 case also has duties that are required of a Chapter 11 trustee. These duties will be ordered by the court, for cause, if requested by a party in interest, the trustee, or the United States trustee. 11 U.S.C.A. § 1202(b)(2). These duties include

1. investigation of the acts, conduct, assets, liabilities, and financial condition of the debtor;
2. operation of the debtor's business and the desirability of continuing the business; and
3. any other matter which is relevant to the case or to the formulation of a plan. 11 U.S.C.A. § 1106(a)(3).

If the trustee conducts an investigation, he or she is required to file a statement on this investigation and to include any information on fraud, dishonesty, incompetence, misconduct, mismanagement, or irregularity in the management of the debtor's affairs, or any cause of action available to the estate. 11 U.S.C.A. § 1106(a)(4).

The trustee must appear and be heard at any hearing concerning the value of property subject to a lien, the confirmation of a plan, the modification of the plan after confirmation, or the sale of property of the estate. 11 U.S.C.A. § 1202(b)(3). The trustee also has a duty to ensure that the debtor begins making timely payments required by a confirmed plan. 11 U.S.C.A. § 1202(b)(4).

Because the trustee's avoidance powers are spelled out in Chapter 5, a universal chapter, the trustee in a Chapter 12 case has most of the same avoidance powers granted to trustees in other types of cases. See 11 U.S.C.A. §§ 544–549. The Bankruptcy Reform Act of 1994 imposes a two-year statute of limitations, running from the date of the order for relief, on the trustee's avoidance powers. Under new 11 U.S.C.A. § 546(a)(1)(B), a trustee elected or appointed before expiration of the two-year period specified in subparagraph (A) has only one year to begin an avoidance action or proceeding. 11 U.S.C.A. § 546(a)(1)(A).

The essential role of a Chapter 12 trustee, however, differs from the role of a Chapter 7 trustee but is similar to that of a Chapter 13 trustee. The primary function of a Chapter 12 trustee is to review the Chapter 12 plan, to advise the court with respect to the plan, and to act as a disbursing agent under the confirmed plan. The fact that the Chapter 12 trustee may choose not to exercise the trustee's avoidance power should not be taken to mean that the trustee does not have the power to avoid fraudulent and preferential transfers.

If the Chapter 12 debtor ceases to be a debtor in possession, the Chapter 12 trustee must file periodic reports and summaries of the operation of the business with the court, the United States trustee, and any governmental unit responsible for collection or determination of taxes arising from the business. 11 U.S.C.A. § 1202(b)(5). This is a duty "borrowed" from the duties of the Chapter 7 trustee. 11 U.S.C.A. § 704(8).

The trustee in a Chapter 12 case in which the debtor is no longer in possession also has other duties performed by a trustee in a Chapter 11 case. These duties include

1. filing the list, schedules, and statement required by section 521(1), if the debtor has not filed them;
2. filing a tax return for any year from which the debtor has not filed a return; and
3. filing reports after the confirmation of a plan. 11 U.S.C.A. § 1202(5).

SECTION 4
MOTIONS AND COMPLAINTS AFTER THE ORDER FOR RELIEF

In most districts the debtor's plan will contain all the important issues relating to the case. The court will consider most issues at the hearing on confirmation of the plan because all of these issues will affect the plan. The Code does, however, provide for various motions and complaints that may be used to resolve issues as they arise in the case.

A. MOTIONS

After the order for relief, the *debtor* may move to convert the case from Chapter 12 to Chapter 7 (11 U.S.C.A. § 1208(a)); to dismiss the case (11 U.S.C.A. 1208(b); Fed. R. Bank. P. 1017); for a change of venue (Fed. R. Bank. P. 1014); or for permission to use cash collateral (11 U.S.C.A. § 363(c)(2)). The motion for permission to use cash collateral is often filed along with the petition. Without use of cash collateral, the debtor may be unable to carry on farming operations. Therefore, it is important to handle this aspect of the case immediately.

The Chapter 12 debtor may exercise 522(f) power to avoid a **judicial lien** on any property to the extent that the property could have been exempted in the absence of the lien and to avoid a **nonpossessory, nonpurchase money security interest** in certain household and personal goods. Fed. R. Bank. P. 4003(d).

In *In re Dykstra,* the debtor moved to avoid the nonpossessory, nonpurchase money lien of Security State Bank, claiming it was on exempt farm equipment. The court discussed the Chapter 12 debtor's power to **avoid a lien** under 522(f).

In re Dykstra
United States Bankruptcy Court, Northern District of Iowa, 1987.
80 B.R. 128.

FINDINGS OF FACT, CONCLUSION OF LAW, AND ORDER RE: LIEN AVOIDANCE
Michael J. Melloy,
Bankruptcy Judge

The matter before the Court is the Debtors' motion to avoid the lien of Security State Bank (Bank). The Court, being fully advised, makes the following Findings of Fact, Conclusion of Law and Order pursuant to Fed.R.Bankr.P. 7052. This is a core proceeding under 28 U.S.C. § 157(b)(2)(K).

FINDINGS OF FACT

The following facts are stipulated by the parties:

1. Henry and Carolyn Dykstra (Debtors), as individuals, filed a petition under Chapter 12 of the Bankruptcy Code on February 24, 1987.
2. The Security State Bank has a valid security interest in farm equipment, described in Exhibit A, owned by the Debtors as of the date of the filing of their petition.
3. The lien of Security State Bank is a nonpurchase-money, nonpossessory interest.
4. The Debtors have claimed an exemption to the extent of $20,000 in the farm equipment subject to the Bank's lien.
5. The Debtors, in their Substituted and Amended Plan of Reorganization, have reduced the Bank's secured claim by $20,000 to reflect avoidance of the lien on the Debtors' property claimed as exempt.
6. On June 10, 1987, the Debtors filed a motion to avoid the Bank's lien to the extent of $20,000 pursuant to 11 U.S.C. § 522(f).
7. The Bank filed an objection to the Debtors' Substituted and Amended Plan, objecting, among other things, to

avoidance of their lien on Debtors' farm equipment.

DISCUSSION

The Bank contends that Chapter 12 does not permit the debtor to avoid a nonpossessory, nonpurchase-money lien pursuant to 11 U.S.C. § 522(f). The issue of applicability of the lien avoidance provision in a Chapter 12 case is one of first impression. Consequently, it must be analyzed on the basis of the following: (1) the purpose behind the lien avoidance provision, (2) applicability of 11 U.S.C. § 522(f) in Chapter 13 cases, and (3) the legislative history of Chapter 12.

Purpose of 11 U.S.C. § 522(f)

The Bankruptcy Act of 1898, which was repealed in 1978, contained no provision for the avoidance of liens by debtors. Under that Act, creditors were permitted to enforce blanket nonpurchase-money security interests in debtor's household goods. These blanket security clauses were used to encumber as much of the debtor's property as possible without regard to the relationship between the values of the property and the loan amount. Note, *Avoiding Liens under the New Bankruptcy Code: Construction and Application of Section 522(f)*, 15 U.Mich.J.L.Ref. 577 n.2 (1982), *citing* Federal Trade Commission, *Report of the Presiding Officer on Proposed Trade Regulation Rules: Credit Practices* 131, 133 (1973). The purpose behind securing these liens was not to provide the creditor with redeemable collateral but to frighten the debtor into repayment by threatening him with the loss of his household belongings. *Id.*

Congress attempted to remedy this situation in 1978 by providing debtors with a lien avoidance right. Section § 522(f) of the Bankruptcy Code provides:

Notwithstanding any waiver of exemptions, the debtor may avoid the fixing of a lien on an interest of the debtor in property to the extent that such lien impairs an exemption to which the debtor would have been entitled under subsection (b) of this section, if such lien is—

(2) a nonpossessory, nonpurchase-money security interest in any—

(A) household furnishings, household goods, wearing apparel, appliances, books, animals, crops, musical instruments, or jewelry that are held primarily for the personal, family, or household use of the debtor or a dependent of the debtor;

(B) implements, professional books, or tools, of the trade of the debtor or the trade of a dependent of the debtor; or

(C) professionally prescribed health aids for the debtor or a dependent of the debtor.

In addition to alleviating pressure from creditors, Congress intended that this provision allow debtors to retain enough property to make a fresh start after discharge. *In re Hall,* 752 F.2d 582, 588 (11th Cir.1985). Congress was also concerned that a balance be maintained between debtors and creditors. *In the Matter of Thompson,* 750 F.2d 628, 631 (8th Cir.1984). The lien avoidance provision was not deemed applicable to all property otherwise exempt, but only to items described in subsections (A), (B), and (C) above. *Id.* It is clear that, if the items claimed by the debtor constitute exempt property, the lien could be avoided to the extent of $20,000 had the case been filed under Chapter 7 of the Bankruptcy Code. *See In re Punke,* 68 B.R. 936 (Bankr.N.D.Iowa1987); Iowa Code § 627.6(11) (1987).

Lien Avoidance in Chapter 13

The courts which have addressed the applicability of § 522(f) in Chapter 13 cases are not in agreement. At least four bankruptcy courts, including this Court, have permitted § 522(f) to apply to Chapter 13 cases without

legal analysis. *In re Hitts,* 21 B.R. 158 (Bankr. W.D.Mich.1982); *In re McKay,* 15 B.R. 1013 (Bankr.E.D.Pa.1981); *In re Graham,* 15 B.R. 1010 (Bankr. E.D.Pa.1981); *In re Clayborn,* 11 B.R. 117 (Bankr.E.D.Tenn.1981); *In re Ulrich,* No. 85–01042C (Bankr.N.D.Iowa March 3, 1986). Other courts have relied solely on Bankruptcy Code § 103(a) in allowing Chapter 13 debtors to avoid liens pursuant to § 522(f). Section 103(a) provides: "Except as provided in § 1161 of this title, Chapters 1, 3, and 5 of this title apply in a case under Chapter 7, 11, 12, or 13 of this title." *In re Jordon,* 5 B.R. 59 (Bankr.D.N.J.1980); *In re Primm,* 6 B.R. 142 (Bankr.D.Kan.1980); *In re Canady,* 9 B.R. 428 (Bankr.D.Conn.1981). Yet another group of courts has gone further to analyze the issue of whether or not there is a conflict between § 522(f) and § 1325(a)(5)(B)(i). A general rule of statutory construction is that where two provisions in a statute conflict, the more specific one will control. *Matter of Thornhill Way I,* 636 F.2d 1151 (7th Cir.1980). Section 1325(a)(5)(B)(i) states that a Chapter 13 plan can only be confirmed if it provides for the retention of liens held by secured creditors.

The overwhelming majority of courts addressing the issue of conflicting code provisions has determined that there is no conflict between § 522(f) and § 1325(a)(5)(B)(i). *Baldwin v. Avco Financial Services,* 22 B.R. 507 (Bankr.D.Del.1982); *In re Mattson,* 20 B.R. 382 (Bankr.W.D.Wis.1982); *Matter of Lantz,* 7 B.R. 77 (Bankr.S.D.Ohio1980); *In re Lincoln,* 26 B.R. 14 (Bankr.W.D.Mich.1982); *In re Mitchell,* 25 B.R. 406 (Bankr.N.D. Ga.1982); *In re Cameron,* 25 B.R. 410 (Bankr.N.D.Ga.1982); *In re Thurman,* 20 B.R. 978 (Bankr.W.D. Tenn.1982). The rationale for this is that once a lien has been avoided pursuant to § 522(f), the once secured claim becomes an unsecured claim, and therefore § 1325(a)(5)(B)(i) does not apply. *Mattson,* 20 B.R. at 384. Additionally, the legislative history was found to be void of any Congressional intent to deny the use of § 522(f) in a Chapter 13 case. *Lincoln,* 26 B.R. at 15. As further support, a finding that § 522(f) does not apply in Chapter 13 cases would make Chapter 7 the more desirable proceeding, thus defeating the efforts of Congress to encourage greater use of Chapter 13. *Baldwin,* 22 B.R. at 510.

The leading case which found that § 522(f) and § 1325(a)(5)(B)(i) conflict is *In re Aycock,* 15 B.R. 728 (Bankr.E.D.N.C.1981). The court stated:

> Although Section 522(f) provides the debtor may avoid the fixing of a lien on the debtor's interest in certain property. Section 1325(a)(5)(B) conflicts by *mandating* that the plan contain a provision for the retention of the lien of a non-accepting holder of a secured claim, provided for in the plan, in order for the court to confirm the plan. (Emphasis added).

This decision has been criticized and is thought to be an incorrect decision. 5 *Collier on Bankruptcy,* ¶ 1300.81, 1300–158 (15th ed. 1987).

Another theory for not allowing a debtor in a Chapter 13 case to avoid liens pursuant to § 522(f) is that he keeps all of his property so there is no exemption which is being impaired. *In re Sands,* 15 B.R. 563 (Bankr.M.D.N.C.1981). However, *Collier's* states that a Chapter 13 debtor is entitled to claim the same exemptions as those allowed a Chapter 7 debtor, though exemptions are of less practical concern in a Chapter 13 proceeding than in a Chapter 7 liquidation. *Collier, supra* at 1300–157. The majority of courts have determined that exemptions are important to a Chapter 13 debtor. *In re Thurman,* 20 B.R. 978 (Bankr.W.D.Tenn.1982); *In re Ohnstad,* 6 B.C.D. 6 (Bankr.S.D.1980).

Legislative History of Chapter 12

The legislative history of Chapter 12 indicates that it was created because Congress felt that the bankruptcy system "did not afford an opportunity of financial rehabilitation to many family farmers since most of them had too much debt to qualify as debtors under Chapter 13 and many of them found the only remaining remedy, Chapter 11, to be needlessly complicated, unduly time-consuming, inordinately expensive, and, in too many cases, unworkable." *Bankr.Service L.Ed.,* Code Commentary and Analysis § 44.1:2 at 7 (1987), *citing* H.R. 958, 99th Cong., 2nd Sess., 132 Cong. Rec. H8986–(H)9002 (1986). Chapter 12 was closely modeled after Chapter 13 with changes being made in those provisions which were inappropriate for family farmers. *Id.*

The provisions of § 1225 are identical to those of § 1325. As the majority of courts have determined that there is no conflict between Code § 522(f) and § 1325(a)(5) (B)(i), it follows that there is no conflict between § 522(f) and § 1225(a)(5)(B)(i). Additionally, exemptions are important to Chapter 12 debtors who file as individuals.[1] J. Anderson and J. Morris, *Chapter 12 Farm Reorganizations,* § 5.16, 5–77 (1987). The legislative purposes of § 522(f) to protect debtors from unnecessary harassment of creditors and provide them with a fresh start should apply in Chapter 12 cases, the same as in Chapter 7 and Chapter 13 cases, where the family farmers are individual debtors.

CONCLUSION OF LAW

The nonpossessory, nonpurchase-money lien of Security State Bank in the Debtors' farm equipment claimed as exempt is avoidable pursuant to 11 U.S.C. § 522(f).

ORDER

Henry and Carolyn Dykstra, as individuals filing under Chapter 12 of the Bankruptcy Code, are entitled to avoid the nonpossessory, nonpurchase-money lien of Security State Bank in exempt farm equipment as described in Exhibit A to the extent of $20,000.

---

[1]Section 522(b) clearly states that only individual debtors may exempt property of the estate. This may explain why this Court could find no case in which a Chapter 11 debtor attempted to avoid a secured creditor's nonpossessory, non-purchase-money lien pursuant to 11 U.S.C. § 522(f).

A *party in interest* may move for relief from the automatic stay (11 U.S.C.A. § 362(d); Fed. R. Bank. P. 4001, 9014); for abstention by the court (11 U.S.C.A. § 305); to dismiss the case (11 U.S.C.A. §§ 1208(c), (d)); for a change of venue (Fed. R. Bank. P. 1014); for disallowance of a claim (11 U.S.C.A. § 502); to convert the case to Chapter 7 (11 U.S.C.A. § 1208(d)); for relief from the codebtor stay (11 U.S.C.A. § 1201(c)); for examination of any person (Fed. R. Bank. P. 2004); or for removal of the debtor as debtor in possession (11 U.S.C.A. § 1204(a)).

The *U.S. trustee* may move to dismiss the case. 11 U.S.C.A. §§ 307, 1208.

A *party in interest,* the *trustee,* or the *U.S. trustee* may move to object to confirmation of the plan. 11 U.S.C.A. § 1224.

B. COMPLAINTS

Proceedings brought by the *trustee* to avoid transfers are classified as adversary proceedings by Rule 7001. The trustee's avoidance powers were discussed in Section 3 of this chapter.

The *debtor* in a Chapter 12 case is granted powers nearly identical to those of a debtor in possession in Chapter 11, with only the investigation and distribution functions assigned exclusively to the Chapter 12 trustee. 11 U.S.C.A. § 1203. Therefore, a Chapter 12 debtor, as debtor in possession, may use the avoidance powers granted to the trustee. 11 U.S.C.A. § 1203.

The *debtor* may file a complaint against third parties to collect accounts receivable or to have property brought back into the estate. 11 U.S.C.A. §§ 542, 543.

A *creditor* may file a complaint objecting to the dischargeability of a debt. 11 U.S.C.A. § 523.

SECTION 5
THE CLERK'S NOTICE

The official forms for the clerk's notice in a Chapter 12 case are B9G and B9H. Official Form B9G is the clerk's notice in a Chapter 12 case filed by an individual or joint debtor family farmer. (See Exhibit 7.2.) Official Form B9H is the clerk's notice for a Chapter 12 case filed by a partnership or corporation family farmer. (See Exhibit 7.3.)

The clerk must give the debtor, the trustee, all creditors, and the indenture trustees not less than 20 days notice by mail of the date, time, and place of the meeting of creditors and of the time fixed for filing proofs of claim. Fed. R. Bank. P. 2002. This notice generally serves as the notice of the order for relief required by 11 U.S.C.A. § 342(a) and may also serve as the notice for the confirmation hearing in a Chapter 12 case if a plan has been filed in the case. In practice, this does not often happen. If this notice is to serve as notice for the confirmation hearing, a copy or a summary of the proposed plan will be included.

SECTION 6
MEETING OF CREDITORS (THE SECTION 341 MEETING)

The meeting of creditors (the section 341 meeting) is held not less than 20 nor more than 35 days after the order for relief. The business of the meeting includes the examination of the debtor under oath by the U.S. trustee, the trustee, and the creditors. Fed. R. Bank. P. 2003.

EXHIBIT 7.2
Notice of Commencement of Chapter 12 Case, Meeting of Creditors, and Fixing of
Dates (Individual or Joint Debtor Family Farmer)

FORM B9G
(Rev. 12/94)

United States Bankruptcy Court

Case Number

_____ District of _____

NOTICE OF COMMENCEMENT OF CASE UNDER CHAPTER 12 OF THE BANKRUPTCY CODE.
MEETING OF CREDITORS, AND FIXING OF DATES
(Individual or Joint Debtor Family Farmer)

In re (Name of Debtor)	Address of Debtor	Soc. Sec./Tax Id. Nos.
	Date Case Filed (or Converted)	
Name and Address of Attorney for Debtor	Name and Address of Trustee	
Telephone Number		Telephone Number

□ This is a converted case originally filed under chapter _____ on _____ (date).

DEADLINE TO FILE A PROOF OF CLAIM
For creditors other than governmental units: For governmental units:

DATE, TIME, AND LOCATION OF MEETING OF CREDITORS

FILING OF PLAN AND DATE, TIME, AND LOCATION OF HEARING ON CONFIRMATION OF PLAN
□ The debtor has filed a plan. The plan or a summary of the plan is enclosed. Hearing on confirmation will be held:
_____ (Date) _____ (Time) _____ (Location)
□ The debtor has filed a plan. The plan or a summary of the plan and notice of the confirmation hearing will be sent separately.
□ A plan has not been filed as of this date. Creditors will be given separate notice of the hearing on confirmation of the plan.

DISCHARGE OF DEBTS
Deadline to File a Complaint to Determine Dischargeability of Certain Types of Debts:

COMMENCEMENT OF CASE. A family farmer's debt adjustment case under chapter 12 of the Bankruptcy Code has been filed in this court by the family farmer named above as the debtor, and an order for relief has been entered. You will not receive notice of all documents filed in this case: All documents filed with the court, including lists of the debtor's property and debts are available for inspection at the office of the clerk of the bankruptcy court.

CREDITORS MAY NOT TAKE CERTAIN ACTIONS. A creditor is anyone to whom the debtor owes money or property. Under the Bankruptcy Code, the debtor is granted certain protection against creditors. Common examples of prohibited actions by creditors are contacting the debtor to demand repayment, taking action against the debtor to collect money owed to creditors or to take property of the debtor, and starting or continuing foreclosure actions, repossessions, or wage deductions. Some protection is also given to certain codebtors of consumer debts. If unauthorized actions are taken by a creditor against a debtor, or a protected codebtor, the court may punish that creditor. A creditor who is considering taking action against the debtor or the property of the debtor, or any codebtor, should review §§ 362 and 1201 of the Bankruptcy Code and may wish to seek legal advice. The staff of the clerk of the bankruptcy court is not permitted to give legal advice.

MEETING OF CREDITORS. The debtor (both husband and wife in a joint case) is required to appear at the meeting of creditors on the date and at the place set forth above for the purpose of being examined under oath. Attendance by creditors at the meeting is welcomed, but not required. At the meeting, the creditors may examine the debtor and transact such other business as may properly come before the meeting. The meeting may be continued or adjourned from time to time by notice at the meeting, without further written notice to creditors.

EXEMPT PROPERTY. Under state and federal law, the debtor is permitted to keep certain money or property as exempt. If a creditor believes that an exemption of money or property is not authorized by law, the creditor may file an objection. An objection must be filed not later than 30 days after the conclusion of the meeting of creditors.

DISCHARGE OF DEBTS. The debtor may seek a discharge of debts. A discharge means that certain debts are made unenforceable against the debtor personally. Creditors whose claims against the debtor are discharged may never take action against the debtor to collect the discharged debts. If a creditor believes a specific debt owed to the creditor is not dischargeable under § 523(a)(2), (4), (6), or (15) of the Bankruptcy Code, timely action must be taken in the bankruptcy court by the deadline set forth above in the box labeled "Discharge of Debts." Creditors considering taking such action may wish to seek legal advice.

PROOF OF CLAIM. Except as otherwise provided by law, in order to share in any payment from the estate, a creditor must file a proof of claim by the date set forth above in the box labeled "Deadline to File a Proof of Claim." The place to file the proof of claim, either in person or by mail, is the office of the clerk of the bankruptcy court. Proof of claim forms are available in the clerk's office of any bankruptcy court.

PURPOSE OF A CHAPTER 12 FILING. Chapter 12 of the Bankruptcy Code enables family farmers to reorganize pursuant to a plan. A plan is not effective unless approved by the bankruptcy court at a confirmation hearing. Creditors will be given notice in the event the case is dismissed or converted to another chapter of the Bankruptcy Code.

Address of the Clerk of the Bankruptcy Court	For the Court:
	Clerk of the Bankruptcy Court
	Date

EHXIBIT 7.3

Notice of Commencement of Chapter 12 Case, Meeting of Creditors, and Fixing of Dates (Partnership or Corporation Family Farmer)

FORM B9H
(Rev 12/94)

United States Bankruptcy Court

_____ District of _____

Case Number

**NOTICE OF COMMENCEMENT OF CASE UNDER CHAPTER 12 OF THE BANKRUPTCY CODE.
MEETING OF CREDITORS, AND FIXING OF DATES**
(Corporation/Partnership Family Farmer)

In re (Name of Debtor)	Address of Debtor	Soc. Sec./Tax Id. Nos.
	Date Case Filed (or Converted)	

☐ Corporation   ☐ Partnership

Name and Address of Attorney for Debtor	Name and Address of Trustee
Telephone Number	Telephone Number

☐ This is a converted case originally filed under chapter _____ on _____ (date).

DEADLINE TO FILE A PROOF OF CLAIM

For creditors other than governmental units: For governmental units:

DATE, TIME, AND LOCATION OF MEETING OF CREDITORS

FILING OF PLAN AND DATE, TIME, AND LOCATION OF HEARING ON CONFIRMATION OF PLAN

☐ The debtor has filed a plan. The plan or a summary of the plan is enclosed. Hearing on confirmation will be held:
_____ (Date) _____ (Time) _____ (Location)

☐ The debtor has filed a plan. The plan or a summary of the plan and notice of the confirmation hearing will be sent separately

☐ A plan has not been filed as of this date. Creditors will be given separate notice of the hearing on confirmation of the plan

DISCHARGE OF DEBTS

Deadline to file a Complaint to Determine Dischargeability of Certain Types of Debts:

COMMENCEMENT OF CASE: A family farmer's debt adjustment case under chapter 12 of the Bankruptcy Code has been filed in this court by the family farmer named above as the debtor, and an order for relief has been entered. You will not receive notice of all documents filed in this case. All documents filed with the court, including lists of the debtor's property and debts, are available for inspection at the office of the clerk of the bankruptcy court.

CREDITORS MAY NOT TAKE CERTAIN ACTIONS. A creditor is anyone to whom the debtor owes money or property. Under the Bankruptcy Code, the debtor is granted certain protection against creditors. Common examples of prohibited actions by creditors are contacting the debtor to demand repayment, taking action against the debtor to collect money owed to creditors or to take property of the debtor, and starting or continuing foreclosure actions or repossessions. Some protection is also given to certain codebtors of consumer debts. If unauthorized actions are taken by a creditor against a debtor or a protected codebtor, the court may penalize that creditor. A creditor who is considering taking action against the debtor, the property of the debtor, or a codebtor, should review §§ 362 and 1201 of the Bankruptcy Code and may wish to seek legal advice. If the debtor is a partnership, remedies otherwise available against general partners are not necessarily affected by the commencement of this partnership case. The staff of the clerk of the bankruptcy court is not permitted to give legal advice.

MEETING OF CREDITORS. The debtor's representative, as specified in Bankruptcy Rule 9001(5), is required to appear at the meeting of creditors on the date and at the place set forth above in the box labeled "Date, Time, and Location of Meeting of Creditors" for the purpose of being examined under oath. Attendance by creditors at the meeting is welcomed, but not required. At the meeting, the creditors may examine the debtor and transact such other business as may properly come before the meeting. The meeting may be continued or adjourned from time to time by notice at the meeting, without further written notice to the creditors.

DISCHARGE OF DEBTS. The debtor may seek a discharge of debts. A discharge means that certain debts are made unenforceable against the debtor. Creditors whose claims against the debtor are discharged may never take action against the debtor to collect the discharged debts. If a creditor believes a specific debt owed to the creditor is not dischargeable under § 523(a) (2), (4), (6), or (15) of the Bankruptcy Code, timely action must be taken in the bankruptcy court by the deadline set forth above in the box labeled "Discharge of Debts." Creditors considering taking such action may wish to seek legal advice.

PROOF OF CLAIM. Except as otherwise provided by law, in order to share in any payment from the estate, a creditor must file a proof of claim by the date set forth above in the box labeled "Deadline to File a Proof of Claim." The place to file the proof of claim, either in person or by mail, is the office of the clerk of the bankruptcy court. Proof of Claim forms are available in the clerk's office of any bankruptcy court.

PURPOSE OF A CHAPTER 12 FILING. Chapter 12 of the Bankruptcy Code enables family farmers to reorganize pursuant to a plan. A plan is not effective unless approved by the bankruptcy court at a confirmation hearing. Creditors will be given notice in the event the case is dismissed or converted to another chapter of the Bankruptcy Code.

Address of the Clerk of the Bankruptcy Court	For the Court:
	Clerk of the Bankruptcy Court
	Date

It is quite common for the trustee to conduct some type of examination of the debtor at the meeting of creditors. The trustee must be assured that all debts and assets have been listed. Creditors with problems will have an opportunity to talk to both the trustee and the debtor.

If a plan has been filed at the time of the meeting, the trustee may ask questions about the feasibility of the plan and may give the debtor some indication of the trustee's recommendation on the confirmation of the plan. The trustee may suggest modification of the plan in an attempt to lead the debtor and the debtor's attorney toward a confirmable plan.

In addition to the meeting of creditors, the Code authorizes the U.S. trustee to convene a meeting of equity security holders if the debtor is a corporation.

SECTION 7
THE CHAPTER 12 PLAN

The debtor must file a **Chapter 12 plan** showing how he or she intends to repay part or all of the creditors' allowed claims from future earnings. The plan must be filed not later than 90 days after the order for relief (i.e., the filing of the petition), although an extension may be granted by the court if substantially justified. Only the debtor may file a plan in a Chapter 12 case. 11 U.S.C.A. § 1221. Creditors cannot file a plan nor can they vote on the debtor's plan. If the debtor does not file a plan within 90 days or within the allowed extension, the trustee or a creditor may request dismissal of the case. 11 U.S.C.A. § 1208(c)(3).

A. CONTENTS OF A CHAPTER 12 PLAN

The contents of a Chapter 12 plan are delineated in the Code. 11 U.S.C.A. § 1222. Some provisions are mandatory; others are permissive. The **mandatory provisions** are noted in the Code by "shall" and the **permissive provisions** by "may." Compare 11 U.S.C.A. § 1222(a) with 11 U.S.C.A. § 1222(b).

1. MANDATORY PROVISIONS
Because Chapter 12 is designed with flexibility in mind, the Code provides only a few mandatory provisions in regard to the contents of the plan.

1. A Chapter 12 plan must provide for the trustee's supervision and control of that portion of the debtor's future income necessary for the implementation of the plan. 11 U.S.C.A. § 1222(a)(1).
2. A Chapter 12 plan must provide for the full payment of all priority claims (11 U.S.C.A. § 507) unless the holder of the claim agrees to a different treatment of that claim. 11 U.S.C.A. § 1222(a)(2).
3. If the Chapter 12 plan divides claims and interests into classes, the plan must provide the same treatment for each claim or interest within a particular claim, unless the holder of a particular claim or interest agrees to less favorable treatment. 11 U.S.C.A. § 1222(a)(3).
4. The payment period under the plan may not exceed three years unless the court, for cause, approves a longer period. If a longer period is approved, it may not exceed five years. 11 U.S.C.A. § 1222(c).

2. PERMISSIVE PROVISIONS

A Chapter 12 plan may

1. designate a class or classes of unsecured claims, but may not discriminate unfairly against a designated class (the plan may treat claims for a consumer debt of the debtor differently than other unsecured claims if there is a codebtor);
2. modify the rights of holders of secured and unsecured claims;
3. cure or waive any default;
4. propose payments on unsecured claims concurrently with payments on any secured claim or any other unsecured claim;
5. provide for curing any default on any secured or unsecured claim on which the final payment is due after the proposed final payment under the plan;
6. provide for assumption, rejection, or assignment of any previously unrejected executory contract, including the debtor's unexpired lease;
7. provide for the payment of all or any part of any claim from property of the estate or of the debtor;
8. provide for the sale of all or any part of the property of the estate or the distribution of all or any part of the property of the estate among those having an interest in such property;
9. provide for payments of allowed secured claims consistent with section 1225(a)(5) over a period exceeding the usual three years of the plan allowed for other payments under the plan;
10. provide for the vesting of property of the estate in the debtor or in any other entity; and
11. include any other provision not inconsistent with other Title 11 provisions. 11 U.S.C.A. § 1222(b).

Unlike Chapter 13, which does not give the debtor a method for dealing with long-term secured debts, Chapter 12 gives the family farmer a method for dealing with long-term secured debts owed on both farmland and equipment. Such secured debts may be paid out after the other payments under the three-year plan have been completed. 11 U.S.C.A. § 1222(b)(9). The length of this extended period is not specified by the Code. Chapter 12 was written specifically to allow the farmer to handle this type of long-term mortgage debt which is so much a part of farm life.

The value of nonexempt property, as of the effective date of the plan, plays a critical role in the confirmation of the plan. For a Chapter 12 plan to be confirmed, it must meet the best interests of creditors test.

In *In re Nielsen,* the Nielsens filed for bankruptcy under Chapter 12 and filed a Chapter 12 plan before the fall harvest. By the time the confirmation hearing was held, the harvest had been completed and the value of the crops exceeded the expected value when the petition was filed. The crops were free from liens. The unsecured creditors objected to the confirmation of the debtors' plan on the ground that it failed to meet the best interests of creditors test. The court discussed the appropriate date for applying the best interests of creditors test.

In re Nielsen
United States Bankruptcy Court, Eastern District of Missouri, 1988.
86 B.R. 177.

MEMORANDUM OPINION
David P. McDonald,
Bankruptcy Judge

INTRODUCTION

Nels and Amy Nielsen are family farmers who filed for bankruptcy pursuant to Chapter 12 of the United States Bankruptcy Code on September 1, 1987. They filed their original Chapter 12 Plan on November 30, 1987 and subsequently filed a First Amended Plan and Second Amended Plan on January 21, 1988 and February 10, 1988, respectively. Objections to the Plan were filed by First Bank of Montgomery County, Trustee, Robert and Mildred Starr and The Federal Land Bank. A confirmation hearing was held on January 21, 1988. The Starrs filed a Memorandum Regarding Section 1225(a)(4) Feasibility Analysis on February 10, 1988. On February 12, 1988, the Trustee filed his objections to the Second Amended Plan. A hearing was held on February 17, 1988.

JURISDICTION

This Court has jurisdiction over the parties and subject matter of this proceeding pursuant to 28 U.S.C. §§ 1334, 151, and 157 and Local Rule 29 of the United States District Court for the Eastern District of Missouri. This is a "core proceeding" pursuant to 28 U.S.C. § 157(b)(2)(B) and (L), which the Court may hear and determine.

DISCUSSION

The Nielsens filed their Chapter 12 case prior to the fall harvest of 1987. However, by the time a confirmation hearing was held, the crops had been harvested and their value was considerably higher than at the inception of this case. These crops were free of any liens. The unsecured creditors objected to the confirmation of the Debtors' plan. They assert that the Debtors failed to meet the requirements of 11 U.S.C. § 1225(a)(4), which provides

§ 1225. Confirmation of plan.
(a) Except as provided in subsection (b), the court shall confirm a plan if—
   (4) the value, as of the effective date of the plan, of property to be distributed under the plan on account of each allowed unsecured claim is not less than the amount that would be paid on such claim if the estate of the debtor were liquidated under chapter 7 of this title on such date;

By including the value of the unencumbered harvested crops in a liquidation analysis, the creditors argue they would be paid more on their claims if the Debtors were liquidated under Chapter 7. The Debtors, on the other hand, have built their plan on the use of the funds generated from these harvested crops and feel it would be unjust to allow a Chapter 12 plan to rise or fall based on the timing of a harvest.

There has been very little case law developed concerning Section 1225(a)(4) and its interpretation and application. The first reported case concerning Section 1225(a)(4) is the case of *In re Fauth,* 79 B.R. 490 (Bankr.Mont.1987). The *Fauth* court found that the claim by the creditors that they would receive more on liquidation under Chapter 7 than by confirmation of the plan was factually without merit. However, the court then went on to say in dicta that even if the creditor's position on liquidation had been correct, the court could still confirm the plan under the best interest of creditors test. *Fauth* stated that an unsecured creditor must be treated in either one of two ways, either its allowed claim must be paid in full or all of the Debtor's projected disposable income must be committed under the plan to payments of claims. If the Debtor's disposable income is committed to the payment of unsecured claims, liquidation of the farm can be avoided regardless of the amount of that disposable income. The *Fauth* court gave as its reasoning for this determination that liquidation is against the clear intent of Congress to keep the family farmer in operation. It is true Congress has exhibited a desire to keep the family farmer in operation, but *only* if the farmer complied with the standards set forth in Chapter 12 and, in particular, Section 1225. This Court specifically rejects the *Fauth* reasoning. A farmer's plan cannot be confirmed if it fails to comply with 11 U.S.C. § 1225(a)(4). *See, In re Willingham,* 83 B.R. 552 (Bankr.S.D.Ill.1988).

Whether or not the Nielsens' plan meets the requirements of Section 1225(a)(4) depends on the meaning of the phrase "on such date," since that is the date value is to be determined for liquidation analysis. It should be noted that the wording of Section 1225 and Section 1325 is identical. In interpreting the provisions of Chapter 12, courts have often turned to Chapter 13 for guidance because Chapter 12 was closely modeled after the existing Chapter 13 with alterations of provisions that are inappropriate for family farmers. *In re Kjerulf,* 82 B.R. 123 (Bankr.D.Ore.1987).

> "Chapter 12 imposes the same requirements as are considered relevant in the Chapter 13 cases: Section 1225(b)(1)(B) provides that the court may not approve a plan over the objection of the trustee or an unsecured creditor unless the plan provides that all the debtor's projected disposable income to be received during the life of the plan will be applied to make payments under the plan, and Section 1225(a)(4) provides that the court shall confirm the plan if the value of the property to be distributed under the plan to unsecured creditors is not less than they would receive under chapter 7 liquidation." *In re Kjerulf,* at 127.

Therefore, this Court looks to the interpretation of Section 1325(a)(4) to give guidance on interpreting Section 1225(a)(4). The Eighth Circuit has held that the language of "on such date" of Section 1325(a)(4) means the date that the petition was filed. *Holytex Carpet Mills v. Tedford,* 691 F.2d 392 (8th Cir.1982). The *Holytex* court cited *In re Statmore,* 22 B.R. 37 (Bankr.Neb.1982) which held that the statutory language of "on such date" referred to the effective date of the plan but not to the assets in existence on the effective date of the plan. The *Statmore* court read the statutory provision to suggest that if the estate of the debtor were liquidated under chapter 7 on the effective date of the plan, the rights of the creditors would refer back to the petition date. The rights to avoid preferences, fraudulent conveyances, and to pursue the debtor for conversion of estate assets would all be fixed as of the original petition date. Following that line of reasoning, the liquidation value to be used when comparing the amount to be paid to allowed unsecured claims, either under the proposed plan or Chapter 7 liquidation is to be determined as of the date of the filing of the petition. If the liquidation amount on the date of the filing of the petition was such that the unsecured claimants would receive more or an equal amount under the plan, the plan can be confirmed.

Therefore, a hearing will be set to give the parties the opportunity to present evidence concerning the liquidation value of the assets as of September 1, 1987, the original petition date.

3. A SAMPLE CHAPTER 12 PLAN

Chapter 12 plans vary from district to district. Exhibit 7.4 is a sample Chapter 12 plan. How does this Chapter 12 plan compare with the Chapter 13 plan in Chapter Six of this text?

B. THE DEBTOR'S PAYMENTS UNDER THE PLAN

As in a Chapter 13 case, the debtor makes payments to the trustee in a Chapter 12 case. There is, however, no time period set for beginning the payments in a Chapter 12. The trustee retains the payments until confirmation or denial of confirmation of the plan. 11 U.S.C.A. § 1226(a).

EXAMPLE

Peter Eckert filed a petition for bankruptcy relief under Chapter 12 on June 1. A Chapter 12 plan was filed along with the petition. The plan called for payments by the trustee to creditors on the first of each month.

On July 15, Eckert began making payments to the trustee. On September 10, the plan was confirmed by the bankruptcy court.

On October 1, the trustee began to pay out under the plan.

C. MODIFICATION OF THE PLAN BEFORE CONFIRMATION

The debtor may modify the plan at any time before confirmation, but the plan, as modified, must meet the same requirements as the original plan. 11 U.S.C.A. § 1223(a). The plan, as modified, becomes the plan. 11 U.S.C.A. § 1223(b). A holder of a secured claim that has accepted or rejected the plan is deemed to have accepted or rejected the plan, as modified, unless the holder's rights have been changed by the modification and the holder has changed the previous acceptance or rejection. 11 U.S.C.A. § 1223(c).

EXAMPLE

On January 1, First Bank loaned Alice Whatley $22,000 so she could buy a John Deere tractor for her farm. On May 1, Whatley filed a petition in bankruptcy under Chapter 12. At the time of filing her petition, Whatley filed her Chapter 12 plan.

On May 10, First Bank accepted the plan. On May 20, Whatley modified the plan, but this modification did not affect First Bank's rights because Whatley's obligation to the Bank was fully secured by the tractor. First Bank, without further action, is deemed to have accepted the plan as modified.

EXHIBIT 7.4
A Chapter 12 Plan

**IN THE UNITED STATES BANKRUPTCY COURT
FOR THE NORTHERN DISTRICT OF OKLAHOMA**

In re Ronald Milton Oliver,
        Debtor

Case No. _____
Chapter 12

CHAPTER 12 PLAN

    COMES NOW Ronald Milton Oliver, debtor, and proposes the following plan under 11 U.S.C.A. §§ 1221, 1222.

    The debtor shall pay to the trustee all disposable income as defined by 11 U.S.C.A. § 1225(b)(2), including tax refunds, for a period of 36 months. The projected amount of disposable income is $45,000.00 per year, to be paid to the trustee in two equal semi-annual installments of $22,500.00 each on approximately April 1 and December 1 each year, beginning April 1, 1996.

    Disbursements from the regular semiannual payment of $22,500.00 shall be as follows until the priority claim is paid:

Administrative Expenses	$ 2,250.00
Priority Claims	1,000.00
Secured Claims	18,278.18
Unsecured Claims	971.82
	$22,500.00

    The trustee shall make the following disbursements from the payments received:

    1. All claims entitled to priority under 11 U.S.C.A. § 507 shall be paid in full in deferred cash payments unless the holder of a particular claim agrees to a different treatment of such claim. Claims entitled to priority and payment to holders of secured claims are:

PRIORITY CLAIMS

Priority Creditor	Est. Amt. of Claim	Semiannual Payment	No. Full Payments	Total Payment
Lonnie D. Eck, Trustee	$xxxxx.xx	$xxxxx.xx	x	$xxxxx.xx
Gary W. Wood	4,000.00	1,000.00	4	4,000.00
Total	$xxxxx.xx	$xxxxx.xx		$xxxxx.xx

    2. Concurrent with priority payments as per 11 U.S.C.A. § 507, if any, payments shall be made as follows:

        a. Creditors holding secured claims which are duly approved and allowed shall retain their lien to the extent their claim is secured and shall be paid modified payments. The total of these payments, representing the value of the security plus reasonable interest, with the balance of their claim is to be paid in accordance with the provisions for unsecured claims.

EXHIBIT 7.4
Continued

b. The claim of Utopia Mutual Life Insurance Company ("Utopia") secured by the debtor's real property shall be treated as a secured claim in the total sum of $198,000.00. By an agreed order entered December 2, 1995, Utopia and the debtor agree that any unsecured claim of Utopia is hereby waived. The secured claim of Utopia is to be paid in 40 equal installment payments of $11,539.44, including interest of 10 percent per annum, beginning April 1, 1996. The first six installments shall be made by the trustee from payments made to the trustee under the plan by the debtor in possession. The remaining 34 installments shall be made directly by the debtor in possession to Utopia, after which Utopia shall be required to release and extinguish of record its mortgage lien on the debtor's real property. If the debtor fails to make any payment on Utopia's claim within 60 days of the date due to the trustee or to Utopia, Utopia shall be entitled to pursue all available remedies for default under its mortgage lien without further action or order from the bankruptcy court, provided, however, the debtor shall retain all rights he may have to request modification of the confirmed plan under the Bankruptcy Code.

c. The secured creditor, First Bank, secured by a second mortgage on real property and a first lien on livestock and farm equipment, shall take notice the debtor proposes to pay the fair market value of the collateral in the sum of $115,627.00 as a secured claim. The debtor has valued the collateral as follows:

(1) Real property in the sum of $186,250.00 subject to a first mortgage to Utopia in the sum of $247,940.00. The value to First Bank's claim is zero.

(2) Livestock in the net sum of $115,627.00 after lien avoidance of nonpurchase money security interest of two horses, five cows, and their calves. The net value to First Bank's claim is $115,627.00.

(3) Farm equipment in the sum of $5,000.00 subject to the lien avoidance powers of the debtor as tools of the trade. The value to First Bank's claim is zero.

3. In accordance with 11 U.S.C.A. § 1222(b)(9), the debtor proposes to pay the secured claim in 40 semiannual installments of $6,738.74, including interest at the rate of 10 percent per annum. The first six installments shall be made by the trustee from payments made to the trustee under the plan by the debtor in possession. The remaining 34 installments shall be made directly by the debtor in possession to First Bank, after which First Bank shall be required to release and extinguish of record its lien or security interest in the livestock. Upon completion of all installments to be made by the trustee during the 36-month term of the plan, First Bank shall be required to release and extinguish of record its mortgage lien on the debtor's real property and the lien or security interest in the farm equipment. The balance of the claim of First Bank in the sum of $164,033.67 shall be relegated to unsecured and treated in accordance with provisions for unsecured creditors.

EXHIBIT 7.4
Continued

MODIFIED PAYMENTS TO
HOLDERS OF SECURED CLAIMS

Creditor	Est. Amt. of Claim	Semiannual Payment	No. Full Payments	Total Payment
Utopia Mutual Life Ins. Co.	$198,000.00	$11,539.44	40	$461,577.60
First Bank	115,627.00	6,738.74	40	269,549.60
Total	$313,627.00	$18,278.18		$731,127.20

UNSECURED CLAIMS

Creditors with unsecured claims are to be paid concurrently with secured claims and priority claims until approximately 5 percent of the unsecured claims are paid, without interest.

INTRODUCTION

On September 24, 1995, Ronald Milton Oliver, the debtor, filed his bankruptcy petition under Chapter 12 of the Bankruptcy Code.

The debtor has been engaged in a ranching operation at his current location since 1966 and was able to successfully operate and conduct his business until divorce proceedings in 1990. As part of those proceedings, the debtor's former wife, Mary Alice Oliver, received certain real property and assets which necessitated refinancing long-term indebtedness at substantially higher rates than the debtor had previously experienced. The refinancing coupled with a decrease in cattle prices resulted in the beginning of the debtor's financial problems. In an effort to resolve these matters, he attempted to negotiate settlement with First Bank related to an indebtedness to First Bank and during a 12-month period paid $91,000.00 to First Bank in contemplation that a settlement agreement had been reached. As a result of the substantial amounts paid to First Bank, the debtor became delinquent with his first mortgage holder, Utopia.

ASSETS

The debtor's primary asset is his homestead, consisting of 1,490 acres legally described as:

The North Half (N/2) of the North Half (N/2) of the Southwest Quarter (SW/4) of the Southwest Quarter (SW/4) and the Northwest Quarter (NW/4) of Section 2;
and
The Northwest Quarter (NW/4) of Section 12;
and
The South Half (S/2) and the Northeast Quarter (NE/4) of Section 13;
and
The Southeast Quarter (SE/4) of the Northwest Quarter (NW/4) and the West Half (W/2) of the Northeast Quarter (NE/4) and the South Half (S/2) of Section 14;
and
The West Half (W/2) of the Northwest Quarter (NW/4) of Section 15.

EXHIBIT 7.4
Continued

All of the above described lands are located in Township 28 North, Range 6 East of the Indian Meridian, Osage County, Oklahoma; contain 1,490 acres, more or less; and have been valued at $198,000.00.

In addition, the debtor has personal property of approximately 286 head of cattle and four horses which have a liquidation value of $115,627.00. The debtor also has farm equipment and machinery which he uses as tools of his trade. Most of it is old and in poor condition and of little value and has been determined to have a total market value of $5,000.00.

The debtor's other assets are a 1986 Chevrolet pickup valued at $800.00, two guns, and his personal property and household goods, with total value of $3,100.00 for all three categories.

LIABILITIES

The debtor has two creditors, other than his monthly living and operating expenses. Utopia Mutual Life Insurance Company, secured by the first mortgage on the debtor's real property and owed approximately $247,940.00, and First Bank, secured by a second mortgage on the debtor's real property, livestock, and farm equipment for the total sum of approximately $279,660.00.

NONFARM INCOME

The debtor has no nonfarm income.

PROJECTION OF ADMINISTRATIVE EXPENSES

It is anticipated there will be administrative fees for the standing Chapter 12 trustee in the sum of 10 percent of the disposable income of approximately $13,500.00 during the term of the plan. This administrative expense is to be paid in semiannual installments of $2,250.00.

Attorney fees for representing the debtor are projected at $4,000.00. The debtor has not paid any attorney fees prior to the filing of the Chapter 12 plan. It is anticipated that all attorney fees will be paid in four semiannual payments of $1,000.00 each.

TAX CONSEQUENCES OF SALE OF ASSETS

No sale of assets is anticipated except through the normal course of business. Income should be offset by operating expenses and interest paid through the plan.

SECURED PROPERTY PROPOSED TO BE RETAINED

The debtor proposes to retain all secured property. The debtor's real property is valued at $198,000.00 and is the collateral for a first mortgage of $247,940.00 and a second mortgage of $279,660.00.

The debtor also proposes to retain the livestock valued at $115,627.00 and farm equipment valued at $5,000.00 which is subject to the debtor's claim of exemption on which $279,660.00 is owed.

EXHIBIT 7.4
Continued

LIQUIDATION ANALYSIS

If the debtor's estate were liquidated as of the date of filing, it is anticipated, without deducting for any cost of sale or other expenses associated with liquidation, the creditor, Utopia Mutual Life Insurance Company, would receive at most $198,000.00 from the sale of the real property and First Bank would receive no sums from the sale. Upon liquidation of livestock and farm equipment, subject to the exemption and lien avoidance powers of the debtor, and without deducting for the cost of other expenses associated with liquidation, First Bank would receive at most $115,627.00. This liquidation analysis assumes no cost of administration and would provide no payment of any unsecured portion of their claim.

INCOME AND EXPENSE PROJECTION

INCOME

Cash flow is projected based on the sale of the debtor's cattle. It is expected that sales will take place twice each year, once during the spring and once during the fall. All income during the plan is anticipated to come strictly from the debtor's farm income and not from any other source. Anticipated sales of livestock are

April 1996	$ 36,810.00
December 1996	36,810.00
April 1997	36,810.00
December 1997	36,810.00
April 1998	36,810.00
December 1998	36,810.00
Total Income	$220,860.00

EXPENSES

Expenses are based on a monthly projection that includes both living and farm expenses for the total sum of $2,385.00 per month. Expenses are itemized and appear as Exhibit A, an attachment to this plan. For the purposes outlined below, those sums have been projected for a six-month period, which will correspond with the income being derived from the sale of the cattle. Expenses are

April 1996	$14,310.00
December 1996	14,310.00
April 1997	14,310.00
December 1997	14,310.00
April 1998	14,310.00
December 1998	14,310.00
Total Expenses	$85,860.00

EXHIBIT 7.4
Continued

DISPOSABLE INCOME

All disposable income of the debtor will be paid to the trustee for distribution even if the amount exceeds the projected payment. Based on the income and expense estimates for each of the six periods, the following disposable income is to be paid:

Semiannual:	
Income	$ 36,810.00
Expenses	−14,310.00
Disposable Income	$ 22,500.00
Terms of the Plan:	
Income	$ 220,860.00
Expenses	−85,860.00
Total Disposable Income	$ 135,000.00

SCHEDULES OF DATES AND AMOUNTS TO BE PAID BY DEBTOR

It is anticipated the debtor will make the following payments to the trustee during the term of the plan. The sum of $22,500.00 semiannually to be paid April 1, 1996, December 1, 1996, April 1, 1997, December 1, 1997, April 1, 1998, and December 1, 1998.

Upon completion of the term of the plan, the debtor will make the following payments directly:

1. to Utopia Mutual Life Insurance Company $11,539.44 on April 1 and December 1 of each year, with the first payment on April 1, 1999, and the last payment on December 1, 2015;
2. to First Bank $6,738.74 on April 1 and December 1 of each year, with the first payment on April 1, 1999, and the last payment on December 1, 2015.

The debtor further represents an ability to carry out his Chapter 12 plan and it is submitted in good faith.

Date: December 23, 1995.

_____

Gary W. Wood
ATTORNEY FOR THE DEBTOR
3223 E. 31st Street, Suite 101
TULSA, OK 74105
(918) 744-6119

CERTIFICATE OF MAILING

I, Gary W. Wood, do hereby certify that a true and correct copy of the above and foregoing instrument was mailed on the 23rd day of December 1995 to: Lonnie D. Eck, 1508 S. Carson, Tulsa, OK 74119; U.S. Trustee, 333 West Fourth Street, Tulsa, OK 74103; and all parties in interest with full and proper postage thereon.

_____

Gary W. Wood

EXHIBIT 7.4
Continued

EXHIBIT A

PROJECTED MONTHLY EXPENSES

Item	Amount
Home Maintenance	$ 40.00
Electric	41.00
Telephone	25.00
Food	150.00
Clothing	60.00
Medical/Dental	21.00
Auto Insurance	66.00
Recreation	30.00
Transportation: Gasoline/Repairs	420.00
Property Taxes	67.00
Veterinary Services	100.00
Salt	33.00
Hay and Cake	916.00
Weed Control/Fertilizer	416.00
Total Monthly Expenses	$2,385.00

SECTION 8
HEARING ON CONFIRMATION OF THE PLAN

The **hearing on confirmation of the plan** must be concluded not later than 45 days after the filing of the plan. This time period may be extended for cause. 11 U.S.C.A. § 1224. Most courts will require the debtor to be present at the hearing on confirmation of the plan. The judge may ask the debtor's attorney to summarize the contents of the plan. The judge will ask the trustee for comments on the plan. The trustee will advise the judge of any problems and of whether or not the plan can be confirmed. The judge may ask questions of the debtor, the debtor's attorney, or the trustee to clarify the information being presented. The trustee may suggest modification to make the plan confirmable. The judge may decide to continue the hearing to give the debtor an opportunity to file an amendment or a supplemental plan.

The trustee, a creditor, or the U.S. trustee may file an objection to confirmation of the plan. 11 U.S.C.A. § 1224. The judge, on his or her own initiative, may determine that the plan is not confirmable. To be confirmed by the court, the plan must comply with the provisions of 11 U.S.C.A. § 1225. Section 1225 contains several requirements:

1. The plan must comply with Chapter 12 and other applicable provisions of the Code. 11 U.S.C.A. § 1225(a)(1).
2. The fees and charges required by Title 28 of the Code or by the plan must be paid. 11 U.S.C.A. § 1225(a)(2).
3. The plan must be proposed in **good faith.** 11 U.S.C.A. § 1225(a)(3).
4. The payments of unsecured claims must fulfill the **best interests of creditors test.** Under this test, each holder of an unsecured claim must receive under the plan not less than it would have received had the claim been paid under Chapter 7 liquidation. 11 U.S.C.A. § 1225(a)(4). In a Chapter 12 case, it is unnecessary to cramdown unsecured creditors because they

have no vote. Although unsecured creditors may object to confirmation of the plan, the plan is confirmable in regard to unsecured claims if the holders of the unsecured claims will receive an amount not less than the claims. The plan is also confirmable if it provides that all of the debtor's projected disposable income for three years from the date the first payment is due will be applied to make payments under the plan. 11 U.S.C.A. § 1225(b)(1).

5. A secured claim in a Chapter 12 plan must be dealt with in one of three basic ways: get the holder of the secured claim to agree to accept the plan; have the debtor surrender the property; or cram the plan down on the creditor. 11 U.S.C.A. § 1225(a)(5). If the holder of a secured claim does not accept the settlement stated in the plan, the debtor may surrender the property securing the claim to the creditor. If the value of the secured property does not fully cover the claim, there will be a deficiency. The deficiency becomes an unsecured claim. The attorney for the debtor may want to obtain a full release from the creditor when the property is surrendered. This may be provided for in the plan and is binding if the plan is confirmed.

If the debtor cannot get a release upon surrender of the property, then the plan must provide that the creditor will retain the unsecured claim. This last option, in which the plan provides that the holder of each secured claim may retain the lien securing the claim and receive not less than the allowed amount of the secured claim, is the **Chapter 12 cramdown** and applies only to secured creditors. 11 U.S.C.A. § 1225(a)(5)(B)(ii).

Cramdown under Chapter 12 is a simple cramdown without application of the fair and equitable doctrine. The debtor can retain everything and need only meet the best interests of creditors test. This may leave the unsecured creditors with little or nothing.

6. The debtor will be able to make all payments under the plan and to comply with the plan. 11 U.S.C.A. § 1225(a)(6).

In *Travelers Insurance Co. v. Bullington,* the Bullington brothers and their now-deceased father operated their individual farms as a constructive partnership. In February 1985, the Bullingtons took out a $520,000 mortgage from Travelers on their farmland and fixtures. Under the mortgage, the Bullingtons were to pay only interest (no principal) for the first four years and all of the principal on the fifth year (February 1990). The interest rate was fixed at 12.50 percent for the first year and one point above the AAA corporate bonds index for the next three years.

In January 1987, the Bullingtons filed for bankruptcy under Chapter 12. Their Chapter 12 plan split Travelers's claim into two parts: (1) a secured claim of $475,000 (the stipulated value of the collateral; i.e., the farmland and fixtures); and (2) an unsecured claim of $170,000 representing the balance (principal and unpaid interest). The Bullingtons's plan converted the five-year floating-rate mortgage into a $475,000 thirty-year fixed-rate (10.75 percent) mortgage. Travelers objected to the confirmation of the plan and the Court of Appeals discussed five issues:

1. Does 11 U.S.C.A. § 1225 prohibit a thirty-year payout to an objecting secured creditor?
2. Does the plan provide a present "value" to the creditor that is not less than the allowed amount of such claim, as section 1225(a)(5)(B)(ii) requires?
3. Did the debtors prove the feasibility of the plan, as section 1225(a)(6) requires?
4. Does Chapter 12 constitute an unconstitutional taking of property without due process?
5. Does Chapter 12 apply retroactively?

Travelers Insurance Co. v. Bullington
United States Court of Appeals, Eleventh Circuit, 1989.
878 F.2d 354.

Before KRAVITCH and COX, Circuit Judges, and MORGAN, Senior Circuit Judge
Phyllis A. Kravitch,
Circuit Judge

This is an appeal by Travelers Insurance Co. from an order affirming the bankruptcy court's confirmation of plan under Chapter 12 (Family Farmer) of the bankruptcy code. 89 B.R. 1010. We affirm.

The Bullingtons were brothers who, together with their now-deceased father, operated their individual farms in a constructive partnership. Because of this the bankruptcy court effectively consolidated their individual petitions for Chapter 12 bankruptcy and their virtually identical reorganization plans are treated as one. [hereinafter the "plan"]

In February of 1985 the Bullingtons took out a mortgage from appellant on certain of their farm properties. It was a balloon-type mortgage under which the Bullingtons received $520,000 and were to pay interest (but no principal) in semi-annual installments for the first four years, and then the entire amount of the principal would be due in February of 1990. The interest rate was fixed at 12 ½% for the first year; the rate then floated at one point above an index of AAA corporate bonds. The mortgage was secured by land and certain fixtures (pumps, motors, etc.). The Bullingtons used the funds from the mortgage loan in their farming operations.

In November of 1986 Congress enacted Chapter 12 of the bankruptcy code to provide special relief for family farmers.

In January, 1987 the Bullingtons petitioned for bankruptcy under Chapter 12. As of the date of the petition, the Bullingtons' debt to Travelers Insurance was $645,929.77, with interest accruing at $300 per day. The value of the land that secured the Travelers loan was stipulated to be $475,000.

The plan, submitted by the Bullingtons and approved over the objections of Travelers, split Travelers claim into two parts: a secured claim of $475,000 (the stipulated value of the collateral) and an unsecured claim of $170,000 representing the remainder. The plan converted the five-year floating-rate mortgage into a $475,000 thirty-year fixed-rate mortgage. The court set the interest rate on the mortgage at 10.75%. The unsecured claim of $170,000 would be treated as any unsecured claim: the Debtors' entire disposable income (if any) would be used over the four-year term of the plan to pay each unsecured claim on a pro rata basis. At the end of the four years of the plan, any part of the unsecured debt that had not been paid off would be discharged.

Travelers appealed the bankruptcy court's order to the district court raising, inter alia, statutory and constitutional issues. The district court affirmed[1] and this appeal ensued. We address each issue in turn.

Unlike Chapter 11, secured creditors in Chapter 12 do not "vote" on a plan. Instead, section 1225 provides that the bankruptcy court "shall" approve the plan if one of three conditions are met in the plan:[2]

with respect to each allowed secured claim provided for by the plan—
(A) the holder of such claim has accepted the plan;
(B) (i) the plan provides that the holder of such claim retain the lien securing such claim; *and*
    (ii) the value, as of the effective date of the plan, of property to be distributed by the trustee or the debtor under the plan on account of such claim is not less that the allowed amount of such claim; or
(C) the debtor surrenders the property securing such claim to such holder; . . .

Because Travelers did not accept the plan, section 1225(a)(5)(A) does not apply. Under § 1225(a)(5)(C) the court may also approve a plan if the debtor surrenders the property subject to the lien, i.e., forfeits the land. Here debtors have not done so, thus our focus is on section 1225(a)(5)(B).[3]

Travelers does not suggest that the plan fails under section 1225(a)(5)(B)(i), which requires that the plan give the creditor a lien in the amount of his secured claim. The allowed secured claim here is $475,000 (the stipulated value of the property) and the plan gives a lien in that amount, so this requirement is satisfied.

Travelers argues, however, that the plan fails to meet the requirements of section 1225(a)(5)(B)(ii) because it stretches out the payments for thirty years and because Travelers does not receive sufficient "value" under the plan.

1. DOES 11 U.S.C. § 1225 PROHIBIT A THIRTY-YEAR PAYOUT TO AN OBJECTING SECURED CREDITOR?

Travelers first objection is that the plan's thirty-year mortgage violates section 1225(a)(5)(B)(ii). Travelers reasons as follows: section 1225(a)(5)(B)(ii) requires that the value of the property distributed under the plan be not less than the allowed amount of the claim, and that it be distributed "under the plan." Yet section 1222(c) provides that—subject to only two exceptions—payments under a plan may never exceed five years. Thus, Travelers suggests that because the thirty-year rescheduled mortgage is longer than five years, the plan violates the code.

Travelers argument is colorable, but it ignores the two express exceptions to section 1222(c) that permit payments to exceed five years. Section 1222(c) provides as follows:

> Except as provided in subsections (b)(5) and (b)(9), the plan may not provide for payments over a period that is longer than three years unless the court for cause approves a longer period, but the court may not approve a period that is longer than five years.

Section 1222(b)(5), the first exception to the section 1222(c) five-year limit, permits a debtor to reinstate an old debt (cure default), and is not applicable to this appeal. Section 1222(b)(9), however, has direct bearing on this case:

> [the plan may] provide for payment of allowed secured claims consistent with section 1225(a)(5) of this title, over a period exceeding the period permitted under section 1222(c).

Thus, section 1222(b)(9), as an express exception to the section 1222(c) five-year limit, permits payments under a plan to extend over five years, but only when "consistent with section 1225(a)(5)."

We find section 1222(b)(9) explicit and dispositive of Travelers' objection: a plan may provide for a payout period greater than five years, provided that it is "consistent with section 1225(a)(5)." Travelers' argument that payments under a plan can never exceed five years would render section 1222(b)(9) a nullity. Thus, the mere fact that the plan provides for a thirty-year payment of Travelers' allowed secured claim does not violate section 1225.

2. DOES THE PLAN PROVIDE A PRESENT "VALUE" TO THE CREDITOR NOT LESS THAN THE ALLOWED AMOUNT OF SUCH CLAIM AS SECTION 1225(A)(5)(B)(II) REQUIRES?

Travelers next argues that the plan does not give it the full value of its allowed secured claim as § 1225(a)(5)(B)(ii) requires. Travelers frames this objection in two ways. First, Travelers stresses that to satisfy this section it must receive value equal to its allowed secured claim "under the plan." Arguing that under the plan means the same as "during the plan," Travelers concludes that the four-year length of the plan that the bankruptcy court confirmed is the proper time frame in which to apply the section 1225(a)(5)(B)(ii) "value" test, i.e., Travelers would have us total up the payments it is to receive over these four years, and if that amount is less than the $475,000 amount of its allowed secured loan, then the plan fails.

This objection need not detain us long. Section 1225(a)(5)(B)(ii) explicitly directs that the "value" is to be determined "as of the *effective date of the plan.*" (emphasis added) Under this section, therefore, we do not total the payments received "during the plan." Instead, the test is simply whether, as of the effective date of the plan, the present value of the property distributed—i.e., the new thirty-year mortgage—is equal to or greater than the amount of the allowed secured claim.

In addition to its argument that the value it receives under section 1225(a)(5)(B)(ii) must be within the term of the plan, Travelers also argues that the thirty-year mortgage itself is not of sufficient value.

Travelers frames this issue in terms of burdens of proof. Travelers asserts that there is insufficient proof to show that a thirty-year 10.75% mortgage is of a value not less than the allowed secured claim of $475,000. From a pure finance perspective, all Travelers seems to be saying is that the term of the mortgage is too long and/or the interest rate is too low.

The debtors presented to the district court a chart of then-current interest rate returns, which tends to support a finding that a 10.75% interest rate on a thirty-year mortgage is within the range of market rates. Travelers, on the other hand, presented no *objective* evidence to demonstrate that the term or interest rate of the mortgage was such that its present value did not equal or exceed $475,000.

Travelers put on a witness who testified that Travelers itself would never lend for a period longer than twenty years, and if it did it would be at a somewhat higher rate of interest. Yet this testimony regarding Travelers' subjective valuation does not sufficiently undermine the bankruptcy courts' implicit factual finding that the present value of the mortgage as of the effective date of the plan was not less than the value of the allowed secured claim.

"Value" must be determined objectively. Simply because a creditor subjectively would not extend a mortgage on the same terms does not mean that objectively the mortgage does not have a given value. Given that

Travelers has pointed to no record evidence to show that the 10.75% interest rate does give the mortgage a present value of $475,000, while the debtors' chart does tend to support that interest rate, the bankruptcy court's finding that the thirty-year mortgage at 10.75% annual interest rate has a present value not less than the $475,000 value of Travelers' allowed secured claim is supported by sufficient evidence.

3. DID THE DEBTORS PROVE THE FEASIBILITY OF THE PLAN AS § 1225(A)(6) REQUIRES?

Travelers also argues that the debtors failed to demonstrate that the plan was feasible, as section 1225(a)(6) requires.

Travelers attacks the bankruptcy court's finding that the plan was feasible by making essentially evidentiary objections. The main objection is that the court apparently relied upon computer projections based on underlying data that has been lost. The debtors gave historical data concerning their farming operations to a government agency (Georgia Extension Service or "GES") which used this information as well as other information from its own data collection efforts and developed a computer projection of the farms' yield. Unfortunately, the debtors' farm data was destroyed in a fire. Travelers, therefore, argues that the GES projections are unreliable hearsay because we can no longer examine the underlying data.

Evidentiary questions such as this are left to the discretion of the bankruptcy court. Thus, we apply an abuse of discretion standard to the court's decision to admit the GES projections.

Because the fire destroyed the Bullingtons' farm data there is no question that the Bullingtons were not able to produce the data. The court admitted the GES projections as *opinion of the debtor.* The court has such power under rule 701 (opinion testimony by lay witness). We cannot say that the court's decision to admit the projections as opinion testimony was an abuse of discretion.

Given that there was no evidence that the debtors' plan was *not* feasible, and given that the GES projections support the conclusion that the plan was feasible, we cannot say that the court erred in determining under section 1225(a)(6) that the plan was feasible.

4. DOES CHAPTER 12 CONSTITUTE AN UNCONSTITUTIONAL TAKING OF PROPERTY WITHOUT DUE PROCESS?

No circuit has yet addressed the constitutionality of Chapter 12 of the bankruptcy code. The courts that have addressed it have found no unconstitutional taking of property.[4] We conclude that the operation of Chapter 12 of the Bankruptcy Code does not operate as an unconstitutional taking of appellant's property.

To put the takings issue in perspective, it is useful to consider the differing treatment of unsecured and secured claims. When the debtors petitioned for bankruptcy they owed Travelers $645,000 but their collateral was worth only $475,000. Under section 506, Travelers' claim was split into a secured claim in the amount of their collateral, and an unsecured claim for the remainder.[5]

As we discussed above, section 1225(a)(5) permitted the court to confirm the plan over the objections of Travelers provided that the value of the new mortgage Travelers received under the plan was not less than the amount of its allowed secured claim—i.e., the $475,000 value of the collateral. Because we affirm the finding that the new mortgage Travelers received under the plan satisfied the requirements of section 1225(a)(5), there is no taking of property with respect to the value of the collateral. The 10.75% interest will adequately compensate Travelers for the longer term of the mortgage.

The plan provided for the debtors to devote for four years all of their disposable income to the satisfaction of the unsecured claims. If we assume *arguendo* that the debtors have no disposable income for the four years of the plan, it may be that the entire $170,000 amount that Travelers's loan was undersecured will be discharged. Where Travelers once had a security interest it may conceivably end up with nothing.

Thus, our takings analysis focuses solely on the amount that the original debt was undersecured.

It is undisputed that the takings clause of the fifth amendment protects certain of the rights of secured creditors. *See Louisville Joint Stock Land Bank v. Radford,* 295 U.S. 555, 55 S.Ct. 854, 79 L.Ed. 1593 (1935) (Frazier-Lemke Act).[6] However, as the Court has observed in *Wright v. Union Central Life Insurance Co.,* 311 U.S. 273, 61 S.Ct. 196, 85 L.Ed. 184 (1940), "[these] safeguards were provided to protect the rights of secured creditors . . . to the extent of the value of the property. There is no constitutional claim of the creditor to more than that." 311 U.S. at 278, 61 S.Ct. at 199–200. A recent pronouncement of the Court in a closely related area of bankruptcy law reflects the same view. *See United Savings Ass'n of Texas v. Timbers of Inwood Forest Assocs., Ltd.,* 484 U.S. 365, 108 S.Ct. 626, 630, 98 L.Ed.2d 740 (1988) (construing section 506(a) "value of such creditor's interest" as "value of the collateral").

In light of the principle that the takings clause of the fifth amendment protects the secured creditor only to the extent of value of the collateral, section 1225 withstands appellant's constitutional challenge.[7] Section 1225(a)(5) ensures that the creditor receives value not less than the amount of his allowed secured claim, i.e., the value of the collateral.

5. DOES CHAPTER 12 APPLY RETROACTIVELY?

Travelers also makes an argument that Chapter 12 should not apply to obligations existing before Congress enacted Chapter 12. Although we will not automatically give bankruptcy laws retroactive effect, *United States v. Security Industrial Bank,* 459 U.S. 70, 82, 103 S.Ct. 407, 414, 74 L.Ed.2d 235 (1982), where it is clear from the language or legislative history of a statute that Congress intended the law to apply retroactively then we must follow Congress's intent.

We have no doubt that Congress intended the provisions of Chapter 12 to apply to debts incurred before its enactment. Although Chapter 12 does not explicitly state that it is to be applied retroactively, any contrary view would render Chapter 12 a triviality. Chapter 12 was enacted as an emergency response to a then-existing farm debt crisis. As Judge Rosenbaum has noted:

> Congress intended the family farmer provisions to be novel, but short-lived. The statute by its terms expires after only seven years. 28 U.S.C. § 581 note. The short lifetime of Chapter 12 suited Congress' desire to 'evaluate both whether the chapter is serving its purpose and whether there is a continuing need for a special chapter for the family farmer.' H.R.Conf.R. at 48, USCCAN at 5249. Common sense suggests Congress was mindful of the farmer' existing loans when it set the seven year limitation.

Dahlke v. Doering, 94 B.R. 569 (D.Minn. 1989).

Accordingly, we reject appellants' statutory and constitutional challenges, and AFFIRM the order of the district court affirming the bankruptcy court's confirmation of the debtors' plan for reorganization.

---

1 In the course of the proceedings the plan was amended slightly, but none of the amendments have anything to do with this appeal.

[2] Section 1225 provides in part:

(a) Except as provided in subsection (b), the court shall confirm a plan if—

  (1) the plan complies with the provisions of this chapter and with the other applicable provisions of this title;

  (2) any fee, charge, or amount required under chapter 123 of title 28, or by the plan, to be paid before confirmation, has been paid;

  (3) the plan has been proposed in good faith and not by any means forbidden by law;

  (4) the value, as of the effective date of the plan, of property to be distributed under the plan on account of each allowed unsecured claim is not less than the amount that would be paid on such claim if the estate of the debtor were liquidated under chapter 7 of this title on such date

[3] The plan does call for the debtors to surrender the personal property collateral, but does not provide for them to forfeit the real property.

[4] Two district courts have addressed this issue, and in well-reasoned opinions have upheld Chapter 12 against constitutional challenges. *See Dahlke v. Doering,* 94 B.R. 569 (D.C.Minn.1989); *Albaugh v. Terrell,* 93 B.R. 115 (E.D. Mich.1988).

[5] § 506. Determination of secured status

(a) An allowed claim of a creditor secured by a lien on property in which the estate has an interest, or that is subject to setoff under section 553 of this title, is a secured claim to the extent of the value of such creditor's interest in the estate's interest in such property, or to the extent of the amount subject to setoff, as the case may be, and is an unsecured claim to the extent that the value of such creditor's interest or the amount so subject to setoff is less than the amount of such allowed claim. Such value shall be determined in light of the purpose of the valuation and of the proposed disposition or use of such property, and in conjunction with any hearing on such disposition or use or on a plan affecting such creditor's interest.

(b) To the extent that an allowed secured claim is secured by property the value of which, after any recovery under subsection (c) of this section, is greater than the amount of such claim, there shall be allowed to the holder of such claim, interest on such claim, and any reasonable fees, costs, or charges provided for under the agreement under which such claim arose.

(c) The trustee may recover from property securing an allowed secured claim the reasonable, necessary costs and expenses of preserving, or disposing of, such property to the extent of any benefit to the holder of such claim.

(d) To the extent that a lien secures a claim against the debtor that is not an allowed secured claim, such lien is void, unless—

(d)(1) such claim was disallowed only under section 502(b)(5) or 502(e) of this title; or

(d)(2) such claim is not an allowed secured claim due only to the failure of any entity to file a proof of such claim under section 501 of this title.

[6] "[T]he famous statement that the bankruptcy power is subject to the fifth amendment must be taken to mean nothing more than that the fifth amendment, through either the due process clause or the takings clause, is the constitutional foundation for the proposition that statutes that

retroactively disrupt settled expectations may be subject to particularly attentive judicial scrutiny." James S. Rogers, *The Impairment of Secured Creditors' Rights in Reorganization: A Study of the Relationship Between the Fifth Amendment and the Bankruptcy Clause,* 96 Harv.L.Rev. 973, 985 (1983).

[7] Such a rule is fully consistent with common sense. Had Travelers foreclosed on the farm property all it could have obtained would be the $475,000 stipulated value. Under Chapter 12, the reason Travelers may not recover the remaining amount of their claim is because the claim was undersecured.

The plan must be specific enough so that the trustee and the debtor know exactly who is to be paid, how much is to be paid, and when it is to be paid.

The **confirmation of the plan** binds the debtor, each creditor, each equity security holder, and each general partner in the debtor to the provisions of the confirmed plan, whether or not the claim is provided for by the plan and whether or not the party has objected to, accepted, or rejected the plan. 11 U.S.C.A. § 1227(a).

The confirmation of a plan vests all of the property of the estate in the debtor except as provided in section 1228(a), in the plan, or in the confirmation order. The property vested in the debtor is free and clear of any claim or interest of any creditor provided for by the plan. 11 U.S.C.A. §§ 1227(b), (c). This allows the debtor to use property not encumbered by the provisions of the plan as collateral for new loans. Although the court can deny confirmation on legal grounds, such as nonpayment of a fee, creditors may object on legal grounds but have no vote on the confirmation itself.

If the plan is confirmed, the trustee will distribute payments to the creditors in accordance with the plan. If the plan is not confirmed, the trustee will return the payments to the debtor, less any unpaid administrative expenses allowed under section 503(b) and the percentage fee fixed for a standing trustee, if a standing trustee is serving in the case. 11 U.S.C.A. § 1226(a).

If the plan is unconfirmable, the debtor may convert the case to Chapter 7 or may request the court to dismiss the case. 11 U.S.C.A. §§ 1208(a), (b). A party in interest may also request the court to dismiss the case. 11 U.S.C.A. § 1208(c)(5).

SECTION 9
MODIFICATION OF THE PLAN AFTER CONFIRMATION

At any time after the confirmation of the plan but before the completion of payments under the plan, the debtor, the trustee, or the holder of an allowed unsecured claim may request modification of the plan. The holder of a secured claim, however, may not request modification. The plan, upon notice and opportunity for a hearing, may be modified to increase or reduce the amount of payments on claims of a particular class provided for by the plan or to extend or reduce the time for such payments. The plan may also be modified to alter the amount of the distribution to a creditor provided for by the plan to the extent necessary to take into account any payment of such claim outside the plan. 11 U.S.C.A. § 1229(a).

In *In re Cooper,* the debtors' Chapter 12 plan, as amended, was confirmed on December 14, 1987. The plan provided for payments of $57,050 to unsecured creditors over the life of the plan. This amount represented the liquidation value of the debtors' unencumbered farm machinery and equipment as of November 1, 1987.

On May 6, 1988, the debtors filed an amendment to their plan in which they proposed to reduce the payments to unsecured creditors to $34,150 because the liquidation value of the debtors' unsecured farm machinery and equipment was only $34,150 as of the time of the proposed modification. The trustee objected on the ground that the liquidation value should not be reevaluated. The court needed to decide whether the unsecured farm machinery and equipment should be reevaluated as of the time of the proposed modification and how this modification would affect the unsecured creditors and their reliance on the confirmed plan.

In re Cooper
United States Bankruptcy Court, Southern District of Illinois, 1989.
94 B.R. 550.

MEMORANDUM AND ORDER
Kenneth J. Meyers,
Bankruptcy Judge

Debtors, Robert and Phyllis Cooper, filed a Chapter 12 bankruptcy petition on December 12, 1986, and filed their original plan of reorganization on March 12, 1987. They subsequently filed a first amendment to their plan on September 14, 1987, and a second amendment on October 13, 1987. On November 24, 1987, debtors filed a third amendment to their plan of reorganization, which was confirmed by order of the Court on December 14, 1987.

Debtors' plan as confirmed provides for payments to unsecured creditors over the life of the plan in the amount of $57,050. This amount represents the liquidation value of debtors' unencumbered farm machinery and equipment as of November 1, 1987. The plan defines the effective date of the plan as the "date the order confirming the plan becomes final and non-appealable," which was assumed to be November 1, 1987, in debtors' liquidation analysis.

On May 6, 1988, debtors filed a fourth amendment to their plan in which they seek to modify the confirmed plan of reorganization with regard to the treatment of unsecured claims. By this amendment, debtors propose to sell a portion of the farm machinery and equipment and to distribute the proceeds to unsecured creditors, after payment of trustee fees and unpaid attorney's fees. The amendment further proposes to reduce the amount of the yearly payments to unsecured creditors.

The trustee has filed two objections to debtors' proposed amendment, one of which—regarding the amount of trustee's fees to be paid under the amendment—has been settled. The trustee's remaining objection is that the amendment proposes to pay unsecured creditors $34,150 over the life of the plan, which is less than the liquidation value of $57,050 provided in the confirmed plan. The trustee prays that the plan as modified provide for total payments of $57,050 to unsecured creditors so as to comply with § 1225(a)(4), which requires that unsecured creditors receive at least as much under a Chapter 12 plan as they would receive in a Chapter 7 liquidation.[1]

In response to the trustee's objection, debtors state that the value of their unencumbered farm machinery and equipment is less than that set forth in their original liquidation analysis of November 1987 and assert that this lesser value should control in determining whether the proposed modification to their plan complies with the liquidation test of § 1225(a)(4). Debtors maintain that the appropriate time for determining the liquidation value of unencumbered assets in a post-confirmation modification is the time of the proposed modification rather than the time the original plan became effective. Debtors contend, therefore, that their modified plan should be approved over the trustee's objection because it proposes to pay unsecured creditors the value of unencumbered assets as of the date of their modified plan.

At hearing on the trustee's objection, debtors informed the court that the $57,050 liquidation value ascribed to their unencumbered farm machinery and equipment in November 1987 was an inflated value based on debtors' own estimates. Debtors have since obtained professional appraisals of this equipment in preparing to sell part of the equipment in order to reduce their farming operation. The liquidation value based on these appraisals is less than that originally estimated, and debtors assert that they are only required to pay the revised value of $34,150 over the life of the plan in order to comply with the confirmation standard of § 1225(a)(4).

Section 1229, dealing with modification of a Chapter 12 plan after confirmation, provides in pertinent part

> (a) At any time after confirmation of the plan but before the completion of payments under such plan, the plan may be modified . . . to—
> > (1) increase or reduce the amount of payments on claims of a particular class provided for by the plan; . . .
> (b) (2) The plan as modified becomes the plan unless, after notice and hearing, such modification is disapproved.

11 U.S.C. § 1229.

Post-confirmation modification under Chapter 12, as under Chapter 13, is intended as a method of addressing unforeseen difficulties that arise during plan administration, and such modification is warranted only when an unanticipated change in circumstances affects implementation of the plan as confirmed. *Matter of Grogg Farms, Inc.,* 91 B.R. 482 (Bankr.N.D.Ind.1988); *In re Dittmer,* 82 B.R. 1019 (Bankr.D.N.D.1988). A debtor seeking to modify a confirmed Chapter 12 plan under § 1229 has the burden of proving that the modifications meet the confirmation requirements. *In re Hart,* 90 B.R. 150 (Bankr.E.D.N.C.1988). Absent a modification under § 1229, the provisions of a confirmed Chapter 12 plan are binding on both the debtor and his creditors. *See* 11 U.S.C. § 1227(a); *In re Grogg Farms, Inc.*

Debtors have cited no authority, and the Court has found none, in which modification of a Chapter 12 plan was allowed based on a lesser liquidation value than existed at

the time of confirmation. Debtors, observing that a modified plan replaces the original plan, assert that modification has the effect of creating a new "effective date of the plan" as of which debtors' estate is to be valued to determine compliance with § 1225(a)(4). The court, however, need not reach this issue under the facts of the instant case. By debtors' own admission, there has been no change in the value of their unencumbered assets in the few months since confirmation. Rather, debtors have determined that their original estimate of value in the liquidation analysis of their confirmed plan was not accurate. While debtors seek to be relieved of the consequences of their mistaken valuation, it would be contrary to the purpose of § 1229 to allow debtors to change a term of their confirmed plan that could have and should have been properly determined at the time of confirmation. *Cf. In re Grogg Farms, Inc.*: confirmation is *res judicata* as to those issues which could and should have been raised prior to or in connection with confirmation.

In considering debtors' proposal to decrease the amount of payments to unsecured creditors, the Court must be aware of the legitimate expectations of the parties to the confirmed plan and the need for finality in determining their rights and duties. *See In re Grogg Farms, Inc.* Once debtors' Chapter 12 plan was confirmed, their creditors could rightfully expect that the new contractual arrangement represented by the plan would be complied with. Absent some unforeseen difficulty leading to debtors' inability to fulfill their obligations under the plan, the plan should be implemented as agreed. The Court finds, therefore, that debtors' proposed modification to their plan providing for payment to unsecured creditors in the amount of $34,150 over the life of the plan fails to comply with § 1225(a)(4) and cannot be approved as proposed.

At hearing, debtors stated that if the Court should find that the payments to unsecured creditors under their proposed fourth amendment to the plan were insufficient, the trustee and debtors have agreed that debtors would increase these payments by $4,500 per year in order to give the unsecured creditors the equivalent of the liquidation value of debtors' equipment as of November 1, 1987. Based upon this representation, the Court will approve debtors' proposed fourth amendment to allow debtors to sell a portion of their farm machinery and equipment and to distribute the proceeds pro rata to unsecured creditors after payment of trustee and attorney's fees. The amount of the trustee's fee to be paid from the sale proceeds is $2,300, as agreed at the time of hearing.

IT IS ORDERED, therefore, that debtors' fourth amendment to their Chapter 12 plan is APPROVED as modified by the agreement between the trustee and debtors regarding payments to unsecured creditors and the amount of the trustee's fee.

---

[1]Section 1225(a)(4)provides

(a) . . . [T]he court shall confirm a plan if—

(4) the value, as of the effective date of the plan, of property to be distributed under the plan on account of each allowed unsecured claim is not less than the amount that would be paid on such claim if the estate of the debtor were liquidated under Chapter 7 of this title on such date.

This requirement is made applicable to postconfirmation modifications by 11 U.S.C. § 1229(b)(1).

SECTION 10
REVOCATION OF ORDER OF CONFIRMATION, CONVERSION, OR DISMISSAL

Upon request of a party in interest, the court may revoke an order for confirmation if the order was procured by fraud. The revocation must occur within 180 days after the order for confirmation and must follow notice and a hearing. 11 U.S.C.A. § 1230(a). The case in which an order for confirmation has been revoked will be dismissed pursuant to section 1208(c)(7), unless within the time fixed by the court the debtor proposes a modification of the plan which is confirmed by the court. 11 U.S.C.A. § 1230(b). A case under Chapter 12 may be converted to Chapter 7 or dismissed upon request of a party in interest only after notice and a hearing to show that the debtor has committed fraud in connection with the case. This is the only provision in the Code that allows for the involuntary liquidation of a farmer's assets. 11 U.S.C.A. § 1208(d).

SECTION 11
DISCHARGE

After the completion of payments under the plan, the debtor receives a discharge. The debtor will not be discharged from allowed claims, secured or unsecured, that were not provided for by the plan, from any debt for the curing of any default on any secured or unsecured claim on which the final payment is due after the proposed final payment under the plan, or from the nondischargeable debts listed in section 523(a). 11 U.S.C.A. § 1228(a).

The court may grant what is called a **hardship** or **compassionate discharge** to a debtor who has not completed payments under the plan. This type of discharge is granted only if the debtor's failure to complete the payments is due to circumstances for which the debtor should not justly be held responsible, the payments to creditors would not be less than they would have received if the debtor's estate had been liquidated under Chapter 7, and modification of the plan is not practicable. 11 U.S.C.A. § 1228(b).

The debtor under a hardship discharge will not be discharged from any allowed secured claims, from allowed unsecured claims that were not provided for by the plan, from any debt for the curing of any default on any secured or unsecured claim on which the final payment is due after the proposed final payment under the plan, or from any nondischargeable claims under section 523(a). 11 U.S.C.A. § 1228(c). Therefore, the effect of a hardship discharge is that the debtor will not be discharged from any secured debts or from unsecured debts not provided for by the plan or that would be nondischargeable under Chapter 7.

A debtor who has received either a full-compliance or a hardship discharge cannot receive a discharge in a Chapter 7 case filed within six years of the date of the Chapter 12 filing, unless payments under the Chapter 12 plan totaled 100 percent of the allowed unsecured claims, or payments under the Chapter 12 plan totaled 70 percent of the allowed unsecured claims and the Chapter 12 plan was proposed by the debtor in good faith and was the debtor's best effort. 11 U.S.C.A. § 727(a)(9). A debtor who has received a discharge in a Chapter 12 case is not foreclosed from filing another Chapter 12 case or a Chapter 11 case or a Chapter 13 case at any time if the debtor is otherwise eligible to file under these chapters.

SECTION 12
REVOCATION OF THE DISCHARGE

A party in interest may request revocation of the discharge for fraud within one year after the discharge is granted if this party did not know about the fraud until after the discharge was granted. 11 U.S.C.A. § 1228(d).

SECTION 13
CLOSING THE CASE AND AFTER THE CASE IS CLOSED

Upon the completion of payments under the plan and the discharge of the debtor, the trustee files a final report and account, certifying that the case has been fully administered. There is a presumption that the case has been fully administered unless the United States trustee files an objection within 30 days. If no objection is filed, the court may discharge the trustee and close the case without reviewing the final report and account. 11 U.S.C.A. § 350(a); Fed. R. Bank. P. 5009.

Even after the case is closed, it is still subject to further action. In certain situations, a case may be amended without being reopened. Clerical errors in judgments, orders, and other parts of the record or errors in the record caused by oversight or omission may be corrected. A closed case may be reopened to add a creditor or to distribute previously undistributed property of the estate. 11 U.S.C.A. § 350(b).

BASIC TERMS AND PHRASES

Adequate protection
Avoid a lien
Best interests of creditors test
Chapter 12 cramdown
Chapter 12 plan
Chapter 12 trustee
Codebtor stay
Confirmation of the plan
Debtor in possession (DIP)
Family farmer

Farming operations
Good faith
Hardship (compassionate) discharge
Hearing on confirmation of the plan
Judicial lien
Mandatory provisions
Nonpossessory, nonpurchase money
    security interest
Permissive provisions

The Voluntary Chapter 11 Bankruptcy (Reorganization)

SECTION 9
A DISCLOSURE STATEMENT OR EVIDENCE SHOWING COMPLIANCE WITH 11 U.S.C.A. § 1126(B)

SECTION 10
HEARING ON THE DISCLOSURE STATEMENT

SECTION 11
HEARING ON CONFIRMATION OF THE PLAN

SECTION 12
EFFECT OF CONFIRMATION OF THE PLAN

SECTION 13
DISTRIBUTION UNDER THE PLAN AND REPORTING BY DEBTOR IN POSSESSION OR CHAPTER 11 TRUSTEE

SECTION 14
REVOCATION OF AN ORDER OF CONFIRMATION

SECTION 15
FINAL DECREE

The voluntary Chapter 11 bankruptcy, called **reorganization,** is covered in this chapter. Not all debtors may file a Chapter 11 petition. A person that may proceed under Chapter 7 may be a debtor under Chapter 11, with two exceptions. Stockbrokers and commodity brokers cannot proceed under Chapter 11, although they can proceed under Chapter 7. Railroads, which are excluded from Chapter 7, may file under Chapter 11.

The complex nature of a Chapter 11 proceeding has always presented an obstacle for small businesses seeking reorganization. A provision of the Bankruptcy Reform Act of 1994 should encourage the filing of more Chapter 11 small business cases. A "small business" can elect the "fast track" Chapter 11 provision. 11 U.S.C.A. § 1121(e). A "small business" is defined as

> a person engaged in commercial or business activities (but does not include a person whose primary activity is the business of owning or operating real property and activities incidental thereto) whose aggregate noncontingent liquidated secured and unsecured debts as of the date of the petition do not exceed $2,000,000 . . . . 11 U.S.C.A. § 101(51C).

The 1994 Bankruptcy Reform Act allows the court to *conditionally* approve a disclosure statement that will be subject to final approval after notice and hearing. 11 U.S.C.A. § 1125(f). The court may also hold a combined hearing on disclosure statement approval and plan confirmation. Any party in interest in a small business case may request that a committee of creditors not be appointed. 11 U.S.C.A. § 1102(a)(3).

The Bankruptcy Reform Act of 1994 provides for some changes in the Bankruptcy Rules that affect Chapter 11 cases. Because there will be a delay in incorporating these changes, the Bankruptcy Rules Advisory Committee has suggested interim local rules to cover small business reorganizations, election of a trustee, and jury trials. The paralegal should consult local bankruptcy court rules in such cases.

The chronological order of a Chapter 11 case is not as fixed as that of the Chapter 7 case because of the more complex nature of the proceedings in a Chapter

11. For example, the reorganization plan may be filed along with the petition or at a much later time. The petition and other documents necessary in a Chapter 11 case are described in this chapter. Possession and control of the property of the estate, operation of the debtor's business, evidence of debtor in possession status along with the form constituting this evidence, and exemptions are covered. This material encompasses the area in which many of the battles are fought in Chapter 11 cases. The ultimate success of a reorganization case will hinge upon the debtor's ability to utilize the Code sections discussed here.

The appointment of committees and their powers and duties are covered. Motions and complaints are discussed.

Material on the order and notice of the Chapter 11 filing, meeting of creditors, and fixing of dates is presented. The meetings of creditors and of equity security holders are described.

Some of the strategies often used in a Chapter 11 plan and the contents of the plan filed by the debtor are included. The Chapter 11 plan filed by parties other than the debtor is also discussed. The requirements for the disclosure statement and the hearing on the disclosure statement are described.

The hearing on confirmation of the plan and the effect of confirmation of the plan, including discharge, are set forth. There are brief discussions of distribution under the plan and of reporting requirements for the debtor in possession or the trustee. Revocation of an order of confirmation is covered as is the final decree. Exhibit 8.1 presents a "road map" for this chapter.

EXHIBIT 8.1
Chapter 11 Reorganization (Voluntary Petition)

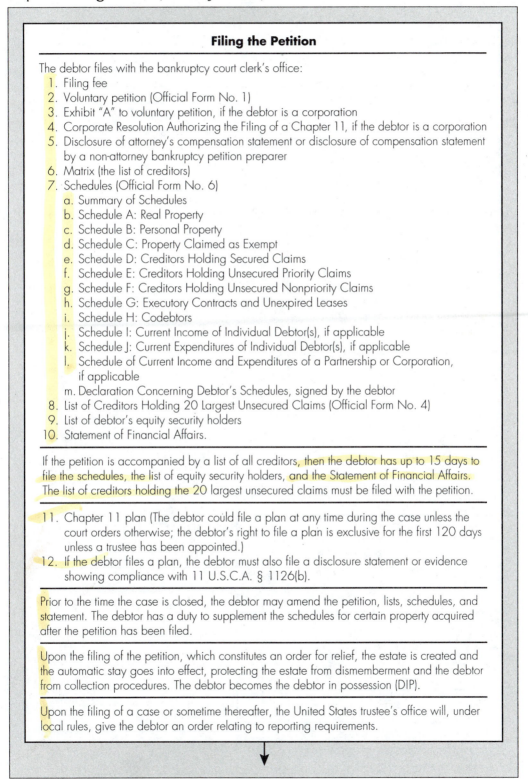

Filing the Petition

The debtor files with the bankruptcy court clerk's office:
1. Filing fee
2. Voluntary petition (Official Form No. 1)
3. Exhibit "A" to voluntary petition, if the debtor is a corporation
4. Corporate Resolution Authorizing the Filing of a Chapter 11, if the debtor is a corporation
5. Disclosure of attorney's compensation statement or disclosure of compensation statement by a non-attorney bankruptcy petition preparer
6. Matrix (the list of creditors)
7. Schedules (Official Form No. 6)
   a. Summary of Schedules
   b. Schedule A: Real Property
   c. Schedule B: Personal Property
   d. Schedule C: Property Claimed as Exempt
   e. Schedule D: Creditors Holding Secured Claims
   f. Schedule E: Creditors Holding Unsecured Priority Claims
   g. Schedule F: Creditors Holding Unsecured Nonpriority Claims
   h. Schedule G: Executory Contracts and Unexpired Leases
   i. Schedule H: Codebtors
   j. Schedule I: Current Income of Individual Debtor(s), if applicable
   k. Schedule J: Current Expenditures of Individual Debtor(s), if applicable
   l. Schedule of Current Income and Expenditures of a Partnership or Corporation, if applicable
   m. Declaration Concerning Debtor's Schedules, signed by the debtor
8. List of Creditors Holding 20 Largest Unsecured Claims (Official Form No. 4)
9. List of debtor's equity security holders
10. Statement of Financial Affairs.

If the petition is accompanied by a list of all creditors, then the debtor has up to 15 days to file the schedules, the list of equity security holders, and the Statement of Financial Affairs. The list of creditors holding the 20 largest unsecured claims must be filed with the petition.

11. Chapter 11 plan (The debtor could file a plan at any time during the case unless the court orders otherwise; the debtor's right to file a plan is exclusive for the first 120 days unless a trustee has been appointed.)
12. If the debtor files a plan, the debtor must also file a disclosure statement or evidence showing compliance with 11 U.S.C.A. § 1126(b).

Prior to the time the case is closed, the debtor may amend the petition, lists, schedules, and statement. The debtor has a duty to supplement the schedules for certain property acquired after the petition has been filed.

Upon the filing of the petition, which constitutes an order for relief, the estate is created and the automatic stay goes into effect, protecting the estate from dismemberment and the debtor from collection procedures. The debtor becomes the debtor in possession (DIP).

Upon the filing of a case or sometime thereafter, the United States trustee's office will, under local rules, give the debtor an order relating to reporting requirements.

EXHIBIT 8.1
Continued

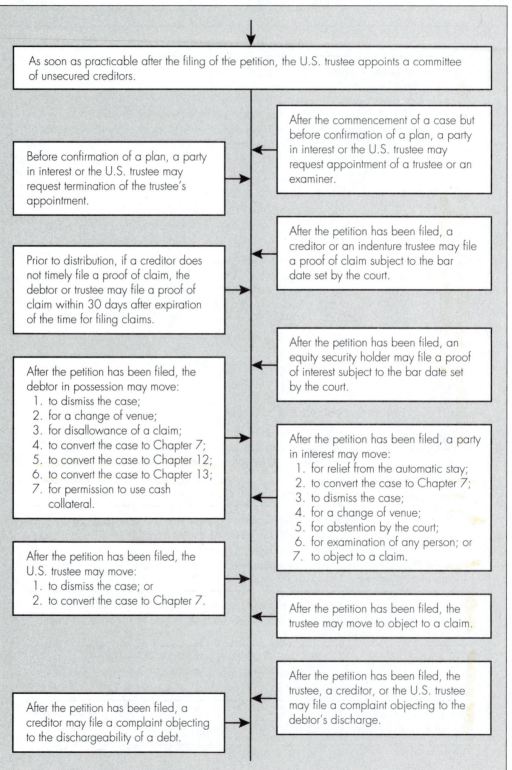

EXHIBIT 8.1
Continued

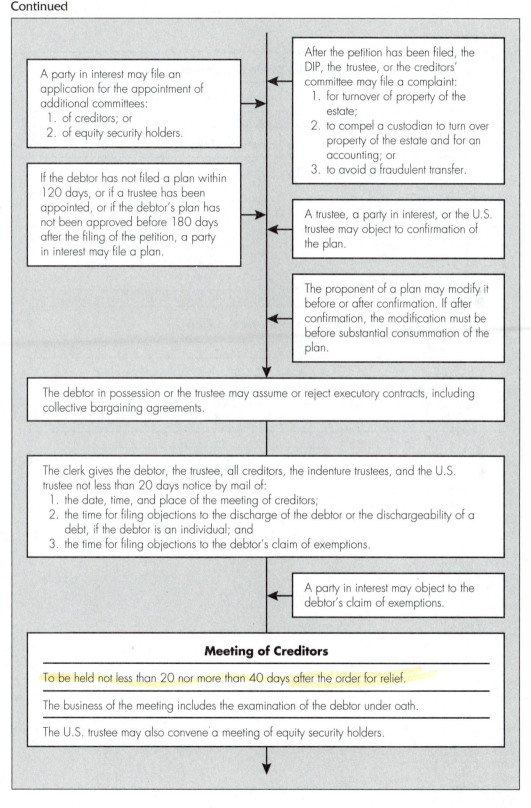

A party in interest may file an application for the appointment of additional committees:
1. of creditors; or
2. of equity security holders.

If the debtor has not filed a plan within 120 days, or if a trustee has been appointed, or if the debtor's plan has not been approved before 180 days after the filing of the petition, a party in interest may file a plan.

After the petition has been filed, the DIP, the trustee, or the creditors' committee may file a complaint:
1. for turnover of property of the estate;
2. to compel a custodian to turn over property of the estate and for an accounting; or
3. to avoid a fraudulent transfer.

A trustee, a party in interest, or the U.S. trustee may object to confirmation of the plan.

The proponent of a plan may modify it before or after confirmation. If after confirmation, the modification must be before substantial consummation of the plan.

The debtor in possession or the trustee may assume or reject executory contracts, including collective bargaining agreements.

The clerk gives the debtor, the trustee, all creditors, the indenture trustees, and the U.S. trustee not less than 20 days notice by mail of:
1. the date, time, and place of the meeting of creditors;
2. the time for filing objections to the discharge of the debtor or the dischargeability of a debt, if the debtor is an individual; and
3. the time for filing objections to the debtor's claim of exemptions.

A party in interest may object to the debtor's claim of exemptions.

Meeting of Creditors

To be held not less than 20 nor more than 40 days after the order for relief.

The business of the meeting includes the examination of the debtor under oath.

The U.S. trustee may also convene a meeting of equity security holders.

EXHIBIT 8.1
Continued

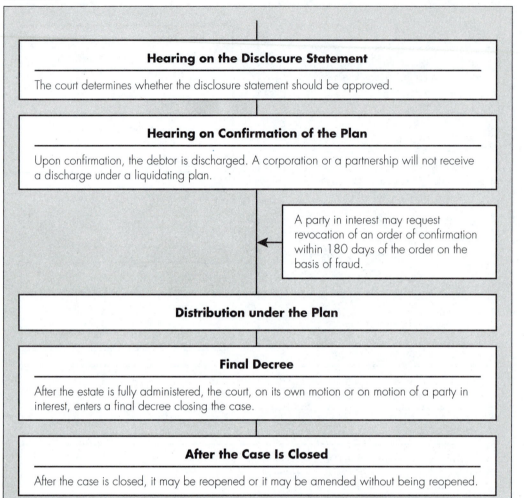

Hearing on the Disclosure Statement

The court determines whether the disclosure statement should be approved.

Hearing on Confirmation of the Plan

Upon confirmation, the debtor is discharged. A corporation or a partnership will not receive a discharge under a liquidating plan.

A party in interest may request revocation of an order of confirmation within 180 days of the order on the basis of fraud.

Distribution under the Plan

Final Decree

After the estate is fully administered, the court, on its own motion or on motion of a party in interest, enters a final decree closing the case.

After the Case Is Closed

After the case is closed, it may be reopened or it may be amended without being reopened.

SECTION 1
THE FILING OF THE PETITION

The same documents necessary for the filing of the petition in a voluntary Chapter 7 case are also necessary in a voluntary Chapter 11 case, with the exceptions of the clerk's notice and a statement of intention, both of which are required in a Chapter 7 case if the debtor is an individual with consumer debts. A Chapter 11 filing also requires Exhibit "A" to the voluntary petition if the debtor is a corporation, a list of the debtor's 20 largest unsecured creditors, a list of equity security holders, a Chapter 11 plan, and a disclosure statement. Therefore, the filing of a voluntary Chapter 11 case requires the following items:

1. Filing fee;
2. Voluntary Petition (Official Form No. 1);
3. Exhibit "A" to voluntary petition, if the debtor is a corporation;
4. Corporate resolution authorizing the filing of a Chapter 11, if the debtor is a corporation;
5. Disclosure of attorney's compensation statement or disclosure of compensation statement by a non-attorney bankruptcy petition preparer;
6. Matrix (the list of creditors);
7. Schedules (Official Form No. 6)
   a. Summary of Schedules
   b. Schedule A: Real Property
   c. Schedule B: Personal Property
   d. Schedule C: Property Claimed as Exempt
   e. Schedule D: Creditors Holding Secured Claims
   f. Schedule E: Creditors Holding Unsecured Priority Claims
   g. Schedule F: Creditors Holding Unsecured Nonpriority Claims
   h. Schedule G: Executory Contracts and Unexpired Leases
   i. Schedule H: Codebtors
   j. Schedule I: Current Income of Individual Debtor(s), if applicable
   k. Schedule J: Current Expenditures of Individual Debtor(s), if applicable
   l. Schedule of Current Income and Expenditures of a Partnership or Corporation, if applicable
   m. Declaration Concerning Debtor's Schedules, signed by the debtor(s);
8. List of Creditors Holding 20 Largest Unsecured Claims (Official Form No. 4);
9. List of debtor's equity security holders;
10. Statement of Financial Affairs;
11. Chapter 11 plan; and
12. Disclosure statement or evidence showing compliance with 11 U.S.C.A. § 1126(b).

If the debtor is a corporation filing under Chapter 11, Exhibit "A" to the voluntary petition must be completed and attached to the petition. (See Exhibit 8.2.)

EXHIBIT 8.2
Exhibit "A" to the Voluntary Petition (Official Form No. 1, Exhibit "A")

Form B1XA
6/90

UNITED STATES BANKRUPTCY COURT
_____ DISTRICT OF _____

In re _____ ,
        Debtor

Case No. _____

Chapter _____

Exhibit "A" to Voluntary Petition

1. Debtor's employer identification number is _____ .

2. If any of debtor's securities are registered under section 12 of the Securities and Exchange Act of 1934, the SEC file number is _____ .

3. The following financial data is the latest available information and refers to debtor's condition on _____ .

		Approximate number of holders
a. Total assets	$ _____	
b. Total liabilities	$ _____	
Fixed, liquidated secured debt	$ _____	_____
Contingent secured debt	$ _____	_____
Disputed secured claims	$ _____	_____
Unliquidated secured debt	$ _____	_____

EXHIBIT 8.2
Continued

Exhibit "A" continued

		Approximate number of holders
Fixed, liquidated unsecured debt	$ _____	_____
Contingent unsecured debt	$ _____	_____
Disputed unsecured claims	$ _____	_____
Unliquidated unsecured debt	$ _____	_____
Number of shares of preferred stock	_____	_____
Number of shares of common stock	_____	_____

Comments, if any: _____
_____
_____
_____

4. Brief description of debtor's business: _____
_____
_____

5. List the name of any person who directly or indirectly owns, controls, or holds, with power to vote, 20% or more of the voting securities of debtor: _____
_____
_____
_____

6. List the names of all corporations 20% or more of the outstanding voting securities of which are directly or indirectly owned, controlled, or held, with power to vote, by debtor: _____
_____
_____
_____

Not all of these documents must be filed at once. If the petition is accompanied by the list of creditors, the debtor has up to 15 days from the date of the filing of the petition to file the schedules, a statement of financial affairs, and a list of the debtor's equity security holders.

In a Chapter 11 case, as in a Chapter 7 case, the debtor has a duty to supplement the schedules. A supplemental schedule is not necessary, however, in a Chapter 11 case for property acquired after the order confirming the plan has been entered. Fed. R. Bank. P. 1007(h). A Chapter 11 debtor also has a right to amend the petition, lists, schedules, and statement of financial affairs. Fed. R. Bank. P. 1009(a).

The List of Creditors Holding the 20 Largest Unsecured Claims (Official Form No. 4) is required to enable the United States trustee to appoint a committee of unsecured creditors. (See Exhibit 8.3.) The information concerning each creditor expedites the formation of the committee and assures adequate creditor representation. 11 U.S.C.A. § 1102; Fed. R. Bank. P. 1007(d).

EXHIBIT 8.3
Official Form No. 4 (List of Creditors Holding 20 Largest Unsecured Claims)

Form B4
11/92

UNITED STATES BANKRUPTCY COURT
_____ DISTRICT OF _____

In re _____,
         Debtor

Case No. _____

Chapter _____

LIST OF CREDITORS HOLDING 20 LARGEST UNSECURED CLAIMS

Following is the list of the debtor's creditors holding the 20 largest unsecured claims. The list is prepared in accordance with Fed. R. Bankr. P. 1007(d) for filing in this chapter 11 [or chapter 9] case. The list does not include (1) persons who come within the definition of "insider" set forth in 11 U.S.C. § 101, or (2) secured creditors unless the value of the collateral is such that the unsecured deficiency places the creditor among the holders of the 20 largest unsecured claims.

(1)	(2)	(3)	(4)	(5)
Name of creditor and complete mailing address including zip code	_Name, telephone number and complete mailing address, including zip code, of employee, agent, or department of creditor familiar with claim who may be contacted_	_Nature of claim (trade debt, bank loan, government contract, etc.)_	_Indicate if claim is contingent, unliquidated, disputed or subject to setoff_	_Amount of claim [if secured also state value of security]_
A	**B**	**C**	**D**	**E**

Date: _____

F
_____
Debtor

I, [the president _or_ other officer _or_ an authorized agent of the corporation] [_or_ a member _or_ an authorized agent of the partnership] named as the debtor in this case, declare under penalty of perjury that I have read the foregoing [list _or_ schedule _or_ amendment _or_ other document (describe)] and that it is true and correct to the best of my information and belief.

Date _____

Signature _____

_____
(Print Name and Title)

Instructions for Completing Official Form No. 4
(List of Creditors Holding the 20 Largest Unsecured Claims)

The **List of Creditors Holding the 20 Largest Unsecured Claims** should not include insiders. Insiders include persons who are related to the debtor, such as relatives, partners, directors, officers, affiliates, or others in control of the debtor. See 11 U.S.C.A. § 101 (31). A creditor holding a secured claim can be listed only if the claim is undersecured and the unsecured portion of the claim would place it among the 20 largest unsecured claims.

A State the name of each of the debtor's creditors holding the 20 largest unsecured claims. State the creditor's complete name and complete mailing address, including zip code. Although the form does not call for a telephone number, a telephone number for each creditor would be helpful.

B For each creditor listed in "A," state the name, telephone number, and complete mailing address, including zip code, of the employee, agent, or department of the creditor familiar with the claim. This information must be complete so the U.S. trustee's office can find the creditors for the creditors' committee.

C State the nature of the claim.

Example: Trade debt for merchadise or supplies
      purchase of computers
      purchase of inventory
   Institutional debt
      bank loan
   Debt based on a judgment
      money judgment from negligence action
      money judgement for breach of contract
   Debt for services
      installation of fence
      maintenance contract
      security services
      repairs to the company's automobile fleet

D Indicate if the claim is contingent, unliquidated, disputed, or subject to setoff. If the claim is not, state "no."

E State the amount of the claim. If the claim is secured, also state the value of the security.

Example: $50,000 claim
      secured by present
      and after-acquired
      equipment valued
      at $40,000

F Have the debtor sign and date the form. The debtor's name should appear as it appears on the petition.

Although there is no official form for the **list of equity security holders,** the list enables the United States trustee to appoint a committee of equity security holders. (See Exhibit 8.4.) An **equity security holder** is a holder of an equity security of the debtor. 11 U.S.C.A. § 101(17). Equity security is defined as

1. the share in a corporation, whether or not transferable or denominated "stock," or a similar security;

2. an interest of a limited partner in a limited partnership; or
3. a warrant or a right, other than a right to convert, to purchase, sell, or subscribe to a share, security, or interest of a kind previously specified. 11 U.S.C.A. § 101(16).

Therefore, the two most common holders of equity security are stockholders of a corporation and limited partners of a partnership.

Rule 1007(3) requires the debtor to file a list of the debtor's equity security holders within 15 days after entry of the order for relief. The list must contain

1. the name of each holder;
2. the last known address or place of business of each holder;
3. the kind of interest registered in the name of each holder; and
4. the number of interests registered in the name of each holder.

See also 11 U.S.C.A. § 1102.

EXHIBIT 8.4
List of Equity Security Holders

UNITED STATES BANKRUPTCY COURT
_____ **DISTRICT OF** _____

In re _____ ,
                Debtor   Case No. _____

                                          Chapter _____

LIST OF EQUITY SECURITY HOLDERS

The following list of the debtor's equity security holders is prepared in accordance with Fed. R. Bank. P. 1007(a)(3) for filing in this Chapter 11 case.

(1) Name of equity security holder and complete mailing address, including zip code	(2) Kind of interest registered in the name of each holder	(3) Number of shares or percentage of ownership	(4) Par value, if applicable
A	**B**		

Date: _____   _____
                                        Debtor

If completed by an individual debtor, or husband and wife filing a joint petition, use the following sworn declaration.

I declare under penalty of perjury that I have read the answers contained in the foregoing list of equity security holders and any attachments thereto and that they are true and correct.

_____   _____
Date   Signature of Debtor

_____   _____
Date   Signature of Joint Debtor (if any)

If completed on behalf of a partnership or corporation, use the following sworn declaration.

I declare under penalty of perjury that I have read the answers contained in the foregoing list of equity security holders and any attachments thereto and that they are true and correct to the best of my knowledge, information, and belief.

_____   _____
Date   Signature

                              _____
                              Print Name

                              _____
                              Title   **C**

Instructions for Completing List of Equity Security Holders

The list of the debtor's equity security holders can be derived from the Debtor-Client Questionnaire and the Statement of Financial Affairs (Official Form No.7). Equity security holders who are limited partners will be listed in the Debtor-Client Questionnaire § VII, question 19.a, and in the Statement of Financial Affairs, question 19.a. Equity security holders who hold 5 percent or more of the voting securities of the corporation will be listed in the Debtor-Client Questionnaire § VII, question 19.b, and in the Statement of Financial Affairs, question 19.b. Equity security holders holding less than 5 percent of the voting securities are listed in the Debtor-Client Questionnaire § VII, question 19.c.

A State the name of equity security holder and complete mailing address, including zip code. The address should be the last known address or place of business of the equity security holder.

B Identify the kind of interest registered in the name of each holder.

Examples: limited partner
preferred stock
common stock

C An individual signing on behalf of a partnership or a corporation must indicate his or her position or relationship to the debtor.

SECTION 2
THE SIGNIFICANCE OF FILING A PETITION

The significance of filing a petition under Chapter 11 is similar in many ways to the significance of filing a petition under Chapter 7. The filing of the case constitutes an order for relief, bringing the automatic stay into effect and creating the bankruptcy estate.

A. POSSESSION AND CONTROL OF THE PROPERTY OF THE ESTATE

The main difference between filing a voluntary Chapter 7 case and filing a voluntary Chapter 11 case lies in possession and control of the property of the estate. The debtor in a Chapter 11 case is called the **debtor in possession** (better known by the abbreviation **DIP** and pronounced D I P) because the debtor retains possession of the property of the estate rather than turning it over to a trustee. Although a trustee may be appointed in a Chapter 11 case, the Code contemplates that the DIP will serve as a trustee would serve. It should be noted that the word "trustee" as used in Chapter 11 of the Code is to be read as debtor in possession *or* trustee.

The DIP has the rights, powers, and duties of a **Chapter 11 trustee** except the right to compensation and the duty to investigate the acts, conduct, assets, liabilities, and financial condition of the debtor. 11 U.S.C.A. §§ 1106(a)(3), (4), 1107(a). The DIP has the powers of a trustee to avoid preferences and fraudulent transfers and to assume or reject executory contracts. There is now a two-year statute of limitations, running from the date of the order for relief, on the trustee's avoidance powers. 11 U.S.C.A. § 546(a)(1)(A). A trustee elected or appointed before expiration of the two-year period specified in subparagraph (A) has only one year to begin an avoidance action or proceeding. 11 U.S.C.A. § 546(a)(1)(B).

One important duty of a DIP is to file quarterly reports of disbursements made and a statement of the amount of the fee required by 28 U.S.C.A. § 1930(a)(6) that has been paid. The reports are filed and transmitted to the United States trustee on or before the last day of the month after each calendar quarter and continue until the plan is confirmed or until the case is dismissed or converted. Fed. R. Bank. P. 2015(a)(5).

B. OPERATION OF THE DEBTOR'S BUSINESS

Unless the court orders otherwise, the DIP continues to operate the debtor's business. 11 U.S.C.A. § 1108. Permitting a business to continue operations allows parties to deal with it as an ongoing business. Any significant period of shutdown might destroy any possible option to pursue a plan for continuing the business.

Several Code provisions figure prominently in the Chapter 11 debtor's powers to remain in control of the property of the estate and continue its business. Adequate protection of the interest of the creditor in property of the estate as required under section 361 plays an important part in section 362 (automatic stay), section 363 (use, sale, and lease of property), and section 364 (obtaining credit). Section 365 (executory contracts and unexpired leases) may make or break a Chapter 11 reorganization. Section 366 (utility service) allows the debtor to obtain utilities necessary for everyday operations.

1. ADEQUATE PROTECTION

Adequate protection is a concept used in bankruptcy law to protect an entity's interest in the property of the estate when the automatic stay goes into effect. A change made by the Bankruptcy Reform Act of 1994 states that the concept of adequate protection also applies to personal property that is leased. 11 U.S.C.A. § 363(e). Unsecured creditors do not receive this protection, but secured creditors are protected. This balances the interests of the debtor and its creditors. The debtor could not remain in business and reorganize if its creditors were not stayed from taking their property when the Chapter 11 bankruptcy petition was filed. It would be unfair to the creditors, however, to allow their property interests to be diminished or destroyed by the debtor's use with no protection. Adequate protection may be provided by a cash payment or periodic payments, an additional or replacement lien, or such other relief as would constitute the **indubitable equivalent** of the entity's interest in the property. 11 U.S.C.A. § 361.

2. USE, SALE, AND LEASE OF PROPERTY

The use, sale, and lease of property enables the DIP to operate its business. An important component of this power concerns the use of cash collateral. Cash collateral means cash, negotiable instruments, documents of title, securities, deposit accounts, or other cash equivalents in which the estate and an entity other than the estate have an interest. One of the debtor in possession's first acts will be to move for court permission to use cash collateral. Without use of cash collateral, the debtor may be unable to operate. Therefore, this motion is often filed along with the petition. If the DIP has obtained court permission to use cash collateral, this power will continue over to the trustee if, for any reason, a trustee is appointed to take over operation of the debtor's business.

3. OBTAINING CREDIT

The DIP or the trustee authorized to operate the business of the debtor may obtain unsecured credit and incur unsecured debt in the ordinary course of business unless the court orders otherwise. Court authorization is necessary, however, for the debtor to obtain unsecured credit or incur unsecured debt out of the ordinary course of business. Creditors in both instances have an administrative expense priority, which makes it easier for the DIP to obtain credit. 11 U.S.C.A. §§ 364, 503(b)(1). If the debtor is unable to obtain unsecured credit allowable as an administrative expense, other more complex alternatives are afforded by the Code. 11 U.S.C.A. §§ 364(c), (d).

4. UTILITY SERVICES
The uninterrupted continuation of utility services is imperative to the survival of a debtor's business. For this reason the Code affords protection from loss of such services that might otherwise occur because of the filing of a bankruptcy case or because the debtor had not paid, when due, a debt owed for service rendered before the order for relief. 11 U.S.C.A. § 366(a). The DIP or the trustee, however, must furnish adequate assurance of payment, in the form of a deposit or other security, within 20 days after the order for relief has been entered. Modification of the amount necessary for adequate assurance may be made by the court, after notice and a hearing, upon request of a party in interest.

5. SHEDDING BURDENSOME COLLECTIVE BARGAINING CONTRACTS
The Chapter 11 DIP or the trustee may, subject to the court's approval, assume or reject any executory contract or unexpired lease of the debtor. 11 U.S.C.A. § 365(a). This provision of the Code has proved invaluable to the DIP in shedding burdensome collective bargaining agreements and in assuming leases of real property essential to a reorganization plan or rejecting such leases that are unnecessary to the plan.

The debtor in possession or the trustee in a Chapter 11 case may assume or reject collective bargaining agreements. This power is not, however, extended to the DIP or the trustee in railroad reorganization cases filed under Subchapter IV of Chapter 11 and may be exercised only in accordance with the provisions of 11 U.S.C.A. § 1113.

After the petition has been filed and before the motion to reject the collective bargaining agreement has been filed, the DIP or the trustee must make a proposal, based on the most complete and reliable information available at the time, to the authorized representative of the employees covered by the agreement. The proposed modifications in employee benefits and protections must be necessary to permit the debtor's reorganization. The proposal must assure that all creditors, the debtor, and all other affected parties are treated fairly and equitably. Relevant information necessary to evaluate the proposal must also be provided to the representative of the employees. 11 U.S.C.A. § 1113(b). This information, however, may be controlled to some extent. If disclosure of information could compromise the position of the debtor with competitors, the court may enter protective orders to prevent such disclosure. 11 U.S.C.A. § 1113(d)(3).

After the proposal is made and before the hearing date on the application for rejection of the collective bargaining agreement, the DIP or the trustee must meet with the authorized representative of the employees at reasonable times. These meetings are for the purpose of conferring in good faith to attempt to reach mutually satisfactory modifications of the agreement. 11 U.S.C.A. § 1113(b)(2).

The court, after notice and hearing, may authorize the DIP or the trustee to make interim changes in the terms, conditions, wages, benefits, or work rules provided by a collective bargaining agreement. This will be done only if it is essential to the continuation of the debtor's business or to avoid irreparable damage to the estate and will not render the application for rejection of the agreement moot. 11 U.S.C.A. § 1113(e).

A hearing must be held on an application for rejection of a collective bargaining agreement not later than 14 days after the application is filed. The time may be extended for no more than seven days if the circumstances of the case and the interests of justice require an extension. Additional periods of time may be allowed if the DIP or the trustee and the employees' representative agree. 11 U.S.C.A. § 1113(d)(1).

The court must rule on the application for rejection within 30 days after the date on which the hearing begins. This time period may be extended for an additional period if agreed upon by the DIP or the trustee and the employees' representative. If the court does not rule on the application within the 30 days or the agreed to extension, the DIP or the trustee may terminate or alter any provisions of the collective bargaining agreement pending the ruling of the court on the application. 11 U.S.C.A. § 1113(d)(2).

The creative use of reorganization under the bankruptcy laws to deal with burdensome collective bargaining contracts is best illustrated by the *Continental Airlines* case. *In re Continental Airlines Corp.,* 38 B.R. 67 (Bankr.S.D.Tex.1984). On September 24, 1983, Continental Airlines filed a petition for reorganization under Chapter 11. Continental admitted that a primary motivation for its filing was a desire to reduce operating costs in addition to its inability to negotiate concessions from its employees' unions. At the time of the filing, Continental was still flying and had substantial net worth and working capital. It had not been forced by a cash flow crisis into a "nonoperating" Chapter 11, as had been the case with Braniff Airways. Upon filing, Continental rejected its collective bargaining agreements with its employees and imposed unilateral wage reductions and work rule changes.

When the unions moved to dismiss the petition, the bankruptcy judge denied their motion. The judge found that Continental was, in fact, in a severe and terminal financial crisis. The judge found that Continental had a long and continuing history of mounting financial losses, was shortly going to run out of operating capital, had no credit or unencumbered assets, and had no prospects for raising cash sufficient to continue operating for a reasonable time. Because management had no alternative to filing the petition, except almost certain operational failure and possible liquidation, the filing of the petition was proper and necessary.

The following case, *In re Royal Composing Room, Inc.,* illustrates how the strategy to reject collective bargaining worked for a smaller company.

In re Royal Composing Room, Inc.
United States District Court, Southern District of New York, 1987.
78.B.R. 671.

OPINION AND ORDER
John F. Keenan,
District Judge

BACKGROUND

New York Typographical Union No. 6 ("Local 6") appeals from an order of the Bankruptcy Court filed by Bankruptcy Judge Prudence B. Abram, 62 B.R. 403. Judge Abram granted the motion of the Debtor, Royal Composing Room, Inc., ("Royal") for approval of its rejection of its collective bargaining agreement with appellant. For the reasons set forth below, the Court affirms Judge Abram's order.

FACTS

This case arises in a changing industry. The appellee is an advertising typography company, and one of the last unionized shops. For most of this century, the advertising typography industry relied extensively on the linotype machine. However, the past decade has seen the industry turn increasingly to the latest computer technology.

It was in this corporate environment that Royal was created in 1975 as a result of the merger of two old unionized typesetting companies. Royal was a party to a collective bargaining agreement with Local 6. Although the company was profitable during its first several years, in 1982 its financial condition worsened. In that year, the annual gross revenues decreased by two million dollars, and it suffered a net loss of $545,236. Over the following three years, Royal lost over $752,900.

When confronted with these difficulties, Royal began to cut expenses. In 1983, Royal sharply cut the compensation of its principal executives, it froze salaries of salesmen and middle management foremen, and it eliminated company automobiles, along with other savings efforts. In 1985, Royal moved its plant to a smaller location to avoid a rent increase. By the end of that year, Royal reduced the number of non-Local 6 employees from 48 to 40.

As of the end of 1985, Local 6 had not yet made any sacrifices or concessions. It became increasingly urgent to obtain some savings from the union when Royal lost its largest customer, Doyle Dane Bernbach Inc., at the start of 1986. Royal was unable to convince the union to forego a 3% wage increase that had already been agreed to, nor would the union alter its arbitration demands.

On March 14, 1986, Royal filed its petition for reorganization under Chapter 11, section 301 of the Bankruptcy Code. Royal then sought to reject its collective bargaining agreement under section 1113(a). However, pursuant to section 1113(b)(1)(A), before rejecting the agreement, Royal was required to make a proposal to the union, "which provides for those necessary modifications in the employees' benefits and protections that are necessary to permit the reorganization of the debtor and assures that all creditors, the debtor and all of the affected parties are treated fairly and equitably." On March 18, a meeting was held between Royal and Local 6 at which the proposal was made. The proposal included a reduction of benefits, changes in work rules, the elimination of the scheduled wage increase, and the elimination of the union's right to arbitration as the way to change the contract. The union rejected the proposal and did not negotiate. Judge Abram noted that, "[t]he small number and short length of the meetings had is attributable to the union. . . . At no time prior to May 5, 1986 did the union make a counterproposal, comment item by item on the Debtor's proposal or the Debtor's financial situation, or state any reasons why it found the Debtor's request to be unfair or inequitable." *In re Royal Composing Room, Inc.,* 62 B.R. 403, 409 (Bankr.S.D.N.Y.1986). On May 5, 1986 the Bankruptcy Court held a final pretrial conference and, for the first time, the union made a counterproposal. Judge Abram found the proposal unacceptable. *See id.* at 410. On May 8, the trial commenced and on June 16, Royal's section 1113 motion was granted. This appeal followed.

DISCUSSION

Focusing on section 1113(c)(1), Local 6 raises two arguments on appeal: (1) the Bankruptcy Court did not apply the proper definition of "necessary" under section 1113, and (2) Royal's proposal did not treat all affected parties fairly and equitably. Both positions are unavailing.

At the outset, it should be noted that a bankruptcy court's interpretation of the statute is a legal conclusion subject to plenary review. *Truck Drivers Local 807 v. Carey Transportation Inc.,* 816 F.2d 82, 88 (2d Cir.1987). If the bankruptcy court's legal interpretations are correct, then its factual determinations can only be disturbed if they are clearly erroneous. *Id.* In this case, Judge Abram's opinion passes muster.

The Second Circuit has indicated that the term "necessary" contained in section 1113(b)(1)(A) does not mean " 'essential' or bare minimum." *See Carey Transportation,* 816 F.2d at 89. In rejecting the Third Circuit's approach which equated necessary with essential, *see Wheeling-Pittsburgh Steel Corp. v. United Steelworkers,* 791 F.2d 1074, 1088 (3d Cir.1986), the Second Circuit ruled that, "the necessity requirement places on the debtor the burden of proving that its proposal is made in good faith, and that it contains necessary, but not absolutely minimal, changes that will enable the debtor to complete the reorganization process successfully." In substance, this is the analysis employed by Judge Abram. Indeed, the Second Circuit in *Carey Transportation* quoted with approval Judge Abram's de-

scription of why a broader definition of "necessary" was required. "As the *Royal Composing Room* court phrased it, 'A debtor can live on water alone for a short time but over the long haul it needs food to sustain itself and retain its vigor.' " *Carey Transportation,* 816 F.2d at 89–90 (*quoting* 62 B.R. at 418).

Applying the standard of necessity later endorsed by the Second Circuit in *Carey Transportation,* Judge Abram found that Royal had, "established that it had in good faith attempted to negotiate for necessary changes but had been unsuccessful because of the Union's unwillingness to engage in serious discussions." 62 B.R. at 618. The record supports this finding. Local 6 was unresponsive and dilatory in the face of management's financial condition and resulting proposal. Likewise, Judge Abram was correct in her analysis of Royal's proposal. She found that Royal had cut non-union management and executive salaries, eliminated trade association memberships and even reused old doorknobs. 62 B.R. at 412. During this time, union labor costs were the only expenses not cut. *Id.* It cannot be concluded that these findings were clearly erroneous. The correctness of Judge Abram's legal conclusion is bolstered by the Second Circuit's statement in *Carey Transportation* that courts "must consider whether rejection [of a collective bargaining agreement] would increase the likelihood of successful reorganization." *Carey Transportation,* 816 F.2d at 89. This Court cannot envision Royal being able to successfully reorganize absent at least enforcement of its proposal under section 1113(b)(1)(A). Rejection clearly increases the likelihood of successful reorganization.

Local 6 further asserts that Royal did not satisfy the statutory requirement that under the pre-petition proposal, "all creditors, the debtor and all affected parties are treated fairly and equitably." Judge Abram correctly found that Royal "had spread the burden of financial sacrifice." 62 B.R. at 411. As noted earlier, Royal cut costs in many ways, including a decrease in executive compensation, the rescinding of raises and freezing of salaries of salesmen and middle level management, the elimination of company cars, and the moving of its premises to smaller quarters. The union's wages were neither frozen nor cut. It is clear that the pre-petition proposal merely sought "to spread the burden of financial sacrifice" a little further, so that it reached the union. *Carey Transportation* again underscores the wisdom of Judge Abram's opinion. The Second Circuit observed that a debtor need not show that managers and non-union employees have their benefits cut to the degree union benefits are cut. 816 F.2d at 90.

In this case, the union's benefits were the last to be cut, and it certainly was not the only constituency in Royal to feel the financial pinch. Royal's proposal satisfied the statute's requirement of fairness and equity.

CONCLUSION

The Bankruptcy Court properly found the pre-petition proposal satisfied the requirements section 1113(b)(1)(A), and that the rejection of the collective bargaining agreement was proper. The opinion of Judge Abram is hereby affirmed.

SO ORDERED.

---

6. DEALING WITH PENDING AND FUTURE LITIGATION

Another creative use of reorganization under the bankruptcy laws is to deal with pending and future litigation. This strategy is best illustrated by the *Manville* case. *In re Johns-Manville Corp.*, 26 B.R. 420 (Bankr.S.D.N.Y.1983). The Johns-Manville Corporation, a Fortune 500 company, was a diversified manufacturing, mining, and forest products company that conducted its business through five principal operating subsidiaries. Manville was the world's largest miner, processor, manufacturer, and supplier of asbestos and asbestos-containing products. After the link between asbestos and cancer became well known, Manville became the target of thousands of products liability claims. By September 1982, 16,500 asbestos-related lawsuits had been filed against the Manville Corporation. The company estimated that this was less than one-third of a projected 52,000 asbestos-related lawsuits that could be brought against it in the next 20 years. Manville projected that the lawsuits could cost the company $2 billion.

On September 2, 1982, Johns-Manville Corporation and 20 of its subsidiaries or affiliates, in an attempt to reduce the burdens placed on them by these suits, filed for reorganization under Chapter 11. At the time of the filing, Manville was a profitable, solvent corporation with 25,000 employees. Its net worth exceeded $1.1 billion, its long-term debt was less than $500 million, its short-term debt was just over $100 million, and its sales for 1981 exceeded $2 billion. By filing for reorganization, the Manville Corporation hoped to find an orderly manner of dealing with these cases and a method of providing a finite sum (a fund) for dealing with the cases arising in the future.

The Manville strategy provided an orderly manner of dealing with the asbestos cases and a cap on its aggregate liability, and saved the company. Some analysts, however, predicted that the cost of the reorganization strategy to the stockholders of the Manville Corporation could be high.

On October 3, 1988, the United States Supreme Court refused to hear the last appeal on Manville's reorganization plan. The plan required Johns-Manville Corporation to establish two trust funds. The first, a trust fund for property damage claims, would start with $330 million in cash and receive $250,000 a year from the Manville Corporation. The second, a trust fund for personal injury claims, would have a role in selecting company directors and would start with $675 million in cash and receive $160 million from Manville's insurers over the next three years; $1.85 billion in notes and bonds, repayable in regular installments by 2014; and 20 percent of Manville's net income, beginning in 1992. If the Manville payments to the fund do not meet claims as they are settled, the trust could claim 50 percent of the outstanding shares in the corporation (estimated at $180 million). The trust's claim could be increased to 80 percent.

The Manville strategy has had a profound effect on all asbestos-related tort claims and has led the way for other solvent companies who face massive tort liability. Industries producing tobacco, chemicals, or pharmaceutical products, if threatened by large-scale products liability claims, may find comfort, however cold, in a reorganization filing to limit the aggregate size of their current and future liability.

The Bankruptcy Reform Act of 1994 includes a procedure for dealing with the future personal injury claims in a Chapter 11 case that arise from exposure to asbestos-containing products. This procedure involves the creation of a trust to pay the future claims, coupled with an injunction to prevent future claimants from suing the debtor. 11 U.S.C.A. § 524(g).

C. EVIDENCE OF DEBTOR IN POSSESSION (DIP) STATUS

The debtor often needs evidence of debtor in possession status to continue business operations. Lending institutions and suppliers may be reluctant to deal with the Chapter 11 debtor without some official assurance of the debtor's status. The clerk of the bankruptcy court may certify the DIP status of the debtor. This certificate constitutes conclusive evidence of such status. Fed. R. Bank. P. 2011. Former Official Form No. 26, Certificate of Retention of Debtor in Possession, has been abrogated as an official form but is still available as Procedural Form No. B207 for this purpose. (See Exhibit 8.5.)

EXHIBIT 8.5
Certificate of Retention of Debtor in Possession

B207
(6/91)

United States Bankruptcy Court

_____ **District of** _____

In re

Bankruptcy Case No.

Debtor*
Social Security No.   :
Employer Tax I.D. No. :

CERTIFICATE OF RETENTION
OF DEBTOR IN POSSESSION

I hereby certify that the above-named debtor continues in possession of its estate as debtor in possession, no trustee having been appointed.

_____
Clerk of the Bankruptcy Court

_____   By: _____
Date   Deputy Clerk

*Set forth all names, including trade names, used by the debtor within the last 6 years. (Bankruptcy Rule 1005). For joint debtors set forth both social security numbers.

D. EXEMPTIONS

Only individuals are eligible for exemptions. Partnerships and corporations are not allowed exemptions. The scheduling and determination of exemptions in a Chapter 11 case are done in the same way as exemptions in a Chapter 7 case. There is, however, an important difference in the way nonexempt property is handled in Chapter 7 and in Chapter 11 cases. In a Chapter 7 case, property that exceeds the limits on exemptions is sold by the trustee, who then uses the proceeds to pay creditors. A DIP in a Chapter 11 case retains possession of *all* property, except as otherwise provided by the plan. The best interests of creditors test, however, must be met before confirmation of a plan. This test is determined by the amount of property that would be nonexempt under Chapter 7 and therefore available for payment of creditors. "Best interests of creditors" means that a creditor or an interest holder whose claim is impaired under a Chapter 11 plan must accept the plan *or* must receive no less under the plan than it would receive under Chapter 7. 11 U.S.C.A. § 1129(a)(7).

SECTION 3

APPOINTMENT OF A COMMITTEE OF UNSECURED CREDITORS AND A COMMITTEE OF EQUITY SECURITY HOLDERS

The Code requires appointment of a **committee of creditors holding unsecured claims** as soon as practicable after the order for relief in a Chapter 11 case. The United States trustee appoints this committee and may appoint additional committees of creditors or of **equity security holders** if they are needed. 11 U.S.C.A. § 1102(a)(1). The appointment of a committee may be deferred indefinitely in a small case because of lack of interest on the part of creditors.

Upon the request of a party in interest, the court may order the U.S. trustee to appoint additional committees of creditors or equity security holders. This would only be done to assure adequate representation of creditors or equity security holders. 11 U.S.C.A. § 1102(a)(2).

A committee of creditors usually consists of the seven persons holding the largest claims of the kinds represented on the committee. 11 U.S.C.A. § 1102(b)(1). Sometimes one or more such persons are unwilling to serve on a committee. When this occurs, another person or persons among those holding the top 20 unsecured claims will be appointed.

Occasionally, a committee has been organized by creditors before the commencement of the Chapter 11 case. This committee, if fairly chosen and representative of the different kinds of claims, will be appointed to serve as the committee in the case.

Selection of a **committee of equity security holders** works in the same way as selection of the committee of creditors. The persons holding the seven largest amounts of equity securities of the debtor will be appointed by the U.S. trustee to the committee, provided they are willing to serve.

An unsecured creditors' committee has several powers and duties. The committee may employ attorneys, accountants, or other agents to represent or perform services for it. The selection and authorization of employment of such persons must, however, take place at a scheduled meeting of the committee and must have court approval. 11 U.S.C.A. § 1103(a). The Code has a conflict of interest provision that prevents an attorney or an accountant from representing any other entity having an adverse interest in the case. 11 U.S.C.A. § 1103(b).

The creditors' committee may play an important role in the case by keeping a sharp eye on the debtor in possession. It may consult with the DIP concerning the administration of the case. The DIP is required to meet with the committee as soon as practicable after the appointment of the committee. The purpose of this meeting is "to transact such business as may be necessary and proper." 11 U.S.C.A. § 1103(d). The committee may investigate the operation of the business and the desirability of continuing the business. Any other matter relevant to the case or to the formulation of the plan may be investigated. The committee may also participate in the formulation of a plan and may request the appointment of a trustee or an examiner. A catchall provision also allows the committee to perform other services that are in the interest of those represented by the committee. 11 U.S.C.A. § 1103(c). The Bankruptcy Reform Act of 1994 allows compensation of actual and necessary administrative expenses of a member of an official committee of creditors or equity security holders for expenses incurred in performance of committee duties. 11 U.S.C.A. § 503(b)(3)(F).

The powers and duties of an equity security holders' committee are the same as those of a creditors' committee.

SECTION 4
MOTIONS AND COMPLAINTS

Unlike a Chapter 7 case, which often is more or less routine, every Chapter 11 case is unique. Therefore, the motions and complaints must be tailored to the individual case. In practice, fewer complaints are filed in some districts in a Chapter 11 case than would appear to be necessary under the Code due to the willingness of attorneys to bypass such filings. Attorneys for both sides may agree to the filing of a motion and response in order to expedite a hearing. This section sets forth both motions and complaints as they appear in the Code. This is not meant to be a comprehensive list.

A. MOTIONS

After the order for relief, the debtor in possession may move to dismiss the case (Fed. R. Bank. P. 1017); for a change of venue (28 U.S.C.A. § 1412); for disallowance of a claim (11 U.S.C.A. § 502); to convert the case from a Chapter 11 to a Chapter 7, 12, or 13 (11 U.S.C.A. §§ 1112(a), (d)); or for permission to use cash collateral (11 U.S.C.A. § 363(c)(2)).

A party in interest may move for relief from the automatic stay (11 U.S.C.A. § 362(d); Fed. R. Bank. P. 4001, 9014); to convert the case to Chapter 7 (11 U.S.C.A. § 1112(b)); to dismiss the case (11 U.S.C.A. § 1112(b); Fed. R. Bank. P. 1017); for a change of venue (28 U.S.C.A. § 1412); for abstention by the court (11 U.S.C.A. § 305); or for examination of any person (Fed. R. Bank. P. 2004).

A party in interest or the U.S. trustee may move to appoint a trustee or an examiner. 11 U.S.C.A. §§ 1104(a), (c). Any time after a Chapter 11 case has been commenced but before a plan has been confirmed, the court may order the appointment of a trustee on request of either a party in interest or the U.S. trustee for cause, including fraud, dishonesty, incompetence, or gross mismanagement, that occurred either before or after the case was commenced. 11 U.S.C.A. § 1104(a)(1). A trustee may also be appointed if it is in the interests of the creditors, equity security holders, and other interests of the estate. 11 U.S.C.A. § 1104(a)(2). Neither the number of holders of securities nor the amount of the debtor's assets or liabilities is to have any bearing on the appointment of a trustee.

The Bankruptcy Reform Act of 1994 provides for the election of a Chapter 11 trustee. The United States trustee must convene a meeting of creditors for this purpose on request of a party in interest made not later than 30 days after the court orders appointment of a trustee. This amendment does not apply to railroad debtors. The election of a Chapter 11 trustee will follow the same procedures provided for the election of a Chapter 7 trustee in 11 U.S.C.A. §§ 702(a), (b), and (c). 11 U.S.C.A. § 1104(b).

Any time before the confirmation of a plan, on request of a party in interest or the U.S. trustee, the court shall appoint an examiner if a trustee has not been appointed. An examiner will be appointed if it is in the interests of the creditors, equity security holders, and other interests of the estate or if the debtor's fixed, liquidated unsecured debts exceed $5,000,000. Exceptions to this are debts for goods, services, or taxes or debts owed to an insider. 11 U.S.C.A. § 1104(c).

If a trustee or an examiner dies, resigns, fails to qualify, or is removed, the United States trustee shall appoint one disinterested person to serve in a case. This appointment is made after consultation with parties in interest and is subject to court approval. The United States trustee may not appoint himself or herself as a trustee or an examiner in a Chapter 11 case. 11 U.S.C.A. § 1104(d).

The U.S. trustee may move to dismiss the case or to convert the case to Chapter 7. 11 U.S.C.A. § 1112(e).

A motion objecting to a claim is usually filed by the DIP or the trustee but can be filed by a party in interest. 11 U.S.C.A. § 502(a); Fed. R. Bank. P. 3007.

B. COMPLAINTS

The trustee, a creditor, or the U.S. trustee may file a complaint objecting to the debtor's discharge in a Chapter 11 case. Fed. R. Bank. P. 4004, 7001. Such a complaint must be filed no later than the first date set for the hearing on confirmation of the plan. This timing is based on the fact that confirmation of the plan discharges the Chapter 11 debtor. 11 U.S.C.A. § 1141(d). A debtor or any creditor may file a complaint to determine the dischargeability of a particular debt in a Chapter 11 case involving an individual debtor. 11 U.S.C.A. § 523; Fed. R. Bank. P. 4007.

A complaint to determine the dischargeability of a debt under section 523(c) must be filed no later than 60 days after the first date set for the meeting of creditors. Fed. R. Bank. P. 4007(c). An objection to discharge may be filed if the plan is a liquidating plan, if the debtor does not continue to engage in business, *and* if the debtor would be denied a discharge under section 727(a) if the case were a case under Chapter 7. A dischargeability complaint will be filed by a creditor and will usually be based on the debtor's fraudulently obtaining goods or services or trying to discharge spousal support or an educational loan. Although the successful dischargeability complaint will deprive the debtor of a discharge of only the particular debt in question, a successful objection to discharge will prevent discharge of any and all debts.

The DIP, the trustee, or the creditors' committee may file a complaint for turnover of property of the estate (11 U.S.C.A. § 542), to compel a custodian to turn over property of the estate and for an accounting (11 U.S.C.A. § 543; Fed. R. Bank. P. 6002), or to avoid a fraudulent transfer (11 U.S.C.A. § 548).

The DIP or the trustee may file a complaint to avoid transfer of property. 11 U.S.C.A. § 544.

The trustee may file a complaint to avoid a preferential transfer of property. 11 U.S.C.A. § 547(b).

SECTION 5
ORDER AND NOTICE OF CHAPTER 11 BANKRUPTCY FILING, MEETING OF CREDITORS, AND FIXING OF DATES

The clerk gives the debtor, the trustee, all creditors, the indenture trustees, and the U.S. trustee not less than 20 days notice by mail of the date, time, and place of the meeting of creditors and the time for filing objections to the debtor's claim of exemptions. This notice also serves as the notice of the order for relief required by 11 U.S.C.A. § 342(a). Fed. R. Bank. P. 2002.

The Bankruptcy Reform Act of 1994 requires that notice be given by the debtor to a creditor (Official Forms No. 9E and 9F, Notice of Commencement of Case Under Chapter 11 of the Bankruptcy Code, Meeting of Creditors, and Fixing of Dates) that contains the debtor's name, address and taxpayer identification number. 11 U.S.C.A. § 342(c). Forms B 205, B 206, and B 207 would also appear to be affected by this requirement. These procedural forms, however, have not been changed.

Official Forms No. 9E and 9F have also been revised for the new period (180 days after the order for relief) allowed under 11 U.S.C.A. § 502(b)(9) for governmental units to file proofs of claim and for the time period (60 days) for filing a domestic relations property settlement dischargeability complaint under 11 U.S.C.A. § 523(c)(1). Fed. R. Bank. P. 4007(c).

Parties in interest, who may object to the debtor's claim of exemptions, will probably begin to do so on receipt of the clerk's notice unless they have had prior notice from the debtor's attorney or from another source.

SECTION 6
MEETING OF CREDITORS (THE SECTION 341 MEETING) AND MEETING OF EQUITY SECURITY HOLDERS

The meeting of creditors (the section 341 meeting) is held not less than 20 nor more than 40 days after the order for relief. The business of the meeting includes the examination of the debtor under oath by the U.S. trustee, the trustee (if one has been appointed), and the creditors. If the debtor is a corporation, the Code authorizes the U.S. trustee to convene a meeting of equity security holders.

SECTION 7
THE CHAPTER 11 PLAN

A **Chapter 11 reorganization plan** must be filed showing how the debtor intends to surmount its financial difficulties so it can once more become a viable business. In a voluntary Chapter 11 case, the debtor may file a reorganization plan along with the petition or at any time after the filing of the petition. 11 U.S.C.A. § 1121(a).

The debtor has the exclusive right to file a plan for 120 days after the filing of the petition (i.e., after the order for relief) unless the court has appointed a trustee or the court, for cause, has reduced or increased this exclusive time period. 11 U.S.C.A. §§ 1121(b)–(d). If the debtor files a plan within this 120-day period, the debtor has an additional 60 days to obtain acceptance of the plan by each class of claims or interests impaired under the plan. Therefore, the debtor's exclusive period expires if the debtor does not file a plan within 120 days after the filing of the petition or does not obtain the required acceptances of the plan within 180 days after the filing of the petition. If the debtor obtains the necessary acceptances within the 180-day exclusive period, no other party in interest may file a plan.

EXAMPLE

Fern Nicholson, dba Fern's Graphics and Design, filed a petition in bankruptcy under Chapter 11 on March 1. Fern has the exclusive right to file a plan through June 28, which is 120 days from March 1. If Fern files a plan on June 1, a date within the 120-day period, she will have through August 27, which is 180 days from March 1, to obtain the required acceptances of the plan.

PROBLEM 8.1   If Fern files a plan on June 28, by what date must she have obtained the required acceptance of the plan?

The filing and acceptance of the plan are independent of the confirmation of the plan. This is important to the debtor because the confirmation hearing may not take place until long after the exclusive period has elapsed.

If a debtor requests an increase in the exclusive filing period for the plan, an increase in the time period for obtaining the acceptances should also be requested to get the full benefit of the extension.

EXAMPLE

Fern Nicholson, dba Fern's Graphics and Design, filed a petition in bankruptcy under Chapter 11 on March 1. Fern has the exclusive right to file a plan through June 28, which is 120 days from March 1. On June 1, Fern requested a 30-day extension in the exclusive filing period. Fern did not request an extension in the time period required to obtain the acceptances of the plan. If Fern files a plan on July 20, she will still have only through August 27, which is 180 days from March 1, to obtain the required acceptances of the plan.

28 U.S.C.A. § 148(a)(2) has been amended to cut down on excessive extensions of the debtor's exclusive 120-day period in which to file a reorganization plan. This amendment allows an immediate appeal to the district court from an extension or a reduction of that period.

A. STRATEGIES UTILIZED IN REORGANIZATION PLANS

A proponent of a reorganization plan may utilize one or more strategies in designing a plan. The strategy or strategies chosen by the proponent should be based on a realistic assessment of the debtor's activities and future. Commonly used strategies are

1. recapitalization by selling some assets, borrowing some money, or issuing securities;
2. rejection or assumption of executory contracts;
3. dealing with pending and future litigation;
4. merger or consolidation;
5. bootstrap; or
6. liquidation of all assets.

Recapitalization may be managed by the sale of some of the debtor's assets or by borrowing more money. For either to be successful, the debtor must have unencumbered assets that may be sold or pledged as security for new loans. If incorporated, the debtor may issue company stock to investors to fund a plan. Stock may also be issued to creditors in lieu of cash payments. If stock is issued, the debtor is exempt from federal, state, or local securities laws under the Code. 11 U.S.C.A. § 1145. For this reason, the debtor is required to file with the court and to transmit to each holder of a claim or interest a disclosure statement providing "adequate information" to allow an informed judgment to be made on the proposed plan. 11 U.S.C.A. § 1125.

Executory contracts, including unexpired leases and collective bargaining agreements, may be rejected by a debtor in possession or a trustee in a nonrailroad Chapter 11 case. 11 U.S.C.A. §§ 365, 1113. If the executory contract is a collective bargaining agreement, the employees affected under an agreement must have an authorized representative to evaluate the proposed modifications. Meetings will be held by the DIP or trustee with the employees' representative to attempt to reach mutually satisfying modifications of the agreement. The application for rejection of a collective bargaining agreement must be ruled on by the bankruptcy court. 11 U.S.C.A. § 1113.

The debtor may seek reorganization to deal with pending and future litigation. The risks that emanate from pending and future litigation might threaten the existence of the debtor. By filing a petition in bankruptcy under Chapter 11, a plan can be developed for controlling the litigation process and a cap can be placed on the debtor's liability.

The debtor might reorganize by a merger with a related or unrelated company or consolidation with a related company. The debtor's net operating losses may benefit the other company as a tax write-off. Tax consequences of a proposed plan should always be determined before going forward.

The bootstrap plan will not require new money from outside sources. As the name implies, a bootstrap plan involves funding a plan through the debtor's ability to produce income either through ongoing activities or by a partial liquidation of assets. This is sometimes called an internal plan and is the most difficult to implement because of the debtor's reluctance to change operating methods. Many debtors engage in a type of magical thinking, imagining that the methods that may have worked in the past will work in the future, even though they are not working in the present.

A plan involving liquidation of all assets will be a last resort in many Chapter 11 cases and will be proposed only if the debtor has no realistic hopes of regaining its status as a viable operation. As a general rule, a debtor clearly has a right to proceed to terminate its business as it wishes, and to use Chapter 11 as the basis for filing a liquidating plan. In most cases there is little prospect of dissent from creditors to the confirmation of the liquidating plan. Creditors rarely, if ever, believe that a business should continue if its managers have concluded otherwise.

Liquidation under Chapter 11 may be more beneficial to creditors than liquidation under Chapter 7. The debtor in possession is in a better position than a trustee would be to collect accounts receivable and to sell assets, particularly such things as inventory. Although the DIP may not be able to get the prices for assets normally available to an operating business, the amount obtained to pay creditors will generally still exceed what might be obtained in a Chapter 7 auction. For this reason, some Chapter 11 cases are filed with the intention of proposing a liquidating plan. This is permitted under the Code even though Chapter 11 is entitled "Reorganization." 11 U.S.C.A. § 1123(b)(4).

There are cases in which some of the assets of the debtor may be sold prior to confirmation of a plan. There may even be distribution of the proceeds from such a sale prior to confirmation if the creditor can establish extraordinary circumstances to justify immediate distribution.

In the following case, *In re Conroe Forge & Manufacturing Corporation,* the debtor filed an emergency motion to sell a piece of heavy equipment, free and clear of liens, and the bankruptcy court granted this request. After the sale, Mellon Bank, a creditor holding an unsecured claim, requested the immediate payment of the proceeds from the sale. The court, in *Conroe,* evaluated whether extraordinary circumstances existed that would require the immediate payment of proceeds.

In re Conroe Forge & Manufacturing Corporation
United States Bankruptcy Court, Western District of Pennsylvania, 1988.
82 B.R. 781.

MEMORANDUM OPINION
Judith K. Fitzgerald,
Bankruptcy Judge

The matter presently before the Court is secured creditor Mellon Bank's oral request, made at a hearing on Debtor's motion to sell free and clear, to receive immediate payment of proceeds of sale of a piece of heavy machinery.

Mellon Bank has submitted a "Memorandum of Law In Support of the Proposition that, When a Secured Creditor's Collateral is Sold Pursuant to 11 U.S.C. § 363 in a Liquidating Chapter 11 Case, the Proceeds of Sale May Be Distributed Immediately to the Secured Creditor." The Court finds the facts to be as follows.

Conroe Forge & Manufacturing Corporation (Debtor) is a corporation formerly engaged in the business of manufacturing die forgings. The Debtor's sole manufacturing facility is located in Conroe, Texas.

Debtor filed a petition for relief under Chapter 11 of the Bankruptcy Code in the United States Bankruptcy Court for the Western District of Pennsylvania on November 6, 1987, after having ceased operations. Debtor is a Debtor-in-Possession and does not intend to resume its manufacturing operations.[1] According to the Debtor's schedules, Mellon Bank holds a security interest in Debtor's land, buildings, machinery and equipment and is owed

$2,254,004.51. The Debtor has valued these assets in its schedules at $1,909,360.77. Of this amount $440,831.69 represents the value of real estate pursuant to a tax assessment which may or may not reflect the fair market value of the realty.

In early December, the Debtor filed an emergency motion to sell certain machinery free and clear of liens, claims and encumbrances and a request that the Court shorten the notice period and conduct an expedited hearing. Mellon Bank did not oppose and the Court granted the requests. A hearing was held on December 23, 1987, because Interstate Drop Forge Company (Buyer) had an immediate need for the equipment and its offer would expire if it was not able to transport the machinery to Wisconsin before the Wisconsin Frost Laws went into effect. The Wisconsin Frost Laws prohibit movement of heavy machinery and the like over Wisconsin roads during certain winter months. From these facts, the absence of any relationship between Debtor and Buyer, the utilization of an independent broker and Mellon Bank's consent to the sale, the Court finds that a bona fide emergency existed and that the Buyer acted in good faith.

The gross sales price offered by Buyer was $149,000.00 which was represented without contradiction to be a fair and reasonable price. There were no other bidders at the hearing. At the request of the Debtor and with the consent of all parties who were present at the sale and hearing on this motion, the Court confirmed the sale and directed that a 10% (ten percent) brokerage commission be paid out of these gross receipts and an additional amount be placed in escrow pending resolution of the broker's claim for reimbursement of expenses.

Also escrowed was $7,200.00 representing a claim by Victoria Machine Works for repair charges allegedly secured by a repairman's possessory lien on a component of one of the presses. Victoria Machine Works agreed to turn over the piece in order that the Buyer would complete the sale inasmuch as the component increases the useful life of the machinery and, therefore, its absence would affect the sale. Debtor filed an adversary action to require Victoria Machine Works to turn over the component. Victoria Machine Works did not have an opportunity to respond to the adversary complaint prior to the sale but did agree to release the component to facilitate the sale. Victoria Machine Works has asserted that its response to the adversary complaint will claim that approximately $43,000 is due for repair work on the machinery sold. Therefore, at the hearing on December 23, 1987, Victoria Machine Works argued that the amount of its entire claim should be escrowed pending the outcome of the trial on the adversary proceeding. Thus, there is a dispute concerning the appropriate disposition to be made of these funds.

Mellon Bank argued that in order to adequately protect its interest, the Court must apply either 11 U.S.C. § 361(1) or the "indubitable equivalen[ce]" language of 11 U.S.C. § 361(3) and must authorize the immediate payment to Mellon Bank of the net proceeds of sale. Mellon Bank did not deny the Court's suggestion that 11 U.S.C. § 361(2), which permits a lien substitution to proceeds, would provide that protection; rather, Mellon Bank's position is that it would benefit more from immediate payment. The motion to sell free and clear specifically provided for the transfer of all liens to proceeds. On January 13, 1988, this Court entered an Order requiring that all proceeds be escrowed except for amounts previously authorized to be paid to the broker.

DISCUSSION

Bankruptcy Rule 3021 provides:

> After confirmation of a plan, distribution shall be made to creditors whose claims have been allowed. . . .

This provision is the successor to former Bankruptcy Rule 10–405(a) which is derived from § 224(3) of the Bankruptcy Act. Rule 10–405(a) provided that ". . . after confirmation of a plan distribution shall be made . . . to . . . creditors whose claims have been allowed. . . ." The problem in the case at bar arises from Bankruptcy Code § 1123(b)(4) which enables Debtors to structure a liquidation through a plan and states, in substance, that a plan *may* provide for the sale of all or substantially all estate assets and the distribution of proceeds.

The general rule is that distribution should not occur except pursuant to a confirmed plan of reorganization, absent extraordinary circumstances. *Abbotts Dairies of Pennsylvania, Inc.,* 788 F.2d 143 (3d Cir. 1986). *See* 6A Collier on Bankruptcy, ¶ 11.14 (14th ed. 1977). *See also* 11 U.S.C. § 1123(a)(5) (plan must provide adequate means for implementation); and Bankruptcy Rule 3021.

It is within the discretion of the Bankruptcy Court to determine whether extraordinary circumstances exist so that sale proceeds may be paid to creditors outside the confines of a plan. *Cf. In re Lilly C. Anderson,* 833 F.2d 834, 836 (9th Cir.1987) (concerning award of postpetition interest but denial of "lost opportunity" compensation to oversecured creditor after sale of collateral by Trustee appointed to conduct sale in apparent Chapter 11 where no plan had been confirmed). *See also, In re Industrial Office Building Corp.,* 171 F.2d 890, 892 (3d Cir.1949) (authorizing interim distribution of funds in excess of those needed for reorganization).

In re Braniff Airways, Inc., 700 F.2d 935 (5th Cir.1983) (rehearing and rehearing en banc denied), concerned a sale of a substantial portion of Debtor's assets before a plan had been confirmed. The appellate court found that the terms of sale would have dictated the plan provisions without circulation of a proposed plan. The sale was not permitted. Although the facts of the case at bar are not on point with those of *Braniff,* this court finds persuasive the Fifth Circuit's opinion that, first, Chapter 11's confirmation requirements (herein a plan and disclosure statement) should not be short-circuited and, second, approval of preplan distributions in liquidating Chapter 11 cases would leave little incentive for completing the requirements of the disclosure statement and plan preparatory to a reorganization by way of liquidation. *Id.* at 940.

The policy behind Chapter 11 reorganization is successful rehabilitation. *NLRB v. Bildisco and Bildisco,* 465 U.S. 513, 527, 104 S.Ct. 1188, 1196, 79 L.Ed.2d 482 (1984). However, the concept of reorganization includes liquidation. *In re Koopmans,* 22 B.R. 395, 398 (Bank.D.Utah1982). *See also In re Industrial Office Building Corp., supra,* 171 F.2d at 892. This Court, therefore, must determine whether the property, herein proceeds, is necessary for an effective reorganization. *See In re Keller,* 45 B.R. 469, 471 (Bank.N.D.Iowa1984). In a liquidating Chapter 11 where Debtor has ceased operations and collateral value is not decreasing, ordinarily all property will be necessary for an effective reorganization. "Necessary" property has been defined as that which "'will contribute' to a plan of reorganization." *In re 6200 Ridge, Inc.,* 69 B.R. 837, 843 (BankE.D.Pa.1987). If, as in this case, circumstances require confirmation of a sale before a liquidating plan has been confirmed, the proceeds, which will be earning interest, are necessary to the plan which presumably will provide for the sale of the rest of Debtor's assets and distribution of proceeds.[2] *Cf.* 11 U.S.C. § 1123(a)(5) (plan must provide adequate means for implementation).

If distribution is made to creditors in a liquidating Chapter 11 before confirmation of a plan there will be little incentive for parties in interest to prosecute the case in an expeditious manner much less to perform the work required to issue and obtain approval of a disclosure statement and plan. *See In re Braniff Airways, Inc., supra,* 700 F.2d at 940; *In re Jartran, Inc.,* 71 B.R. 938, 942 and n. 6 (Bank.N.D.Ill.,E.D.1987) (court rejected argument that because debtor's case was a liquidating Chapter 11 it should be treated as a Chapter 7 for distribution purposes). In addition, if distribution of assets occurs before confirmation, there will exist no means by which a plan may be implemented. Such a course would violate § 1123(a)(5).

Moreover, Bankruptcy Rule 3021 provides that distribution pursuant to a Chapter 11 plan is authorized only with respect to *allowed* claims. The amount of Mellon Bank's allowed claim has not been determined and could depend on many factors, including, *inter alia,* the terms of a proposed plan, whether or not the plan is accepted, and whether or not the case suffers conversion to a Chapter 7.

The crux of Mellon Bank's argument is that even if it eventually receives the proceeds of sale plus interest it would receive a much greater return if it is paid the proceeds now and is able to use them in the ordinary course of its business. In support of this position, Mellon Bank relies on *In re American Mariner Industries, Inc.,* 734 F.2d 426 (9th Cir.1984), where, in deciding a motion for relief from stay, the court held that the secured creditor was entitled to compensation for the delay it had suffered in enforcing its rights in order to give it, as nearly as possible, the benefit of its bargain.

The United States Supreme Court recently discussed the concept that an undersecured creditor is not entitled to compensation for the delay occasioned by the automatic stay provisions of the Code. In *United Savings Association of Texas v. Timbers of Inwood Forest Associates, Ltd.,* ___U.S.___, 108 S.Ct. 626, 98 L.Ed.2d 740 (1988), the Court stated that "the undersecured petitioner [creditor] is not entitled to interest on its collateral during the stay to assure adequate protection under 11 U.S.C. § 362(d)(1)." *Id.* at ___, 108 S.Ct. at 635. In the case at bar, as in *Timbers of Inwood,* the undersecured creditor has not sought relief from stay under § 362(d)(2) or on any other ground, but merely raised the issue of what constitutes adequate protection.[3] To the extent that *Timbers of Inwood* discussed the payment of interest for use of an undersecured creditor's collateral during the automatic stay period, this Court finds it apposite to the instant case, and finds that *American Mariner,* which discussed a similar premise after a creditor applied for relief from stay, to be inapposite.[4] Even so, Mellon Bank's interest in the value of its collateral is preserved because the sale itself determined the value of the collateral and the sales proceeds, to which Mellon Bank's lien now attaches, are escrowed.

At the hearing in the instant matter Mellon Bank's counsel indicated that it was his opinion that Mellon Bank is undersecured and not secured in all assets and probably would sustain a deficiency. Furthermore, counsel did not know whether Debtor's obligation to Mellon Bank had been accelerated by reason of default. These factors, coupled with those discussed above, lead the Court to find that escrowing the proceeds at interest adequately protects Mellon Bank's interest. In addition, Mellon Bank has shown no basis upon which immediate payment of the net proceeds of sale would be required to afford it adequate protection nor why substitution of liens denies adequate protection. Whether or not Mellon Bank receives the indubitable equivalent of its claim, as argued at the hearing, is a matter for determination at the time of plan confirmation, *Timbers of Inwood, supra,* ___U.S. at ___, 108 S.Ct. at 632–33, especially where the value of its security has not been determined and where there is, as in this case, Debtor's assurance that it has prepared a liquidating plan.[5]

This Court also notes that case law in the Third Circuit which construed certain provisions of former Chapter XI of the Bankruptcy Act established that a sale of assets before confirmation of a plan is permissible only on the basis of a demonstrated emergency. "Emergency" was defined as an "imminent danger that the assets of the ailing business will be lost if prompt action is not taken." *In re Solar Manufacturing Corp.,* 176 F.2d 493, 494 (3d Cir.1949). *Compare In re White Motor Credit Corp.,* 14 B.R. 584, 4 C.B.C.2d 1562 (Bank.N.D.Ohio1981). *And see Matter of Mesta Machine Co.,* 30 B.R. 178 (Bank. W.D.Pa.1983) (concerning a Code case filed in the Western District of Pennsylvania pursuant to Chapter 11).[6] If the sale itself is permissible only in the most exigent circumstances absent confirmation of a Chapter 11 plan, distribution of the proceeds will require, at minimum, a showing of similar immediate need. That a creditor could receive a better return through immediate payment does not mean that the creditor is not adequately protected by substitution of liens to proceeds especially where the proceeds are escrowed at interest pending confirmation of a liquidating plan, and when the secured creditor agreed to the Debtor's motion for sale providing for transference of liens to proceeds.

Mellon Bank cites various Code provisions in support of its argument that this Court may order immediate payment; however, whether or not the Court may so order is not the issue. The issue is whether the best interests of all parties in interest will be served by the course of action requested. *See Matter of Realty Associates Securities Corp.,* 58 F.Supp. 220 (E.D.N.Y.1944) (regarding distribution of excess cash). *See also In re Industrial Office Building Corp.,* 171 F.2d at 893. At the time of the hearing on the sale a creditor's committee had not been appointed in this case. Furthermore, this case was only a few weeks old and, in this Court's view, an adequate opportunity to examine Debtor's affairs and/or negotiate and/or form a plan of reorganization had not been provided. There is no dispute that the sale was for a fair and reasonable price and in the best interest of creditors because a delay would have meant either the loss of the sale or a postponement until after the winter months with corresponding loss to the value of the collateral itself. In addition, a liquidating plan has been proposed which includes suggested distribution of proceeds to classes of creditors. Thus creditors are provided an opportunity to examine the proposal for liquidation pursuant to the plan and disclosure statement in accordance with the policy and spirit of Chapter 11 of the Bankruptcy Code. *See* H.R. No. 95–595 (1977), U.S.Code Cong. & Admin.News 1978, p. 5787 (Chapter 11 "incorporates the essence of the protection features of . . . Chapter X").

Furthermore, § 1106 provides, in pertinent part:

(a) A trustee shall—

(5) . . . file a plan . . . a report of why the trustee will not file a plan, or recommend conversion . . . or dismissal. . . .

Pursuant to § 1107(a) a debtor-in-possession is charged with the obligations of a trustee. No justification exists, based on the instant facts and the provisions and policies of the Bankruptcy Code, to order remittance of proceeds to Mellon Bank before confirmation of a plan or reorganization.

CONCLUSION

In accordance with the foregoing, this Court holds that in this liquidating Chapter 11 case where there has been a sale of assets prior to confirmation of a plan and an undersecured creditor has not established that immediate payment to it of proceeds of sale is required for adequate protection, there will be no distribution until a plan is confirmed. *See* H.R. No. 95–595, 95th Cong., 1st Sess. (1977) (the purpose of reorganization "is to form and have confirmed a plan of reorganization").

If Mellon Bank believes that it is suffering unduly through the pendency of this Chapter 11, it has many courses of action to choose from under the Bankruptcy Code. At this point and in this particular matter Mellon Bank is adequately protected by the

substitution of liens to proceeds and payment of proceeds prior to plan confirmation will be and hereby is denied in accordance with the Order of this Court dated January 13, 1988.

---

[1]In fact, albeit after the sale involved herein, Debtor filed a disclosure statement and a liquidating Chapter 11 plan. As yet, there has been no hearing on the disclosure statement or plan.

[2]The plan proposed by Debtor but as yet uncirculated to creditors does precisely this.

[3]The Court emphasizes that this issue was raised by the creditor after it consented to a sale free and clear of liens and encumbrances with transfer of liens and encumbrances to proceeds.

[4]Of further note is that the Bankruptcy Court for the Eastern District of Pennsylvania has chosen to disagree with *American Mariner* insofar as that case may require compensation for delay to every undersecured creditor in every case. *In re Grant Broadcasting of Philadelphia, Inc.,* 71 B.R. 376, 388 (Bank.E.D.Pa.1987). This court agrees that adequate protection depends on the circumstances of each case.

[5]Debtor's liquidating plan was filed with the court while this opinion was pending.

[6]This Court is aware of the opinion of the Bankruptcy Court for the Eastern District of Pennsylvania in *In re Industrial Valley Refrigeration and Air Conditioning Supplies, Inc.,* 77 B.R. 15 (Bank.E.D.Pa.1987), which held that the Third Circuit's decision in *Abbotts Dairies* implicitly overruled *Solar Manufacturing* and that therefore "the Third Circuit has . . . abandoned the 'emergency-only' standard . . . enunciated in *Solar Manufacturing,*" adopting instead a test which includes as an element a showing of a "sound business purpose." 77 B.R. at 20, 21. This Court's examination of *Abbotts Dairies* revealed that an emergency sale was the event which triggered the appeal, 788 F.2d at 144–45, that the question of exigent circumstances was not at issue having been found by the district court to exist, and that the only issue before the Third Circuit and on remand was the existence of good faith between Debtor and Buyer. Nonetheless, this Court finds that the more stringent test of *Solar Manufacturing* was met in the case at bar, and it is not necessary to choose between the two standards. *McLaughlin v. Arco Polymers, Inc.,* 721 F.2d 426, 430 n. 5 (3d

Cir. 1983) (Third Circuit panel is bound by reported circuit opinions "unless and until they are reversed by the in banc court"); *Gardner v. Com. of Pa. Dept. of Public Welfare,* 685 F.2d 106, 108 (3d Cir.), *cert. denied,* 459 U.S. 1092, 103 S.Ct. 580, 74 L.Ed.2d 939 (1982) (a panel of the Third Circuit "is not free . . . to overrule a governing precedent in this circuit"). *See Penn Central*

Transportation Co., Inc. v. Celotex Corp., 403 F.Supp. 70, 74 (E.D.Pa.1975), *aff'd,* 538 F.2d 320 (3d Cir.1976) (on a statute of limitations question, the court stated "to overrule prior [judicial] authority is not lightly to be presumed, especially an overruling *sub silentio")* (citations omitted).

B. CONTENTS OF A PLAN

The contents of a Chapter 11 reorganization plan are delineated in the Code. 11 U.S.C.A. § 1123. Some provisions are mandatory while others are permissive. The **mandatory provisions** are noted in the Code by "shall" language. 11 U.S.C.A. § 1123(a). The **permissive provisions** are set forth in "may" language. 11 U.S.C.A. § 1123(b).

1. MANDATORY PROVISIONS

A plan must divide the creditors into classes of claims and classes of interests. 11 U.S.C.A. § 1123(a)(1). A creditor holding an undersecured claim will have two claims, one secured and the other unsecured, and thus will be in two classes of claims. 11 U.S.C.A. § 506.

> **EXAMPLE**
>
> The XYZ Corporation borrowed $1,000,000 from First Bank and gave First Bank a perfected security interest in all of its present and after-acquired inventory. Shortly thereafter, XYZ Corporation filed a petition in bankruptcy under Chapter 11. At that time, XYZ's inventory had a value of $750,000. First Bank's secured claim for $750,000 will be in one class, and its unsecured claim for $250,000 will be in another class.

The usual classification of holders of claims or interests will include creditors holding secured claims, creditors holding unsecured priority claims, creditors holding unsecured nonpriority claims, and holders of equity security interests. In order to formulate a reorganization plan, it is necessary to classify the claims or interests. The Code has a general rule and an exception for classification. As a general rule, claims or interests may be included in a particular class only if substantially similar to the other claims or interests in that class. 11 U.S.C.A. § 1122(a). The exception to the general rule provides for a plan to designate a separate class of smaller claims for administrative convenience. This class would consist of every unsecured claim that is less than an amount, or that is reduced to an amount, that the court approves as reasonable and necessary for administrative convenience. 11 U.S.C.A. § 1122(b); Fed. R. Bank. P. 3013.

> **EXAMPLE**
>
> The XYZ Corporation has filed a petition in bankruptcy under Chapter 11. XYZ has 10 creditors with claims of $2,000 or more and 100 creditors with claims under $2,000. If XYZ were required to classify both groups of claims together, it could ruin a plan. In the plan, XYZ could utilize the exception and designate a separate class of smaller claims.

The plan could then pay cash in full to the 100 creditors holding claims under $2,000 whose claims are in one class and give stock to the 10 creditors holding claims of $2,000 or more whose claims are in the other class.

This exception was provided as a practical matter. A Chapter 11 plan must be accepted by a majority in number of claims and two-thirds in amount of claims. A plan in a case with many small claims that were not to be paid in full might experience difficulty in gaining acceptance by a majority in numbers if only substantially similar claims were included in a class.

The ultimate meaning of the general rule that a claim or interest may be placed in a particular class only if substantially similar to the other claims or interests of the class is best demonstrated by security interests in specific assets or judgment liens. Each of these will usually be in a class by itself.

The next class, creditors holding unsecured claims whose claims are entitled to priority, is set forth in the Code. 11 U.S.C.A. § 507.

Creditors holding unsecured claims are third in the line-up. They hold a claim only against the general assets of the bankruptcy estate.

Equity security holders are last in line in the classification and payoff of creditors. They may consist of one or more classes depending on ownership, that may be at more than one level.

EXAMPLE
The XYZ Corporation has issued 1,500 shares of common stock and 1,000 shares of preferred stock. The claims of holders of the common stock will be in one class, and the claims of holders of the preferred stock will be in another class.

The Chapter 11 plan must specify any class of claims or class of interests not impaired under the plan. 11 U.S.C.A. § 1123(a)(2). The plan must also specify the treatment of any class of claims or interests impaired under the plan. 11 U.S.C.A. § 1123(a)(3). The Code describes when a class of claims or interests is impaired. 11 U.S.C.A. § 1124. As a general rule, a class of claims or interests is treated as impaired (i.e., when contractual rights of creditors or interest holders are affected by the plan) unless it falls within one of two enumerated exceptions.

1. If the plan proposes not to alter the legal, equitable, or contractual rights to which the claim or interest entitles its holder, the claim or interest is unimpaired. 11 U.S.C.A. § 1124(1).
2. If the plan proposes to restore a holder of a claim or interest to his or her original position by curing the effect of a default or by reinstating the original terms of an obligation when maturity was brought on or accelerated by the default, the claim or interest is unimpaired. 11 U.S.C.A. § 1124(2).

Each claim or interest within a class must be provided the same treatment unless the holder of the claim or interest agrees to a less favorable treatment. 11 U.S.C.A. § 1123(a)(4).

The plan must provide adequate means for implementation of its provisions. The Code sets out examples of such means:

(A) retention by the debtor of all or any part of the property of the estate;
(B) transfer of all or any part of the property of the estate to one or more entities, whether organized before or after the confirmation of such plan;
(C) merger or consolidation of the debtor with one or more persons;
(D) sale of all or any part of the property of the estate, either subject to or free of any lien, or the distribution of all or any part of the property of the estate among those having an interest in such property of the estate;

(E) satisfaction or modification of any lien;

(F) cancellation or modification of any indenture or similar instrument;

(G) curing or waiving of any default;

(H) extension of a maturity date or a change in an interest rate or other term of out-standing securities;

(I) amendment of the debtor's charter; or

(J) issuance of securities of the debtor, or of any entity referred to in subparagraph (B) or (C) of this paragraph, for cash, for property, for existing securities, or in exchange for claims or interests, or for any other appropriate purpose, ... 11 U.S.C.A. §§ 1123(a)(5)(A)–(J).

The means of implementing the plan will vary greatly from debtor to debtor, and the plan must be designed to fit the particular situation.

The plan must stipulate that certain provisions will be included in the charter of the debtor and in the charter of any corporation acquiring assets of the debtor or merging with or consolidating with the debtor. These provisions are designed to prohibit issuance of nonvoting equity securities and to provide an appropriate distribution of voting power among the classes having such power, including provisions for the election of directors representing preferred stockholders in the event of default in payment of preferred stock dividends. 11 U.S.C.A. § 1123(a)(6).

Every provision of the plan must be consistent with the interests of creditors and equity security holders and with public policy in the selection of any officer, director, or trustee (or their successors) under the plan. 11 U.S.C.A. § 1123(a)(7).

2. PERMISSIVE PROVISIONS

A Chapter 11 plan may impair or leave unimpaired any class of claims (secured or unsecured) or interests. 11 U.S.C.A. § 1123(b)(1).

EXAMPLE

The XYZ Corporation provided its president with a company car, which was financed by First Bank. Several weeks before XYZ filed its petition in bankruptcy under Chapter 11, the president's car was involved in an accident. The car was repaired by Joe's Body Shop. At the time of the filing of the petition, the body shop's $1,500 bill had not been paid.

The plan placed First Bank's secured claim in one class and the body shop's unsecured claim in another class. In the plan, if the XYZ Corporation continues its payments to the creditors in the secured class, the bank's claim is unimpaired. If the plan provides for less than full payment to the class of unsecured claims, the body shop's claim is impaired under the plan.

A Chapter 11 plan may provide for the assumption or rejection of executory contracts. 11 U.S.C.A. § 1123(b)(2). In a Chapter 11 case, the debtor or the trustee may, at any time before the plan is confirmed, assume or reject an executory contract, including an unexpired lease of the debtor. The court, however, on request of a party to the contract or lease, may order a decision on rejection or assumption to be made within a specified time period. 11 U.S.C.A. § 365(d)(2).

EXAMPLE

The XYZ Corporation leased a warehouse from the ABC Property Company and subsequently filed a petition in bankruptcy under Chapter 11. In its plan, the XYZ Corporation decided to consolidate its operation, and the leased warehouse became expendable. The XYZ Corporation could reject the unexpired lease of the warehouse.

Under the Code, a Chapter 11 plan may provide for settlement or adjustment of any claim or interest belonging to the estate or for the retention and enforcement of any such claim or interest. 11 U.S.C.A. § 1123(b)(3).

EXAMPLE
The XYZ Corporation sold the ABC Company goods on credit. The ABC Company subsequently refused to pay, claiming that the goods failed to comply with the contract. Shortly after this, the XYZ Corporation filed its petition in bankruptcy under Chapter 11. XYZ negotiated with the ABC Company concerning the settlement of its claim. The settlement agreement provided that ABC would pay XYZ 75 percent of the original purchase price. XYZ's Chapter 11 plan may provide for settlement of XYZ's claim along the lines of the settlement agreement worked out between the parties.

Under the Code, a plan may be a liquidating plan, providing for sale of all or substantially all of the property of the estate with the proceeds of the sale to be distributed among the holders of claims or interests. 11 U.S.C.A. § 1123(b)(4).

Under the Bankruptcy Reform Act of 1994, a plan may modify the rights of holders of secured claims, with the exception of a claim secured only by the debtor's principal residence. The plan may also modify the rights of holders of unsecured claims or leave unaffected the rights of holders of any class of claims. 11 U.S.C.A. § 1123(b)(5).

A plan may also include any appropriate provision that is not inconsistent with Code provisions. 11 U.S.C.A. § 1123(b)(6).

3. A SAMPLE CHAPTER 11 PLAN

Exhibit 8.6 presents a sample Chapter 11 plan. Most Chapter 11 plans are much longer and more complex than the one shown here. This plan has been selected because it is relatively short but still shows what a Chapter 11 plan might look like. It may be helpful to compare the Chapter 11 plan with the Chapter 12 and Chapter 13 plans. How are they the same, and how do they differ?

This Chapter 11 plan, like all Chapter 11 plans, is accompanied by an extensive disclosure statement. (See Exhibit 8.7.)

EXHIBIT 8.6
A Chapter 11 Plan

UNITED STATES BANKRUPTCY COURT
DISTRICT OF _____

In re *[debtor's name]* _____)_____
    [set forth here all names including)
    married, maiden, and trade names,)
    used by debtor within last 6 years])
)   Case No. _____
                Debtor   )
)   Chapter 11
Address _____)
Social Security No. _____)
Employer's Tax Identification Nos. [if any])
_____)

PLAN OF REORGANIZATION

    The debtor in possession, *[debtor's name]*, dba *[name of debtor's business]* ("debtor"), a sole proprietorship, proposes the following plan pursuant to Chapter 11 of the Bankruptcy Code of 1978, as amended.

ARTICLE I
DEFINITIONS

    For the purposes of this plan of reorganization ("plan"), the following terms shall mean:

    1.01. *Allowed Claim* shall mean a claim (a) in respect of which a proof of claim has been filed with the Court within the applicable period of limitation fixed by Rule 3001; or (b) scheduled in the list of creditors prepared and filed with the Court pursuant to Rule 1007(b) and not listed as disputed, contingent, or unliquidated as to amount, in either case as to which no objection to the allowance thereof has been interposed within any applicable period of limitation fixed by Rule 3001 or an order of the Court, or as to which any such objection has been determined by an order or judgment which is no longer subject to appeal or certiorari proceeding and as to which no appeal or certiorari proceeding is pending.

    1.02. *Allowed Secured Claim* shall mean an allowed claim secured by a lien, security interest, or other charge against or interest in property in which the debtor has an interest, or which is subject to setoff under 11 U.S.C.A. § 553, to the extent of the value (determined in accordance with 11 U.S.C.A. § 506(a)) of the interest of the holder of such allowed claim in the debtor's interest in such property or to the extent of the amount subject to such setoff, as the case may be.

    1.03. *Allowed Small Claim* shall mean an allowed claim (a) the amount of which (prior to any subdivision or assignment thereof after the petition date) is not more than $300.00 or (b) the holder of which has irrevocably elected prior to the confirmation date to reduce the amount thereof to $300.00 and to have such allowed claim included in Class 4 by indicating such election on the form utilized for purposes of acceptance or rejection of the plan.

EXHIBIT 8.6
Continued

1.04. *Claim* shall mean any right to payment, or right to an equitable remedy for breach of performance if such breach gives rise to a right to payment, against the debtor in existence on or as of the petition date, whether or not such right to payment or right to an equitable remedy is reduced to judgment, liquidated, unliquidated, fixed, contingent, matured, unmatured, disputed, undisputed, legal, secured, or unsecured.

1.05. *Class* shall mean any class into which allowed claims or allowed interests are classified pursuant to Article III.

1.06. *Class 1 Claims, Class 2 Claims, Class 3 Claims, Class 4 Claims,* and *Class 5 Claims* shall mean the allowed claims so classified in Sections 3.01 through 3.05 of this plan.

1.07. *Code* shall mean the Bankruptcy Code, 11 U.S.C.A. § 101 et seq., as amended.

1.08. *Confirmation Date* shall mean the date upon which the order of confirmation is entered by the Court.

1.09. *Court* shall mean the United States Bankruptcy Court for the *[name the district]* District of *[name the state]*, in which the debtor's Chapter 11 case, pursuant to which this plan is proposed, is pending, and any court having competent jurisdiction to hear an appeal or certiorari proceeding therefrom.

1.10. *Debtor* shall mean the debtor sole proprietorship, the debtor in this Chapter 11 case, or any successor thereto or any transferee of all or substantially all of its assets.

1.11. *Distribution Account* shall mean the consideration to be distributed to holders of allowed claims and allowed interests on the distribution date (and the corresponding consideration payable to holders of claims and interests which have not been allowed as of the distribution date) and any account or accounts into which such consideration has been deposited.

1.12. *Distribution Date* shall mean the date upon which the order of confirmation is no longer subject to appeal or certiorari proceeding, on which date no such appeal or certiorari proceeding is then pending and on which date all of the conditions to the effectiveness of the plan expressly set forth in the plan have been satisfied fully or effectively waived.

1.13. *Fiscal Year* shall mean the fiscal year of debtor and its subsidiaries, which is the 12-month period ending December 31.

1.14. *Indebtedness* as applied to any person shall mean:

(a)   all indebtedness or other obligations of the person for borrowed money or for the deferred purchase price of property or services;

(b) all indebtedness of the person, contingent, direct, or otherwise, secured (or for which the holder of such indebtedness has an existing right (contingent or otherwise) to be secured) by any mortgage, pledge, lien, security interest, or vendor's interest under any conditional sale or other title retention agreement existing on any property indebtedness secured thereby shall have been assumed by the person (hereinafter "secured"); or

(c) all indebtedness of others, secured or unsecured, directly or indirectly guaranteed, endorsed, or discounted with recourse by the person, or in respect of which the person is otherwise directly or indirectly liable, including without limitation, indebtedness in effect guaranteed by the person through any agreement (contingent or otherwise) to purchase, repurchase, or otherwise acquire such indebtedness or any se-

EXHIBIT 8.6
Continued

curity therefor, or to provide funds for the payment or discharge of such indebtedness (whether in the form of loans, advances, stock purchases, capital contributions, or otherwise), or to maintain the solvency or any balance sheet or other financial condition of the obligor of such indebtedness, or to make payment for any products, materials, or supplies or for any transportation or services, regardless of the nondelivery or nonfurnishing thereof.

1.15. *Order of Confirmation* shall mean the order entered by the Court confirming the plan in accordance with the provisions of Chapter 11 of the Code, which order is no longer subject to appeal or certiorari proceeding and as to which no appeal or certiorari proceeding is pending.

1.16. *Person* shall mean an individual, corporation, partnership, joint venture, trust, estate, unincorporated organization, or a government or any agency or political subdivision thereof.

1.17. *Petition Date* shall mean [month, day,] 19__, the date on which debtor filed its Chapter 11 petition with the Court.

1.18. *Plan* shall mean this Chapter 11 plan, as amended in accordance with the terms hereof or modified in accordance with the Code.

1.19. *Prorate* shall mean, with respect to any holder of plan debt, in the same proportion that the amount of such plan debt bears to the aggregate amount of the plan debt.

1.20. *Rules* shall mean the Federal Rules of Bankruptcy Procedure as supplemented by local rules as are adopted by the Court.

ARTICLE II
ADMINISTRATION AND PRIORITY CREDITORS

Unless otherwise ordered by the Court, the administrative expenses of the debtor's Chapter 11 case allowed pursuant to 11 U.S.C.A. § 503(b) and each allowed claim entitled to priority pursuant to 11 U.S.C.A. § 507(a)(2) or (6) shall be paid in full in cash on the distribution date or as soon thereafter as is practicable.

ARTICLE III
CLASSIFICATION OF CLAIMS AND INTERESTS

The claims and interests are classified as follows:

3.01. *Class 1*. Class 1 shall include the allowed secured claims of *[name the mortgagees]*.

3.02. *Class 2*. Class 2 shall include the allowed secured claims of *[name the claimants]*.

3.03. *Class 3*. Class 3 shall include the allowed secured claims of *[name the claimants]*.

3.04. *Class 4*. Class 4 shall include the allowed small claims.

3.05. *Class 5*. Class 5 shall include all allowed claims other than those claims included in Classes 1 through 4.

EXHIBIT 8.6
Continued

ARTICLE IV
TREATMENT OF CLAIMS AND INTERESTS

4.01. *Class 1.* The Class 1 claims are impaired and shall be fully satisfied by execution of a deed in lieu of foreclosure or consent to an *in rem* decree of foreclosure with respect to the real property which secures the Class 2 claims. The holders of Class 2 claims shall have no recourse directly against the debtor or his spouse.

4.02. *Class 2.* The Class 2 claims are not impaired and shall be paid in accordance with the terms of the notes or contracts evidencing such claims.

4.03. *Class 3.* The Class 3 claims are not impaired and shall be paid in full in deferred cash payments which, as of the distribution date of the plan, equal the allowed amount of such claims. The Class 3 claims shall be paid as follows:

Claimant	Amount of Secured Claim	Payment Terms
[name of claimant]	$_____	____ consecutive monthly installments of principal and interest (at ____ Bank's prime plus ____ percent), commencing on the first day of the calendar month following 30 days from the distribution date
[name of claimant]	$_____	____ consecutive monthly installments of principal and interest; interest rate on $____ is ____ Bank's prime plus ____ percent; interest rate on balance of principal is *[name the city]* prime less ____ percent; payments commence on the first day of the calendar month following 30 days from the distribution date

4.04. *Class 4.* Each holder of a Class 4 claim is impaired and shall be paid ____ percent of the amount of such claim upon the distribution date.

4.05. *Class 5.* Each holder of a Class 5 claim is impaired and shall be paid ____ percent of the amount of such claim, which payments shall be made by deferred cash payments commencing *[month, day]*, 19____ and thereafter at *[specify the intervals]* month intervals for a period of *[specify the total number]* years, without interest.

ARTICLE V
RETENTION OF JURISDICTION

The Court shall retain jurisdiction of this Chapter 11 case pursuant to and for the purpose set forth in 11 U.S.C.A. § 1127(b) and to
1. hear and determine objections to claims and interests;
2. fix allowances of compensation and other administrative expenses allowable under the Code;
3. hear and determine causes of action by or against the debtor arising prior to the commencement of or during the pendency of this proceeding;

EXHIBIT 8.6
Continued

4. hear and determine disputes arising under or relating to this plan;
5. hear and determine causes of action by or against the debtor relating to questions of what constitutes property of the estate; and
6. for such other matters as may be set forth in the order of confirmation or as may be appropriate under the Code.

ARTICLE VI
EXECUTORY CONTRACTS

6.01. *Assumption of Certain Executory Contracts.* The debtor hereby assumes, pursuant to 11 U.S.C.A. § 1123(b)(2), the executory contracts set forth on Exhibit "A" attached to this plan.

6.02. *Rejection of Certain Executory Contracts.* The debtor hereby rejects, pursuant to 11 U.S.C.A. § 1123(b)(2), the executory contracts set forth on Exhibit "B" attached to this plan.

ARTICLE VII
MISCELLANEOUS

7.01. *Headings.* The headings in the plan are for convenience of reference only and shall not limit or otherwise affect the meanings hereof.

7.02. *Notices.* All notices required or permitted to be made in accordance with the plan shall be in writing and shall be delivered personally or by telex or other telegraphic means or mailed by registered or certified mail, return receipt requested:

(a) if to the debtor at *[mailing address]*, Attention: *[debtor's name]* with a copy to the debtor's counsel, *[debtor's attorney's name]*, *[mailing address]*;

(b) if to a holder of an allowed claim or allowed interest, at the address set forth in its proof of claim or proof of interest or, if none, at its address set forth in the debtor's schedules prepared and filed with the Court;

(c) notice shall be deemed given when received. Any person may change the address at which it is to receive notices under the plan by sending written notice pursuant to the provisions of this paragraph 7.02 to the debtor, with a copy to the debtor's counsel.

7.03. *Paragraph and Article References.* Unless otherwise specified, all references in the plan to paragraphs and articles are to paragraphs and articles of the plan.

7.04. *Reservation of Rights.* Neither the filing of this plan, nor any statement or provision contained herein, nor the taking by any creditor of any action with respect to this plan shall (a) be or be deemed to be an admission against interest and (b) until the distribution date, be or be deemed to be a waiver of any rights which any creditor might have against the debtor or any of its properties or any other creditor of the debtor, and until the distribution date all such rights are specifically reserved. In the event that the distribution date does not occur, neither this plan nor any statement contained in it, may be used or relied upon in any manner in any suit, action, proceeding, or controversy within or outside of the reorganization case involving the debtor.

[city], [state] _____

EXHIBIT 8.6
Continued

Dated this ____ day of ____, 19____

[debtor's name], dba _____
[debtor's business name] _____
By: [signature of debtor] _____

[name of debtor's attorney], Esq. _____
[firm name] _____
[mailing address] _____
[telephone number] _____

ATTORNEY FOR THE DEBTOR

EXHIBIT "A" TO PLAN OF REORGANIZATION
OF [debtor's name], dba [debtor's business name]

ASSUMED EXECUTORY CONTRACTS

1. Lease agreement dated [month, day], 19____, from [name the creditor] to debtor covering a 19____ [make, model] [automobile, truck].

EXHIBIT "B" TO PLAN OF REORGANIZATION
OF [debtor's name], dba [debtor's business name]

REJECTED EXECUTORY CONTRACTS

1. Lease agreement dated *[month, day]*, 19____, from *[name the creditor]* to debtor covering a 19____ *[make, model] [automobile, truck]*. (Assigned to *[name the assignee].*)

C. MODIFICATION OF A CHAPTER 11 PLAN

A Chapter 11 plan may be modified by the proponent at any time before confirmation. The modified plan must meet the Code's requirements regarding the classification of claims or interests and the contents of a plan. 11 U.S.C.A. §§ 1122, 1123. After a modification is filed, the plan as modified becomes the plan. 11 U.S.C.A. § 1127(a).

EXAMPLE

The XYZ Corporation filed a petition in bankruptcy under Chapter 11. At the time of filing the petition, the XYZ Corporation filed its Chapter 11 plan. Prior to filing the plan, the XYZ Corporation hired an appraiser who valued XYZ's real property at $2,000,000, which was the market value listed in the plan. The real property was mortgaged to First Bank. When First Bank had the real property appraised, its appraiser valued the property at $2,500,000. XYZ and First Bank negotiated an agreed upon value of $2,200,000. XYZ filed a modification of the plan, amending the value of the real property to $2,200,000. The plan as modified became the plan.

The proponent of a Chapter 11 plan may file a modification of the plan after acceptance but before confirmation. The modification may not adversely change the rights of a creditor or an equity security holder, as those rights were fixed in the accepted plan before modification, unless the entities adversely affected have accepted the modification in writing. This rule allows for minor modifications to be made without submission to creditors and equity security holders if their rights are not affected. The modification is deemed accepted by all creditors and equity security holders who have previously accepted the plan. Fed. R. Bank. P. 3019.

Although not often done, the proponent of a plan or the debtor may modify the plan after confirmation but before substantial consummation of the plan. Such a modification must also meet the Code's requirements. 11 U.S.C.A. §§ 1122, 1123. This modified plan becomes the plan only if circumstances warrant the modification and if the Court, after notice and a hearing, confirms the plan as modified. 11 U.S.C.A. §§ 1127(b), 1129.

The proponents of a modification must meet the Code's disclosure requirements. 11 U.S.C.A. §§ 1125, 1127(c). This would require an amended disclosure statement unless an amendment to the disclosure statement met the requirements.

Any holder of a claim or interest that has accepted or rejected a plan is deemed to have accepted or rejected the modified plan unless this holder changes its vote within the time fixed by the court. 11 U.S.C.A. § 1127(d). The creditor or stockholder whose interests have been materially and adversely affected by the modification therefore has an opportunity to change its vote. This opportunity is necessary to meet the requirements regarding disclosure and solicitation of votes. 11 U.S.C.A. § 1125.

SECTION 8
CHAPTER 11 PLAN FILED BY PARTIES OTHER THAN THE DEBTOR

Parties in interest, other than the debtor, may file a Chapter 11 plan under certain conditions. Parties who may file a plan include the trustee, a creditor, a creditors' committee, an equity security holder, an equity security holders' committee, or an indenture trustee. These parties may file a plan only if

(1) a trustee has been appointed under this chapter;
(2) the debtor has not filed a plan before 120 days after the date of the order for relief under this chapter; or
(3) the debtor has not filed a plan that has been accepted, before 180 days after the date of the order for relief under this chapter, by each class of claims or interests that is impaired under the plan. 11 U.S.C.A. §§ 1121(c)(1)–(3).

The 120-day period or the 180-day period may be reduced or increased by the court for cause upon request by a party in interest and after notice and a hearing.

SECTION 9
A DISCLOSURE STATEMENT OR EVIDENCE SHOWING COMPLIANCE WITH 11 U.S.C.A. § 1126(b)

A **disclosure statement** (see Exhibit 8.7) must provide "adequate information" to enable those voting on the plan to make an informed judgment about the plan. A disclosure statement is a written document that must be transmitted to each holder of a claim or interest, along with the reorganization plan or a summary of the plan, before acceptance of the plan may be solicited. The disclosure statement, however, must be approved by the court, after notice and a hearing, before it is transmitted to the creditors. The court will only approve a disclosure statement if it is found to contain **adequate information.** Adequate information can mean different things for different classes of creditors. The Code definition of "adequate information" is set forth in 11 U.S.C.A. § 1125.

> (a) In this section—
> (1) "adequate information" means information of a kind, and in sufficient detail, as far as is reasonably practicable in light of the nature and history of the debtor and the condition of the debtor's books and records, that would enable a hypothetical reasonable investor typical of holders of claims or interests of the relevant class to make an informed judgment about the plan, but adequate information need not include such information about any other possible or proposed plan; and
> (2) "investor typical of holders of claims or interests of the relevant class" means investor having—
> > (A) a claim or interest of the relevant class;
> > (B) such a relationship with the debtor as the holders of others claims or interests of such class generally have; and
> > (C) such ability to obtain such information from sources other than the disclosure required by this section as holders of claims or interests in such class generally have. 11 U.S.C.A. §§ 1125(a)(1), (2).

Although the same disclosure statement must be transmitted to each holder of a claim or interest of a particular class, different disclosure statements may be sent to other classes. Adequate information for one class may differ in amount, detail, or kind from that required for another class. 11 U.S.C.A. § 1125(c).

EXAMPLE

The debtor's plan provides for issuing stock to one class of unsecured creditors and paying cash in the full amount of the claim to another class of unsecured creditors. The class of creditors receiving stock will receive an extensive disclosure statement that looks like a prospectus but is not as detailed and would not meet securities regulations. The class of creditors receiving cash will receive only a brief disclosure statement that basically discloses the source of the cash that will be used to pay these creditors.

What adequate information consists of is not governed by any otherwise applicable nonbankruptcy law, rule, or regulation. An agency or official charged with administering or enforcing such a law, rule, or regulation may be heard on the subject but may not appeal an order approving a disclosure statement.

One of the areas most likely to cause problems for the proponent of a plan involves the issuing or transferring of stock. Adequate information may be difficult to glean from the records available. For this reason, the Code has what is known as the "safe harbor" provision. This provision permits freedom from liability for violations of securities laws made by a person, in good faith and in compliance with Code provisions, in the offer, issuance, sale, or purchase of a security under the plan. 11 U.S.C.A. § 1125(e).

In spite of the fact that the debtor issuing or transferring stock under the plan need not comply with state and federal securities laws to have a disclosure statement approved by the court, it may be desirable to do so. If the securities are to be traded soon after confirmation, they will have to meet securities regulations to be registered for trading. Preparation of a disclosure statement by the debtor issuing or transferring stock will be time and resource consuming if it is to be approved by the court. The extra effort expended at this time to meet securities regulations could pay off if the stock is ready to be registered for trading immediately upon certification.

A disclosure statement should contain a section stating the nature of the business and enough of the debtor's history to show why a Chapter 11 petition was filed. There should be a full discussion of any changes to be made that will permit the debtor to reorganize. Both financial data and a narrative discussion should be included. The creditor or the equity security holder must be able to determine from the disclosure statement if it will receive "not less" under the plan than it would receive under Chapter 7 liquidation. The best interests of creditors test is required for confirmation of the Chapter 11 plan. 11 U.S.C.A. § 1129(a)(7).

The plan will not be confirmed unless sufficient financial information is presented in the disclosure statement to show that the plan is a feasible one and will not be followed by liquidation or another attempt at reorganization.

The debtor may have solicited acceptances of a plan before the commencement of the Chapter 11 case. The holder of a claim or interest that has accepted or rejected the plan before the debtor has filed the case is deemed to have accepted or rejected the plan if

(1) the solicitation of such acceptance or rejection was in compliance with any applicable nonbankruptcy law, rule, or regulation governing the adequacy of disclosure in connection with such solicitation; or

(2) if there is not any such law, rule, or regulation, such acceptance or rejection was solicited after disclosure to such holder of adequate information, as defined in section 1125(a) of this title. 11 U.S.C.A. §§ 1126(b)(1), (2).

If the debtor has complied with these requirements and can provide evidence of this fact to the court, it will not be necessary to file any further disclosure statement.

EXHIBIT 8.7
A Chapter 11 Disclosure Statement

UNITED STATES BANKRUPTCY COURT
_____ **DISTRICT OF** _____

In re [*debtor's name*] _____)_____
     [Set forth here all names including)
     married, maiden, and trade names,)
     used by debtor within last 6 years])
)   Case No. _____
            Debtor   )
)   Chapter 11
Address _____)
Social Security No. _____)
Employer's Tax Identification Nos. [if any])
     _____)

DISCLOSURE STATEMENT
FOR
[NAME OF THE DEBTOR]

The creditors should read the Disclosure Statement and the Plan carefully to determine into which class their claims are classified and how their claims are treated under the Plan. Classes 1, 4, and 5 are impaired under the Plan and therefore are entitled to vote on the Plan. A ballot accompanies this Disclosure Statement. Each creditor in the classes entitled to vote should properly complete the ballot and return it to the Bankruptcy Court as instructed on the ballot.

    Capitalized terms used in this Disclosure Statement have the meanings as defined herein or in Article I of the Plan.

I.   *PURPOSE*

A.   *Introduction*

On [*month, day*], 19____, the Debtor in Possession, [*debtor's name*], dba [*name of business*] ("Debtor"), a sole proprietorship, filed its Voluntary Petition for Reorganization under Chapter 11 of the United States Bankruptcy Code. The Debtor has proposed a plan of reorganization which is provided simultaneously for your review.

B.   *Acceptance of the Plan*

The Bankruptcy Court has set the ____ day of [*month*], 19____ at _____ o'clock __.m. for hearing on acceptance of the Plan. A creditor may vote to accept the Plan by filling out and mailing the ballot which is provided with this Disclosure Statement to [*name and mailing address of debtor's attorney*]. A creditor may also vote in person at the hearing on acceptance, which will be held at the above time and date in Room _____ of [*name of the building or address*] in [*city, state*]. Whether a creditor votes on the Plan or not, the creditor will be bound by the terms and treatment set forth in the Plan if the Plan is accepted by the requisite majorities of creditors and is confirmed by the Court.

EXHIBIT 8.7
Continued

Absent objection, any claim timely filed is deemed allowed. However, absent an affirmative act constituting a vote accepting or rejecting the Plan, a nonvoting creditor and that creditor's claim will not be included for purposes of determining whether or not the requisite number of votes is obtained. (Allowance or disallowance of a claim for voting purposes does not necessarily mean that all or a portion of the claim will not be allowed or disallowed for distribution purposes.)

In order for the Plan to be accepted by creditors, a majority in number and two-thirds in amount of claims filed and allowed (for voting purposes), and actually voting, of each affected class of creditors must vote to accept the Plan. You are therefore urged to complete, date, sign, and promptly mail the enclosed ballot. Please be sure to properly complete the form and legibly identify the name of the claimant.

C.   *Solicitation*

The Debtor may solicit your vote. No one soliciting votes shall receive any compensation for any solicitation.

No representations concerning the Debtor or the Plan of Reorganization are authorized, other than those set forth in this Disclosure Statement. Any representations or inducements made by any person to secure your vote, other than those contained in this Disclosure Statement, should not be relied upon, and such representations or inducements should be reported to counsel for the Debtor, who shall deliver such information to the Bankruptcy Court.

D.   *Requirement of Disclosure Statement*

Pursuant to the terms of the Code, this Disclosure Statement has been presented to and approved by the Bankruptcy Court. Such approval is required under the Code to provide assurance that this Statement contains information adequate to enable the holders of claims to make an informed judgment about the Plan. Court approval does not, in any way, constitute a judgment by the Court as to the desirability of the Plan or as to the value of any consideration offered thereby. Interested parties are referred to Section 1125 of the Bankruptcy Code (11 U.S.C.A. § 1125), which reads, in part

(b) An acceptance or rejection of a plan may not be solicited after the commencement of a case under this title from a holder of a claim or interest with respect to such claim or interest, unless, at the time of or before such solicitation, there is transmitted to such holder the plan or a summary of the plan, and a written disclosure statement approved, after notice and a hearing, by the court as containing adequate information. The court may approve a disclosure statement without a valuation of the debtor or an appraisal of the debtor's assets.

(c) . . . .

(d) Whether a disclosure statement required under subsection (b) of this section contains adequate information is not governed by any otherwise applicable nonbankruptcy law, rule, or regulation, but an agency or official whose duty is to administer or enforce such a law, rule, or regulation may be heard on the issue of whether a disclosure statement contains adequate information. Such an agency or official may not appeal from, or otherwise seek review of, an order approving a disclosure statement.

(e) A person that solicits acceptance or rejection of a plan, in good faith and in compliance with the applicable provisions of this title, or that participates, in good faith and in compliance with the applicable provisions of this title, in the offer,

EXHIBIT 8.7
Continued

issuance, sale, or purchase of a security, offered or sold under the plan, of the debtor, of an affiliate participating in a joint plan with the debtor, or of a newly organized successor to the debtor under the plan, is not liable, on account of such solicitation or participation, for violation of any applicable law, rule, or regulation governing solicitation of acceptance or rejection of a plan or the offer, issuance, sale, or purchase of securities.

E.   *Limitation of Disclosure Statement*

The Debtor has prepared the Disclosure Statement in order to disclose that information which, in the opinion of Debtor, is material, important, and necessary to an evaluation of the Plan. The information herein contained is intended to be used solely for the use of known creditors of the Debtor and, accordingly, may not be relied upon for any purpose other than the determination of how to vote on the Plan. In addition, materials contained in this Disclosure Statement are not intended to be adequate for the formation of a judgment by any creditor as to the preferability of any alternative to the Plan. Materials referring to alternatives to the Plan are limited by both the practical considerations of space and the opinion of the Debtor regarding same.

Certain of the materials contained in this Disclosure Statement are taken directly from other, readily accessible instruments or documents or are digests of other instruments or documents. While the Debtor has made every effort to retain the meaning of such other instruments or the portions thereof, it urges that any reliance on the contents of such other instruments should depend on a thorough review of the instruments themselves.

II.   *BACKGROUND INFORMATION*

A.   *Organization of Debtor*

Debtor is a sole proprietorship operated by *[debtor's name]*. *[Debtor's name]* purchased *[name of business]* from *[name of former owner]* on *[month, day]*, 19___, for a purchase price of $xxx,xxx.xx. Debtor's place of business is located at *[street address]*.

B.   *Business of the Debtor*

Debtor is in the business of *[describe debtor's business]* in the *[geographic]* market area.

C.   *Economic Factors Affecting the Plan*

The Debtor believes that the Plan as proposed is fair and equitable and that each class of creditors will receive at least what it would realize if the Debtor were liquidated.

EXHIBIT 8.7
Continued

1. *Value of Debtor's Assets.* The Debtor has business assets having the liquidation values set forth below:

Asset	Liquidation Value
Land and buildings [address]	$xxx,xxx.xx
Office equipment	x,xxx.xx
Machinery, fixtures, equipment (excluding office equipment, and supplies	xx,xxx.xx
Inventory	xx,xxx.xx
Accounts receivable	x,xxx.xx

The Debtor has non-business, personal assets owned by himself and his spouse having the liquidation values set forth below:

Asset	Liquidation Value
Residence [address]	$xxx,xxx.xx
Bank deposits	x,xxx.xx
Household goods	xx,xxx.xx
Wearing apparel and personal possessions	x,xxx.xx
[description of motor vehicle]	x,xxx.xx
[description of motor vehicle]	x,xxx.xx
[description of motor vehicle]	x,xxx.xx

2. *Liens and Debts.* The Debtor's business real property, inventory, and equipment are subject to claims of lien held by [name of creditor] in a total sum of approximately $xxx,xxx.xx. [Name of creditor] holds a lien in the approximate amount of $x,xxx.xx against Debtor's 19___ [make, model] automobile. [Name of creditor] holds a lien on Debtor's 19___ [make, model] automobile in the approximate amount of $x,xxx.xx. [Name of creditor] holds a lien on Debtor's 19___ [make, model] truck in the approximate amount of $x,xxx.xx. [Name of creditor] holds a lien on Debtor's telephone system in the approximate amount of $x,xxx.xx. [Name of creditor] holds a lien on Debtor's pneumatic forklift in the approximate amount of $xxx.xx. The Debtor owes approximately $xx,xxx.xx on unsecured, prepetition indebtedness.

   The personal residence of Debtor and his spouse is encumbered by two mortgages, one held by [name the mortgagee] in the approximate sum of $xxx,xxx.xx, and one held by [name the mortgagee] in the approximate sum of $xx,xxx.xx.

   Since the filing of the petition, Debtor has paid for its inventory on a prepaid basis. Wages and taxes have been timely paid. Debtor has not borrowed any funds or incurred any credit after the petition date.

   Expenses of administration, including professional fees of attorneys and accountants, have been incurred and either have been or will be entitled to priority by the Bankruptcy Court. As of this date, counsel for the Debtor has incurred unpaid legal fees and expenses of approximately $x,xxx.xx. Incurred and unpaid accounting fees are presently in the sum of approximately $x,xxx.xx.

EXHIBIT 8.7
Continued

It should be emphasized that the above estimates of debts and expenses are estimates only. The final determination of claims against the Debtor will be made by the Bankruptcy Court. There may be legitimate claims which are not reflected on the Debtor's books of account. In addition, final allowed claims may be more or less than the amounts shown on the books. The Debtor has accrued additional expenses since the preparation of this disclosure statement and will continue to accrue expenses in the future.

D.   *Summary of Debtor's Assets and Liabilities*

The business assets of the Debtor have a total liquidation value of approximately $xxx,xxx.xx. Of this sum, $xxx,xxx.xx represents the value of land and buildings constituting Debtor's place of business at *[street address]*. The value of such real estate was established by *[name]* of *[name of company]*, who testified as to the value of such property on behalf of *[name the creditor]* at a hearing in Bankruptcy Court to determine if *[name the creditor]* should be allowed relief from the automatic stay to foreclose its real estate mortgages and security agreements.

The Debtor's business liabilities are in the total sum of approximately $xxx,xxx.xx, of which $xx,xxx.xx is due to unsecured creditors and $xxx,xxx.xx is due to holders of asserted secured claims. Debtor has filed objections to the secured claims of *[name the creditor]*. If such objections are upheld by the Court, $xxx,xxx.xx of asserted secured claims would be classified and treated as unsecured claims.

The personal assets of the Debtor and his spouse are approximately equal in value to their joint liabilities.

E.   *Events Leading to the Bankruptcy Proceeding*

In *[month]* 19__, *[name the mortgagee]* commenced an action in the *[name the court]* to foreclose its second real estate mortgage and security agreements on the business assets of the Debtor. At that time, the interest of *[name the mortgagee]* in the assets was subordinate to the lien of *[name the mortgagee]* in the amount of approximately $xxx.xxx.xx. *[Name the mortgagee]* paid the Debtor's indebtedness to *[name the mortgagee]* and became subrogated to the first lien position held by *[name the mortgagee]*.

As stated previously, the Debtor had purchased *[name of business]* from *[name the seller]* in *[month]* of 19__ for $xxx,xxx.xx. Debtor paid $xx,xxx.xx of the purchase price down, and the balance of $xxx,xxx.xx was financed through *[name the creditor]* and *[name the creditor]*. Because the business of the Debtor is seasonal and Debtor had the burden of servicing substantial indebtedness, Debtor was unable to timely pay the sums owing to *[name the creditor]* in late 19__ and early 19__.

To avert *[name the creditor's]* foreclosure action and to reorganize his financial affairs, the Debtor filed for relief under Chapter 11 of the Bankruptcy Code on *[month, date]*, 19__.

F.   *Events Subsequent to Filing*

The Debtor has continued to operate his business as a debtor in possession since the date of the filing of the Petition, *[month, date]*, 19__. A committee of unsecured creditors was appointed by the Court. The names, addresses, and phone numbers of the members of the committee are shown on Exhibit "A" to this Disclosure Statement.

EXHIBIT 8.7
Continued

On *[month, date],* 19___, the Debtor obtained an order of the Bankruptcy Court authorizing the Debtor to use cash collateral in the operation of his business during the bankruptcy proceeding. The effect of the order was to allow the Debtor to use inventory and accounts receivable, and the proceeds thereof, in the operation of his business notwithstanding the security interests of *[name the creditor]* in such assets. On *[month, date],* 19___, the Bankruptcy Court denied the motion of *[name the mortgagee]* for relief from the automatic stay provided that the Debtor pay to *[name the mortgagee]* the accrued interest on the first mortgage indebtedness of approximately $x,xxx.xx previously held by *[name the mortgagee]* and subsequently transferred to *[name the mortgagee].*

On *[month, date],* 19___, *[name the second mortgagee]* moved for removal of the automatic stay to allow *[name the second mortgagee]* to foreclose its second mortgage on the Debtor's personal residence. With the consent of the Debtor, the Bankruptcy Court subsequently entered an order allowing *[name the second mortgagee]* to proceed with a foreclosure action in state court. Under the order of the Bankruptcy Court, *[name the second mortgagee]* could not proceed to establish a personal judgment against the Debtor, but may only assert its interest against the Debtor's property. The Debtor consented to the Order Granting Relief from the Stay because Debtor's total monthly mortgage payments amount to approximately $x,xxx.xx. By surrendering the residence to the mortgage holders, Debtor can acquire replacement housing at a substantially lower cost, which will in turn allow the Debtor to reduce his compensation from *[name of business]* and facilitate the performance by the Debtor of his obligations under the Plan of Reorganization.

G. *Development of the Plan*

The Plan has been discussed by the Debtor in a general fashion with the committee of unsecured creditors and the Debtor's primary secured creditor, *[name the creditor].* Such parties were advised by the Debtor that the purchase price which the Debtor paid for *[name of business]* was excessive in view of the value of the assets and earning potential of *[name of business].* The Debtor advised such parties that his secured debt would have to be adjusted to conform to the true value of the assets which constituted the collateral for the secured indebtedness. The primary objective of the Plan is to reduce the Debtor's secured indebtedness, which will necessarily result in an increase of the Debtor's unsecured indebtedness. However, the unsecured indebtedness can then be paid on the basis of an amount which exceeds what the unsecured creditors would obtain in the event of a liquidation.

III.   THE PLAN

A. *Principal Elements of the Plan*

The Plan essentially provides that secured creditors will receive payments equalling 100% of the allowed amount of their secured claims. Unsecured claims of $300.00 or less will be paid 15% of their claims, and other unsecured creditors will be paid 10% of their claims. Since there are no priority claims other than claims for administrative expenses, only the professional fees incurred by the Debtor and approved by the Court will have to be paid prior to making the payments to secured and unsecured creditors.

EXHIBIT 8.7
Continued

B.   *Classification of Creditors*

The claims of the Debtor's creditors are divided into five classes: Class 1, Class 2, Class 3, Class 4, and Class 5. The following table shows the approximate amount of the claims in each class as reflected on the amended schedules filed in the chapter 11 proceeding by the Debtor, exclusive, unless otherwise noted, of: (i) interest, if any; (ii) amounts paid previously pursuant to court order; and (iii) contingent, disputed, or unknown portions of claims. These amounts are for illustration only and do not include all claims.

Class Number	Claims Included	Unless Otherwise Indicated, Approximate Class Amount as of *[month, day]*, 19__
1	*[name of creditor]*, *[name of creditor]*	$xxx,xxx.xx
2	*[name of creditor]*, *[name of creditor]*, *[name of creditor]*, *[name of creditor]*	xx,xxx.xx
3	*[name of creditor]*, *[name of creditor]*	xxx,xxx.xx
4	Unsecured creditors having claims less than or equal to $300.00	xxx.xx
5	Unsecured claims in excess of $300.00	xxx,xxx.xx

C.   **Treatment of Various Classes**

Article 4 of the Plan details the treatment of the various classes under the Plan. It is important to realize that the Plan, if accepted and confirmed, binds each creditor and in some cases, in particular with regard to the holders of Class 4 and 5 claims, may result in the reduction and settlement of their claims for less than the full amount thereof. However, the liquidation of the Debtor would, in the opinion of the Debtor, result in settlement of these claims for far less than the full amount thereof and would result in Classes 4 and 5 receiving less than they would under the Plan.

Generally, the Plan impairs the Class 1, 4, and 5 Claims. Class 1 claims shall be satisfied by a deed in lieu of foreclosure or an agreed judgment of foreclosure with respect to the real property which secures such claims. Class 4 and Class 5 claims will be satisfied by the payment of a percentage of the full amount of such claims which, as to Class 5 Claims, shall be paid on a deferred basis.

The Class 2 Claims are not impaired and will be paid in accordance with the terms of promissory notes or contracts evidencing such claims. The Class 3 Claims shall be paid in full in deferred cash payments equal to the allowed amount of the claims plus accrued interest at the rates of interest specified in the notes evidencing the Class 3 Claims.

EXHIBIT 8.7
Continued

IV.   *EFFECT OF ACCEPTANCE OF PLAN*

If a majority in number and two-thirds in amount of claims filed, allowed, and actually voting of each affected class of creditors vote to accept the Plan, the Plan will become effective and will be confirmed by the Court. Upon confirmation, all of the prepetition debts of the Company will be modified into the indebtedness as described in the Plan with respect to each class of claims.

The allowed amounts of Class 3, Class 4, and Class 5 Claims have not been completely resolved, and some objections to such claims have been or may be asserted. No final determination of the validity of these objections will be made until after the date of confirmation. Accordingly, some of the claims may be totally or partially disallowed.

Attached to this Disclosure Statement as Exhibit "B" is a projection of the Debtor's income and expenses for the period of *[month]* 19__, through *[month]* 19__. The projection reflects the payments to secured and unsecured creditors under the Plan. The sales projections are based upon actual sales for 19__, less __%. The projections reflected in Exhibit "B" are based upon estimated revenues of the Debtor, and, while such projections are based upon the most reliable sources available, they are only estimates.

V.   *GENERAL CONSIDERATIONS IN ACCEPTING A CHAPTER 11 PLAN*

A.   *Operation of Chapter 11*

The confirmation of a Plan of Reorganization is the ultimate goal of a Chapter 11 proceeding. Consequently, the decision of the creditors to accept the Plan must be made in the context fixed by the law for Chapter 11 proceedings.

In a Chapter 11, the Debtor is the only possible proponent of a Plan of Reorganization during the initial 120 days of the proceedings unless certain special conditions, not present in this case, are met. After that 120-day period (unless the Bankruptcy Court extends it), any party in interest may propose a Plan of Reorganization. In this case, the 120-day period has expired.

Chapter 11 of the Bankruptcy Code permits the adjustment of secured debt, unsecured debt, and equity interests. A Chapter 11 plan may provide less than full satisfaction of senior indebtedness and payment to junior indebtedness or may provide for return to equity owners absent full satisfaction of indebtedness so long as no impaired class votes against the Plan. ("Impaired" is defined in § 1124 of the Bankruptcy Code.)

If an impaired class votes against the Plan, this does not necessarily make implementation of the Plan impossible so long as the Plan is fair and equitable and the affected class is afforded "adequate protection." Adequate protection may be very broadly defined as providing to a creditor (or interest holder) the full value of his claim. Such value is determined by the Court and balanced against the treatment afforded the creditor. If the protection afforded to the creditor under the Plan is equal to or greater than the protection which the creditor otherwise has, the Plan may be confirmed over the dissent of that class. In the event a class is unimpaired, it is automatically deemed to accept the Plan. A class is unimpaired, in essence, if (1) its rights after confirmation are equal to what existed (or would have existed absent defaults) before the commencement of the Chapter 11 and any existing defaults are cured or provided for and the class is reimbursed actual damages, or (2) the class is paid its full claim as though matured.

EXHIBIT 8.7
Continued

If there is not a dissenting class, the test for approval by a court of a Chapter 11 plan (i.e., confirmation) is whether the Plan is feasible and is in the best interests of creditors and interest holders. In simple terms, a Plan is considered by the court to be in the best interests of creditors and interest holders if the Plan will provide a better recovery to the creditors than they would obtain if the Debtor were liquidated and the proceeds of liquidation were distributed in accordance with bankruptcy liquidation priorities. In other words, if the Plan provides creditors with money or other property of a value exceeding the probable distributions in liquidation bankruptcy, then the Plan is in the best interests of creditors. The Court, in considering this factor, is not required to consider any alternative to the Plan other than liquidation bankruptcy.

In considering feasibility, the court is only required to determine whether the obligations of the Plan can be performed. This entails determining: (1) the availability of cash for payments required at confirmation; (2) the ability of the Debtor to generate future cash flow sufficient to make payments called for under the Plan to continue in business; and (3) the absence of any other factor which might make it impossible for the Debtor to accomplish what is proposed in the Plan.

B.   Alternatives to the Plan

Although this Disclosure Statement is intended to provide information to assist in the formation of a judgment whether to vote for or against the Plan, and although creditors are not being offered through that vote an opportunity to express an opinion concerning alternatives to the Plan, a brief discussion of alternatives to the Plan may be useful. These alternatives include: (1) continuation of the Chapter 11 proceedings and development of another, different Plan; (2) transfer to liquidation bankruptcy; or (3) dismissal of these proceedings. The Debtor believes the proposed Plan to be in the best interests of creditors and the Debtor. Thus, it does not favor any of the alternatives to the proposed Plan discussed below. In arriving at that conclusion, the alternative courses are assessed as follows:

1. Continuation of the Chapter 11 proceedings would be advisable if greater advantage could thereby be attained by improving the position of the Debtor and arranging a better plan of operations. While continuation of the Chapter 11 proceedings may result in an alternative Plan of Reorganization being developed, the Debtor does not believe, based upon his experience in the *[name the business]* business, that there can be material changes in the operation of *[name of company]*. The payments provided for under the proposed Plan are consistent with the past and projected income of *[name of company]*. Accordingly, the Debtor is unaware of any benefits that might result from continuation of the Chapter 11 proceedings and is unaware of any improvements which could be made to the Plan of Reorganization.

2. It is believed that liquidation proceedings would be contrary to the best interests of all interested parties. Market prices for assets of the Debtor are somewhat depressed at this time. Based upon the information available to the Debtor, the creditors will receive more under the Plan than they would recover in a liquidation.

3. Dismissal of the proceedings would lead to an unsatisfactory result. Should the proceedings be dismissed, secured creditors would pursue foreclosure actions against the Debtor which would ultimately result in the termination of the Debtor's business with no distribution to its unsecured creditors and a reduced distribution to secured creditors.

EXHIBIT 8.7
Continued

The assessment of these alternatives is provided solely for the purpose of full disclosure, and creditors are cautioned that a vote must be for or against the Plan. The vote on the Plan does not include a vote on alternatives to the Plan. There is no assurance of what results will occur if the Plan is not accepted. If you believe one of the alternatives referred to above, or some other alternative, is preferable to the Plan and you wish to urge it (them) upon the Court, you should consult counsel as to the appropriate action.

C. *Additional Specific Considerations in Voting*

All of the foregoing give rise in the instant case to the following implications and risks concerning the Plan.

While the Plan provides for some payments at or shortly after confirmation, such payments will be limited to Allowed Claims. Under the Bankruptcy Code, a claim may not be paid until it is allowed. A claim will be allowed in the absence of objection. A claim, including claims arising from defaults, which has been objected to will be heard by the Court at a regular evidentiary hearing and allowed in full or in part or disallowed. While the Debtor bears the principal responsibility for claim objections, any interested party, including the Creditors' Committee, may file claim objections. Accordingly, payment on some claims, including claims arising from defaults, may be delayed until objections to such claims are ultimately settled or a decision is made not to object to such a claim.

VI. *BINDING EFFECT UPON CREDITORS; DISCHARGE*

Upon confirmation, the Plan will bind all creditors and interest holders, including their heirs, successors, and assigns. All such creditors and interest holders will be legally obligated to execute and deliver any and all documents that may be required to effectuate the Plan. All debt, whether liquidated, contingent, or disputed and whether scheduled by the Debtor, except as provided in § 1141 of the Bankruptcy Code and except as same either is not impaired under the Plan or is payable as provided in the Plan, shall on confirmation of the Plan be discharged and thereby released and no longer recoverable from the company.

VII. *RELEVANT INFORMATION—FURTHER INFORMATION*

In addition to the Exhibits attached hereto, the following additional documents pertain to the Debtor, or to the Plan and its implementation, and are referred to in order that any creditor who so desires may review a part or all of such documents in addition to the summaries or descriptions of them as contained in this disclosure statement:

1. Initial Financial Report filed with Bankruptcy Court by Debtor; and
2. Monthly Financial Reports filed in *[month]*, *[month]*, and *[month]* of 19__.

Copies of the foregoing documents (or, if they are not yet in final form, then copies of the latest available drafts thereof) may be obtained from

[Name of Debtor's Attorney] _____
[mailing address] _____
[telephone number] _____

EXHIBIT 8.7
Continued

In addition, any creditor who desires any further information of any type regarding the Company or the Plan should direct his or her inquiry to the above address and telephone number. No person, other than Debtor and Debtor's counsel, is authorized to furnish any information on which a creditor is entitled to rely in connection with such creditor's acceptance or rejection of the Plan.

CONCLUSION

This disclosure statement contains information intended to assist the Debtor's creditors in evaluating the Plan of Reorganization. If the Plan is accepted, all creditors of the Debtor will be bound by its terms.

The Debtor urges each creditor to read the plan carefully and to use this Disclosure Statement, the other exhibits hereto, and such other information as may be available to the creditor in order to make an informed decision on the Plan.

[city], [state] _____

Dated this ____ day of _____, 19____

[debtor's name], dba _____
[debtor's business name] _____
By: *[signature of debtor]* _____

[name of debtor's attorney], Esq. _____
[firm name] _____
[mailing address] _____
[telephone number] _____

ATTORNEY FOR THE DEBTOR

EXHIBIT "A" TO DISCLOSURE STATEMENT
OF *[name]* **dba** *[name of business]*

UNSECURED CREDITORS' COMMITTEE

[Name]	*[Name]*
[mailing address]	*[mailing address]*
[telephone number]	*[telephone number]*
[Name]	*[Name]*
[mailing address]	*[mailing address]*
[telephone number]	*[telephone number]*
[Name]	*[Name]*
[mailing address]	*[mailing address]*
[telephone number]	*[telephone number]*

SECTION 10
HEARING ON THE DISCLOSURE STATEMENT

At the **hearing on the disclosure statement,** the court will set the time for the hearing on the confirmation of the plan, set the time for filing objections to confirmation, and may set a bar date for the filing of the claims and the requests for payment of administrative costs. Exhibit 8.8 is the official notice of the hearing on the disclosure statement. Votes on the plan may be solicited along with transmission of the approved disclosure statement and plan or summary of the plan, or they may be solicited later. Votes may not be solicited prior to transmission of these documents. Exhibit 8.9 is the official order approving the disclosure statement and fixing the time for filing acceptances or rejections of the plan.

EXHIBIT 8.8

Official Form No. 12 (Order and Notice for Hearing on Disclosure Statement)

Form B12
6/90

UNITED STATES BANKRUPTCY COURT
_____ DISTRICT OF _____

In re _____ ,)
     Set forth here all names including married,)
     maiden, and trade names used by debtor within)
     last 6 years.])
                                  Debtor) Case No. _____
)
Address _____)
)
              _____) Chapter _____
Social Security No(s). _____ and all)
Employer's Tax Identification No(s). *[if any]*_____)
_____)

ORDER AND NOTICE FOR HEARING
ON DISCLOSURE STATEMENT

To the debtor, its creditors, and other parties in interest:

    A disclosure statement and a plan under chapter 11 [*or* chapter 9] of the Bankruptcy Code having been filed by _____ on _____ ,
IT IS ORDERED and notice is hereby given, that:

    1. The hearing to consider the approval of the disclosure statement shall be held at: _____ , on _____ , at _____ o'clock ___.m.

    2. _____ is fixed as the last day for filing and serving in accordance with Fed. R. Bankr. P. 3017(a) written objections to the disclosure statement.

    3. Within _____ days after entry of this order, the disclosure statement and plan shall be distributed in accordance with Fed. R. Bankr. P. 3017(a).

    4. Requests for copies of the disclosure statement and plan shall be mailed to the debtor in possession [*or* trustee *or* debtor *or* _____] at * _____ .

Dated: _____

                                   BY THE COURT

                                  _____

*   State mailing address
                                   United States Bankruptcy Judge

EXHIBIT 8.9

Official Form No. 13 (Order Approving Disclosure Statement and Fixing Time for Filing Acceptances or Rejections of Plan, Combined with Notice Thereof)

Form B13
6/90

UNITED STATES BANKRUPTCY COURT
_____DISTRICT OF_____

In re _____,   )
    Set forth here all names including married,)
    maiden, and trade names used by debtor within)
    last 6 years.])
                     Debtor)   Case No. _____
)
)
Address _____)
)
)   Chapter _____
    _____)
)
Social Security No(s). _____ and all)
Employer's Tax Identification No(s). *[if any]*_____)
_____)

ORDER APPROVING DISCLOSURE STATEMENT AND FIXING TIME
FOR FILING ACCEPTANCES OR REJECTIONS OF PLAN,
COMBINED WITH NOTICE THEREOF

    A disclosure statement under chapter 11 of the Bankruptcy Code having been filed by _____, on _____ *[if appropriate, and by* _____, on _____ *]*, referring to a plan under chapter 11 of the Code filed by _____, on _____ *[if appropriate, and by* _____, on _____ respectively] *[if appropriate*, as modified by a modification filed on _____ *]*; and

    It having been determined after hearing on notice that the disclosure statement *[or statements]* contains[s] adequate information:

    IT IS ORDERED, and notice is hereby given, that:

    A. The disclosure statement filed by _____ dated _____ *[if appropriate*, and by _____, dated _____ is *[are]* approved.

    B. _____ is fixed as the last day for filing written acceptances or rejections of the plan *[or plans]* referred to above.

    C. Within _____ days after the entry of this order, the plan *[or plans]* *or* a summary *or* summaries thereof approved by the court, [and *[if appropriate]* a summary approved by the court of its opinion, if any, dated _____, approving the disclosure statement *[or statements]*], the disclosure statement *[or statements]*, and a ballot conforming to Official Form 14 shall be mailed to creditors, equity security holders, and other parties in interest, and shall be transmitted to the United States trustee, as provided in Fed. R. Bankr. P. 3017(d).

    D. If acceptances are filed for more than one plan, preferences among the plans so accepted may be indicated.

    E. *[If appropriate]* _____ is fixed for the hearing on confirmation of the plan *[or plans]*.

    F. *[If appropriate]* _____ is fixed as the last day for filing and serving pursuant to Fed. R. Bankr. P. 3020(b)(1) written objections to confirmation of the plan.

    Dated: _____

                                   BY THE COURT

                                     _____
                                   United States Bankruptcy Judge

    [If the court directs that a copy of the opinion should be transmitted in lieu of or in addition to the summary thereof, the appropriate change should be made in paragraph C of this order.]

In re Scioto Valley Mortgage Company involves a hearing on a disclosure statement and the problems the court found with the debtor's disclosure statement.

In re Scioto Valley Mortgage Company
United States Bankruptcy Court, Southern District of Ohio, 1988.
88 B.R. 168.

ORDER ON FIRST AMENDED DISCLOSURE STATEMENT
R. Guy Cole, Jr.,
Bankruptcy Judge

I.　PRELIMINARY CONSIDERATIONS

This matter is before the Court upon the request of Scioto Valley Mortgage Company (the "Debtor") for approval of its First Amended Disclosure Statement ("Disclosure Statement"). Objections to the Debtor's request for approval have been filed by William G. Hayes, Jr., Trustee for Beacon Securities, Inc. and its consolidated affiliates; R. Dale Smith; BancOhio National Bank; and the United States Trustee. Upon conclusion of an actual, evidentiary hearing, the Court ruled orally that the Disclosure Statement omits adequate information as that term is defined in 11 U.S.C. § 1125(a). The Court hereby supplements its oral ruling with this Order.

The Court has jurisdiction over this matter pursuant to 28 U.S.C. § 1334(b) and the General Order of Reference entered in this judicial district. This is a core proceeding which the Court may hear and determine. 28 U.S.C. § 157(b)(1) and (2)(A). The following opinion constitutes the Court's finding of fact and conclusions of law pursuant to Bankruptcy Rule 7052.

II.　FACTS

No interest would be served by the recitation of the numerous facts which were adduced at the nearly four-hour hearing on this matter. Suffice it to say, testimony was elicited from several witnesses and numerous documents were introduced into evidence. On the basis of the record made at the hearing, the Court finds that the Disclosure Statement does not contain information of a kind, and in sufficient detail, as far as is reasonably practicable in light of the nature and history of the Debtor and the condition of the Debtor's books and records, that would enable a hypothetical reasonable investor typical of the holders of claims or interests to make an informed judgment about the plan.

III.　DISCUSSION

One of the fundamental policies underlying the Chapter 11 reorganization process is disclosure. The disclosure statement was intended by Congress to be the primary source of information upon which creditors and shareholders could rely in making an informed judgment about a plan of reorganization. *See In re Egan,* 33 B.R. 672, 675 (Bankr.N.D.Ill.1983). No simple method exists for determining whether a disclosure statement contains adequate information. A determination as to what constitutes adequate information in any particular instance must occur on a case-by-case basis under the facts and circumstances presented. Generally, the disclosure statement should set forth "all those factors presently known to the plan proponent that bear upon the success or failure of the proposals contained in the plan." *In re The Stanley Hotel, Inc.,* 13 B.R. 926, 929 (Bankr.D.Colo.1981). Although the term "adequate information" is not susceptible to precise definition, 11 U.S.C. § 1125 provides the framework for the Court's determination. Section 1125(b) of the Bankruptcy Code provides as follows:

> (b) An acceptance or rejection of a plan may not be solicited after the commencement of the case under this title from a holder of a claim or interest with respect to such solicitation, unless, at the time of or before such solicitation, there is transmitted to such holder the plan or a summary of the plan, and a written disclosure statement approved, after notice and a hearing, by the court as containing adequate information. The court may approve a disclosure statement without a valuation of the debtor or an appraisal of the debtor's assets. (emphasis added)

"Adequate information" is defined in 11 U.S.C. § 1125(a)(1) to mean:

> . . . information of a kind, and in sufficient detail, as far as is reasonably practicable in light of the nature and history of the debtor and the condition of the debtor's books and records, that would enable a hypothetical reasonable investor typical of holders of claims or interests of the relevant class to make an informed judgment about the plan, but adequate information need not include such information about any other possible or proposed plan.

A number of courts have provided a list of the type of information which should be addressed by a disclosure statement. Such information includes the following:

1. The circumstances that gave rise to the filing of the bankruptcy petition;
2. A complete description of the available assets and their value;
3. The anticipated future of the debtor;
4. The source of the information provided in the disclosure statement;
5. A disclaimer, which typically indicates that no statements or information concerning the debtor or its assets or securities are authorized, other than those set forth in the disclosure statement;
6. The condition and performance of the debtor while in Chapter 11;
7. Information regarding claims against the estate;
8. A liquidation analysis setting forth the estimated return that creditors would receive under Chapter 7;
9. The accounting and valuation methods used to produce the financial information in the disclosure statement;
10. Information regarding the future management of the debtor, including the amount of compensation to be paid to any insiders, directors, and/or officers of the debtor;
11. A summary of the plan of reorganization;
12. An estimate of all administrative expenses, including attorneys' fees and accountants' fees;
13. The collectibility of any accounts receivable;
14. Any financial information, valuations or *pro forma* projections that would be relevant to creditors' determinations of whether to accept or reject the plan;
15. Information relevant to the risks being taken by the creditors and interest holders;
16. The actual or projected value that can be obtained from avoidable transfers;
17. The existence, likelihood and possible success of non-bankruptcy litigation;
18. The tax consequences of the plan; and
19. The relationship of the debtor with affiliates.

See In re Inforex, Inc., 2 C.B.C.2d 612 (Bankr.D.Mass.1980); *In re William F. Gable Co.,* 10 B.R. 248, 249 (Bankr.N.D.W.Va.1981); *In re A.C. Williams Co.,* 25 B.R. 173, 176 (Bankr.N.D.Ohio1982); *In re Malek,* 35 B.R. 443, 444 (Bankr.E.D.Mich.1983); *In re Metrocraft Publishing Services, Inc.,* 39 B.R. 567, 568 (Bankr.N.D.Ga.1984); *In re Jeppson,* 66 B.R. 269, 292 (Bankr.D.Utah1986).

Disclosure of all the aforementioned information is not necessary in every case.

Conversely, the list is not exhaustive; and a case may arise in which disclosure of all the foregoing type of information is still not sufficient to provide adequate information upon which the holders of claims or interests may evaluate a plan. Nevertheless, this list provides a useful starting point for the Court's analysis of the adequacy of information contained in the Disclosure Statement under review. *See In re Metrocraft Publishing Services, Inc.,* 39 B.R. at 568 (Bankr.N.D.Ga.1984).

While complete disclosure is integral to the Chapter 11 process, "overly technical and extremely numerous additions" to a disclosure statement suggested by an objecting party may be rejected if such additions decrease the clarity and understandability of the disclosure statement to the claimholders who will be called upon to accept or reject the plan. *In re Waterville Timeshare Group,* 67 B.R. 412, 413 (Bankr.D.N.H.1986). Further, it is noteworthy that a creditor only has standing to object to the adequacy of a disclosure statement as to its own class and not as to the adequacy of the statement as it affects another class. *In re Adana Mortgage Bankers, Inc.,* 14 B.R. 29, 30 (Bankr.N.D.Ga.1981). And, as one author warns, "reorganization is not to be doomed by meaningless disclosure paperwork." Trost, *Business Reorganization under Chapter 11 of the New Bankruptcy Code,* 34 Bus. Law. 1309, 1339 (1979).

Obviously, it would be impossible for the Court to instruct any plan proponent as to the entire spectrum of information which should properly be included in a disclosure statement. As a starting point, however, the Court directs the Debtor to the aforementioned types of information which numerous courts have noted are most often included in a disclosure statement. The Court also refers the Debtor to the various objections filed by the parties since, for the most part, they contain valid complaints about the adequacy of the information contained in the Disclosure Statement. The use of such guideposts would appear to mandate, at a minimum, the disclosure of the following information: (1) matters pertaining to an Agreement and Note entered into by and between the Debtor and an entity known as Quail Marsh Partnership, including the status of the parties' relationship and the existence and collectibility of a possible account receivable from Quail Marsh Partnership; (2) a more-detailed liquidation analysis, including the potential impact upon claimholders in the event of a hypothetical Chapter 7 liquidation (particularly if the sale of a partnership property were treated as an event of dissolution under the particular partnership agreements); (3) additional information concerning the status of various partnerships in which the Debtor may have an interest, including the nature and extent of any such interest or relationship; (4) the status of negotiations with KinderCare regarding future business opportunities of the Debtor; (5) information regarding the future ownership and management of the Debtor, including compensation to be paid to any insiders, directors, and/or officers of the Debtor; (6) all significant assets of the Debtor, including payments—whether they are periodic, lump-sum, or "balloon" payments—which the Debtor is entitled to receive in the future pursuant to any agreements with corporations, partnerships, individuals and other entities; (7) more detailed information concerning the Debtor's ability to make the payments proposed in the plan; (8) all accounting and valuation methods used in the preparation of the Disclosure Statement; (9) whether the Debtor can sell or alienate its interest in various partnerships, as proposed by the plan; and (10) whether the Debtor has any executory contracts it intends to assume under the plan.

The Court-suggested list is, by its very nature, nonexhaustive. In reality, the Debtor and affected creditors are better situated than is the Court to assess the extent of disclosure needed to satisfy the standard imposed by § 1125 because they possess a breadth of information which is unavailable to the Court. It is not the Court's intention to require the disclosure of burdensome and unnecessary information. Nor is it the

Court's desire to give any holder of a claim or interest a strategic advantage by making it difficult for the Debtor to obtain ultimate review of a proposed plan. It is imperative, however, that the Debtor disclose all pertinent information so that such holders can cast an informed vote accepting or rejecting the plan. That is all the Code requires. If the creditors oppose their treatment in the plan, but the Disclosure Statement contains adequate information, issues respecting the plan's confirmability will await the hearing on confirmation. Therefore, the Debtor need not obtain the creditors' approval of the plan; it need only provide them with adequate information as that term is defined in 11 U.S.C. § 1125(a)(1).

Based upon the foregoing, the First Amended Disclosure Statement is hereby DISAPPROVED. The Debtor shall have forty-five (45) days from the entry of this Order to file a second amended disclosure statement. Failure to file a second amended disclosure statement in the time provided may result in the imposition of sanctions, including dismissal of the case, conversion to a case under Chapter 7, or appointment of a Chapter 11 trustee or examiner.

IT IS SO ORDERED.

SECTION 11
HEARING ON CONFIRMATION OF THE PLAN

After notice, the court holds a **hearing on confirmation of the plan.** The trustee, a party in interest, or the U.S. trustee may object to confirmation of the plan. 11 U.S.C.A. § 1128(b). The plan will be confirmed only if it meets all of the following requirements of the Code.

1. The plan and the proponent of the plan must comply with all of the applicable provisions of Title 11.
2. The plan must be proposed in good faith.
3. Any payment for services or for costs and expenses in connection with the case or the plan is subject to approval by the court as reasonable.
4. The identity and affiliation of any individual who is to serve as a director, an officer, or a voting trustee, after confirmation of the plan, must be disclosed and must be consistent with the best interests of creditors and equity security holders and with public policy. The identity of, and compensation for, an insider to be employed or retained by the reorganized debtor must be disclosed.
5. Any rate change provided for in the plan that is subject to approval of any governmental regulatory commission must be approved.
6. The plan must meet the best interests of creditors test by demonstrating that the creditor or equity security holder will not receive less under the plan than it would under a Chapter 7 liquidation.
7. The plan may not discriminate unfairly and must be fair and equitable with respect to impaired classes of claims or interests that have not accepted the plan. 11 U.S.C.A. § 1129.

At the hearing on confirmation of the Chapter 11 plan, the court reviews the case for acceptance by ballots or rejection by ballots and whether the plan can be "crammed down." **Cramdown** is a concept that permits confirmation of a plan if certain standards of fairness are met, even if some creditors or equity security holders do not accept the plan. The plan must be fair and equitable and may not dis-

criminate unfairly. 11 U.S.C.A. § 1129(b)(1). For a Chapter 11 plan to be fair and equitable, it must meet certain criteria for each dissenting class.

1. The holder of a secured claim must retain its lien and receive deferred cash
   payments of at least the allowed amount of the claim. If the value of the
   claim is determined as of the effective date of the plan, the lien of the creditor attaches to the proceeds, or the holder of a claim may receive the indubitable equivalent of its claim. 11 U.S.C.A. § 1129(b)(2)(A).
2. The holder of an unsecured claim must receive property of a value equal to
   the allowed amount of the claim. The value of the claim is determined as
   of the effective date of the plan. If the holder of an unsecured claim does
   not receive property of a value equal to the allowed amount of its claim,
   the holder of a junior claim or interest receives nothing. This is called the
   absolute priority rule. 11 U.S.C.A. § 1129(b)(2)(B).
3. There is also an absolute priority rule for interest holders. 11 U.S.C.A. §
   1129(b)(2)(C). The holder of an interest receives or retains property of a
   value (as of the effective date of the plan) equal to the greatest of the allowed amount of any fixed liquidation preference, any fixed redemption
   price, or the value of such interest. If this requirement is not met, the holder
   of any junior interest will not receive or retain anything.

The mere threat of cramdown appears to obviate the need for its actual use in
most cases. The risks inherent in a possible cramdown tend to encourage settlement.
Negotiations by the debtor, creditors, and equity security holders facilitate the development of a plan that can be accepted by all classes. Thus, the purpose of cramdown (to secure confirmation of a plan in spite of the dissent of one or more classes
holding impaired claims or interests) is often accomplished through compromise and
settlement. Exhibit 8.10 presents the ballot used in confirmation of the plan.

EXHIBIT 8.10
Official Form No. 14 (Ballot for Accepting or Rejecting the Chapter 11 Plan)

Form B14
6/90

UNITED STATES BANKRUPTCY COURT
_____DISTRICT OF_____

In re _____,   )
   Set forth here all names including married,   )
   maiden, and trade names used by debtor within   )
   last 6 years.]   )
           Debtor   )   Case No. _____
)
)
Address _____   )
)
   _____   )   Chapter _____
)
Social Security No(s). _____ and all   )
Employer's Tax Identification No(s). *[if any]*_____   )
_____   )

BALLOT FOR ACCEPTING OR REJECTING PLAN

Filed By_____
on *[date]* _____   .

The plan referred to in this ballot can be confirmed by the court and thereby made binding on you if it is accepted by the holders of two-thirds in amount and more than one-half in number of claims in each class and the holders of two-thirds in amount of equity security interests in each class voting on the plan. In the event the requisite acceptances are not obtained, the court may nevertheless confirm the plan if the court finds that the plan accords fair and equitable treatment to the class or classes rejecting it and otherwise satisfies the requirements of § 1129(b) of the Code. To have your vote count you must complete and return this ballot.

[If holder of general claim] The undersigned, a creditor of the above-named debtor in the unpaid principal amount of $ _____ ,

[If bondholder, debenture holder, or other debt security holder] The undersigned, the holder of *[state unpaid principal amount]* $ _____ of *[describe security]* _____ of the above-named debtor, with a stated maturity date of _____ ,

[if applicable] registered in the name of _____ ,

[if applicable] bearing serial number(s) _____

EXHIBIT 8.10
Continued

[If equity security holder] The undersigned, the holder of *[state number]* _____ shares of *[describe type]* _____ stock of the above named debtor, represented by Certificate(s) No. _____, *[or* held in my/our brokerage Account No. _____ at *[name of broker-dealer]* _____.]

[Check One Box]

[ ] Accepts

[ ] Rejects

the plan for the reorganization of the above-named debtor proposed by
[name of proponent] _____,

and *[if more than one plan is to be voted on]*

[ ] Accepts

[ ] Rejects

the plan for the reorganization of the above-named debtor proposed by
[name of proponent] _____.

[If more than one plan is accepted, the following may but need not be completed.] The undersigned prefers the plans accepted in the following order.

[Identify plans]

1. _____ .

2. _____ .

Dated: _____

Print or type name: _____

Signed: _____

[If appropriate] By: _____

as: _____

Address: _____

Return this ballot on or before _____ to: _____
                                          (date)   (name)

Address: _____

_____

In *In re Edgewater Motel, Inc.,* the debtor sought confirmation of its Chapter 11 plan. The court discussed the best interests of creditors test, the feasibility requirement, and cramdown.

In re Edgewater Motel, Inc.

United States Bankruptcy Court, Eastern District of Tennessee, 1988.
85 B.R. 989.

MEMORANDUM
Richard Stair, Jr.,
Bankruptcy Judge

The debtor seeks confirmation of its "Amended Plan of Reorganization" (Plan) filed August 6, 1987. Union Planters National Bank (Union Planters), holder of the first mortgage indebtedness encumbering the debtor's real property in Gatlinburg, Tennessee, filed "Objections To Confirmation" on September 25, 1987. A hearing on confirmation was held October 1, 1987.[1]

This is a core proceeding. 28 U.S.C.A. § 157(b)(2)(L) (West Supp. 1987).

I

The debtor, Edgewater Motel, Inc., a corporation, owns and operates a motel in the resort town of Gatlinburg, Tennessee. Subsequent to the 1983 tourist season, the debtor demolished its 39-unit motel and commenced construction of its present facility—a 209-room mid-rise resort hotel[2] known as the Edgewater Motel. Union Planters loaned the debtor the construction money for this project; Security Federal Savings and Loan Association, Nashville, Tennessee, was to provide permanent financing and "take out" Union Planters at the conclusion of construction.

In connection with its construction loan, the debtor executed a promissory note in favor of Union Planters on March 1, 1984, in the original principal amount of $7,605,000 bearing interest at the rate of one and one-half percent (1 1/2%) above the Union Planters prime rate.[3] This note, secured by a mortgage encumbering the debtor's real es-

tate, matured on September 30, 1985. Construction of the Edgewater Motel was substantially completed on April 30, 1985; however, conditions essential to the funding of the permanent financing were not met and the commitment of the permanent lender expired. No permanent financing was obtained by the debtor prior to the filing of its voluntary petition under Chapter 11 on March 24, 1986. Union Planters' fully matured claim as of October 1, 1987, approximated $8,400,000.[4] It is undisputed that Union Planters is a fully secured.[5]

In its Plan the debtor designates ten classes of claims and interests. Union Planters is the sole creditor comprising Class II. Class I, consisting of administrative expense claims, represents the only unimpaired class under the Plan. All impaired classes, excepting the Class II creditor, Union Planters, have accepted the Plan.[6] The claim of Union Planters is dealt with under the Plan as follows:

Treatment of Class II Creditors. The only creditor under Class II of the Plan is Union Planters National Bank. The Debtor proposes to amortize the debt due to Union Planters National Bank on a twenty five (25) year amortization schedule at nine (9%) percent interest with a ten (10) year balloon payment for all principal remaining due and owing at the end of the said period of time. As indicated above, the first payment shall be due on October 1, 1987 and the balloon payment would be due on September 30, 1997.

During the first year of the Plan the Debtor shall pay Union Planters only One Hundred Eighty Thousand ($180,000.00)

Dollars of the amount that would be due to Union Planters under the provisions of Paragraph 1 of this Subsection. Debtor will defer the remaining portion of the first year's payments to be paid in the eight year of the Plan in equal monthly installments. Interest will be paid on the deferred portion of first year's payments at nine (9%) percent per annum. Interest on this deferred portion will accumulate for the first Plan year and will be paid in equal monthly installments during the second year of the Plan. Interest for the second year and interest thereafter until the deferred portion of payments due for the first year of the Plan are paid in full will be paid on a monthly basis at nine (9%) percent per annum.

During the second year of the Plan Union Planters will be paid only Six Hundred Thousand ($600,000.00) Dollars of the amount that would otherwise be due under Paragraph 1 of this Subsection. This deferred portion of the second year's payments shall be paid in the eighth year of the Plan. Interest on the deferred payment for the second year of the Plan shall be paid in equal monthly installments during the second year of the Plan. Interest on the deferred portion of the second year's payments under the Plan for the third year and successive years until paid in full shall be paid in equal monthly installments at the rate of nine (9%) percent per annum.

During the third year of the Plan Union Planters will be paid only Seven Hundred Thousand ($700,000.00) Dollars of the amount that would otherwise be due under Paragraph 1 of this subsection. The deferred portion of the third year's payments will be paid in the eighth Plan year. Interest on the deferred payment for the third year of the Plan shall be paid in equal monthly installments during the third year of the Plan. Interest on the deferred portion of the third year's payment for the fourth year and successive years shall be paid in equal monthly installments at the rate of nine (9%) percent per annum.

Beginning with the fourth year of the Plan and thereafter until the balloon payment is due, the Debtor shall pay payments in accordance with the amortization schedule set forth in Paragraph 1 above.

Union Planters National Bank shall retain its security interest and all security which it presently holds for payment of its claim. Union Planters National Bank is impaired under the terms of the Plan.

It is undisputed that the claim of Union Planters is impaired within the meaning of § 1124 of the Bankruptcy Code.

Union Planters grounds its objections to confirmation on the following allegations: (1) the Plan does not meet the best interest of creditors test required by § 1129(a)(7); (2) the Plan does not offer a reasonable prospect of success and therefore does not meet the feasibility standard required by § 1129(a)(11); and (3) the Plan discriminates unfairly against Union Planters and does not meet the "fair and equitable" test required by § 1129(b)(2)(A).

II

The debtor's Plan can be confirmed only if the court determines that the debtor has complied with all the requirements of Bankruptcy Code § 1129. The salient provisions of § 1129 which are at issue as a result of the Union Planters' objections are as follows:

§ 1129. Confirmation of plan.

(a) The court shall confirm a plan only if all of the following requirements are met:

. . . .

(7) With respect to each impaired class of claims or interests—

(A) each holder of a claim or interest of such class—

(i) has accepted the plan; or

(ii) will receive or retain under the plan on account of such claim or interest property of a value, as of the effective date of the plan, that is not less than the amount that such holder would so receive or retain if the debtor were liquidated under chapter 7 of this title on such date; or

. . . .

(11) Confirmation of the plan is not likely to be followed by the liquidation, or the need for further financial reorganization, of the debtor or any successor to the debtor under the plan, unless such liquidation or reorganization is proposed in the plan.

(b)(1) Notwithstanding section 510(a) of this title, if all of the applicable requirements of subsection (a) of this section other than paragraph (8) are met with respect to a plan, the court, on request of the proponent of the plan, shall confirm the plan notwithstanding the requirements of such paragraph if the plan does not discriminate unfairly, and is fair and equitable, with respect to each class of claims or interests that is impaired under, and has not accepted, the plan.

(2) For the purpose of this subsection, the condition that a plan be fair and equitable with respect to a class includes the following requirements:

(A) With respect to a class of secured claims, the plan provides—

(i)(I) that the holders of such claims retain the liens securing such claims, whether the property subject to such liens is retained by the debtor or transferred to another entity, to the extent of the allowed amount of such claims; and

(II) that each holder of a claim of such class receive on account of such claim deferred cash payments totaling at least the allowed amount of such claim, of a value, as of the effective date of the plan, of at least the value of such holder's interest in the estate's interest in such property;

(ii) for the sale, subject to section 363(k) of this title, of

any property that is subject to the liens securing such claims, free and clear of such liens, with such liens to attach to the proceeds of such sale, and the treatment of such liens on proceeds under clause (i) or (iii) of this subparagraph; or

(iii) for the realization by such holders of the indubitable equivalent of such claims.

11 U.S.C.A. § 1129 (West 1979 & Supp.1987).

III. BEST INTEREST OF CREDITORS TEST: § 1129(A)(7)

Under the provisions of § 1129(a)(7)(A)(ii), the court, if it is to confirm the Plan, must find the Union Planters, the holder of a secured claim which has not accepted the Plan, "will receive or retain under the plan on account of such claim . . . property of a value, as of the effective date of the plan, that is not less than the amount that [Union Planters] would so receive or retain if the debtor were liquidated under chapter 7 of this title on such date."

The House Report describes § 1129(a)(7) as follows:

Paragraph (7) incorporates the former "best interest of creditors" test found in chapter 11, but spells out precisely what is intended. With respect to each class, the holders of the claims or interests of that class must receive or retain under the plan on account of those claims or interest property of a value, as of the effective date of the plan, that is not less than the amount that they would so receive or retain if the debtor were liquidated under chapter 7 on the effective date of the plan.

H.R. Rep. No. 595, 95th Cong., 1st Sess. 412 (1977), U.S.Code Cong. & Admin.News 1978, p. 5787.

In summary, the court must compare what Union Planters would receive upon liquidation to what it will receive under the Plan. Absent a determination that the Plan provides for Union Planters to receive as much as or more than it would receive upon liquidation under Chapter 7, the confirmation requirements of § 1129(a)(7) will not be met and the Plan cannot be confirmed.

Upon liquidation of the debtor under the provisions of Chapter 7 of Title 11, Union Planters would receive in cash the value of its fully secured claim, $8,400,000.[7]

The effect of the debtor's treatment of Union Planters under the Plan is to totally restructure the Union Planters loan. The debtor's obligation to Union Planters matured on September 30, 1985; the Plan provides that Union Planters will be paid on a twenty-five year amortization schedule at nine percent (9%) interest, with a balloon payment in the tenth year consisting of the remaining unpaid balance. However, the Plan further provides that actual payments to Union Planters during the first three years of the Plan will be substantially less than those required by the debtor's proposed twenty-five year amortization schedule: $180,000 will be paid in the first year; $600,000 will be paid in the second year; and $700,000 will be paid in the third year. The payment deficiencies in the first three years are deferred to the eighth year of the Plan and interest at nine percent (9%) on these deficiencies is to be paid monthly beginning in the second year of the Plan. The debtor's Plan payments to Union Planters, actual and deferred, are summarized as follows:[8]

Payments Due Union Planters under Plan

First Year—October 1, 1987 –
      September 30, 1988

Due in Year 1	$845,909.88	
Paid in Year 1	180,000.00	
Deferred to Year 8	665,909.88	
Total Paid		$180,000.00

Second Year—October 1, 1988 –
      September 30, 1989

Due in Year 2	$845,909.88	
Paid in Year 2	600,000.00	
Deferred to Year 8	245,909.88	
Interest Paid On	104,799.03	
Deferred Payments—(two years interest on Year 1 deferral; one year on Year 2 deferral)		
Total Payment		704,799.03

Third Year—October 1, 1989 –
      September 30, 1990

Due in Year 3	$845,909.88	
Paid in Year 3	700,000.00	
Deferred to Year 8	145,909.88	
Interest Paid On	89,176.60	
Deferred Payments		
Total Payment		789,176.60

Fourth Year—October 1, 1990 –
      September 30, 1991

Due and paid	$845,909.88	
Interest Paid On	95,195.67	
Deferred Payments[9]		
Total Payment		941,105.55

Fifth Year—October 1, 1991 –
        September 30, 1992

Due and paid	$845,909.88	
Interest Paid On	95,195.67	
Deferred Payments		
Total Payment		941,105.55

Sixth Year—October 1, 1992 –
        September 30, 1993

Due and paid	$845,909.88	
Interest Paid On	95,195.67	
Deferred Payments		
Total Payment		941,105.55

Seventh Year—October 1, 1993 –
        September 30, 1994

Due and paid	$845,909.88	
Interest Paid On	95,195.67	
Deferred Payments		
Total Payment		941,105.55

Eighth Year—October 1, 1994 –
        September 30, 1995

Due and paid	$845,909.88	
Deferred Payments	1,057,729.64	
Years 1, 2, and 3		
Interest Paid on	52,270.60	
Deferred Payments		
Total Payment		1,955,910.12

Ninth Year—October 1, 1995 –
        September 30, 1996

Due and paid		845,909.88

Tenth Year—October 1, 1996 –
        September 30, 1997

Due and paid	$845,909.88	
Balloon payment due		
September 30, 1997	6,950,096.16	
Total Payment		7,796,006.04

The dispositive issue for resolution by the court in determining whether the Plan meets the best interest of creditors test as to the Class II claim of Union Planters is the present value of the stream of payments provided Union Planters under the Plan. Most of the cases concerning present value arise in the context of "cram down" under the provisions of § 1129(b)(2)(A)(i) or under § 1325(a)(5)(B). Nonetheless, the principle is the same under § 1129(a)(7).

The court has determined that within the context of this Chapter 11 case present value assumes a current market rate of interest on Union Planters' claim based on comparative loans as distinguished from a rate of interest, as argued by the debtor, established pursuant to 28 U.S.C.A. § 1961(a) (West Supp.1987), or in reliance upon the Federal Reserve Bulletin for September, 1987, containing the weighted average during the week of May 4–8, 1987, for long-term loans with a fixed rate where the loan was for $1,000,000 or more. As has recently been noted by Judge Morton, Senior District Judge for the United States District Court for the Middle District of Tennessee:

Sections 1129(a)(7)(A)(ii) and 1129(b)(2) (A)(i) require the Bankruptcy Court to analyze the present value of the stream of payments or other consideration provided by a plan. This concept of present value assumes the use of *market* rates of interest (as distinguished from the rate specified in the contract) for loans of similar duration, with similar security, and with similar risks. 5 *Collier on Bankruptcy* (15th ed. 1985) ¶ 1129.03[i]; *see Memphis Bank & Trust Co. v. Whitman,* 692 F.2d 427 (6th Cir. 1982) (construing 11 U.S.C. § 1325(a)(5)(B), the language of which is virtually identical to that contained in § 1129).

In determining the allowed amount of the claim of a full-secured creditor, the creditor is entitled to his contract rate of interest up the effective date of the plan by virtue of 11 U.S.C. § 506(b), ... But this rule has no application to the present value analysis required by § 1129, or to the interest payable on claims after the effective date of a plan. 3 *Collier on Bankruptcy* (15th ed. 1985) ¶ 506.05 at 506–43.

Federal Land Bank of Louisville v. Gene Dunavant and Son Dairy (In re Gene Dunavant and Son Dairy), 75 B.R. 328, 335–36 (U.S.D.C.M.D.Tenn.1987) (emphasis in original).

The debtor's Plan contemplates the payment of interest on any deferred amounts at nine percent (9%). In support of its contention that nine percent (9%) represents a current market rate of interest, the debtor elicited testimony from Michael L. Harmon, a certified public accountant and president of a concern known as TexLaMiss Corp. (TexLaMiss). Mr. Harmon testified that TexLaMiss purchased the River Terrace Hotel in Gatlinburg, Tennessee, on July 8, 1987; that the purchase price was $8,850,000; that $20,000 was paid down; and that the sum of $8,830,000 was financed for a period of five (5) years at nine and four-tenths percent (9.4%) interest with the interest rate to be renegotiated at the end of the five year period.

Mr. Harmon further testified as to the involvement of TexLaMiss in negotiating several projects throughout the South with interest rates ranging from four percent (4%) fixed for five years to eleven percent (11%). Of the various loans discussed by Mr.

Harmon, it is apparent that the only loan bearing any similarity to the debtor's proposed treatment of Union Planters' claim under the Plan is that loan involving the River Terrace Hotel. The basic similarity between the River Terrace loan and the debtor's proposed treatment of Union Planters' claim under its Plan are the amounts of the two obligations and their identical geographic locations. However, the debtor's own proof, through Mr. Harmon, establishes a current market rate of nine and four-tenths percent (9.4%), four-tenths percent (.4%) higher than the nine percent (9%) envisioned under the Plan.[10]

Mr. James G. Howell, a partner in the certified public accounting firm of Pannell, Kerr and Forster, testified that the prevailing market rate on October 1, 1987, for a twenty-five year loan with a ten year call providing a payout similar to that set forth in the debtor's Plan for the Union Planters' claim, approximated twelve percent (12%). Richard K. Howarth, a senior consultant with Pannell, Kerr and Forster, testified that the present value of the payments proposed to be made to Union Planters under the Plan, based upon the debtor's nine percent (9%) interest factor, assuming a market rate of twelve percent (12%) for similar loans, approximates $7,000,000.

This court doubts the availability under any current market setting of a loan envisioning the deferred repayment plan such as is provided Union Planters under the debtor's Plan. Nonetheless, considering the criteria espoused by Judge Morton in *In re Gene Dunavant and Son Dairy, supra,* the court, having considered the use of a market rate of interest for "loans of similar duration, with similar security, and with similar risks" concludes that the market rate of interest testified to by Mr. Howell, i.e., twelve percent (12%), represents a current market rate of interest for comparable loans.

As is noted in a leading treatise on bankruptcy:

It is submitted that deferred payment of an obligation under a plan is a coerced loan and the rate of return with respect to such loan must correspond to the rate which would be charged or obtained by the creditor making a loan to a third party with similar terms, duration, collateral, and risk. It is therefore submitted that the appropriate discount rate must be determined by reference to the "market" interest rate.

5 Collier on Bankruptcy, ¶ 1129.03, at 1129–62, 63 (15th ed. 1987) (footnote omitted).

As the debtor's Plan contemplates interest at nine percent (9%), the Plan's discount rate is nine percent (9%). The Plan cannot be confirmed because it does not meet the best interest of creditors test required under § 1129(a)(7)(A)(i).

IV. FEASIBILITY REQUIREMENT:
§ 1129(A)(11)

As a confirmation requirement, § 1129(a)(11) mandates a determination by the court that "the plan is not likely to be followed by the liquidation, or the need for further financial reorganization, of the debtor. . . ." The court will not expend a considerable amount of time analyzing the debtor's projections in support of its claim of feasibility. The lack of feasibility appears to be self-evident by the deferred payment method provided in the Plan for payment of the Class II Union Planters claim, the Class III claim of Borg-Warner Leasing, and the Class IV claims of Blaine-Hays Construction Company and First National Bank of Gatlinburg.[11]

The debtor proposes a ten year Plan at the conclusion of which it will sell the Edgewater Motel or refinance the first mortgage claim of its largest creditor, Union Planters. At the end of the ten year Plan period the principal balance of Union Planters' claim will have been reduced by $1,449,903.84, from $8,400,000 to $6,950,096.16. During this ten year period the debtor will defer $1,057,729.64 in payments due in Plan years one through three to Plan year eight.

"[T]he longer a debtor intends to take in retiring plan obligations, the more difficult it may be to prove feasibility." *In re White,*

36 B.R. 199, 204 (Bankr.D.Kan.1983). The ability of the debtor to retire the claim of its major secured creditor is at best speculative. While the debtor projects a sufficient income to meet the payments proposed to various classes of creditors, the court, in view of the substantial amount of payments deferred by the debtor to Plan years six through eight, is not satisfied as to the ability of the debtor to meet these projections. The court cannot make a finding that confirmation "is not likely to be followed by the liquidation, or the need for further financial reorganization, of the debtor. . . ." 11 U.S.C.A. § 1129(a)(11) (West 1979).

The debtor's Plan does not meet the confirmation requirements of § 1129(a)(11).

V. CRAM DOWN: § 1129(b)(2)(A)

The court also finds that the Plan violates the "fair and equitable" standard of § 1129(b)(2)(A)(i). The § 1129(b) "cram down" provisions are available to a debtor only "if all of the applicable requirements of subsection (a) of . . . [§ 1129] other than paragraph (8) are met with respect to a plan, ..." Under such circumstances, § 1129(b) further provides that if all the confirmation requirements of § 1129(a) are met except that of § 1129(a)(8) "the court . . . shall confirm the plan notwithstanding the requirements of . . . [§ 1129(a)(8)] if the plan does not discriminate unfairly, and is fair and equitable, with respect to each class of claims or interests that is impaired under, and has not accepted, the plan."

Although the court's finding that the debtor's Plan does not meet the confirmation requirements of § 1129(a)(7) and (11) precludes the debtor from proceeding to "cram down," the court will nonetheless consider the debtor's Plan within the confines of § 1129(b)(2)(A).

For the debtor's Plan to be "fair and equitable" under the provisions of § 1129(b)(2)(A)(i), the Plan, with respect to the impaired non-accepting Class II claim of Union Planters, must provide (1) that Union Planters retain the lien securing its claim; and (2) that Union Planters receive on account of its claim "deferred cash payments totaling at least the allowed amount of such claim, of a value, as of the effective date of the plan, of at least the value of . . . [Union Planters] interest in the estate's interest in [the Edgewater Motel]. . . ."

As has been discussed within the context of the best interest of creditors test under § 1129(a)(7)(A), the inquiry to be made by the court is that of present value:

> If the proponent of a plan attempts to cram down a class of secured claims by means of making deferred cash payments under section 1129(b)(2)(A)(i), the court is required to value the future cash stream so as to establish the present value of the deferred payments provided for under the plan.

5 Collier on Bankruptcy, ¶ 1129.03[f], at 1129–60 (15th ed. 1987). Thus, if the Plan proposes to pay interest on the fully secured claim of Union Planters at a rate less than the current market rate, the Plan does not satisfy the "fair and equitable" requirement of § 1129(b)(2)(A)(i). *In re Sullivan,* 26 B.R. 677 (Bankr.W.D.N.Y.1982) (debtor's nine and one-half percent (9 1/2%) interest rate on mortgage balance did not satisfy the "fair and equitable" requirement in a market where the prime rate of interest was in excess of sixteen percent (16%)).

As is further noted in *5 Collier on Bankruptcy,* ¶ 1129.03, at 1129–62 (15th ed. 1987):

> The concept of "present value" is of paramount importance to an understanding of section 1129(b). Simply stated, "present value" is a term of art for an almost self-evident proposition: a dollar in hand today is worth more than a dollar to be received a day, a month or a year hence. Part of the "present value" concept may be expressed by a corollary proposition: a dollar in hand today is worth exactly the same as (1) a dollar to be received a day, a month or a year hence plus (2) the rate of interest which the dollar would earn if invested at an appropriate interest rate.

While the debtor's Plan provides that Union Planters will retain the lien securing its claim, the Plan, as has been noted in the court's discussion of the § 1129(a)(7)(A) confirmation requirement, does not meet the "fair and equitable" test of § 1129(b)(2)(A)(i). The current market rate of interest on October 1, 1987, the date of the hearing on confirmation, approximated twelve percent (12%); the debtor's Plan proposes to pay Union Planters interest at a rate of nine percent (9%). Further, the Plan does not provide for Union Planters to receive the "indubitable equivalent" of its claim under § 1129(b)(2)(A)(iii). "[T]reatment which is less favorable than the treatment specified in section 1129(b)(2)(A)(i) and (ii) would not satisfy the ["indubitable equivalent"] test." *5 Collier on Bankruptcy,* ¶ 1129.03[c], at 1129–56 (15th ed. 1987).

The court further notes that § 1129(b)(2), in defining the requirements utilized by the court to determine whether the Plan is "fair and equitable," uses the word "includes." Bankruptcy Code § 102(3) entitled "Rules of construction" provides that "includes" is not limiting. 11 U.S.C.A. § 102(3) (West 1979). The implication in reference to the "fair and equitable" doctrine of § 1129(b)(2) is that the use of the term "includes" is open-ended. The court accordingly finds, irrespective of the statutory definition of "fair and equitable," that the debtor's Plan, in its treatment of the claim of Union Planters, is not "fair and equitable."

Union Planters' claim matured on September 30, 1985. The debtor's Plan converts the Union Planters construction loan to a twelve year loan (two years since the September 30, 1985, maturity of its loan plus ten years under the Plan) with Union Planters to occupy substantially the same position at the end of the ten year life of the Plan as it occupies today. The debtor presently owes Union Planters $8,400,000; at the end of the ten year Plan period it will owe Union Planters $6,950,096.16 against resort property subject to the use and abuse of the public, which at that time will be almost thirteen years old. In the interim, the debtor will defer until the eighth year of the Plan payment of more than forty-one percent (41%) of those payments due Union Planters during the first three Plan years. In fact, the Plan requirements for liquidating the Union Planters Class II claim, while a panacea for the debtor, causes Union Planters' claim to increase from $8,400,000 on October 1, 1987, to $9,149,393.30 at the end of Plan year three, with a modest reduction to $8,585,401.98 at the end of Plan year seven.[12] Only at the end of Plan year eight, after satisfaction of those payments deferred from Plan years one through three, will the Union Planters prepetition claim of $8,400,000 reflect a reduction.

The debtor's Plan does not meet the "fair and equitable" test with respect to the claim of Union Planters and thus cannot be confirmed under the "cram down" provisions of § 1129(b).

For the reasons set forth herein, confirmation of the debtor's "Amended Plan Of Reorganization" filed August 6, 1987, will be denied.

This Memorandum constitutes findings of fact and conclusions of law as required by Fed.R.Bankr.P. 7052.

---

1 In addition to the evidence introduced at the confirmation hearing, the court has also considered portions of the debtor's amended disclosure statement filed August 6, 1987, approved as containing adequate information on September 4, 1987.

[2] The terms "hotel" and "motel" are used interchangeably by the debtor in its amended disclosure statement and Plan and also by witnesses testifying at the hearing on confirmation. The court draws no distinction between the use of these two terms.

[3] Under the permanent financing arrangement contemplated by the debtor, Union Planters, and Security Federal Savings and Loan Association, the permanent loan was to bear interest at a minimum rate of fourteen and one-half percent (14 1/2%).

[4] In its pre-hearing memorandum Union Planters reflects a principal and interest balance on October 1, 1987, amounting to $8,329.857.30. The debtor estimates an additional liability for attorney fees approximately $75,000. The parties agree that $8,400,000 represents the amount of Union Planters claim.

[5] This court in a Memorandum filed October 29, 1986, after consideration of a motion filed by Union Planters seeking relief from the automatic stay and abandonment, determined the fair market value of the Edgewater Motel, including land and improvements, to be not less than $11,500,000. At the October 1, 1987, confirmation hearing, Jack Mann, an MAI appraiser, testified that the fair market value of the debtor's property is $11,000,000.

[6] Pursuant to the provisions of 11 U.S.C.A. § 1126(f) (West Supp.1987), the holders of unimpaired Class I claims are conclusively presumed to have accepted the Plan.

[7] Jack Mann, the MAI appraiser testifying on behalf of the debtor, testified that liquidation value "severely restricted to, say, two weeks or a month . . . will run between 60 and 75 percent of market value." As has been noted, Mr. Mann testified that the market value of the Edgewater Motel is $11,000,000. The issue of liquidation value was not further explored by the debtor's attorney on direct examination and was only briefly alluded to by the attorney for Union Planters on cross examination. The debtor, in its amended disclosure statement and at the hearing on confirmation, has consistently represented that Union Planters is fully secured. The court cannot and will not now conclude from the undeveloped testimony of Mr. Mann that the liquidation value of the debtor's real estate is less than $8,400,000.

[8] This analysis has been prepared from an exhibit to the testimony of Stuart Rispler, controller of The LeConte Company, entitled "Projected Payments Under Amended Plan as Modified." The LeConte Company has managed the Edgewater Motel since mid-1986.

[9] Payments deferred during Plan years one through three total $1,057,729.64. These deferred payments remain unpaid through Plan year seven. Interest on these deferred payments is reflected in this chart for Plan years four through eight; the total amount of deferred payments is not reflected except in Plan year eight, the year of payment.

[10] The court further notes that the nine and four-tenths percent (9.4%) interest rate testified to by Mr. Harmon is not truly indicative of the current market rate of interest. Mr. Harmon testified that TexLaMiss purchased the River Terrace Hotel from First Federal Savings and Loan Association, which had acquired the hotel through foreclosure proceedings. As acknowledged by Mr. Harmon, the River Terrace Hotel was financed

by a seller with an apparent need to divest itself of property due to regulations requiring it to charge that property off against its earnings. The court also notes that Mr. Harmon is the vice-president for finance for The LeConte Company, the entity presently managing the Edgewater Motel.

[11] In addition to the $1,057,729.64 due Union Planters during Plan years one through three, payment of which is deferred to Plan year eight, the debtor defers payment of the Borg-Warner Leasing Class III claim totaling $372,240.72 to Plan year six, and payment of Blaine-Hays Construction Company and First National Bank of Gatlinburg's Class IV claims totaling $410,000 and $375,000, respectively, to Plan year seven.

[12] Under the twenty-five year amortization schedule proposed by the debtor, Union Planters will be entitled to receive $845,909.88, inclusive of principal and interest, during each Plan year, for a total of $2,537,729.64 during Plan years one through three. However, the Plan provides that $1,057,729.64 of the first three years payments will be deferred for payment in Plan year eight. This will affect the amount of the Union Planters claim as follows:

End of Plan Year	Amortized Balance	Deferred Payment	Total Claim
1	$8,306,287.03	$698,372.70 (includes deferred payment of $665,909.88 and interest on deferred payment of $32,462.82)	$9,004,659.73
2	8,203,783.13	911,819.76	9,115,602.89
3	8,091,663.66	1,057,729.64	9,149,393.30
4	7,969,026.63	1,057,729.64	9,026,756.27
5	7,834,885.37	1,057,729.64	8,892,615.01
6	7,688,160.75	1,057,729.64	8,745,890.39
7	7,527,672.34	1,057,729.64	8,585,401.98
8	7,352,129.03	1,057,729.64	8,409,858.67
9	7,160,118.54	—0—	7,160,118.54
10	6,950,096.16	—0—	6,950,096.16

SECTION 12
EFFECT OF CONFIRMATION OF THE PLAN

Upon **confirmation of the Chapter 11 plan,** the property of the estate, except as otherwise provided in the plan or in the order confirming the plan, vests in the debtor. 11 U.S.C.A. § 1141(b). The confirmed plan is a contract that binds the debtor, creditors, and interest holders. 11 U.S.C.A. § 1141(a). The payment or issuing of stock by the debtor to its creditors under the plan is a substitute for the debtor's legal obligation to these parties prior to the filing of the bankruptcy petition.

The confirmation of a Chapter 11 plan discharges the debtor and releases it from all claims and interests of creditors, equity security holders, and general partners, whether or not the claims and interests are impaired or whether or not their holders have accepted the plan. 11 U.S.C.A. § 1141(a). This is a very broad discharge which includes all debts arising prior to the filing of the Chapter 11 and some debts arising after the filing. Corporations and partnerships will not, however, be discharged under a liquidating plan. This prevents the corporate or partnership debtor from accomplishing a discharge under Chapter 11 that would be forbidden under Chapter 7. The individual debtor will be discharged whether it remains in business or liquidates its assets, unless it would be denied a discharge under section 727(a).

It will not be discharged from any debt that is excepted from section 523 of the Code. 11 U.S.C.A. § 1141(d). These exceptions include spousal or child support, educational loans, and debts incurred through fraud.

The court shall hold the discharge or reaffirmation hearing not more than 30 days following the confirmation of a plan in a Chapter 11 reorganization case concerning an individual. Fed. R. Bank. P. 4008. The form used to confirm a Chapter 11 plan appears in Exhibit 8.11.

EXHIBIT 8.11
Official Form No. 15 (Order Confirming the Chapter 11 Plan)

Form B15
6/90

UNITED STATES BANKRUPTCY COURT
_____DISTRICT OF_____

In re _____,   )
    Set forth here all names including married,   )
    maiden, and trade names used by debtor within   )
    last 6 years.]   )
                     Debtor   )   Case No. _____
)
)
Address _____   )
)
     _____   )   Chapter _____
)
Social Security No(s). _____ and all   )
Employer's Tax Identification No(s). *[if any]*_____   )
_____   )

ORDER CONFIRMING PLAN

The plan under chapter 11 of the Bankruptcy Code filed by _____,
on _____ [*if applicable*, as modified by a modification filed on _____,]
or a summary thereof, having been transmitted to creditors and equity security holders; and

It having been determined after hearing on notice that the requirements for confirmation set forth in
11 U.S.C. § 1129(a) [*or, if appropriate*, 11 U.S.C. § 1129(b)] have been satisfied;

IT IS ORDERED that:

The plan filed by _____, on _____, [*If*
appropriate, include dates and any other pertinent details of modifications to the plan] is confirmed.
A copy of the confirmed plan is attached.

Dated: _____

                                           BY THE COURT

                                           _____
                                           United States Bankruptcy Judge.

SECTION 13
DISTRIBUTION UNDER THE PLAN AND REPORTING BY DEBTOR IN POSSESSION OR CHAPTER 11 TRUSTEE

Upon confirmation of the plan, distribution is made to creditors and equity security holders whose claims have been allowed under the confirmed plan. Either the debtor in possession or the trustee in the case will usually handle distribution under the plan. The court, however, may appoint a person designated as agent to handle the money. In some cases, the court appoints a "trustee" to administer the plan. This is not the trustee in the Chapter 11 case. The court might also place some conditions on how the money is to be handled, who will handle it, and in what manner it is to be handled.

The debtor in possession or the trustee, after confirmation of the plan, is required to file such reports as are necessary or as the court orders. 11 U.S.C.A. § 1106(a)(7).

SECTION 14
REVOCATION OF AN ORDER OF CONFIRMATION

A party in interest may request revocation of an order of confirmation within 180 days of the order on the basis of fraud. 11 U.S.C.A. § 1144; Fed. R. Bank. P. 7001.

SECTION 15
FINAL DECREE

After an estate is fully administered in a Chapter 11 case, the court, on its own motion or that of a party in interest, enters a final decree closing the case. The form used to enter a final decree is shown in Exhibit 8.12.

Even after the case is closed, it is still subject to further action. In certain situations, a case may be amended without being reopened. For example, clerical errors in judgments, orders, and other parts of the record or errors in the record caused by oversight or omission may be corrected without reopening the case. A closed case may be reopened to add a creditor or to distribute previously undistributed property of the estate.

EXHIBIT 8.12
Sample Final Decree

B271
(Rev. 7/94)

United States Bankruptcy Court

_____District of_____

In re

Bankruptcy Case No.

Debtor*

Social Security No.   :
Employer Tax I.D. No.:

FINAL DECREE

The estate of the above named debtor has been fully administered.

☐ The deposit required by the plan has been distributed.

IT IS ORDERED THAT:

☐ _____
(name of trustee)
is discharged as trustee of the estate of the above-named debtor and the bond is cancelled;

☐ the chapter _____ case of the above named debtor is closed; and

☐ [other provisions as needed]

_____   _____
Date   Bankruptcy Judge

*Set forth all names, including trade names, used by the debtor within the last 6 years. (Bankruptcy Rule 1005). For joint debtors set forth both social security numbers.

BASIC TERMS AND PHRASES

Adequate information
Adequate protection
Bootstrap plan
Chapter 11 reorganization plan
Chapter 11 trustee
Committee of creditors holding
  unsecured claims
Committee of equity security holders
Confirmation of a Chapter 11 plan
Debtor in possession (DIP)

Disclosure statement
Equity security holder
Hearing on the confirmation of the plan
Hearing on the disclosure statement
Indubitable equivalent
List of Creditors Holding 20 Largest
  Unsecured Claims
List of equity security holders
Mandatory provisions
Permissive provisions

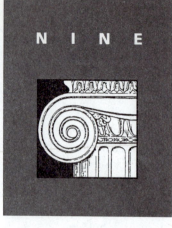

N I N E

The Involuntary Bankruptcy: Chapter 7 or Chapter 11

Not all petitions in bankruptcy are filed by the debtor. Those petitions filed by the debtor are known as voluntary petitions. A creditor may force a debtor into bankruptcy by filing an **involuntary petition.** Because involuntary petitions constitute less than 1 percent of all bankruptcy petitions filed in a given year, discussion here will be confined to the basic requirements for filing or controverting an involuntary petition.

SECTION 1
LIMITATIONS ON FILING AN INVOLUNTARY PETITION

There are limitations on the chapters in which an involuntary petition may be filed, as well as limitations on the debtors against whom an involuntary case may be commenced. The numbers of holders of claims and the amounts of such claims necessary to the filing of an involuntary petition are also circumscribed by the Code.

A. THE CREDITORS' OPTIONS IN BANKRUPTCY COURT

The creditors' options in bankruptcy court are limited to an **involuntary Chapter 7 (liquidation)** or an **involuntary Chapter 11 (reorganization).** In addition, there are limitations regarding the debtors against whom such a petition may be filed. An involuntary case may be commenced only against a person that may be a debtor under the chapter in which the case is filed. Furthermore, an involuntary case may not be filed against a farmer, a family farmer, or a corporation that is not a moneyed, business, or commercial corporation. 11 U.S.C.A. § 303(a).

In *In re United Kitchen Associates, Inc.,* 15 employees of United Kitchen Associates, Inc., filed a petition to put the debtor corporation into involuntary bankruptcy. The court investigated whether an eleemosynary (nonprofit) corporation was exempt from involuntary bankruptcy.

In re United Kitchen Associates, Inc.
United States Bankruptcy Court, Western District of Louisiana, 1983.
33 B.R. 214.

FINDINGS OF FACT
LeRoy Smallenberger,
Bankruptcy Judge

The issues at question are . . . and second, is the entity in question an eleemosynary corporation, and therefore exempt from involuntary bankruptcy?

On April 22, 1983, fifteen employees of United Kitchen Associates, Inc., debtor corporation, filed a petition to put debtor corporation into involuntary bankruptcy. The

claims of these employees are past due wages, and the claims aggregate to $19,504.87.

These petitioning creditors claimed in their petition that United Kitchen Associates, Inc. was a Louisiana non-profit corporation. Now those petitioning creditors disclaim that United Kitchen Associates, Inc., is a non-profit corporation.

These petitioning creditors set forth two principal reasons why they believe that debtor corporation should not be classified as an eleemosynary corporation. First, these creditors allege that the debtor corporation has not filed an exemption number for status as a non-profit corporation with the Internal Revenue Service. Second, these creditors claim that United Kitchen Associates, Inc., has only received contributions from the Council of the Aging in six different parishes, and not from the general public.

United Kitchen's articles of incorporation, dated June 10, 1980, state that the corporation was incorporated as a non-profit corporation. The stated purpose in the articles is to provide meals to the elderly. The corporation was organized on a nonstock basis with only issuances of membership allowed for a $5.00 fee to each member. As issuance of membership entitled the member to vote at general membership meetings. The articles state that none of the profits of the corporation, if any, shall ever be disbursed to a holder of a membership certificate.

An audit report of the debtor corporation by James Orr, certified public accountant, showed that the accounts payable by the debtor corporation exceed the cash and accounts receivable of the debtor corporation by more than $14,000, on June 20, 1982. There were no formal books of accounting produced for periods subsequent to June 30, 1982, because debtor corporation claimed none could be located. The bank statements for the period August 1, 1982, through March 31, 1983, showed deposits exceeded disbursements by $1,960.35 for the eight month period.

CONCLUSIONS OF LAW

. . . .

Issue No. 2: Is United Kitchen Associates an Eleemosynary Corporation, and Therefore Exempt From Involuntary Bankruptcy?

Under 11 U.S.C. 303(a) an involuntary case in bankruptcy may not be commenced against a "corporation" that is not a moneyed, business, or commercial corporation. Such eleemosynary institutions as churches, schools, and charitable organizations and foundations are, thus exempt from involuntary bankruptcy. *H.Rept. No. 95–595, p. 322, Bk-L. Ed., Legislative History Section 82:16.*

The exemption granted these institutions is a continuation of earlier bankruptcy law. The pertinent provisions of the Bankruptcy Act of 1898 were phrased somewhat differently. Section 4 thereof (former 11 U.S.C.S. Section 22) stated that, " . . . any moneyed, business, or commercial corporation . . . may be adjudged an involuntary bankrupt. . . . " Hence, it was by judicial interpretation that eligibility for involuntary bankruptcy was limited to corporations organized for profit, and that charitable or educational institutions were excluded, at least unless transactions indicated otherwise.

9 Am.Jur.2d, Bankruptcy Section 227.

The bankruptcy courts have not been consistent in their results. In the case of *In re Elmsford Country Club* (1931, D.C.N.Y.) 50 F.2d 238, The court found a country club not to be subject to involuntary bankruptcy. In the case of *In re Allen University* (1974, C.A.4 S.C.) 497 F.2d 346, a university was found to be exempt, even though it carried on a number of commercial activities. In the case of *In re Weeks Poultry Community, Inc.,* (1931, D.C. Cal.) 51 F.2d 122, a corporation organized on a co-operative basis for the purpose of packing and marketing agricultural products for members and others to facilitate profitable marketing, was held not to be a moneyed, business, or commercial corporation. In the case of *In re Dairy Marketing Assn.* (1925, D.C. Ind.) 8 F.2d 626, a dairy marketing association was held not to be a moneyed, business, or commercial corporation. However, in the case of *In re American Grain and Cattle, Inc.,* (1976, N.D. Tex.) 415 F. Supp. 270, 2 B.C.D. 823, the court found that co-operative associations were within the intendment of former 11 U.S.C. 22(b), and the court has jurisdiction over the bankrupt.

The disparity in results seem to flow from a conflict among the courts as to whether the "state classification rule" should apply, or the "bankrupt rule." The former gives a corporation the same status under the bankruptcy laws as it has under state law. The latter permits the bankruptcy courts to examine both the corporation's character and its activities to determine whether it should enjoy the immunity afforded charitable institutions. The 1978 Bankruptcy Code, as enacted, and its legislative history, does not appear to resolve this conflict.

9 Am.Jur.2d, Bankruptcy Section 227.

In deciding this case, the court does not need to decide between the "state classification rule" or the "bankruptcy rule," for both will yield the same result. Under state law the debtor corporation was a non-profit corporation, and based on the corporation's character and the nature of its activities the court finds that it is a non-profit corporation.

The facts indicate that the debtor corporation was incorporated under the laws of the State of Louisiana as a non-profit organization, for the stated purpose of providing meals to the elderly. The debtor corporation was organized on a nonstock basis. The corporation did issue memberships, which were not ownership interests in the corporation, but instead were only rights to vote in the general membership meetings. The articles plainly state that none of the profits of the corporation, if any, shall ever be disbursed to a holder of membership certificate. It is not a requirement that disbursements equal or exceed contributions in order to retain the status of a non-profit corporation, but a review of the available financial data indicates that over the life of

the debtor corporation disbursements have exceeded contributions.

The petitioning creditors argue that because the debtor corporation has not filed an exemption number for status as a non-profit corporation with the Internal Revenue Service then the court should not recognize the debtor corporation as a non-profit corporation. This is a procedural matter for tax considerations to contributors, and does not change the status of the corporation under state law, nor does it change the character or the nature of the activities of the corporation.

The petitioning creditors allege that the debtor corporation has only received contributions from the Council of Aging in six different parishes, and not from the general public. Even if this allegation were proved, there was no evidence introduced that the debtor corporation would not accept contributions from the general public; in fact membership fees of $5.00 are a form of contribution from the public. However, the fact of the matter is that accepting or not accepting contributions from the general public is not a determinative factor in the classification of a corporation as either a for profit corporation or an eleemosynary corporation under the "state classification rule" or the "bankruptcy rule."

To summarize, though fifteen employees with claims in excess of $5,000.00 may file a petition of involuntary bankruptcy against an employer, United Kitchen Associates, Inc., is an eleemosynary corporation, and therefore is exempt from involuntary bankruptcy under 11 U.S.C. 303(a).

B. WHO MAY BE A PETITIONER

An involuntary petition to be filed against a debtor who has more than 12 creditors requires that three creditors must join in the petition. Indenture trustees are considered creditors for this purpose. The claims of the three creditors must aggregate at least $10,000 more than the value of any lien on the debtor's property securing these claims. The claims must not be contingent or the subject of a bona fide dispute. 11 U.S.C.A. § 303(b)(1). If the debtor has fewer than 12 creditors, one or more creditors may file an involuntary petition with aggregate claims of at least $10,000. 11 U.S.C.A. § 303(b)(2). After the petition has been filed but before relief is ordered or the case is dismissed, a creditor holding an unsecured, noncontingent claim who was not one of the original petitioning creditors may join in the petition. This will have the same effect as if the joining creditor had been one of the original petitioners. 11 U.S.C.A. § 303(c); Fed. R. Bank. P. 1003(b). This can prevent dismissal of a case, if the claim of one of the original petitioners is disallowed, by enabling the petition to meet the requirements of three creditors and $10,000 in claims.

The trustee of a single general partner may file an involuntary petition against the partnership if all of the general partners of the partnership are in bankruptcy. Fewer than all of the general partners in a partnership may file against the partnership. 11 U.S.C.A. § 303(b)(3). A foreign representative of the estate in a foreign proceeding may file an involuntary petition in order to administer assets in this country. 11 U.S.C.A. § 303(b)(4).

In *In re Hopkins,* an involuntary petition was filed by the debtor's former wife and his three minor children. The debtor challenged the petition on the ground that the children did not hold judgments against him and therefore were ineligible to serve as petitioning creditors. Therefore, the three or more entities required for the filing of the petition did not exist and the petition should be dismissed.

In re Hopkins
United States Bankruptcy Court, District of Maine, 1995.
177 B.R. 1.

MEMORANDUM OF DECISION
James A. Goodman,
Chief Judge

Before the Court is a motion by the Debtor to dismiss his involuntary bankruptcy proceeding because of an insufficient number of petitioning creditors. As discussed below, the motion is denied.

On May 2, 1991, the marriage of Debtor William Hopkins, IV, ("Hopkins") and creditor Linda Cady ("Cady") was dissolved by a judgment in Maine state court. Pursuant to this judgment, Hopkins was ordered to pay Cady $500 per week as alimony, and $500 per week as child support for the couple's three minor children (the "Children"): William Hopkins, Kevin Hopkins and Eileen Hopkins.[1] On July 6, 1994, Cady on behalf of herself and the Children filed an involuntary petition for bankruptcy against Hopkins. The petition listed four petitioning creditors; Cady and each of the three Children.

On October 12, 1994, Hopkins filed a motion to dismiss the involuntary petition. Hopkins maintains that because the Children do not hold judgments against

Hopkins, they are ineligible to serve as petitioning creditors, and therefore, there are not the required three petitioning creditors needed to commence an involuntary case under 11 U.S.C. § 303(b)(1).[2] This Court disagrees with Hopkins. Under Section 303(b)(1) of the Bankruptcy Code, a party can be a petitioning creditor if that party holds a "claim" against the debtor. Pursuant to 11 U.S.C. § 101(5), one has a "claim" if one has "a right to payment." In the instant case, the Children whether through Cady, or through another third party, have a right to payment for their support from Hopkins. Because there are at least three petitioning creditors as required under 11 U.S.C. § 303(b)(1), Hopkins' motion to dismiss is denied. The foregoing constitutes findings of fact and conclusions of law pursuant to F.R.Bky.P. 7052.

---

[1] The divorce judgment stated that "[t]he Defendant is ordered to pay to Plaintiff the sum of $500.00 per week, toward the support of the parties three (3) children: William K. Hopkins, V, ... Kevin P. Hopkins ... Eileen C. Hopkins ... " The parties agree, however, that the children

were not named parties to the divorce action and do not hold any separate judgments against the Debtor.

[2] Section 303(b)(1) states in pertinent part:

An involuntary case against a person is commenced by the filing with the bankruptcy court of a petition under chapter 7 or 11 of this title—

(1) by three or more entities, each of which is either a holder of a claim against such person that is not contingent as to liability or the subject of a bona fide dispute, or an indenture trustee representing such a holder, if such claims aggregate at least $5,000 more than the value of any lien on property of the debtor securing such claims held by the holders of such claims;

SECTION 2
"ROAD MAPS" FOR THE INVOLUNTARY PETITIONS

Exhibits 9.1 and 9.2 are "road maps" for the involuntary Chapter 7 case and the involuntary Chapter 11 case, respectively.

EXHIBIT 9.1
Chapter 7 Liquidation (Involuntary Petition)

The creditor files with the bankruptcy court clerk's office:
1. Filing fee
2. Creditors' petition

Upon filing of the petition, the estate is created and the automatic stay goes into effect, protecting the estate from dismemberment. Unless the court orders otherwise, any business of the debtor may continue to operate as usual until the court issues an order for relief.

Upon the filing of the petition, the clerk issues a summons along with the petition on the debtor.

After a case is filed, the debtor may move:
1. for a change of venue; or
2. to contest the petition.

After the case is filed, a party in interest may move:
1. to dismiss the case; or
2. for a change of venue.

Before an order for relief is entered, a party in interest may request appointment of an interim trustee.

The court determines the issues of a contested petition at the earliest practicable time and enters an order for relief or dismisses the petition.

Promptly after the order for relief, an interim trustee is appointed by the U.S. trustee.

EXHIBIT 9.1
Continued

The debtor must file within 15 days after entry of the order for relief:
1. Disclosure of attorney's compensation statement
2. Matrix (the list of creditors)
3. Schedules (Official Form No. 6)
   a. Summary of Schedules
   b. Schedule A: Real Property
   c. Schedule B: Personal Property
   d. Schedule C: Property Claimed as Exempt
   e. Schedule D: Creditors Holding Secured Claims
   f. Schedule E: Creditors Holding Unsecured Priority Claims
   g. Schedule F: Creditors Holding Unsecured Nonpriority Claims
   h. Schedule G: Executory Contracts and Unexpired Leases
   i. Schedule H: Codebtors
   j. Schedule I: Current Income of Individual Debtor(s), if applicable
   k. Schedule J: Current Expenditures of Individual Debtor(s), if applicable
   l. Schedule of Income and Expenditures of a Partnership or a Corporation, if applicable
   m. Declaration Concerning Debtor's Schedules, signed by the debtor(s)
4. Statement of Financial Affairs
5. An individual debtor with consumer debts must file a statement of intention within 30 days after the date of the order for relief or by the date of the meeting of creditors, whichever is earlier.

Prior to the time the case is closed, the debtor may amend the lists, schedules, and statement. The debtor has a duty to supplement the schedules for certain property acquired after the petition has been filed.

From the date of the order for relief, the case proceeds in exactly the same manner as a voluntary Chapter 7 case.

EXHIBIT 9.2
Chapter 11 Reorganization (Involuntary Petition)

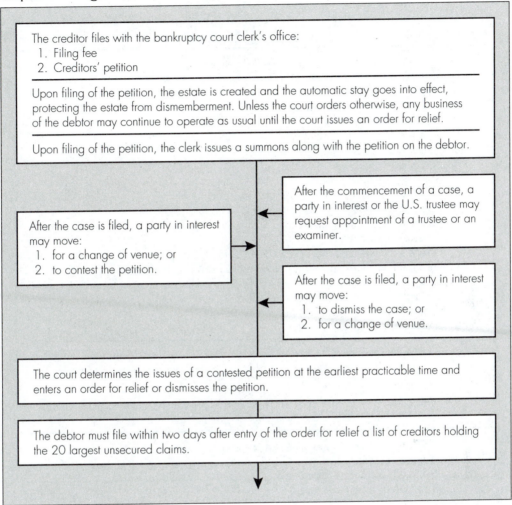

The creditor files with the bankruptcy court clerk's office:
1. Filing fee
2. Creditors' petition

Upon filing of the petition, the estate is created and the automatic stay goes into effect, protecting the estate from dismemberment. Unless the court orders otherwise, any business of the debtor may continue to operate as usual until the court issues an order for relief.

Upon filing of the petition, the clerk issues a summons along with the petition on the debtor.

After the case is filed, a party in interest may move:
1. for a change of venue; or
2. to contest the petition.

After the commencement of a case, a party in interest or the U.S. trustee may request appointment of a trustee or an examiner.

After the case is filed, a party in interest may move:
1. to dismiss the case; or
2. for a change of venue.

The court determines the issues of a contested petition at the earliest practicable time and enters an order for relief or dismisses the petition.

The debtor must file within two days after entry of the order for relief a list of creditors holding the 20 largest unsecured claims.

EXHIBIT 9.2
Continued

The debtor must file within 15 days after entry of the order for relief:
1. Disclosure of attorney's compensation statement
2. Matrix (the list of creditors)
3. Schedules (Official Form No. 6)
   a. Summary of Schedules
   b. Schedule A: Real Property
   c. Schedule B: Personal Property
   d. Schedule C: Property Claimed as Exempt
   e. Schedule D: Creditors Holding Secured Claims
   f. Schedule E: Creditors Holding Unsecured Priority Claims
   g. Schedule F: Creditors Holding Unsecured Nonpriority Claims
   h. Schedule G: Executory Contracts and Unexpired Leases
   i. Schedule H: Codebtors
   j. Schedule I: Current Income of Individual Debtor(s), if applicable
   k. Schedule J: Current Expenditures of Individual Debtor(s), if applicable
   l. Schedule of Income and Expenditures of a Partnership or a Corporation, if applicable
   m. Declaration Concerning Debtor's Schedules, signed by the debtor(s)
4. Statement of Financial Affairs
5. List of debtor's equity security holders

Prior to the time the case is closed, the debtor may amend the lists, schedules, and statement. The debtor has a duty to supplement the schedules for certain property acquired after the petition has been filed.

From the date of the order for relief, the case proceeds in exactly the same manner as a voluntary Chapter 11 case.

SECTION 3
THE FILING OF THE CREDITORS' PETITION

Because a creditor or a group of creditors, rather than the debtor, is filing the petition in an involuntary case, the filing of the petition to commence an involuntary case requires fewer documents. The petition must conform substantially to Official Form No. 5. (See Exhibit 9.3.) The creditors' petition is filed in the bankruptcy court clerk's office along with the filing fee.

EXHIBIT 9.3

Official Form No. 5 (Involuntary Case: Creditors Petition)

FORM B5
(6/90)

FORM 5. INVOLUNTARY PETITION

United States Bankruptcy Court	INVOLUNTARY PETITION
_____ District of _____	

IN RE (Name of Debtor—If Individual, Last, First, Middle)	ALL OTHER NAMES used by debtor in the last 6 years (Include married, maiden, and trade names.)

SOC. SEC./TAX I.D. NO. (If more than one, state all.)

STREET ADDRESS OF DEBTOR (No. and street, city, state, and zip code)	MAILING ADDRESS OF DEBTOR (If different from street address)
COUNTY OF RESIDENCE OR PRINCIPAL PLACE OF BUSINESS	

LOCATION OF PRINCIPAL ASSETS OF BUSINESS DEBTOR (If different from previously listed addresses)

CHAPTER OF BANKRUPTCY CODE UNDER WHICH PETITION IS FILED

☐ Chapter 7   ☐ Chapter 11

INFORMATION REGARDING DEBTOR (Check applicable boxes)

Petitioners believe:
☐ Debts are primarily consumer debts
☐ Debts are primarily business debts (complete sections A and B)

TYPE OF DEBTOR
☐ Individual
☐ Partnership
☐ Other: _____

☐ Corporation Publicly Held
☐ Corporation Not Publicly Held

A. TYPE OF BUSINESS (Check one)

☐ Professional   ☐ Transportation   ☐ Commodity Broker
☐ Retail/Wholesale   ☐ Manufacturing/   ☐ Construction
☐ Railroad   Mining   ☐ Real Estate
                        ☐ Stockbroker   ☐ Other

B. BRIEFLY DESCRIBE NATURE OF BUSINESS

VENUE

☐ Debtor has been domiciled or has had a residence, principal place of business, or principal assets in the District for 180 days immediately preceding the date of this petition or for a longer part of such 180 days than in any other District.

☐ A bankruptcy case concerning debtor's affiliate, general partner or partnership is pending in this District.

PENDING BANKRUPTCY CASE FILED BY OR AGAINST ANY PARTNER OR AFFILIATE OF THIS DEBTOR (Report information for any additional cases on attached sheets.)

Name of Debtor	Case Number	Date
Relationship	District	Judge

ALLEGATIONS
(Check applicable boxes)

1. ☐ Petitioner(s) are eligible to file this petition pursuant to 11 U.S.C. § 303(b).
2. ☐ The debtor is a person against whom an order for relief may be entered under title 11 of the United States Code.
3.a. ☐ The debtor is generally not paying such debtor's debts as they become due, unless such debts are the subject of a bona fide dispute;

or

b. ☐ Within 120 days preceding the filing of this petition, a custodian, other than a trustee, receiver, or agent appointed or authorized to take charge of less than substantially all of the property of the debtor for the purpose of enforcing a lien against such property, was appointed or took possession.

COURT USE ONLY

EXHIBIT 9.3
Continued

	Name of Debtor _____
FORM 5 Involuntary Petition	Case No. _____
(6/92)	(court use only)

TRANSFER OF CLAIM

☐ Check this box if there has been a transfer of any claim against the debtor by or to any petitioner. Attach all documents documents evidencing the transfer and any statements that are required under Bankruptcy Rule 1003(a).

REQUEST FOR RELIEF

Petitioners(s) request that an order for relief be entered against the debtor under the chapter of title 11, United States Code, Code, specified in this petition

Petitioner(s) declare under penalty of perjury that the foregoing is true and correct according to the best of their knowledge, information, and belief.

X _____	X _____
Signature of Petitioner or Representative (State title)	Signature of Attorney Date
Name of Petitioner Date Signed	Name of Attorney Firm (If any)
Name & Mailing Address of Individual _____ Signing in Representative Capacity _____	Address
	Telephone No.
X _____	X _____
Signature of Petitioner or Representative (State title)	Signature of Attorney Date
Name of Petitioner Date Signed	Name of Attorney Firm (If any)
Name & Mailing Address of Individual _____ Signing in Representative Capacity _____	Address
	Telephone No.
X _____	X _____
Signature of Petitioner or Representative (State title)	Signature of Attorney Date
Name of Petitioner Date Signed	Name of Attorney Firm (If any)
Name & Mailing Address of Individual _____ Signing in Representative Capacity _____	Address
	Telephone No.

PETITIONING CREDITORS

Name and Address of Petitioner	Nature of Claim	Amount of Claim
Name and Address of Petitioner	Nature of Claim	Amount of Claim
Name and Address of Petitioner	Nature of Claim	Amount of Claim
Note: If there are more than three petitioners, attach additional sheets with the statement under penalty of perjury, petition(s) signatures under the statement and the names(s) of attorneys(s) and petitioning creditor information in the format above.	Total Amount of Petitioners' Claims

_____ continuation sheets attached

SECTION 4
THE SIGNIFICANCE OF FILING A PETITION

The significance of filing a petition is somewhat different in an involuntary case. The filing of the petition does not constitute an order for relief.

Upon the filing of the petition in an involuntary case, however, the estate is created and the automatic stay goes into effect, protecting the estate from dismemberment just as it does in a voluntary case. This prevents the more aggressive creditors from taking what is owed to them to the detriment of other creditors. The creditors filing the involuntary petition are attempting to protect their interests from the actions of the other creditors as well as from the actions of the debtor. The involuntary petition also gives the debtor relief (albeit unsolicited) under the automatic stay from harassment by creditors. 11 U.S.C.A. § 362(a).

A. THE ORDER FOR RELIEF

The court will enter the order for relief against the debtor if the petition is not timely converted or after a trial on the petition. At any time during what is called the gap period—the time between the filing of an involuntary petition and the order for relief—the debtor may concede and convert the case to any other chapter of the Bankruptcy Code for which it is eligible or may choose to file its own voluntary petition.

Unless the court orders otherwise, until an order for relief has been entered in an involuntary case, any business of the debtor may continue to operate and the debtor may continue to use, acquire, or dispose of property as if the case had not been filed. This means the debtor in an involuntary case is not limited by the constraints of Section 363 until the order for relief has been entered. 11 U.S.C.A. § 303(f).

B. APPOINTMENT OF A TRUSTEE

An interim trustee is always appointed upon the order for relief in a Chapter 7 case. In a voluntary case, the order for relief is entered upon the filing of the case. If a party in interest is concerned that the assets of the estate may be in jeopardy during the gap period, he or she may request appointment of an interim trustee in a Chapter 7 involuntary case. 11 U.S.C.A. § 303(g). No special provision is necessary for appointment of a trustee in a Chapter 11 involuntary case because an interim trustee is never appointed in a Chapter 11 case. Under the Code, a trustee may be appointed in a Chapter 11 case at any time after the commencement of the case. 11 U.S.C.A. § 1104(a).

C. GAP PERIOD CREDITORS

Creditors who hold claims that arise between the filing of an involuntary petition and the order for relief are called **gap creditors.** This group may be comprised of both existing creditors and creditors who have only begun to deal with the debtor post-petition.

Unless an interim trustee has been appointed in an involuntary Chapter 7 or a trustee has been appointed in an involuntary Chapter 11, creditors may remain unaware of the petition until the order for relief has been entered. These creditors do have some protection under the Code. If their claims arise in the ordinary course of the debtor's business or financial affairs after the commencement of the case but before the earlier of the appointment of a trustee or the order for relief, they are given a second priority and their claims are treated as if they had arisen before the date of the filing of the petition. 11 U.S.C.A. §§ 502(f), 507(a)(2).

If creditors have claims that arise from extending credit to the trustee in a case, their claims are given first priority as an administrative expense.

SECTION 5
THE CLERK'S SUMMONS

Upon the filing of an involuntary petition, the clerk issues a summons to be served on the debtor. The summons must conform to the appropriate Official Form. Old Official Form No. 13, Summons to Debtor in Involuntary Case, has been abrogated as an Official Form but is available as Administrative Form B 250E. A copy is served with a copy of the petition. (See Exhibit 9.4.) The manner of service is provided by Rule 7004(a) or (b), which is personal service or service by first class mail. If service cannot be accomplished in this manner, the court may order service by mailing copies of the summons and petition to the party's last known address and at least one publication, as directed by the court. The summons and petition may be served on the party anywhere. Fed. R. Bank. P. 1010.

EXHIBIT 9.4
Summons to Debtor in Involuntary Case

B250E
(6/91)

United States Bankruptcy Court

_____ **District of** _____

In re

Bankruptcy Case No.

Debtor*
Social Security No.   :
Employer Tax I.D. No.:

SUMMONS TO DEBTOR IN INVOLUNTARY CASE

To the above named debtor:

A petition under title 11, United States Code was filed against you on _____

(date)

in this bankruptcy court, requesting an order for relief under chapter _____ of the Bankruptcy Code (title

11 of the United States Code).

YOU ARE SUMMONED and required to submit to the clerk of the bankruptcy court a motion or

answer to the petition within 20 days after the service of this summons. A copy of the petition is attached.

Address of Clerk

At the same time you must also serve a copy of your motion or answer on petitioner's attorney.

Name and Address of Petitioner's Attorney

If you make a motion, your time to serve an answer is governed by Bankruptcy Rule 1011(c).

If you fail to respond to this summons, the order for relief will be entered.

_____
Clerk of the Bankruptcy Court

By: _____

_____
Date

Deputy Clerk

*Set forth all names, including trade names, used by the debtor within the last 6 years. (Bankruptcy Rule 1005). For joint debtors, set forth both social security numbers.

EXHIBIT 9.4
Continued

Case No. _____

CERTIFICATION OF SERVICE

I,   ,

of**   ,

certify:

That I am, and at all times hereinafter mentioned was, more than 18 years of age;

That on the   day of   , 19   ,

I served a copy of the within summons, together with the petition filed in this case, on

,

the debtor in this case, by [*describe here the mode of service*]

the said debtor at

I certify under penalty of perjury that the foregoing is true and correct.

Executed on _____   _____
                         [Date]   *[Signature]*

_____

**State mailing address.*

SECTION 6
THE DEBTOR'S ANSWER

The debtor named in an involuntary petition may contest the petition. In an involuntary petition against a partnership, a nonpetitioning general partner, or a person who is alleged to be a general partner but denies the allegation, may contest the petition. Fed. R. Bank. P. 1011(a). Defenses and objections to the petition must be presented in accordance with Rule 12 of the Federal Rules of Civil Procedure and are to be filed and served within 20 days after service of the summons. If service is made by publication on a party or partner not residing or found in the state in which the court sits, the time for filing and serving the response is fixed by the court. Fed. R. Bank. P. 1011(b). No claim may be made in the answer against a petitioning creditor except for the purpose of defeating the petition. Fed. R. Bank. P. 1011(d).

If the debtor claims to have 12 or more creditors in its answer to a petition filed by fewer than three creditors, the debtor must file a list of all creditors with the answer. The list must include addresses, a brief statement of the nature of the claims, and the amounts of the claims. Fed. R. Bank. P. 1003(b).

SECTION 7
HEARING AND DISPOSITION OF AN INVOLUNTARY PETITION

If the petition in an involuntary case is not timely controverted, the court will enter an order for relief without a trial. Fed. R. Bank P. 1013(b). However, if the debtor contests the petition, a trial will be held on the matter. Fed. R. Bank. P. 1013(a).

A. THE ORDER FOR RELIEF

Relief against the debtor will be ordered after the trial only if

(1) the debtor is generally not paying such debtor's debts as such debts become due unless such debts are the subject of a bona fide dispute; or
(2) within 120 days before the date of the filing of the petition, a custodian, other than a trustee, receiver, or agent appointed or authorized to take charge of less than substantially all of the property of the debtor for the purpose of enforcing a lien against such property, was appointed or took possession. 11 U.S.C.A. §§ 303(h)(1), (2).

In *In re Lough,* Peoples Bank & Trust, a single entity, filed an involuntary petition against Bette Mae Lough claiming that she owed the bank on several notes. Mrs. Lough contended that there was a bona fide dispute concerning the bank's claim against her. Therefore, the involuntary petition against her should be dismissed.

In re Lough
United States Bankruptcy Court, Eastern District of Michigan, 1986.
57 B.R. 993.

MEMORANDUM OPINION
Steven W. Rhodes,
Bankruptcy Judge

The Peoples Bank & Trust of Alpena filed this involuntary petition against Bette Mae Lough pursuant to 11 U.S.C. § 303 arising from two debts which the bank claims that Mrs. Lough owes to it. For the reasons stated in this memorandum opinion,[1] the Court concludes that there is a bona fide dispute concerning the bank's claim, and that therefore the involuntary petition must be dismissed.

I.

The first debt upon which the bank claims liability arose from a joint note which Mrs. Lough signed with her husband on April 30, 1973; this note has a balance of approximately $75,000. The second debt allegedly arose from a guaranty which Mrs. Lough signed on November 30, 1967 relating to her husband's various sole obligations with the bank; these obligations were consolidated into one note executed by Mr. Lough on February 19, 1981, in the approximate amount of $135,000. Thus, the bank claims a total indebtedness by Mrs. Lough in the approximate amount of $210,000. In its petition, the bank alleged that there are fewer than twelve creditors and that Mrs. Lough was not generally paying her debts, especially the debt to the bank, as they became due.

In her amended answer, Mrs. Lough admitted signing the April 30, 1973 joint note but nevertheless denied any liability on that note. She claims that this note was secured by a mortgage on property held by her and her husband as tenants by the entirety; that this property was deeded to the bank in lieu of foreclosure; and that if the proceeds from the bank's sale of this property had been applied to this note, rather than to a note on which Mr. Lough was obligated on solely, as required, then the proceeds would have been sufficient to extinguish the joint note.

In her amended answer, Mrs. Lough further alleged that although she signed the November 30, 1967 guaranty, she has no further liability on it in regard to her husband's note of February 19, 1981. She claims she has no liability on it because in 1967 she did not intend to guaranty what arose some fourteen or fifteen years later as a $135,000 note. She also contends that there was no consideration for this guaranty and no reliance upon it by the bank.

Mrs. Lough contends that because there is a bona fide dispute about the bank's claim against her, the bank does not qualify under 11 U.S.C. § 303 as a proper entity to file an involuntary petition in bankruptcy against her.

To this contention, the bank responds that there are no genuine issues of fact and that on the facts it is or would be entitled to a summary judgment against Mrs. Lough. Therefore, the bank argues, because there is no bona fide dispute, the bank is qualified to file this involuntary petition against Mrs. Lough.

II.
A.

11 U.S.C. § 303(b) provides that an involuntary case against a person is commenced by the filing with the bankruptcy court of a petition, pursuant to either subparagraph (1), "by three or more entities, each of which is . . . a holder of a claim against such person that is not contingent as to liability or the subject [of] a bona fide dispute," or subparagraph (2) if there are fewer than 12 such holders, excluding employees and insiders, "by one or more of such holders." The phrase "such holders" in subparagraph

(2) refers to holders of claims which are "not contingent as to liability or the subject [of] a bona fide dispute."

The Court notes that the phrase "bona fide dispute" also arises in subsection (h) of Section 303, which provides:

If the petition is not timely controverted, the court shall order relief against the debtor in an involuntary case under the chapter under which the petition was filed. Otherwise, after trial the court shall order relief against the debtor in an involuntary case under the chapter under which the petition was filed only if—(1) the debtor is generally not paying such debtor's debts as such debts become due unless such debts are the subject of a bona fide dispute.

The parties cited three cases[2] interpreting the phrase "bona fide dispute," and these cases are not entirely consistent.

In *In re Johnston Hawks, Ltd.,* 49 B.R. 823 (Bankr.D.Hawaii1985), the court noted that there had been a statutory change implemented by the Bankruptcy Amendments Act of 1984. After reviewing the pre-1984 law, the court noted that the 1984 amendments to the bankruptcy code made significant revisions regarding disputed claims. 49 B.R. at 830. First, the test for the standing of petitioning creditors was revised to provide that holders of claims which are subject to bona fide disputes are barred from being petitioning creditors. Second, debts which are subject to bona fide disputes were excluded from the test provided in section 303(h), which provides that the court shall order relief if the debtor is not paying debts as such debts become due. The court further stated:

It is evident that under the 1984 amendments, creditors holding claims which are subject to bona fide disputes cannot be petitioning creditors under the threshold test of Section 303(b)(1). As stated in Colliers, "[t]his does not mean of course that the debtor can assert any defense to a claim and be successful. Presumably, there must be a 'bona fide dispute' which a bankruptcy judge must find either on a motion

to dismiss or at trial." 2 Collier's on Bankruptcy ¶ 303.08(b) (1985). . . .

A bona fide dispute is a conflict in which an assertion of a claim or right made in good faith and without fraud or deceit on one side is met by contrary claims or allegations made in good faith and without fraud or deceit on the other side.

49 B.R. at 830.

Then the court listed the following factors to determine whether the claims or defenses are subject to a bona fide dispute:

1. The nature of the dispute;
2. The nature and the extent of the evidence and allegations presented in support of the creditor's claim and in support of the debtor's contrary claims.
3. Whether the creditor's claim and the debtor's contrary claims are made in good faith and without fraud or deceit.
4. Whether on balance the interests of the creditor outweighs those of the debtor.

In re Henry, 52 B.R. 8 (Bankr.S.D.Ohio 1985), reviewed at length the legislative history relating to the addition of the "bona fide dispute" language to Sections 303(b) and 303(h). The Court stated:

The reason for the introduction of this additional language in the statute was explained by its proponent as follows:

The problem can be explained simply. Some courts have interpreted section 303's language on a debtor's general failure to pay debts as allowing the filing of involuntary petitions and the granting of involuntary relief even when the debtor's reason for not paying is a legitimate and good-faith dispute over his or her liability. This interpretation allows creditors to use the Bankruptcy Code as a club against debtors who have bona fide questions about their liability, but who would rather pay up than suffer the stigma of involuntary bankruptcy proceedings.

My amendment would correct this problem. Under my amendment, the original filing of an involuntary petition could not be based on debts that are the subject of a good-faith dispute between the debtor and his or her creditors. In the same vein, the granting of an order of relief could not be premised solely on the failure of a debtor to pay debts that were legitimately contested as to liability or amount.

I believe this amendment, although a simple one, is necessary to protect the rights of debtors and to prevent misuse of the bankruptcy system as a tool of coercion. I also believe it corrects a judicial misinterpretation of existing law and congressional intent as to the proper basis for granting involuntary relief. 30 Cong.Rec. S7618 (June 19, 1984) (comments of Senator Baucus). 52 B.R. at 9–10.

In *In re Stroop,* 51 B.R. 210, 212 (Bankr. D.Colo.1985), the court stated:

This Court has concluded that an appropriate standard in determining whether a claim is subject to a bona fide dispute for purposes of 11 U.S.C. § 303(b)(1) is that applicable on motions for summary judgment. If the defense of the alleged debtor to the claim of the petitioning creditor raises material issues of fact or law so that a summary judgment could not be rendered as a matter of law in favor of the creditor on a trial of the claim, the claim is subject to a bona fide dispute.

B.

This Court concludes that none of these standards for determining whether there is a bona fide dispute concerning a debt is entirely appropriate. The standard set forth in the *Johnston Hawks* case is unsatisfactory for two reasons. First, it improperly gives consideration to the balance of interests as between the creditor and the debtor. These considerations were carried forward from the pre-1984 Amendments Act cases, but there is no basis for this in the statute as amended.

Second, the inquiry into "good faith," "fraud," and "deceit," as mandated in *Johnston Hawks* involves subjective considerations as to the parties' respective intentions. For example, the *Johnston Hawks* test would disqualify a creditor when a debtor has a defense which he or she offers in subjective good faith but which objectively has little or no merit. This Court simply cannot conclude that Congress intended to invoke any such considerations in the language "bona fide dispute." Accordingly, the Court rejects the *Johnston Hawks* test.

Likewise, the Court rejects the test of *In re Stroop*. Under that test, if the alleged debtor's defense to the claim of the petitioning creditor raises material issues of fact so that a summary judgment could not be entered as a matter of law in favor of the creditor, the claim is subject to a bona fide dispute. The difficulty is that the test does not fully address a case where there is a substantial dispute as to the proper application of law but no substantial issue of fact. It might be argued that *Stroop* would then require the Court to resolve the question of law as if on a motion for summary judgment and simply determine whether the alleged debtor is liable to the creditor.

Yet, this Court concludes that, given the previously quoted legislative history, *In re Henry, supra,* if there is a bona fide dispute as to either the law or the facts, then the creditor does not qualify and the petition must be dismissed. The legislative history makes it clear that Congress intended to disqualify a creditor whenever there is any legitimate basis for the debtor not paying the debt, whether that basis is factual or legal. Congress plainly did not intend to require a debtor to pay a legitimately disputed debt simply to avoid the stigma of bankruptcy. Accordingly, if there is either a genuine issue of material fact that bears upon the debtor's liability, or a meritorious contention as to the application of law to undisputed facts, then the petition must be dismissed.

In this regard, the Court must emphasize that in deciding whether there is a bona fide dispute, it must not resolve any genuine issues of fact or law. If the Court concludes that there is a bona fide dispute on any issue of fact or law, this must not be interpreted as any indication of how the Court would resolve that issue of fact or law.

III.

A.

With regard to the joint 1973 note on which the bank claims liability against Mrs. Lough, the Court finds that the debtor's defenses do create a bona fide dispute and that therefore she should not be required as a result of that dispute to pay that debt in order to avoid bankruptcy. As noted, Mrs. Lough claims that the issue involves the application of the proceeds from the sale of jointly held property, which the bank undertook following a deed in lieu of foreclosure. It is reasonably clear that if these proceeds had been applied to the 1973 note rather than the subsequent 1981 note, then there would be no liability on the 1973 note.

The bank contends that in the absence of instructions from Mrs. Lough and her husband, the bank could apply the proceeds as it saw fit and therefore it was proper for it to apply these proceeds to the later sole note of Mr. Lough. Although the bank has cited numerous cases which hold to that effect, the Court concludes that there is substantial merit (without resolving the issue) in Mrs. Lough's argument that the proceeds should have been applied to the joint 1973 note. There is substantial merit in this position because the proceeds which came into the bank's possession were the result of the sale of a joint asset and thus Mrs. Lough could reasonably argue that therefore it should have been applied to the joint note rather than to her husband's sole note. In support, Mrs. Lough could reasonably argue that otherwise, there would have been no consideration to her for the deed in lieu of foreclosure which she executed in the bank's favor.

Moreover, there is a genuine issue of material fact as to whether the bank was given instructions as to how to apply the proceeds of that sale. The parties stipulated that if the Lough's former attorney were called to testify, he would testify that in the time period prior to the deed in lieu of foreclosure, it was the Loughs' position that the proceeds from the sale should be applied to the joint 1973 note. This plainly raises an issue of fact about whether the bank was aware of the Loughs' intent as to the proceeds of this sale.

Finally, the Court finds that there is substantial merit in the Loughs' alternative position that as a matter of law the proceeds should have been applied on a pro rata basis between the two distinct obligations, the result of which would likewise extinguish Mrs. Lough's liability on the 1973 note.

The Court finds, therefore, that there are genuine issues of fact and substantial, nonfrivolous arguments as to the applicable law. Therefore, the Court finds that there is a bona fide dispute as to Mrs. Lough's liability on the 1973 note.

B.

Likewise, the Court finds that there is a bona fide dispute as to her obligation on the guaranty. The bank has taken the position, and has cited case law, to the effect that this guaranty was an open-ended and continuing guaranty which, until revoked by Mrs. Lough, would apply to all obligations incurred by Mr. Lough after 1967. In response, however, Mrs. Lough has alleged that she simply never intended in 1967 when she signed this guaranty to guaranty her husband's debts for as long a period of time as fifteen years and to the extent of $135,000. The Court finds that there may be substantial merit to this position. It must be noted that on the day the guaranty was executed, Mr. Lough's only obligation was a rollover of an existing obligation in the amount of $20,000. In addition, credence is given to this argument by the fact that subsequently when the parties so intended, they entered into joint notes as to which then there would be no dispute about Mrs. Lough's obligation.

Perhaps most importantly, a legal issue arises as to whether there was consideration for the guaranty to the extent that the bank seeks to assert it now. In a guaranty circumstance, there is hardly ever, if ever, consideration which flows directly to the guarantor. In the circumstances of a guaranty, consideration most often consists of the reliance that the obligee, in this case the bank, places upon the guaranty. There is a substantial issue here about whether the bank relied upon this guaranty throughout this fourteen or fifteen year time period during which Mr. Lough continued to increase his borrowing for his business.

In this regard, the Court notes the testimony that the guaranty was buried in the files of the bank and apparently was located only in connection with preparation for this litigation. Thus, there is a substantial dispute about whether in February of 1981, when the note on which liability is now asserted was signed, the bank officers involved even knew about the guaranty. Finally, on Plaintiff's Exhibit 1, an account ledger card from this time period, the indication that there was a loan guaranty agreement signed by Mrs. Lough was crossed out; the question arises as to what inferences are to be drawn from that.

Therefore, the Court must conclude that there is a bona fide dispute as to whether Mrs. Lough is obligated on this guaranty.

IV.

Because there is a bona fide dispute concerning both of the bank's claims against Mrs. Lough, the bank is ineligible to file an involuntary petition against her. 11 U.S.C. § 303(b).

Accordingly, the petition must be dismissed.

---

[1] This memorandum opinion supplements a bench opinion given at the conclusion of trial.

[2] The parties also cited *In re Matter of Cinnamon Lake Corporation,* 48 B.R. 70 (Bankr. M.D.Fla.1985). However, that case was decided under Section 303 as it existed prior to the 1984 Bankruptcy Amendments Act. Accordingly, it cannot be considered in resolving the legal question at issue here.

An order for relief must substantially conform to Procedural Form No. B 253, Order for Relief in an Involuntary Case. (See Exhibit 9.5.) After an order for relief has been entered, the debtor has 15 days to file the schedules, lists, and statements that would have been filed by the debtor in a voluntary case. From the date of the order for relief, the case proceeds in exactly the same manner as a voluntary case.

EXHIBIT 9.5
Order for Relief in an Involuntary Case

B253
(6/91)

United States Bankruptcy Court

_____ **District of** _____

In re

                                      Bankruptcy Case No.

Debtor*

Social Security No.   :
Employer Tax I.D. No.:   Chapter No.

ORDER FOR RELIEF IN
AN INVOLUNTARY CASE

On consideration of the petition filed on _____ against the

(date)

above-named debtor, an order for relief under chapter __ of the Bankruptcy Code (title 11 of the United

States Code) is granted.

_____   _____
          Date   Bankruptcy Judge

*Set forth all names, including trade names, used by the debtor within the last 6 years. (Bankruptcy Rule 1005). For joint debtors set forth both social security numbers.

B. DISMISSAL OF AN INVOLUNTARY PETITION

The court may dismiss an involuntary petition after notice and a hearing on the motion of a petitioner, on consent of all petitioners and the debtor, or for want of prosecution. 11 U.S.C.A. § 303(j); Fed. R. Bank. P. 1017.

Dismissal of an involuntary petition may be a costly business for the petitioners. This serves as a deterrent to creditors who might otherwise file an involuntary petition merely to harass the debtor. After notice and a hearing, and for cause, the court may require petitioning creditors to post a bond to indemnify the debtor against damages the court may allow later if the petition is dismissed under section 303(i). 11 U.S.C.A. § 303(e). If the court dismisses an involuntary petition for any reason other than on consent of all petitioners and the debtor, and if the debtor does not waive the right to judgment, the court may grant judgment against the petitioners for costs or a reasonable attorney's fee. 11 U.S.C.A. § 303(i)(1). The court may grant judgment against any petitioner found to have filed the petition in bad faith for any damages proximately caused by the filing or for punitive damages. 11 U.S.C.A. § 303(i)(2).

The following case illustrates a situation in which the petitioner was found to have acted in bad faith. Ackerman filed a collection action in state court seeking payment for a debt he claimed the Runyons owed. A month after the state court granted the Runyons a continuance in that action, Ackerman filed an involuntary petition in the bankruptcy court against the Runyons, using an identical debt to support his standing in the involuntary action. The bankruptcy court found Ackerman had acted in bad faith and entered judgment against him for punitive damages and attorney's fees.

In re Runyon
United States Court of Appeals, Ninth Circuit, 1994.
1994 WL 259770.

MEMORANDUM[1]
Before: D. W. Nelson and Beezer,
Circuit Judges
and J. Spencer Letts,[2]
District Judge

Ackerman appeals the Bankruptcy Appellate Panel's affirmance of a bankruptcy court's order awarding the Runyons $15,000 in attorney's fees and $10,000 in punitive damages for Ackerman's "bad faith" filing of an involuntary petition within the meaning of 11 U.S.C. § 303(i). Ackerman challenges the punitive damages award, arguing that the bankruptcy court erred in finding that he filed in "bad faith." He also challenges the award of attorney's fees, contending that the bankruptcy court abused its discretion by holding him solely responsible for all of the fees, including those incurred after he withdrew from the involuntary bankruptcy action. The Runyons seek the imposition of sanctions for a frivolous appeal. We have jurisdiction pursuant to 28 U.S.C. § 158(d). We affirm.

I

Ackerman challenges the bankruptcy court's award of punitive damages, contending that the court erred in finding that he filed the petition against the Runyons in "bad faith" within the meaning of § 303(i). Specifically, Ackerman argues that the record does not support the predicate findings that he knew or had reason to know that he was an ineligible creditor, that he failed to disclose the disputed nature of his debt to his co-petitioners, and that he wrongfully induced petitioner Garaway to participate by misrepresenting material facts. He concludes that absent these challenged findings, the remaining facts cannot sustain the bankruptcy court's ultimate finding of "bad faith."

We review de novo decisions of the Bankruptcy Appellate Panel. *In re Dewalt,*

961 F.2d 848, 850 (9th Cir.1992). We review de novo the bankruptcy court's conclusions of law and its findings of fact for clear error. *Id.* We review the finding that an involuntary petition was filed in "bad faith" for clear error. *See In re Wavelength,* 61 B.R. 614, 620 (9th Cir.BAP1986).

Ackerman's argument is without merit. Even absent many, if not most, of the challenged findings, the record amply supports the bankruptcy court's ultimate finding of "bad faith." Ackerman filed an involuntary petition only one month after the state court granted the Runyons a continuance in a pending collection action seeking payment for the identical debt Ackerman relied on to support his standing in the involuntary action. The Runyons had filed a general denial to Ackerman's complaint, and trial was already set when Ackerman filed. At a minimum, Ackerman reasonably should have known that he would be required to demonstrate that the debt was not subject to a "bona fide dispute" or face dismissal. *See In re Rubin,* 769 F.2d 611, 615 (9th Cir. 1985) (burden on petitioner to prove that a claim is not subject to a "bona fide dispute"); *cf. In re Nordbrock,* 772 F.2d 397, 399 (8th Cir.1985).[3] Despite this requirement, Ackerman supported his standing by claiming an unliquidated and contested debt of $356,000 rather than the $37,000 that Runyon had previously admitted he owed. This factor, considered in tandem with the fact that the unliquidated sum Runyon admitted owing was far smaller than the funds already subject to Ackerman's writ of attachment, provides ample support for the bankruptcy court's inference that Ackerman filed the petition with an eye toward harassing the Runyons or for gaining an advantage in the settlement of the collection action. *See In re Johnston Hawks, Ltd.,* 72 B.R. 361, 366 (Bkrtcy.D.Haw.1987). There was ample record support for the position that Ackerman's participation in the filing was merely another battle in his personal war with the Runyons. *See In re Willow Lake Partners II,* L.P., 156 B.R. 638, 644–45 (W.D.Mo.1993).

In reaching this conclusion we reject Ackerman's argument that the lack of clarity in the case law on whether the "bona fide dispute" requirement of § 303(b) attached to the liability or to the amount of the alleged debt undermined the ultimate finding of "bad faith." Although Ackerman is correct that the case law was unclear at the time of filing, *see In re Dill,* 731 F.2d 629, 631 (9th Cir.1984), his argument is a red herring. Any lack of clarity in the case law regarding the eligibility of creditors fails to negate the inference of "bad faith" established by the facts recited above.

A

We also reject the contention that res judicata principles barred the bankruptcy court's predicate finding concerning the existence of a written retainer agreement between Ackerman and Runyon.

We review de novo the question of the availability of res judicata and collateral estoppel. *Clark v. Bear Sterns & Co., Inc.,* 966 F.2d 1318, 1320 (9th Cir.1992). Ackerman provides no basis for the proposition that the state collection action and the instant adversary proceeding to determine whether he filed an involuntary petition in "bad faith" involved the same "claim." *See Parklane Hosiery Co. v. Shore,* 439 U.S. 322, 326, n.5 (1979); *Hulsey v. Koehler,* 218 C.A.2d 1150, 1157 (1990). The judgment entered pursuant to the settlement agreement did not, moreover, incorporate any findings pertaining to the existence of a written retainer agreement. Collateral estoppel cannot bar a matter that was not actually litigated in a prior proceeding. *Shore,* 439 U.S. at 326, n.5; *Lucido v. Superior Court,* 51 Cal.3d 335, 341 (1990).

II

Ackerman challenges the bankruptcy court's award of attorney's fees. He argues that the award is excessive because it singles Ackerman out as being solely responsible for all of the Runyons' attorney's fees. He contends that he is, at most, responsible for one-third of the fees incurred for the period between the filing of the initial and the amended petitions.

We uphold the bankruptcy court's award of attorney's fees unless the court abused its discretion or erroneously applied the law. *Southwestern Media, Inc. v. Rau,* 708 F.2d 419, 422 (9th Cir.1983).

In *In re Reid,* 854 F.2d 156, 160 (7th Cir. 1988), the Seventh Circuit concluded that the bankruptcy court may properly employ a prior determination that a petitioner filed in "bad faith" to guide its discretion in imposing costs and fees pursuant to § 303(i)(1)(A) and (1)(B). We adopt this reasoning in concluding that the bankruptcy court did not abuse its discretion by holding Ackerman solely responsible for all of the fees incurred. The instant facts, moreover, support the award. Ackerman explained the value of filing an involuntary petition to Wiens and Gordon when they met to discuss their options. Ackerman also helped induce Garaway to join the petition by telling him that he had paid a retainer large enough to see the matter through to the end.

III

Although Ackerman has already had one proverbial bite at the apple before the Bankruptcy Appellate Panel, *see In re Nordbrock,* 772 F.2d at 400, the Panel did not fully address the question concerning the scope of the bankruptcy court's discretion in awarding attorney's fees pursuant to § 303(i)(1)(B). We consequently deny the Runyons' apparent request for Rule 38 sanctions. This appeal was not frivolous. *See McConnell v. Critchlow,* 661 F.2d 116, 118 (9th Cir.1981).

AFFIRMED.

---

[1]The panel unanimously finds this case suitable for decision without oral argument. Fed. R. App. P. 34(a); Ninth Circuit Rule 34–4.

This disposition is not appropriate for publication and may not be cited to or used by the courts of this circuit except as provided by Ninth Circuit Rule 36–3.

[2] The Honorable J. Spencer Letts, United States District Judge for the Central District of California, sitting by designation.

[3] We are not convinced by Ackerman's attempt to feign ignorance of federal bankruptcy law.

The record establishes that Ackerman was the attorney of record in the motion to dismiss the Runyons' personal Chapter 11. The record also supports the inference that Ackerman had at least some familiarity with the involuntary bankruptcy process, insofar as he explained the value of using this procedure to Wiens and Gordon.

BASIC TERMS AND PHRASES

Gap creditor
Involuntary Chapter 7 (liquidation)

Involuntary Chapter 11
  (reorganization)
Involuntary petition

GLOSSARY

Abandonment of Property of the Estate
The trustee's release of property from the estate that is burdensome or of inconsequential value to the estate.

Absolute Priority Rule The requirement that a class of creditors be paid or satisfied in full before the next lower ranking class of creditors receives anything.

Abstention The decision by a United States district court or a bankruptcy court to refrain from determining an issue raised during a bankruptcy proceeding that should be heard in another court, such as a state court or a tax court, until the other court has had an opportunity to consider the issue.

Accounts (Accounts Receivable) A right to payment for goods sold or leased or for services rendered that is not evidenced by an instrument or chattel paper. UCC § 9–106.

Adequate Information The information necessary for creditors holding secured claims and holders of equity interests to make an informed decision concerning assent to a Chapter 11 plan.

Adequate Protection Protection given to a creditor with a secured claim entitled to have the value of the collateral securing the claim, as determined as of the date of the filing of the petition, protected against depreciation beyond the point where the value of the collateral would no longer protect the creditor's claim. The determination of whether a creditor with a secured claim is adequately protected must be considered in light of all the facts surrounding the case and the equitable considerations to which those facts give rise.

Administrative Cost Claim A claim or a reasonable and necessary expense of the estate that arises after the petition has been filed.

Adversary Proceeding An action in bankruptcy that is commenced by the filing of a complaint. Fed. R. Bank. P. 7001.

Assignment A transfer of a right.

Assignment for the Benefit of Creditors A voluntary transfer by a debtor of all of his or her property to a trustee of his or her own selection for administration, liquidation, and equitable distribution among his or her creditors. It is distinguishable from a bankruptcy proceeding in that the debtor may not require a discharge from his or her obligations to creditors. Such an assignment is regulated by state statute.

Assumption of Executory Contracts An agreement after filing bankruptcy to perform or continue with the performance of a contract.

Attachment The prejudgment seizure of property by legal process.

Attorney's Compensation Statement A statement to be filed with a bankruptcy petition in which the debtor's attorney specifies the amount and source of compensation paid or agreed to be paid for his or her services in connection with the debtor's bankruptcy case.

Automatic Stay Upon the filing of the bankruptcy petition, the preclusion of any effort by a creditor to satisfy a claim.

Avoidance Powers The authority to vacate a prior transaction.

Bankruptcy A federal system whereby the debtor is given a "fresh start" and the creditors receive an equitable distribution of the debtor's nonexempt assets.

Bankruptcy Act The previous bankruptcy law, the Bankruptcy Act of 1898, replaced by the Bankruptcy Code of 1978.

Bankruptcy Code Title 11 of the United States Code. This title was Title I of the Bankruptcy Reform Act of 1978. It was amended in 1984, 1986, 1990, and again in 1994.

Bar Date The last date for filing proofs of claim as set by the bankruptcy court.

Best Interests of Creditors Test The requirement that creditors holding unsecured claims receive no less in a Chapter 11, 12, or 13 plan than what they would have received had the case been filed under Chapter 7 and the bankruptcy estate liquidated.

Bootstrap Plan A plan that utilizes only the resources of the debtor that existed at the time of the filing of the case.

Cash Collateral Cash or other cash equivalents in which the estate and an entity other than the estate have an interest. 11 U.S.C.A. § 363(a).

Change of Venue Moving a bankruptcy case or proceeding from one bankruptcy court to another.

Chapter 7 A liquidation case under the Bankruptcy Code.

Chapter 9 The adjustment of debts of a municipality or a governmental unit under the Bankruptcy Code.

Chapter 11 A reorganization under the Bankruptcy Code whereby a plan is developed for the payment of debts.

Chapter 12 An adjustment of debts by a family farmer with regular annual income that is accomplished through a plan under the Bankruptcy Code.

Chapter 13 An adjustment of debts of an individual with regular income that is accomplished through a plan under the Bankruptcy Code that generally runs for three years.

Chattel Paper A writing or writings which evidence both a monetary obligation and a security interest in or a lease of specific goods. UCC § 9–105(1)(b).

Claim A right to payment or a right to an equitable remedy for breach of performance if such breach gives right to payment.

Clerk's Notice Notice given by the clerk of the bankruptcy court of the filing of the case. It includes the dates for filing proceedings to object to discharge and dischargeability, the time for filing claims, and the date and time of the 341 meeting.

Codebtor Stay Under Chapters 12 and 13, upon the filing of the petition, creditors are prohibited from beginning or continuing any action to collect a claim against any individual jointly liable with the debtor on a consumer debt or any individual who secured such debt even though that individual is not the debtor in the bankruptcy petition.

Cognovit Note (Confession of Judgment Note) A note containing a provision appointing the creditor as the debtor's agent to admit liability and to confess judgment.

Collateral The property that may be repossessed by the creditor if the debtor does not meet the terms of the agreement.

Collective Bargaining Agreement A contract between an employer and a labor union that regulates the terms and conditions of employment.

Complaint A pleading that commences an adversary proceeding in a bankruptcy court.

Composition An agreement between the debtor and his or her creditors whereby the creditors agree to accept in full satisfaction something less than the amounts of their original claims.

Confirmation Hearing The hearing before the bankruptcy court to determine whether the plan in a Chapter 11, 12, or 13 case will be put into effect.

Confirmation of the Plan The determination by the bankruptcy court that the proposed plan in a Chapter 11, 12, or 13 case meets the requirements of the Bankruptcy Code.

Consensual Lien A lien created by agreement of the parties.

Consideration The "price" paid for a promise. A contract has two "considerations"—the "price" sought by the promisor for his or her promise and the "price" sought by the promisee for his or her promise or performance.

Consolidation Loan A large loan that allows a debtor to pay off all of his or her debts.

Consumer Debt Debt incurred by an individual primarily for a personal, family, or household purpose. 11 U.S.C.A. § 101(8).

Contested Matter A disputed matter that is not an adversary proceeding and that is brought by motion rather than by complaint. Fed. R. Bank. P. 9014.

Contingent Claim A claim that is dependent on the occurrence of a future event that may never happen.

Conversion The changing of a bankruptcy case from one chapter to another.

Core Proceedings Proceedings in bankruptcy in which the bankruptcy judge may order a disposition order. 28 U.S.C.A. § 157(b)(1). Examples of core proceedings are found in 28 U.S.C.A. § 157(b)(2).

Corporate Shell An entity that has a corporate identity but not a corporate purpose.

Cramdown The confirmation of a plan over the objections of creditors holding secured claims. Cramdown will differ, depending on whether the plan is a Chapter 11, Chapter 12, or Chapter 13 plan.

Credit Counseling Centers Licensed and bonded agencies that analyze the debtor's obligations and negotiate with creditors for the repayment of the debtor's bills on a schedule the debtor can manage. Credit Counseling Centers do not lend money but only educate the debtor and distribute the debtor's money to the debtor's creditors.

Creditor An entity that has a claim against the debtor that arose prior to or at the time of the filing of the bankruptcy petition. 11 U.S.C.A. § 101(10).

Creditor's Bill An action in equity by a judgment creditor to reach property which could not be reached by execution at law.

Creditors' Committee The committee that is formed in a Chapter 11 case from the list of creditors holding the 20 largest unsecured claims. The function of the committee is to consult with the trustee, the U.S. trustee, and the debtor's attorney regarding the bankruptcy estate.

Debtor In bankruptcy, a party for or against whom a case has been filed. 11 U.S.C.A. § 101(13). In nonbankruptcy, the party who owes payment or other performance of an obligation.

Debtor Engaged in Business A self-employed debtor who incurs trade credit in the production of income from this employment. 11 U.S.C.A. § 1304.

Debtor in Possession (DIP) A Chapter 11 debtor unless a trustee has been appointed to serve in the case. 11 U.S.C.A. § 1101(1). A Chapter 12 debtor unless removed. 11 U.S.C.A. § 1204(a).

Default The failure to perform a legal duty, such as the failure to pay a debt when it becomes due.

DIP An abbreviation for debtor in possession and pronounced D I P.

Discharge The bankruptcy court's release of a debtor from his or her debts.

Disclosure of Attorney's Compensation Statement A form that must be filed along with the petition stating how much, when, and how the debtor's attorney will be paid. The form may also contain a statement of what services the attorney will perform for the debtor.

Disclosure Statement A written document containing adequate information to enable those voting on the reorganization plan to make an informed judgment about the plan.

Dismissal The termination of a bankruptcy case or proceeding by the court.

Disputed Claim A claim that is challenged as to either its existence or its amount.

Disputed Matter A matter concerning a proceeding that has been filed in the bankruptcy court or the determination of the rights of the parties.

Entity Includes a person, estate, trust, governmental unit, or U.S. trustee. 11 U.S.C.A. § 101(15).

Equitable Lien A right, not recognized by law, to have a fund or a specific property or its proceeds applied, in whole or in part, to the payment of a particular debt or class of debts.

Equity Securities Shares of stock or other evidence of an ownership interest in a firm.

Estate The name given to the property of the debtor when it comes under the jurisdiction of a bankruptcy court upon the filing of a bankruptcy case.

Examiner An individual appointed by the bankruptcy court to investigate the financial affairs of a Chapter 11 debtor in possession. 11 U.S.C.A. § 1104.

Execution The process of carrying a judgment into effect.

Execution Lien A lien acquired by a judgment creditor upon the service of an execution.

Execution Sale A sale under judicial process.

Executory Contract A contract in which performance has not been completed by either party.

Exemptions Property of the bankruptcy estate that the debtor has a right to claim under state or federal law and that is free from claims of creditors.

Ex Parte An application made by one party to a proceeding in the absence of and without notice to the other party.

Fair and Equitable Test See 11 U.S.C.A. § 1129(b).

Family Farmer See 11 U.S.C.A. § 101(18).

Family Farmer with Regular Annual Income A family farmer whose annual income is sufficiently stable and regular to enable the family farmer to make payments under a Chapter 12 plan. 11 U.S.C.A. § 101(19).

Farmer A person that receives more than 80 percent of such person's gross income during the taxable year immediately preceding the taxable year in which the case was filed from a farming operation owned or operated by that person. 11 U.S.C.A. § 101(20).

Farming Operation Activities include farming; soil tilling; dairy farming; ranching; producing or raising crops, poultry, or livestock; and producing poultry or livestock products in an unmanufactured state. 11 U.S.C.A. § 101(21).

Federal Rules of Bankruptcy Procedure 28 U.S.C.A. § 2075 provides that the United States Supreme Court has the power to prescribe rules for the bankruptcy court practice. These rules apply to all bankruptcy courts and must be read along with the applicable Bankruptcy Code section. Each United States District Court and United States Bankruptcy Court must also issue local rules. The Federal Rules of Bankruptcy Procedure were formerly entitled the Bankruptcy Rules.

The Supreme Court has delegated the power to prescribe Official Forms to the Judicial Conference of the United States. Fed. R. Bank. P. 9009.

Fed. R. Bank. P. The Federal Rules of Bankruptcy Procedure, which were formerly called Bankruptcy Rules.

Final Decree An order by the bankruptcy court holding that the case has been fully administered, that the trustee in the case has been discharged, and that the case is closed.

Fixtures Goods that have become so related to real estate that an interest in them arises under real estate law. UCC § 9–313(1)(a).

Fraudulent Transfer A prepetition transfer of property by the debtor made within one year of the date of the filing of the petition that is done without consideration or renders the debtor insolvent. A fraudulent transfer may be avoided by the trustee under 11 U.S.C.A. § 548.

Fresh Start The concept of relieving the debtor from burdensome and unmanageable debt to assure his or her return to full productivity.

Gap Period Creditors The creditors in an involuntary case whose claims arise between the filing of the petition and the order for relief.

Garnishment The legal or equitable procedure through which the earnings of an individual are required to be withheld for payment of any debt.

General Intangible The catchall classification for personal property. Personal property is classified as a general intangible if it is not goods, accounts, chattel paper, documents, instruments, or money. UCC § 9–106.

Good Faith Honesty in fact.

Goods All things which are movable but not including money, documents, instruments, accounts, chattel paper, general intangibles, or minerals (including oil and gas) before extraction. UCC § 9–105(1)(h).

Indenture See U.S.C.A. § 101(28).

Indenture Trustee A trustee under an indenture. 11 U.S.C.A. § 101(29).

Indubitable Equivalent A form of adequate protection, which is a creative substitute for the usual surrender of collateral or its cash equivalent, that will result in the creditor's realization of the value of its interest in the property involved.

Insider A party who has a close relationship to the debtor and includes those parties listed in 11 U.S.C.A. § 101(31).

Insolvency Under the Bankruptcy Code, when the sum of an entity's debts is greater than a fair valuation of all the entity's property, exclusive of property exempted or fraudulently transferred, including a general partner's nonpartnership property in a partnership. Under the Uniform Commercial Code, when an individual or an organization ceases to pay its debts in the ordinary course of business, cannot pay its debts as they become due, or is insolvent under the Bankruptcy Code.

Instrument A writing which evidences a right to the payment of money and includes a negotiable instrument (check, note, draft, or certificate of deposit) and a certificated security (stocks and bonds). UCC § 9–105(1)(i).

Interim Trustee The trustee appointed in a Chapter 7 case after the filing of the petition who will continue on as the trustee, unless a different trustee is elected at the meeting of creditors.

Involuntary Petition A bankruptcy petition that is filed against a debtor by its creditors.

Judicial Lien A lien obtained by judgment, levy, sequestration, or other legal or equitable process or proceeding. 11 U.S.C.A. § 101(36).

Jurisdiction The power of a court to hear and decide the issues raised in a case.

Lien A claim against property to secure payment of an obligation. 11 U.S.C.A. § 101(37).

Limited Partner A partner whose liability for partnership debts extends only to the amount of his or her investment.

Liquidated Claim A claim, the amount of which is undisputed and certain.

Liquidation Sale of the bankruptcy estate (those assets of the debtor that are neither nonexempt nor abandoned by the trustee) by the trustee in a Chapter 7 case.

Local Bankruptcy Rules The set of rules issued by a United States district court or by a United States bankruptcy court relating to bankruptcy court practice and procedure. These rules apply only to the court issuing the rules.

Matrix The list of creditors compiled in a prescribed format and required to be filed along with the petition.

Meeting of Creditors The section 341 meeting. A meeting at which the creditors or other parties in interest may examine the debtor concerning matters that relate to the bankruptcy estate and to the debtor's discharge.

Meeting of Equity Security Holders A meeting at which the equity security holders can discuss their rights and methods for enforcing those rights.

Mortgage A grant of an interest in real estate to secure payment of a debt.

Motion A request made to a court to obtain an order or a ruling. A motion is used in a contested matter that is not an adversary proceeding.

Noncontingent Claim A claim that is not dependent on the occurrence of a future event that may never happen.

Nonpossessory, Nonpurchase Money Security Interest A security interest in which the creditor neither retains possession of the collateral nor advances the purchase price to the debtor so the debtor could acquire the collateral.

Notice and a Hearing A notice appropriate for the particular circumstances and an opportunity for a hearing. 11 U.S.C.A. § 102.

Official Forms Forms prescribed by the United States Supreme Court as part of the Federal Rules of Bankruptcy Procedure.

Operative Chapters The chapters of the Bankruptcy Code under which petitions in bankruptcy are filed. The operative chapters are Chapters 7, 9, 11, 12, and 13.

Opt Out The power granted to a state to refuse the federal scheme of exemptions under 11 U.S.C.A. § 522(b)(1) and to thereby limit its residents to the state's scheme of exemptions and federal nonbankruptcy exemptions.

Order for Relief Occurs automatically upon the filing of a petition in bankruptcy, creating the estate of the debtor and triggering the automatic stay.

Party in Interest A party who has an interest in a bankruptcy case or a bankruptcy proceeding.

Perfected Security Interest A security interest as to which notice is given so as to give a creditor protection against interests acquired by third parties.

Person Includes an individual, a partnership, and a corporation, but does not include a governmental unit. 11 U.S.C.A. § 101(41).

Personal Property Property that is not real property and includes goods, documents, instruments, general intangibles, chattel paper, and accounts (accounts receivable).

Petition The document filed by a debtor to initiate a voluntary bankruptcy case or by creditors to initiate an involuntary bankruptcy case.

Plan The document filed in Chapter 11, 12, or 13 that sets forth the financing and structure for payments to creditors by the debtor.

Postpetition Transfer A transfer of property of the estate that occurs after the filing of the bankruptcy petition.

Preference A transfer of property of the debtor, made prior to the filing of the bankruptcy petition, that gives one creditor an advantage over other creditors. 11 U.S.C.A. § 547.

Priority Claim An unsecured claim, such as a claim for administrative expenses or wages, that is to be paid before other unsecured claims. 11 U.S.C.A. § 507.

Proof of Claim A pleading filed in the bankruptcy court by a creditor stating the nature and amount of the claim.

Proof of Interest A pleading filed in the bankruptcy court by equity security holders stating the nature and amount of the interest.

Property of the Estate All of the legal and equitable interests in property of the debtor at the time of the filing of the petition in bankruptcy. Property remains property of the estate unless it is exempt or abandoned.

Purchase Money Security Interest A security interest taken by a party furnishing funds for the purchase of the collateral by the debtor.

Reaffirmation Agreement An agreement to pay a debt notwithstanding the discharge or prospective discharge of a debt in bankruptcy. Reaffirmation contemplates a continuation of payments over a period of time.

Real Property Land and whatever is erected or growing on the land.

Receivership A state court proceeding in which a fiduciary is appointed to hold in trust and administer property that is in litigation.

Redemption The process by which the debtor pays the secured interest of the creditor in a lump sum for release of the security interest.

Rejection of Executory Contracts When the debtor in possession or the trustee disaffirms a contract that has not been fully performed on both sides.

Relief from Automatic Stay An adversary proceeding in the bankruptcy court in which the creditor requests that the court modify the automatic stay to allow the creditor to proceed against the property of the estate.

Reorganization The restructuring of the debtor's business to enable it to become a viable business.

Replevin The proceeding in which a party holding a special interest in personal property seeks to gain possession of that property from another party.

Revocation of Discharge The bankruptcy court's rescission of its order discharging the debtor from its debts.

Schedules The debtor's schedules, Official Form No. 6, begin with a Summary of Schedules and include the following:

Schedule A—Real Property

Schedule B—Personal Property

Schedule C—Property Claimed as Exempt

Schedule D—Creditors Holding Secured Claims

Schedule E—Creditors Holding Unsecured Priority Claims

Schedule F—Creditors Holding Unsecured Nonpriority Claims

Schedule G—Executory Contracts and Unexpired Leases

Schedule H—Codebtors

Schedule I—Current Income of Individual Debtor(s)

Schedule J—Current Expenditures of Individual Debtor(s)

Although not an Official Form, a partnership or a corporation will need to complete a Schedule of Current Income and Current Expenditures of a Partnership or Corporation.

Secured Claim The claim of a creditor holding a lien against property of the estate.

Secured Party A lender, seller, or other person in whose favor there is a security interest. UCC § 9–105(1)(m).

Security Agreement An agreement that creates or provides for a security interest in personal property or fixtures under the Uniform Commercial Code. 11 U.S.C.A. § 101(50); UCC § 9–105(1)(1).

Security Interest A lien created by an agreement. 11 U.S.C.A. § 101(51); UCC § 1–201(37).

Self-Help Repossession A procedure by which a creditor with a secured claim takes possession of the collateral upon the default of the debtor without the aid of a judicial proceeding. UCC § 9–503.

Setoff The crediting of one claim against another without an actual exchange of money between the parties.

Standing Trustee A trustee with a permanent appointment to serve in all Chapter 12 or Chapter 13 cases.

Statement of Financial Affairs A statement made on a prescribed official form giving information concerning the debtor's financial transactions.

Statement of Intention Individual consumer debtor's notification of the court, the trustee, and the parties in interest of whether he or she will surrender or retain property of the estate that secures his or her consumer debts.

Statutory Lien A lien arising solely by force of a statute on specified circumstances or conditions. 11 U.S.C.A. § 101(53).

Straight Bankruptcy A Chapter 7 liquidation.

Subordinated Claim A claim that the bankruptcy court orders postponed in deference to another claim.

Summons A legal notice giving the defendant in an adversary proceeding notification of an action filed against him or her and specifying the time given in which to file a response.

Title 11 The title in the United States Code that contains the Bankruptcy Code.

Transfer Every mode of disposing of or parting with property or an interest in property, whether it be direct or indirect, absolute or conditional, voluntary or involuntary. 11 U.S.C.A. § 101(54).

Trustee A person appointed by the bankruptcy court to administer the estate.

Uniform Commercial Code (UCC) A code drafted by the American Law Institute and the National Conference of Commissioners on Uniform State Laws that includes the sale of goods, commercial paper, bank deposits and collections, letters of credit, bulk transfers, documents of title (bills of lading and warehouse receipts), investment securities, and secured transactions. Articles on leases of goods and fund transfers were recently added to the official text. In order for the UCC to become state law, the state's legislature must enact it. The District of Columbia, and the Virgin Islands have enacted the UCC. Louisiana has enacted articles 1, 3, 4, 4A, 5, 7, 8, and 9 of the UCC. Each state has its own variations to the official text.

United States Code (U.S.C.) The official edition of federal statutes. U.S.C. is printed and sold by the United States Government Printing Office.

United States Code Annotated (U.S.C.A.) West Publishing Company's version of federal statutes.

United States Trustee A person appointed by the attorney general of the United States to oversee the progress of bankruptcy cases and to appoint and supervise the trustees.

Universal Chapters Chapters 1, 3, and 5 of the Bankruptcy Code, which contain definitional and administrative provisions that generally apply to all operative chapters of the Code.

Unliquidated Claim A claim in which the amount owed is uncertain.

Unperfected Security Interest A security interest as to which notice has not been deemed to have been given so as to notify third parties of the secured party's interest in the collateral.

Unsecured Claim A claim that is not protected by a lien on property.

Unsworn Declaration An unsworn statement made under penalty of perjury.

Usury An interest rate charged for the use of money that exceeds the interest charge permitted by law.

Venue The proper court in which to hear a bankruptcy case or proceeding.

Voidable Preference A transfer of property of the debtor, made prior to the filing of the bankruptcy petition, that gives one creditor an advantage over other creditors and that may be avoided by the trustee to bring the property back into the estate. 11 U.S.C.A. § 547.

Voluntary Petition A bankruptcy petition that is filed by a debtor.

Workout A noncourt arrangement between the debtor and his or her creditors to satisfy the debtor's obligations.

INTERVIEW QUESTIONNAIRE FOR THE DEBTOR-CLIENT

For us to properly handle your case, it is necessary that you complete this questionnaire. It is essential that you list every debt that you owe and every claim that any person or entity asserts that you owe.

Please list all real and personal property you own or own an interest in, including property you believe is exempt. If a bankruptcy petition is filed on your behalf, we will claim, in the schedules which will be prepared for you, the proper exemptions. We will discuss this with you before filing your case.

In listing real property, it is necessary that you include the full legal description. This may require you to search for deeds or other legal documents, but it is important that this information be furnished.

Each item on the following parts of the questionnaire must be answered. Complete these parts only:

- ☐ **I. A.** General Information—Individual Debtor and a Husband and Wife Filing a Joint Petition
- ☐ **I. B.** General Information—Partnership Debtor
- ☐ **I. C.** General Information—Corporate Debtor
- ☐ **II.** Assets
- ☐ **III.** Debts
- ☐ **IV.** Executory Contracts and Unexpired Leases
- ☐ **V.** Current Income and Current Expenditures of Individual Debtor(s)
- ☐ **VI.** Current Income and Current Expenditures of a Partnership or Corporation
- ☐ **VII.** Statement of Financial Affairs
- ☐ **VIII.** Property Status—Real and Personal

If additional space is needed, write the information on a separate sheet of paper and attach it to this questionnaire. Indicate to which question this information relates.

If your answer to any question should change during the period when we are handling your case, you must contact this office and advise us of any such change. Our paralegal, _____, will be assisting you in completing this questionnaire.

by _____
Attorney at Law

Complete all parts of this questionnaire. If a question does not apply to you, indicate "n.a."

I. GENERAL INFORMATION

If the debtor is an individual or the debtors are a husband and wife filing a joint petition, complete question A.

If the debtor is a partnership, complete question B.

If the debtor is a corporation, complete question C.

At times a debtor may file as both an individual and a partnership or a corporation. If this may be your situation, complete question A and either question B or C, depending on whether you are a partnership or a corporation.

A. If the debtor is an individual or a husband and wife filing a joint petition, complete this question.

1. Information concerning the debtor

   a. State your full name (last name, first name, middle name):

     Debtor: _____

          Last   First   Middle

   b. Telephone number: _____ (home)

                               _____ (work)

   c. Have you used, or been known by, any other name or names within the immediately preceding six years?

     yes _____ no _____

     If yes, give particulars. Include maiden names, prior married names, nicknames, and trade names.

     _____

     _____

     _____

   d. Social Security Number: _____

   e. Tax ID No., if any: _____

   f. Address: _____

            street

     _____

     city   state   zip code

     _____

     county of residence

   g. Have you lived there longer than three months?

     yes_____no_____

   h. Mailing address if different from the street address:

     _____

     _____

     city   state   zip code

i. If business debt, briefly describe the nature of the business.

_____

_____

j. Marital status:

_____ single

_____ married

  date: _____

  place of marriage: _____

_____ divorced

  date: _____

  place of divorce: _____

_____ widowed

  date: _____

  place of spouse's death: _____

2. Information concerning the debtor's spouse

  a. State your spouse's full name (last name, first name, middle name):

  Spouse: _____

  Last   First   Middle

  b. Telephone number: _____ (home)

  _____ (work)

  c. Has your spouse used, or been known by, any other name or names within the immediately preceding six years?

  yes_____ no_____

  If yes, give particulars. Include maiden names, prior married names, nicknames, and trade names.

  _____

  _____

  _____

  d. Social Security Number: _____

  e. Tax ID No., if any: _____

  f. Address: _____

    street

  _____

  city   state   zip code

  _____

  county of residence

  g. Has your spouse lived there longer than three months?

  yes_____ no_____

  h. Mailing address if different from the street address:

  _____

  _____

  city   state   zip code

  i. If business debt, briefly describe the nature of the business.

  _____

  _____

B. If the debtor is a partnership, complete this question.

  1. State the name of the partnership:

  _____

  2. Name of the individual authorized to file the petition:

  _____

3. Title: _____

4. Telephone number (include area code): _____

5. Is the partnership known, or has it been known, by any other name or names within the immediately preceding six years?

yes _____ no _____

If yes, state the names and dates when the names were used.

_____

_____

_____

_____

6. Partnership's Tax ID No.: _____

7. Street address of the partnership:

_____

street

_____

city   state   zip code

8. County of principal place of business: _____

9. Mailing address of the partnership if different from the street address:

_____

10. Location of principal assets of the partnership if different from the street address: _____

_____

11. Nature of the partnership's business: _____

_____

12. If a prior bankruptcy case has been filed within the last six years, provide the following information:

a. Location where filed: _____

b. Case number: _____

c. Date filed: _____

13. If a pending bankruptcy case has been filed by a partner or an affiliate of the partnership, provide the following information.

a. Name of the debtor: _____

b. Case number: _____

c. Date filed: _____

d. Relationship: _____

e. District where case was filed: _____

f. Judge: _____

C. If the debtor is a corporation, complete this question.

1. State the name of the corporation:

_____

2. Name of the individual authorized to file the petition:

_____

3. Title: _____

4. Telephone number (include area code): _____

5. Is the corporation known, or has it been known, by any other name or names within the immediately preceding six years?

yes _____ no _____

If yes, state the names and dates when the names were used.

_____

_____

_____

_____

6. Corporation's Tax ID No.: _____

7. Street address of the corporation:

_____

street

_____

city   state   zip code

8. County of principal place of business: _____

9. Mailing address of the corporation if different from the street address:

_____

10. Location of principal assets of the corporation if different from the street address: _____

_____

11. Is the corporation publicly held or privately held?

_____

12. Nature of the corporation's business:

_____

13. If a prior bankruptcy case has been filed within the last six years, provide the following information.
    a. Location where filed: _____
    b. Case number: _____
    c. Date filed: _____
14. If a pending bankruptcy case has been filed by an affiliate of the corporation, provide the following information.
    a. Name of the debtor: _____
    b. Case number: _____
    c. Date filed: _____
    d. Relationship: _____
    e. District where case was filed: _____
    f. Judge: _____

II. ASSETS

All debtors must complete this Part. Complete each question based on the assets of the debtor. All questions must be answered.

> If you are answering as an individual, provide information for all questions that relate to you as an individual. Use "none" or "n.a." as your answer to a question if you have no assets or if the question is inapplicable to you as an individual.
> If you are answering for a partnership, provide information for all questions that relate to the partnership. Use "none" or "n.a." as your answer to a question if the partnership has no assets or if the question is inapplicable to the partnership.
> If you are answering for a corporation, provide the information for all questions that relate to the corporation. Use "none" or "n.a." as your answer to a question if the corporation has no assets or if the question is inapplicable to the corporation.

A. REAL PROPERTY

State the legal description and the mailing address of all real property in which you have an interest, including all equitable and future interests, estates by the entirety, community property, life estates, leaseholds, and any power exercisable for your own benefit relating to real property. State the nature of your interest in each item of real property. If the debtor is an individual or a husband and wife filing a joint petition, state whether the property is owned by the husband, the wife, jointly, or as community property. State the current market value of your interest in the real property without deducting the mortgages or exemptions. If the property is mortgaged, state the amount of the mortgage.

If you do not have an interest in any real property, indicate "none."

1. Legal description

    _____
    lot #, block #   addition

    _____
    city   county   state
2. Mailing address

    _____
    street

    _____
    city   state   zip code
3. The nature of the debtor's interest in the property (e.g., fee simple, option to purchase, three-year lease, life estate)

    _____

4. If the debtor is an individual who is married or a husband and wife filing a joint petition, check who owns the property:
    _____ husband
    _____ wife
    _____ jointly
    _____ community property
5. State the current market value of the debtor's interest in the property. (Do not deduct any secured claim or exemption.)
    $ _____
6. If the real property has a secured claim (e.g., a mortgage), state the amount of the claim.
    $ _____

B. PERSONAL PROPERTY

If the debtor is an individual or a husband and wife filing a joint petition, list your personal property and, if married, your spouse's personal property, and its location. If the debtor is married, indicate who owns the property (e.g., husband, wife, jointly, community) by circling the appropriate letter. Also state the current market value of your interest in the property, without deducting for secured claims or exemptions. If the property normally spends part of the day at your residence, list "at residence." EACH BLANK MUST BE FILLED IN.

If the debtor is a partnership or a corporation, list all personal property of the partnership or the corporation.

If the assets are a mixture of individual and partnership or corporate assets, list all assets and designate whether they are individual, partnership, or corporate assets.

Description	Location	Ownership	Market Value of Debtor's Interest
1. Cash on hand	_____	H W J C	$_____
2. Checking, savings, and other financial accounts			
a. Banks			
_____	_____	H W J C	$_____
_____	_____	H W J C	$_____
b. Savings and loans			
_____	_____	H W J C	$_____
_____	_____	H W J C	$_____
c. Credit unions			
_____	_____	H W J C	$_____
_____	_____	H W J C	$_____
d. Brokerage houses			
_____	_____	H W J C	$_____
_____	_____	H W J C	$_____
e. Others			
_____	_____	H W J C	$_____
_____	_____	H W J C	$_____
3. Security deposits			
a. Public utilities			
_____	_____	H W J C	$_____
_____	_____	H W J C	$_____
b. Telephone company			
_____	_____	H W J C	$_____
c. Landlord			
_____	_____	H W J C	$_____
_____	_____	H W J C	$_____
d. Others			
_____	_____	H W J C	$_____
_____	_____	H W J C	$_____
_____	_____	H W J C	$_____
4. Household goods and furnishings			
a. Living room, dining room, and family room			
1) sofa	_____	H W J C	$_____
2) chairs	_____	H W J C	$_____
3) tables	_____	H W J C	$_____
4) TVs	_____	H W J C	$_____
5) VCRs	_____	H W J C	$_____
6) stereos	_____	H W J C	$_____
7) lamps	_____	H W J C	$_____
8) carpets	_____	H W J C	$_____
9) bookcases	_____	H W J C	$_____
10) piano	_____	H W J C	$_____
11) other musical instruments	_____	H W J C	$_____
12) radios	_____	H W J C	$_____
13) buffet	_____	H W J C	$_____
14) china closet	_____	H W J C	$_____
15) china	_____	H W J C	$_____
16) silverware	_____	H W J C	$_____
17) sewing machine	_____	H W J C	$_____
18) other	_____	H W J C	$_____
b. Kitchen			
1) table and chairs	_____	H W J C	$_____
2) stove	_____	H W J C	$_____

3) microwave _____ H W J C $_____
4) refrigerator _____ H W J C $_____
5) freezer _____ H W J C $_____
6) dishwasher _____ H W J C $_____
7) washer _____ H W J C $_____
8) dryer _____ H W J C $_____
9) telephones _____ H W J C $_____
10) misc. appliances _____ H W J C $_____
11) misc. furnishings _____ H W J C $_____

c. Bedrooms and study
1) bedroom suites _____ H W J C $_____
2) cedar chest _____ H W J C $_____
3) bureaus _____ H W J C $_____
4) desks _____ H W J C $_____
5) computer equipment _____ H W J C $_____
6) TVs _____ H W J C $_____
7) VCRs _____ H W J C $_____
8) CD player _____ H W J C $_____
9) radios _____ H W J C $_____
10) stereos _____ H W J C $_____
11) lamps _____ H W J C $_____
12) telephones _____ H W J C $_____
13) other _____ H W J C $_____

d. Garage
1) tools _____ H W J C $_____
2) bicycles _____ H W J C $_____
3) other _____ H W J C $_____

e. Other areas, including storage facilities
_____ _____ H W J C $_____
_____ _____ H W J C $_____
_____ _____ H W J C $_____

5. a. Books, pictures, and other art objects
1) books _____ H W J C $_____
2) pictures _____ H W J C $_____
3) other art objects _____ H W J C $_____

b. Collections and collectibles
1) antiques _____ H W J C $_____
2) stamps _____ H W J C $_____
3) coins _____ H W J C $_____
4) records _____ H W J C $_____
5) tapes _____ H W J C $_____
6) compact discs _____ H W J C $_____
7) other collections or collectibles _____ H W J C $_____

6. Wearing apparel (exclude furs and jewelry)
List any item that exceeds $200 in market value.
_____ _____ H W J C $_____
_____ _____ H W J C $_____
Other clothing _____ H W J C $_____

7. Furs and jewelry
List any item that exceeds $200 in market value.
_____ _____ H W J C $_____
_____ _____ H W J C $_____
_____ _____ H W J C $_____
_____ _____ H W J C $_____
Other jewelry _____ H W J C $_____

8. a. Firearms

		Ownership	Value
_____	_____	H W J C	$_____
_____	_____	H W J C	$_____
_____	_____	H W J C	$_____
_____	_____	H W J C	$_____

b. Sports equipment
   List any item that exceeds $200 in market value.

		Ownership	Value
_____	_____	H W J C	$_____
_____	_____	H W J C	$_____
_____	_____	H W J C	$_____
_____	_____	H W J C	$_____
Other sports equipment	_____	H W J C	$_____

c. Photographic equipment

		Ownership	Value
_____	_____	H W J C	$_____
_____	_____	H W J C	$_____
_____	_____	H W J C	$_____

d. Other equipment
   List any item that exceeds $200 in market value.

		Ownership	Value
_____	_____	H W J C	$_____
_____	_____	H W J C	$_____
_____	_____	H W J C	$_____

9. Interests in insurance policies (list the surrender or refund value of each policy)

Type of insurance	Insurance company	Location	Ownership	Surrender or refund value
_____	_____	_____	H W J C	$_____
_____	_____	_____	H W J C	$_____
_____	_____	_____	H W J C	$_____
_____	_____	_____	H W J C	$_____
_____	_____	_____	H W J C	$_____

10. Annuities

Type of annuity	Name of fund	Location of fund	Ownership	Current market value
_____	_____	_____	H W J C	$_____
_____	_____	_____	H W J C	$_____
_____	_____	_____	H W J C	$_____
_____	_____	_____	H W J C	$_____
_____	_____	_____	H W J C	$_____

11. Interests in IRA, ERISA, Keogh, and other pension or profit sharing plans

Description	Location of institution	Ownership	Current market value
_____	_____	H W J C	$_____
_____	_____	H W J C	$_____

12. Stock and interests in incorporated and unincorporated businesses

Shares or interests	Name of business	Location of business	Ownership	Current market value
_____	_____	_____	H W J C	$_____
_____	_____	_____	H W J C	$_____
_____	_____	_____	H W J C	$_____
_____	_____	_____	H W J C	$_____

13. Interests in partnerships or joint ventures

Interest	Name of partnership	Location	Ownership	Current market value
_____	_____	_____	H W J C	$_____
_____	_____	_____	H W J C	$_____

14. Government and corporate bonds and other negotiable and non-negotiable instruments

Description	Location	Ownership	Current market value
_____	_____	H W J C	$_____
_____	_____	H W J C	$_____

15. Accounts receivable

Description (account no.)	Name of account debtor	Date first due	Ownership	Current market value of the amount due
_____	_____	_____	H W J C	$_____
_____	_____	_____	H W J C	$_____
_____	_____	_____	H W J C	$_____
_____	_____	_____	H W J C	$_____

16. Alimony, maintenance, support, and property settlements to which the debtor is or may be entitled

Description of the obligation	Address of the person owing the obligation	Ownership	Current market value of the total amount due or the amount of the monthly payments and duration
_____	_____	H W J C	$_____
_____	_____	H W J C	$_____

17. Other liquidated debts owing debtor, including tax refunds

Description of the debt	Address of the entity owing the obligation	Ownership	Current market value of the amount due
_____	_____	H W J C	$_____
_____	_____	H W J C	$_____

18. Equitable or future interests, life estates, and rights or powers exercisable for the benefit of the debtor, other than those listed under "Real Property"

Description of the interest	Address of the trustee, if any	Ownership	Current market value of the interest
_____	_____	H W J C	$_____
_____	_____	H W J C	$_____

19. Contingent and noncontingent interests in estate of a decedent, death benefit plan, life insurance policy, or trust

Description of the interest	Address of the administrator	Ownership	Current market value of the interest
_____	_____	H W J C	$_____
_____	_____	H W J C	$_____

20. Other contingent and unliquidated claims of every nature, including tax refunds, counterclaims of the debtor, and rights to setoff claims

Description of the claim	Address of the defendant	Ownership	Current market value of the claim
_____	_____	H W J C	$_____
_____	_____	H W J C	$_____

21. Patents, copyrights, and other intellectual property

Description of the property	Address where documentation is kept	Ownership	Current market value of the property
_____	_____	H W J C	$_____
_____	_____	H W J C	$_____

22. Licenses, franchises, and other general intangibles

Description of the property	Address where documentation is kept	Ownership	Current market value of the property
_____	_____	H W J C	$_____
_____	_____	H W J C	$_____

23. Automobiles, trucks, trailers, and other vehicles

	Location	Ownership	Current market value
a. Automobile Year: _____ Make: _____ Model: _____ Serial No.: _____	_____	H W J C	$_____
b. Automobile Year: _____ Make: _____ Model: _____ Serial No.: _____	_____	H W J C	$_____
c. Automobile Year: _____ Make: _____ Model: _____ Serial No.: _____	_____	H W J C	$_____
d. Automobile Year: _____ Make: _____ Model: _____ Serial No.: _____	_____	H W J C	$_____
e. Automobile Year: _____ Make: _____ Model: _____ Serial No.: _____	_____	H W J C	$_____

f. Recreational Vehicle   _____   H W J C $_____
    Year: _____
    Make: _____
    Model: _____
    Serial No.: _____

24. Boats, motors, and their accessories

Description of the property	Address where the property is kept	Ownership	Current market value of the property
_____	_____	H W J C	$_____
_____	_____	H W J C	$_____

25. Aircraft and their accessories

Description of the property	Address where the property is kept	Ownership	Current market value of the property
_____	_____	H W J C	$_____
_____	_____	H W J C	$_____
_____	_____	H W J C	$_____

26. Office equipment, furnishings, and supplies

Description of the property	Address where the property is kept	Ownership	Current market value of the property
_____	_____	H W J C	$_____
_____	_____	H W J C	$_____
_____	_____	H W J C	$_____
_____	_____	H W J C	$_____
_____	_____	H W J C	$_____
_____	_____	H W J C	$_____

27. Machinery, fixtures, equipment, and supplies used in business

Description of the property	Address where the property is kept	Ownership	Current market value of the property
_____	_____	H W J C	$_____
_____	_____	H W J C	$_____
_____	_____	H W J C	$_____
_____	_____	H W J C	$_____
_____	_____	H W J C	$_____
_____	_____	H W J C	$_____

28. Inventory

Description of the inventory	Address where the inventory is located	Ownership	Current market value of the inventory
_____	_____	H W J C	$_____
_____	_____	H W J C	$_____
_____	_____	H W J C	$_____
_____	_____	H W J C	$_____

29. Animals (including pets)

Description of the animal(s)	Address where the animal is located	Ownership	Current market value of the animal
_____	_____	H W J C	$_____
_____	_____	H W J C	$_____
_____	_____	H W J C	$_____
_____	_____	H W J C	$_____

30. Crops—growing or harvested

Description of the crops	Address where the crops are located	Ownership	Current market value of the crops
_____	_____	H W J C	$_____
_____	_____	H W J C	$_____
_____	_____	H W J C	$_____
_____	_____	H W J C	$_____

31. Farming equipment and implements

Description of the equipment or implements	Address where located	Ownership	Current market value of the equipment or implements
_____	_____	H W J C	$_____
_____	_____	H W J C	$_____
_____	_____	H W J C	$_____
_____	_____	H W J C	$_____

32. Farm supplies, chemicals, and feed

Description of the supplies, chemicals, or feed	Address where located	Ownership	Current market value of the supplies, chemicals, or feed
_____	_____	H W J C	$_____
_____	_____	H W J C	$_____
_____	_____	H W J C	$_____
_____	_____	H W J C	$_____

33. Other personal property of any kind not already listed

Description of the property	Address where located	Ownership	Current market value of the property
_____	_____	H W J C	$_____
_____	_____	H W J C	$_____
_____	_____	H W J C	$_____
_____	_____	H W J C	$_____

III. DEBTS

All debtors must complete Part III of the questionnaire. Complete each question based on the debts of the debtor. All questions must be answered.

> If you are answering as an individual, provide information for all questions that relate to you as an individual. Use "none" or "n.a." as your answer to a question if you have no debts or if the question is inapplicable to you as an individual.
>
> If you are answering for a partnership, provide information for all questions that relate to the partnership. Use "none" or "n.a." as your answer to a question if the partnership has no debts or if the question is inapplicable to the partnership.
>
> If you are answering for a corporation, provide information for all questions that relate to the corporation. Use "none" or "n.a." as your answer to a question if the corporation has no debts or if the question is inapplicable to the corporation.
>
> If the debts are a mixture of individual and partnership or corporate debts, list all debts and designate whether they are individual, partnership, or corporate debts.

A. SECURED CREDITORS

List in alphabetical order the name, mailing address, account number, if any, and telephone number of each secured creditor, the date when the security interest (lien) was given, the nature of the lien (i.e., judgment lien, garnishment, mechanic's lien, real estate mortgage, deed of trust, UCC art. 9 security interest), a description of collateral subject to the lien, the market value of the collateral, and the amount of the claim without deducting the value of the collateral. Do not deduct the value of the collateral from the balance owed.

Creditor's name: _____

Creditor's mailing address: _____

                   street

_____

city   state   zip code

Account number, if any: _____

Telephone number (including area code): _____

Date claim was incurred: _____

Nature of the lien: _____

Name of codebtor, if any: _____

Address of codebtor: _____

                street

_____

city   state   zip code

Whose debt: H   W   J   C   (circle one)

Description of the property subject to the lien:

_____

Value of the property subject to the lien: $ _____

Amount of the claim (do not deduct the value of the collateral): $ _____

Creditor's name: _____

Creditor's mailing address: _____

street

_____

city   state   zip code

Account number, if any: _____

Telephone number (including area code): _____

Date claim was incurred: _____

Nature of the lien: _____

Name of codebtor, if any: _____

Address of codebtor: _____

street

_____

city   state   zip code

Whose debt: H   W   J   C   (circle one)

Description of the property subject to the lien: _____

_____

Value of the property subject to the lien: $ _____

Amount of the claim (do not deduct the value of the collateral): $_____

Creditor's name: _____

Creditor's mailing address: _____

street

_____

city   state   zip code

Account number, if any: _____

Telephone number (including area code): _____

Date claim was incurred: _____

Nature of the lien: _____

Name of codebtor, if any: _____

Address of codebtor: _____

street

_____

city   state   zip code

Whose debt: H   W   J   C   (circle one)

Description of the property subject to the lien: _____

_____

Value of the property subject to the lien: $ _____

Amount of the claim (do not deduct the value of the collateral): $_____

B. PRIORITY CREDITORS

1. Has an involuntary petition in bankruptcy been filed against you?
   yes _____ no _____
2. Do you owe any wages, salaries, or commissions, including vacation, severance, or sick pay, to any employee which were earned within the immediately preceding 90 days or within 90 days of the cessation of business?
   yes _____ no _____
   If yes, provide the following information for each creditor and each claim.

Creditor's name: _____

Creditor's mailing address: _____
                                   street

_____

city   state   zip code

Account number, if any: _____

Telephone number (including area code): _____

Name of codebtor, if any: _____

Address of codebtor: _____
                          street

_____

city   state   zip code

Whose debt: H   W   J   C   (circle one)

Date claim was incurred: _____

Consideration for the claim: _____

Amount of the claim: $ _____

3. Do you owe any contributions to employee benefit plans for services rendered by your employees within the last 180 days or within the last 180 days prior to the cessation of business?

yes _____ no _____

If yes, provide the following information for each creditor and each claim.

Creditor's name: _____

Creditor's mailing address: _____
                                   street

_____

city   state   zip code

Account number, if any: _____

Telephone number (including area code): _____

Name of codebtor, if any: _____

Address of codebtor: _____
                          street

_____

city   state   zip code

Whose debt: H   W   J   C   (circle one)

Date claim was incurred: _____

Consideration for the claim: _____

Amount of the claim: $ _____

4. Do you owe any claims to farmers or fishermen?

yes _____ no _____

If yes, provide the following information for each creditor and each claim.

Creditor's name: _____

Creditor's mailing address: _____
                                   street

_____

city   state   zip code

Account number, if any: _____

Telephone number (including area code): _____

Name of codebtor, if any: _____

Address of codebtor: _____

            street

_____

city   state   zip code

Whose debt: H W J C (circle one)

Date claim was incurred: _____

Consideration for the claim: _____

Amount of the claim: $ _____

5. Have you received any deposits from any individual for the purchase, lease, or rental of property or services for personal, family, or household use that were not delivered or provided?

   yes _____ no _____

   If yes, provide the following information for each creditor and each claim.

Creditor's name: _____

Creditor's mailing address: _____

            street

_____

city   state   zip code

Account number, if any: _____

Telephone number (including area code): _____

Name of codebtor, if any: _____

Address of codebtor: _____

            street

_____

city   state   zip code

Whose debt: H W J C (circle one)

Date claim was incurred: _____

Consideration for the claim: _____

Amount of the claim: $ _____

6. Do you owe an obligation to a spouse, a former spouse, or a child for alimony, maintenance, or support in connection with a separation agreement, divorce decree, or other order of a court of record?

   To a spouse: yes _____ no _____

   To a former spouse: yes _____ no _____

   To a child: yes _____ no _____

   If yes, provide the following information for each claimant.

Claimant's name: _____

Claimant's mailing address: _____

            street

_____

city   state   zip code

Nature of the claim: _____

Amount of the claim: $ _____

7. Do you owe taxes to any of the following entities?

   To the United States: yes _____ no _____

   To any state: yes _____ no _____

To any other taxing authority: yes _____ no _____
If yes, provide the following information for each creditor and each claim.

Creditor's name: _____

Creditor's mailing address: _____
                                                    street

_____
city   state   zip code

Account number, if any: _____

Telephone number (including area code): _____

Name of codebtor, if any: _____

Address of codebtor: _____
                                      street

_____
city   state   zip code

Whose debt: H   W   J   C   (circle one)

Date claim was incurred: _____

Consideration for the claim: _____

Amount of the claim: $ _____

8. Have you made a commitment to the Federal Deposit Insurance Corporation, the Director of the Office of Trust Supervision, the Comptroller of the Currency, or the Board of Governors of the Federal Reserve System, or their predecessors or successors, to maintain the capital of an insured depository institution? yes _____ no _____
If yes, provide the following information for each creditor and each claim.

Creditor's name: _____

Creditor's mailing address: _____
                                                    street

_____
city   state   zip code

Account number, if any: _____

Telephone number (including area code): _____

Name of codebtor, if any: _____

Address of codebtor: _____
                                      street

_____
city   state   zip code

Whose debt: H   W   J   C   (circle one)

Date claim was incurred: _____

Consideration for the claim: _____

Amount of the claim: $ _____

C. UNSECURED CREDITORS

List in alphabetical order the name, address, and account number, if any, of each unsecured creditor, the date the debt was incurred, the consideration for the claim, whether the claim is subject to setoff, and the amount of the claim. Include all open accounts with book and record clubs, credit cards, department stores, doctors, gasoline companies, hospitals, mail order houses, utilities, and signature loans at banks, savings and loan associations, credit unions, and finance companies. Show the exact name and address of the creditor, including zip code, and the creditor's telephone number. If a creditor has turned the account over to a collection agency or an attorney for collection, show the name, address, and telephone number of the collection agency or attorney and any additional amounts known to be owed to the collection agency or attorney for collection fees or costs.

Creditor's name: _____

Creditor's mailing address: _____
                                    street

_____

city   state   zip code

Account number, if any: _____

Telephone number (including area code): _____

Name of codebtor, if any: _____

Address of codebtor: _____
                              street

_____

city   state   zip code

Whose debt: H   W   J   C   (circle one)

Date claim was incurred: _____

Consideration for the claim: _____

Was the claim subject to a setoff? yes _____ no _____

Amount of the claim: $ _____

Creditor's name: _____

Creditor's mailing address: _____
                                    street

_____

city   state   zip code

Account number, if any: _____

Telephone number (including area code): _____

Name of codebtor, if any: _____

Address of codebtor: _____
                              street

_____

city   state   zip code

Whose debt: H   W   J   C   (circle one)

Date claim was incurred: _____

Consideration for the claim: _____

Was the claim subject to a setoff? yes _____ no _____

Amount of the claim: $ _____

Creditor's name: _____

Creditor's mailing address: _____
                                    street

_____

city   state   zip code

Account number, if any: _____

Telephone number (including area code): _____

Name of codebtor, if any: _____

Address of codebtor: _____

                    street

_____

city   state   zip code

Whose debt: H W J C (circle one)

Date claim was incurred: _____

Consideration for the claim: _____

Was the claim subject to a setoff? yes _____ no _____

Amount of the claim: $ _____

IV. EXECUTORY CONTRACTS AND UNEXPIRED LEASES

For each executory contract (a contract that has duties still to be performed by both contracting parties) and unexpired lease, provide the following information.

Name of the other party to the contract or lease: _____

Mailing address of the other party: _____

                                    street

_____

city   state   zip code

Telephone number (including area code): _____

Description of the contract or lease: _____

Nature of the debtor's interest: _____

If a lease, is it for nonresidential real property? yes _____ no _____

If a government contract, state the contract number: _____

Name of the other party to the contract or lease: _____

Mailing address of the other party: _____

                                    street

_____

city   state   zip code

Telephone number (including area code): _____

Description of the contract or lease: _____

Nature of the debtor's interest: _____

If a lease, is it for nonresidential real property? yes _____ no _____

If a government contract, state the contract number: _____

Name of the other party to the contract or lease: _____

Mailing address of the other party: _____

                                    street

_____

city   state   zip code

Telephone number (including area code): _____

Description of the contract or lease: _____

Nature of the debtor's interest: _____

If a lease, is it for nonresidential real property? yes _____ no _____

If a government contract, state the contract number: _____

V. CURRENT INCOME AND EXPENDITURES OF INDIVIDUAL DEBTOR(S)

Complete Part V if the debtor is an individual or if the debtors are husband and wife filing a joint petition.

    A. Estimated average monthly income of the debtor and spouse, if applicable

        1. Total average monthly income for the debtor

            a. Net monthly take-home pay

                1) Gross monthly take-home pay

                    a) Current monthly gross wages, salaries, and $ _____
commissions (pro rate if not paid monthly)

                    b) Estimated monthly overtime $ _____

                2) Payroll deductions

                    a) Payroll taxes, including Social Security $ _____

                    b) Insurance $ _____

                    c) Union dues $ _____

                    d) Other: Specify _____ $ _____
                             _____ $ _____

            b. Other monthly income

                1) Regular income from operation of business,
profession, or farm $ _____

                2) Income from real property $ _____

                3) Investment income, including interest and dividends $ _____

                4) Alimony, maintenance, or support payments
payable to the debtor for the debtor's use $ _____

                5) Support payable to the debtor for the support
of another person
Specify name: _____ $ _____
Specify name: _____ $ _____

                6) Social Security benefits $ _____

                7) Other governmental assistance
Specify the type of assistance:
     _____ $ _____
     _____ $ _____

                8) Pension and other retirement income $ _____

                9) Income from ownership of personal property $ _____

                10) Money provided by debtor's spouse to the debtor,
excluding amounts listed above $ _____

                11) Other monthly income:
Specify: _____ $ _____
Specify: _____ $ _____

        2. Total average monthly income for the debtor's spouse, if the debtor is
married

            a. Net monthly take-home pay

                1) Gross monthly take-home pay

                    a) Current monthly gross wages, salaries, and $ _____
commissions (pro rate if not paid monthly)

                    b) Estimated monthly overtime $ _____

    2) Payroll deductions

        a) Payroll taxes, including Social Security $ _____

        b) Insurance $ _____

        c) Union dues $ _____

        d) Other: Specify _____ $ _____

        _____ $ _____

b. Other monthly income

    1) Regular income from operation of business, profession, or farm $ _____

    2) Income from real property $ _____

    3) Investment income, including interest and dividends $ _____

    4) Alimony, maintenance, or support payments payable to the debtor for the debtor's use $ _____

    5) Support payable to the debtor for the support of another person

        Specify name: _____ $ _____

        Specify name: _____ $ _____

    6) Social Security benefits $ _____

    7) Other governmental assistance

        Specify the type of assistance:

        _____ $ _____

        _____ $ _____

    8) Pension and other retirement income $ _____

    9) Income from ownership of personal property $ _____

    10) Money provided by debtor's spouse to the debtor, excluding amounts listed above $ _____

    11) Other monthly income:

        Specify: _____ $ _____

        Specify: _____ $ _____

B. Estimated average current monthly expenditures of the debtor and the debtor's family, if the debtor has a family. Exclude payments on debts owed as of this date unless a debt is specifically listed below.

If the debtor is married, does the debtor's spouse maintain a separate household?

yes _____ no _____

If the debtor's spouse maintains a separate household, include those current expenses in B.2 rather than in B.1.

1. Estimated average current monthly expenses.

    a. Rent or home mortgage payment (include lot rented for mobile home and condominium fee) $ _____

        Are real estate taxes included? yes_____ no _____

        Is property insurance included? yes_____ no _____

    b. Utilities:

        1) Electricity $ _____

        2) Gas, oil, or coal $ _____

        3) Water $ _____

        4) Sewer $ _____

        5) Telephone $ _____

        6) Refuse removal $ _____

        7) Other _____ $ _____

   c. Routine home maintenance (repairs and upkeep) $ _____

   d. Food $ _____

   e. Clothing $ _____

   f. Laundry and dry cleaning $ _____

   g. Medical and dental expenses (include drugs) $ _____

   h. Transportation, excluding automobile payments $ _____

   i. Recreation, clubs, and entertainment $ _____

   j. Newspapers, periodicals, and books, including school books $ _____

   k. Religious and charitable contributions $ _____

   l. Insurance not deducted from wages or included in home mortgage payments

      1) Homeowners or renters insurance $ _____

      2) Life insurance $ _____

      3) Medical insurance $ _____

      4) Automobile insurance $ _____

      5) Other _____ $ _____

  m. Taxes that are not deducted from wages or included in home mortgage payments

     Specify: _____ $ _____

     Specify: _____ $ _____

   n. Installment payments:

      1) Automobile: _____ $ _____

      2) Automobile: _____ $ _____

      3) Home improvements:_____ $ _____

      4) _____ $ _____

      5) _____ $ _____

      6) _____ $ _____

      7) _____ $ _____

   o. Alimony, maintenance, or support paid to others $ _____

   p. Other payments for support of additional dependents not living at your home $ _____

   q. Regular expenses from operation of business, profession, or farm $ _____

   r. Union, professional, social, and other dues that are not deducted from wages $ _____

   s. Other expenses: _____ $ _____

    _____ $ _____

    _____ $ _____

    _____ $ _____

2. Estimated average current monthly expenses for the debtor's spouse who maintains a separate household.

   a. Rent or home mortgage payment (include lot rented for mobile home and condominium fee) $ _____

    Are real estate taxes included? yes _____ no _____

    Is property insurance included? yes _____ no _____

b. Utilities:
　　1) Electricity .... $ _____
　　2) Gas, oil, or coal .... $ _____
　　3) Water .... $ _____
　　4) Sewer .... $ _____
　　5) Telephone .... $ _____
　　6) Refuse removal .... $ _____
　　7) Other .... $ _____
c. Routine home maintenance (repairs and upkeep) .... $ _____
d. Food .... $ _____
e. Clothing .... $ _____
f. Laundry and dry cleaning .... $ _____
g. Medical and dental expenses (include drugs) .... $ _____
h. Transportation, excluding automobile payments .... $ _____
i. Recreation, clubs, and entertainment .... $ _____
j. Newspapers, periodicals, and books, including school
　　books .... $ _____
k. Religious and charitable contributions .... $ _____
l. Insurance not deducted from wages or included in
　　home mortgage payments
　　1) Homeowners or renters insurance .... $ _____
　　2) Life insurance .... $ _____
　　3) Medical insurance .... $ _____
　　4) Automobile insurance .... $ _____
　　5) Other _____ $ _____
m. Taxes that are not deducted from wages or included in
　　home mortgage payments
　　Specify: _____ $ _____
　　Specify: _____ $ _____
n. Installment payments:
　　1) Automobile: _____ $ _____
　　2) Automobile_____ $ _____
　　3) Home improvements:_____ $ _____
　　4) _____ $ _____
　　5) _____ $ _____
　　6) _____ $ _____
　　7) _____ $ _____
o. Alimony, maintenance, or support paid to others ...... $ _____
p. Other payments for support of additional dependents
　　not living at your home .... $ _____
q. Regular expenses from operation of business,
　　profession, or farm .... $ _____
r. Union, professional, social, and other dues that are not
　　deducted from wages .... $ _____
s. Other expenses: _____ $ _____
　　_____ $ _____
　　_____ $ _____
　　_____ $ _____
　　_____ $ _____

VI. Current Income and Current Expenditures of a Partnership or a Corporation

Complete Part VI if the debtor is a partnership or a corporation.

1. How are the debtor's accounting records kept?
   cash basis _____ accrual method _____
   If the debtor's accounting records are kept on a cash basis, complete question 2.
   If the debtor's accounting records are kept on an accrual method, complete question 3.
2. Summarize the debtor's cash flow for a 90- to 120-day period which ends no more than 30 days prior to the commencement of this case.
   a. Beginning date: _____
   b. Ending date: _____
   c. Cash balance at the beginning date: $ _____
   d. Cash disbursements during this period: $ _____
   e. Cash balance at the ending date: $ _____

3. Summarize the debtor's revenue and expenses on an accrual method for a 90- to 120-day period which ends no more than 30 days prior to the commencement of this case.

   a. Beginning date: _____
   b. Ending date: _____
   c. Revenue during this period: $ _____
   d. Expenses during this period: $ _____
   e. Net gain or (loss) during this period: $ _____

4. Attach to this questionnaire a copy of the most recent financial statement (audited or unaudited) which has been prepared by or for the debtor.

VII. Statement of Financial Affairs

Questions 1–15 must be completed by all debtors.

1. Income from employment or operation of business.

   Question 1.a. applies to the debtor. Question 1.b. applies to the debtor's spouse, if a joint petition is filed. Answer question 1.b. only if a joint petition is filed.
   a. Debtor's gross income
      1) Debtor's financial records
         a) How are your financial records maintained or how have they been maintained?
            (1) fiscal year basis? yes _____ no _____
            (2) calendar year basis? yes _____ no _____
            If your answer is fiscal year, you may report fiscal year income.
         b) If fiscal year, identify the beginning and ending dates of your fiscal year.
            (1) beginning date: _____
            (2) ending date: _____
      2) For this calendar [fiscal] year to the date this case was commenced

a) Beginning with this calendar [fiscal] year to the date this case was commenced, did you receive gross income from
   (1) employment
   (2) trade
   (3) profession or
   (4) operation of your business?
   yes _____ no _____

b) If yes, state the gross amount of income you received during this period and the source of this income.

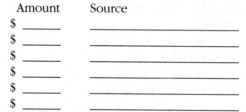

Amount   Source
$ _____   _____
$ _____   _____
$ _____   _____
$ _____   _____
$ _____   _____
$ _____   _____

3) For the two years immediately preceding this calendar [fiscal] year
   a) During the two years immediately preceding this calendar [fiscal] year, did you receive gross income from
      (1) employment
      (2) trade
      (3) profession or
      (4) operation of your business?
      yes_____no_____
   b) If yes, state the gross amount of income you received during this period and the source of this income.

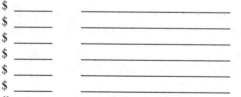

Amount   Source
$ _____   _____
$ _____   _____
$ _____   _____
$ _____   _____
$ _____   _____
$ _____   _____

b. The following questions apply to the debtor's spouse, if a joint petition is filed.
   1) Debtor's spouse's financial records
      a) How are your spouse's financial records maintained or how have they been maintained?
         (1) fiscal year basis? yes _____ no _____
         (2) calendar year basis? yes _____ no _____
         If your answer is fiscal year, you may report fiscal year income.
      b) If fiscal year, identify the beginning and ending dates of the spouse's fiscal year.
         (1) beginning date: _____
         (2) ending date: _____
   2) For this calendar [fiscal] year to the date this case was commenced
      a) Beginning with this calendar [fiscal] year to the date this case was commenced, did your spouse receive gross income from
         (1) employment
         (2) trade

(3) profession or
(4) operation of your business?
yes_____no_____
b) If yes, state the gross amount of income your spouse received during this period and the source of this income.

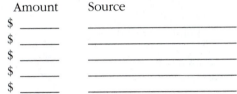

Amount   Source

$ _____   _____
$ _____   _____
$ _____   _____
$ _____   _____
$ _____   _____
$ _____   _____

3) For the two years immediately preceding this calendar [fiscal] year
    a) During the two years immediately preceding this calendar [fiscal] year, did your spouse receive gross income from
        (1) employment
        (2) trade
        (3) profession or
        (4) operation of your business?
           yes_____no_____
    b) If yes, state the gross amount of income your spouse received during this period and the source of this income.

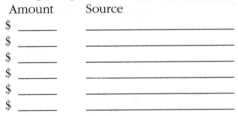

Amount   Source

$ _____   _____
$ _____   _____
$ _____   _____
$ _____   _____
$ _____   _____
$ _____   _____

2. Income other than from employment or operation of business.

Question 2.a. applies to the debtor. Question 2.b. applies to the debtor's spouse, if a joint petition is filed. Answer question 2.b. only if a joint petition is filed.
    a. The following questions apply to all debtors.
    During the two years immediately preceding the commencement of this case, did you receive income *other than from*
    1) employment
    2) trade
    3) profession or
    4) operation of your business?
        yes _____ no _____
    If yes, state the amount of income you received during this period and the source of this income.
    Amount   Source

$ _____   _____
$ _____   _____
$ _____   _____

b. The following questions apply to the debtor's spouse, if a joint petition is filed.

During the two years immediately preceding the commencement of this case, did your spouse receive income *other than from*

1) employment

2) trade

3) profession or

4) operation of your business?

    yes_____no_____

If yes, state the amount of income your spouse received during this period and the source of this income.

  Amount   Source

$ _____ _____

$ _____ _____

$ _____ _____

3. Payments to creditors.

  a. Within 90 days immediately preceding the commencement of this case

    1) Within 90 days immediately preceding the commencement of this case, did you make any payments of

      a) loans

      b) installment purchases of goods or services

      c) other debts

        aggregating more than $600 to any creditor?

        yes_____no_____

    2) If yes, provide the following information.

Name of creditor: _____

Address: _____

Dates of payment: _____

Amount paid: $ _____

Amount still owing: $ _____

Name of creditor: _____

Address: _____

Dates of payment: _____

Amount paid: $ _____

Amount still owing: $ _____

Name of creditor: _____

Address: _____

Dates of payment: _____

Amount paid: $ _____

Amount still owing: $ _____

  b. Within one year immediately preceding the commencement of this case

    1) Within one year immediately preceding the commencement of this case, did you make any payments to or for the benefit of creditors who are or were insiders?

    yes _____ no _____

    The term "insider" includes but is not limited to

    a) relatives of the debtor;

    b) general partners of the debtor and their relatives;

c) corporations of which the debtor is an officer, director, or person in control;

d) officers, directors, and any persons in control of a corporate debtor and their relatives;

e) affiliates of the debtor and insiders of such affiliates;

f) any managing agent of the debtor.

2) If yes, provide the following information.

Name of creditor: _____

Address: _____

Relationship to the debtor: _____

Dates of payment: _____

Amount paid: $ _____

Amount still owing: $ _____

Name of creditor: _____

Address: _____

Relationship to the debtor: _____

Dates of payment: _____

Amount paid: $ _____

Amount still owing: $ _____

4. Suits, executions, garnishments, and attachments.

a. Lawsuits

1) Pending lawsuits

a) At the present time, are you a party to any lawsuit?

yes_____no_____

b) If yes, provide the following information.

Caption of the suit: _____

Case number: _____

Nature of the proceeding: _____

The Court: _____

The Court's location: _____

The status of the suit: _____

Caption of the suit: _____

Case number: _____

Nature of the proceeding: _____

The Court: _____

The Court's location: _____

The status of the suit: _____

2) Suits no longer pending

a) Within one year immediately preceding the filing of this bankruptcy case, were you a party to any lawsuit that is no longer pending?

yes_____no_____

b) If yes, provide the following information.

Caption of the suit: _____

Case number: _____

Nature of the proceeding: _____

The Court: _____

The Court's location: _____

The disposition of the suit: _____

Caption of the suit: _____

Case number: _____

Nature of the proceeding: _____

The Court: _____

The Court's location: _____

The disposition of the suit: _____

b. Attachments, seizures, and garnishments

1) Within one year immediately preceding the filing of this bankruptcy case, has any of your property been attached or seized under any legal or equitable process or subjected to garnishment? yes_____no_____

2) If yes, provide the following information.

Name of the. person for whose benefit the property was attached, seized, or subjected to garnishment: _____

_____

Address: _____

_____

_____

Date of attachment, seizure, or garnishment: _____

Description of the property: _____

Value of the property: $ _____

Name of the person for whose benefit the property was attached or seized or subjected to garnishment: _____

_____

Address: _____

_____

_____

Date of attachment, seizure, or garnishment: _____

Description of the property: _____

Value of the property: $ _____

5. Repossessions, foreclosures, and returns.

a. Within one year immediately preceding the commencement of this case, has any of your property been repossessed by a creditor, sold at a foreclosure sale, transferred through a deed in lieu of foreclosure, or returned to the seller? yes_____no_____

b. If yes, provide the following information.

Name of the creditor or seller: _____

Address: _____

_____

Date of repossession, foreclosure sale, transfer, or return: _____

Description of the property: _____

Value of the property: $ _____

Name of the creditor or seller: _____

Address: _____

_____

Date of repossession, foreclosure sale, transfer, or return: _____

Description of the property: _____

Value of the property: $ _____

6. Assignments and receiverships.
   a. Assignments
      1) Within 120 days immediately preceding the commencement of this case, has any of your property been assigned for the benefit of creditors?

         yes_____no_____
      2) For each assignment, provide the following information.
         Name of assignee: _____
         Address: _____
         Date of assignment: _____
         Terms of assignment or settlement: _____

         _____

         _____

         Name of assignee: _____
         Address: _____
         Date of assignment: _____
         Terms of assignment or settlement: _____

         _____

         _____

   b. Receiverships
      1) Within one year immediately preceding the commencement of this case, has any of your property been in the hands of a custodian, receiver, or court-appointed official?

         yes_____no_____
      2) For any such property, provide the following information.
         Name of custodian: _____
         Address: _____
         Name of the Court: _____
         Location of the Court: _____
         Case title: _____
         Case number: _____
         Date of the order: _____
         Description of the property: _____
         Value of the property: $ _____

7. Gifts.
   a. Gifts
      1) Within one year immediately preceding the commencement of this case, have you made any gifts other than ordinary and usual gifts to family members totaling less than $200 in value per individual family member?

         yes_____no_____
      2) For any such gift, provide the following information.
         Name of the person receiving the gift: _____

         _____

         Address: _____

         _____

         Relationship to the debtor, if any: _____
         Date of the gift: _____
         Description of the gift: _____
         Value of the gift: $ _____

Name of the person receiving the gift: _____

_____

Address of the person receiving the gift: _____

_____

Relationship to the debtor, if any: _____
Date of the gift: _____
Description of the gift: _____
Value of the gift: $ _____

b. Charitable contributions

1) Within one year immediately preceding the commencement of this case, have you made any charitable contributions other than charitable contributions totaling less than $100 per recipient?
yes_____no_____

2) For any such contribution, provide the following information.
Name of the recipient receiving the charitable contribution:

_____

Address: _____

_____

Relationship to the debtor, if any: _____
Date of the contribution: _____
Description of the contribution: _____
Value of the contribution: $ _____

Name of the recipient receiving the charitable contribution:

_____

Address: _____

_____

Relationship to the debtor, if any: _____
Date of the contribution: _____
Description of the contribution: _____
Value of the contribution: $ _____

8. Losses.

a. Within one year immediately preceding the commencement of this case, have you suffered any losses from fire, theft, other casualty, or gambling?
yes_____no_____

b. For each such loss, provide the following information.
Description of the property: _____
Value of the property: $ _____
Description of the circumstances surrounding the loss: _____

_____

Date of the loss: _____

Description of the property: _____
Value of the property: $ _____
Description of the circumstances surrounding the loss: _____

_____

Date of the loss: _____

c. Was the loss covered in whole or in part by insurance?
yes_____no_____

d. Give particulars of the insurance coverage.

_____

_____

9. Payments related to debt counseling or bankruptcy.
   a. Payments made
      1) Within one year immediately preceding the commencement of this case, have payments been made by you or on your behalf to any persons, including attorneys, for
         a) consultation concerning debt consolidation
         b) relief under the bankruptcy law
         c) preparation of a petition in bankruptcy?
         yes _____ no _____
      2) For any such payment, provide the following information.
         Name of the payee: _____
         Address: _____

         _____

         Date of payment: _____
         Name of payor, if other than you: _____
         Amount of money paid: $ _____
   b. Property transferred
      1) Within one year immediately preceding the commencement of this case, has property been transferred by you or on your behalf to any persons, including attorneys, for
         a) consultation concerning debt consolidation
         b) relief under the bankruptcy law
         c) preparation of a petition in bankruptcy?
         yes _____ no _____
      2) For any such transfer, provide the following information.
         Name of the transferee: _____
         Address: _____

         _____

         Date of transfer: _____
         Name of transferor, if other than you: _____

         _____

         Description of the property transferred: _____
10. Other transfers.
   a. Within one year immediately preceding the commencement of this case, have you transferred any other property, either absolutely or as security, which was not transferred in the ordinary course of your business or financial affairs?
      yes _____ no _____
   b. For such transfers, provide the following information.
      Name of the transferee: _____
      Address: _____

      _____

      Relationship to you: _____
      Date of the transfer: _____
      Description of the property transferred: _____

      _____

      Value received for the property: $ _____

Name of the transferee: _____

Address: _____

_____

Relationship to you: _____

Date of the transfer: _____

Description of the property transferred: _____

_____

Value received for the property: $ _____

11. Closed financial accounts.

    a. Within one year immediately preceding the commencement of this case, were there any financial accounts or instruments (including checking accounts, savings accounts, other financial accounts, certificates of deposit, shares and share accounts held in banks, credit unions, pension funds, cooperatives, associations, brokerage houses, and other financial institutions) held in your name or for your benefit which were closed, sold, or otherwise transferred?

    yes_____no_____

    b. For any such financial account or instrument, provide the following information.

Name of the institution: _____

Address: _____

_____

Name under which the account was carried: _____

_____

Type and account number: _____

Amount of the final balance: $ _____

Amount and date of sale or closing: $ _____

Name of the institution: _____

Address: _____

_____

Name under which the account was carried: _____

_____

Type and account number: _____

Amount of the final balance: $ _____

Amount and date of sale or closing: $ _____

12. Safe deposit boxes.

    a. Within one year immediately preceding the commencement of this case, have you kept or used for your cash, securities, or other valuables a safe deposit box or other depositories?

    yes _____ no _____

    b. For each box or depository, provide the following information.

Name of the bank or other depository: _____

_____

Address: _____

_____

_____

Name and address of every person who had the right of access to the box or depository: _____

_____

_____

_____

_____

Brief description of the contents: _____

_____

_____

If the box or other depository has been transferred, state the transfer
date: _____

If the box or other depository has been surrendered, state the date of
surrender: _____

13. Setoffs.
   a. Within 90 days preceding the commencement of this case, were there
      any debts you owed to any creditor, including any bank, which were
      setoff by that creditor against a debt or deposit the creditor owed you?
      yes _____ no _____
   b. If there has been such a setoff, provide the following information.
      Name of the creditor: _____
      Address: _____

      _____

      Date of setoff: _____
      Amount of the debt you owed the creditor: $ _____
      Amount of the setoff: $ _____

      Name of the creditor: _____
      Address: _____

      _____

      Date of setoff: _____
      Amount of the debt you owed the creditor: $ _____
      Amount of the setoff: $ _____

14. Property held for another person.
   a. Do you hold or control property that is owned by another person?
      yes _____ no _____
   b. For such property held or controlled by you, provide the following in-
      formation.
      Name of the owner: _____
      Address: _____

      _____

      Description of the property: _____

      _____

      Value of the property: $ _____
      Location of the property: _____

      _____

      Name of the owner: _____
      Address: _____

      _____

      Description of the property: _____

      _____

      Value of the property: $ _____
      Location of the property: _____

      _____

Name of the owner: _____

Address: _____

_____

Description of the property: _____

_____

Value of the property: $ _____

Location of the property: _____

_____

15. Prior address of debtor.
    a. Within the two years immediately preceding the commencement of this case, have you moved from one address to another?
       yes _____ no _____
    b. For each such address, provide the following information.
       Former address: _____

_____

       Name under which the premises was occupied: _____

_____

       Dates of occupancy: _____

_____

       Former address: _____

_____

       Name under which the premises was occupied: _____

_____

       Dates of occupancy: _____

_____

       Former address: _____

_____

       Name under which the premises was occupied: _____

_____

       Dates of occupancy: _____

_____

    c. If a joint petition, also provide separate addresses of either spouse during this period.
       Separate address: _____

_____

       Name under which the premises was occupied: _____

_____

       Dates of occupancy: _____

_____

       Separate address: _____

_____

       Name under which the premises was occupied: _____

_____

       Dates of occupancy: _____

_____

Questions 16–21 are to be completed by every debtor that is

(a) a corporation;

(b) a partnership;

(c) an individual debtor who is or has been, within the two years immediately preceding the commencement of this case, any of the following:

    (1) an officer, director, managing executive, or owner of more than 5 percent of the voting securities of a corporation;

    (2) a partner, other than a limited partner, of a partnership;

    (3) a sole proprietor or otherwise self-employed.

16. Nature, location, and name of business.

    a. Answer this question if you are filing your petition as an individual.

        1) Within the two years immediately preceding the commencement of this case, were you

           a) an officer

           b) a director

           c) a partner

           d) a managing executive of

               (1) a corporation

               (2) a partnership

               (3) a sole proprietorship or

           e) a self-employed professional?

           yes _____ no _____

        2) For each operation, provide the following information.

        Name of the operation: _____

        Address: _____

        _____

        Nature of the business: _____

        _____

        Beginning date of operation: _____

        Ending date of operation: _____

        Name of the operation: _____

        Address: _____

        _____

        Nature of the business: _____

        _____

        Beginning date of operation: _____

        Ending date of operation: _____

        3) Within the two years immediately preceding the commencement of this case, did you own 5 percent or more of the voting or equity securities of a business?

        yes _____ no _____

        4) For each business in which you owned 5 percent or more of the voting or equity securities, provide the following information.

        Name of the business: _____

        Address: _____

        _____

        Nature of the business: _____

        _____

        Beginning date of ownership interest: _____

        Ending date of ownership interest: _____

Name of the business: _____

Address: _____

_____

Nature of the business: _____

_____

Beginning date of ownership interest: _____

Ending date of ownership interest: _____

  b. Answer this question if you are filing your petition as a partnership.

    1) Within the two years immediately preceding the commencement of this case, were you a partner in a business?

      yes _____ no _____

    2) For each business, provide the following information.

      Name of the business: _____

      Address: _____

      _____

      Nature of the business: _____

      Beginning date of operation: _____

      Ending date of operation: _____

      Name of the business: _____

      Address: _____

      _____

      Nature of the business: _____

      Beginning date of operation: _____

      Ending date of operation: _____

    3) Within the two years immediately preceding the commencement of this case, did the partnership own 5 percent or more of the voting securities of a business?

      yes _____ no _____

    4) For each business, provide the following information.

      Name of the business: _____

      Address: _____

      _____

      Nature of the business: _____

      _____

      Beginning date of ownership interest: _____

      Ending date of ownership interest: _____

      Name of the business: _____

      Address: _____

      _____

      Nature of the business: _____

      _____

      Beginning date of ownership interest: _____

      Ending date of ownership interest: _____

  c. Answer this question if you are filing your petition as a corporation.

    1) Within the two years immediately preceding the commencement of this case, was the corporation a partner in a business?

      yes _____ no _____

2) For each business, provide the following information.
Name of the business: _____
Address: _____

_____

Nature of the business: _____
Beginning date of operation: _____
Ending date of operation: _____

Name of the business: _____
Address: _____

_____

Nature of the business: _____
Beginning date of operation: _____
Ending date of operation: _____

3) Within the two years immediately preceding the commencement of this case, did the corporation own 5 percent or more of the voting securities of a business?
yes _____ no _____

4) For each business, provide the following information.
Name of the business: _____
Address: _____

_____

Nature of the business: _____
Beginning date of ownership interest: _____
Ending date of ownership interest: _____

Name of the business: _____
Address: _____

_____

Nature of the business: _____

_____

Beginning date of ownership interest: _____
Ending date of ownership interest: _____

17. Books, records, and financial statements.
 a. Bookkeepers and accountants
  1) Within the six years immediately preceding the filing of this bankruptcy case, did you use a bookkeeper or an accountant to keep or supervise the keeping of your account books and records?
yes _____ no _____
  2) For any such bookkeeper or accountant, provide the following information.
Name: _____
Address: _____

_____

The dates the services were rendered: _____
 b. Audits and preparation of financial statements
  1) Within the two years immediately preceding the filing of this bankruptcy case, has a firm or an individual audited your books of account and records or prepared a financial statement for you?
yes _____ no _____

2) For any such services, provide the following information.
Name: _____
Address: _____
_____
The dates the services were rendered: _____
_____

c. Possession of books and records
1) Provide the following information concerning the firms or individuals who currently have possession of your books of account or records.
Name: _____
Address: _____
_____

2) Are any of these books or records unavailable?
yes _____ no _____
3) Explain the circumstances surrounding the unavailability of these books or records: _____
_____
_____
_____
_____
_____
_____

d. Financial statements
1) Within the two years immediately preceding the commencement of this case, have you issued any written financial statements?
yes _____ no _____
2) For the persons to whom written financial statements have been issued (including mercantile and trade agencies), provide the following information
Name of the person receiving the written financial statement: _____
_____
Address: _____
_____
Date the financial statement was issued: _____
Name of the person receiving the written financial statement: _____
_____
Address: _____
_____
Date the financial statement was issued: _____

18. Inventories.
a. The last two inventories of your property
1) The last inventory of your property
Date of the last inventory: _____
Name of the person who took the inventory or under whose supervision the inventory was taken: _____
Dollar amount of the inventory: $ _____
Basis for the inventory: cost, market, other (specify): _____
2) The next-to-last inventory of your property
Date of the next-to-last inventory: _____
Name of the person who took the inventory or under whose supervision the inventory was taken: _____

Dollar amount of the inventory: $ _____

Basis for the inventory: cost, market, other (specify): _____

b. Custodian of the inventory records

1) The last inventory

Name of the custodian of the inventory records: _____

Address: _____

2) The next-to-last inventory

Name of the custodian of the inventory records: _____

Address: _____

19. Current partners, officers, directors, and shareholders.

If the debtor is a partnership, answer question a. If the debtor is a corporation, answer question b.

a. For each member of the partnership, provide the following information.

Name of the partner: _____

Address: _____

Nature of the partner's interest: _____

Percentage of the partnership interest: _____ %

Name of the partner: _____

Address: _____

Nature of the partner's interest: _____

Percentage of the partnership interest: _____ %

Name of the partner: _____

Address: _____

Nature of the partner's interest: _____

Percentage of the partnership interest: _____ %

b. For each officer or director of the corporation and each stockholder who directly or indirectly owns, controls, or holds 5 percent or more of the voting securities of the corporation, provide the following information.

Name of the officer, director, or stockholder: _____

Address: _____

Title: _____

Nature of stock ownership: _____

Percentage of stock ownership: _____ %

Name of the officer, director, or stockholder: _____

Address: _____

Title: _____

Nature of stock ownership: _____

_____

Percentage of stock ownership: _____ %

Name of the officer, director, or stockholder: _____

_____

Address: _____

_____

Title: _____

Nature of stock ownership: _____

_____

Percentage of stock ownership: _____ %

c. For each officer or director of the corporation and each stockholder who directly or indirectly owns, controls, or holds less than 5 percent of the voting securities of the corporation, provide the following information.
Name of the officer, director, or stockholder: _____

_____

Address: _____

_____

Title: _____

Nature of stock ownership: _____

_____

Percentage of stock ownership: _____ %

Name of the officer, director, or stockholder: _____

_____

Address: _____

_____

Title: _____

Nature of stock ownership: _____

_____

Percentage of stock ownership: _____ %

Name of the officer, director, or stockholder: _____

_____

Address: _____

_____

Title: _____

Nature of stock ownership: _____

_____

Percentage of stock ownership: _____ %

20. Former partners, officers, directors, and shareholders. If the debtor is a partnership, answer question a. If the debtor is a corporation, answer question b.
a. Partnership
1) Has a member of the partnership withdrawn from the partnership within one year immediately preceding the commencement of this case?
yes _____ no _____
2) For each member of the partnership who withdrew from the partnership within one year immediately preceding the commencement of this case, provide the following information.
Name of the former partner: _____
Address: _____

_____

Date of withdrawal from the partnership: _____

Name of the former partner: _____
Address: _____

_____

Date of withdrawal from the partnership: _____

Name of the former partner: _____
Address: _____

_____

Date of withdrawal from the partnership: _____

b. Corporation
   1) Did an officer or a director of the corporation terminate his or her relationship with the corporation within one year immediately preceding the commencement of this case?
      yes _____ no _____
   2) For each officer or director of the corporation whose relationship with the corporation terminated within one year immediately preceding the commencement of this case, provide the following information.
      Name of the officer or director: _____
      Address: _____

      _____

      Title: _____
      Date of termination of the relationship: _____

      Name of the officer or director: _____
      Address: _____

      _____

      Title: _____
      Date of termination of the relationship: _____

      Name of the officer or director: _____
      Address: _____

      _____

      Title: _____
      Date of termination of the relationship: _____

21. Withdrawals from a partnership or distributions by a corporation.
   a. During one year immediately preceding the commencement of this case, were there any withdrawals of money or distributions of property credited or given to an insider, including compensation in any form, bonuses, loans, stock redemptions, options exercised, or any other perquisites?
      yes _____ no _____
   b. For each insider recipient, provide the following information.
      Name of the recipient: _____
      Address: _____

      _____

      Relationship to the debtor: _____
      Date of the withdrawal: _____
      Purpose of the withdrawal: _____
      Amount of money withdrawn: $ _____
      Description and value of the property distributed: _____

      _____ $ _____

      Name of the recipient: _____

Address: _____

_____

Relationship to the debtor: _____
Date of the withdrawal: _____
Purpose of the withdrawal: _____
Amount of money withdrawn: $ _____
Description and value of the property distributed: _____
_____ $ _____

Name of the recipient: _____
Address: _____

_____

Relationship to the debtor: _____
Date of the withdrawal: _____
Purpose of the withdrawal: _____
Amount of money withdrawn: $ _____
Description and value of the property distributed: _____
_____ $ _____

VIII. PROPERTY STATUS—REAL AND PERSONAL

A. REAL PROPERTY

1. Real property debtor would like to surrender
   a. _____
      Description of the property

      _____
      Creditor's name
   b. _____
      Description of the property

      _____
      Creditor's name
   c. _____
      Description of the property

      _____
      Creditor's name
   d. _____
      Description of the property

      _____
      Creditor's name

2. Real property debtor would like to retain
   a. _____
      Description of the property

      _____
      Creditor's name
   b. _____
      Description of the property

      _____
      Creditor's name
   c. _____
      Description of the property

_____

Creditor's name

d.   _____

Description of the property

_____

Creditor's name

B. PERSONAL PROPERTY

1. Personal property debtor would like to surrender

a.   _____

Description of the property

_____

Creditor's name

b.   _____

Description of the property

_____

Creditor's name

c.   _____

Description of the property

_____

Creditor's name

d.   _____

Description of the property

_____

Creditor's name

2. Personal property debtor would like to retain

a.   _____

Description of the property

_____

Creditor's name

b.   _____

Description of the property

_____

Creditor's name

c.   _____

Description of the property

_____

Creditor's name

d.   _____

Description of the property

_____

Creditor's name

e.   _____

Description of the property

_____

Creditor's name

f.   _____

Description of the property

_____

Creditor's name

g.   _____

Description of the property

_____

Creditor's name

APPENDIX B

INTERVIEW QUESTIONNAIRE FOR THE CREDITOR-CLIENT

1. Name, address (including zip code), and telephone number (including area code) of the creditor.
   Creditor's name: _____
   Address: _____
   _____
   city   state   zip code
   Telephone number (including area code): _____
2. What is the nature of the creditor's business? _____
   _____

3. Name, address (including zip code), and telephone number (including area code) of the debtor.
   Debtor's name: _____
   Address: _____
   _____
   city   state   zip code
   Telephone number (including area code): _____
4. When and how did the claim arise? _____
   _____
   _____

5. What is the amount of the claim?
   Original amount: $ _____
   Current amount: $ _____
6. Is the claim secured?
   yes _____ no _____
   If yes, state the collateral. _____
   _____

7. Is the claim secured by collateral that is not the debtor's?
   yes _____ no _____
   If yes, provide details. _____
   _____
   _____

8. Is there a guarantor or co-obligor to the debt?
   yes _____ no _____
   If yes, provide details. _____
   _____
   _____

9. Have there been transfers of money or property from the debtor to the creditor?
   yes _____ no _____
   If yes, give the dates of each transfer and describe what was transferred.
   _____
   _____
   _____
   _____

10. Does the debtor have counterclaims?
    yes _____ no _____
    If yes, explain. _____
    _____
    _____

11. Does the creditor have an insider relationship with the debtor?
    yes _____ no _____
    If yes, explain. _____
    _____
    _____

12. Does the creditor have evidence or even suspicions that the debtor is hiding assets?
    yes _____ no _____
    If yes, explain. _____
    _____
    _____

13. Has the debtor filed for bankruptcy?
    yes _____ no _____
    If yes, under which chapter did the debtor file, when, and in which Court?
    Chapter _____ Date of filing: _____
    Court where filed:United States Bankruptcy Court for the _____
    District of _____

14. Describe any attempted settlement. _____
    _____
    _____
    _____
    _____
    _____
    _____

APPENDIX C

CHAPTER 9—DEBTS OF MUNICIPALITIES

Chapter 9, a rarely used chapter, applies to financially troubled municipalities. A municipality is defined as a "political subdivision or public agency or instrumentality of a State." 11 U.S.C.A. § 101(40).

The Chapter 9 bankruptcy has a history of its own, apart from the rest of the Code. There were no bankruptcy provisions for the adjustment of debts of municipalities prior to 1934. Because of the problems created by the Great Depression, emergency legislation entitled "Provisions for the Emergency and Temporary Aid of Public Debtors" was passed in 1934. This was the beginning of what would ultimately become Chapter 9.

In 1936, the United States Supreme Court, in *Ashton v. Cameron County Water Improvement District No. 1,* 298 U.S. 513 (1936), found this statute unconstitutional on the ground that it "might materially restrict respondent's control over its fiscal affairs." Under pressure by distressed cities, Congress enacted a new statute the following year. It was entitled Chapter IX, "Composition of Indebtedness of Certain Taxing Agencies or Instrumentalities." The United States Supreme Court, in *United States v. Bekins,* 304 U.S. 27 (1938), held the new law constitutional because it provided for no restrictions on the control of the fiscal affairs of a state. This statute, due to expire in 1940, was extended several times. Finally, in 1946, Chapter IX became a permanent part of bankruptcy law.

The municipal bankruptcy chapter remained in the same form from 1946 until it was amended in 1976. Improved economic conditions after the Depression brought about a decline in municipal debtors, and Chapter IX apparently was sufficient for municipalities that found it necessary to file during this intervening period.

The financial crisis of New York City in the early 1970s caused renewed congressional interest in municipal bankruptcy. In 1975, New York City was near default several times due to a large bureaucracy, tuition-free open enrollment at City University, and high payments and services for welfare recipients. Default was avoided only by bailouts from the city teachers' pension fund, the New York state government, and the federal government.

The requirements of Chapter IX would have been cumbersome or even impossible for a large city such as New York to meet. The 1976 amendments facilitated a bankruptcy filing by such a city. The requirement to file the plan (to be accepted by creditors prior to filing the petition) along with the petition was changed to "with the petition or thereafter, but not later than a time fixed by the court." Bankruptcy Rule 9–22. The Bankruptcy Code contains a provision that is quite similar to this 1976 amendment to the Bankruptcy Act. 11 U.S.C.A. § 941.

It was also necessary under Chapter IX of the Act to file a list of creditors by names and addresses, with a description of each claim or type of securities held, at the time of filing the petition. The filing of such a list, along with the petition, could become an overwhelming clerical burden for a large city, which might have hundreds or even thousands of creditors, and could substantially delay filing of the petition. The 1976 amendments required filing of the list of creditors "within such time as the court may fix." Bankruptcy Rule 9–1. Under the Code, the list of creditors and equity security holders "shall be filed by the debtor in a Chapter 9 municipality case within such time as the court shall fix." Fed. R. Bank. P. 1007(e).

Although these changes in filing requirements have considerably lessened the burden of a municipality wishing to file a Chapter 9 bankruptcy, it is statistically remote that a paralegal will ever be involved in such a case. Between 1978 and 1988, the number of municipal bankruptcies filed nationwide averaged less than three per year.

Index